PENGUIN BOOKS
CHASING THE MONK'S SHADOW

Mishi Saran was born in Allahabad in 1968, but has not lived in India since the age of ten. She graduated with a degree in Chinese studies from Wellesley College, USA, and spent two years in Beijing and Nanjing. In 1994 she moved to Hong Kong, where she worked as a news reporter until she became more interested in travel writing and fiction. She is currently working on her next book.

Chasing the Monk's Shadow

A Journey in the Footsteps of Xuanzang

MISHI SARAN

PENGUIN BOOKS

PENGUIN BOOKS

Published by the Penguin Group

Penguin Books India Pvt Ltd, 11 Community Centre, Panchsheel Park, New Delhi 110 017, India
Penguin Group (USA) Inc., 375 Hudson Street, New York, New York 10014, USA
Penguin Group (Canada), 90 Eglinton Avenue East, Suite 700, Toronto, Ontario, M4P 2Y3, Canada (a division of Pearson Penguin Canada Inc.)
Penguin Books Ltd, 80 Strand, London WC2R 0RL, England
Penguin Ireland, 25 St Stephen's Green, Dublin 2, Ireland (a division of Penguin Books Ltd)
Penguin Group (Australia), 250 Camberwell Road, Camberwell, Victoria 3124, Australia (a division of Pearson Australia Group Pty Ltd)
Penguin Group (NZ), 67 Apollo Drive, Rosedale, North Shore 0632, New Zealand (a division of Pearson New Zealand Ltd)
Penguin Group (South Africa) (Pty) Ltd, 24 Sturdee Avenue, Rosebank, Johannesburg 2196, South Africa

Penguin Books Ltd, Registered Offices: 80 Strand, London WC2R 0RL, England

First published in Viking by Penguin Books India 2005
Published in Penguin Books 2008

Copyright © Mishi Saran 2005

10 9 8 7 6 5 4 3 2 1

Excerpts from *Old Path White Clouds: Walking in the Footprints of the Buddha* (1991) reprinted by permission of Parallax Press, Berkeley, California, www.parallax.org.

ISBN 9780143064398

Typeset in Sabon by Mantra Virtual Services, New Delhi
Printed at Chaman Offset Printers, New Delhi

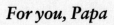

For you, Papa

Contents

AUTHOR'S NOTE ix

THE ROAD TO INDIA 1

JOURNEY TO THE WEST 9

CITY OF THE FLYING HORSE 31

THE JADE GATES 38

RIVER OF SAND 50

FIRE CITY 61

TWIN CONVENTS 68

WHITE WATER 84

HEAVENLY MOUNTAINS 92

PERPETUAL SNOWS 110

NINE *LEPIOSHKAS* 124

SOGDIANA 129

RIVER OF GOLD 141

CROSSING THE RIVER 153

LOCKING THE SEA IN A BOX 164

UNHAPPY VALLEYS 182

SIKANDER AND PORUS 187

KINGDOM ENCLOSED BY PEAKS 195

TREE NYMPHS 205

TOO MANY WOMEN 209

HOLY CONFLUENCE 223

SCHISM IN THE SANGHA 231

SARKARI INTEZAM 235

WRONG KIND OF LOVE 244

LABOUR PAINS 255

FATAL MUSHROOMS 261

DEER PARK 265

BUDDHIST IVY LEAGUE 271

VULTURE'S PEAK 280

PEEPUL LEAF AND PERFECT WISDOM 284

LAND OF THE EASTERN LIGHT 292

REUNITED 301

FLOWER MOUNTAIN 304

OCEAN'S EDGE 311

HIDDEN BUDDHAS 318

STONE ELEPHANTS 324

HILL OF RISHIS 329

LIMBO 335

PURE LAND 337

CITY OF DRESSED STONE 345

MOUND OF THE KING 354

LOTUS CITY 362

SILK ROAD GRAFFITI 368

LISTENING POST 375

INSHALLAH 381

SACRIFICE COUNTRY 387

SAD SECRETS 402

FLEA IN YOUR CLOTHES 418

TOOTI-PHOOTI AFGHANISTAN 425

AFTERWARDS 431

ACKNOWLEDGEMENTS 432

NOTES 434

BIBLIOGRAPHY 440

INDEX 443

Author's Note

In AD 627, the Chinese Buddhist monk Xuanzang* set off from China on a journey from which he returned only eighteen years later, in AD 645.**

At that time Chinese translations of Buddhist texts were garbled and imperfect, particularly those of the Yogacara school, which most interested Xuanzang. Driven by a hunger to know exactly what the texts said, and perhaps also by a sense of adventure, Xuanzang travelled 10,000 miles, and spent about ten years in India. He studied with the great philosopher Silabhadra at Nalanda University in Bihar, and carried 657 sutras back with him.

China was then under the rule of the great emperor Taizong of the Tang dynasty, while much of northern and central India was under the rule of the great king Harshavardhana, who was a patron of Buddhism, although by then Buddhism in India was in decline. Xuanzang notes the many dilapidated and abandoned monasteries he found in the country, in contrast to the accounts of another visiting Chinese monk, Fa Xian, 200 years earlier.

Xuanzang's records of his travels provide an extraordinarily comprehensive account of western China, Central Asia, Afghanistan, the Gandharan regions and India in the seventh century, just before Islam became a dominant influence in some of these areas. On his

---

*   Xuanzang was earlier spelled as Hsuan Tsang or Hiuen Tsang. I have spelled his name according to the modern Pinyin system, adopted by China in 1958. It is pronounced 'Shwenzang'.

**   Though the exact dates are debatable, I have used the timeline suggested by scholars at the Chinese Academy of Social Sciences in Beijing.

return to China, Xuanzang set up his own, short-lived, school of Buddhist thought, and his greatest service to Buddhism in China was translating the texts he carried back from India. Many no longer exist in Sanskrit but are preserved in their Chinese translation.

We are lucky to also have a biography of Xuanzang, penned by a contemporary monk, the Shaman Hui Li. It is likely that the two spent much time discussing the travels and, despite his hagiographic bent, Hui Li's accounts are often more vivid than Xuanzang's own records.

Xuanzang's epic journey has become the stuff of legend in China and has inspired considerable literature. In the sixteenth century, Chinese author Wu Chengen created a splendid mythical journey based on Xuanzang's voyage—*Journey to the West*. Wu added a monkey king with magical powers and threw in demons and battles. The account is so popular that people in China today often confuse the fictional monk—a rather spineless, trembling creature protected by the heroic monkey—and the real Xuanzang.

To follow the monk's route to India, I set off from my home in Hong Kong in May 2000. That summer, I took the train across China and continued overland into Kyrgyzstan. From the capital, Bishkek, I flew to Tashkent, Uzbekistan, and then hired a car to take me south to the Afghan border. As it was still closed and I did not have a Pakistan visa, I returned to Tashkent, from where I flew to Delhi to begin retracing Xuanzang's journeys in India. From November to June 2001, I travelled around India by bus, train, car and occasionally by plane. When I finally got my visa to Pakistan in the summer of 2001, I took the bus across the Wagah border to Lahore and travelled through northern Pakistan by road. From there I went to Afghanistan in August 2001, through the Khyber Pass. My journey in Xuanzang's footsteps ended in Kabul, then still under Taliban rule, just a month before 9/11.

chapter one

The Road to India

AD 600.

One chilly morning deep in a village in China, a woman
gave birth as snowflakes fell over fallow fields and the river
Chen purled and looped. She sweated and pushed, screamed and
cursed under cotton quilts. Her fourth child came with crunched
eyes, bunched fists, slippery with blood. She named him Chen Yi.
Outside, they say, a phoenix flapped its wings and settled in a tree.
It dripped gold light from the tips of its feathers, shuffled along a
branch and twittered softly. *What is born must suffer and then die,
this is the law.*

When the time came, Buddhist monks knelt the child on the floor
to shave his head, and dark, silky hair fell in piles. They inducted
him as a novice and changed his name to Xuanzang.

Before he died, a journey took shape, a tale penned by the fragile
light of candles, a brush lifted, a wrist poised for the first stroke of
history. The story was one man's truth, about his travels to India in
search of scriptures, a journey as he chose to tell it, written in the
classical Chinese of the Tang dynasty.

Xuanzang's account was precise. It consisted of directions, the
number of days he walked, distances, crops, rivers, kings and customs.
He recorded information from the conversations he heard in monastic
corridors, from traders roughened by travel and accustomed to risk.

Ta Tang Xi You Ji, Xuanzang's *Records of the Western World
(written in) the Great Tang Dynasty*, was completed in AD 648 by
order of the Tang emperor Taizong. The Chinese tome was translated
into English by the Reverend Samuel Beal, professor of Chinese at

the University College London, and first published in 1884. It was an erudite work in several volumes. It had explanatory footnotes with cross-references to Greek historians and Sanskrit specialists.

So exact had the monk been in his directions, that archaeologists in each of the countries he traversed had used his pointers to fix and then dig up the old cities of the seventh century. As for historians seeking a picture of the Indian subcontinent in medieval times, it was a rare source of information. Between its pages lay the road to India.

80

I flipped through Xuanzang's records almost 1400 years later, and thought that the written word was a fragile truth. His records were meticulous, but there was a vastness left unsaid. There were spools of thought that fell through the cracks and were swallowed by time. I hungered to know if he ever lost sight of his training, if on empty mountain roads loneliness crept into the sides of his mind till he thought he was mad, if in foreign marketplaces he succumbed to desire or greed or temper.

I knew I stood on some concealed cusp. Each event in my life had led to this point, this collision with a monk and his memories. I was made in India, born where two rivers meet. There were mangoes in summer, the smell of fresh-boiled rice. I held these early years close and quiet, for the unspooling years scattered me from continent to continent. By the time I fumbled through thirty years, destiny had dropped me in six countries, drawn me through multiple languages, a confirmed expatriate child, a hopscotch chameleon. I moved from man to man, restless and solitary like the misplaced joker in a deck of cards, though it was a woman who told me, 'Your men are like your search for a country.'

I washed up in Hong Kong. In its mixed-up, cosmopolitan porridge I found a society of refugees and misfits and decided to stay. Along the way, China had ensnared me. I fell for it like a teenage girl falls for an older man. There was nothing it could not teach me. I drank it in, awed by its enormity, somehow at home. The small, patient movements of a street sweeper in those sleeve covers, hands rough and red on a Beijing winter morning; the creak of a bicycle down a back lane; the quilted army coats we wore, for they were cheap and held some imagined defiance or Maoist chic. I was a foreign student studying the language, but I was at the edge of a prolonged frenzy. Years later, on Hong Kong subways, my index finger still traced Chinese characters against my handbag. The language had first held me, my eyes caught in a web of brush-strokes.

And there was India, always India.

Swinging between countries, mine was a split life. My worlds never met. I eased in and out of cultures, switched tongues, I held together with string, tape and staples. Stuck in the space between one language and the next, lost among continents, unjoined dots. All of a sudden, I wanted to shut my eyes and rest. I wanted to go home.

Who else in this whole world? Who else was caught thus between India and China?

૪૭

AD 645, Chang An.

Xuanzang, Master of the Law, returned to China from his travels to India. It had taken him eighteen years. He was not quite an old man. Yet, his knees ached at the onset of winter. A whole generation had been born and had grown up in his absence. Eighteen years of voyage clung to him in a cloud, a silent but palpable aura of other worlds. He had trod the soil of faraway India.

His dreams plagued him. He saw the flash of a sand dune in barbarian deserts, the crossing of a mountain pass, a sunrise over the Ganga. His nights were filled with jarring shadows of dacoits, the mustard fields in northern India. And, most of all, he remembered the Buddhist holy places, where the Perfect One himself had walked. Once, Xuanzang had collapsed in a well of tears, unable to bear the nearness of the event and his own lack of perfection.

These days there were moments, before ink brushed paper, when Xuanzang sat with his face half in darkness and wondered who would understand. He had to force himself to trace the words on paper. When he closed his eyes he saw with another vision a rivulet in a village where a boy bent to poke the bed and dig for snails. Or a figure running, but away, so that he saw small heels kick up dust in a lane. He heard the child panting and, as if in sympathy, his own lungs tightened. Then the apparition vanished. The monk picked up his brush again, but then rested his chin on his hand and stared at the sky outside his cell window. The setting sun had turned it lilac, streaked with orange and pink and gold.

China had moved on, carried without resistance on the rollers of time, imperceptible up close. Only those who returned from long journeys saw. How changed the people from his past looked, at least those that remained. They were reminders of their youthful selves, but someone had pencilled in grey hair, drawn a flap of skin at a throat, shaded under eyes, traced lines on the sides of a mouth, painted sorrow over pupils. Did they mirror his own ageing?

He felt his way around the city like a blind man, groping for signs and textures vanished into memory. The city and he were like strangers meeting at a tea house, glancing up for a sign of recognition and finding none, staring back at their cups. This would be his curse, to lose something vital and be unable to explain what he had gained.

He came back to China a hero. They hailed him.

Or did they flock from curiosity? Did they come to his feet to bow and learn, glean wisdom from the dust on his hem, or to gape in secret at this quiet shaven man with the horizon in his eyes and the oddest gestures picked up from his Indian friends?

That head waggle. The monks of Chang An caught him scooping rice from a bowl with his fingers. Eyes flicked in surprised glances, but nothing was said in deference to his greatness.

India had drenched the monk, transformed him. Leaving India, he thought he had lost what he needed to breathe, he was caught between worlds, born of one space, imbued now with others. It came to him that he would be an outsider for the rest of his days.

There were lighter moments. He lifted chopsticks, dropped one through lack of practice. He smiled as he bent to pick it up. A child could do better.

He tested the cadences of his mother tongue. For years now he had dreamed, spoken, written in Sanskrit, and to hear Chinese again in the streets was like spring rain on a rooftop.

He drew comfort from his Buddhist doctrines, his mind sharpened and made edgy by daily reflection on death and emptiness. The monk had studied with the Indian masters, forged friendships.

'Silabhadra, my teacher.' Xuanzang's vision blurred.

∞

It had to have happened this way. I needed it to have happened this way. History had been a troublesome deficiency throughout my life. Of Indian history, I knew nothing. It is not on the syllabi of international schools in South-East Asia or American undergraduate colleges, nor can one find it in airline magazines.

In my dismembered state, I realized I would have to seek it myself. How did Indians know they were Indian? Their hearts swelled at the sight of the tricolour. They stood with their hands on their hearts and sang the national anthem with a tear at the corner of their eyes. They loved cricket. Most of all, they knew what had happened in their country in the years before they were born. For my Indianness, there was one single bit of evidence. Over the years, I had never relinquished the blue passport with the four lions stamped on it, hanging on to the document like a last bit of straw. History seemed the key.

At age thirty-one, I shook off the grime and found that when I looked in a mirror I no longer knew my eyes. They were underlined, undefined, my outlines smudged like an ink drawing left in the rain. There were things I had to do before I died a splintered sheet of glass.

An Indian woman with a China craze, a Chinese monk with an Indian obsession; we had the same schizophrenia, the monk and I. It seemed logical to take the same road. In this quest I would dig into the rubble of the past, sift through 1400 years and forage for the debris of the monk's journey. On that road between China and India, perhaps I could find a history that belonged to me, a past and a present. What was true? What was false? And what did it have to do with me? Is not history one woman's truth—as she chooses to tell it? I thought again of India, of a city where two rivers meet. But there was a third river, subterranean, hidden.

In the beginning, the desire was a persistent monotone at the back of my head, like a mosquito swooping on a summer night, an urgent need, not a conscious plan. Sometimes the explanation comes later for events that unfold now.

∞

Stumbling for clues to Xuanzang, picking up threads of submerged stories, I snatched time from the Hong Kong job and flew to Beijing. I was sniffing for the monk's trail, for my student days, for a road to India. That day in April, the poplars showed off tight, new shiny leaves. Through the haze of traffic fumes and dust blown in from western deserts, spring struggled. As it happened, there was a society in Beijing devoted to the study of Xuanzang.

'Why didn't you come to us before?' The Chinese scholars were stooped, white-haired.

'I came as soon as I knew you existed.'

Off a trafficked boulevard, Beijing turned on itself, vanished, leaving a lane with willow trees, a bicycle bell trill, a hint of coal dust. Huang Xinchuan and Sun Baogang, China's *éminences grise* of Indology, ushered me through plastic flaps that kept out April sandstorms. In a restaurant, by a window, we sipped jasmine tea in bowls.

'I remember India,' Sun said. 'The parrots in the trees. Hundreds of them.'

'Xuanzang is very important to China.' Huang looked stern. 'He came back from India to serve our country. He was a patriot.' *Aiguo.*

I explained the problem.

'We can help you,' Huang said.

He reached into his bag and handed over a photocopied sheaf. It was a timeline of the monk's life, a breakdown of his route to India, a list of places—their seventh-century names and their current ones.

I sipped the jasmine tea and felt its delicacy in my throat. I thought of my Hong Kong studio where at dusk I watered the dieffenbachia on the tiny balcony and at night watched the lights shine off the harbour water. The persistent hum of the mosquito at the back of my head grew stronger, like interference on a radio.

My hosts explained that kingdoms, even rivers, had swelled, shrunk and shifted after the monk went west. Cities had collapsed, left crumbs. The monk's journey now meant facing China's western deserts, broken-off Soviet republics, warring Muslim nations, one Himalayan kingdom and a great swing through India.

The scholars were persistent.

'Make sure you mention he was a philosopher and a great traveller.'

'Please add that he was an expert in causality, in logic. Also, don't forget, a geographer. And a skilled debater.'

The old Chinese men thought back on their days in India.

'To understand China you must see India's influence,' Huang said. 'Many, many Sanskrit roots and concepts have shaped us.'

'Xuanzang is the spine of China.' Sun leaned over the table and prodded his back to illustrate.

Outside, the wind bobbed red round lanterns strung along the street; their tassels whipped and swung. Huang rummaged once more in his bag for telephone numbers across China, contacts, handwritten with a fountain pen on sheets of paper saved from conferences.

'These people will assist you once you get there.' He paused. 'But beyond China's borders, we cannot help.'

Dusk settled. The tail end of winter carried a snapping wind. The two men waved goodbye and walked into the dark. Through a park, boys bent elbows and raced on roller skates. On an overhead pass, headlights swept by. I scrambled for certainty but found only phantoms, and one monk's words left for history to ponder. In these lay the faintest of beginnings. I realized a decision had been made without my knowledge.

When I returned to Hong Kong, I telephoned a storage company. I donated my dieffenbachia plant to a neighbour. I packed a flashlight, a few T-shirts, a jacket, a sun hat, a compass, maps, some medicines and a copy of Xuanzang's writings.

'When will you be back?' my boss asked.

'I'm not sure.'

The windows at the news agency where I worked framed the harbour. Across, a rash of flats leaned from hills. A phone rang and keyboards clattered. The water was a murky shade of jade. The horizon bled into the sea and a few ships floated forgotten. There were pale streaks where other boats had passed and this too was a beginning. I felt the twinge of passing thirty, and when I ran my hands through dark hair, underneath were streaks of grey, a first whiff of death.

How did one pack a life, shut a door and head west in the tracks of a monk? I watched, nervous, as the packers emptied my small flat and loaded the cartons onto a blue truck, for storage, at least for now.

chapter two

Journey to the West

It was a familiar rail hop from Hong Kong into mainland China, but the rest shivered in the unknown. It was May. I was flattened by the tearing sensations of leaving, the aches of departure and the fight with fear—there were so many fears, of the unknown, of the dark, of a stranger's squeaky black shoes. On the phone from Switzerland, my father said, 'At the banquet of this journey, you're the guest, not the cook.' Flap open your napkin, dab your mouth and enjoy, he meant. But I sobbed and wept like a little girl, struggling with the helplessness of leaving. What if something happened? What if I died? There was so much I did not know.

I was flattened too at leaving S., with his eyes like hazel marbles, the way he checked on me, point by point like a dive buddy. Have you packed? Maps. Rain gear. Train tickets. Passport. Traveller's cheques. Write to me. We had clung together through the years, on and off, across distances, on the phone. We had broken up and reconciled, we fought, we circled each other across time zones and datelines, more warriors than lovers. We were unable to acclimatize and remained addicted to each other.

'You didn't consult me about this,' he grumbled. He had flown into Hong Kong for work. In between meetings he helped with final arrangements, heaved plants out, carried my backpack to his hotel, waited as I handed the keys back to the landlord.

I conceded that I had acted alone.

'It's just that if I manage to do this, I can die happy.'

I did not mention the future. How could I? Besides, he was

Californian and he rollerbladed and, being a designer, liked shiny chrome buildings. He did not at all fit into my solemn search for the past.

The train pulled out of Hong Kong and rolled towards Guangzhou on the mainland. Outside, amidst the rice fields, a parade of grey brick skeletons—empty factories—glided by. Cantonese businessmen on the train bought cognac bottles from trolleys, paid with credit cards and consulted glittering watches.

I left Guangzhou, the Pearl River delta, and its preoccupations behind, to press north-west, to a village not far from Luoyang in Henan province, where one chilly morning in AD 600, a woman gave birth as snowflakes fell and the river Chen purled and looped.

The city of Luoyang sat south of the banks of the Yellow River. After flowing past Luoyang, the river swerved north for about 500 kilometres until it spilled into the Yellow Sea, into a vast bay sheltered on the east by the Korean Peninsula. Dynasty after dynasty had found the city an ideal location for a capital.

As the train to Luoyang rattled north, travellers fished for jars, dropped in tea leaves and began trips to the hot water boiler at the end of the carriage. They shook out face towels and hung them on rails, they peeled boiled thousand-year eggs and cracked melon seeds. A baby smiled up, toothless in its wrappings. The mother wiped her eyes. She mopped and coped and pulled out tissue after tissue as her infant beamed and tested the newness of things. The train intercom crackled. 'We are heading to Luoyang and we begin our life as travellers. Be clean, be orderly. Please.' Don't have small tragedies. But in our section of the train the mother wept and sighed.

'It's not convenient to travel with a baby.' She wiped her eyes again but her woes trickled out. *Bu fangbian.* Inconvenient.

She held the baby over a blue basin. Like all Chinese babies, it wore pants split at the crotch for easy excretion. My companions looked at me. I shrugged.

'Kids' poop doesn't smell,' a man from Luoyang said after a pause. But he moved to the window seat. The world stayed as it was. Nothing cracked, nothing shifted. I was on a train speeding through a China night, dreaming of nothing at all.

Tentatively, I began to savour it. I read Hui Li who said that
Xuanzang grew to be a serious boy who

> . . . did not mix with those of his own age, or spend time at market-
> gates. Although cymbals and drums, accompanied by singing,
> resounded through the public streets, and the girls and boys
> congregated in crowds to assist in the games, singing and shouting
> the while, he would not quit his home.[1]

When I got off the train at Luoyang and crossed the street to
check into a local hotel, it was as though I left an imprint in the air.
The town froze for a moment to register the arrival of a stranger with
a backpack. An averted glance, an open stare, a comment to a friend.
But then things shifted and settled, as though the place rearranged
itself to make room for one more person. China's smaller towns wear
a sleepy cloak, their streets are quieter, for more people use bicycles.
Luoyang dwellers sat on small pavement stools outside their shops or
at a restaurant, to relish the summer evenings. Their curiosity rose
like a physical need.

'Which is your country?' they called out.

Funny you should ask, I wanted to say. That's exactly what I
wonder all the time.

⁊

Around AD 547, more than five decades before Xuanzang was born,
Luoyang's graceful Buddhist monasteries lay deserted. The city's inner
and outer walls were ruined, palaces toppled and monasteries burnt
down. The walls were overgrown with vines after invasions and wars.
Only in the early years of the seventh century, after Xuanzang's
birth in the nearby village, did the ill-fated emperor Yang Di of the
Sui dynasty engage two million men to labour on a capital west of
the old ruins, creating the city to which the young Xuanzang arrived.

The monk might have learned the city's stories—how the Indian
monk Bodhiruci arrived in Luoyang in AD 508 and stayed at the
grand Yung-ning Monastery by order of the emperor, how he
translated thirty-nine texts including the *Lankavatara Sutra*, the *Lotus*

Sutra and the *Diamond Sutra*, along with many works by the brothers Asangha and Vasubandhu, the two scholars who founded the Yogacara school of Indian Buddhism.[2] The Yogacara school believed that everything we perceive is an illusion. Therefore, why be attached to material things? This freedom from attachment, the Buddha taught, was the key to release from rebirth and suffering.

Here in Luoyang, Xuanzang, though still very young, might have also heard for the first time how, nearly half a century earlier, Emperor Wu of the Liang dynasty (AD 502–49) had asked Paramartha, a Brahmin from western India, to visit his court. Perhaps with growing excitement he heard that in the years AD 563 to 567 this Indian monk had managed to translate a key Mahayana Buddhist text of the Yogacara school, the *Mahayanasamgraha*, written by Asangha in the fourth century and annotated by his brother, the great Buddhist philosopher Vasubandhu. [3]

એ૦

I slept soundly at the small hotel not far from the railway station. I was reassured, as I would be at every stop in China, by the multitude of *fuwuyuan* at the front desk, on each floor. These were women in matching pastel pants and cotton jackets who held bunches of room keys, refilled thermoses with hot water, swept the rooms, brought blankets. They were present all the time and missed nothing. It was inbuilt security. In case they hesitated, seeing my foreign passport, for in more remote parts of China the old habit of ghettoizing foreigners in expensive hotels still lingers, I pulled out my Hong Kong identity card and reminded them that Britain had handed Hong Kong back to China in 1997. Therefore, I pointed out, I was a resident of China.

China was familiar territory from my student days. I was pleased to see I still knew how to navigate its streets. Small things I had forgotten about China leapt out, the way split-second expressions do on an old friend's face. A whiff of garlic, the silences between traffic noise, a child's eyes. I rolled the language in my mouth and tested the weight of words.

Xu Jinxing arrived the next morning to take me to Xuanzang's village. Professor Huang had telephoned from Beijing and Xu had been expecting me. We went south from Luoyang that dusty May morning, a film of sand flying up from China's loess plateau. Acacia trees and fa guo wu tong trees lined the city roads. The base of gritty cliffs still showed dark mouths, cave-dwellings dug out many moons ago. I sat in the back seat of the navy-blue Volkswagen Santana used by local cadres. Liu, our chauffeur, drove with verve, flicked on the siren when it suited him and leaned on the horn to swerve past peasants on donkey carts.

There was a hint of heat about to bloom. On the roadsides peasants in blue coats unloaded cabbage, and wheat fields flew by. The crop here would be ready in two weeks, Xu said from the front seat. We crossed the Luo River, a sluggish thing with mudbanks in the middle. It waved a lazy turn and brought us to the Xuanzang Industrial Area, off Xuanzang Main Road. More swirls of dust churned under wheels. In Goushi county, the road shrank to a street through a marketplace, with piles of bricks and sand for construction. Through a track we bounced into the Chen River village to meet Xuanzang's descendants. The river that purled and looped, it turned out, had dried up.

Chen Zhiwei was the forty-eighth generation of the Chen family, descended from the oldest brother of the Master of the Law. The youth was a very grand nephew, a skein of blood and genes that trickled into a different China, a flesh link to Xuanzang, to the journey that loomed around the corner.

Chen Zhiwei stared hard at his feet. His white shirt hung from bony shoulders and from his belt a bunch of keys dangled. Did he feel the pressure of representing his illustrious Buddhist uncle? In the quiet of the village, a breeze ruffled celadon wheat stalks. A radio somewhere spilled Mandarin pop music—*Tebie de ai gei tebie de ni.*

'*Ni hao,*' I said and put out my hand.

He shook it, a shy, limp exchange. '*Ni hao.*'

Together, Chen Zhiwei and I stepped through fields to the graves in which Xuanzang's mother and father lay. They had died in AD 604 and 609 respectively, when Xuanzang was still a boy. They were buried side by side opposite the family home tucked away in a sheltered loess basin with steps cut into the hills for farming. The grave was a mound of earth, surrounded by wheat stalks over which paper-white butterflies flitted. It was a landscape cremated of colour, reduced to a wash of brown and olive, crowned by a sometimes blue sky. A brief wind rustled the grass on the graves of Xuanzang's parents.

There was scant information on the monk's mother. She was thought to have been Buddhist, a counterpart to his Confucian father. Such are history's holes. Perhaps she had held her son on her knee as she uttered prayers. He watched her mutter charms and heard her ghost stories and grew up to believe them. Years later, when he wrote his *Records*, he filled the spaces between level-headed geographical reports with tales of dragons living at the bottom of lakes, shadows that spoke, monsters that attacked travellers made defenceless by fatigue and hunger.

At noon, China stopped for lunch. The heat roared, flattening the outlines of the fields. We sat in a side room at a restaurant by a county road and ate a bowl each of rice noodles with spikes of cucumber doused in vinegar, with chunks of garlic and a dab of chilli sauce. We picked at spicy tofu bits and at steamed eggplant lathered in garlic. In Xuanzang's honour, I was making a brave attempt to be vegetarian. Liu, the driver, could not help ordering a plate of crisp broiled pork chops and a bottle of beer. He tucked in, as my guide explained how Xuanzang might have coped with going west.

'Many monks in Chang An knew tongues of Western lands, many monasteries in the capital had monks from those areas. Monks came and studied Chinese so they could speak their own language as well as Chinese,' Xu said. 'When the foreign monks went back, they acted as interpreters. Relations were very close between Tang-dynasty China and those areas.'

Later that afternoon, we drove to a garden partitioned with hedges. It sat off National Highway 207. In the middle, a pagoda with cracked sides leaned, and at the back was a heap of earth overgrown with stalks of grass where sparrows hopped.

'Xuanzang's clothes and food bowl are buried here,' Xu Jinxing explained. 'Parts of Xuanzang himself were buried in Taiwan, Japan and Xian.'

It was only later, when I began to discover the story of the Buddha, that I realized his relics had been divided in the manner of the Buddha himself.

Goods trucks rattled past, horns blaring, on the way south to Guangzhou. In the garden the birds sang. Rose and peony bushes grew within the borders of the hedges, and one shrub of nine-*li*-fragrance flowers.

'Because you can smell them nine *li* away,' Xu said.

The 1980s were hard times for much of China. Inflation soared. Goushi county, off the beaten track, demanded that the government promote the area's sole point of fame, Xuanzang's birthplace, to attract tourists. The provincial administration scraped together funds and built a Xuanzang theme park. My guides ushered me into a hall with onion domes. It was a toy once begged for, now forgotten in the dust. The halls were filled with wooden and plastic life-size dolls and a stage set with neon lighting and creaky mechanics.

I felt a little dizzy from lunch, from garlic, from the afternoon heat.

We walked through dark corridors sprayed with concrete to emulate rocks, and watched scenes of Xuanzang's birth. The kneeling figure of a boy monk stood in the shadows. Another monk leaned over him to shave his head, a spooky clacking of wooden clappers spilled from hidden speakers and the mechanical arm swung back and forth, back and forth.

Outside the theme park, two old women sold fizzy orange drinks. We sat on stools under a tree.

'Oh, so you're from the place where Xuanzang went to get the scriptures,' one said.

'Amazing.' They looked me up and down. 'What are you doing here?'

෨

At night, in my hotel room, under a neon light, I consulted Hui Li. We all paint the picture we need, and the monk's biographer was prone to panegyric. Hui Li of the glittering eyes would not be stopped.

This story was his destiny. He needed miracles and applause. He wrote:

> By hearing a book only once, [Xuanzang] understood it thoroughly,
> and after a second reading he needed no further instructions, but
> remembered it throughout.[4]

Yes, the monk was brilliant, blessed with a blade-like memory. He
loved the texts, the arcane discussions of non-being. They seemed
important, the void in his childish heart filled by the discussion of
emptiness.

But I was possessed with doubt, unable to keep to the text. In my
unruly mind, other scenes kept leaping up—a little boy, not yet a
monk, orphaned at a young age, bewildered at his loss. The child's
older brother had already left the village for the big city nearby and
entered a monastery. What if he followed in his brother's footsteps?
It would be the sole choice open to him. Perhaps as a novice in
Luoyang, following his brother around the monastery, Xuanzang
heard of the White Horse Temple and its legends, felt them tugging
him towards India, sending a shiver through him as he pondered the
very first journey to the west.

One night, maybe during kitchen duty at the monastery in Luoyang,
as the youth sat chopping vegetables, an older monk told him the
story of how Buddhism came to China, how Emperor Han Mingdi,
around AD 68, dreamed a gossamer dream and saw a figure in a
distant land speaking words of luminous wisdom, how Chinese
emissaries were sent to Central Asia to investigate, how they packed
the scriptures into panniers, tightened the saddles of white horses and
returned to Luoyang, how the emperor built China's first Buddhist
monastery and set it with the Mang Mountains to the north, facing
the Luo River to the south, and called it the White Horse Temple.

Maybe the older monk explained that from then on Buddhist texts
were translated into Chinese in increasing numbers, with varying
degrees of accuracy and success, while Confucian China looked on
in consternation. Buddhism was a disturbing idea. It encouraged young
people to leave their families and join bands of roving monks. Filial
piety destroyed! And if the basic family unit was under threat, could
the breakdown of civil society be far behind?

Xuanzang might have learned then too how Central Asian monks, and some Indian ones, were travelling back and forth, bringing Buddhist texts with them to China's courts, translating them as best as they could into Chinese, like Kumarajiva, the famous half-Indian, half-Chinese monk who in the fifth century translated volumes of Buddhist texts.

Slowly, the youthful monk may have come to realize that although translation centres churned out Chinese versions of Sanskrit texts, because of the vast difference between the languages and ways of thinking, it was a tedious, erratic process. New words had to be invented for concepts that had no name in Chinese.

He must have learned that in his day and age, hundreds of translations existed of a variety of texts. Nobody agreed on which one was the most authoritative. The Buddhist Church in China had split into a number of factions that disagreed on doctrine.

৪৩

In Luoyang, with some help from Xu, who scribbled a name on a piece of paper and handed it to me, I stood at the White Horse Temple's side entrance. The nuns were busy with a fasting ceremony, but sent me to the main temple which had accommodation for visitors.

I found myself sharing a dormitory room with three elderly village women and a nun from Nanyang. Perhaps somewhere in these temple grounds lay hints to another seventh-century cloister that once stood nearby, the one in which Xuanzang spent his younger days. I doubted that the routines of Buddhist monasteries had changed much over the centuries.

Just after 4 a.m., I pushed sleep from my eyes as voices rose and swirled around the beams and walls at the White Horse Temple and a full moon set on the other side of the sky. The clapper sounded single beats, monks filed in adjusting their robes. Senior monks wore yellow silk, sleeves that dangled almost to the ground, a dark brown cloth pulled under a right arm and fastened with a loop above the left breast. They shaved their heads and some had burnt spots on their scalps, jabbing raw skin with lit incense sticks. It was part of an induction ceremony.

We walked to the central prayer hall in measured steps and ordered ranks. The nuns followed, then the laity. Other monks lined up and began an arioso chant. One struck a bell for a thick dull sound and, on the other side of the prayer hall, another hammered a vast drum for a low, slow growl. The chanting broke off and changed rhythm. A novice yawned. Another picked his nose. The day lightened. When we filed outside, the monks sang *Na-mah A-mi-to-fo*, a mellifluousness filtered around the courtyard trees in the grey morning. It was too early for birds and cool enough for goosebumps. Incense, candles flickered, we marched around the yard and then back into the hall to circumambulate the big Buddha.

He was Avalokiteshvara, the lord who regards the cries of the world. Indian Buddhism was stern, cerebral stuff, but ordinary housewives in China needed something more accessible, somewhere to turn to when their husbands beat them, when they couldn't conceive, when the rice got burnt, when their children grew up to become drunks.

As the ancient, graceful *Lotus Sutra*, a key text of the Mahayana Buddhist faith says, Avalokiteshvara could help.

> And the terrors of the untoward and bad rebirths,
> In hells, in brute creation, and in Yama's kingdom,
> And the oppressions from birth, old age and sickness,
> Will slowly come to an end for living beings.[5]

The cult of Avalokiteshvara swelled and spread in China after the seventh century. To pull him closer to earth, to reach for a more comfortable figure, the Chinese melded him into older Taoist and even older shamanist traditions. They made him female and called him Guanyin. Everybody needs the divine feminine. One form of Guanyin has a thousand arms. She is weaponed to the teeth, like the Indian goddess Kali. It was a startling resemblance. Was I imagining links where there were none? Or was I closer to home than I imagined?

The nun from Nanyang pulled a plastic gold medallion from her pocket and strung it on a red thread. She tied the ends together and reached up to loop it around my neck.

'Here, wear this. It will protect you on your journey.'

It was Guanyin, for good luck, and I kept it on.

At 6 a.m., the just-risen sun poured yellow light. A monk swept the flagstones, bus number 56 was parked outside the temple gates and the first tourists lined up.

Luoyang shimmered with history. Where were the hints to how Xuanzang spent his youthful days in this city? I looked for them in the present, seeking a foothold in his life, an entry into his journey.

The young Xuanzang must sometimes have sneaked away from Luoyang's Tsing-tu Monastery, surer now of the city, thirsty for novelty, and too impatient for permission. He must have missed a meditation session and crept off one day to see the riverside Buddhas, and received a beating as a result. It fitted. He would venture out of other city gates later and set off much further without authorization.

Longmen, or Dragon Gate, lay thirteen kilometres south of Luoyang. On the soft sandstone cliffs that rise from the Yi River, successive dynasties had carved Buddha after Buddha. I did not believe that a young Buddhist novice could have missed the spectacle, a few hours' walk from where he lived.

One morning, I boarded the bus from Luoyang's main terminal for the half-hour ride through low hills out to the caves. At a quarter to seven, the sun slanted across the Yi's waters and lit up the river bed. The light spilled over the caves, touched the recesses, brushed the knees of the Buddhas carved deep in the rock face.

The three Binyang caves were there that morning when Xuanzang skipped his meditation. The Middle Binyang Cave dated from the Northern Wei dynasty, around AD 500–53, and perhaps young Xuanzang knelt before one of the Buddhas and admired the elegant lines of the Wei sculptors, how the robe knotted at the chest, in flowing rippled folds at the bottom, showing off the sculptors' great skill and obsession with how cloth falls, the broad smile, the echoes (though I did not know it then) of India's Gupta art. The errant, youthful monk missed his step and stumbled, as his head was tilted back to take in Longmen's extraordinary creations. He pondered on a prince who gained enlightenment in a faraway land.

What on earth do they eat there?

A thought flew by that day, fleeting (so quick, he hardly knew it). What would it be like to see that place? He turned his head to follow its trail, thinking of somebody's name, somebody he had once met, a long time ago.

'There's nothing to see up there,' a little woman in a straw baseball cap called out to me, nodding towards the upper stairs near the end of the cliff. She was seventy-six and from Shanghai.

'It's all been destroyed, by the KMT, by the Cultural Revolution. Didn't you think the Buddha in the Feng Xian Cave looked like Empress Wu Zetian? Bits and pieces were taken by museums in Britain and the US. By the way, has India entered the WTO?' She stopped for a moment to draw breath.

'Do you know we have a monk who went to India?'

Yes, I said. I had heard.

ॐ

There were tough times ahead for the monk growing up. He was older now, his voice had broken. He could meditate for hours without interruption and yet, he found in himself a dissatisfaction he could not name. He could see the weaknesses and inconsistencies in the texts. He whispered these things to his brother, in passing, as they lowered a bucket into the well, foreheads touching. His brother told him to keep his head down and practise his sutras.

But history was at work. Things would shatter soon around the young men. The Sui dynasty was lurching to an end, drowned by vast impractical public works and expensive wars that required higher and higher taxes.

Nine batches of rebellious forces licked their lips and edged in on a weakened Sui emperor. The duke of Tang, Li Yuan, governor of the city of Taiyanfu in Shaanxi province, began to move south along the river Fen, down towards Chang An, which the Tangs declared would be their capital. He was helped by his sons Li Jiancheng and Li Shimin[6] and, in a combination of near-misses and luck, the Tangs snatched Chang An. Yang Di, the last emperor of the Sui dynasty, was assassinated in AD 618 by his own guards.

The biographer Hui Li eloquently describes the political confusion, the robbers swarming through Chang An where Xuanzang and his brother first took refuge after fleeing Luoyang. Wild beasts roamed the river banks and the population, including the monastic body, fled, leaving the streets filled with bleached bones and the skeletons of burnt buildings. From Chang An the brothers fled to Sichuan like 'two horses from the Chen family'. There they found teachers from their old convent in Chengdu and stayed a few years.

That's where Xuanzang met the monk Tao-Chi. Tao-Chi, who had learned from Ching-Sung, who had studied at the feet of Fa-Tai, who had learned it straight from the drooping, dismayed mouth of the Indian monk Paramartha, whom the winds blew back to China's shores. Xuanzang and Tao-Chi read and talked, and dissected the texts and wondered at the mental acrobatics it required. Yogacara was unwieldy stuff in Sanskrit, gossamer folds of metaphysics parsed by the muscled minds of the brothers Asangha and Vasubandhu. In the *Mahayanasamgraha II*, the brothers sought to illustrate how the world was simply a construct of the mind. They used the example of shadows, of dreams, of the moon reflected in water, of magical creations, of mirages.

> One may ask, 'how can thought and mental acts arise without an object?' To remove this doubt, there is the comparison to a mirage . . . Here thought and mental acts correspond to the mirage, and the object to the water. When a mirage makes its appearance, no real water is there, and yet the notion of real water arises . . .[7]

Entranced by these notions Xuanzang stayed in Chengdu until AD 622, studying the *Mahayanasamgraha* and the *Abhidharmakosa*. But he wanted to find the major text, the *Yogacarabhumi Shastra*. Was consciousness pure or impure? Was the mind being pure or impure?

Xuanzang had certainly studied Paramartha's texts too, for those were the ones he sought out in India, in the original Sanskrit, and retranslated into Chinese, anxious for accuracy, enamoured of the Yogacara school.

The Indian origins of Xuanzang's beloved Yogacara tradition are lost. It is impossible to reconstruct with any precision the reasons why

Indian Buddhist texts dating from some time after the second century AD began to emphasize the problems of the nature of consciousness.[8]

Nevertheless, the idea that we imagine the universe troubled Xuanzang, raised urgent questions, as the Chinese translations disagreed with each other on the finer points. The monk was in search of nothing less than a perfect translation of the nature of enlightenment: What do we perceive that is real?

After Sichuan, Xuanzang wandered east, to Jiangsu and Henan. He preached at Buddhist establishments, studied with the current masters of the land. He picked at the words, honed in on cracks in the arguments that had been haphazardly translated. Hui Li said he gained fame for his ability to debate, tearing apart opponent after opponent.

Perhaps it was during those years that he acquired a taste for wandering. Travel eased the disquiet in his belly. When he walked at dawn, or rode on horses through back roads by a river, hitched rides on carts, some shroud fell away and he saw an approach to truth, a truth that no sutra described. On one level, it was a straightforward addiction to see what the next town brought, what lay behind a hillock up ahead, a breezy freedom into which his cares vanished and he felt something akin to bliss. There was a simplicity in putting one foot before the other. He began to yearn for a journey that did not end quite so soon, to breach his own limits.

In AD 625, Xuanzang returned to Chang An. He found room at the Mahabodhi Monastery and settled there with his meagre possessions. The very next year, AD 626, the duke of Tang's son Li Shimin ambushed his brothers outside the city's north gate. His supporters displayed their severed heads from the wall. A few weeks later, Li Shimin made his father abdicate.[9] He was the new Tang emperor, Tang Taizong. The unrest in China ebbed, and in the birth pains of the Tang dynasty lay the seeds of China's golden age.

The city's monasteries were abuzz with the news, monks gathered in courtyards with bent heads and discussed in whispers whether Taizong would favour Buddhists, despite the Tang clan's Taoist lineage. Xuanzang fiddled with rosary beads. He was restless. The city's monks irritated him, with their scheming and obsession with the Imperial courts.

When he acknowledged it, he realized it had always been there, waiting to be perceived. He could say it out loud now, the thought that lived between one breath and the next, the knowledge that had coursed through his veins all these years. Now he could voice it, couched in exemplary motives, pointing at precedence. Hui Li scribbled it down, the way Xuanzang told it:

> 'Fa-hien and Chi-yen, the first men of their age, were both able to search after the Law for the guidance and profit of the people; should I not aim to preserve their noble example so that their blameless character may not be lost to posterity?'[10]

'I will translate the *Yogacarabhumi*. I will have to, however, get it from the source.'

There. He'd said it. Not yet pronounced the word 'India'; it was too far, it was too big, too much like death. It meant a very long tramp, to see if it was true that everything is false. But it came to him that a decision had been made without his knowledge.

§

I scrambled to pack my bag and follow the monk to Chang An—now called Xian—before the story surged ahead of me. For the brief four-hour journey towards Xian, the train headed west, up the Yellow River, crossing from Henan into Shaanxi province. I would see what was left of the Tang capital, pinpoint the start of the monk's journey, and its end too; and somehow begin to find my own way home.

The fertile arc of land in southern Shaanxi is known as Guangzhong. Here, the Jing River meets the Wei River. In the east rises Mount Taihua and in the south the Zhongnan Mountains guard the region. Because of its strategic location, no fewer than thirteen dynasties chose to build their capital here, the first one in the eleventh century BC.[11] The city of Chang An rose and fell again and again, but its Han dynasty avatar, between 202 BC and AD 8, became the prototype for later emperors. The Han adviser Zhang Liang strode through the elevated plain known as Dragon's Head and pronounced it a fine place for a capital, shielded by nature 'like metal walls of a thousand *li*'.[12]

It was from here that Xuanzang would leave on his journey, and where he would return, a triumphant hero.

ᔡ

Xian's streets were crammed with bicycles and taxis and buses. The great Sui and Tang capital had become a hot spot for China's new Internet giants, their banner advertisements hung across avenues. By the old bell tower at the crossroads lay a beggar with a bump on his back, rolling on his stomach on the pavement. He balanced on a small contraption, a wooden platform with wheels, pulling himself inch by inch. There was the wall, the inner city palace wall which made my heart leap with its nonchalant presence, a thick slap across the road, heavy with age and stories.

Under its archways, cars and buses honked and swerved. There were steps to climb the wall and look out at the moat surrounding the Forbidden City, for the Tang emperors, like all emperors, preferred to keep their distance. At night, fairy lights outlined its crenulated boundaries. The wall was broad enough for a dozen men to march abreast above the city. Somebody had set up loudspeakers and Chinese couples waltzed in the semi-darkness, as though it was the most natural thing to waltz on a wall fourteen centuries old.

A string of lights showed up the eaves of the guardhouses that punctuated the wall's stolid lengths. In the strip of garden between the base and the moat, there was an entertainment ground. I leaned between the notches, where archers once aimed their weapons, and looked down upon a Chinese opera solo performance, a man trilling into a wincing microphone. There were bright bulbs, loudspeakers. Tables were set up for drinks, and hawkers sold hand fans.

ᔡ

What an injection of adrenalin Chang An must have given the monk as he wandered amongst the crowds. Did he flatten himself against a wall as a camel perhaps strolled by, eyes half-closed and mouth in a pout, on its back a posse of eight musicians and a woman standing to sing, her robes flowing? On rich tapestry in blue, gold and orange, they sat cross-legged, hair bound high on foreheads in topknots, facing outward, backs to each other. One played the flute, one a mandolin, a moustachioed fellow held a harp-like stringed instrument, another a conch, blowing into it with gusto. The camel swayed, the singer stood in the middle, and in a high flutey voice she sang of heroes and kings. Her dress swung with the camel's thudding pads.

I saw the ensemble, shrunken and frozen now in ceramic glaze, under a glass case in the Shaanxi History Museum.

Did the monk stare in the western marketplace at a man with eyes that protruded, a high nose, a beard and a smile from distant parts, a man closing a sweetheart deal on a cargo of silk, a merchant gesturing with his fingers and hand? Perhaps the young monk picked up from the dust a dropped silver coin, turned it over to examine it, the currency of the Persian Sassanian dynasty all the way from Iran, and the weight of it on his palm set his heart beating like a drum one wild.

Fa Xian, Sung Yun, Hui Sheng. He muttered the names of the monks who had been to India as he swept the yard in the monastery and then fingered his rosary in meditation.

ॐ

I was having trouble with my beginnings and endings. They knotted into skeins of wool, crossed and recrossed the lines of time and sequence. I began here and did not know where my end would be. I needed some sign from beyond death, some hint, some help. It seemed important to pin a point, hold a baton passed across the centuries from traveller to traveller, so that Xuanzang's resolve could seep through the years and guide my unsure, searching feet.

Sometimes beginnings happen in the middle, in a muddle. Two monks drove me to where Xuanzang's remains had been moved. And I found my start. I began at his graveside one heated day in May.

They had buried him in a courtyard, under a pagoda. It was an edifice of five levels, five angles of mud brick up on a hill, cocooned in the 'shush' of pine trees and the sound of cicadas. The monk and his journey to India lay furled beneath; the scent of a sense of him hovered, but faintish.

The Future Buddha carved in bas-relief looked south from the tower's belly and at the bottom sat a wooden door with nails and a box for donations. It held a few coins. A turtle dove called. The courtyard wall glowed blood-red. Flies buzzed and settled in the languid noon and a woman's voice floated from the grounds below. It was threshing time in Shaanxi. China's farmers stripped their fields, piles of wheat tinged with old gold sat by the roads.

There were three knotted-cloth rugs to kneel on before the Master of the Law. An incense-holder sat empty. It seemed an end of memory. The day held its breath. I listened for an omen but none came, I had to make do with the sigh of bamboo groves, the written and unwritten things that tumbled Xuanzang to India and back. This monk, this pile of bones under a tower. He was just dust.

What drifted in his eyes when he paused and looked up at the seventh-century sky?

I had argued with the two monks who escorted me. It was not a good start. They were sulking behind the pagoda, holding sotto voce discussions in the local Shaanxi dialect.

'Maybe one can imagine what went through Xuanzang's mind,' I responded to a query, without thinking. It was silly. I knew quite well that the Chinese these days are attached to their heroes and dislike modern interpretations.

'What do you mean "imagine"?' the younger monk said. I could tell he was feeling less friendly. 'Everything is written.'

'Yes, but maybe things happened, maybe the monk felt things he did not write.'

'*Bu keneng*,' the monk muttered. Not possible. 'Everything is written.'

I dropped the discussion, but the air stayed prickly and they glared at me throughout the meal with the monastery's abbot, Chang Ming.

The old monk moved slowly and looked at the world through watery eyes. He was inducted in 1937 and had tended Xuanzang's grave for forty years. The attendant monks stopped glaring long enough to translate the abbot's dialect into Mandarin.

'Xuanzang wanted a quiet place for his burial. So the emperor Gao Zong had his remains moved here in 669,' he said.

On the road back from the Xingjiao Temple, I drank in the sight of wheat being harvested. A hand-held threshing machine rolled across the field, sliced the stalks off in a spray. On the road, two women had spread a carpet of grain. We drove right over the bounty and raised a dust of chaff. From behind the clouds, the sun came out; dogs played in the market, a straw hat tilted.

There was the crunch of car wheels as we drove over patches of grain. Dusk fell quickly now, the sounds of a day crumpling into night.

ಬಿ

Xuanzang raised his head. The sun had set and crickets conquered the cool night. The bamboo groves rustled outside. He walked to the well, pulled up a bucket of water and splashed some over his face. He drank, taking care not to touch the edge of the bowl to his lips. Indian habits. After he returned from India, he worked for almost twenty years, translating the Sanskrit sutras into Chinese. It eased the confusion in him, of being doubly homesick, for a China that existed in his past and for an India which he could never reach again and which had transformed him.

He was head of the capital's most famous monastery, guiding 300 monks and priests. But the traffic tired him, the visitors, the administration. He held his head and longed for the moments when he could return to the translating, longed for the day's work to be over so he could retire to his cell and meditate and, for the skimmed, hollow moments before sleep, think of India.

ಬಿ

The Wild Goose Pagoda, built to store the scriptures Xuanzang brought from India, was now run by the Abbot Zeng Qin. The head monk was busy when I went to see him, but he ushered me to a seat and asked for tea to be sent in. He wore the customary grey tunic, the calf-high binding of cloth shoes and he sat at a large desk. The Abbot Zeng Qin signalled to an attendant and signed a cheque for a large amount of yuan. Renovations were in progress.

'So, you're from India,' he said. 'You're most welcome. We get many visitors. I have accompanied the king of Nepal.'

'I'm an ordinary traveller,' I said.

'Sometimes that's more interesting,' the abbot replied.

We sipped tea and talked.

He pressed upon me the Chinese copy of Xuanzang's records, in fine calligraphy. But it ran into several volumes and would not fit in my backpack. I ran my hands over the package with great regret, for I could not accept it.

Visitors to the Wild Goose Pagoda compound were still flooding in. There were groups from China, Japan, Germany, America. At the main entrance there was a motley crew of worshippers; one woman brought a bag of incense wrapped in plastic, but she tried to set the entire bag alight from the wrong end.

The tower used to be five floors, built Indian-style. Up in the structure sat a stone carving of the Buddha's footprints. There were chisel marks on the pads of his big toes—a conch, two fish, a trident. A chakra.

I mingled with others to walk the narrow steps up to each floor, slowing behind a group of American high-school students jostling each other.

'Wanna cigarette?' a lanky youth with baggy shorts and a crew cut offered his classmate, hopeful.

'Just breathe the damn air,' the girl snapped.

A thick, soupy haze hung over Xian, a cocktail of dust and pollution. After days of heat, the city had a blowy, overcast day. The taxi driver said rain was forecast. Wind blew across Xian, clouds scudded around the sky, but there was not a drop of water. Still, the heat eased.

A man wheeled his bicycle, its back hung with a garland of garlic. I dodged him, flagged a taxi and went to see Wang Yarong, a specialist on Tang dynasty Buddhism. His office was room number 404, near the back stairs of the Shaanxi Academy of Social Sciences. There were shelves piled high with books on the Tang dynasty. Beyond the wooden door, his desk was placed on blocks to suit his height. He was a thin man, he stooped, he wore large glasses and smiled a quick smile.

There were two leather chairs with wooden arms, a thermos for hot water. Thin green curtains hung from windows nobody had dusted.

Empty inkpots sat in a metal tray. There is something instantly recognizable about a Chinese scholar and his surroundings—a dishevelled look, the ink-stained fingers, the tea leaves floating in hot water in an old coffee jar. It reminded me of my student days in China and I relaxed into the comfort of it.

'Xuanzang was very clever,' he said, as we slipped into a discussion of the monk. 'He was a part of society, his relationships were important, he established relationships for his *yuan zi*, principles. And in this process he was very clever. Xuanzang knew very clearly what Taizong was all about. Taizong understood Xuanzang. They were two heroes; it was a treaty between heroes.'

And smack in the middle of their lives one hero defied the other. It was a question of Turks, of closed borders, of injunctions against crossing abroad for safety reasons, for the emperor Taizong was having trouble with the Turks. In fact, it was the same old problem of Chinese foreign policy, the clash between the settled, farming Han and the horse-mounted nomads who wandered the Mongolian steppes and northern Central Asia. They raided and looted and pillaged. The Great Wall had been built centuries ago to defend against this. Emperor Tang Taizong had to be vigilant about those borders of his empire. Xuanzang was denied permission three times to venture into the troublesome regions so that, finally, he left in secret, like a thief.

Wang Yarong, thin and professorial, leaned over to my map of Xian and drew a small circle at the crossroads, the place where the old city wall used to be, the western gate that Xuanzang likely departed from. The city of Xian considered this to be the start of the Silk Road.

We shook hands. He waved, a lone figure standing behind the gates, arm raised.

Bus number 606 stopped after Labour Road, beyond Peach Garden Road, west of the Forbidden City. There was a small park with hedges and peony flowers. Buses ran on either side of the park, trucks roared. I checked the map and Wang's inked circle.

Here perhaps, at one time, within the city gates, were a plethora of eateries, places to water camels coming in from the western routes. The noise of bazaars, traders unloading packs, the exchange of foreign coins, the mumble of different languages, and if a Sogdian merchant from Samarkand turned into a lane, he could surely ask for a discreet madam and choose a girl for a few hours.

Now, there was a trading caravan sculpted in vast clumps of porous pink stone, a string of camels, horses and a couple of dogs that faced west, the setting sun glancing off the surface. Chunky socialist realism met the Tang dynasty. On the middle camel's hind legs, somebody had reached up to scribble in chalk two hearts, an arrow and a scrawl in English: 'I love you Zhang Lu.' Three teenagers pushed bicycles into the small park and leaned them against the base of the sculpture. They clambered up, dusting their hands. At the gate of the park a man sat on a chair, selling soft drinks. He wore a vest, his trousers were rolled up to his knees, he smoked a cigarette, listened to the radio on earphones.

Long-distance buses rolled by, leaving town with bags piled high on the roof, secured with nets and ropes. And on the other side of the road, other buses clattered into Xian, covered in dust from the counties.

There was the oddest sense of a threshold.

From here, one moonless autumn night in AD 627, a monk clutched his robes, hefted a pack. From here somewhere, he stole outside the gates and set his course westwards.

Yes, it was possible, I told myself. What I had undertaken was possible. I felt filthy. I looked it too, swathed in city dust. For a single moment I felt lonely and sad, but it passed, and that felt like a lesson of sorts. Things pass. Forget about it, I told myself. You have a long way to go.

chapter three

City of the Flying Horse

The train from Xian left central China, crossed the Yellow River at Lanzhou and pushed into the north-west, into bone-shaped Gansu province, tucked under Inner Mongolia. I would cross the Hexi corridor, the key trade link between central China and the deserts of the west.

In 121 BC, under the rule of the Western Han, this district was conquered by General Huo Qubing sent by Emperor Han Wu and was named Wuwei. A few hundred years later, between AD 220 and 280, it served as the capital of the Liang state and thus got its present name, Liangzhou. It was an important vassal state during the subsequent Sui, Tang, Song, Yuan, Ming and Qing dynasties.

I fought with my overloaded pack, heaving it onto buses and trains. Despite the lure of history, I had grown weary of modern Xian, more an assault than a city. The sheer numbers of people pressed at me, I felt claustrophobic and detected a slight wheeze in my lungs from the pollution.

On the train, I felt an essential rightness about being in this particular place at this particular time. I was glad to be rolling through flat landscapes, grey and dry, heading towards Liangzhou. I had longed for great empty distances and flat horizons. Flakes settled in the glass ball and a scene appeared in the middle, serene. That was my life.

The Yellow River was a natural boundary of sorts, separating the western regions from all that was Han and civilized. It was dark when the train crossed it. Beyond, the Zhuanglang River coursed at the foot of the thick western spur of the Qilian Mountains. The train tracks followed the river, until they broke free of the mountain range in the north and reached Liangzhou.

There were no natural boundaries to protect Liangzhou. To the north spread the plains of Inner Mongolia. A curve of the Great Wall swept down here in an attempt to shelter the city and stave off over-eager nomads. To the south rose the foothills of the Qilian Mountains.

I argued (was I to argue my way through China?) with the train attendants, who made it clear that no sleeper berths would be sold until passengers forked over five yuan for a magazine published by the army.

'It's all about Jiang Zemin and taking over Taiwan,' the attendant said.

'What if I don't buy the magazine?' I said, irritated by this transparent sales ruse and also by how everyone was playing along.

'It's patriotic,' she barked.

'I'm not Chinese, it's useless to me.'

A younger man shook his head. 'Foreigners should complain. If we complain, nobody listens. This is corruption.'

I remembered all of a sudden why I had wearied of China. It was not China at all that had so captured my imagination, it was some imagined construct, a place that I needed it to be. I only saw what I wanted to and ignored the rest. In my mind, I edited the world, airbrushed its faults and painted in the parts I would have preferred.

I refused to part with the paltry sum of five yuan for the magazine, which meant that I passed the night shifting and stretching on a seat, leaning against my bag, or putting my head against it to try and get some sleep. You bear the consequences of your actions.

By morning there were cornfields flying by outside, bottle-green in colour. We were still in a flat place and light spilled over the mountain, there was a peace of sorts in this empty landscape. The sun slid in from the window, a silence slid in. In its wake, slim poplar trees flashed past. There were more peasants in the rural vistas outside, the temperature had dropped. Along the low-stepped mountains, by the river, a flock of sheep picked their way, a herder followed behind.

An old man teased my story from me in accented Mandarin, little by little.

'Which country? Name?'

I scribbled notes, chewed on the back of my pen and tried to make sense of things. The oddest things about the world wormed their way into my days and I could not shake them off.

'You are writing a noodle soup, mixed-up, confused,' my travel companion commented. I looked up and caught the tinge of humour in his faded eyes.

Some thirty years ago, archaeologists unearthed from a tomb near Liangzhou the bronze sculpture of a horse in full gallop, poised on a swallow. It dated from the second century AD and was the city's current claim to fame. But of Xuanzang nothing specific was left.

∽

Hui Li held his hand up.

Wait, he begged the Master. He had run out of ink. He put the brush down, rubbed his aching hand against his thigh. Glued to the monk's narrative, he had written:

> Now Liang-Chow is the place of rendezvous for people dwelling to the West of the River: moreover merchants belonging to the borders of Si-Fan (Tibet) and countries to the left of the T'sung-Ling Mountains, all come and go to this place without hindrance.[1]

Xuanzang, Master of the Law, was enjoying this. It was more fun to dictate to the younger monk than write out his diaries for the emperor. He composed his expression into the gravitas befitting a senior monk who had been to India, though sometimes he wanted to yell at Hui Li, 'Go, leave this cursed city and its machinations, hit the road. It is better than any wine you will ever drink.'

He cleared his throat. Monks are not, he remembered, supposed to know about wine.

∽

The taxi driver at the station took me to a civilized hotel in Liangzhou called, naturally, the Flying Horse Hotel, but I woke up feeling weak, shaky, running a slight fever, fighting the low-grade burble in my lungs. I had no idea where to start looking for Xuanzang. I staggered to the post office, determined to lighten my absurdly full bag. Besides, I discovered this persistent affection for Chinese post offices, for their green symbol and for what happened within, the nosiness of who was sending what. I tried to sew a bag to mail off the extra stuff.

'Here, let me do it for you,' the woman at the counter said kindly. 'Can't even sew, aren't you a stupid melon.'

That's when I saw the Buddhist monk, in grey robes and cloth shoes and an almost shaven head. It was as though he had been waiting for me to show up.

'Which temple are you from?' I sidled up to ask.

'Luoshi Temple, down the road. There's a pagoda, you can see it from the road.'

Looking for Xuanzang had been easy in capital cities of yore like Xian and in Luoyang. The Chinese are obsessed with history and the monk had played an ample role in Xian. Here, in China's smaller towns, the records were less precise. I knew from Huang's timeline that Xuanzang had stopped in this city, but where? Where were the Buddhist monasteries, the pagodas? In the absence of any pointers, it made sense to look for Buddhist ruins that dated from the seventh century or before.

I walked right past the Luoshi Temple and had to be directed back. In a yard, off the road, there was a dusty opening, a low shack where the monks lived. Behind the yard, three attendants lazed on short stools by the stairs. One got up to unlock the door to the pagoda. And there it was, a twelve-storey structure, redone recently, but dating from AD 382. It was a quiet, mud-coloured tower, with a brick base and a pagoda, the ruins of what used to be an enormous temple complex. If it had survived until the seventh century, it may have been where Xuanzang stayed when he stopped here. I looked up at the pigeons flapping among the stones on the sixth level. They fluttered and circled and came to rest.

Along the boundary of the temple rose a wall with turrets. A guard dressed in a thick green coat and low cap paced, hugged a rifle and shifted once in a while. Gansu province was where China had set up many of her labour camps. This was the edge of the world, after all—if they escaped there would be nowhere to go.

'How many people are in there?' I asked the temple watchman.

'Around three hundred.'

'From Gansu?'

'From all over China.'

The guard turned to stare across the courtyards and walls and hitched up his rifle. I edged around the pagoda until it stood between him and me.

The Luoshi Temple, like any other self-respecting Buddhist organization, was trying to raise money for renovations. I had come to China in the wake of newly constructed temples smelling of fresh paint and bright with new colours. From a ghostlike vanished froth in the air, it seemed, the Buddhist faith—or what it had become in China— was thickening, solidifying and taking shape in these monks who wandered the cities, in the repainted temples and in unforgotten ceremonies.

A day or two later, in a quiet temple by the old bell tower to the north of the city, I climbed the wide steps, thrilling to the cast-iron bell with its scalloped edges like a narrow umbrella. There was a wide view of the city, bathed in the afternoon light, the hazy presence of the Qilian Mountains in the distance, and the sharp smell of fermenting wine at a nearby factory. In the main hall of the temple was a row of seated Buddhas wearing cloth cloaks. Candles flickered in rows in front, there were bundles of incense. A young woman knelt on the wooden bench, her head covered with a red cotton scarf.

I had stumbled on some sort of folk ritual.

The wise woman of the village, her head covered in a blue scarf, shook a smoky incense bundle over the girl's head. She did a stepped dance, backwards and forwards, chanting rhythmically, and waved thin sheets of paper inscribed with characters. She muttered about a *wa wa* (baby) and walked around the girl.

The mother, dressed in her best outfit, held a large plastic bag full of the giant swollen dumplings known as *mantou*s. Buns in the oven. It was a fertility offering, scrambled with leftover Buddhist practices, sprinkled with whatever worked for the moment. Outside, in the temple hall, they burned paper money and the mother tossed bits of the *mantou* into the fire.

'This girl, it's a problem trying to find her a husband,' they confided to me later.

The girl's expression revealed nothing, but something about her kneeling, the intensity of her bowed head, showed that it mattered.

As I was still trying to decipher the faded, handwritten legend on the wall, a nun wearing a black cap staggered up. She was unable to speak. 'Hhnnnnn, hnnnn, hhhhnnnn' was all she could say, but she grabbed the Guanyin amulet around my neck and stuck up her thumb. She settled on the bench outside to sleep.

Sonic jets were zooming overhead, as they had been all morning. I had woken to the sound of these jets, the rolling noises after they flew by, the sonic boom. I looked up and counted several deep-V wings, flat noses and boomerang tails heading west.

Once a garrison town, always a garrison town. The emperors of the East still had to cope with the minorities at the western frontiers; other alliances beckoned, as they always have. China's emperors still send armies westwards across vast territories, it is still a tenuous peace.

It struck me that I was, for a moment, free from all the dusty ties that bound me. Here, queueing up for the Internet at a small shop in Liangzhou, behind small-town schoolboys in China, I was anonymous, a body moving through space. Ties of love and friendship existed, but only in my head.

I closed my eyes from momentary dizziness. Reality and memory wobbled, inflated and tilted in this remoteness. I had not spoken English in days. My dark hair and Chinese language helped me blend with the crowd. People stared when it emerged I was different, but it took a few seconds. Often they refused to believe I was a foreigner, and argued.

A common language smashed the walls between worlds, blurred boundaries, turned the concept of foreignness on its head. I spoke a language and sensed sometimes the secret life of a people. In some small way it made me more like them. Or like them more.

There was an openness, a pleasant ease about Liangzhou that perhaps Xuanzang also felt. Something to do with the Qilian Mountains, the desert so close. This feeling of being at the edge of the world, as a Chinese poet put it. The city's south gate was being rebuilt: it was a stout base, broad enough for six horses to pass abreast through the arches, high enough for military banners held up.

଼ୠ

Somewhere within these walls, nearly 1400 years ago, the religious conference at Liangzhou was going well for Xuanzang. As the priest from the capital with something of a reputation, he was given a platform and attention. He was far enough from the Imperial guards to be more open about his purpose, although the emperor's stringent travel restrictions applied here too.

He bragged. A little bit.

'I'm going to seek the Law in the country of the Brahmans.'

They bowed and wished him well. They gave him packets of gold and silver and white horses. He accepted half. With the rest he had all the lamps of the convents lit, and distributed the money among the numerous religious establishments. Word reached Li Daliang, the governor of Liangzhou.

Li Daliang made inquiries at the monasteries and found the Master of the Law without much difficulty. He summoned the monk.

'I wish to go to the west to seek the Law,' Xuanzang told him.

'I'm afraid, sir, that I cannot let you do that. Please return to the capital where you belong. The road is dangerous, the Imperial mandate is strict. This is not wise.'

Xuanzang bowed, but said no more.

Li Daliang shook his head, and took up the brush that rested on the table. He felt as if the air had shifted, that something had flitted past but he had missed it. Something about the monk's flinty eyes.

Later that night, two muffled figures escorted Xuanzang away from Liangzhou and its dangers. Hwui-Lin and Taou-Ching were disciples of Hwui-Wei, a monk who admired Xuanzang. The trio hid by day in wilder mountain regions where they would not encounter armed mounted patrols; at most they might bump into a goatherd or two. They travelled by night, kept to smaller roads and skirted dwellings where lamplights flickered. In due course they arrived at the garrison town of Kwa-chow, at the western edge of modern Gansu province.

chapter four

The Jade Gates

On a train between Liangzhou and Anxi, on the western tip of Gansu province, I watched relentless, flat desert shrubland fly by, broken by tufts of dusty green, and in the distance snaked the Qilian Mountains, the same barren range.

The woman in front of me ate non-stop, snacked on a sort of sticky dried vegetable she took out of a plastic packet. She pulled chunks off with her teeth and ate with her mouth open, making loud smacking noises. The train was quite empty.

There was nothing outside either, no villages, no cultivation, just the desert, deserted. Behind a hillock spread a thick, brief smear of velvet. Green slashes, white poplars and phoenix trees flashed by, and then a sudden swatch of emerald. Some thought yawned and stretched and vanished into the past. A goods train clattered by.

The family seated across seemed content and at peace. The little girl was bright and chirpy and played cards with her father, a placid fatty who plainly loved his daughter.

Another goods train crashed past, one carriage laden with net sacks full of potatoes. To the north spread the Badain Jaran desert and to the south, the foothills of the Qilian Mountains. There were sand dunes, barren dust whirling up. Just then the Qilian Mountains got higher, the peaks now covered with snow, and at the bottom the river edged on.

Train 96 was the Beijing–Urumqi line. The staff, at least in this carriage, took great pride in its cleanliness. An attendant tenderly swept the floor with a damp mop and straightened a towel hanging askew.

The fatty across the aisle commented, 'But you just cleaned.'

'Still have to clean.' The attendant was a burly fellow, unusual in a Chinese man. He had a gentle face. A policewoman who stepped on for an inspection ordered a passenger to straighten a bunch of scallions he had tossed on the luggage rack.

The train pushed west. A thick mist trickled over the mountain tops, a flank curved and dusted with snow. I could not tire of this spectacular scenery. I imagined Xuanzang here, going from stop to stop. He walked this very path, at the foothills of the Qilian Mountains, hiding by day and walking by night, by moonlight. What happened on cloudy nights? At Jia Yu Guan floated the last bit of the Great Wall, its western crumbling edges. After this, there was nothing. Just the setting sun, sandy tones, and fear.

The unknown.

China was torn apart by the desert. There were mountains of grey rock streaked with red, a sudden turquoise lake by this grey-grim outcrop and not a tree in sight. The bitter paysage unrolled and in the desert, like inadequate insects, trucks buzzed through, back and forth, miniaturized. A wind bowed all the poplars west, as though pointing the way.

૪૭

By the time Xuanzang and his two companions arrived in Kwa-chow, news had travelled by word of mouth and reached the governor, To-Kiu. He was delighted. After the three travellers had washed and eaten, To-Kiu provided Xuanzang with provisions.

'You have travelled a long way.'

'This is just the beginning.' The monk smiled. The last leg of the journey had been exhausting, the monk's horse had died. He was tanned already, his feet calloused, his muscles firmer from carrying his pack.

'What is the road I should take from here?'

To-Kiu took a willow stick and traced the route in the sand.

'Roughly fifty *li* north of here you will come to the river Hu-lu. The lower part is wide, upstream is narrower. The water is rough and suddenly deep, so it's difficult for boats.'

The two disciples glanced at each other.

To-Kiu reached further, absorbed in his drawing.

'On the upper part there is the Jade Gate barrier. You'll have to pass by it, it is the key to the western frontiers. North-west, beyond the barrier, there are five signal towers. Army officers live in each one. They are 100 *li* apart, and in between there is nothing, no water, no grass.'

To-Kiu paused as he measured equal spaces between the watch-towers, one pace, one pace, one pace. A circle for each watchtower.

'Here. Beyond is the desert of Mo-Kia-Yen.' He drew diagonal lines to indicate sand.

He looked up to see dismay on the faces before him. One of the two disciples suddenly remembered urgent business in Liangzhou and left the very next day. The other stayed on, but looked so unhappy that eventually Xuanzang sent him off too.

The monk's courage faltered. Late at night, he sat with his head in his hands and wondered if he was making a terrible mistake. He sat with his rosary and meditated and then thought about life in the capital. It repulsed him still. He could not go back, but he was terrified of going forward. It paralysed him.

Another month went by. There were spies around. Would he leave on a skinny roan horse, as a fortune teller in Xian had forecast?

∽

Li Qunyuan, at the provincial museum in Anxi, was enthusiastic. 'Xuanzang, why he's famous all over the world! When he came through Anxi, in October 629, it was as though Clinton himself were here!'

Li Qunyuan explained how Xuanzang met Duguda, an inveterate horseman, a Mongolian who showed the monk how to muffle the collar of the horse and wrap the hooves with bunches of fresh grass so they wouldn't clink against stones. I liked the way Li told stories. He got a faraway look and spoke with such certainty, as if he had seen it with his own eyes.

I was not familiar with this version of the story and listened with interest. Was it real, or just another example of how locals expand on history to include themselves and the rhythm of their days? Certainly it was plausible. This area was so close to Mongolia, and horsemen abounded.

'They carried a type of dry flour on their journey,' he said. 'You just add water for a sort of paste. They had goatskin to carry water and grass for the horse.'

The five watchtowers were the Muxu Feng, the Baidun Zi, the Han dynasty Feng, the Da Quan Feng and the Leng Quan Yi Feng.

'That last one is at the 3384-kilometre mark of the National Highway 312,' he said. 'Keep an eye out for it. Between Leng Quan Yi and Hami, there was no water, there were just the bones of people . . .'

I stared at him, absorbed in his tale, not wanting him to stop.

Nie Hua drove a tough bargain, a small car, and did not brake for potholes or goats. She was one of Anxi's five women taxi drivers and we settled on a price the next morning for the ride to Suoyang Cheng, which in the Tang dynasty was called Kwa-chow. It was 160 kilometres there and back from modern-day Anxi city. I had checked into a sparse hotel right by the bus station in this straggly half-hearted town that was still just an overgrown village.

'Before, this used to be all grassy, now it's too hot, it's all gone,' she explained. We were bouncing along a pitted road. There were wide spaces on either side, a thin fuzz of green and clumps of camel grass. The horizon was an uneasy edge, clouds hung low.

We were heading towards the final boundary of the Tang empire. Xuanzang spent anxious days somewhere here before crossing the desert into barbarian lands beyond Imperial jurisdiction.

'Last year all the cotton froze to death,' Nie Hua muttered, pressing the accelerator. 'Yesterday, the *sabo* blew in from the east. They had just planted cotton and a whole lot was destroyed, the wind split open melons.'

'Really?' I said. She was making me nervous.

Yesterday, the air had been tight with urgency. The innkeepers and shopkeepers rattled their shutters down, running with their coats around them, as the dust storm built at the lower edge of the sky and tents of sand gusted across the road. I just made it back to my hotel, diving in through the plastic flaps, the steel doors banging closed behind me, everywhere, one after the other. I was coated with the light brown Gobi desert. The girls with the keys, bunches of them, offered to fill the bathtub, haul steel cans filled with steaming water from the central heater down the corridors. They tipped the hot water into the bathtub.

Outside, the wind had jostled and chided; somewhere, something crashed. The bathroom had no electricity and the flush pulled with a twig tied to a string, but sitting in scalding water in the dark was akin to heaven.

How far away that comfort felt, strapped into this small red taxi, bumping along. The road unpeeled before us, a thin grey triangle with its apex in the sky. Nie Hua swerved a corner, through a village, a picture of pastoral calm. We skidded through a herd of goats, their rumps popping skywards, heads dipped low. To the north, a man sat tall on a thin chestnut horse. He wore a blue coat and a turban: a reminder. Xuanzang left on a lean brown horse. Because this is horse country, the graceful animals were everywhere, swishing silken tails. Perhaps one of these villagers' ancestors, 1400 years ago, supplied a roaming monk with a ride.

There were low earthen pens to lock the goats in, secured with gates of thorny brush, but nothing else for miles and miles. The Inner Mongolian steppes were just 100 kilometres north of these desolate plains. The garrison town of Suoyang Cheng rose from the plains, more or less preserved through the centuries, protected by the region's extreme dryness. It was an imposing structure of adobe, a uniform dun colour.

Above the fortification, a swallow fought the wind, dived and bucked, but went nowhere, tossed like a crumpled letter. I climbed to the top from a bricked slope. Lu Pin, the guide, shouted above the gale's noise and pointed to crumpled bumps within the walls.

'Here, on the east, was the administrative section, smallish, because this was a military operation. Here, to the west, the army, the military city.'

The beacon tower used to be eighteen metres high and the walls much higher than their present nine metres, now overgrown with camel grass which never dries, not even in the greatest heat. The wind snatched Lu Pin's hat off her head and she scrambled down an incline to fetch it. My shirt flapped and I shivered as the temperature dropped. The winter temperatures here reached −15°C. The sky was a flat soupy blanket.

From the walls of the fortification, Lu Pin pointed at two leftover structures. 'That's where they put the misbehaved soldiers,' she said over the wind. It was easy to imagine the soldiers, far away from their women and their land, stuck in a border garrison town where the wind blew cracks in their heads. The Tang generals could not afford a rebellion in their ranks. They threw mutinous men into a chamber made of dried earth, with only one small opening which was plugged. There were no exits. There they were left to die. I was looking at a 1400-year-old death row.

The temple where Xuanzang would have lodged was one kilometre away. Lu Pin shook her head and pointed at the sky. But I was itching with curiosity and delighted in the brewing storm.

'I'll be back soon,' I yelled across to her.

&

Xuanzang sat morose and miserable.

He heard there were spies from Wuwei filtering through the remote encampment and thought that this could be the end of the journey.

Li-Chang was the governor of Wuwei, and perhaps the lonely posting and howling winds had made him a pious man. He knew perfectly well that the Master of the Law had entered his turf and secretly he wished him well. Li-Chang had heard the rumours and read the mandate:

> There is a priest called Hiuen-Tsiang who is purposing to enter on the Si-Fan territory. All the governors of provinces and districts are ordered to detain him.[1]

It passed through his mind that Chang An was very far away. News from these desolate western barracks took time and it would be months before the emperor found out. Then he could plead ignorance, just a harmless monk he let pass. Early one morning, he headed alone to the temple where Xuanzang was staying. The Master had just finished his morning meditation and was sweeping his small cell.

Li-Chang unrolled the mandate.

'Is this not about you?'

Xuanzang was silent. 'You should tell me the truth, your disciple will make some plan for you to escape,' Li-Chang said softly.

Xuanzang snapped his head up in disbelief.

'You are capable of this journey,' Li-Chang told him. 'I will destroy the document for your sake.' Then he tore the paper into small pieces and scattered them into a soft wind. They danced and spread and vanished. 'Now, sir, you must depart in all haste.'

Xuanzang mumbled his thanks for this unexpected generosity in this unexpected place.

෨

I walked east, one kilometre through scrabbled terrain, picking my way through thorny camel grass. The bushes scratched through my pants, and on my forearm a red jag spread. For the first time I was alone in China, in a landscape of mud, thorny clumps and the wind. From a ridge I could see the pagoda in the distance. It disappeared in the saddles and I had to consult my compass to ensure I was still heading east. Here, in this broken, tilted ruin of a temple, Xuanzang stayed a month. There was a gaping hole which seemed like the shape of a seated Buddha with the *ushnisha*, the bump on the Buddha's head, a sign of his wisdom. A bank of fine sand spilled from the caved-in pagoda, the bricks and the mixed straw—the adobe of the time.

I walked up the incline and around the base of the pagoda, hugging the side. There, at the back, I looked down at the remains of four stupas. It took a few moments to sink in. They were dome-shaped stupas, not pagodas. It was a first architectural hint of India. I stood and stared in quiet delight. Home was not that far.

A furious wind from the west surged and swilled. From this height, I could see the plains all around, for miles and miles. The sky was grey, turbulent. A hawk of some sort was trying to fly west, but it just bobbed up and down, pinioned by the wind.

At the foot of the broken tower, there was scattered pottery. I could make out the clay roof tiles, a square piece with an aquamarine glaze, a carved bit of a statue with bottle-green colour still stuck on in parts. As I flipped a peacock-blue tile over, a drop of water streaked across it, washing the sand off. Wet spots pattered across the earth. I turned back, keeping the ancient city wall dead ahead, bending my head against the slapping wind. Soon the rain was steady and insistent, and by the time I reached the ticket office I was soaked.

Nie Hua opened the door, anxious, even before I got there. Back in the small office, by the kitchen fire blazing with twigs shoved under a stove, I took off my shirt, held it up against the warmth and watched steam rise from it.

๛

Xuanzang needed a guide for his journey to I-Gu, his next destination.

As he sat and prayed in the temple, a foreigner came in and introduced himself as Pan-to. Seeing that he was in the presence of a Buddhist priest, Pan-to asked to be inducted into the five rules of a lay disciple, which Xuanzang did. Xuanzang took in the man's strong build and intelligence and on the spur of the moment revealed his destination and his need for a guide. Pan-to said he would be happy to help. He knew the region, he said. The two agreed to meet the next day at sundown by the bush and the monk pulled out some clothes and other belongings to exchange for a horse. That evening Pan-to arrived in the company of an old man with a grey beard. The man, he said, had crossed the desert to and from I-Gu over thirty times, he should know. The old man nodded. He explained that the roads to the west were terrible, that evil spirits and heated winds cursed the passage, that men got lost.

Xuanzang replied that he'd rather die trying to reach the land of the Brahmans than return east. The old man was aghast.

> If, sir, you will go you must ride this horse of mine: he has gone to and fro to I-gu some fifteen times. He is strong and knows the road; your horse, sir, is a small one and not suitable for the journey.[2]

The horse was lean and reddish, its varnished saddle bound with iron. The animal was exactly as the fortune teller in Xian had predicted. The two men exchanged horses. Having packed his baggage, the monk went on through the night with the young foreigner. In the third watch they came to the river and spotted the guardhouse called the Yuh-men, the Jade Gate, still a good way off.

സ

There was definitely the remains of a beacon tower of some sort a short drive outside Anxi. As I clambered up the hill, I could see for miles around. If a fire burned here, its smoke would be visible for kilometres on end, signals to the first watchtower in the desert. What a lonely, dangerous job this would have been. Just the wind screaming over the desolate plains and rocky sand, an outcrop of hills and this clump of adobe. I could still see the ancient straw poking out from underneath the layers of mud. This was all that was left of the Jade Gate, the last boundary of Tang power outside Anxi city. It was not to be confused with the Jade Gate near Dunhuang, which dated from a much earlier (Han) time.

Had there been anybody on watch that night, they would have seen a hunched monk and his guide on horses, quietly and illegally clip-clopping towards the barbarian lands beyond the river.

The Su Le River used to lie north of Anxi, the British explorer Sir Aurel Stein wrote. And after this the road headed north, crossing a bare *sai*, a desert of stone or gravel, low Gobi hillocks, low ridges of detritus before getting to I-Gu.

Stein's affair with China's western deserts took place in the early part of the twentieth century. He traced its lines as he might have brushed a loved face, feeling its landscape of scrub and low jungles, its hard salt crusts, drift-sand areas, its sandy tracts, poplars and perpetual snows. He was enamoured of its wild empty skies. He called Xuanzang his Chinese patron saint and read the monk's words for directions. Stein's detailed maps were published in 1919, while the British still ruled India. That is how a pile of maps of Chinese Turkestan and Gansu, from surveys made during Stein's explorations, came to rest in a dusty archaeological library in New Delhi, where I found them many months later.

In Anxi, from a red plastic roadside phone in a booth manned by a woman, I phoned S. to let him know I was still alive, to hear his voice.

'Has anything happened in the world that I should know about?' I asked.

'The LA Lakers won.' His voice, bouncing across satellites, was clear and warm. I began to laugh. Next to me, small trucks honked.

I returned to a Muslim restaurant I had discovered for an alfresco dinner. 'Oh, we're out of your favourite dumplings,' the cook said, rueful. I had a yen for those steamed bite-sized dumplings, stuffed with fresh chopped spinach. They floated in a broth, with an edible fungus and miniature shrimps, topped with a sprinkle of fresh coriander. But I was beginning to grit my teeth against the endless local fascination with me.

Over dinner, as I scribbled notes, three people leaned over my shoulder to watch me write in English, the tap of China's commentary turned on.

'Aren't you afraid of writing something wrong?'

'I thought you were Chinese.'

'No,' another disagreed. 'Look at her, see, big eyes, high nose.'

I sighed and bit back bad temper.

Despite the intrusions, I went often to the restaurant run by the Hui Muslims, where Chen Haixiao showed off her baby's six teeth. Chen shared her reluctance to go back to her husband's home.

'What if you didn't go back?' I asked her.

'They telephoned me already,' Chen said. 'They've called, screaming for me to go back.' She paused. 'When will you come back to Anxi?'

'Don't know, it could be years,' I said.

The women clustered around me, they felt my hands. So soft, they chirped. Theirs were red and roughened, with thick fingers, the joints thicker, as though at one point they had broken. One girl carried a surging burn mark on her upper arm.

'Don't you do any work?' they asked me in amazement.

'I, er, type.' General hilarity.

They bent my fingers and looked at my rings, thin bands bought as an afterthought years ago, trinkets from some New Delhi market. I took one off and gave it to the kitchen girl. She refused, shook her head from side to side, but her eyes were begging 'yes'. I put it down on the table, and the talk turned to Islam—the fasting, the customs, the five-times-daily prayers at the mosque—and I wanted to ask about circumcision but I didn't know the Chinese for it and could not even begin to act it out.

Life in a small town is lived on its pavements. Opposite the restaurant, pool tables were set up at dusk and the sharp clickety-clack of cues hitting balls filled the falling night. The local toughs played under lights strung between thin trees.

The little boy at the next table was doing his homework with the utmost reluctance. He sat at the far end, a quiet child with thin wrists. He kept his eyes downcast, the back of his head was as flat as a board. He wrote in his notebook, one square for each Chinese character. But then the lead of the pencil became problematic. Was it time to change it? The boy pulled out a stick of lead, then dropped it. He wiggled flat onto his tummy on the chair, waving both legs in the air, then, arms outstretched, balancing on the chair, he reached for the lead. I looked under the table at him. He looked back at me.

Behind me, somewhere, the radio played in English. *I'm a big big girl in a big big world.*

The clack of goh tiles resounded through dusk. I thought of Gansu's slanting golden sunlight, the rich chocolate-coloured desert, blue skies, wafting clouds and the monk's bad luck with his guides.

✿

Xuanzang slept, exhausted from the tension of the river crossing, the relief of making it to the other side and fear of what still lay ahead.

Just ten *li* from the Yuh-men barrier, the upper stream of the river was not much more than ten feet wide; on each side there was scrub composed of the wu-tung tree. Pan-to had cut wood, made a bridge and spread branches over it, filling it up with sand. They led the horses over the water and went on.[3]

There was a peculiar moment, the monk half-thought he dreamt it. He saw Pan-to approaching him with a drawn knife; he made a small sound, prayed to Guanyin, muttered scriptures. Pan-to retreated, slept too. Finally, shifty Pan-to abandoned the monk, like many had before, and Xuanzang faced the desert utterly alone.

chapter five

River of Sand

It was a beautiful day as I set off on the mini bus westwards, surprised that I could feel a twinge to leave a dump like Anxi. But the sky was a clarified, satiny blue and I loved these fresh Gansu mornings. Well into the desert, before switching to a bigger bus, I bought a small packet of raisins and almonds to nibble at from an ancient Uighur sitting outside. *Kishmish, badam.* The language of India already. I felt a silent satisfaction seep into my ribs, a reminder of some enormous childhood comfort.

National Highway 312 sliced west across the sands, cutting through dark, pointed, stony hills. A road slashing through this terrain showed the determination of a government. This expansion westwards was nothing new; the communists merely cemented what the Tang dynasty had begun. I dozed off in the punishing midday heat and awoke when the bus bumped to a halt at a truck pit stop right at the border of Xinjiang province. There were ancient remains of watchtowers on the surrounding hills. But judging from their condition they were more recent structures.

Otherwise, the stop was a hellhole in the desert. There were oily gas stations, dark with petroleum, the backs piled with rusted pipes. A massive ceramic pillar announced: THE FIRST RESTAURANT IN XINJIANG. When the bus moved on, I saw that I had missed the last watchtower that Lu Qunyuan at the Anxi museum had told me to look out for. A man in rags, matted dark blue coat, carrying a patched bag, was walking west, solo in the noonday sun. Had anything ever been this forsaken?

The hills got higher. Some furious ancient heaving had thrown up this sulky crop of jagged peaks. There was not a tree for miles in this gravelled and grim landscape. This was no place for living creatures. I dozed off in the heat again. A nap, and then a startled awakening.

Here in the wasteland, to my amazement, I saw a stretch of water, and a crashing herd of horses, galloping, dust clouds swirling under their hooves. Then I felt a slow touchdown, a refocus: it was more desert trickery, the mix of heat and distance, a sun-picture.

&

Xuanzang too was tricked by the heat and light as he felt his way across, guided by heaps of bones and dried horse dung. He saw troops, hundreds of them, wrapped in fur and felt. They advanced. They stopped. He saw camels and horses, standards and lances. Then they vanished.

He thought they were robbers first. But they dissolved into nothing. His heart pounded, thinking they were demons. The desert sands sniggered and quivered. A jocular wind shrieked.

He heard voices—'Do not fear! Do not fear!'—and so, he pushed himself over the next eighty *li* and spotted the first watchtower.

He hid from the guards in sandy hollows, found the water west of the tower, knelt to wash and drink. He drenched a corner of his robe and wiped his neck. His lips were parched. He held his gourd by the neck in the water and watched the liquid burble into the empty container. An arrow whistled and grazed his knee. More angry than startled, made braver by his ordeal, he yelled out: 'Don't shoot, I'm a priest from the capital!'

He got to his knees and tugged at his horse as the roughened men on guard at the tower clanged the gate open. They led him to their chief, Wang-siang, who ordered a fire built for a proper inspection. Wang's face was leathery from a life in the open, eyes narrowed from watching the desert horizon.

In the flickering light of a roaring fire, he examined the silent monk. A tall, good-looking man, he thought, noting how his shaved head highlighted his features. The flames bounced and danced off the walls and painted the monk's face a dull orange.

'What are you doing here, and where, sir, are you going?'

'Haven't the men of Liangzhou talked about a priest called Xuanzang who was about to proceed to the country of the Brahmans and seek the Law?'

Wang-siang frowned.

'I heard that Xuanzang returned to the east. But what of him?'

Xuanzang took him out to his horse, unpacked belongings with his name and title on them. Wang kept shaking his head. In a low voice he tried to dissuade the monk, but it was a futile effort.

'I will never return one step to the east or give up my purpose,' Xuanzang said. Filled with emotion, his voice rose and then wobbled. Wang-siang touched the monk's arm.

'You are tired. Sleep before the sky lightens. I will show you the proper route myself.'

He unrolled a mat for the monk to sleep on and Xuanzang surrendered, drained, huddling against the sudden cold of the desert night. The desert he crossed next, the one they called the River of Sand for its shifting, treacherous ways, was one of the worst experiences of his journey. He muttered mantras to drive away demon shapes and strange goblins which seemed to surround him.

'Guanyin, Guanyin,' he mumbled under his breath, and then another, more powerful sutra. But he was lost, confused. Somewhere, he had wandered off the track and missed the water fountain of Ye-ma, where he was supposed to refill his depleted water gourd.

He shook it and listened to the water sloshing inside. He had to fill it soon. He lifted it to drink, tilting his head back, but the horse stumbled. The monk's hand slipped and he watched in horror as the gourd fell, as though in slow motion, bounced once against the horse's flanks and then away, and lay limp as the contents sighed and trickled out, staining the sand. Gone. It was over.

His vow, he thought, his vow, feverishly invoked, that it was better to die in the attempt than return to the east and face the life he had left. He yanked the horse's bridle to the north-west and pummelled his heels into the animal's side. Startled, the horse set off at a trot.

'Guanyin!' he shouted, but his voice came out as a croak. 'Do something.' He felt hot tears course down his face in frustration and helplessness. But not defeat.

Thirst made him limp, he felt death at the back of his seared throat. Four nights and five days, not a drop of water to wet his throat or mouth; his stomach was wracked by a burning heat, his skin blistered, his lips cracked. His memory dissolved, there was nothing left but the will to take one more step. He slid off his horse and crumpled in the sand.

Dizzy and faint, he prayed until night fell and the stars rose.

Suddenly a cool wind fanned his body, cold and refreshing like an icy bath. He sank into sleep and dreamed of a mighty being who approached him and said, 'Why are you asleep and not pressing on with all your might?' In the dark, Xuanzang roused himself, crawled to the horse and hoisted himself up. The animal set off at a walk but soon stopped. It let out a soft whinnying and tugged to the left. It would not budge, not even when the monk thwacked its flanks. It pulled and reared and the monk slumped, forced to let the creature wander. And then, it was as though the air rearranged itself, as though the molecules spaced themselves further apart, as though the cosmos relaxed. There were acres of green grass, a pool of sweet water, bright as a mirror. He dismounted and lurched towards it. Man and horse slaked their thirst side by side. They made small ripples and slapping sounds. The monk laughed, a rough, raucous sound. Water dripped from his face. He laughed till his belly hurt. We made it, he shouted to the horse, but the animal had moved off, cropping juicy weeds with scritch-scritch noises. Xuanzang filled his gourd and cut a pile of grass for his mount.

The monk arrived in I-Gu two days later, where he stopped at a temple and found three Chinese priests. One of them was an old man, barefoot, without a girdle, who ran out with his arms outstretched. Recognizing a fellow Chinese, Xuanzang embraced him. He felt his eyes fill with tears, the tears of a man who has pulled himself up by the roots and feels them dangling, bloodied, wandering amongst strangers, struggling with fear in a vast alien landscape.

৪০

It was another ninety-eight kilometres to Hami, the blue sign said in Arabic and Chinese. Hami, the first oasis in this other, different country.

As the bus rounded a bend through reddish sandstone hillocks, I spotted the mountains. The surprise and pleasure, a trick. I first thought it a mere rag of clouds, below the line of cumulus against the azure, but it was the snowed peaks of a mountain that reached the skies.

Tian Shan, 'heavenly mountains' in Chinese, Tangri Tagh or 'god mountain' in Uighur. It had probably acquired god-like properties by being the main source of water. The melting snows streaked into the desert, channelled into an ancient underground irrigation system and fed oasis after oasis. The sweet mountain water leached into melons and grapes that swelled into their famed sugary ripeness.

It was 38°C as we bounced along a back road into Hami. We turned off into a route through villages lined with poplar trees and running streams, vineyards with ripening grapes and kids biking back from school. Suddenly, the bus sighed to a stop and all the men got off and pushed it, heaved it, until the motor juddered to a start again and we rolled into what used to be the kingdom of I-Gu.

ஐ

Further west, in the next oasis city of Gaochang, King Qu Wentai had already heard of Xuanzang's presence. He sent a cavalry of horses, officers and ministers to welcome the monk and accompany him to Gaochang.

The monk and his troupe crossed the southern desert towards Gaochang. These were men who knew the shifting sands. They led the monk across ridges and dunes, across rocky patches filled with prickly grasses. Banners flew, hooves sent up puffs of dust. A magistrate leaned forward to point out some feature of note. After six days they reached Pih-li on the borders of Gaochang. The sun was setting, throwing a lilac and orange stain across the skies. At midnight the party reached the city gates and the officer of the guard shouted for the gates to be flung open.

As the massive doors creaked open, Xuanzang saw that King Qu Wentai had come himself to receive him. He was surrounded by attendants carrying lighted torches that threw giant shadows and lit the foreign faces. Qu Wentai was beside himself with delight. His words tumbled out. He was a devout Buddhist, this was a rare opportunity for solace, for guidance. The king, hungry for talk, kept the monk awake until dawn.

Please, the monk begged, rubbing his eyes. He needed desperately to be alone, to sleep. Please.

The king dragged his feet, but he left, assigning eunuchs to wait on his precious guest. Trouble trickled through the monk's dreams and he awoke exhausted, bleary and certain of nothing.

ॐ

Anxious to reach Turfan, I did not stop long in Hami. A train left that very night and I purchased a sleeper berth. Dawn broke as the train pulled into the station, an hour away from Turfan and the remains of Gaochang city. The day promised to be a broiler despite the cloud cover. I was among the Uighurs, a Turkic Muslim minority, and Turfan was a cultural centre. Over the days, I struck up a slow friendship with Abdullah, a young Uighur guide, the kind of friendship made on travels—an exchange of views, in which both sides for a while ignore their vast differences, forget for a time how little each knows of the other's life, all for the sake of a complicity, a sense of alliance, in which you part with the knowledge that you are unlikely to meet again.

Perhaps the ease with the Uighurs had something to do with how much like them I looked. How powerful is the natural ease among people who resemble one another. We all had rounder eyes, different bones, something non-Chinese. The women had heavy waists, square jaws and thick legs, their heads were covered with scarves. The men's darker features were topped with stiff square caps with four peaks that rose to a point in the middle. It was in the company of Uighurs, Abdullah and his friends, that I took a long drink of my first beer in weeks. And lit a cigarette. Though we were still speaking in Mandarin, it felt like a different country. It felt more like home. In the days that followed, I learned more words of Uighur.

Rachmad. Thank you.

It was a natural alliance between me and the Uighurs—Han fatigue. I felt relief at being out of Han China (did I say that?). How tiresome I found the Chinese, in the end.

Here was a welcome whiff of unpatterned passions, a deep belief in Allah for one, which changed many things. I found more traces of home in the language: *badam, waqat, adam*. Almond, time, man. The names of people were music to my ears too. Alim-Jaan.

People gnawed at grey mutton chops. Steamed or boiled, it made a thin soup and they tore off chunks of naan and dipped it in the mutton soup. I could now pinpoint the vague smell of mutton fat that hung in the air, sticky, fly-attracting. Shops sold mutton in chunks, or a glistening row of flesh hanging on carts, four legs splayed, head dangling.

∞

King Qu Wentai was a man of drama and tantrums. The site of Gaochang city, where Qu Wentai met the monk, lay south of modern Turfan. It was 10.40 a.m. (or 8.40 a.m. in Xinjiang time) and the heat was gathering strength in the silence of this baked earth. Gaochang was a vast complex of wind-blown shapes, worn down to stumps, an entire ghost city crumbling from its former glory into dried lumps of mud.

In the north-central part of the inner city, there was a Khan's castle, possibly where some of Xuanzang's travails occurred. Inside the castle, on a high terrace, stood a pagoda of rammed earth. The south-western part of the outer city was a temple, built around AD 518. There was an arched gate, a courtyard, a main hall, a lecture hall, monks' dormitories. Around it, there were the remains of workshops and market sites, the beginnings of the quintessential Central Asian city.

Groups of Chinese tourists from Shanghai had hired donkey carts to ride the three kilometres there and back. Little Uighur children held bunches of metal bells on keychains for them to buy. On the way back, an Uighur driver offered me a ride on his cart with a smile, a jerk of his chin towards the platform. He snapped the reins and the donkey lurched forward. A couple of the Shanghainese started grumbling until they worked out I was a foreigner, at which point their attitude somersaulted into a smiling welcome.

About a decade after Xuanzang tried to get some sleep as the

Khan chattered on, the Tang emperor in Chang An sent the powerful general Hou Junji to march across the desert, take over Gaochang and set up the western region, divided into five counties. Qu Wentai quailed when he saw the dust on the horizon raised by the Chinese army and sank to his knees before the general, bowed his head and died of fright, although that might just be the version of some smug Chinese historian. General Hou Junji rolled his eyes and set about conducting a census in which he found the population of Gaochang to be 37,000.

It would be another 200 years or so before the Uighurs migrated to this region, practising Buddhism before Islam began to creep into China. But for the time being in the seventh century, Gaochang was still Buddhist. To the east of Gaochang there were caves where artisans had carved and painted scenes from the life of a quiet man from India.

Down narrow steps one pale morning, we followed the hush of the river below, the sough of poplar trees swaying. A hoopoe called down in the gorge. These caves in the flat face of a flaming mountain, faced north. There were smaller caves too, as though crouching to escape the heat and the vastness of this desert around, kneeling by the river.

Entire statues had been knocked off and all that remained was the outline of a body and the shape of what must have been a reclining Buddha. A thread of vengeance and greed ran through these caves— sharp hammers or axes had gouged out the faces of the Buddhas.

One cave dated from the eleventh century and carried a doleful legend: 'The back part of the eastern wall was stolen by Stein in the winter of 1914, it is empty now.'

Stein had ripped off chunks of the back part of the eastern wall. The entire middle of the eastern wall had been yanked off too, but whoever took that hadn't bothered to stoop, so that the bottom strip still showed Sakyamuni's sandalled feet, turned outwards, and the lower part of the robe: folds of thick yellow, blue and a warm ruby. The strappy sandals had toeholds for the big and little toes, a loop across the top of the foot, another around the heel. The toes curled, as though the Buddha was leaning backwards and gripping the ground for a hold on his lotus.

Here, on this translucent morning with the sound of the river through the gorge and the hoopoe calling, you could almost hear the monks chanting. Those who came with their packing cases or guns were sacrilegists, not thieves.

The Uighur donors were painted in the finest line drawings. These splendid drawings were delicate, rich draped cloth painted line by loving black line along the russet robe, more lifelike than in Dunhuang. A warrior sat at the foot of the Buddha. At the back, figures paid their respects to the disappeared Buddha, offering their awe to an elliptical muddy gash. Another hint of India, already: a subcontinental man, full, round cheeks, rounded eyes, high nose and curly black moustache. There was a lightness to these drawings, an expressiveness around the eyes and mouths, a hint of a feel I saw a year later at the Ajanta caves in India.

In these deserts, Buddhism succumbed to Islam. Fights among Buddhist and Muslim kings raged for decades. Arabs in Central Asia were losing power by the ninth century due to local opposition. But Islam had made a strong entrance, and a king of the Khas Khan dynasty had three big clashes with the Buddhist kings of Gaochang. In AD 998, over 300 years after Xuanzang passed through, the Buddhists were defeated and from then on, in the western Tarim Basin, Islam became the dominant religion with Kashgar as its centre. In AD 1209, the Uighurs declared their suzerainty to Genghis Khan.

The clash between the two seemed to freeze in time at Togoyu, some distance outside Turfan, the site of a holy Muslim shrine.

The gravel road to Togoyu followed dun mountains. Far in the distance, a lone donkey cart pulled north; there were tufts of camel grass, the desert everywhere. As the minivan bumped along, the honeyed voice and tugging melodies of the popular Uighur singer, Abdullah, wobbled on the rickety player.

Abdullah the guide—everyone called him Abla-Jaan—translated for me into Mandarin.

'It's about a tree and a pool of water and two lovers Leili . . .'

'And Majnun!' I interrupted. Laila and Majnun! I knew this story, of Majnun, mad with love for Laila, tearing his hair out, losing his mind and wandering. Every other Hindi film song made a reference to Laila and Majnun. How odd and yet unsurprising to find it here.

We bumped along a mud road and ground up an incline. The wall around the shrine followed the mountain slope, a brick necklace around an olive dome.

'This is like going to hajj,' Abla-Jaan said.

Through a hall covered in carpets, we walked up dingy narrow steps at the back of the mosque that led into a cave in the hillside. The floor was covered in black felt. Piles of small change, cash, a plastic water bottle filled with oil for the lamp, sat near the wall.

Abla-Jaan knelt, sat back on his heels and put both hands in front of his face. Then he wiped his hands across his face. There was an extraordinary feeling of stumbling into a different world, a network of Muslim scholars and teachers, schooled in the worship of Allah, filled with a different faith, unmindful and quite independent of those who did not worship their god.

ഇ

Xuanzang's troubled dreams were spilling into his days. Qu Wentai, the king of Gaochang, went to see him again, as soon as courtesy permitted. He was tearful, emotional.

He fussed and ordered simple vegetarian food to be brought to the monk. He assigned fresh eunuchs to look after his guest. He made the resident monk, Tun, go to visit Xuanzang. Tun had studied in Chang An. They chatted.

Qu Wentai summoned Buddhist Master Kwo-tong-wang, who was eighty years old, and instructed him to persuade the monk to stay. Ten days went by. The king himself went to see Xuanzang and made his request. But Xuanzang looked at his hands and bowed his head. The king begged, on his knees now. He wept. He abandoned all dignity. 'I'll do anything you want. All the priests of this kingdom will be at your service. Please don't go on with this journey.'

The monk began to get angry. 'I pray your majesty to change your mind and do not overpower me with an excessive friendship.'[1]

The king lost his temper. You will stay! he shouted. I will detain you by force and send you back to your country, you obstinate man! How dare you disobey me!

Xuanzang folded his arms and refused. He sighed and sighed and could not speak another word. The monk stopped eating. He sent his food back untouched and sat silent and stubborn for three days. He became faint and pale, his cheeks sank in enough to alarm the king and make him feel ashamed.

Okay, okay, the king said. But on your way back you have to stop three years and you have to stay one more month to preach every day. The monk agreed. Repentant, Qu Wentai sat and bowed his head to the ground so the monk could climb on his curved back daily to reach the podium from where he delivered his religious lectures.

In preparation for the monk's departure, the king had thirty different robes stitched for the monk. The western regions were cold, so he ordered the royal tailors to make face-coverings, padded caps, gloves, leather boots and so on. He gathered 100 ounces of gold, three myriad (30,000) pieces of silver, 500 rolls of satin and taffeta, enough to fund the outward and homebound journeys of the Master over twenty years. He went to the stables himself to select thirty horses. He picked twenty-four of his best servants and assigned Hun-Sin, one of the Imperial censors, to conduct the monk to the Khan Yeh Hu who ruled in present-day Kyrgyzstan across the icy mountains.

Altogether, Qu Wentai wrote twenty-four letters of introduction for his beloved priest. He asked that the different rulers conduct the priest through their countries, that they provide relays of horses.

The day came when the two men parted company. The king ordered the queen to stay home. But he and his closest religious advisers travelled with the monk for a distance towards the west, towards the kingdom of 'O-ki-ni.

The king stood still and watched for hours as Xuanzang's figure, surrounded by his escort, grew smaller and smaller and finally vanished. Perhaps he already had a sense, in the way one sometimes does, that life would spin from his hands, his plans would float off in the wind, and he would not live to see his monk again.

chapter six

Fire City

From Turfan, the old Silk Road swung south-west to cross a mountain range that the Uighurs named Qol Tag. The road skirted the Bostang Lake and led to Yanqi, the place Xuanzang refers to as the kingdom of 'O-ki-ni. It was here that I began to pay attention to the names of places.

Yanqi, it seemed, was the local derivation of *yanghi*, the Turkish word for fire. The city had possibly once been called Yanghi-shaher or Fire City. Xuanzang, a stickler for precision and partial to India, had used the Sanskrit word for fire, *agni*, and transliterated this into Chinese, yielding 'O-ki-ni.[1]

I consulted my list from my Beijing scholars. All it said was to go to the Yanqi Administrative Area.

The local bus from Turfan to Yanqi was stuffed with rural travellers. A little Uighur girl sat on the fold-down seat in the aisle, her hard little head leaning against my arm as we groaned along a rough road. The river had worked down the rock. By the river bed may have been the old path where Xuanzang rode on his horse, along with the small group of travellers, but now the water had dried into a sheen of wetness in the sun.

A bird wheeled overhead by the high rocks. A hawk flew so close to a sand dune, its shadow loomed large. The gorge rose steeper and steeper, rocky crags and grey slatey stuff right up near your face.

☙

Xuanzang leaned forward, waving his arms, jabbing a finger in the air to stress the point for Hui Li. The hair on the back of his neck lifted with the memory, stinging like daylight, the dread returned for a flash.

'We climbed the Silver Mountain,' Xuanzang said. The mountain had been mined and provided these countries with their silver currency.

Hui Li nodded.

'Our troupe was on the western flank of the mountains.'

The robbers came out of nowhere, armed to the teeth, shouting and cursing, dislodging pebbles. They wore tattered clothes, their faces were masked. The travellers handed over valuables, dropping things, wordless. They scrabbled amongst baggage and folds of clothing for offerings. White sheets of fear swept silently across the caravan.

The group managed to continue unharmed, hearts pounding. The robbers had evaporated, carting off goods, shoving dried food into their mouths. They stuffed coins into pouches. The monk could hear the blood rush through his veins. He imagined his throat being slit, drops of blood arcing in the sunlight.

How tenuous life was.

Not far from 'O-ki-ni, the monk and his caravan banded with a group of twenty or thirty foreign merchants, perhaps Central Asians returning home after a lucrative stop in Chang An. There was safety in numbers.

The party bivouacked together by a stream for a few hours of sleep. In the middle of the night, Xuanzang thought he heard muffled hooves and soft neighing and footsteps. He was wrapped in threads of fatigue and unable to investigate.

It turned out the foreign merchants had left, anxious to hit the city's market and set up their stalls early. But ten *li* from the campsite, the monk's caravan came across a terrible sight. The bodies of the merchants lay slaughtered by the roadside. Jewellery had been torn off their ears and bodies, their clothes ripped off, there was blood everywhere. The horses were gone, along with the piles of merchandise.

Xuanzang walked to the side of the road, leaned over and retched. His hardier escorts from Gaochang glanced over their shoulders, muttered, shook their heads and said they must press on to the safety of the city walls at 'O-ki-ni.

လ

The bus rolled down a gentle incline; a swatch of green appeared, an oasis. The lake spread like a thin blue wash at the foot of the mountain and yet another ambience dawned. Here the mosques were more elaborate, prouder, out in the open, not hidden in marketplaces like in China. I kept doing this without thinking—referring to China as another country.

To the north-east, the snow-dusted peaks of the Tian Shan lifted. Rushing water flooded the roads, so abundant that reeds grew through a clear burble over pebbles. I tried to shake off the malaise of Xuanzang's violent encounter, described sparsely in Hui Li's account and not at all in Xuanzang's own records.

My own bus journey surrounded by Uighur peasants was a genteel passage in comparison; my hardest task lay in locating the seventh-century ruins of 'O-ki-ni. The thrill of that grew. The dusty piles of brick had become for me lighthouses, shining beads in a necklace that stretched all the way to India. The cracked walls of mud stupas and foundations of old monasteries enthralled me. The surmise that the monk walked here brought them alive.

The sense of being in a right moment ballooned inside me. In Yanqi, I looked for transport that would take me to the kingdom of 'O-ki-ni. But three taxi drivers gave blank looks.

'You know,' I said weakly. 'History. Ruins, old places.'

Bu zhi dao. I don't know.

Mei you. There aren't any.

One morning, I wandered through the small town. I drank some coffee, strolled to where the Bank of China was opening shop and a woman cleaned the steps before the half-raised shutters. Inside, a clerk leaned over and pointed. She suggested I consult the Wenhua Ju, the cultural bureau, down the road, on the left-hand side. I thanked her. A ladder of inquiry led me to Xu Weishen's office, right at the top of the building.

Xu hemmed and hawed and fussed and peered at my map.

'The kingdom of 'O-ki-ni? Yes, I know where it is.'

'Can you show me the place?'

'Well, it's not open to the public.'

I raised my eyebrows, but said nothing.

He cavilled.

'There are no buses. It's all arranged from Urumqi.' He glanced to see my reaction. 'You have to hire a car.' That was his trump card. The final obstacle.

'What about Xuanzang's route?' I said, keeping the crossness at the periphery of my voice. Nothing irritated me more than bureaucrats. Besides, I could see him tussle with his own curiosity.

'I need to find out where the monk stopped,' I pressed home my advantage, 'where the remains of the kingdom of 'O-ki-ni are. I can hire a car. It won't take long at all.' I sugared my smile to urge him along, as one does a child who refuses to eat.

Silence. He fiddled with papers.

'Okay, okay. How about I go with you?'

'Yes, what a wonderful idea.'

He paused.

'I haven't had breakfast yet. I must have breakfast.'

He sighed and got up and walked off.

In a small taxi arranged by him, we crossed the Kai Du River. It was a perfect morning. There were cirrostratus clouds in fine torn veils across the sky. Above the mountains cumulus floated, flat-bottomed with thick puffs on top, indicating rising hot air currents. And this, the Tian Shan's particular trick, a whole mountain that vanished in a smoke-blue brume, so that all I saw were dabs of snow right under the clouds.

Until now, I had relied on Hui Li's story. 'O-ki-ni was where the monk's own account began:

> On all sides it is girt with hills. Numerous streams unite, and are led in channels to irrigate the fields. The soil is suitable for red millet, winter wheat, scented dates, grapes, pears and plums and other fruits . . . The air is soft and agreeable; the manners of the people are sincere and upright.[2]

Here, the written letters were almost like those of India, the monk wrote. The people did not wear headdresses. They used gold, silver and copper coins for commerce. The country had no annals, no set laws, he noted.

I sensed unwritten shock. Xuanzang of China would be accustomed to his country's meticulous records, volumes of dynastic histories and genealogies, all copied and recopied for posterity. He could not know that his own record, inked for the Chinese emperor, would provide modern Indian historians with one of the few sources of information about the subcontinent in the seventh century.

King Lung-Tuk'ichi of 'O-ki-ni and his ministers rode out to meet Xuanzang—perhaps with all the to-and-fro that took place between the oases, everyone knew that the famous monk from Chang An was heading this way. At 'O-ki-ni, Xuanzang wrote, he found ten or more monasteries, with a collection of about 2000 priests. They used the same books as in India to study the sutras. The king was a coward, he noted. A decade after Xuanzang's passage, Lung-Tuk'ichi secretly abandoned allegiance to the Tang court and made a deal with the western Turks to irk China. The fuming Emperor Taizong dispatched an invading army in AD 643–4 and imprisoned Yanqi's spineless king.[3]

We drove by cornfields, rolling along this road flanked by white poplars. My world had shrunk, my past had crumpled, people I knew had evaporated. I had been travelling for one month. Only this road existed, these poplars, this destination. We passed the occasional brick factory, tall chimney stacks rose in the distance. We drove through Qi Gi Xin village, graced with its soft Mongolian name. The wheat here too was still pastel green and the heat would begin in July and August.

'The lake cools things down,' Xu said, amicable. His earlier reluctance had vanished and he seemed to be in a good mood.

Half an hour later, we stopped by a walled gate by the roadside. Invisible dogs barked in a huddle of poplars. The wind rustled the leaves. Xu disappeared to get the key, set off a crescendo of barking, and reappeared with the keys dangling. He pushed open the rusted gate and there, among hillocks, were the remains of what used to be the main Buddhist temple of the kingdom of 'O-ki-ni, built sometime between the fifth and sixth centuries.

We crossed the courtyard, overgrown with grasses and thistle and dandelions, to the source of this wild bounty—a small, clear natural spring, near the hillock in the middle.

Perhaps this was the site of the main pagoda, with a clear view to the north of the Tian Shan. The base of a stupa was made of the now-familiar earth mixed with straw, baked dry and painted over. To the south-east a block spread out—a living area, with rooms and corridors. It was a considerate architect's model, laid out for all to see. There were three halls on the incline, possibly the main prayer areas. An arched door led to a hollowed corridor, where there were still faint red and black remnants of what was once resplendent with paint.

'A long time ago they all worshipped fire,' Xu explained. 'That's why it's called *agni*, "fire" in Sanskrit.' If the desert satraps of old called this spot Fire City, there had to be a very good reason. Central Asia's Zoroastrian fingers spread all the way here!

We walked up the sandy path. Xu offered a hand and pulled me up. In the silences between sentences, I could see him wrestle with the idea of me, this odd foreign woman alone in the middle of Xinjiang.

'Are you married, by the way?' he asked, right on cue.

I invented an alternative domestic universe for him. It was a more acceptable one, with a husband, some children, a garden, a dog. Somewhere deep inside, perhaps, it was a world I wanted for myself. Except that I was in Xinjiang, following a monk. Without a flat, I was homeless. I hung on to my journey, sank into it, because for the time being it was all I had.

I shielded my eyes against the rising sun. The inhabitants of this ancient city I stood on had spoken Tocharish. How had I managed to live this long without ever hearing about the Tocharians? I practised saying the word. Scholars still wrestled with its identification, but believed the language to be a close cousin of Celtic, German, Italian or Greek possibly spoken by an Indo-European people. They had found remains of these Indo-European people in tombs. The Tocharians played a key role in transmitting Buddhism across Central Asia. All the Tocharian documents unearthed from Dunhuang's cache of treasures related to Buddhism or Buddhist scriptures.

Outside, in the flanks of the hill to the north, up a rough muddy incline, caves appeared. They were painted with apsaras, motifs from India or Sassanid Iran. Brick walls had collapsed, the doors had vanished.

'See, they even steal the doors,' Xu said, disconsolate.

There were traces of paint on the wall, delicate circles on the ceiling of the middle cave. Here the Buddha wore an ochre overcoat, a white circle traced around the figure. In an arched shallow pit on the wall, there was the faint outline of a Buddha statue.

On the floor lay a smashed green beer bottle. At the end of the 1950s and in the 1960s, the caves were used as army barracks. Relations with the Soviet Union were '*bi jiao jin zhang*', Xu said, 'relatively strained', understating the case as only the Chinese can.

How close I was to China's western edge. Across the mountains lay Russia, the former military glory of the Soviet Union reduced to a motley collection of floundering countries, but the border paranoia lingered.

හ

Xuanzang paused to let Hui Li finish writing.

'Then, let's see, after the kingdom of 'O-ki-ni, to get to Kucha, I had to . . .' He scrunched up his eyes, conjuring up that journey, that desert, until he could see the distances, the horizons, the sandstorms. He felt sand rasp the back of his throat, bunch under his skin, coat the inside of his belly until he was gripped by a nameless cafard. He could see each grain in his mind's eye obscuring the destination. India.

All he said was this: 'I climbed a small mountain range, crossed two large rivers and then travelled along a level valley for several hundred *li*.'*

---

*   One *li* is approximately half a kilometre.

chapter seven

Twin Convents

To get to Kucha, I sat at the dusty little bus station in Yanqi for what seemed like hours for the buses would not move until they had filled. The station had a computerized ticketing system but still the conductors hung out of stationary buses yelling 'Korla, Korla' to attract passengers. Korla was the midway stop before Kucha.

A Muslim beggar in a white cap held a bulging pink plastic bag that swung from his wrist. A newspaper seller stopped by the bus, a man bought an army paper which was all about beating up Taiwan.

A long, loud yawn emerged from the back of the bus, followed by, 'Allah! Why isn't this bus moving? It was supposed to have left ages ago.'

An ample Uighur woman yelled for tickets, shepherded stragglers into the bus and walked around to the left side. She opened the door, lifted her dress, clambered into the driving seat and shifted into first gear.

It was an overheated morning. We splashed into streams by the road. They must have flowed from glaciers and minipools, creating entire ecosystems, with ducklings, gulls and reeds. It made me think of Xuanzang's description of many streams uniting into one in the magic of an oasis. After drives through the desert, the water was a sign—the heat gods had forgiven humanity after all.

But then we rolled out into the forbidding black rocks of the desert, a range of knobbly hills. The oil-filling stations were massive tent-like structures with bright orange pipes so you could see them for miles. After changing to a bigger bus at Korla, we moved along the foothills of the mountains, the Tian Shan, inching west.

The driver handed me a warm Feichang Kele, the cheaper Chinese version of Coca-Cola, and flicked the tape on. Abdullah, the Mohammad Rafi of western China's deserts, must be the perfect accompaniment to the sands, this blank rolling flatness, the emptiness—a soulful voice to make up for the oceans of sand.

There was a lunch break. The Chinese grumbled at yet another delay, but the Uighurs paid no attention. They filed out to a small roadside stall and waded into grilled mutton on skewers, sprinkled with salt and cumin and chillies. They waved to me to join them and I did.

It was a long journey through the desert, about 360 rough kilometres. On the bus, listening to that rusty cassette recording of Abdullah, things felt torn and broken. Perhaps it was the singer's lambent voice. Perhaps it was the desert, so flat and miraculous, rolling through the horizon, so absolute in its emptiness.

Strange things happen in the desert. I missed nobody. I could be a tumbleweed forever, I could keep going. At the same time, it seemed the juddering of the bus shook up old memories. I felt saddened, as though the jolting ride scraped open forgotten wounds and reminders of broken loves came wafting to the surface.

Why was the past bubbling up now of all times? I felt tears gather as I looked out of the window, tears for M., a man I knew a decade ago. It had been intense and wholehearted between us. Once he wrote me a letter in green ink. I never forgot that. The green ink burned itself into the back of my heart. I still mourned the death of this youthful love. Or perhaps this is what the desert did, uncovered things I had thought long-vanished.

Can one mourn for a decade without knowing? All those years ago, I didn't think M. had loved me at all. But I saw now that he had. It was I who couldn't believe it at the time. I needed so many tokens. It was a failure of imagination. And of faith.

A full moon hung low over faraway Kucha. Something settled, something intangible floated in the dusty air around the streets. Was it the ether of a dead civilization? When grandeur dies does it leave a whiff, a hint? At any rate, my curiosity was roused and I stayed to savour the days.

೫

'Kucha.' The monk began. Then he stopped, frowning as his weeks in Kucha uncoiled in his mind, so quick, so furious, it left him a little breathless. Why was he cursed with such a memory? It was such a long time ago, but it still burned. He was young and unforgiving then. Would he have said the same things, done the same things now?

Hui Li scratched his neck. He waited for the Master to continue. Xuanzang seemed perturbed. Hui Li sensed that these sessions pulled out old ghosts from muddy depths. Buried things that were dislodged and fell into the present often disturbed the Master's peace of mind.

'I suppose I should tell you about that monk, Mokshagupta,' Xuanzang said, half under his breath. It was a way of easing the guilt. He had misbehaved. He felt it now, older and kinder. Could he have been an entirely different man? A rogue, a drunkard, a man who seduced women, then left them pining? A man who sought extremes as a solution? Wasn't this journey an extreme solution?

> The country of K'iu-chi is from east to west some thousand *li* or so; from north to south about 600 *li* . . . The capital of the realm is from 17 to 18 *li* in circuit. The soil is suitable for rice and corn, also (a kind of rice called) keng-t'ao, it produces grapes, pomegranates, and numerous species of plums, pears, peaches, and almonds, also grow here. The ground is rich in minerals—gold, copper, iron, and lead, and tin.[1]

King Bai of the oasis kingdom of Kucha rode out to meet Xuanzang in the style of desert potentates. He brought with him a learned Buddhist priest, Mokshagupta, while thousands of other priests waited at the city's eastern gate where they erected a pavilion and bands played.

'How beautiful the music was!'

Xuanzang rapped his fingers on the window sill, as though the slight, dry sound could conjure up a symphony in the desert for Hui Li.

'Perhaps it was the ache, the harshness of the surrounding deserts. Ah, the sweet, yearning melodies. Do you know, in the mountains there is a stream that flows, drop by drop. Do you know that they collect the sounds and make a tune of it?'[2]

'But what shall I write, Master?' Hui Li urged.

Xuanzang, chastened, dictated, 'They excel other countries in their skill in playing on the lute and pipe.'

At the grand reception thrown by the king and monks of Kucha, Xuanzang accepted bouquets of flowers, worshipped at a statue of the Buddha and moved from tent to tent, greeting priests and sipping grape juice.

There were monks from Gaochang who had migrated to Kucha and lived in one particular temple in the south-east section of the desert city. They insisted that Xuanzang spend the night with them first, for they were hungry for news of their native city.

ॐ

With such natural wealth, on a major trade route, Kucha had become a flourishing desert civilization with an appreciation for the good life. The hints of India were stronger the further west I went. One morning, leaning into a dusty museum glass case, I saw the Indian style of writing. On a broken piece of pottery inscribed in the Han dynasty with the Qiuci language, the artist had brushed a clear stroke and indeed the script looked familiar, curved like a bell jar.

When Xuanzang came through, the Turks were yet to filter into this region and the inhabitants were still of an Indo-European race who were devout Buddhists. Here too, they spoke Tocharish.

Xuanzang wrote that the people wore ornamental garments of silk and embroidery and, in the fashion of the day, flattened the backs of their children's heads with a wooden board. It wasn't until Central Asia, in a museum in Samarkand, that I saw a small skull behind a glass case with a flat back and remembered his words.

Xuanzang referred to one particular monastery in Kucha and it turned out, to my delight, that the ruins of Chau-hu-li were a historic landmark of this oasis. The spot was painted on every city map as being located in the old town of Su Bashi.

About 40 *li* to the north of this desert city there are two convents close together on the slope of a mountain, but separated by a stream of water, both named Chau-hu-li, being situated east and west of one another, and accordingly so called.[3]

At 8.15 a.m. one misted morning, the sun had not yet slashed the sky. A People's Liberation Army garrison was out jogging. I was learning to start at dawn, retire at midday when possible and set off again when the sun eased. In a little red taxi driven by Li Jianjun, a Han taxi driver I had hired to take me around, we passed a Uighur village on a gravel road where women were splattering water from mugs across mud front yards so the earth became damp and tamped down. We had bargained. I grumbled at his prices, for that was expected; he had protested and assured me of his fairness.

Inside the mud houses there were flashes of courtyards with trellises and flowers. The mountains were a shadow in the distance of this cool dawn. Buddhist monasteries were always in the hills. It was a few kilometres outside the main city, a bumpy ride on gravel and stone, over a rough track traced by car tyres. There was a small brick house with an inner courtyard, a watchman and his motorcycle. Two boys sat on a bench outside, swinging their legs, wearing Uighur caps. It seemed a parody of what they would be like when they got old, sitting on a bench wearing Uighur caps, but not swinging their legs. The rays of the sun spilled in thin streaks from behind a deep grey quilt of clouds to the sound of the river. A dog tied to the motorcycle yapped and a puppy wagged its tail.

Two convents close to each other on the slope of a mountain.

My sense of symmetry and concord settled into contentment. There was an ocean of satisfaction in this simple task of matching the past with the present.

Always there was the drama of the mountain range, the Tian Shan, to the north. The morning shivered in the light breeze and I walked over to the place where Xuanzang stood and nodded his approval, perhaps pausing to scribble notes that night.

(Here there is) a statue of Buddha, richly adorned and carved with skill surpassing that of men. The occupants of the convents are pure and truthful, and diligent in the discharge of their duties.[4]

But the shush of monkish feet shod in cloth hurrying across flagstones had long gone. There was a main temple with niches, perhaps for statues, or to store rolled-up sutras written on silk or birch bark. A corner of a chamber was still intact, maybe an assembly hall. A wall extended, for defence, for it was thick, with the 'horse face' structure—narrow on top, broad at the base. Wooden electricity poles now ran through the monastery, strung together with wires.

In the gravelly earth, there were sprays of green camel grass. Some flower with creamy petals and long pistils grew in abundance low on the ground, as though origami butterflies had alighted on the thorny grass. There were flat lands by the river where possibly the monks cultivated grain. Inside an archway of the main stupa, there was the graffiti of visitors. There was always such a need to leave a mark, fight mortality.

Kucha was a very old state. According to an old Buddhist text, Ashoka, the Indian king who converted to Buddhism, mentions it as a part of his empire that he wished to hand to his son Kunala.[5] Given that Ashoka's influence extended here, it is unsurprising that Xuanzang recorded the grand Buddhist ceremonies Ashoka instituted.

Outside the western gate of the chief city, Xuanzang remarked on two erect figures of the Buddha, both ninety feet high. Between these statues, the oasis city got busy with its Buddhist ceremonies, including the *panchvarsha*. It was a grand five-yearly ceremony instituted by King Ashoka, an event historians placed somewhere in the third century BC. Glitter and pomp vanished, like dispersing incense smoke.

The melting snows of the Tian Shan had engorged the river and it was impossible to cross to the other monastery. The water was a thick coffee-brown, swirling with mud. It was an overcast day, but already heat curled through the clouds.

I was absorbed in the business of finding the monk and his route, in the work of specificity. Was the imagined past like a different country, where I could stay a long time, find a job, friends, a residence permit, and never come back to the present? That, at least, would solve my homelessness. At the same time, I felt a glad consolation. Here was a story that had begun to belong to me, the drama of this region, this history, the story of a long-ago journey.

Being in one Kucha hotel for a stretch of days meant that I was easier to reach by phone. S. and I chatted more often, with expensive disregard for international phone bills between Xinjiang and California.

His voice was my link, however tenuous, to the things I had needed to shrug off, like a moulting snake leaving its skin on a warm stone to look for a new home. But snakes grew their own new skins.

'Send me something from there,' S. said a few days later.

I headed to the post office and mailed off a few cassettes of Abdullah's music and an Uighur hat.

છ

'I don't know what the problem was with that old man in Kucha,' Xuanzang muttered.

Hui Li nodded. He had learned to wait for explanations.

'It was after the meal. I was taken north-west to a temple called O-she-li-ni to where Mokshagupta lived.' Xuanzang looked most unhappy. 'Mokshagupta had travelled in India for over twenty years. I thought I might learn something.'

Hui Li bent his head and began to write.

> Addressing the Master of the Law, [Mokshagupta] said: 'In this land we have the Samyuktabhidarma, the Kosha, the Vibhasha, and other Sutras; you can gain sufficient knowledge by studying these here, without troubling yourself to voyage to the West, encountering all sorts of dangers.'
>
> The Master of the Law replied: 'And have you here the Yoga-Sastra or not?'
>
> [Mokshagupta] answered: 'What need ask about such an heretical book as that? The true disciple of Buddha does not study such a work!'[6]

Xuanzang argued with Mokshagupta over the superiority of the Yoga Shastra school of Buddhist thought. Mokshagupta said Xuanzang's view was heretical. Xuanzang was furious. Mokshagupta's challenge called into question the whole point of his trip.

'How dare you call the *Yoga Shastra* heretical, are you not afraid of the bottomless pit?'

Mokshagupta snapped back, 'You don't even understand the Vibhasha and the Kosha. How can you say they don't contain the deepest principles of religion?'

'Of course I understand them.'

Xuanzang began to recite them. Then he stopped.

'Why don't you pick it up from here?'

'I . . . er,' Mokshagupta began to recite, but then stuttered, blundered and stopped. He turned bright red. He could remember nothing, it turned out, from any of the sutras.

Xuanzang was stuck in Kucha for two months more, waiting for the snowbound passes of the mountains ahead to open.

৯০

I snapped Hui Li's *Life* shut.

Other than that argument, in his account there was nothing further on the public humiliation of a doddering old monk by a younger, brighter man, more up to date with the fashionable philosophies of the day. I was impressed with Xuanzang, wielding esoteric Buddhist concepts like spears, charging at opponents.

The city of Kucha wrapped itself around my ankles. I tasted its life and basked in the textures of a new land. The summer wore on, hotter and hotter, but there were apricot trees thick with leaves and bursting with fruit. Unable to resist, Li Jianjun clambered up one and shook it till it rained pebbly fruit. We washed the mud off, and when I bit into one in the taxi the juice squirted out and made my fingers sticky.

A group of Uighur women were carrying baskets of fruit to market. Uruk, apricots in Uighur. We had breakfast in the old city; I wandered as Li Jianjun slurped his noodles at a stall. A spice seller advertised twelve yuan per kilo for asafoetida.

'How much for a handful?' I asked in my baby Uighur.

'Point five mon,' the man said, weighing.

I was proud of managing this little bit, breathless with the effort of an untried tongue. He poured saunf into a paper cone, fashioned from a newspaper. The pleasure of this linguistic familiarity rose through me. Zeera, mirch, cupped in bags. There were also dried lizards and desiccated snakes, coiled in baskets.

For breakfast, I chose a *samsa*, wrapped in elastic squares of dough. The man made a pat of a meat mixture, flipped the triangular dough pouch shut, slapped it onto the sides of a tandoor oven till it puffed, the pastry turning flaky and golden brown and soft and fragrant with mutton and onion. The baker refused to take money. My resolve to be vegetarian weakened, and then died, as I bit into the delicacy.

I wanted to study Uighur, fascinated by the sounds of this Indo-Turkic tongue, with the way I sometimes heard words and already knew what they meant. In these consonants I found the sounds of India. It was a roundabout way home, and how bizarre to be speaking bits of Hindi in China.

One day, somewhat lost behind a market, I wandered into a school and found Aixem, an Uighur schoolteacher who said she would be delighted to teach me some basics. She gave me a child's primer of the Arabic script, in which the Uighur language is written. It had been years since I'd tried to learn a new language. This one slipped in and out of shadows, I grasped some Persian-based words and others eluded me. I battled and felt like a child.

Standard Chinese, which I spoke with Li Jianjun, began to sound boxed and dissonant, with no room for manoeuvre, that ugly, 'h'-at-back-of-the-throat sound, a language made for platitudes in conversation. And with that came a lassitude, the despair of something changed: what was once enchanting was now suffocating. The passions of my twenties were waning in my thirties.

I reverted to Xuanzang.

Why did he not mention the Buddhist caves at Kizil, north of Kucha? Was he too busy proving himself at the city? Did he go to the caves and sit unmoved by wall paintings? Was it too far away and too much of a drain on resources? Did he get busy with preparations to cross the mountains?

Nobody knew.

An hour or so from Kucha, the Kizil caves sat on a cliff above the Muzart River. Li Jianjun took me there in his taxi. He told me tales of fisticuffs, Hong Kong-ers who refused to pay the arbitrary, inflated entrance fees. Cameras snatched and broken. A Japanese woman assaulted by two Uighurs and a Chinese man.

I controlled a flash flood of fear. I had become complacent, perhaps too complacent, about my own safety. The truth was, I could not afford to think too much of the dangers, for I would quail, lose my balance, crumple, and give up. I did not allow myself to contemplate what could happen; except at moments like this, when it hit me like an insidious virus that there was nothing to stop Li from pulling over the taxi and raping or murdering me. We were doing eighty kilometres per hour, and then 100 along this thin flat streak through the desert.

Kumarajiva (AD 344–413) sat in a lotus position at Kizil, his birthplace, frozen in stone. The half-Indian master translator shifted to Chang An after years in captivity and beavered away with a group of monks there, translating.

'Life is a kind of suffering,' the tour guide said crisply in Chinese.

It was a rattled, memorized spiel; a group of army cadres listened, leaning forward.

The caves were smaller, more compact than at Turfan, the paintings often a blue and turquoise of ground lapis lazuli from Afghanistan. There were also thick black lines and white swirls where the lead had discoloured.

In one cave, the Buddha was painted in turquoise, the faces were delicate, smiling, and drawn with finesse: there were apsaras over the front doors, holding an ochre mandolin, looking down from a background of blue and cream.

Another cave held evidence of the thirteenth century and its onslaught of Islam. Muslims destroyed clay statues with human faces, for only Allah could make representations of living things. Kizil, which means red, was also in the earthquake belt; the fragile statues had clattered and spilled and smashed. This was a three-part cave with a central column where visitors walked around three times clockwise. This was the closest thing I had seen to Indian stupas and their *pradakshinapath*, the path for circumambulation around it.

My guide, Su Yumin, was a grave young woman who spoke faultless English. She was Beijing-trained and yawned with the heat, or the routine. Dangling keys, she opened one cave door after another. It was in one of the Kizil caves that I saw on an inside column the painting of the Buddha's first speech in the Deer Park. The Buddha's face was gouged out, but I could make out the deer at the bottom.

In Cave 176 of the seventh century—most of it collapsed—in a narrow passageway, inches from my nose, I saw detailed line drawings. Indian lips, a dark prince with arched eyebrows. He was a most handsome creature with bright red ornaments encircling his upper ‚arms and a supercilious look down his nose.

It was amazing that this Indian man should be here, sitting cross-legged, the index and thumb of his right hand touching, dressed in a blue undershirt and light brown robe over the shoulder, that he should be painted here, deep in a Chinese cave, sitting on a stone pedestal preaching in the Deer Park.

I lingered, awed at how far the tales had travelled to lodge themselves in this cave wall. This one was about the first time, after his enlightenment, that the Buddha spoke to his disciples about the Middle Way.

'From inscriptions we know that Syrian painters, or those whose teachers were from India, Pakistan, Afghanistan, came here to paint,' Su Yumin said. 'They copied their teachers again and again and again and then they became painters, hired by Kucha court noblemen—the king and queen and their relations, for example—by donors, rich patrons who liked the South Asian style.'

The Buddha reached nirvana, but as a bedtime story his tale left much to be desired. Illustrious prince sees death and sickness and old age. Prince leaves home. Prince fasts but gets no results. Prince comes up with Middle Way. Wanders and preaches across North Indian plains for the rest of his life. Dies.

And so there were the Jatakas, folk tales about the Buddha's previous lives, which gave licence to the popular Indian imagination to embroider and weave the qualities and compassion of the beloved prince into something more tellable. It made a much better story to graft tales of compassion, stories of rabbits jumping into fires to offer themselves as meals, elephants offering their own tusks to be ground into medicine, birds flying over fires.

Here, in Kizil, was the story of a prince who sacrificed himself to the hungry tiger. The tiger was a jumbled scribble in the sandy wall, a hint of a man tumbling backwards.

Li Jianjun sulked under a tree, I had taken far too long.

Good, I thought, maybe he'll stop talking. But I had no such luck. The midday heat swung like a gong against my head, and Li chatted about Tiananmen Square, the way it was in the summer of 1989.

'It was an enormous loss of face, for Gorbachev was visiting. If you are a mother and your kids are misbehaving in front of an important visitor, wouldn't you chastise them? Yes, some were killed, they killed some soldiers too. But a country can't be too disorderly.'

Back in Kucha, there was a tightening in the air, a thin curtain of fear that hung in the city, dividing its citizens; there were whisperings of killings in Aksu, further west. Han Chinese done in by Uighurs, Uighurs done in by Uighurs.

The longer I stayed in the city, the more enmeshed I got in its troubles. Everybody warned me.

'Watch your money, watch yourself, don't go out after dark, be careful, you, a woman, alone.'

It was infectious, this nameless dread of your neighbour; I began to look over my shoulder, but there was nothing there. A walk through the Xinhua bookstore showed a book screaming from the shelves: *Separatism*. There was a sense of hunkering down before some threat of lese-majesty.

The donkey carts in the streets were not for tourists, but for the Uighurs themselves. The old market, the streets, the melons. There was a sense of the Uighurs having been here for centuries, a sense of belonging. It hung thick in the air, it was quite different from any other place. A de jure possession, the proprietoriness of it all. The instinct ran here, that the Han were the outsiders.

The mosques, the poorer sections of the cities, these were what I was looking for without even knowing it. China's fraying edges were what interested me.

There was a susurration of 'those who want a separate Xinjiang', who yanked kids from the schools and taught them treason. 'We have to work hard against this,' my Uighur teacher said, 'to enforce socialism and towards nationalism.'

Speaking Chinese, and being a foreigner, I mingled with the Han with ease. My Indian looks were similar to the Uighurs, and I understood bits of their tongue too. And so my days in Kucha passed, slipping in and out of each different world, seeking signs of a third, past, lost one.

It was intriguing. I decided to stay a few more days. I had already been in Kucha a week. An Uighur woman befriended me, a tall, stately woman. She was nearly forty, with long braids, plaits that came to her calves. Sometimes she wound them into an enormous bun behind her head. She had high cheekbones, a high, aristocratic nose. She wore heels and dressed with care. I shall call her Zulpia-gul.

Every day she told me her stories, how she adopted a child when he was one day old, how she had yearned to have a child but the doctors said that her husband could not. It caused fights between them, she wanted a divorce.

'It's upsetting to me.' She wiped a couple of tears from her eyes.

A few days later, we drove across to her house on her two-wheeled scooter. How proud she was, announcing 'Mehman' to her neighbours, although they didn't ask.

'We all have money,' she told me, 'we lack for nothing.'

I could see that was true—the fridge, the toaster, the thick, coloured carpets from Altai hanging on the walls and floors, the pictures. But her childlessness hunted her down. 'When my mother dies, I'll have nobody, I'll have nobody, I'll have nobody.' She twisted and untwisted the cap of her juice bottle. 'Husband, brother, father, they're all outsiders. It's a mother and sisters that are really close.'

She spoke with bitterness about her workplace.

'The danwei has ten Uighurs and 100 Chinese, and this is Xinjiang. How the Chinese women wear short skirts.' She wrinkled her nose in disgust. 'I wouldn't go to their house if they invited me. Their food has a funny taste. And they eat donkey meat and dog meat. And we don't know about our pension, will we get any? My husband is educated and holds such a low position in the bank, but a Chinese with a high-school degree can get promoted, and promoted again.

We should leave all this. I will open a restaurant and he will drive a taxi.'

She hinted at Uighur sons getting arrested, at people fleeing to Pakistan and being hauled back.

I watched as she kneaded the dough for noodles, sprinkled it with salt. Knead and fold and knead and fold and pass through a machine that flattened the dough and then, this long flat piece sliced into noodles and dropped into boiling water.

She made a sauce of tomatoes and beans and bits of mutton, a delicious stew, and at the end she threw in a handful of raw garlic. I slurped it up, taking out the mutton bits. I was trying to be a vegetarian again.

Earlier in the day she had fed me bits of naan. It had sesame seeds and onion flakes embedded in it. Smeared with honey, topped with walnuts and washed down with bowls of tea, the repast made me feel like a queen.

The boiler had broken down, I couldn't bathe. Despite the inconvenience, public baths were sensible. Who said you need a private bathroom for luxury? I sensed, with a small jolt, the absence of loneliness. It was the warmth of the Uighurs. I had been lonely in Han China, where the current Chinese view of the world could not expand enough to include an outside concept. And this was the beginning of the process of going home. Acceptance, and this link. To acquire a country and be at home.

If you hang around long enough, people want to hook you up. A woman said, 'I have a young handsome son, come to San Ya and marry him.'

I said I was married already.

'Divorce him,' she smiled.

A woman is measured by the men in her life. Otherwise, too much is left open to the imagination. I sat at the marketplace with my language teacher. She shovelled in sheep innards, the corners of her mouth stained with the oil from the large intestine.

Aixem ate as though she couldn't stop. As she ate, she told me the names. *Bettakhsah*: sheep innards. Sheep stomach, the fatty part: *oepka*. Sheep stomach lining: *khosak*. Sheep tripe, boiled sheep large intestine: *hassib*. You wash it, soften with water, mix with flour, add oil, spices, chillies, and cook. Sheep oesophagus: *kharek*, which swells after boiling with fat. 'My father said if you eat the *kharek* you'll get a big voice, it's not good for women,' Aixem said. 'But I think he said that because he wanted to eat it himself.'

The bazaar was the biggest this side of Kashgar—cows, sheep, horses all traded briskly. At namaz time, a man climbed onto the roof of the mosque between the towers, put his hands to his ears and yelled, 'It's almost time.' The authorities had taken down the loudspeakers. The worshippers faced west because that's where Mecca was. A beggar woman, her feet bound with cloth and with large bumps on her calves, had come for Friday charity.

Under the khariyakhash trees outside, rows of men spread prayer mats and knelt, heads covered, putting their hands by their ears as though to better hear what Allah had to say. There were all these words I already knew: *jumaat, akhbaar, malum, rang*.

The roads were full of peasants. Fat horses with jingling harnesses pulled simple carriages. These were a large plank on wheels with four poles over which a cloth was stretched against the sun, bunting fluttering.

A baker kneaded naan dough into a circle, slapped it into the sides of an underground tandoor, a hollow in the ground, then pulled it up with a hooked iron stick and swirled it through the air so that it landed on a table with a light thud, floating a tail of warm aromas. It was hot and soft and irresistible, embedded with roasted cumin and onion flakes. I broke off a piece and the naan steamed in the light.

I walked down to a spice vendor who had the same dried lizards and saunf, and bought a small bottle of honey. It was in a glass bottle, sealed with a rubber stopper. It was so fresh that a bee wing floated in the clarity.

Roads were blocked off all over the city. Friday was the day for the bazaar, and in June it was also exam time at the school; anxious parents swarmed outside the gate awaiting their kids. I took a horse cart all the way back. The market had swelled and expanded like the universe—cabbages, turnips, shoes. The whole city was out eating ices, all dressed up for the outing. Further out, there were shops with carved chests, furniture, door grills, sofas and beds. I had sunk into Kucha, as into a comfortable armchair, but there was now a vague whisper at my heels, a certain restlessness. The days thinned and it was time to move again.

chapter eight

White Water

For the monk, there was a royal send-off from Kucha. The king gave him servants, camels, horses. Monks and laymen from the desert city walked with him a fair distance. He travelled about 600 *li* to the west, a two-day journey crossing a small sandy desert, to arrive at Poh-lu-kia.

On the way, the caravan stumbled on a camp of 2000 Turkish robbers on horseback. From a distance, the travellers heard the sound of squabbling. Then zinging arrows rose from behind the sand dunes and fell by the monk.

The group came to a halt, hidden by the dunes, frozen with fear, but they need not have worried. The Turks were too busy arguing over the spoils of a raid. The previous caravan had been pillaged and had yielded a rich haul.

The yells grew fainter, the robbers had dispersed without noticing Xuanzang and his retinue. The group plodded through the sands of the desert and spent one night at Poh-lu-kia. It was not that different from Kucha, the monk wrote.

෫

Poh-lu-kia, by the foothills of the Tian Shan range, was reborn in the twentieth century as Aksu. *Ak-su*, 'white water' in Turkish. The monk had continued west from Aksu, heading to the Bedel Pass high in the mountains—the actual border with the old Soviet Union.

A two-carriage train started the previous year from Kucha to Aksu was almost empty. There was no air-conditioning, it was broiling.

Everybody slept. Someone further back, with a deep voice, awoke just long enough to beg the carriage attendant to turn on the ceiling fans which glared, unmoving, from small wire boxes. The attendant did nothing. The voice sighed and went back to sleep.

The apricots were ripe, boughs bent with the weight of the fruit. Threshed wheat lay around fields in neat piles. A hare raced across the fields, with long ears, a light brown body, hopping lightly.

A sudden dust sprang up. The windows of the train were slammed shut. The wind rose and sand flew into the carriage. There was dust in every crease of my clothes, my hair, between my teeth, sand between pen and paper.

Where did Xuanzang sleep? There was not even a tree to hide under. Now we were in the middle of a vast grassy plain. There must be a river somewhere; as I wrote that, we crossed it.

The wind swelled to an enormous sandstorm blowing across the plain, a low rush at a small train station; the guard's blue shirt flapped wild as he unloaded cartons of drinks. We could see nothing beyond 100 metres or so. We were on the periphery of the storm, then we were in it. I travelled in a thin veil of sand all the way to Aksu.

Sometimes you burn out, and so that night I felt a burning heat crawl over my body. I tossed through the restless night, trying to cool off with cold water from the shower, but mosquitoes hovered.

The crashing loneliness was back, the tiresomeness of being in a very Chinese town and being a foreigner, the ominousness of border areas and the blandness of Aksu. I missed my Kucha companions. I longed to meet other travellers, but there were none here. Instead, the place was crawling with policemen. There was nothing here to see, it seemed. Placards on the streets gave away the city's biggest problems.

ETHNIC UNITY IS THE LIFE PATH OF EVERY ETHNIC GROUP
OPPOSE ETHNIC SPLITTISM
THE ARMY IS HERE TO PROTECT YOU
NATIONAL UNITY AND WORLD PEACE

A country's fears writ large on street placards, sponsored by the Agricultural Bank of China. But I was tired of other people's conflicts.

Aksu had no Buddhists left nor any Buddhist remains that I could find, but the food was excellent. At lunch, I had a sweet-and-sour eggplant dish, with shredded garlic, chopped spring onions and the barest hint of chilli in it. I scooped up the sauce with a spoon and learned that the cook was from Sichuan. All these Sichuanese stuck in the desert, nostalgic for the green mountains and rivers of their native province, poured their wistfulness into the cooking at the restaurants they came here to open.

It rained one morning and cooled things down. To check about crossing the Tian Shan from the Bedel Pass, I went to the city police, who said to go to the regional police, who said to ask the border police. This one was an impressive building. I was not even allowed inside. Things had to be done through a window, bending at the waist.

'Sorry, no foreigners allowed in this area. You need permission from the highest security levels. Beijing has to approve this. Without that nobody here will dare approve anything.'

Bu kai fang. Not open.

I had expected this, so I accepted it.

The tensions felt close to the surface here. At the street food square, a Han Chinese woman reached for a skewer and pointed it at a man in an Uighur food stall. Luo Hong, a businesswoman from Sichuan, stomped out of the dormitory room and snapped at the concierge.

'How come you've put me in the same room as an Uighur?'

'She's not an Uighur, she's Indian.'

Luo Hong came back and smiled.

'You know, you can get great food across the road, but hurry.'

Later that night, she fished out recent wedding pictures and reached across to my bed to show me. I was scribbling notes leaning on the headboard.

She confided, 'Sichuan is much better than here. I don't like the Uighur.'

I said nothing and she took this as encouragement.

'The more you give him, the more he wants. He's never happy. You know, China has a liberal policy towards minorities, they can have several kids, they get all these concessions, and the Uighur is still not satisfied.'

'Some of them are nice.' Her tone became filled with her own largesse. 'If an Uighur likes you, he'll bring out the nicest things in his house to give you, but really there is nothing between the two. But you know, Uighurs, they won't wash, they smell. It's not that they don't have water, they're just not used to washing.'

Jiang Xing, another Sichuanese at the restaurant, was so unhappy she could not eat her lunch and said if she had known Xinjiang was like this she would never have come.

'It's horrible, it never rains. They said it was a good place. How much is a plane ticket to Guangzhou, do you know?' she asked me mournfully.

'No,' I said, 'but if you call 114 you can get the number for the ticketing office.' We pored over train routes to Guangzhou on my map.

She smiled with a faint ray of hope, poor sad woman. I began to reassess who the foreigner was here.

I gave up on the idea of crossing the mountains from Aksu into Kyrgyzstan. It appeared the only way was from the Torugart Pass much further south. And this meant, I looked at my map, a detour south of over 400 kilometres to Kashgar. I wasted no further time and purchased a train ticket for the next morning.

I had to fight my favourite worry that somehow I was on the wrong train making excellent progress to the wrong place. But it was always the right train to the next destination, as though some creamy invisible thread guided me.

Rolling into Kashgar was a warm surprise—the surroundings were rural, but in the fields outside wheat was piled in a great golden heap in the middle and farmers hefted great bundles of it into the air. I watched a fine dust lift, thinking this is what I had to learn too—to separate the wheat from the chaff. By now I could have sworn I was in a different country. At the Chinibagh Hotel, on the third floor, three Pakistanis aligned their prayer mats west and bowed down and prayed.

I shared a dormitory room with an Israeli woman and her New Zealand travel companion. Another traveller, Axel, was German.

Small groups formed and fell apart. The comfort for me of speaking English was like exercising unused muscles. The illusion of closeness was temporary, but real while it lasted; we clicked and then scattered like marbles.

'China is a strange country,' Axel said. He talked rapidly, entertaining us with tales of a Pakistani embassy official who wanted to spend the night with him in exchange for a visa. It was Axel who pointed out that the Pakistani traders came over the Khunjerab Pass, along the Karakoram Highway, to Kashgar to sell their merchandise and buy the favours of slim Chinese women. We all leaned over the banisters one warm evening to watch a bulky man from Peshawar follow into a back room a twiggy, elegant girl in a skirt that barely covered her buttocks.

Axel swigged his beer. He had been trying to get his bicycle fixed for days to cycle along the Karakoram. But it seemed a Kafkaesque drama of one thing getting fixed and another breaking.

At least he hadn't that edge of Jim from Northern Ireland, who talked of Pakistan's Dera Adam Khel, guns made of ceramics, not detectable by X-rays. He knew all about missile cones made of fused aluminium or silica.

There was Imran Bhatt, a Pakistani from Peshawar, who bought electronic goods in Kashgar and sold them in Peshawar: a new version of the Silk Road. He invited me for tea. I declined, but regretfully, torn between curiosity and bound by the limits of a social web we both understood. As travellers, we were all on some threshold, trembling on the brink of our own separate journeys, a fragile coalition.

I was not having much luck heading to Kyrgyzstan, across the mountains. Loyuk, a lanky, sad-faced Tajik who was supposed to arrange these things, did little to help. Help me find the way, I muttered, and I could have sworn I felt the monk reach out a hand through the centuries, for the way to Kyrgyzstan opened one day.

I asked at John's Cafe. 'How do I get to Kyrgyzstan?'

'There, behind you,' the man said.

He meant Bernard and Constance, a young German student-couple who were also going to Kyrgyzstan. Bernard had straight-up thick curly hair and a frank, open face. Constance, his girlfriend, was shyer, more reserved. There was also Alex, a Frenchman, who was heading home to France via Turkmenistan and Iran.

Word gets around: travellers nosing for like-minded people heading the same way, safety in numbers, costs reduced. Bernard was good at this. He had contacted the Kyrgyz travel agent to meet our latter-day caravan at the border and accompany it to the capital, Bishkek.

I could sink back into my dreamy state and ignore the logistics for once. It would take a few days to complete the paperwork, organize a suitable car for the drive to the Kyrgyz border. I was more or less on schedule, but geographically I was off-track. I missed the monk's trail; its residual heat nagged at me. Off the path, I felt distracted and restless, a broken concentration waiting to return to a chosen task.

But the delay meant there was time to see Kashgar's famous Sunday market, and our little Chinibagh group set off early. The dust was already in eddies around hooves in the market where sheep, their behinds bobbing, were fat with extra wool. Trade thickened the air at 8 a.m. local time.

A buyer, a squat man in loose trousers tied with a belt, stood by three black sheep he intended to purchase. He undid his belt, pushed his pants below his belly, pulled up his shirt and eased out a woman's stocking tied around his middle. Caught in the middle of the stocking was a bundle of 100-yuan notes from which he peeled off ten. He handed over the money, the farmer counted it and, satisfied, parted with the rope tying the three sheep together.

There was a makeshift stable with horses restless and edgy. Beyond, a boy so small he could ride without a saddle sat high on the animal's withers, his grubby bare feet swinging loose. Whip in hand, he galloped the horse up and down the dusty lane: a test drive for all to see. The tight shoulders, fleshy flanks, gaskin, hocks and hooves. He made the horse stop, wheel, and set off again. Later, he leaned forward and with tiny hands tightened a strap below the horse's right ear: a slow, tender movement in the hubbub and sweat, under a kingfisher-blue sky.

A row of barbers shaved and scraped with sharp knives. A barber pulled up a client's upper lip to trim the moustache, a delicate region. The bearded man closed his eyes. Stall after stall of men leaned back, their torsos covered with wide cloths, heads bare, while another army of men listed forward with their lethal edges.

An unhappy donkey, upper lip quivering, let out a bray—a painful inward breathing sound. Peaches were in season, juicy, a tinge of pink on a pale fuzzy background. And figs, small and flat and light green and pulpy, thick with seeds, sold in a large leaf. Wrinkled old women sold yoghurt, fresh and tart, set at home in bowls, to be eaten on the spot so the bowl could be returned. The yoghurt sold out fast, cooling customers in the heat. A man sliced a wine-dark liver and two sheep hearts leaned against each other. The donkey was sold for 1500 yuan.

In this camaraderie, a farmer from Shaanxi in China (I did it again), walnut-brown face, blue shirt, bargained. He had driven 4500 kilometres to Kashgar from central China to buy cattle in the oldest game on the Silk Road: buy low, sell high. He would load the cattle onto his truck and drive them all back. An Uighur strained, pulled his cow's mouth open, showing him the teeth, but the Shaanxi farmer demurred, 'It's too old, it's too small. Still, can I come by your house in the afternoon? Maybe we can talk more.' The second oldest game on the Silk Road: disparage what you intend to buy.

At the fowl market, they lifted the wings of cocks for signs of disease, checked the eyes, squatted in a circle, held the bird down with both hands, tossed corn and watched it peck. The fowl skipped between feet. Someone lunged to capture it.

Two pigeons sat in a basket slung over a bicycle. A handsome man rested a foot on the saddle, sure of his goods. Another Uighur examined the pigeons, folding the bird's feet and feathers in one deft hand, the index of his right hand pulling down the skin below a round eye, a shiny glistening bead with clear whites.

Small boys held charcoal baby birds with sharp yellow beaks opened wide, a tongue showing at the back of its throat when the boy imitated with his finger a parent bird swooping with food. The small claws curled on his other index finger.

Grey rabbits in plastic flour sacks, held up by their ears, waved paws in the air.

In the back alleys there were pelts, fox furs, minks, bolts of cloth, hats, knives, tyres, electronic goods and a crude anti-Nato T-shirt with Clinton's head drawn on it.

A woman walked back cradling a lamb, her husband tugged at a sheep. They had the air of proud parents. Or satisfied customers. By noon the market had wound down.

We too wandered back tired and satisfied.

It would be hard to leave China–not China and cross the mountains into the unknown.

chapter nine

Heavenly Mountains

When the snows had melted a little in the lower reaches of the range, the monk and his retinue headed west from Aksu to tackle the crossing at the Bedel Pass, high among the hills. China lay behind a desert and then behind a serried curtain of peaks, veiled and lost to him. He took deeper breaths, shook off memories. He saw each detail of the landscape around him, as though he were looking for the first time.

He fingered his rosary. One step at a time. After each *li* he recited a sutra under his breath; when his breath failed, he said it in his mind. *Guanyin* . . . He got off his horse to give it a rest, slipped and fell against the ice. For a brief moment he laid his face against the slab and felt the heat of his cheek melt the surface. He closed his eyes until he felt his breath even and lose its ragged edge and found the strength to ease to his knees, then to his feet.

Around him, men groaned and panted, pack animals heaved. Think of the next step, he schooled himself.

Men began to die. Three, four, then five. They starved or froze in the seven days of the crossing. Many more oxen and horses perished. The cold closed punishing fingers around the men's bones. The monk thought he would shiver for the rest of his life; if he lived through this, he would shiver forever though he had on all the fur-lined clothing from the king of Gaochang.

Six, seven men died.

The company leaned into the wind and felt it scrape their noses. At night there was no shelter, not a dry place to be found. They hung their cooking pots exposed and unrolled mats on the ice. In the morning they counted their dead, grey faces with frozen lashes, covered in a film of ice under their blankets. When the caravan pushed on, they did not look back at the bundles left in the snow.

Twelve, fourteen dead.

After seven days they descended below the snowline on the other side, they had crossed the cursed mountains, which closed over the shattered caravan without a murmur as the monk and his companions sank into a new world.

ℰℴ

From Kashgar, the peacock-blue four-wheel-drive Toyota Land Cruiser with its tinted windows swept west across flat deserts through the light burn of a morning, with slim poplar trees in a valley. Bernard, Constance, Alex and I hunched inside, a little nervous, pleased to have each others' company and to be on our way after days of delay.

There were graves by the roadside, tilted reminders of those who had died so long ago in Xuanzang's party. Who was now buried in the desert, by the rocks, in the lonely ground? There was nothing around, no humans came to lay flowers; there was only the wind and the road and the tombs at the foot of the mountain.

Immigration, baggage checks, security checks at the Torugart Pass took the four of us one hour. The staff was nervy, the security high. The enterprise felt unknown. They had never seen an Indian at this border crossing.

'Please take off your dark glasses,' the official said, craning from his post. I whipped them off and smiled. I aimed for a mix of beguiling and bored.

'Which city in India are you from? Which part of the city is this address in? Who's the President?'

He examined the photo, turned the passport this way and that, flipped through the pages. I hoped he would not make me sing the national anthem, because I only knew the first two lines. He shook his head in amazement.

'First Indian.' He made an entry in his ledger. The thump of a stamp, that glad noise.

Exit. Torugart Pass. Dozens of Uighurs were travelling to

Kyrgyzstan. One, an Uighur cloth merchant, was going to a bazaar in Bishkek on this, the new Silk Road, an easy continuance of the old route's primary purpose.

Beyond customs, there was a great pile of debris on the road from a dynamited mountain and the driver, nervous, had to wheel off the gravel right down into the river bed, bounce along and then crawl up again, easing into first gear.

We turned hairpin bends. Mists hung around the mountain tops. At the foot of the mountain, by the roadside, a brick mosque sat at an angle. Behind it rose barren hills, rocky outcrops, villages with low mud walls.

There were herds of horses and, already, the yurts—round felt tents the nomads used—which we would see hundreds of in Kyrgyzstan. We began to climb up to the actual pass. The temperatures dropped, it began to drizzle. For the first time since leaving the desert, we donned our sweaters. At a checkpoint, a bus from Kyrgyzstan stopped to unload carpets. Our driver fished out two watermelons and handed them to the official who, after a look at our passports and the car, waved us through.

Massive, articulated trucks, filled with metals—aluminium, copper, Central Asia's metal riches—stopped for checks. A miasma of gloom settled over the final checkpoint on the Kyrgyz side. It was a grand stone arch, with CCCP and the hammer and sickle still engraved on it, as though news of the USSR's demise had not travelled this far.

'Do you have any rolls of film?' the Chinese guard asked.

'*Mei you*,' I lied. Our driver handed over a packet of developed pictures to the officers, collected on a previous trip. Small favours grease the wheels.

On the other side of the arch Zhenya waited, as Bernard had arranged. Zhenya had driven fro..1 the capital, Bishkek, a two-day journey, to meet us here and take us back. There was no other way for foreigners to get from Kashgar in China to Bishkek in Kyrgyzstan. Authorities banned foreigners from using the public bus. Zhenya was middle-aged and his hands were calloused, his expression unreadable. His thinning strawberry-blond hair and blue eyes came as a shock after months of Chinese faces.

We were unable to communicate; even with six languages between the four of us we could not tell Zhenya the simplest thing. Constance pulled out a small pocket Russian–German dictionary. She looked up the Russian, translated it into German, then into English.

We gestured and pointed and loaded our bags, and the four of us squeezed into the white Lada, a Russian jeep with strong tyres. A short drive further, the Kyrgyz immigration gates had yet to open and we waited on the road, hopping up and down to keep warm, and looked at the marmots sitting on their haunches with their forefeet in the air. They had sharp faces. They looked at us and dove back into their holes. The weather was dismal.

I was hundreds of kilometres south of where the monk had crossed this border. Compared to what Xuanzang endured crossing the icy mountains, his companions dying one by one, this was a breeze. Still, removed from his track, I felt a climbing unease, like a toothache. He was history, but he was a familiar beacon in the midst of strange new things. I relied on his company.

An hour later, big guards in military fatigues with Kalashnikovs slung over their shoulders pulled open metal gates. They wore thick black leather boots, a whiff of something Russian. They had donned thick fur hats with earflaps and coats against the cold and rain. One restrained a leashed German Shepherd at the guard tower, which was protected by rolls of barbed wire.

Water dripped from the peak of a guard's camouflage hat as he leaned into the car window and checked passports, one by one. The water pooled on passport pages causing Alex no end of anxiety as visa stamps ran colour and inked signatures blotched.

The car had to be left on a dual track, as if it were at the garage for repairs, so that the police could check for bombs and weapons underneath the carriage while we filed into a shed to have our papers checked. We fiddled with declaration forms in Russian, blowing on our fingers, guessing and leaning over to see what the others were doing.

There were tilted mirrors behind the queue, so the guard could see behind the person being checked. The guards were everywhere, in black-and-white camouflage gear for snow, as well as in uniforms with olive and black splodges. Their faces were startlingly varied.

Fine-boned Kyrgyz with dark hair, tall blond Russians, in-betweens. It was my first taste of Central Asia and its ethnic khichdi.

'Good luck,' they kept saying in English. 'Good luck.'

Laden with fears, unsure of what lay ahead, I was unprepared for Kyrgyzstan. Unprepared for the grasslands that met us, the ease of cantering roadside horsemen with their white felt hats striped with black, hats that mirrored snow-capped mountains and rivers flowing down them. Bathed in mists and rain, Kyrgyzstan was a breathlessness, beauty veiled in a numinous whisper.

The Lada broke down and had to be towed by another van. Dinner late at night was pulao, which they called *pollov*, a soup with chunks of mutton and boiled potatoes, seasoned with dill. A dollop of cream floated on top. It was a delicate, delicious flavour which would become a familiar staple in Central Asia. We tucked into peanuts and walnuts, naan, black tea with sugar, apples fallen straight from the tree judging by the bruises, bowls of yoghurt lightly seasoned. Here was the beginning of India, a sweet whimper of recognition in the yoghurt.

At the half-way stop, we slept in a yurt. It had four beds arranged against the round wall. We fell into our beds, hunger sated, dulled with fatigue. It was warm and comfortable and so absolute in its darkness that not a chink of light fell in to disturb our sleep.

∞

In the silent recesses of his Xian monastery, Xuanzang lay in his cell, unable to move. Sweat poured from his body, soaking the mat he lay on. Rags of dreams flitted behind his eyes, pushing sibilant sounds from his throat.

'Master,' Hui Li muttered. 'Master, you are ill.'

'The mountains,' Xuanzang breathed. 'We crossed the mountains. But they died.'

'Hush,' Hui Li said, placing his fingers over the monk's dry lips.

'There was nothing I could do,' Xuanzang wept in his delirium. Tears dripped from the sides of his eyes. 'They died. I had to leave them lying there so I could reach the city of Su-yeh. I had to keep going.'

The words sounded more like a confession than a narrative.

ॐ

It would take a day-long drive north-west to Bishkek where I would try and rejoin the monk's journey, although, having looped south and then north-west to avoid the mountains, I had missed a section.

For now, Kyrgyzstan gently prised open my senses. We had woken feeling fresh and filled with hope. The grass smelled sweet, dandelions grew and birds chirped. There were blue flowers with pale mauve petals, five of them, and hundreds of flowers with thin yellow petals spread on the mountain flanks. There were wisps of clouds and butterflies. It was like some dreamy state I did not want to wake from.

Zhenya pulled a rope across our luggage atop the Lada. Three little Kyrgyz boys played in the grass. I asked their names, to relish the sound of a new language. Norbek, Tashi and Itoi. The roses were bright splashes of colour, vermilion, cream and pink. The sun soaked into me and sucked the last bits of fatigue from my bones.

Zhenya stopped for fermented mare's milk, *kimiz*, ripened in sheepskin bags, sold from yurts by the roadside. I wrinkled my nose at its taste, a tart, tangy slap on my tongue. Small Kyrgyz children with rough red cheeks ran up begging for pictures to be taken. Clear glacial streams. Fields, smears of bright yellow flowers against the snow-and-blue of hills and sky, the fuchsia flowers called kislichka in Russian. Lenin's face, made in looped and bent metal wire, stood atop a hill, a face filled with sky. Lenin. I was travelling through a whole different history.

The Kyrgyz too had built tombs by the road. Kyrgyz cemeteries were the only elaborate structures in the landscape, as though it took death to build something permanent in the mountains. They were wire cages with a Muslim crescent on top, a wire bent and cut into shape. Or brick, with a face painted on a stone at the top. Sometimes, a stone falcon was perched on top, its wings spread as though ready for flight, the structure gripped in its talons as though the whole tomb would lift off.

Stalin moved much of Russia's heavy industry to Kyrgyzstan during the Second World War. Many soldiers were recruited from here too. And so, in this forgotten corner of the world there lingers mourning for a war that ended over half a century ago. Every Kyrgyz village we passed held war memorials, monuments to the heroes who died, great socialist men with muscles of stone and determined jaws.

When we drove into Bishkek it was late afternoon. Bernard, Constance, Alex and I clung together like small, lost children. We banded together, unwilling to separate, petrified by the thought of going our own ways. We found a dormitory, a Kyrgyz guest house or *mehmankhana*, with a few hostile-looking Kyrgyz hunched outside. When we paid off Zhenya, it was as though we were sending off our guardian angel.

The place was near Tsirk, the circus, now boarded-up and closed. The *mehmankhana* had cracked and broken windows, it had a cubicle for a bathroom, a flush that did not work. The days had turned hot, mosquitoes and flies hovered. Small items disappeared from the room.

Through the fog of fear, it came as clear as a bell, a small pocket of delight, that this word in Kyrgyz, *mehmankhana*, was the same in Uighur and in Persian. We found public showers at the place next door for ten som. Socialism had died in China, and now in Russia, but had left its public baths everywhere. They were not unlike the Chinese ones with the single stream of hot water, the steam, the cubicles to change in. Next door, at the Azerbaijan Cafe, sunlight filtered through massive oak trees.

Azerbaijan, I said to myself. Azerbaijan. The name conjured up new worlds I thrilled to. The four of us sat around a table alfresco and flapped open the English-language *Times of Central Asia*. It was a moment of normality in this disconcerting town.

For the third time since I was ten years old, I found myself in a country where I did not speak the local language. As before, it made me curious to know what people were saying. I had never even come across the Kyrgyz national flag where on a flaming red background a yellow centre spread like an egg yolk: the *tunduk*, or top of a yurt, they say, with the surrounding forty rays representing the forty wives of the legendary Manas, who gave rise to the forty tribes of Kyrgyzstan.

I hunted down details to satisfy this sudden craving. Bishkek was a couple of hours' flight from New Delhi. How was it that I knew nothing about a country that sat in India's backyard? The Kyrgyz, those Turkish-derived tribes, first wrote in an ancient runic lettering which remained till the tenth century, but with the spread of Islam, the upper levels of Turkish society became Islamic and the runic lettering gave way to Arabic. In 1927, the Arabic system was changed to the Latin alphabet for a short time between 1939 and 1940, and then the land's new Russian masters shifted it to Cyrillic, which is still used.

In modern Bishkek, the beauty of the mountains had ebbed. Leafy avenues and parks of oak trees filled the city, but it was plastered with something dubious. The roads were full of stolen cars still bearing the stickers of European countries. Money-changing kiosks abounded and lovely leggy women wearing the bare minimum bent into car windows, negotiated, and then stepped into the back seat.

On our first day in Bishkek, we managed, with the help of Constance's Russian dictionary, to order boiled eggs, *iran*—a cold yoghurt drink like lassi—coffee with milk, cheese. We went, all together, to change money at a Kyrgyz bank. It took the better part of the morning. Our taxi driver had a snake tattooed on his upper arm, scratches on his face, several gold teeth. The head of his gear shift was a cobra. He was obviously an apparition, which perfectly fit the mood of the day.

Still, our panic lost its edge. We ventured further, laughed at our own fears. We stopped to try a glass of *shoro* among the oak trees. It was liquified cereal, oatmeal, barley and corn mixed, with a salty–tangy aftertaste. It was like the nation, such a mixture, a veritable Bishkek Benetton advertisement: Russians, Mongolians, Kyrgyz, Uzbeks, Uighurs, Koreans.

We even went out to a nightclub, because oddly, after dark, dour Bishkek's ill-lit streets filled with music, bass and drum beats. *I wish that you would hold me like a Spanish guitar.*

At W, a discotheque in an open-air park, Latin beats filled the night as couples danced; the women in the skimpiest dresses showed off their tight Slavic bodies like medals. I began to think I had been mistaken about the other women I'd seen climbing into cars. Perhaps they were not negotiating business. They just dressed this way.

'Zees fashion, it's the eighties. Zeez women, zey all look like prostitutes.' Alex said what we were all thinking.

The music throbbed, the strobe lights bounced. In the clammy darkness there were burly Russians with shaved heads, rich Kyrgyz with moustaches. A Pakistani man sat close to a Chinese woman, his arm around her. Both were drunk. At the next table they drank whisky out of a decanter, empty bottles of vodka were strewn everywhere. A crimson BMW was parked on the pavement.

A day or so later, our little group split, three segments of an orange. Bernard and Constance went on to Uzbekistan. Alex headed off to explore the region. And I collected my wits to try and reconnect with Xuanzang's journey. Bishkek was right on the Silk Road; one section of northern Bishkek was called Ipak Yole, 'Silk Road' in Kyrgyz, because it ran through there.

But the vast Central Asian town where Xuanzang stopped, after he crossed the mountains and followed the route along the southern shore of Lake Issykul, was called Su-yeh. I only knew it was somewhere near a city called Tokmak, some kilometres east of Bishkek. It was where the monk had met the great Khan of the Turks, Yeh Hu.

∞

That day Yeh Hu was setting off on a hunting expedition, and he invited the Buddhist monk to rest a few days until he returned. For a bunch of barbarians, the Turks put on quite a show, Xuanzang admitted to Hui Li, who wrote down this description of that day:

> The horses of these barbarous people are very fine; the Khan's person was covered with a robe of green satin, and his hair was loose, only it was bound round with a silken band some ten feet in length, which was twisted round his head and fell down behind. He was surrounded by about 200 officers who were all clothed in brocade stuff, with their hair braided. On the right and left he was attended by independent troops all clothed in furs and fine spun hair garments; they carried lances and bows and standards, and were mounted on camels and horses. The eye could not estimate their numbers.[1]

They agreed that the Khan's chief officer, Ta-mo-chi, would conduct the tired and very relieved monk to a large tent (a yurt!) and arrange things for his comfort, that the Khan and the monk would speak at length in a few days.

Xuanzang could rest, shave the stubble on his face, his head, tend to chilblains and frostbite, meditate at dawn, wash his robes in the river and hang them up to dry. The caravan could feed the horses, repack the shifted contents of saddlebags, trade bolts of silk and dried rations for fresh supplies.

And mourn the dead.

∞

Who was this hunting Khan who lived in the Chuy River valley and received the roaming Chinese Buddhist priest? Yeh Hu was possibly a Chinese version of the Turkish title *Yabgu* or 'secondary ruler', rather than a proper name. The Khan had fierce antecedents. A hundred-odd years before the monk crossed the Tian Shan range, somewhere in Mongolia, they say from a base in the Altai Mountains, a proud Turkic chieftain called Bumin revolted against his overlords in Siberia[2] known as the Juan-juan.

By AD 556, the band of Turks had smashed Juan-juan power and set up a Turkic empire on the steppes.[3] Was it through war? A more pragmatic version in the Kyrgyz History Museum suggested too that when the Turks led by Bumin stumbled on territories rich in iron, they paid taxes to the Juan-juan and bought the right to capture other tribes and make them slaves. Thus they won over western Siberia.

Dramatic changes were nothing new in this part of the world, I learned.

Tribes rose and fell, fought and won, or lost. Clans and bands stuck together, nominating their brothers or their sons to positions of power. No outsider held power for long in this unruly region. Not Alexander the Great, who marched as far as Śamarkand in 329 BC but did not quite make it to the Chuy River valley; not the Iranians who eyed the region from Persepolis. And in the eighth century the Arabs faced tough campaigns as they grappled to extend their dominion here.

Many of these Central Asian dramas did not have much in the way of written records. We know that the old Turkish Khanate founded by Bumin in the sixth century split into two sections, East and West. We know from Chinese sources that Xuanzang's Khan belonged to the Western Turks and ruled the region from AD 619 to 630.[4]

We also know that from his home in this picturesque valley, the Turk had allied with a powerful neighbour to the west, Emperor Heraclius, to fight the Sassanian king Khusrau II. Perhaps, like his ancestors, the Khan adopted the nomenclature of 'On Ogbudun', People of Ten Arrows.

Yeh Hu was proud and ambitious. A rebellion arose, led by another Turkic tribe called the Karluks, and the Khan who met Xuanzang under blue Central Asian skies was murdered not long after their meeting.[5] Perhaps as the Khan lay slumped against his horse's neck, his bow and arrow tumbling to the grass and blood mingling with sweat, a conversation with a foreign monk flashed through his mind.

The shamanist Khan Yeh Hu and the Buddhist Chinese monk spoke through an interpreter. Somebody was found who happened to have spent time in Chang An and spoke both Chinese and the local language. The monk handed the Khan letters and presents from the king of Gaochang. Khan Yeh Hu was delighted to hear from the Buddhist king of Gaochang across the mountains, to whom he was related by marriage. Yeh Hu had always liked the king in the Tarim Basin, and any friend of his was welcome, even a Buddhist monk from China, for whom Yeh Hu himself perhaps had little use.

A celebration was in order. The Khan ordered wine and music.

Xuanzang, being a monk, sipped simple grape juice while the Turks around him proceeded to get quite drunk. They toasted each other, challenged each other, filled and emptied their cups in rapid succession. The music clanged louder and louder. Xuanzang had to admit, once more, that although the music was the common sort that barbarians liked, it was good. 'Diverting both to the ear and the eye, pleasing the thoughts and the mind.'[6]

As the party heated up, the food was brought on. Boiled mutton quarters and veal were heaped before the guests. In deference to the monk's religion, the Turks served him rice cakes, sugar candy, honey sticks, raisins.

After dinner, more wine was drunk. At length, past midnight, in a post-prandial haze, the Khan asked the monk to expound on this religion of his. Somewhat stiff, the monk launched into an explanation. He cleared his throat. Hui Li, faithful scribe, wrote:

> Then he, with a view to admonish them, spoke upon the subject of the ten precepts (Dasasilam), love of preserving life, and the Paramitas, and works that lead to final deliverance.[7]

Do not kill, do not steal. No adultery, slander, greed, cherish the lives of other creatures.

It sounded good to the Khan. He felt he could use some deliverance, especially from his head, which was beginning to throb. Perhaps it was the drink and the satiation of food, perhaps he was stirred or amused by his visitor's resolve; his type was hard to come by in the Valley of the Seven Rivers, this hint of something beyond a rude life of hunting, falcon-raising and roasting mutton on spits.

At any rate, the Khan raised his hands and humbly prostrated himself to the ground (that, or he stumbled and fell on his face) and accepted the teachings of the Master.

At least that is what Hui Li said. And that is all we have to go on.

෴

I snapped into action. I telephoned the Indian embassy and said I had reached Bishkek. Months ago in Delhi, preparing for the trip, I had met my own king of Gaochang. I too needed a little help from the powers that be. I turned to the Indian ministry of foreign affairs. A joint secretary dispatched a friendly message to the Indian embassies in Central Asia: a traveller will be passing through in a few months, nothing important, a known quantity, most grateful if you could help her find accommodation, keep an eye on her in case she runs into trouble. That kind of thing.

The Indian embassy in Bishkek sent a shiny taupe Mercedes to pick me up from the Kyrgyz *mehmankhana*. It was with unspeakable relief that I dropped my backpack into its padded trunk. Soon, I had swapped the filthy guest house for a small private apartment rented from Russian pensioners, payable from my stash of US dollars. It was clean and comfortable, not far from the Indian embassy.

The embassy also put me in touch with Stalina, an interpreter, without whose enterprising ways and ability to translate from three Central Asian languages into English nothing would have happened. Stalina was Uzbek, many of her relatives were in Uzbekistan. She was my age. She had fine, dark features, a long Persian nose and a noble mouth, pulled down at the corners. I relied on her utterly. She too welcomed the change from routine translation work. Stalina made inquiries at the Kyrgyz State National University about the location of the ancient site. Where were the ruins of the city of Su-yeh where the Chinese monk had met the Khan?

One fine Saturday morning we drove towards Tokmak, past the Lenin Museum, which had become the History Museum when Kyrgyzstan came into being in 1991, past the White House, which used to house the Communist Party and was now used by President Askar Akaev and his executive.

In front of Bishkek's marbled square stood a statue of Lenin. At 10 a.m. sharp, the fountains started and three guards goose-stepped across the square. Lenin's right foot was kicked out, his right hand outstretched south, his left held his coat back, his chest thrust out, as though he had sighted the mountains and exclaimed, 'What a fine view!'

Stalina painted a rough impression of Kyrgyzstan, filled with bits and pieces, brush-strokes that made up a whole—the commerce with Turkey, the gas imported from Uzbekistan. We drove by the Ataturk petrol pump, the symbol of a wolf stamped on its sides. The Turkish influence persisted in Bishkek.

'The Grey Wolves in Turkey,' said Stalina, 'are a fascist movement.' But the wolf harked back to an ancient legend of a band of Turkish warriors from the Altai Mountains. The Turks have a story about a young boy who survived the massacre of his tribe and was nursed back to health by a she-wolf. He impregnated the she-wolf, who produced ten boys. The boys grew tall, wedded human females. One of them, A-shih-na, founded the tribe of Turks.[8]

In twenty-first-century Bishkek there were leftovers from more recent histories—a Russian Orthodox Church stood on the outskirts of the city, not too far from a Turkish neighbourhood. The mixed-up nature of the city's inhabitants made my head spin.

Outside Bishkek, we bumped through fields of sunflowers. Corn and more sunflowers at the excavations at Krasnaeritchka (Red River), funded by Belgian and Japanese grants. We got out of the car and looked at the trenches where students crouched and dug. Stalina and I, followed by the driver, looked down into the dig.

'Are we in the right place?' I asked, wavering.

Stalina tapped a digger crouched in the mud. With some reluctance, the youth looked up from his work. He stood up, dusted his hands and glared at us. He introduced himself as Assan Torgoyev, a postgraduate student at Bishkek's Scientific Research Institute, aged all of twenty-five. He wore a stripy black-and-white tank top over his skinny frame, trousers rolled at the bottom and glasses with thick black frames.

Assan was not given to smiles. Also, we had interrupted his work. Somewhat grudgingly he explained that this town was called Navarikat, translated from Persian *navarikat*, or 'new city'. There were references to it in Persian and Arabic manuscripts in Iran and Afghanistan.

On the lower levels, dating from the fifth and sixth centuries AD, they had found Buddhist temples. It was one of the largest towns in the Chuy River valley during the middle ages. The town was established in the sixth or seventh century AD by Sogdians who came from present-day Uzbekistan and Tajikistan.

Through Stalina, who translated into English from Russian, he told us how in this region in 1962 they found an eighth-century clay twelve-metre-high Buddha which was now in the Hermitage in St Petersburg.

'But is this where Xuanzang met the Khan?' I asked, confused.

Su-yeh itself was a little further along the way. He said he'd show us the way.

In the car he stuck his nose to the window, looking for the rusted hull of an old truck, the signal of where to turn, a village outside Tokmak. There were beetroot fields, more sunflower fields.

'Everything is lying around, there's no money for excavations, we're doing everything from our own pockets,' Assan said. 'We're running out of grants, but most important is to finish excavation. If you don't have workers, you dig it yourself. I will do this my whole life,' he beamed. 'And it will still not be finished.'

The thought delighted him. Warming to his unsolicited role as a tour guide, he informed us that in the twelfth century somehow the valley was abandoned. There was some mysterious catastrophe in Central Asia, perhaps the water dried up.

Safflower fields glowed gold-orange and reeds called *kamish* sprouted by the roadside. The car rolled up between two hillocks, at the city gate. We had entered Su-yeh, the town on the river Chuy. In the distance, a thin line of fire flickered where somebody was clearing the scrubland of grass. Smoke rose, and through the heat waves the landscape misted.

࿐

> The Turks worship Fire: they do not use wooden seats, because wood contains fire, and so even in worship they never seat themselves, but only spread padded mats on the ground and so go through with it. But for the sake of the Master of the Law they brought an iron warming-pan covered with a thick padding, and requested him to be seated thereon.[9]

Veolutova Lubov Mikhailovna was the archaeologist on site. She wore a checked red shirt, the breast pocket held shut by a safety pin. A straw hat sat low on her head against the sun. She had flaxen hair in a blunt cut. Pale blue eyes looked out from her face, a net of wrinkles. She wore black canvas shoes and cotton pants, she held a chisel and was pointing at something.

It was my destiny to interrupt archaeologists.

'Xuanzang passed here in AD 629, the Valley of the Seven Rivers,' Mikhailovna said, gracious, though with Russians it is so very hard to tell. 'There were Hu people, Sogdians, mixed with Turks. It was the most settled valley in Central Asia.'

Alim Dononbaev, historian and philosopher at the Kyrgyz State

National University, had added a few details. When Xuanzang came through, Iranians as well as Nestorian Christians were established here, though the Turkic leaders remained shamanists. But some excavations showed Manichaeism in these parts. They had also found many fire-worshipping dishes.

There was water, plenty of it, from the seven rivers.

Here, on the site of that drunken banquet, archaeologists had dug up a Christian place of worship, clay tablets, a Nestorian Christian cross. But the style of architecture was Buddhist.

'There, look at that long hill,' Mikhailovna pointed. 'It could also be a temple. It was a very well-developed city, with two Buddhist temples beyond the city wall. Because the Buddhist temples were usually found outside the city walls, it reinforced the belief that Buddhism was an add-on, a result of this trading back and forth. Perhaps a rich merchant sponsored a temple.'

And if they were there when Xuanzang came through, he did not mention them. He was a meticulous chronicler of monasteries, monks and which Buddhist doctrine prevailed.

Inside the walls of the ancient city there was a *chachistan*, where merchants and the wealthy administration resided. The *rabat* section of the city housed the army, labourers, traders and peasants. In a corner rose the citadel or ark, from where the ruler governed, fortified, safe. These were the basic structures of old cities in Central Asia.

Archaeologists found water pipes made of baked clay, tubes that were seventy centimetre in diameter, narrower at one end than at the other for water movement: it was simple, but still it was engineered to provide a seven per cent gradient.

I was no expert, but I found myself getting absorbed in the way archaeologists decode history. Tramping over a buried city produced a lingering joy, particularly as some of its story lived on above the earth.

Communication between towns flew thick and fast, Mikhailovna said. Since ancient times, towns had been at a distance of twenty or forty kilometres, because everybody travelled on animals and that was the limit to get fresh animals.

'From Chimkent to Bam, it was all like this,' she said. 'There was a saying that from Chimkent to Bam a cat could travel the Silk Road jumping from roof to roof and never touch the ground.'

It was cultivated. The whole valley was once populated by craftsmen, a lot of food was probably grown on the mountains, because that is where archaeologists had found parts of a canal system for irrigation.

Very often bowls and jars with traces of wheat, grapes and apricot seeds were found, and at one spot they found a place to make wine. There were thirteen big jars for wine. There was a vat for grapes, but they didn't open it for fear that it would fall apart. I wanted to believe that these were the very same ingredients of a long-ago party attended by a visiting Chinese monk and a group of drunken Turks.

This city too was founded by Sogdians from the Samarkand region, and later the Turks came. In summer, the nomads went to the mountains and in winter they came down.

That, at least, had not changed.

There were fire-darkened niches where people had burned lamps. Even here, among the Turks, Zoroastrian hints remained. Historians say there was a complicated system of fire worship, each house had a method.

సా

'Stay,' the Khan begged the monk.

He was beginning to like this wiry, tonsured man who acted older than he looked, who kept to himself and fiddled with prayer beads and did not mind lecturing his hosts.

'Sir,' the Khan said, 'you have no need to go to India; that country is very hot, the tenth month there is as warm as our fifth month: as I regard your appearance I am afraid you will succumb under the climate. The men there are naked-blacks, without any sense of decorum, and not fit to look at!'[10]

The monk raised an eyebrow.

Drunken fool, he thought. What they have you will never understand.

Perhaps the Khan sensed some disdain, for he did not insist and, after making inquiries, found a proper translator from among his army ranks—a young man who spoke Chinese and several other regional tongues. He had spent many years in Chang An.

The youth was promoted on the spot and instructed to prepare letters of commendation for hosts in the scattered countries. A special letter was needed for Yeh Hu's eldest son in Afghanistan and for his wife, the sister of the Buddhist king of Gaochang. He commended the monk to their care, a fragile precious cargo handed from Turk to Turk.

Yeh Hu presented Xuanzang with a brand new set of robes in red satin and fifty pieces of silk. And when the day came, together with some officers, he accompanied the monk westwards for a distance of ten *li* or so.

chapter ten

Perpetual Snows

Visiting the old city of Su-yeh, I was filled with this new history, adding the Kyrgyz bead to my story. Still, a small point of incompletion nagged. What happened after the monk and his bedraggled, shrunken troupe crossed the snowy mountains at the Bedel Pass into Kyrgyzstan, before they got to Su-yeh and watched the Khan get drunk?

I had failed to get to the Bedel Pass from the Chinese side, but could I get to it from this side of the mountain range? By now, I knew enough of Kyrgyzstan to understand that things could be 'arranged'. Everything was for sale, from university degrees to medical degrees, to passports. For the right price.

I talked it over with Stalina. She looked at me as though I had lost my mind, but put the word out. A few days later, a friend phoned saying she knew somebody who knew somebody who could do the drive into the mountains, to the Bedel Pass. But it wasn't 'allowed'. It was a military zone. I shrugged, obsessed. Stalina shook her head.

'You're mad. Do they even have food there? I'm going to pack you some, just in case.'

A day or so later, I boarded a rickety public bus to Tamga, a small holiday town on the southern shores of Lake Issykul, where the driver would meet me and take me up to the Bedel Pass. The bus was full of poorer Russian families heading out of the city for a weekend by the lake. There were four teenage Russian girls with their boyfriends, the girls all dressed up (or down) for the beach. They had flowers tattooed on their shoulders. To my alarm, I was the only foreigner on the bus.

'Tamga,' I said brightly to the bus driver. 'Tamga. Tamga.' I hoped to convey that he should tell me when to get off. Already, I regretted the absence of Stalina, my right hand, my crutch in this strange land. Perhaps this was a mistake.

I missed the stop and stood with my backpack on the side of an abandoned country road by the lake. It was lovely, a soft blue, and the water lapped at the shores.

Xuanzang described it to Hui Li thus:

> The circuit of this lake is 1400 or 1500 *li*, longer from east to west, narrower from north to south. Looking at the watery expanse, the wind suddenly arising swells the waves to a height of several *chang*.[1]

In his own records, the monk gave further details.

> On all sides it is enclosed by mountains, and various streams empty themselves into it and are lost. The colour of the water is a bluish-black, its taste is bitter and salt. The waves of this lake roll along tumultuously as they expend themselves (on the shores). Dragons and fishes inhabit it together. At certain (portentous) occasions scaly monsters rise to the surface, on which travellers passing by put up their prayers for good fortune. Although the water animals are numerous, no one dares (or ventures) to catch them by fishing.[2]

The ban on fishing was no longer true; the trout from Lake Issykul are delicious, they say. But in the meantime I had no idea what to do. I sat and waited. A few Kyrgyz men from the village sauntered up and inspected me.

'Tamga?' I said, more cheerfully than I felt.

Niet. Niet. They pointed west. I had come from there.

I offered them Stalina's apples, which they accepted and bit into. We waited.

There was brief fruitless conversation via the dictionary. They examined my shoes. I wore dusty hiking boots, but theirs were ragged and worn out. I wondered if people had been killed for less. More Kyrgyz boys trickled out of the village. A small group gathered.

'Tamga,' I said, wavering.

They flagged down a bus going in the opposite direction and put me on it.

'Tamga,' they told the bus driver.

'*Spaciba*,' I said, a little breathless with relief.

Miraculously, I got there.

Somehow, Zhenya of the Tamga guest house (were all Russians called Zhenya?) found me. I began to babble like an idiot, making conversation, though he understood not one word. He took my backpack from me and smiled kindly. His hair was gelled and one lock fell artfully over his forehead. He wore a leather jacket. He walked me through a few back lanes of Tamga, nothing more than a village, but it turned out to be dotted with sanatoriums—something about proximity to the warm lake, Russians escaping Siberian winters and holidaying in their colonies. We turned into a small private house converted into a guest house, and it was a piece of heaven.

Zhenya was a Russian peasant, tanned, with brown eyes and thick ropes of muscle. He felt trustworthy. He kept smiling at me and asked if I was single and did I play an instrument, all picked from a phrase book he pored over, pointing at words one by one. He scratched his head and announced ungrammatically that he played the guitar and also sang Russian songs—sometimes, a little. Not English songs.

I gathered that the sauna would be ready for my use at 6 p.m. and dinner was at 7.30 p.m., and then I had to retire early because I was setting off the next morning at 5 a.m. to go to the Bedel Pass.

There were rose bushes, buzzing bees. Somebody loved this garden. The trees were thick with cherries and there were raspberry bushes. Zhenya served raspberries, tart and ripe, fresh off his raspberry plant, three salads, and hot strong black tea with sugar.

Pavel, the driver who knew the Bedel Pass, dropped in with a tall blonde Russian woman who spoke some English. He was a giant of a man, bulky in his checked felt shirt. He wore glasses with the thickest, roundest lenses I had ever seen. He stomped around in black gumboots. Sitting at the garden table, he proceeded to open up a map on the table. He unfolded and unfolded and unfolded until the map spilled over the edges. I learned he was a retired geologist and that's how he owned the map. And because he studied the rocks of the region, he knew the area inside out. He took his glasses off and leaned over the table into the map until his eyelids brushed the paper. He stretched a thick finger.

'I can take you to the pass, but there are soldiers there. We can take bottles of vodka,' he said, 'and see what happens. We'll see how far we get.'

I nodded. I did not mind zigzags and backtracks across Kyrgyzstan if I eventually had a straight line, approximating the monk's route. We negotiated a price in US dollars.

Warmed and relaxed by the sauna, showered and fed, I fell into a baby-sleep under woollen blankets and didn't dream of the monk and his icy mountain crossing.

❧

This mountain is steep and dangerous, and reaches to the clouds (heaven). From the creation the perpetual snow which has collected here in piles, has been changed into glaciers which melt neither in winter nor summer; the hard-frozen and cold sheets of water rise mingling with the clouds; looking at them the eye is blinded with the glare, so that it cannot long gaze at them. The icy peaks fall down sometimes and lie athwart the road, some of them a hundred feet high, and others several tens of feet wide. On this account the extreme difficulty of climbing over the first, and the danger of crossing the others.[3]

❧

The mountains around Tamga were etched against the dawn, a flock of pigeons quivered in the sky. We veered south-east, away from the lake, backtracking onto the monk's route. There were warning signs— 'Proceed with caution'—on the thin thread of a road. The snow on the mountain passes was tinged pink with the rising sun, and Pavel's mustard Niva jeep growled uphill.

I sat in front. Pavel was at the wheel and his son Ivan in the back seat. I held the Russian–English dictionary open in my lap, snug in my down jacket. *Khitai* for China. Xuanzang—*Khitaisky monakh*— and how he crossed the *perival* I wanted to see.

Yuri Gagarin once came to the sanatorium in Tamga, it turned out. Along the mountain roads there was a great rock chiselled in the shape of an astronaut's visor. It was a tantalizing brush with the Soviet Union, a glimpse of Moscow far to the north, of this other texture.

The mountain flanks were covered with pines and horses grazed in the dawn light. The farmers were up, and a woman walked with plastic buckets swinging empty, taking long strides towards her cows. The Saramainol Pass at 3442 metres was draped in ice, a black ridge. We climbed in a slow zigzag. NO STOPPING, a sign said, AVALANCHE AREA. It advised a twelve per cent climbing gradient for six kilometres. Up at this height there were 'mag', yellow flowers, and purple ones, snowdrops. The Barskoon Pass at 3819 metres headed towards the Tian Shan. There were cairns to mark the passes, four thigh-high stone piles. The road was parallel to the bottoms of the tongues of glaciers. To be precise, the road had been reduced to rubble by passing glaciers; high up there were seracs. All my scepticism about Pavel vanished. His eyesight may have been short, but he manoeuvred his jeep like a magician, as though he felt the road through his vehicle. He worked the slippery, icy bits like a master, easing in and out of gears, almost crooning at the car.

The Soyuk Pass at 4028 metres means 'bone pass' in Kyrgyz, for here many perished in wars and in winter. It was aloof, packed with ice. And in the distance, as the road tumbled below, a chain of the snow-capped Heavenly Mountains became visible. As when seen from the Chinese side, they hovered in the sky.

'That,' said Pavel, 'is the border with China.' He inquired tenderly about my breathing, was my head light?

The graves of soldiers who died at this border made lonely spots among the grass. At an old checkpoint the roof had blown off, a rusted caravan sat empty, nobody seemed to be around. In a small sheltered saddle between the mountains, the Kyrgyzstan Greenpeace had made a shed its office. The mountains were rich with wildlife. Marco Polo mountain sheep wandered, marmots dived and vast vultures with wings like tents glided in the sky.

The mountains yielded gold, and here the Canadians had established a Kyrgyz joint venture. A rabbit skidded off into the bushes on the flank, zigzagging, its white tail bobbing, fur streaked with white. An ariol—a kite, brown with black-tipped wings and a pale beige tail—flew far above. We drove alongside a wide grass-filled river. Up ahead, a bank of grey clouds emerged, thick with snow, swirling low and around the mountains; rain spattered the windshield. The entire range had now vanished under the cloud. Their favourite disappearing trick seen up close.

When the Niva sputtered to a stop on a mud track in a grassy field, my heart sank. Pavel got out to fiddle under the bonnet. He emptied a thick black bottle of grease into some compartment, black blood. The car sucked it up. He tossed the empty bottle into the wilderness. In the calf-high dry grass, a fox spun and raced to the foot of the mountain and an eagle swooped towards the icy-grey river, disturbed in its watch by the cough of the Niva. The road sighed and gave up and became gravel and mud, deep potholes. Pavel eased the jeep through, always keeping his extraordinary control.

We crossed a rickety wooden bridge sewn together with wires, I gripped the car handle. An eagle sat by the mud track, majestic, yellow-footed. There were patches of jade-green lichen, and the carcass of a bulldozer that had tumbled down years ago.

We crossed another river, but this one had no bridge and we splashed and skidded through the water. There were wires strung across, presumably to indicate the shallowest points. It was slippery. The jeep moaned and gasped across the stones, water licked the tyres and we edged up a mud bank. Somehow we made it up the hill on the other side, twisting in the wet earth. I glanced at Pavel. He had not batted an eyelid, but my throat was dry. My palms sweated, crinkling the pages of the dictionary.

The sullen beauty of these mountains held an edge of danger, of ruthlessness.

We passed rolls of barbed wire, marking the edge of the country, and at the vast shed of the isolated military garrison, Pavel got out for a brief conversation with the soldier. A bottle of vodka changed hands. It began to drizzle, and then stopped.

'A senior general is coming for an inspection,' Pavel said, half in Russian, half in English, leaning into the window of the jeep. 'We'd better hide until they leave.'

I could not believe I was doing this. We drove around a bend in the river, behind a hillock. Pavel flung a checked blanket over the car, black-and-white to soften the metallic glint, to prevent an edge catching the sunlight and giving us away. He held it down with stones from the river.

We sat in the Niva, we dozed, and then ate a quick lunch in the grass, an afternoon picnic by the Bedel River—slices of salty pork fat, raw onions, cloves of garlic, sausage and cheese on thick unbuttered brown bread. There were carrots from the garden and sweet crunchy green peas, boiled eggs, a sack of cherries from the trees and a bag of apples. Everything here was only one step removed from the soil. Nobody had shopped at a supermarket in days. Even the round *lepioshka* bread, the Russian naan, was home-made.

We dozed and occasionally talked through the dictionary and then got back into the car. Pavel picked a small bunch of edelweiss, combined it with dotted blue flowers, and handed it to me with a smile. There was the hush of the river, and a sort of calm descended.

Two hours later, we drove into the garrison. The soldiers clanged the door behind us and parked the Niva out of sight in a vast garage. Dogs barked on a leash, straining against their wire cages. Doberman Pinschers and German Shepherds. Up on a hill, though it was almost invisible, I could see a guardhouse with the tip of some weapon that was swivelling. It was misty and very cold in the late afternoon.

The barracks were headed by a tall blond Russian youth, Vassily. He was handsome, with parched lips. Be careful, my instincts said. The instinct of how to behave at border areas, with foreign military, especially if they were armed to the teeth.

'Firstly,' Vassily said, in broken English, 'the Bedel Pass, well, it is not possible to go today, it is too late. The weather in the mountains changes quickly. You will have to stay the night.'

And before that, he said, he would sample the vodka we had so kindly brought.

'You will have some too,' he said. It was a statement. He sat at his desk in the command room and barked orders into a black bakelite phone. One or two of the officers had families, I noted with relief. The Kyrgyz ones had children.

'Why do you want to see the Bedel Pass?' Vassily asked.

I explained about the *Khitaisky monakh*, about the journey. They brought out a tourist map. To my immense relief, there was a cartoon figure of the monk drawn above the Bedel Pass.

'See, here,' I jabbed at the picture. 'This is the man. From Khitai. To India.'

Pavel said little, but he looked nervous. His son, however, was beginning to relax as the alcohol flowed. Vassily became oddly formal the more vodka he drank.

'It is isolated here,' he said, 'but we have many pleasures. Like the sauna. Do you have the custom where men and women go to the sauna together?'

'No,' I said gravely. 'We do not have this custom.'

He gulped another thimble-sized cupful. He really was handsome, with his fine jawline, his face flushed and lips cracked with the cold. The Kyrgyz wives prepared a meal of *pollov*. There was more drinking.

'Without vodka, things are tight,' Vassily said. In my head I corrected him, *you're* tight. But I knew what he meant.

'Drink up,' he said. 'Any vodka left at the bottom of your cup is the tears you will shed.'

I drank up and was glad for its warmth. Strangely, it did not go straight to my head.

There was some humming and hawing about the sleeping arrangements. Pavel and his son were given beds with the soldiers. And I was to sleep in Vassily's small bunker. What made me shrug and agree? What made me think that there was any wisdom in this insane venture? What was I doing here on this high lonely mountain pass with a bunch of drunken Russian soldiers?

Late that night, Vassily made an extraordinarily polite, drunken attempt at seduction. He leaned against the door on his own porch because he could barely stand. I opened the door a crack.

'Are you afraid of the dark?' he muttered.

'Er, not really.'

'Not even a little bit? I could come in and, ah, protect you.'

He weaved a little.

'That's very kind of you, but I think it's okay.'

'Do you have a boyfriend?'

'Yes.'

'He won't know,' Vassily said cunningly.

'But I would,' I said. I put my hand over my heart and gazed at the starless sky in what I hoped was a lovelorn manner. 'And I love him.'

'Oh, I'm sorry,' Vassily said. And vanished into the dark.

I shut the door and leaned against it as my knees turned to water. I had to sit down.

The next morning, the soldiers decided they might at least have some fun hunting on the short trip to the Bedel Pass. Rifles were oiled and loaded. Three soldiers took out the vast olive Russian-made GAZ, a sort of massive army truck; when its engine started, it sounded like firecrackers, as there appeared to be no muffler. We discussed the price of petrol.

'Yes, yes, I am aware that prices are high,' I said, trying not to sound snappy. I was getting impatient with the delay. I knew what was coming, I wondered how much it had to do with my night-time refusal of Vassily. I counted out the money.

This would take me to as near the Bedel Pass as possible. Ivan was to come along too.

There was the flat Bedel River, the rush and the mountain pass that curved into China. The GAZ tilted and sloshed but made it across the river, the water nearly reaching the windshield. The grass grew thick and green, and young birch trunks were implanted into the earth with barbed wire. We came to a barbed wire fence across the river.

'That's China,' one soldier said. 'Can't go any further.' The pass itself was hidden in swirling mists.

'*Khitai, boukh, boukh.*' I gathered it was Russian for 'bang, bang', that if we crossed into no-man's-land, the Chinese would begin to shoot. So instead they opened another bottle of vodka and emptied it. I refused when they held it out to me. They nibbled on tomatoes and thick slices of bread and cracked jokes.

And then Ivan walked to the end and stood the bottle onto a post 100 metres away. They unslung their Kalashnikovs and fired at it. The ringing noise of bullets ricocheting off rocks echoed thunderously among the mountain-tops. They gestured to me to have a go. I declined. I had lost interest now that I saw this was as close to the pass I would ever get.

A mist gathered around the mountains, it was cold. I climbed up onto the GAZ. I had no desire for this game. Besides, in fifteen rounds of bullets, not one had hit the bottle. I sulked.

'*Sobaka*,' Pavel said, pounding his fist into an open palm, when I told him, after the short drive back, that I hadn't actually *been* to the Bedel Pass. The soldiers—to mollify me—had pointed out the famous spot to which the Chinese army had reached on one incursion, but I was unable to tell whether they meant in recent history or during the time of the Tang dynasty, for the Chinese had tried then too. It did not matter.

In their own wild way, they were showing me a little bit of their world. Now I wished I had been a little more gracious, maybe even taken a potshot at the glass bottle.

We rolled into Tamga late that night. Pavel drove like a hero, easing back through shallow rivers, uneven roads, the gravel and shale of disintegrating glaciers, spits of ice melting underneath, dripping like the tears at the bottom of a vodka glass. The Soyuk Pass again, sinister and not conducive to smiles, although we stopped in the freezing driving rain and took a quick picture—it was a memento.

Back at the guest house, it was almost midnight. A group of Danes had stopped for the night. I sat in the kitchen with Pavel and the guest house owners, Sasha and Luba, and learned that the Danes were heading back to Bishkek, via Lake Son Kul.

There was a Danish ornithologist, an odd, silent blond man called Hans. Come with us, he said, with half-lowered eyes, staring at his cup of tea. 'You cannot leave Kyrgyzstan without seeing Son Kul.'

The kitchen was warm, I could feel my fingertips again. I felt a little giddy from being safe and thinking how Tamga, which two days earlier had been an alien town, now felt like a safe house. And Bishkek, how it was an urban metropolis filled with conveniences.

How soon world views flip.

'You cannot leave Kyrgyzstan without seeing the lake,' Hans said again. For some reason, I believed him. Perhaps because he said little, what he said mattered. He was kind. As luck would have it, this also solved my logistical problem of how to get back to Bishkek. Pavel arrived the next morning with books, of birds and flowers and their names.

I felt a quiet squeeze of affection for this man who had risked so much. There was a joy too in seeing people you think you've said farewell to. Who knew when I'd ever see him again, that vast bulk of a man, my peasant-professor, in his checked lumber shirt, his gumboots. He explained about the no-man's-land for two kilometres on either side of the border, the barbed wire. Perhaps he sensed my disappointment.

'*Spaciba*,' I said. 'I'm sorry it took an extra day. I know your family was worried about you.'

'Yes, but I enjoyed it,' he said, through the dictionary. 'It was an adventure. Better than growing old and bored.' I wanted to hug him for saying that, but I wasn't sure about the etiquette.

So the Danes and their kindness was how I found myself seated by Lake Son Kul on a foldable stool, surrounded by flapping tents and Danish grandmothers scribbling postcards home and dreaming of summer in Copenhagen.

'What are you writing?' Hans asked.

'About the landscape,' I said.

You name the things you love. But half of the velvety carpet spread out before us like some spilled treasure had yet to be named and researched. There were Siberian poppies, edelweiss everywhere. The delicate flowers are protected in Europe and the well-behaved, eco-minded Danes stumbled over themselves trying not to step on them, but here it was hopeless, the fields were littered with the stuff. Gentians, kislichka, asters with their fine violet petals and brilliant yellow middles; there was light grey lichen, thick on the ground, it had serrated edges and veins. Miniature wild tulips, delphinium, aconitum.

Hans said, for he knew about these things, the flora was a mixture of southern Siberian species, and typical Eurasian species, and some typical of the Himalaya. Under his tutelage, I learned there were red-billed choughs, charcoal-bodied with sharp red bills; red-fronted serins; scarlet rose finches; grey-necked buntings; mistle thrushes; greenish warblers; the sandy-beige Isabelline Wheatear. He pointed out a common sandpiper fluting across a river.

Kyrgyzstan held me captive in a surreal intoxication. It was as though the land's beauty had injected itself into my veins and addled my mind. Anything was possible in the rarefied atmosphere of the mountains. Perhaps I was dreaming.

Hans had his own tent and offered to share it. It did not even occur to me to refuse. Where else would I sleep on this grassy plateau? Like experienced mountaineers, he slept in a sleeping bag, stripped to his underwear.

I was shivering and could not stop. Hans said, in his English full of cracks, that if I was cold, he would with a kind heart share his sleeping bag. He said this carefully, so as not to frighten me, in the most tender of ways. My teeth chattering, I nodded and edged closer to him and he delicately turned his back to me.

At midnight I crawled out of the tent, freezing. It was cosmic, to squat and pee in the grass in this setting. A vast moon and my cold bottom. The Kyrgyz saying, I thought, made perfect sense: *There are only two paths—the Silk Road and the Milky Way.*

There had been a car accident, on the way up here.

A dirty white local car overtook the Danes' convoy, skidded and as though in slow motion, flipped over and came to rest on its roof against the trees. For a horrific moment, nothing happened.

'Kyrgyz!' spat Sasha, our driver, his Russian face blank. The word sounded like an expletive.

Then the moment broke and Sasha yanked the car door open and ran out, and I found myself on the road, along with Hans, running as fast as I could, *towards* the accident. Only later did I think, what on earth did I know about first aid, or death, or safety? Only later did I imagine that the fuel tank could have blown into a bright orange ball. There could have been burnt bodies carried out from smouldering cinders. But none of that happened.

In fact, a small child was crawling out of the wreckage, the wheels still spinning, the car body so crushed it was a miracle anybody was alive. The child was moaning, a car door was opening skywards. The debris of a ruined holiday scattered all around. Fruit, bathing suits, handbags covered in dust were strewn under the roadside trees. We leaned a mother against a whole car seat spat out by the impact.

There were broken ribs, bloodied faces. The Danish men pulled out hurt, broken bodies. Hans sprinted back to the van and pulled out Band-Aids and first-aid kits. He bandaged the old woman's face full of blood, a white T-shape across her face against a red background, the Swiss flag. She was in shock. I was too appalled and unqualified to do anything but hold another woman's hand as she lay immobile and weeping, tears rolling out of her eyes, eyeliner dark and nails painted. She couldn't move her neck. She faded in and out.

'She mustn't go into shock,' Hans snapped. 'Keep her awake.'

Squatting beside her, I tapped her cheeks.

'Hey, what's your name?'

'Chulpon,' she whispered.

I made serious conversation, half in English, half in Russian, as though we were meeting at a tea party.

Many days later I had lunch with a Russian journalist.

'You know,' she said, 'the Kyrgyz, they drive their cars like they ride their horses. You get very drunk on a horse and fall on her neck, never mind, she keeps going. But they don't understand a car is different, you can't get drunk and fall asleep and keep going.'

The driver had indeed turned out to be drunk—a family gathering, a reunion celebrated with an all-night vodka session. At any rate, the drink explained his attitude, watching his family devastated and bleeding, the mother moaning in pain, unclear what was broken and what could be fixed.

It shattered me to wipe the tears from Chulpon's eyes as she lay immobile, covered up to keep warm. Her daughter Regina bawled and bawled, her upper lip a bloody mess and face bruised. She kept spitting blood. I held Chulpon's hand, stroked her forehead and gave her small slaps on her cheeks when her eyes rolled back in her head. Her chin quivered, she pressed her neck, her head hurt.

The police came, and the village doctor with a bag that held a single stethoscope. He wore a brimmed hat. The Kyrgyz police sauntered around.

I saw Chulpon lifted onto a stretcher and into a van (they had to unscrew seats to make space for the three stretchers). And as I leaned in for a final check of her eyes, she pressed my hand and whispered '*Spaciba, spaciba, spaciba.*' I shook my head and burst into tears, and could not stop.

But at Son Kul, the accident faded as black-headed gulls swooped and dived for fish. And then time broke into a gallop and snatched me from this glow.

Bishkek was already hot and would get hotter. One night, we were all dancing the night away to Uzbek music, stamping our feet, including the Danish grannies, who knew how to party. The group would fly home to Denmark the next day.

Back at my room rented from the Russians, S. phoned from California at midnight.

'I was so worried,' he said. 'I hadn't heard from you.' Hearing his voice and the gladness that spread through me, I knew, even as I half fell in love with Hans, that this was ephemeral, confined to a moment in the mountains, and that what sustained me was the constancy of S. Hans was a passing mist. What a relief.

'I'm fine,' I said, smiling into the phone in the dark. 'I can't wait to see you. Did you get my letter? I miss you.'

And the monk.

I yanked myself from what already felt like the shred of a dream and went to check on my visa to Uzbekistan. I felt the breath at my heels and knew it was time, like the end of a movement in a piece of music, a natural pause in events.

chapter eleven

Nine *Lepioshkas*

The Uzbeks had refused my visa, no reason given. I phoned the Indian embassy in Tashkent. Yes, His Excellency would intervene. They would write a letter. It would take a few days. I was relieved. I had no desire to leave Kyrgyzstan and I could not fight the way the days unfolded. When I was ready to go, a great palm shoved me back on my bottom and made me wait some more. I was at a loose end in Bishkek, but I was learning that loose ends dangle in space and carry their own beginnings. I wandered around Bishkek and saw the city now with different, affectionate eyes. I was no longer afraid.

Instead, I savoured the feel of the open-air cafes in the summer, the street stalls where boys sold single cigarettes for a som. Summer's watermelons were piled in the mini market along with trays, spare parts. Here too they conserved hair clips, metal parts, old buttons, pipe elbows, string ends. Hoarding, storing, saving, using and reusing, plastic bags smoothed out and folded, broken toys stashed because they can be fixed, torn clothes mended—the habits of those who know need or have lived amidst it. Like in India.

Bishkek must be the only place where taxi drivers sit under the shade of oaks and read tomes instead of plying the roads hunting down fares. Music-mad Bishkek, with its potholed roads and *mariadchy* that wobbled along to destinations written on cardboard balanced on the windshield. But by the time I tried to decipher the Cyrillic they had whizzed passed and I never found out where they were going.

The mountain yearning eased somewhat when Stalina's sister,

Tahmina, and her German boyfriend, Stephen, took me with them on a hike up the Ala Archa glacier not far from Bishkek. In the icy rush of a grey river, we plopped in a watermelon so it could cool. Then we sat by the stream and looked at the mountains.

The climb to the glacier began step by step, out of breath, huffing and puffing with screaming legs and aching feet. We sometimes counted steps, now only a hundred, counting and counting until we finally reached the top where, across the base camp, around the hillock, the glacier, the ice monster, lived.

Outside Bishkek, I had found the ghost of the monk's nightmarish crossing of the Heavenly Mountains and I hadn't even been looking. The glacier was covered with great cracks and crevices. It was dirt and debris, but icy underneath, and hissing and cracking and moving and speaking below its breath. It was a being that talked on the top of the mountain; perhaps it cursed me, perhaps it blessed me, but it felt like a presence, an immense power, and I felt humbled and small and a little bit afraid. I understood now what the monk had written of his own climb:

> Both hills and valleys are filled with snowpiles, and it freezes both in spring and summer; if it should thaw for a time, the ice soon forms again. The roads are steep and dangerous, the cold wind is extremely biting, and frequently fierce dragons impede and molest travellers with their inflictions. Those who travel this road should not wear red garments or carry loud-sounding calabashes. The least forgetfulness of these precautions entails certain misfortune. A violent wind suddenly rises with storms of flying sand and gravel; those who encounter them, sinking through exhaustion, are almost sure to die.[1]

Exhausted with the climb, we lay on the rocks and fell asleep. All through the day, fit Russians were jogging, jogging up and down, carrying laden packs for the base camp at the glacier. Food supplies, matches, clothes. They ran an alpine camp to head up the glacier.

And then came the descent, with my wobbly, aching legs and smashed knees and rubble that slipped and slithered. I was devastated by the walk, sleepy in Bishkek, unable to get up, pressed, oppressed by the heat. Tossing in bed, nursing my knees, I was conscious of how the city had crept under my skin.

I went to see Beksultan Jakiev, a Kyrgyz writer. Stalina came along. He had wiry eyebrows and the movements of the elderly. He wore a half-sleeved white shirt and had been appointed state writer by President Akaev.

That sunny Bishkek morning, in his office, with Stalina translating from Russian into English, he made me see a grassy plateau, like the one I'd left, a whole lifetime of things I could barely begin to understand. A yurt, a time of war, a nine-year-old boy with a rumbling stomach looking after a horse. A little boy who lived with his grandfather in the mountains during the summer holidays and was so fond of riding wild horses bareback that he had problems with his hands and legs the rest of his life. How deprived people had been in the Soviet Union, Jakiev mused, thinking on his boyhood, the days of the war, the source of his plays.

'I remember,' he said. 'I was hungry, waiting for the sun to move a little bit, time for food, we would boil water and beat wheat and mix it in. Suddenly I saw my uncle galloping on his horse, he was very excited and people came out of their yurts. He was gesturing and talking and some were crying and some were laughing. I also ran towards him and came to know the war was finished. People were saying thanks to god, everyone will come back from the battlefield.'

He paused. 'None of my relatives came back from the war.'

The most impressive development that long-ago morning, for the little boy, Beksultan Jakiev, was that one of his aunts, who was preserving barley for the new harvest—the family had forgotten what bread was, there was no food—when she heard the good news, milled the flour and made nine *lepioshkas*.

'That is the tradition when something nice happens,' Jakiev smiled.

The boy, after hearing this good news, ran to the centre of the village thinking everyone would come back immediately.

'Lots of people didn't come back, and from my family nobody came back. My grandfathers, grandmothers, parents, till the end of their lives, were expecting these people to come back and I was also doing the same. And this feeling I have expressed in my first play. So we are children of the war, we didn't have enough food, bad clothes.'

Jakiev had explained the Manas, the epic about the big-hearted Kyrgyz warrior hero, betrayed, stabbed in the back by Kongur Bai as he knelt to pray. The story was four times longer than the Ramayana, sixteen times longer than the Iliad and the Odyssey combined, an amalgam of ideas of tribal honour and conduct, the threadless, clothless fabric that held a people together: when history fails, we turn to legend. Epics were passed down from generation to generation, and at difficult times in history people got braver from hearing an epic, Jakiev explained.

Manas was the spiritual backbone that supported the nation. It was a substitute for religion.

But stories like the Manas's spread ideas of liberty and sovereignty, so the Soviet authorities attacked the epic, said it was harmful for people's thoughts. The Manas was forbidden. There was repression in the 1930s of those who were researching the Manas. Scholars were imprisoned and killed.

How far we were from Moscow, how long ago the Soviet Union had died, but here people still remembered how the planning of one nation above others meant hiding the history of people from them.

Jakiev's eyes wafted far away as he spoke names that meant the world to him and that I was hearing for the first time. Kasiatiev. How Palivanov was also shot: he had translated the Manas into Russian, it was considered the best translation. And Karsaev, a collector of Manas epics who escaped from prison—his friends hid him in Moscow and Kazakhstan. He died at 101 years, an encyclopaedia. He was Jakiev's teacher.

From the origins of the Manas, thought to be about 1000 years old, I thought it was a hop and a skip to Xuanzang's Khan of the Turks. There would certainly have been similar stories for the nomads of the region. How old is a story, after all? If it is said to be 1000 years, could it be 1400 years old?

Kyrgyzstan in the summer. Buckets of apples by the roadside, clear pale green ones, red-streaked rosavayastalovka, pears, tomatoes on tables as though they had descended straight from heaven, onions, potatoes, watermelons: an entire neighbourhood sat by the road on low stools, selling the fruit of their gardens.

One fine day I did get my visa to Uzbekistan. I boarded the Russian Tupelov to Tashkent and watched Kyrgyzstan get smaller and smaller until it vanished in a haze.

chapter twelve

Sogdiana

By AD 628 Xuanzang was deep in Sogdiana, amongst clans and bands who lived in fortified castles, arks and citadels, with small settlements around them. Here was the land of the Sogdians, renowned merchants who thought nothing of packing up cargoes and travelling for months, east to China's Tang empire or west to Persia where in the seventh century the Sassanids held sway.

Buy low, sell high—the Sogdians in the middle were the acknowledged masters of the Silk Road trade. They owned warehousing rights all along the Silk Road, they had established small colonies along the entire way, even in faraway Chang An, to ease trade along. They were loyal only to their businesses, though the powerful Persian rulers to the west of Sogdiana had long tried to bring these clannish Central Asians into their fold. To some extent, they had succeeded. The Sogdian alphabet was derived from Aramaic, the language of the great Achaemenians.[1] These Central Asians paid taxes to Persepolis. A steady trickle of semi-precious stones, carnelian, turquoise, lapis lazuli and gold, found its way west to the Persian courts.[2]

A thousand years before Xuanzang, in the spring of 329 BC, Alexander the Great and his army, in their push eastwards, crossed the Hindu Kush Mountains to hunt down Bessus, the satrap of Sogdiana and Bactria in north Afghanistan. Bactria bowed down to Alexander. A Bactrian duke called Oxyartes even offered Alexander his daughter's hand in marriage.[3]

But to the north of the Oxus River, the stubborn Sogdians dug their heels in, resisting, as they would in the face of the Arabs nearly a century later. Still, Alexander managed to establish a garrison in Samarkand, the Sogdian heartland, not far from the Zerafshan River.

In AD 673, barely half a century after Xuanzang passed through Sogdiana, a storm of Arab armies forded the Oxus into neighbouring Bukhara. An Arab became the governor of Khurasan. The Sogdians battled, but were unable to unite with other Central Asian states to meet the invading forces. Still, ever practical, the Sogdians soon began to switch sides to join the Arabs. They loaned them money for the military ventures.[4] Muslim armies, fighting far away from Arabia, began to use the local Persian language in the east, which became a bridging tongue, for it was not so hard for the Sogdians to learn.[5] Naturally, Sogdian words filtered into the eastern Caliphate's language.[6]

Soon, these adaptable Central Asian states became a bedrock of Islamic Sunni learning and early Arab history is filled with wise men from Sogdiana called Samarkandi or Bukhari or Balkhi or Termezi.[7] For the time being, in the pre-Islamic seventh century, things were peaceful in Sogdiana. The dwellings of merchants in settlements like Panjikant or Samarkand were gracious, with elegant wall paintings that showed a liking for elongated, graceful forms.[8]

When Xuanzang passed through Sogdiana, the land was at the height of its prosperity and culture. If he was disappointed at the notable lack of Buddhist monasteries, he did not say so.

෨

From Bishkek it was barely a two-hour flight to Tashkent, in Uzbekistan, and yet it felt a long time to be aloft. Somewhere below me coiled the waters of the Amu Darya and the Syr Darya, what the Greeks called the Oxus and the Jaxartes, names that susurrated.

Darya was another word that lingered in the shadows until months later, when one evening in Delhi my sister-in-law, Maya, sat on the bed and began to sing in Hindi, a wafting song of dusk and a boat floating down a *darya*. *Darya*. River.

My Hindi came and went, like waves on a shore, swelled and strengthened when in India and weakened abroad. There were words I had learned as a child and forgotten, there were words I never knew. And each time I heard one I liked, I picked it off and held it to my ear like a seashell to hear the sound of rushing blood. *Darya*.

From the window of the plane I could make out the fields and grasses of Uzbekistan and a thick slab of water. In the sixteenth century AD, much after Xuanzang, Babur rode across the Hindu Kush, galloped through Kabul in Afghanistan, crossed the Indus in Pakistan and set up the Mughal dynasty on the Indian plains, so that as a child I picnicked next to the domed sandstone tomb of his son and thought nothing of it. I did not imagine that his forefather was a Central Asian on a horse who hunted the fattened partridges of Ferghana in Uzbekistan. Babur was ours, I had thought, until I arrived in Uzbekistan and saw that he was theirs. Here in Uzbekistan I was practically home. At least Uzbekistan held the roots of India as I knew it.

The Indian ambassador received me in his office. The wall behind his desk was covered with maps and flags. His desk had a glass top on the wood and it had been cleared of all papers. He was Bengali, I could tell from his name, and generous with his influence, as he had been from the start.

'Ah yes, Xuanzang.' He got right to the point.

I gathered from the way he discussed the monk's route that he had, during his tenure in Tashkent, developed a deep personal interest in the region and its history.

'Don't,' he said to me, 'try and take a stand on the history. It's too tricky, too complex.'

'That is not my objective,' I said.

I started to explain, then stopped and shrugged. I was a traveller, not a podium-thumper, pointer of index fingers, leaning into crowds shouting neo-Marxist or postmodern agendas.

The ambassador made recommendations. He pressed a buzzer and a peon glided in, bowing slightly. A brief exchange, a few more phone calls. He scribbled things on a pad and handed me names and numbers.

Tashkent's Indian embassy took me under their wing. They pointed me to a Bengali couple, long-time Tashkent residents, who could host me in their home as a paying guest. The embassy also provided me with the names of a couple of Russian scholars who could help me pinpoint Xuanzang's route across Sogdiana. Here was exactly the help I needed. I would not have known where to begin. This section of the journey was particularly hard for scholars to decipher. The monk had included the names of places that he heard about, but never visited.

Uzbekistan was taut in the summer of 2000. The air clenched and loosened like some sinister heartbeat. The staff at the Indian embassy were keyed up, restless. It was a contagious disease. A Russian translator made a few phone calls, she helped me set up meetings. I had a few days to kill in Tashkent.

One evening, I sat in the garden at the home of one of the Indian diplomats. It was a pleasant evening in a lawn shaded with trees. The phone rang sharply through the Tashkent dusk and there was no way to avoid hearing half the conversation.

'What? Are you sure?' The diplomat's voice tensed.

'How many people?'

'Where exactly? Is this confirmed?'

There was bruitage of fighting, of guerrilla action by Islamic militants. The diplomat returned to the lemon drink and sighed. The trouble had started at the beginning of August. Local papers reported that a 100-strong band of terrorists had infiltrated into the south of Uzbekistan from neighbouring Tajikistan. Their aim was to establish bases from which to harass Uzbekistan and organize channels for transportation of arms and drugs.

Uzbekistan began to evacuate civilians from the region. As August wore on, the authorities sent in the military, blocking the militants in a gorge. There was a shoot out. Eventually, around thirty terrorists were killed, so were Uzbek guards. Later, sappers neutralized mines laid by the guerrillas. Servicemen blew up an ammunition dump. Uzbekistan's President Islam Karimov cancelled a trip to the Crimea.

'Is it still okay to cross Uzbekistan?' I asked nervously.

The diplomat shrugged.

Termez, Xuanzang's last stop in Uzbekistan, was in the province of Surkhan Darya, where I was heading, where the tension was. My unease grew. Tashkent was a hard city to navigate. Power, old and new, whispered in its buildings. This was a place with clout, a place that knew itself, threw its weight around and hissed unfriendly currents to the lone traveller. I could not get anywhere, I knew no landmarks, was unable to read the signs or speak the language. Smaller, friendlier Bishkek, how I missed it now, the chaotic land of the horse-riding Kyrgyz and the magical mountains with the myths of Manas.

In India's remoter Central Asian consular outposts there is not much traffic from New Delhi. My arrival in Tashkent created a small stir. Here, at least, was temporary amusement amid the tedium of daily embassy tasks. The diplomat offered to take me on a tour of Tashkent, in between his official duties. In the dead of the afternoon, we paused for a cooling drink of Coca-Cola.

It dawned on me that his unstated duties included intelligence gathering. He was far too informed, far too sharp for his clerkish work. Or was it the paranoia of the region that was creeping into my ears, and tightening its net around my brain?

Uzbekistan's key dilemma, I learned, was this: asserting its own identity after the break-up of the Soviet Union had equalled embracing a Muslim heritage. Under the Soviet government, Uzbeks practised Islam in secret, behind closed doors. But things had gotten terribly out of hand with the new openness, and Uzbekistan's President Karimov, Central Asia's sharpest, shrewdest politician, found himself in the unexpected position of fighting Islamic extremists. What a complicated place Sogdiana had become. Or maybe it had always been this way, situated as it was at the crossroads of everything.

I needed an immediate visa extension if I was to have enough time for the journey across Uzbekistan. I accepted without protest the moonlight services of a car and driver for a negotiated fee. After months of public transport, it was a relief. All was cocooned and cushioned. I gazed out at Tashkent from the tinted windows of the Nexias and BMWs and sleekly glided away, but I felt cut-off, isolated, imprisoned and blocked from the country around me.

Frustration at the delays in the visa extension had set in, eating me up. I was unable to sleep, a prisoner of my own requests for help. I was so used already to wandering at will, rambling through the streets collecting dust on my shoes. I wanted to see things at eye level.

Finally, I met my Russian scholars. Following the ambassador's instructions, with the help of the Uzbek driver Rustam, I found an underground room in the basement of the Fine Arts Institute of Tashkent and asked for Dr Rtveladze. It was a casual meeting place lit with neon lights. Black-and-white photographs hung on the walls, arty pictures of nodular roots and cobwebs. On the side sat an enlarger. By the door was a long table covered with a plastic sheet. Somebody had made tea and poured it into bowls. There was the obligatory jar of cherry jam to be eaten with a spoon.

Rtveladze was an archaeologist and numismatist. He was born in 1942 and so was fifty-eight the year I met him. He was a Georgian, born by the Caucasus Mountains, a wiry man with a shock of white hair and bright blue eyes that saw whole histories in dented old copper coins and gleamed with the delight of it. Once, leafing through an old book of his in Russian, I caught a glimpse of the jacket photograph of him, a much younger man, and sucked in my breath at the rakish good looks, the dark eyebrows, the challenge in his look thrown out in an old snapshot. He had been smoking for forty-five years and preferred the harsh Astra cigarettes found only in Tashkent.

'I don't like filters,' he muttered in his hesitant English.

Years and years of digging in the Central Asian dirt had given him a meticulousness I found pleasing, a preoccupation with untangling the puzzles of the past. Later, on another occasion, I visited his house, met his wife, also an archaeologist, greeted his many children.

'Ah yes, Xuanzang. Of course, Xuanzang.'

The Russians read him in the Beal translation, snatching clues from throwaway lines, gleaning hints of fallen empires. They quoted the monk verbatim, from memory.

The country of Che-shi is 1000 *li* or so in circuit. On the west it borders on the river Yeh (Syr Darya) . . . There are some ten towns in the country, each governed by its own chief; as there is no common sovereign over them, they are all under the yoke of the Tuh-kiueh.[9]

'I found many coins with separate rulers,' Rtveladze had said that other day at his house. 'You know that part about ten towns, each with its own ruler.'

He climbed onto the bed to reach higher shelves and pull out yet another publication in Russian.

'Not Buddhist, not Buddhist,' he said, shaking his head. 'In Sogdiana, when Xuanzang passed through, Zoroastrianism was in firm place.'

The people in this region had at least partially adopted the Zoroastrian faith, but with Sogdian characteristics. Unlike the Zoroastrianism in Iran proper, here there was a cult of ossuaries, an obsession with lamenting the dead, and there were goddesses with four arms, like in India. The mother goddess Nana on a lion had nothing to do with Zoroastrianism at all.

There were stories of Rustam and Sohrab, some of them incorporated into Firdosi's *Book of Kings* completed in the eleventh century AD.

The Sogdians tolerated the presence of Zoroastrian priests, but the holy men did not have the kind of power or status they held in Persia.[10] The merchants were polygamous. There was the institution of *chakar*, which in Central Asia referred to slaves bought and trained to guard the homes of merchants travelling on long journeys.[11]

Chakar. The word was familiar. I could not yet exactly put my finger on it.

'Che Shi is Chach, in the modern Tashkent region,' Rtveladze told me, following Xuanzang's description in his *Records*. 'The river Yeh is the Syr Darya. Each of those Turkish chiefs minted their own coinage, indicating independent small states. The Sogdian inscriptions on the coin were hard to decipher.'

'But I read it.' This, he said with glee, pronouncing it 'reed'. At the same time there was a humility, as though he was bowed by the awe and weight of time.

'I read it, the names are difficult. Like Shchaniaback or Zatakh or Yazatpir or Tarnavch or Sochakh. Maybe divine Zoroastrian names.'

He had a bone to pick with the monk. The monk had been less than forthcoming on this section of his trip. Rtveladze wished they could talk across the corridors of the centuries. Archaeologists, even in Central Asia, are still the most passionate fans of the monk of China, their most faithful guide to lost cities and hidden eras.

He lit another cigarette. The room swirled with smoke.

'Xuanzang said something about "paying allegiance to Tuh-kiueh", maybe he meant somebody in south Kazakhstan, or maybe Xuanzang made a mistake, maybe each ruler was in Chach and not under the yoke of Turks at all.'

It was another mystery to be solved.

'There were many Sogdians from Central Asia. They were everywhere, the diaspora. Sogdian inscriptions were in Aramaic, but Bactrian inscriptions were in Greek letters. There were many towns and villages, small settlements, on the north of the Syr Darya.'

He knew the others too, a whole necklace of Silk Road stops sprinkled down to the Amu Darya, on the border with Afghanistan. These men of mud and pottery pieces had pieced the route together, matched the Chinese terminology of Turkish terms translated into English. But how was I to travel to them?

Now, in the basement of the Fine Arts Institute, Rtveladze pointed to a map on the wall. Uzbekistan and its truncated ex-Khanates.

'There is war here, here and here,' Rtveladze said. There were three military flashpoints in Uzbekistan that summer. The first was close by, an area 100 kilometres from Tashkent. There was trouble also in the Surkhan Darya province and, finally, in Batken, the Kyrgyz bulge in Uzbekistan. It was spreading.

Rtveladze introduced me to a younger colleague, Leonid Sverchkov, an Ukrainian, a tall and lanky man with blue eyes and a striking jawline. He looked down on things, not always because of his height. He took me on a tour of the museum.

'You know the legend of Zeus and Athena, of course,' he said. His English mostly held together, though sometimes I waded through his ideas and thought he was saying something quite else. Then we had to backtrack.

'Of course,' I said, politely.

He pointed out old wall paintings of Athena springing from the head of Zeus and then traced parallels with Indian legends of the river Ganga springing from the head of the Hindu god Shiva. I was impressed.

'Here in Central Asia, many ideas meet,' he said to me kindly, pitying my lack of knowledge.

The Russian archaeologists were excited by the idea of following Xuanzang's route. I had envisioned a leisurely ramble through

Uzbekistan, but I now saw that if I was to hit the correct spots I needed their help, and these were men with a mission to uncover the debris of history. Their obsession with the accidents of survival began to communicate itself to me.

Leonid looked at the map. According to his own information, he said, the situation had cooled, although half a Japanese excavation team had returned from Surkhan Darya in the south where they were conducting a dig. There was more talk of the southern province being closed off to foreigners, of the Uzbek military pouring into Surkhan Darya to fight the Muslims. The south had always been a little shaky, what with its proximity to Afghanistan and its civil war still raging. Muslim agitators spilled over into Uzbekistan. That border on the Amu Darya had been closed since 1998.

'I'm inclined to go,' I said. 'I don't have that much time. I'm having visa trouble. We could prepare letters with official letterheads and stamps. If the army stops us, well, we come back.'

Leonid shrugged. He agreed with my assessment. He would take me across the country. He often took Germans on digs. We retired to the stairwell so that Leonid could smoke while we discussed the logistics. To my surprise, the tall man simply hitched up his jeans, sat on his haunches and lit up a cigarette. I had never seen a white man do that. But these were Russians. I was learning they were different from other westerners. They were nothing like anybody I had met before.

We tied up the details of fuel, car, driver and weather conditions. Summer had set in for real and it was blisteringly hot. Some of the central regions would go up to 50°C later in the month.

'Think about what you need,' Leonid said. 'Like your toothbrush.'

He kept a straight face.

'Or my Kalashnikov,' I said.

'Or your Kalashnikov.'

He finally smiled.

'The driver is an archaeologist too,' he said. 'Though he's into the Stone Age.' Leonid managed to look supercilious again. 'It's more geology than archaeology.'

I had to get used to this rivalry amongst specialists. And to Russians having this odd, slow way of absorbing everything—you don't know when they will react or how. Very often, you've finished speaking and they still haven't reacted.

We agreed to leave as soon as Leonid's archaeologist wife returned from her dig so she could be with their children. In the meantime, it was the Indian Independence Day and I found myself early on the morning of 15 August at a small gathering at the ambassador's residence in Tashkent. I had been on the road for exactly three months. The women in their saris nodded to each other, the unspoken but ironclad caste system of the Indian Foreign Service hierarchy inherited intact from the British Foreign Office.

The ambassador pulled on the flag so that it fluttered open and rose petals floated to the garden below. He read the President's speech in a firm voice, his delivery flawless. It was a gloomy outline of the ills that India still faced fifty-three years after independence.

We all sang the national anthem, a thready tune, the words of which I mumbled, pulled out from that fourth-grade memory, locked into a fourth-grade understanding.

My visa extension was still being processed. Fortunately, a happy coincidence brought an old friend, Nadia, to Tashkent on United Nations work. We sat in a *chaikhana* and polished off a bottle of mineral water, drank tea and ate slices of melons, and caught up on the past few years. Among the turtle doves, the large Uzbek women glided around in headscarves and served us. There was always a river, or a body of water, by Tashkent restaurants.

Nadia was a British-born Pakistani given to drama and entangled, complex relationships. Men fell for her vitality and then couldn't handle the wake.

'What a strange man,' Nadia was saying of my monk, half-laughing, in her very pucca voice. She was all deadlines, reports, bosses, work politics. Even in oven-hot Tashkent she managed a corporate crispness. And I was travel-stained, with my single pair of dusty boots. I was taking the long way home. I had stopped fighting time. In Nadia's company I felt speechless, caught in my own travel-spell, where space unspooled and each moment slowed to the exact rhythm of my heartbeat. Her world, which used to be my world, had receded into the distance. I looked at it as I would at an interesting insect frozen in formaldehyde.

'Why did your monk come all the way here? Why not go over the Himalaya to India? Maybe he didn't know there was a route. I'm not so impressed,' she said, 'with your monk.'

I laughed. It was typical of Nadia to ask the obvious question nobody had asked. At least I hadn't.

Patience had never been my forte, but it was rammed down my throat at every turn. I had to learn to wait. There was a phone number where S. could reach me and we talked often. 'How happy you look after you talk to him,' my host Mrs C. noted. She hovered to listen, pretending to clear the table or do her nails.

'Really?' I said innocently. But I was. He made me laugh. He was my bedrock.

One hot afternoon in Uzbekistan, he phoned and read me the resignation letter he had drafted.

'You're giving up your job?' I was flabbergasted. 'But you love it.'

'It's not entirely convenient. There are things that don't work. I can't live here any more,' he said.

'But what will you do?' I said. The question was still 'what will you do', not 'what will we do'.

'I have tickets to the Sydney Olympics. After that I want to go skiing in New Zealand. Why don't you meet me there?'

'You have gone quite mad,' I said kindly.

'Look who's talking,'

'Have you looked at a map lately? Do you see Uzbekistan and then do you see New Zealand?'

'Think about it.'

I put it right out of my mind.

Qamar Rais\ headed the Indian Cultural Centre in Tashkent. Rais was from Lucknow. His old face was now like Auden's 'wedding cake left out in the rain' but traces of his handsome past lingered in his cheekbones and in the slick lock of hair that fell across his forehead, the fine nose, the belated vanity of dyed hair.

He organized meetings of illustrious Uzbeks who had studied Indian culture and history. They were Muslims who held their hands up to their faces in prayer before the gathering and again afterwards.

There was desultory talk of Raj Kapoor. His films were greedily watched in a swathe across Russia, Central Asia and China. Raj Kapoor had done more for Indian diplomacy than anyone since, which goes to show that art, not policy, is the greatest binder.

An elderly Uzbek with gold teeth sang Indian love songs with gusto in a fine baritone. He held the tune steady and sang with feeling: *Yeh mera prem patra padhkar, ke tum naaraaz na hona.* I had come so far to listen to the beauty of my own language. To hear my own blood (can language seep into blood?) echoed and spoken in this foreign land by this kind Uzbek man was a little overwhelming. Maybe it was the heat combined with tiredness, but I was close to tears the whole evening.

chapter thirteen

River of Gold

By the last week of August, all my papers were in order. We could leave the following day to pick up Xuanzang's trail.

President Karimov was on the news that morning, looking drawn and tired, though his grey suit was sleek and his navy-blue tie immaculate. There were television shots of troops picking their way down a rocky hillside, and of a helicopter that issued a black streak of smoke.

There was a long speech from this man fighting a battle on three fronts, though he could not actually declare war. Karimov was shown talking to troops in military fatigues, gesturing with both hands. 'Dushman' was his most frequently uttered word, a word from my own linguistic past. Enemy. I thought, glancing at the television, that President Karimov looked afraid for his life that summer. The terrorists had already tried once to kill him one spring day in 1999.

Country alert or not, Leonid and I were on our way. Early summer mornings in Tashkent were a gift, still dew-drenched from the night, and there were drops of condensation on the vast cream GAZ that came bearing Leonid and the driver, Ravshan.

I tossed my backpack into the trunk and Ravshan backed into a main road. With relief, I sank into the seventh century. We swung by north Tashkent first, Khanabad, Xuanzang's Nujkend. There was a row of buses waiting to grind into their day's routine. There were empty tramlines, few cars; it was too early for the morning rush. Khanabad had been destroyed in the 1966 earthquake and there was not much to see in that corner of town.

Tashkent was the old site of Chach. But centuries before the 1966 earthquake, Genghis Khan, the ancestor of Timur the Lame, had already taken a shot at flattening the place.

South-west of Tashkent lay the modern city of Chinoz, the old crossing of the Syr Darya. The ancient Sogdian name was Chinachket, or 'town of Chinese merchants'. It was tempting to pinpoint it as the place where Xuanzang crossed. Many have done so. But Leonid had other ideas.

We headed south-west along an old Tashkent road to the ruins at Kanka, what would have been a possible stop on the way from Chach to Samarkand. I had to mentally erase the modern cities from maps, abolish international boundaries, to see instead, smaller kingdoms with settlements of vanished names along natural defiles, kingdoms that paused when the landscape changed to a range or a river. Thinking in seventh-century terms, Chach was in the mountains and valleys snuggled in the U of the Syr Darya. Ustrushan unfolded south of the Syr Darya, contained by the Turkestan range to the south. Further west lay Sughd, with the Zerafshan River running through it. Far south spread the ancient kingdoms of Kesh and Termez and Tukharistan.

There were green-uniformed police milling around a traffic booth. The traffic into Tashkent had been stopped for inspection. Already on the fringes of the city, buckets of aubergines and apples were being sold on the roadside. We passed cotton fields, and more cotton fields. Four Uzbek women sat on a bed under a Chinar tree selling watermelons. The sun was rising higher, heating up. Ravshan braked for a boy driving five cows across the road. We crossed the Circik River, overgrown with weeds. It used to be thick with forest.

Leonid twisted from the front seat to deliver neat packages of information in his special English that I was beginning to understand quite well.

We passed a small fortress by the roadside, now a cemetery, a mound or *tepa* which means 'up' or 'high' in Uzbek. It was the first of many such *tepa*s that dotted the region, a whole history reduced to bumps under fields. We were on the left bank of the Ahangaran River, 'ironsmith' in Farsi or Middle Iranian. But they only found silver, gold and copper and two iron furnaces.

'Very bad iron,' Leonid said, curling his lips at some imagined foul odour. But already he was telling me about the famous silver mines of Central Asia from which the coins of Austria and Germany were fashioned.

We passed a grass-filled cart, drawn by a horse, heading to the bazaar. The corn in fields flanking the road was higher than a man's head. We drove through the rural backyards of Uzbekistan, through more cotton fields and past the mulberry trees that lined the roads.

Kanka lay on a rolling hillock, the city wall still visible.

'Attention please,' said Leonid, chuffed. This was his territory. He was the guru and I, a humble student. The morning was still cool.

The remains of the fortress were shaped like a shoe. The moat was now a sluggish weed-ridden puddle. Leonid leaned in the dirt and drew a profile of a boot with a stone. Here, the dungeon, the big tower, the last line of defence. The *kioshk*, or castle, appeared in the middle of the seventh century, as big houses of *dikhans*—small feudal lords, landowners, rich traders. Nowadays, *dikhan* simply means farmer.

Leonid lit another cigarette and said that the city had existed until the beginning of the thirteenth century, till Genghis Khan. The earliest layers here were from the third century BC.

Ducks splashed through water at the moat. Xuanzang, arriving from a northerly direction, would have seen the citadel in the distance, as he would in most Central Asian towns. A city with four gates, 'claw-footed' towers that stuck out on two sides, for defence with bows and arrows. The kingdom of Chach had been crowded, urbanized. A stork landed and flapped off again over the cotton fields.

The sun was no longer playful. I adjusted my hat, sipped water from the bottle and pulled out my shades. We drove to our next stop, the crossing of the Syr Darya at Binaket, which Leonid suggested was the monk's route. It was a more natural route south to Ustrushan and then west across the desert to Sughd.

Travellers on these ancient Silk Road routes covered between thirty-five and forty kilometres a day, which was close to what the archaeologist in Kyrgyzstan had told me. Sheep grazed with white ducks at their feet. There were flocks of crows on a poplar, and eight geese waddled on the side of the road. We pushed further south-west, stopped to ask more directions from an old man with gold teeth.

Soft cotton bolls flashed bright under green leaves. In between, Leonid related a long, sad story about his Russian friend, an expert in the Bengali language, who now had to work as an auto mechanic.

'This is Soviet Union now,' he lamented.

On the east bank of the Syr Darya, over half of the old city of Binaket had been swallowed up by the river which has shifted three kilometres east in the past thirty to forty years.

'This strange river of Central Asia, it moves a lot,' Leonid said. He seemed delighted at the river's vagaries. We clambered up the plateau, on the remains of the old city, moving naturally towards the river. There was shucked corn, with pale cream leaves, lying in golden piles.

Leonid pointed out layers of animal bones and a clunk of rusted iron. This was obviously an ancient garbage pile, he said.

'Obviously,' I muttered. Gasping in the midday heat, I looked down at the Syr Darya from a height of about twenty metres. It was flat and sluggish, a net of white bubbles floated on it. The river clogged and clotted. It was slow and shrunken in summer, its banks choked with grass.

'What did Xuanzang do for money?' I asked the omniscient Leonid.

'Sogdians carried skins with an imprint of Tamga, and this they could change at a Jewish money-changer's. Jewish money-changers controlled the trade from Kirim to Khaim,' Leonid explained. Xuanzang, I reflected, could also have exchanged his bolts of silk from the king of Gaochang.

The structure of the old road interested Leonid. It was three to four metres in depth, like a canal. Security would patrol on horses on either side, hooves raising a cloud of dust. There were caravanserais for those who wished to rest during the day; for the night there was food for the animals and travellers.

We retired to the shade of an apricot tree. A turtle dove gurgled. Bees buzzed. Leonid shared a cigarette with the keeper of the archaeological site. There was a Muslim holy shrine not far away; there would be ram sacrifices until the afternoon. Leonid exhaled smoke.

'At Binaket, archaeologists found a gold earring, snake-shaped, maybe of Indian tradition.'

The idea set him off. Before the Arabs, there was Zoroastrianism, but the Central Asian practice was different from the Sassanid Iranian one. Zoroastrianism was grafted onto older Central Asian practices, but never quite wiped out a few habits here and there.

Sitting under the shade of the trees, deep in rural Uzbekistan, I was hearing these stories for the first time in my life. Why had nobody told me? Perhaps this was why I had to make this journey, to meet Leonid and learn these things from him. If I died the next day, I would be a happy woman, my head stuffed with Central Asian miscellany, these clues to home.

Central Asians liked to use wooden sculptures, they had gods and goddesses like Ordosho or Faro, Leonid explained. They had the cult of *haoma*, or *ephedra*, from which came ephedrine, which acts on the central nervous system. They are red berries, boiled for two hours to make a powerful biological stimulant.

There was devil worship, evidenced in the text *Videvdat*, or text against *dev*.

Dev. Devil.

'Do you see?' Leonid stared at me as though addressing a dull child.

'Deva means god in Hindi,' he added.

'Yes, I know that much,' I said.

Leonid explained that in India, deva is a good god, asura is evil. In Iran, it was the other way round.

'One city's good god is another city's bad god.' He grinned in happiness. 'You know the three Magi who came from the East when Christ was born?'

I nodded. Gaspar, Melchior and Balthasar.

'They were of the Zoroastrian tradition. Magus is the singular noun, it is old Persian for Zoroastrian priest. Magus, magic, man of magic. Same thing.'

Leonid took a drag of his cigarette. 'Balance,' said Leonid, exhaling another cloud of smoke, already on a tangent, following some internal reel of thought.

'It's all about balance. The Taoist Dao Dejing, the proto-Zoroastrian philosophy, the *Rig Veda*, the early Upanishads, they all have a single origin—the Yasht. It was a small part of the early Avesta.'

The merciless heat of the day gripped my head. Leonid seemed not to notice it. I was beginning to wilt. I sipped my bottle of water. There was so much I had not learned about my own past. There was something surreal about being taught it by a blue-eyed Ukrainian scholar, under the trees in the middle of summer in Uzbekistan.

'And look at the system of oral question and answers as a way of teaching. The Greek, the Hindu, the Celtic tradition, they all use the same method.'

'Because what you speak remains in the air. Writing is nothing!' I blinked.

Beyond the Syr Darya, stagnant and green, spread the country of Ustrushana, which Xuanzang called Su-tu-li-sse-na. He said,

> On the east it borders on the Yeh river (Jaxartes). This river has its source in the northern plateau of the Tsung-ling range, and flows to the north-west; sometimes it rolls its muddy waters along in quiet, at other times with turbulence. The products and customs of the people are like those of Che-shi.[1]

The ruins of the kingdom's capital city were at Bunjikat, south of the modern town of Shahristan—all of which lay inconveniently in next-door Tajikistan.

So we did the next best thing and stopped at Khavast, on the Uzbekistan side, a few kilometres from the Tajik border. It was so hot that the road looked wet. Something had died, for eagles circled overhead and two vultures waited for that perfect degree of putrefaction.

The mercury soared, producing a white glare. The flat Uzbek countryside dissolved behind heat waves, but Leonid barely paused, striding ahead with his long legs. I stumbled behind him, not sweating, for it was so dry that any liquid evaporated instantly. But I was sure my muscles were baked. I was a piece of meat cooking in the sun.

I followed Leonid to the railway lines and the remains of walls on a dry mud heap. My curiosity was thinning under the ruthless heat. I was getting cross with these Central Asian heaps of mud and their besotted archaeologists. The magic was withering. The more I drooped, the more energetic Leonid seemed to get.

He lit a cigarette and began to explain.

Khavast was the first point of what used to be the ancient kingdom of Ustrushana. It was a city that lasted from the first or second century BC to around the seventeenth century AD. He sketched a quick diagram in the sand, the walls of the fortress about 200 by 300 metres. Ustrushana was Leonid's baby. He had written a doctoral thesis on the Myk settlement in the mountains of Ustrushana. Ustrushana emerged as an independent country around the sixth and seventh centuries, as the monk was passing through. But my mind was singed shut.

As we drove through what had been Ustrushana, Leonid grew happier and happier, recalling his days of research in the field. I was a small heap, unable to focus under the punishing sun. I saw our next *tepa* westwards in a blur. Zomin lay at the foot of the Turkestan range, sandwiched by the desert to the north and the Turkestan range to the south, Xuanzang's directional guide.

There was no other road to Samarkand, Leonid said. 'You had the mountains to the south, the desert to the north. There was just one way.' And then he launched into something about iron arrowheads for hunting boars and black dirhams on the upper levels, how he had excavated here and how *shahristan* was Farsi for 'city'.

Now only the Hungry Steppes, or the eastern tongue of the Kizil Kum, Desert of Red Sand, lay between the monk and Samarkand.

∞

The monk leaned back. The recollections tired him. The journey had tired him to the soul, sapped him. No, he shook his head. It had soaked into his bones. He had given his life to it. Had it in turn breathed life into him? He was not sure.

Hui Li wrote quickly. His fingers were, as usual, stained with ink by now.

'The desert, Master,' Hui Li said, looking up. 'You were getting to the desert.'

'Yes,' Xuanzang muttered. 'Another desert.'

In his own *Records*, he wrote,

> Northwest from this we enter on a great sandy desert, where there is
> neither water nor grass. The road is lost in the waste, which appears
> boundless, and only by looking in the direction of some great mountain
> and following the guidance of the bones which lie scattered about,
> can we know the way in which we ought to go.[2]

There were things he did not say. There was no need. How would
it serve history to record these other moments? There was no need to
write of the spinning flashbacks, to that first desert crossing so many
moons ago, hideous flashbacks to the time when the sands of other
deserts flew into the corners of his eyes till they watered and reddened,
his first shock on seeing a pile of human bones. Something had changed
in him by the time he reached the road to Samarkand. There was a
new steel thread through his mind. It held him steady. He had learned
to fight fear. By the time Samarkand gleamed in the distance, he
brushed sand from his face and smiled with one side of his mouth.

ॐ

My head lolled on the car's back seat, I dozed in the heat, immensely
relieved to be heading to Samarkand. I caught Leonid saying that
modern Farsi was very similar to Sogdian. He said that Sogdians
were like a river, they had to move or die, that they were middlemen
on the great trade routes, they themselves owned nothing. I fell asleep.

On the borders of Samarkand at dusk, traffic piled up for checks,
trucks filled with melons lined the road. Police had fluorescent
truncheons swinging at their waists. They checked papers, looked in
the boot of cars and leaned in to smell for alcohol breath.

Leonid persuaded a staff member of the Institute of Archaeology
to put us up for a day or so in faculty apartments. Ravshan had
friends in Samarkand from his student days.

We were to visit Afrasiab, the ancient site of Samarkand, the
place Xuanzang referred to as Sa-mo-kien. When Xuanzang arrived,
Samarkand was a grand city with established international relations.
It had ties with the Chinese emperor; indeed, the city's dancing girls

graced the Imperial Chinese courts along with the dance troupes from Chach, Kish and Maimurg,[3] and Tang officials too, might have dreamed of Samarkand. It was a trade centre, a warehouse of merchandise. The Chinese called it Kang, 'blessed country'.

> The capital of the country is 20 *li* or so in circuit. It is completely enclosed by rugged land and very populous. The precious merchandise of many foreign countries is stored up here. The soil is rich and productive and yields abundant harvests. The forest trees afford a thick vegetation, and flowers and fruits are plentiful. The Shen horses are bred here. The inhabitants are skilful in the arts and trades beyond those of other countries. The climate is agreeable and temperate . . . The king is full of courage, and the neighbouring countries obey his commands.[4]

Like all successful cities, it had a mighty defence, strong soldiers, numerous horses. The army comprised men of Chih-kia, warlike, naturally brave and fierce, Xuanzang said. When they attacked, nobody could stand their onslaught. I remembered Rtveladze, poised on his toes atop his bed, reaching for a book, saying that we don't know his name, the name of Xuanzang's 'king full of courage'. We don't know who he was. But there was a finding, a coin from AD 642, of a Sogdian king called Shushpir. And another thing, Rtveladze's eyes sparkled as though removing a velvet cover from a diamond. The 'men of Chih-kia' that Xuanzang refers to was not a separate ethnic term, as Beal thought, but simply from *chakar*, a Sogdian term for 'soldiers'. I was as delighted as him. A sliver of a piece of the puzzle, nudged into place with a tweezer. *Chakar*. I remembered the word now.

I thought, though it was a massive leap, that the Hindi expression *naukar–chakar* means servants, and possibly the *chakar* part comes from the Sogdian for 'soldiers', via the Persian dilution of the word to mean servant.

Old Samarkand was a city with three walls delineating the separate areas. At the museum, there was the shock of an artist's representation, for in the image, greenery abounded. How would a city be liveable without its trees? Chinars and water canals, the pleasantest things imaginable. A moist earth pushed out trees hung with golden peaches, shaded thickets for hunting, gardens laid out like feasts.

It was a city so alluring that when the Arabs arrived from the desert, sweating, chanting Allah's name, they dropped their swords and thought for fragments of minutes that they had found paradise. But Qutaiba bin Muslim's forces loomed in AD 712 to besiege and take the city. The Arabs built mosques over the fire temples and monasteries, bribed citizens with dirhams, one for each time they attended Friday prayers; they waived land taxes for those who believed in Allah.

Historically speaking, the monk missed the Muslims by a whisker.

Atop another mound, Leonid expounded on a favourite theme. 'Chinese traders were rare, traders on the Silk Road were usually Sogdian.'

It made perfect sense that trade along these routes was dominated by Sogdians. Some people did certain things, by tradition or habit or training. Chinese laundries, Patel Motels, or Jews in banking.

'But,' he continued, 'it is *wrong* to say that silk and iron all came from China. In Samarkand, they knew how to make silk by the fifth century.'

August in Uzbekistan was an attrition of the senses. Summer was at its height and the sun merciless, now that the vegetation was gone, now that the desert had crept up and choked rivers.

At Afrasiab, Russian and French archaeologists sat with their noses buried deep in the dust, stripped to the waist, bronzed and burnt, their shirts tied around their waists and white kerchiefs around their heads to keep at least a measure of sanity. We panted and puffed to the top of the citadel of old Samarkand.

Leonid hitched his jeans up and squatted in the dirt, catching up on archaeologist gossip in Russian. I waited patiently, trying to keep pace with the levels of the dig. To dive into the seventh century, I juggled Samanids, Karakhanids, Shaybanids and Timurids and their cities, buried, squashed in sections the archaeologists dug through with patience, sighs of pleasure at their discoveries. At my feet, an old city unpeeled its secrets, and in the hazy distance a Timurid skyline glittered, with its massive blue domes, the bold architecture of Central Asia. The mighty Timur was buried here. They say that

Timur asked his wazirs to cut up three sheep and hang one each in Bukhara, Shahrisabz and Samarkand. After three days, the healthiest meat was in Samarkand. And so he built a crypt for himself here.

I looked down to where the archaeologists were digging in an ancient vanished city. To my untrained eye, it seemed reckless to shovel dirt and then squat with a brush to tickle away a few particles. What if some rare manuscript fragment was caught in the debris off to the side?

What these men and women found here would make or break careers in Central Asian archaeology. It was a peaceful dig, but it was a war zone. A silent, tacit competition thickened the air.

I ducked through the fire lines and hoped for a glimpse of Xuanzang's ghost heels, a waft of incense, the flap of a robe as he turned a corner, a rosary bead that dropped and rolled to my feet to hint that, yes, he was here. My head buzzed with the tangled threads of Central Asian history, a past reflected in the faces of the present: Turkic bones, Persian noses, Mongol foreheads, mixed in with the angles of a more Slavic time.[5] I was drooping from all the newness, the facts, the rivers, the old historical names, the Arab conquest, the beginning and the end of one phase and another, the slow and perfect evolution of history.

'Everything moves, it's dialectics,' said Leonid.

This much was clear: Xuanzang arrived in Central Asia, and found only remnants and shadows of Buddhism, monasteries that were no longer alive.

☙

The monk was shocked, a little alarmed perhaps, but carried on towards India on a well-worn route.

At first the king of Samarkand was disdainful and then, hearing the doctrines, he had a change of heart. Or so Hui Li said. But according to Hui Li, rulers, warriors and laymen dropped to their knees and became Buddhists with great regularity in Xuanzang's wake. How much could be believed?

Although, Hui Li did admit that

The king and people do not believe in the law of the Buddha, but their religion consists in sacrificing to fire. There are here two religious foundations, but no priests dwell in them. If stranger-priests seek shelter therein, the barbarians follow them with burning fire and will not permit them to remain there.[6]

Who were these barbarians? Were they guards at a fire temple, incensed at this foreign intrusion, high on *haoma*? They chased two of Xuanzang's new disciples, waving flaming torches, angry perhaps at a betrayal of their faith. The pair turned and ran, carrying an impression of wide-open mouths gleaming in the firelight. But the monk would not allow the king of Samarkand to have the aggressors' hands cut off. He begged for leniency and they were let off with a beating. And I was left wondering, tangentially, about the punishment of hands being cut off. Wasn't that what they did in Saudi Arabia and other Muslim countries? What if the custom was much older than Islam?

We stayed a night with Tajik friends of Leonid in their home, a caravanserai converted into living quarters, with a giant tree and a small pond in the middle. Rahima cooked *pollov* as I sat in the kitchen and tried to help, slicing carrots. A few chickens wandered through the door and pecked at the mud earth. Rahima spoke no English and I spoke only the barest Russian or Uzbek, but we smiled and gestured. The men sat outside and sipped vodka from bowls. Leonid was threatening to kill somebody. Then there was a loud crash and as Rahima and I rushed outside we saw it was Leonid falling over from too much vodka. He was like a wooden upright doll that simply toppled over. He slept straight through till the morning.

The rest of us ate the *pollov* and conversed as best as we could, stripped of our translator, pretending that what had happened had not actually happened.

chapter fourteen

Crossing the River

After his ambiguous meeting with the king of Samarkand, Xuanzang turned south-west towards Kesh, which he called Ki-Shwang-Na, and said merely that it resembled Samarkand in customs and produce and that reaching there required a journey of 300 *li*.

We left Samarkand early next morning and drove south to old Kesh, with its capital at modern-day Shahrisabz. Green city. As the monk indicated, it was a relatively short journey. We passed a giant clock marking the time zones, a two-hour difference between Samarkand and Moscow, so that the Russian masters in Central Asia would always know what time it was at home.

Leonid was unshaven. He sipped beer from an empty Coke bottle as we drove. I felt quite unhappy. I thought so highly of Leonid and all that he was teaching me. It was my own fault, putting him on a pedestal. But the alcohol seemed to have made no difference whatsoever to Leonid's blade-like historical focus. It was I who had to add 'drunken' to the epithet of 'professor-guide'.

Shahrisabz, known as Kesh in Xuanzang's time, sat south of Samarkand, across the Zerafshan River, cupped in the curve of mountains—to the north and east a spur of the Zerafshan range and to the south, the rise of the Hisor hills. We drove uphill immediately after Samarkand, passing a donkey cart loaded with fodder, curving around roads. The road was flanked by *tepa*s. I was beginning to be able to differentiate a landscape's undulation from a buried *tepa*, a mound of history; sometimes I knew a particular bump to be the rise of a boundary wall, to Leonid's delight. His pleasure was like that of a parent watching a toddler take its first steps.

The monk was staring ahead at what was to come, the barren mountain range tinged rust-red, soil filled with iron. Did he miss the dreamy feel of the region he had left? Did he see that up in the mountains of southern Uzbekistan, the poplar leaves were already turning yellow, a reminder that it was the end of August, that it was autumn at higher altitudes, among the archa trees?

As we rolled into Shahrisabz at the bottom of the hills, at another checkpoint, we stopped to the rustle of thorn bushes. A dog was tied to the roadside where the military examined papers. The car papers needed a stamp, technical reasons. There was a cost, an odd delicacy to the corruption.

At the bottom of the pass, Leonid's sharp eyes picked out another mound, a fortress shaped like a boot. He pointed it out from the front seat, but I missed it entirely, in a moment of inattention.

The settlements and fortresses of Kesh.

Salt of many hues—red, green, black—went to China from here. Tabibs, healers, used the salt against skin diseases. Even now the mines were being explored.

We crossed the Kashka Darya (Kashka River), parched and dead in the heat, reduced to a gravel bed, drove past Kitob and into the green city where archaeologists had found layers from the second century BC.

Shahrisabz was the kind of city where I was desperate to wander the streets; it was a quieter version of Samarkand. I wanted to shed my focussed guides and dip into the juicy figs in season, wander the markets at ease and at my own pace. But then I wouldn't have learned from Leonid that the word for market, *chor-su*, came from *chor*, four, and *su*, water, streams, and from that, streets. Four streets meeting equals a bazaar, the concept had not changed from pre-Islamic times in Central Asia. The Sogdian word for bazaar is 'souk', I had always thought it was from Arabic, but the Arabs likely got it from Central Asia.

It was quite possible that when the monk passed through Kesh there was some version of this bazaar already in existence. The bazaar was subdivided into sections—for textiles, for food, for metal goods—

placed along the shady streets, where the locals looked up in interest to watch the tall, lanky Russian striding ahead and the smaller Indian woman trotting to keep pace.

Leonid was hunting for a modern Muslim cemetery which marked the spot of a medieval settlement, one which would have stood high when the monk went through. Each layer had yielded to archaeologists several coins, indicating a centre of some import. It had existed right till the Arab conquest.

Kesh was the strongest state in the region, helped by its excellent natural defences of mountains and the Kashka Darya, which flowed to the exposed west. We dodged through the back streets of Kesh; I practically walked backwards, looking over my shoulder as Leonid's relentless search continued. But when we found the spot where the cemetery was supposed to be, a small residential neighbourhood had sprung up over it.

It was not far from the Kok Gumbaz, the blue dome. Other layers of history that grew like mould. Once again, a lurch of recognition— *kok*, blue in Uighur, and *gumbaz*, well I knew the word *gumbaz* from India. Built by Ulugh Beg in 1435, the Kok Gumbaz was a place for artisans—archaeologists had found glazed bricks with gold ornamentation. The entry tickets were still printed in Russian and still insisted that the price of entry was twenty kopeks.

An old imam at the madrasa grumbled at more recent historical invasions. Shahrisabz had ninety-six mosques, he said, but the communists had destroyed them and now there were ten.

It was in Shahrisabz that Leonid explained why Xuanzang might have bothered to come through here instead of taking that shorter route to India across the Karakorams, the Pamirs.

'Famous translators of Buddhist texts were from Samarkand, Kang to the Chinese, and so the monk and his contemporaries might have thought the region rich in Buddhism. They were not aware, perhaps, that by the end of the sixth century AD Buddhism had died here.'

Leonid puffed on a cigarette. We were sitting in the shade of a local chaikhana, sipping a sour, cooling yoghurt mix from bowls. My insides were beginning to waver in the iron afternoon heat, but I held strong till the next story.

'Your monk,' Leonid was saying, 'he came to look at Buddhism in Central Asia, he found nothing. So on the way back he took the shorter route.'

That night we stayed in an Uzbek household, friends of Ravshan's family. Like traditional Indian houses, it had an open courtyard in the centre with a pond. In the back, a full bathhouse with a sauna hinted at Russian influences.

Bakhriddin and his family laid out a sumptuous welcome, though the women were separate and we hardly saw them. We sat cross-legged at a low table laden with grapes, apples, pears. There was rock sugar for tea, walnuts, peanuts, sliced watermelon. Outside, thick grape trellises grew. And finally, there was mutton *pollov*, with garlic cooked in its skin and chilli, which we ate with our fingers from the plate. That night in Shahrisabz, there was vodka too, in small bowls. I eyed Leonid nervously. But he was on his best behaviour.

'I had a dream,' Bakhriddin was saying in Uzbek, through Ravshan who translated. 'I had a dream a few days ago that we would have visitors.'

I smiled and raised my bowl of vodka to him, and bowed my head. I slept badly that night, slapping away mosquitoes, tossing and turning. The mutton *pollov* induced an internal breakdown and cramping, so that all of the next day Ravshan had to pull over every half hour so that I could skip over behind rocks by the side, hardly caring whether I was in full sight of passing busloads, overcome by the typhoon gurgling in my belly. The two men delicately turned their backs and smoked as my head whirled in the sun and buses roared by at angles.

80

The monk stared at what was ahead, the barren mountain range tinged rust-red, soil filled with iron, the arid landscape he would have to cross to pass the Iron Gates and enter Tokharistan. He wrote:

> . . . the mountain road is steep and precipitous, and the passage along the defiles dangerous and difficult. There are no people or villages, and little water or vegetation. Going along the mountains

300 *li* or so south-east, we enter the Iron Gates. The pass so called is bordered on the right and left by mountains. These mountains are of prodigious height. The road is narrow, which adds to the difficulty and danger. On both sides there is a rocky wall of an iron colour. Here there are set up double wooden doors, strengthened with iron and furnished with many bells hung up.[1]

&

So it was, clutching my stomach, bleary and weary, that I heard Leonid inform me that this desolate sight the sun was pounding, the rolling softened hills, was landscape typical of the bottom of the ocean. We passed a donkey and herds of sheep, and as I tested the image of being at the bottom of some ancient ocean, Leonid pointed, there, see, the site of the Iron Gates.

I lifted my head and then dropped it back, registering only clumps of rock and the glare of the heat. Then I closed my eyes, for the belly-churning had returned as we swung around the hills, climbing and then descending into the valley of the Surkhan Darya.

There was a house and a garden in Gagarin, in southern Uzbekistan, and the sun, by some miracle, was low and the light pleasant. Leonid had a table set up with apples and grapes. My body sagged, caught on an unseen wire. I crumpled on the dusty bed, too weak to move, my intestines still in mutiny. This was the archaeologists' base, for general use, and in the corner of unswept rooms fragments of pottery were piled up.

At the bottom of the tangled garden, a shed served as a washroom and to the side stood an outhouse. Leonid set about making it as clean and as comfortable as possible. He urged down my throat a bowl of vodka, with a bullet of salt. It would, he said, stop the gurgles and leaks. He pressed his lips to my forehead.

'This is how I check on my children. You have no fever,' he announced tenderly.

The military presence, the regular checkpoints, had spooked both my companions. We were now only a few kilometres from the Afghan border. The guards here wore black military uniforms, black leather boots and green berets with gold badges. They wore bulletproof jackets and knives in sheaths in their breast pockets. This was certainly upgraded from the military camouflage.

It was the second time I had dragged other people into the possibility of danger. Leonid's papers had some technical hitch to them, something about being born in Ukraine but being a Tashkent resident and still not being allowed a passport to leave the country.

But Leonid rolled down his window at the men in dark glasses and joked in Russian, and cajoled, and refused to be cowed. The Uzbek police saw his handsome profile and breezy manner, the letters in Russian with the stamps on them, and waved us on. But it was an act. Leonid was tense too.

'We are Russians,' he said sombrely. 'We have worries.' He refused to elaborate. Ravshan, younger, newly married, thought of his wife and his eyes filled with tears over dinner. His lower lip trembled.

In the morning, we headed towards old Termez, near the Afghan border. In the morning haze, I stood on the remains of Kampyr Tepa, a buried Central Asian city dating from Kushan times, excavated only in bits and pieces. The truth lay here, under the piles of dirt and mounds.

Leonid thought Kampyr Tepa worth seeing. Perhaps this was one of the sites Xuanzang visited when he wrote of Tami, or Termez. From Tarmata, Place of Crossing the River.

❧

Finally, what Xuanzang yearned for. Company.

> There are about ten sangharamas with about one thousand monks. The stupas and the images of the honoured Buddha are noted for various spiritual manifestations.[2]

He left it at that. After all, to him, that was the most important thing.

❧

Dating from the second or third century BC, Termez was a city poised on a river, offering its citizens easy travel. It was a part of the Kushan empire, which straddled the millennium and was best known for its wise king Kanishka, patron of Buddhism. There were tower remains, with a depression for a moat and slits in the walls for bows. The defences were impressive: at the low levels, the walls were three metres wide and ten metres high, with three or four levels for bows. A berm slanted down from the wall outside to prevent the use of battering rams. Here they found papyrus, with inscriptions in Bactrian. We walked across a divide and jumped on to a low wall.

Here, said Leonid, was a temple of fire dating from the beginning of the second century AD. The evidence was two round pits, a stairway to the second floor. A fire always burned, for prayer, but also to light the point of crossing on the Amu Darya, for caravans. The Amu Darya, like its northern counterpart, the Syr Darya, had moved south.

I would have deduced nothing of this if Leonid had not pointed out the small room for sacred ash, a chimney, a small square where a fire could be lit, for breath is polluting and bad for fire.

'In Surkhan Darya, only about five per cent of the findings are related to Buddhism, but there are very few actual traces. All archaeologists have a fad of Buddhism,' he said, lighting his zillionth cigarette. 'Kanishka is Kanishka, introducing Buddhism, but for the normal population, the tradition was fire-praying from the early bronze age in Bactria.'

Maybe Kanishka, the Scythian king who ruled in the first century AD, thought the Buddhist ideology had a role for his empire, but maybe he didn't succeed. It was a very mixed population—many nations, many languages; he needed something to tie it all together.

Leonid stubbed out his cigarette. There was only one small plaquette from the north of the city with the Buddha on it. Leonid kneeled to draw it on the ground. It was a small icon in the shape of a sitting person. 'It's not clear at all. Maybe it's not Buddha at all. You see what you want to see.'

In no-man's-land, inaccessible, was Kara Tepa, excavated by the French. There were the remains of a Buddhist temple beyond the southern courtyard. But a fire altar stood in an attached niche: 'the existence of a fire altar in a Buddhist structure is most striking'.[3] It seemed to reinforce Leonid's point.

There were rice fields visible from this height and, far south, a blue smudge, the Amu Darya, and beyond, a shadow in the early morning, Afghanistan. Though I did not know it then, this was the closest I would get to Balkh, in Afghanistan, which I could see across the river, a dusty maze.

The Amu Darya, this wild river. I had wanted to swim in it, watch the sun flatten its edges, but it flowed beyond the electrified border fence with Afghanistan.

Perhaps it was here somewhere that the legendary hero Rustam unknowingly fought his own son Sohrab. They met on the banks of the Amu Darya. Rustam and Sohrab came face to face and launched into battle. Both fought valiantly till Rustam inflicted a deadly blow on Sohrab.

Dying on the banks of this river, Sohrab whispered, 'If my father comes to know that you have killed his son, then you will not survive.'

Kneeling, suddenly cold, Rustam asked why.

'He is a big warrior, his name is Rustam.'

'Prove that you are the son of Rustam,' the older man said, his voice chilled at the edges, as though he were falling over a cliff, far, far below. Sohrab, in pain, pulled out the *tabiz dhaga* that identified him. Rustam's hot tears fell on Sohrab's face, but his son died in his arms.

At Termez they buried a man who, they say, lived over a hundred years, who died in AD 932—the scholar Al-Khakim-at-Termezi, who penned over 400 works on science and on the history of Islam, examined the secrets of praying and fasting, wrote tracts on trade, arts and crafts.

It was a quiet Muslim mausoleum. But the reason Leonid brought me here was to show me, in the backyard of the tomb, four underground Buddhist cells for meditation that dated from about the first half of the second century AD. Maybe the main stupa was under the mausoleum, Leonid suggested. Being underground avoided the searing summer heat and the monks could focus on the Buddha in an alien land. These were ancient cave habitations. Monks lived in caves in the mountains; here, on this side of the river without the rock faces, they had dug out caves and built rooms for meditation.

We ducked underground into the dark hollows, through uneven

rocks, and emerged on the other side of the compound. Muslims adopted Buddhist meditative techniques and ideas of cleansing the spirit and body. And when building mosques, the Arabs simply chose old holy places, Leonid noted.

And perhaps, when the Muslims finally did reach Central Asia, a certain sect was born who called themselves the Sufis, from the rough woollen garments that they wore. Islam must have felt the impact of Buddhism exactly in this region, giving birth to mystical Sufism.

Here, at Al-Khakim-at-Termezi's tomb, right on top of old Buddhist cells, the idea made utter sense, although scholastically speaking this is a controversial idea. Across the Amu Darya, in Afghanistan's Balkh, one of the earliest Sufis called Ibrahim ibn Adham (*d*. AD 777) had established a school whose ascetic curriculum strangely resembled that of Buddhist monks. After all, when the Arabs conquered the region, Balkh was a centre of Buddhism. It had a well-known monastery that Arabic sources refer to as Naubahar.[4]

There was one more *tepa* to see, a single stupa above ground at the Fayaz Tepa. This is where we went next. We had to drive past more border guards and a gun tower near the border. Cars were backed up five-deep at a checkpoint. There was a radio tower. It was a landscape littered with remnants of the Soviet invasion of Afghanistan.

The Fayaz Tepa was a kilometre from old Termez. There were more high watchtowers, armed guards. This was the southern tip of the Soviet Union's might, before it shivered and splintered, an oak that crashed. This old Buddhist monastery was the launch pad of a ten-year war in Afghanistan. There were dish antennae, revolving radars poised atop trucks. The revolution set off a low whine. There were missile detectors cocooned in barbed wire.

A few metres from this bristling arsenal stood a simple stupa of mud bricks, dun-coloured, each brick thirty centimetre by thirty centimetre by ten centimetre. These are, Leonid said, typical Kushan bricks, which placed the structure roughly at the turn of the millennium. There was a sunken square courtyard, with the outlines of monastic cells still visible around it. It was so small and quiet, this gentle structure of mud, I felt a blossom of tenderness towards it. Was it here that Xuanzang counted some of his 1000 monks? How did it survive the bombings, the low-swooping planes? All those years, it waited for me.

My eyes kept swivelling towards the accoutrements of war, the outdated Russian equipment of the 1980s. The radar's whine distracted me, like a dog who hears high-pitched noises. Why was I constantly in somebody's war zone?

Leonid watched me watch the war tools. He yelled above the whine, the transmitters on trucks.

'You can call India from here, but it would be your last phone call.' He thought this extremely funny. At this spot, we had reached the end of Xuanzang's route in Uzbekistan. It was not possible to cross the Amu Darya into Afghanistan, I was once again face to face with my old problem of the visa to Pakistan and Afghanistan, and I had no idea how to tackle it.

We settled into a last meal with an old caretaker, who sighed into his hands, *bismillahar rahmanar rahim*, before we dug into *kattik*, yoghurt-sauce sprinkled with coriander, *zueraboi*, meat with tomatoes, garlic and chillies, and herbs and naan.

'Don't turn the *lepioshka* upside down,' Leonid corrected me. 'You only do that at funerals.' He had decided to expand beyond his archaeological mandate and instruct me in *all* things. 'No tea leaves for the guest's cup, the tea must be clean. And only give them a small amount, so the cup can be refilled many times. It shows respect, a desire for them to stay longer.'

I *did* want to stay longer, drink in strange new things. But it was time to leave, to swing back for the long two-day drive north to Tashkent. There were further worries: would Tashkent be closed off for Uzbekistan's National Day? We stopped on the way to buy apples from the roadside and bottles of fresh jam.

I stared out of the window at the dry, heated countryside rolling by.

'What are you thinking of?' Leonid asked kindly from the front seat.

'My family, my boyfriend,' I said, sniffing a little.

'I am your family here,' he said. Russian, possessive. 'You'll see,' he said. 'Just like you miss them here, you will miss me there.'

He was right, he was always right.

Back in Tashkent, I shook off the seventh century and Leonid with difficulty. It was like a drug, learning so many new things with him. But I had to figure out my next step. I thought I would visit the Afghans in Tashkent. Sections of Afghanistan were controlled by the Northern Alliance. Perhaps they could secret me across the border with Uzbekistan.

Mohammad Gafoorie sat in his office looking slightly nervous. He wore dark socks and loafers, his legs were crossed. He looked at me interestedly. He spoke excellent English.

'A Northern Alliance commander has come back from the war zone with updates and news,' Gafoorie explained. 'At the moment, the Taliban are leading a major offensive. They began that offensive on 3 August. The final decision is to capture Afghanistan completely. It was planned with Musharraf and the generals in the fighting ground. The final decision was made when Musharraf came to Kabul, secretly, just before August,' he said.

A big man entered the room. He leaned over the desk to pick up a folder from the window sill and flashed me a smile. He was from Bamiyan, he said. My heart bounded at the city's name. Would I see the massive Buddhas of Bamiyan that Xuanzang mentioned? This war in Afghanistan was really most inconvenient. Things did not look good for a trip across the border. There was nothing left to do but head home, to New Delhi.

The door of the Uzbek Airlines office was guarded by a blond Russian tough who let people in one at a time. The crowd pressed and leaned towards the door, but nobody complained. Home was a two-and-a-half-hour flight away, but it felt like defeat.

chapter fifteen

Locking the Sea in a Box

After fording the Amu Darya, Xuanzang crossed the mountains of the Hindu Kush in Afghanistan. He made his way through Gandhara, across the Indus River, and then reached the Hunza Valley in Pakistan-Occupied Kashmir. He walked by rock carvings on the cliff walls, passed over narrow iron bridges that swayed in the wind, linking one mountain flank to the other. He grabbed at rails. The iced metal stung his palms. He was dizzy from the height; the waters far below were a dream, a thin whistle to remind him of death. He imagined himself falling, a stick figure splayed, pinned upon the wind, wheeling and turning to the bottom. He followed the course of the Jhelum River, he pressed against the sides of the mountain as a herd of goats jostled by, and watched a clod of earth dislodge and fly. He crossed the Baramula Pass. There were villages, signs of habitation. At first the stone gates were hidden by a clump of pines. But the guards stopped him and the monk understood he must have reached the western entrance of the kingdom of Kashmir.

When news reached the palace, the king's mother and younger brother rushed to the borders in chariots and horses to greet the priest from China. Desultory crowds collected, then dispersed as the group passed. Children fell silent at the sight of the foreign monk.

Xuanzang was shown monasteries on the way, and then when dusk settled they escorted him to an establishment at Hushkara, where the Kashmiri monks would look after him for the night.

It was the end of AD 628. He had been on the road for a year. He had traversed twenty-four kingdoms and covered 13,800 *li*.

જી

It was good to be home, in India. I decided to set aside the monk's route in Pakistan and Afghanistan for now, waiting for a solution. My family was worried about my plans to go to Kashmir in the meantime.

'I don't think you should go to Kashmir,' my bua said. 'You can go to every other place on the Indian map, but not Kashmir.'

'I have to at least try,' I said. But I waited a little longer to book a plane ticket to Srinagar. The day before I was supposed to leave, an uncle dropped in on the way back from work.

'How are you, my darling?' he said.

'I'm off to Kashmir tomorrow,' I told him.

'Who's receiving you?' he asked.

'Uh, nobody. I thought I would go and work it out.'

I could see distress settle on his forehead. 'Beta, Kashmir is not that kind of place. Let me make a few phone calls.'

He did. A few key phone calls, it turned out, so that when I landed in Srinagar, an armed police escort materialized.

In the autumn of 2001, nobody was going to Kashmir, no podgy Punjabi families riding horses at a safe pace and eating Kwality ice creams, or honeymooning couples leaning towards the lake, awkward and anticipating, the women dressed in gold-bordered saris, coy but knowledgeable because they have been practising for this moment all their lives.

The Srinagar airfield was in the control of the Indian Air Force. There were camouflaged bunkers for fighter jets, barbed-wire fences on rollers that could be pulled across a runway. A mist slid across the mountains, a gloomy November blanket pulled over flanks. Raindrops smeared the plane windows.

'This is no longer paradise, it's hell on earth,' the Srinagar police officer said to me, matter of fact, as though this was something he might think every day.

He handed me over to my PSO (Personal Security Officer), my first acronym. He was a Kashmiri, with a sharp nose, a thin moustache and two deep lines etched on the sides of his mouth. He was dressed in a discreet jacket and trousers and had a black service revolver tucked into his belt. I smiled, nervous.

Driving into the city, filled with bunkers and armed men, I was gripped with unease. My uncle knew what he was talking about. Kashmir was not that kind of place. We bumped along in a white Ambassador through the jumble of Srinagar streets. The city was thick with knots of armymen with Kalashnikovs slung over their shoulders. The square of flak jackets pushed out the cloth of uniforms. Amongst the army, there were faces from all over the country. BSF, CRPF, SSB—more acronyms of acrimony in the happy valley.

There were the smooth solid trunks of Chinar trees, the trees planted by homesick Central Asians. Autumn had tinted the leaves a pale red, a hint of green still at the edges. Dried leaves piled up and a few scratched across the road in a breeze. The leaves of the walnut trees had already turned a bright yellow. In the wide sky above the river, eagles churned and circled. The Jhelum River sagged, it looked tired and sunken.

I lay awake in Kashmir's dense autumn night, when the dogs barked and a city under curfew bristled with guns in shadowed corners. But when morning came, fear evaporated with the dew. I blew on my hands and rubbed them together and waited among the damp roses in the front garden of the guest house for a contact at the Archaeological Survey of India (ASI) to fetch me.

This had taken some doing. The ASI's central office in Delhi had helpfully directed me to their Jammu office. From the Jammu office, on a long-distance line, government archaeologist B.R. Mani patiently explained the Buddhist locations that archaeologists had pinpointed as Xuanzang's stops in Kashmir. He had to spell them out, letter by letter, on a phone line that kept getting cut off so that I had to book a call again and again.

'When you get up here, somebody can show you the exact spot,' B.R. Mani said, before the line died out one last time. His colleagues in Srinagar were to take me to the remains of the monastery where Xuanzang spent his first night in the kingdom of Kashmir.

෪

The climate is cold and stern. There is much snow but little wind. The people wear leather doublets and clothes of white linen. They are

light and frivolous, and of a weak, pusillanimous disposition . . . the
people are handsome in appearance, but they are given to cunning.
They love learning and are well instructed.[1]

There were 100 religious centres, 5000 priests. There were four stupas,
built by King Ashoka, stupas of height and magnificence.

King Durlabhavardhana waited for the monk with his ministers
and the priests, with incense and parasols. They bowed and threw
flowers at his feet. They helped him onto an elephant and in this way
he approached the capital.[2]

Durlabhavardhana would remain the ruler until AD 663 and be
known as the king who organized the feast and threw the floor open
to a religious discussion for the monk. He fully sponsored the monk
from China during his two-year stay in Kashmir, offered him men to
help translate and transcribe the scriptures, and, most important,
introduced him to the sage Sanghayasas and an entourage of nine
monks. This new teacher of Xuanzang's was no Kuchean
Mokshagupta who stumbled and stuttered and forgot his texts. The
seventy-year-old scholar schooled his youthful disciple till the monk
felt full and fattened with knowledge. Before noon, the pair tackled
the *Abhidharmakosa*, a luminous work that delineates with merciful
clarity the different schools of thought of early Buddhism, a
compendium that is intended to explain the words of the Buddha and
help one understand the world according to the great Master. It is a
work preserved primarily in its Chinese and Tibetan translations.
Very little of it exists in Sanskrit. After noon, the Chinese monk studied
the *Nyaya-anusara Shastra*, a critique of the *Abhidharmakosa*. After
the first watch of the night, the scholars turned to the Sanskrit education
system. Xuanzang was introduced to grammar and Indian logic. He
learned the use of valid arguments. He perfected his elocution. He
learned the rules of debate, that he must speak pure Sanskrit, that he
must not show nervousness, that he must not speak out of turn.[3]

Xuanzang was naturally all praise for his guru. He told Hui Li:

He observed with the greatest strictness the religious rules and
ordinances. He was possessed of the highest intelligence, and acquainted
with all the points of a true disciple. His talents were eminent; his
spiritual powers exalted; and his disposition affectionate . . .[4]

And in return, the ageing man complimented the foreign monk.

> This priest of China possesses wonderful (vast and immeasurable)
> strength of wisdom. In all this congregation there is none to surpass
> him. By his wisdom and his virtue he is competent to join in succession
> to the fame of the brother of Vasubandhu.[5]

ॐ

The ruins of the monastery of Hushkara lay beyond the border town
of Baramula (from Varahamalas, the boar, Vishnu's incarnation).
The name Hushkara was twisted from Hushkapura, named after
Huvishka, the great Kushan king from the second century AD. The
city prospered in medieval times because it sat on the main trade
routes linking Kashmir and north-western India.[6]

Further down from Hushkara was an ancient watch station which
has been called Drang for centuries, and which, the Kashmir historian
Ram Chandra Kak wrote, 'served the double purpose of a customs
post and frontier outpost where traffic could be controlled and all
suspicious characters apprehended'.[7]

We gathered early that morning in Srinagar at the guest house to
catch the light and make it back to the city before curfew. My troops
rallied faithfully—the driver Ghulam Rasool, Faisal and Mohammad,
who knew the location of the ruins of Hushkara. We had an added
escort that morning—an open jeep with six armed security men, rifles
nestling on their laps. It followed us to the city limits. The jeep
following us gave an irked edge to the Kashmiri voices in the car,
resentful of the security because it threw a problem into high relief.
But on that gracious morning, the horse tongas clopped along the
roads and full buses zoomed and swerved and honked their horns.
We passed fields of mulberry trees, bare in the autumn.

'You should have come in spring, Kashmir is beautiful then.'

'You should have come one month earlier.'

'You should have come last week.'

But I had come in November, the cusp of seasons, when the army
stepped up security, when the militants watched for snowfall, deciding
if they would winter in Pakistan or Kashmir. We passed almond

orchards and bumped along a side road to Parihaspur surrounded by apple and cherry orchards, all bare; and on the remains of an eighth-century city, a snake had shed its skin and left a dried case, a shadow of a passing.

Militants in this region destroyed government property, they burned cars and blasted bridges. There are hundreds of groups, so if one slips from the grasp of Pakistanis, there is always another. Sometimes hard-core militants become MLAs and are treated as VIPs by the government.

Traffic jolted to a halt. Line after line of cars and trucks and buses pulled over to the side, passengers milled outside. There was firing going on up ahead, word passed through the crowd like a malignant breeze.

Shooting. An encounter with the army. I held my breath. I did not have the faintest clue what to do. Yet again, I felt responsible for putting other people in situations of such unpredictability.

Ghulam Rasool opened the car trunk and fished out a red light with a magnet bottom and clacked it to the roof. He flicked a switch to set it flashing. Then, he yanked the steering wheel to the right, leaned on the horn and pressed the accelerator. The crowds skittered out of our way. At the bridge, a policeman in khaki flagged us down, leaned into the window and barked, 'We've got orders, absolutely nobody can go through.'

Ghulam Rasool nodded, crossed the bridge and pulled over for exactly three minutes. He had recognized the car in front as carrying a local militant-turned-government official. He shook hands with the driver through the window, conversed, and we were moving again. The road was deserted, we were twenty-eight kilometres outside Baramula. Deep green bulletproof vans were parked on either side of the road and military forces dotted the fields. At Pattan, a South Indian guard held his gun pointed at us.

'Go no further, there's firing ten metres ahead.'

His skin was ebony but his face was pale and fearful. In the thin Kashmiri sun, the road through the village was clogged with military vans and dozens of men in fatigues on the right. My teeth were chattering with fear. I clenched them to try and make them stop, but they wouldn't.

On the left, the whole village had been evacuated. Men, women and children huddled silently under a shed. Somebody had rolled shut shop doors and a few men in phirans collected on the steps with a devastating fatalistic obedience, an inevitability, stamped on their faces. They squatted and waited in pale planks of sunlight while armed men acted out history.

There had been a tip-off—four militants were hiding in the village. The security forces had swarmed in to flush them out. A soldier glanced at the flashing red light on the roof of our car.

'It's a VIP,' Ghulam snapped, popping his head out of the window like a ferocious turtle with a password. The man hesitated, then waved the tip of his gun.

'Don't stop anywhere.'

Barely out of Pattan, Ghulam slowed down, swung open the door, raised his body off the seat. Keeping one arm on the wheel, he stretched the other hand to the roof and yanked off the flashing light in one lithe movement. The lights were to negotiate *army* checkpoints.

The next day's *Kashmir Monitor* reported that militants hiding in a house in Pattan had lobbed hand grenades on a search party of the Twenty-Ninth Rashtriya Rifles. Captain Atul Sharma and three men had died, houses were burned, the area was cordoned off. It was like Uzbekistan, only this time I was right in the middle of it and this time it was not an isolated incident.

It was just another morning as Kashmir prepared for winter. For the traveller, it was a baptism into life in the Valley. The men in the car with me had said little, but the brush pulled us closer. We were fish hauled into the same net. It made us comrades. Barriers softened and crumpled, they talked more freely, as though words that spilled from their lips could be arranged to ward off death.

'You see, madam,' Mohammad said. 'You see what we have to live with.' He begged me to 'talk to somebody' in Delhi so that he didn't get transferred.

'I have to be here to look after my family. How can I leave them in this? I have to be here in case something happens. There are hospitals, but doctors have left, migrated.'

His plea turned on a tap in the car; the habits of unhappiness dripped and stained the air. There would be other conversations as my days in Kashmir slipped by, snatched moments in other vehicles, a lunch here, a cup of tea there, moments in between my search for Xuanzang. Those were grey days, a gunmetal sky that hung low after a morning sun flashed and then hid.

'Please do not mention my name.'

I swept the piles of words into the centre of the page where they lay ragged and rent like pieces of a puzzle that wouldn't fit.

'We hate the security forces, the constant checks, the way they block traffic while they break for lunch.'

'The security forces line us up outside, our women are inside, there is no guarantee what happens.'

'*Hum aam log do bandook ke beech me phuss gaye.*' (We ordinary people are caught between two guns.)

'Who are these militants?' I asked again and again.

'The militants are Pakistanis, Afghanis, Kashmiris.'

'The militants could be our brothers and uncles, they could be our friends.'

'The militants have broken our backs. Whatever we have built they have destroyed.'

'Would you rather be a part of India or Pakistan?'

'India.'

'Pakistan.'

'It's not that simple. I'm from here, but most of my family lives across the border in Pakistan, we are brothers torn apart by boundaries.'

'Why does faithless India think that if there was a vote we would choose Pakistan?'

On that bright gun-filled morning, after Pattan, we stopped for tea to strengthen our nerves and then pulled up at the bottom of a village where stood the monastery of Ushkar, or what was left of it.

From the calm of Kainil Bagh, the hills spread to the north. The village was flanked to the east by hillsides that grew maize, whose western slopes cupped apple and walnut trees. In the valley, the Jhelum flowed towards Uri, the Pakistan border.

The village kids wore torn phirans, their hair was scruffy, they smelled of poverty. Poverty and old age have their own sour stink.

They wielded cricket bats and threw a green plastic ball. The wicket was a tower of three stones.

They dropped their game and clambered onto the rubble of the Buddhist stupa, lining up to watch the visitors. We walked around the remains of the stupa. It spilled from what may have been a proud height, the ruins of a monastic past, now just mud and scattered bricks, a broken curve for the children to play hide-and-seek around.

I had not imagined it would be quite like this, the journey to see the place where Xuanzang slept once in Kashmir. We edged up the village for a view, to the roofs covered with corrugated galvanized iron sheets. There was the sound of a cow mooing, and a few chicks. A couple of puppies tumbled and scratched in the dust.

The men wandered into a discussion of military strategy.

'If we cover the two main bridges on the Jhelum, we're okay.'

The children followed the strangers at a safe distance, not knowing that in their backyard fourteen centuries ago a monk from China had passed through, lain down for a night's rest to ease his aching muscles. The same monk who led me to this, as though he held me by the scruff of my neck to rub my nose in the shambles of my own history. Not for the first time, I felt daunted, utterly unequipped. I wanted to pass the baton to someone wiser, braver, stronger. I wanted to drop to my knees and say, 'Enough. I've had enough.' I hated the monk briefly, but I felt chained to him, shackled to this route.

'Okay,' I growled over my shoulder at him. 'What next?'

'Look around you,' he was saying. Layers of time deposited to change the landscape while players came and went. Buddhism had settled deep into the Valley, where Xuanzang found it, only to be rattled and replaced hundreds of years later by Hindu kings and then, still later, by Islam.

Unlike in Central Asia, Islam came to Kashmir peacefully. It was brought by fakirs or dervishes and the ulema or theologians, among whom were Ismailian preachers from the province of Dailam in Iran.[8]

But it was Sharaf-ud-Din Sayyid Abdur Rahman Turkistani (localized to Bulbul) who converted Rinchen, a Tibetan king of Kashmir, to Islam. The wandering pious man of Turkistan had stayed in Baghdad for years and died in 1327, after creating the first Muslim king in Kashmir. Tens of thousands in the Valley converted to Islam following Rinchen's example. Hearing of a waiting audience in a valley famed for its lakes and mountains, other Muslim sages journeyed to Kashmir from Bukhara, from Simnan in Iran. There was a Mir Sayyid Ali Hamadani from Hamadan, a province and a town in Iran just 400 kilometres north-west of Isfahan.

But it was a strange kind of Islam, blended perhaps with Buddhism and, here, interlaced too with Hinduism. The blend gave a texture to Kashmir's Islam which more orthodox Muslims saw as decidedly seditious.

According to a sixteenth-century observation on Kashmir, penned by one Mirza Muhammad Haidar Dughlat, so many heretical customs had been accepted that nobody knew any longer what was legitimate. The so-called pirs (spiritual guides) and sufis (mystics), he wrote, are

> forever interpreting dreams, displaying miracles and obtaining from the unseen, information regarding either the future or the past . . . Consider the Holy Law (Shari'at) second in importance to the True 'Way' (Tariqat) and that, in consequence, the people of the 'Way' have nothing to do with the Holy Law.[9]

There were echoes here for me of what had happened to Islam in Central Asia, and I felt intrigued by the idea of Islam colliding with a Buddhist past to give birth to Sufism.

Not far from the Buddhist stupa at Hushkara was a shrine of one Said Mohammad who, the imams said, had come from Iran some 700 years ago. In the quiet enclosure, two cooks stood by a *deg*. In a narrow copper vessel that came up to their shoulders, the duo in rhythm stirred an offering. Sometimes people spent as much as Rs 15,000 on a *deg*, they told us.

Two quintals of rice, thirty kilos of mutton, six kilos of ghee, ten kilos of dal, one kilo of ginger, three kilos of turmeric, six kilos of salt, fifteen kilos of onions. It was an anonymous thanks, a wish fulfilled, a job done. Sunlight filtered through smoke and steam, blurring the image, lending them an ethereal look. Had they vanished in the breeze, I would have shrugged and thought it natural.

The imams of the shrine welcomed us into the inner sanctum— green cloths, a Koran—and ushered me in too, to my surprise, unveiled as I was and obviously not a local. The old men were toothless and insistent on telling their tales. I tried to keep up with their Urdu, which flowed like an elegant waterfall.

'It was in the time of Badshah Zain-al-abedin, who came from Isfahan, preached and then when his time was up, ordered an arrow to be released from a bow and declared he would die where it landed. In the eleven years of trouble, nothing has happened here. All come and do *salaam* here. In 1947, during Pakistani raids, the central administration bombed this place with four planes. Nothing was hit. Later the pilots came and asked for pardon.'

'As for Pakistan,' they said, 'why not divide it up? Kashmir to Pakistan, Jammu to India, Ladakh to India.'

But then the sterner imam changed his mind about the discussion. 'This is a question for the Hurriyat. Here, in this *ziarat*, we sit, we welcome visitors, we give them honour, we do not talk *siyasat*—politics.'

I bowed in silent apology. My curiosity about the inside of other people's minds sometimes made me clumsy. I had not appreciated the moment and the imams had rightly, lightly, rapped me on the knuckles.

I relearned Kashmir. To the memories of my childhood were added these new images.

Back in Srinagar, one evening, followed by the PSO, I panted up the steep stairs to the top of the hill nearby. Smoke from burning chinar leaves drifted over the city and two women in black burkhas walked by a wall, rustling leaves underfoot. Eagles still wheeled through the dusk sky—something had died.

Perhaps it was the city.

As was inevitable, I chatted with the PSO. He took his work seriously and never, ever left my side. He had a wry take on events, which I appreciated.

He became my window into Kashmir's idiosyncrasies, like its fondness for the crunchy, wispy lotus root cut from the Dal Lake, sliced and fried in a chickpea batter. It was Lalla, he said—the poetess combed her hair and what fell into the lake became *nadroo*.

In the old town, to the south-east of the city, we clambered onto the old wall built by Akbar in 1526. In green paint on the outside somebody had scrawled: INDIAN FORCES GO BACK.

ॐ

How different it must have been when Xuanzang came through here, when he wrote these words:

> The soil is fit for producing cereals, and abounds with fruits and flowers. Here also are dragon-horses and the fragrant turmeric, the *fo-chüu*, and medicinal plants . . . There are about 100 sangharamas and 5000 priests. There are four stupas built by Ashoka Raja.[10]

Kushan history permeated the Valley. Xuanzang wrote in great detail of how Kanishka the Scythian king himself studied Buddhism in between royal duties and, finding the schools split and contradictory, issued a call for Buddhist monks to gather. Xuanzang said Kanishka culled 500 of the wisest sages from the multitudes that swarmed like bees and they put their heads together and came up with a Buddhist canon.

Was Kanishka really a pious king, or a clever ruler from distant parts who saw that he could cement his Central Asian Scythian–Saka connection with this land he ruled over, and gain legitimacy with his Buddhist subjects? 'Think about it,' Leonid had said. 'Sakya.' Kanishka wanted to emphasize that he belonged to the same tribe as Sakyamuni.

Xuanzang wrote of a great mountain with a ruined monastery left with only a small double tower and relic stupas of Arhats where strange miraculous things happen, where

> wild beasts and mountain apes gather flowers to offer as religious oblations . . . Sometimes a stone barrier is split across; sometimes on the mountaintop there remain traces of a horse . . .[11]

All around him were monasteries where learned Buddhist monks had composed this sutra or that one. There was such subcutaneous glee in his words that his delight at his discoveries hovered across the centuries, through the classical Chinese translation.

൬

All around the Kashmir Valley, the Kral Sangar hills (*kral* is pottery) spread. There were rice paddies, terraced fields, now dried up and fallow in autumn. There were hills to the south; to the north the valley unfolded rich with poplar trees like strokes of paint. There was somewhere the sigh of water from a spring. The sun heated up quickly, burning off the morning mists.

Not far from Srinagar, we stopped by the road and climbed up to Harwan, the Buddhist site where perhaps Xuanzang spent his two years living and studying. It was backed by hills filled with deodar, the Himalayan cedar. A shred of mist still crouched around one rocky peak. Walnut trees at the lower terrace had turned yellow-gold and the stump of an almond tree had blackened with rot. There was mulberry too. Each step up to the stupa had a retaining wall built behind it, to prevent erosion.

There was a Buddhist prayer hall at the base of the hill. A bulbul fluttered and called in a bush.

'If the bulbul calls on your window sill, expect a guest,' my PSO said. 'It's true, it's happened many times.'

They found no relics of the Buddha here; instead history left broken fingers and toes and terracotta curls that came from Buddha images. Most amazingly, it left a courtyard lined with large brick tiles intricately illustrated. There were, says Ram Chandra Kak, water plants from the Dal Lake, geese flying in rows, deer looking back at the moon. They had been left undisturbed because, when found, each tile was stamped with a number in Kharoshti and the tiles lay in consecutive order.

'The potter,' wrote Kak, 'who made the tiles and stamped them with decorative figures numbered them before baking, to prevent the comparatively unskilled layer from making mistakes and thereby spoiling the design. Incidentally it shows that in ancient India, over fifteen centuries ago, labourers were expected to know at least the rudiments of writing and reading.'

The Kharoshti script also dated the tiles, wrote Kak. If labourers were expected to know Kharoshti, it must have been a commonly used script. Since Kharoshti died out around the fifth century AD, Kak placed the monument's creation at AD 300 or so. So it was entirely possible the monument existed when Xuanzang came through Kashmir. Kak's enthusiasm was infectious:

> Their facial characteristics bear close resemblance to those of the inhabitants of the regions round about Yarkand and Kashgar, whose heavy features, prominent cheekbones, narrow sunk and slanting eyes, and receding foreheads, are faithfully represented on the tiles. Some of the figures are dressed in trousers and Turkoman caps. The only period when Kashmir had any intimate connection with Central Asia was during the supremacy of the Kushans in the early centuries of the Christian era, when Kashmir formed part of the Kushan empire, which extended from Mathura in India to Yarkand in Central Asia. Indeed, then, as now, it appears to have occupied a pre-eminent position; inasmuch as Kanishka (circa AD 125) the greatest of Kushan emperors, is said to have convened here his great council of Buddhist divines. It may be that some pious and prosperous Kushan built this shrine at Harwan, where, according to the ancient history of Kashmir, resided the great Buddhist patriarch Nagarjuna. Further perhaps to increase his religious merit, and to show his humility, the builder had the image of his own face and that of his wife stamped on the tiles so that the commonest people might tread on them. Among the other decorative motifs which reveal foreign influence are the figures of mailed horsemen with flying scarves tied to their heads, which are strongly reminiscent of the contemporary Sassanian art of Persia.[12]

At the top of the hill, the remains of a grand stupa were surrounded by barbed wire to prevent theft. On the lower terrace were the thigh-high walls of four residential rooms.

On a small wooden table at the bottom of the hill, the Kashmiri caretakers laid out biscuits and cake and served tea from plastic jugs. We drank it hot and sweet, at the foot of the ruins of a Kushan Buddhist monument on a crisp autumn morning. Behind us, a wild black crow hopped on the wall of the residential rooms. The hill crows were larger, louder, blacker. Following my gaze, the irrepressible PSO piped up, pointing to his throat, 'You see, their speakers are bigger.'

A levity had settled on our group. We were, despite the city's sombre mood, enjoying the outings. My companions wanted to show off their land, the bits not buried under dust and gunfire. And so, driving through deserted Srinagar, our small band dismounted at Nishat Bagh, the old Mughal garden which lay empty, carpeted with autumn leaves, the fountains silent, with pools of old water that carried a dull sky and mirrored us leaning over.

Guards patrolled the gardens, carrying Lee–Enfield bolt-action rifles, leftovers from the British Raj. What a city of guns this was. Self-Loading Rifles (SLRs), carbines, light machine guns, Kalashnikovs. My PSO was dreamy for a more innocent time. 'Our biggest weapon used to be the *kangri* in winter or stones in summer.'

An old Kashmiri at the gardens came up and presented me with a rose. I thought he was trying to sell it, but he pushed it gently into my hand.

'*Mehman*,' he said. We have a guest.

I would have to leave Srinagar soon, but it was as though the city had infected my dreams. It mesmerized and repelled me. I had no answers. I was confused. Something had gone terribly wrong in these mountains in my country. How far things had floated from the peaceful scenes of Xuanzang poring over Buddhist texts under the guidance of a septuagenarian monk.

I dropped in to see Ahmed, a passionate, eloquent Kashmiri. Over cups of tea, he became gradually more and more excitable. His tone rose and fell with each betrayal and accusation.

'You,' he said, meaning India, meaning the government, but that small word was the shadow of a vast divide. 'You Indians. Us Kashmiris.'

I had come to Kashmir to see an old monastery or two and perhaps, in the light of a sunset amidst the mountains, catch the whisper of a childhood memory. I wanted to untangle myself from this army, this government, these killings. Indeed, Kashmir was another story in the newspaper that I skimmed over in a vaguely regretful way. I had bumbled into the Valley a simpleton.

At Ahmed's urging, I found myself in a Srinagar alley one morning, outside the green metal gates of the All Parties Hurriyat Conference, knocking on a screen door. A group of elderly men with beards sat on the floor sipping *kahwa* and one showed me upstairs to a meeting room.

The Hurriyat's secretary politely sat me down. He steepled his fingers, indexes, on his chin. I learned yet again that morning that the colour of light depends on how you turn the prism. What happened, what really happened, depends on who tells it.

Professor Abdul Ghani Bhatt came in, wrapped from head to toe. He was a man with a dignified profile, an extraordinary Persian nose that hooked and drooped. He was not feeling well.

'Excuse me,' he said, 'I have a slight fever.' I expressed my sympathy for the ailing old man, offered to come back another time. But he waved it away and coughed. He too was determined to say his piece.

'Kashmir is a broken family. Broken hearts, broken relationships, we are literally a broken people and we want to put the pieces back together. We have an agenda, but at the negotiating table we are ready for concessions.'

I saw something calculating flash in the old eyes, akin to a politician judging his pitch. But he did not know that I was no match for him, caught like a creature in night lights, unarmed. Bhatt hugged a hot-water bottle to himself under his wraps. He wore a white cap, and his nose, powerful, curved, overhanging, dominated his face. The bristle on his chin was white. His eyes had reddened with the fever or the cold, and he held his chin in his fingers. Under the blanket, on the floor, I could see the tip of his slipper tapping. I searched for the sensitive professor of Persian language and literature, but that man now served a political purpose.

'We (the Hurriyat) represent the sentiment of the people,' he said. 'Like Mandela in South Africa and Yasser Arafat in Palestine. We never contested elections, but you can never say the Mahatma did not represent the sentiments of the people. We feel the pulse of the people. When you still say Kashmir is not a dispute, I can only say "God help you".'

Before we left Srinagar, there was an incident that could have imploded. It reminded me what a powder keg the city was. A Nepali guard stopped the driver as we walked to the car.

'Hey you.'

It was an unpleasant tone. The guard was wearing yellow plastic slippers.

'Hey you. Why are you parked here? I'll kill you. Talk properly. Why do you tell lies?'

He was slightly incoherent. Voices rose, people jostled, a small crowd gathered, the guard grabbed a handful of Ghulam's shirt. The small Nepali in fatigues and the tall Kashmiri eyed each other.

'Get inside the car, madam,' Ghulam said quietly. He turned to the guard. 'Who is your superior? I will talk to him.'

The Nepali let loose a verbal machine gun. Ghulam's silence was flinty.

Another guard walked up and separated the two. The tension ebbed. It had been unprovoked. Pressing my nose against the window, I felt angry on Ghulam's behalf. These sandbags, these bunkers, these fortifications and hostile words. I was in a war zone.

೫

When Xuanzang's two years were up, he bade a reluctant farewell to his teacher and packed his bags. He was now well-versed in the niceties of contradictory Buddhist doctrines. He looked over his shoulder as he set off from the valley, towards the giant Pir Panjal range he would have to cross to reach the kingdom of Punach, now Poonch.

೫

The papers were grimmer each day. The *Kashmir Monitor* of 15 November reported that intelligence picked up from wireless intercepts suggested that Pakistan-aided suicide squads had been assigned the task of targeting the Indian Army's unit headquarters in Jammu and Kashmir in the coming days and weeks. Especially, the reports said, the districts of Srinagar, Baramula and Kupwara in the Kashmir Valley and the districts of Poonch and Rajouri in the Jammu region.

The monk had criss-crossed footpaths that cut westwards across the sweep of the Pir Panjal range, down into the kingdom of Poonch, and then south into the kingdom of Rajouri. Those were the trade routes the Mughals later used and that was the name that stuck, the 'Mughal Road'. That route across the mountains was not motorable. To get to Poonch, I had to head all the way south to Jammu, skirt the Pir Panjals and then drive north again on the single winding road that linked Jammu to Rajouri and Poonch.

Outside Srinagar, there were fields of saffron crocuses close to the ground, the flower a pale-eggplant colour with a bright orange stigma. These would be harvested and dried and added to rice dishes for that heavenly flavour. We stopped the car and, by the road, I plucked a couple. I pressed them carefully into a book. Six petals of a purple flower. I was haunted by a sense that I might never come back, that this might be my last glimpse of these mountains, this lake. The Valley had pulled me underwater into its muddy depths and asked me to look below. This is what happened here, this is what this means, this is your history and therefore this is you.

It was, my PSO said, too much to handle. *Samunder ko kuzeh meh bandh karna.* It was like locking the sea in a box, but I was distracted and relished only how the word *samunder* carried waves within it. I would miss the PSO and his running commentary.

It was mid-morning and already the climate softened as we descended from Kashmir's heights. No wonder the *darbar*—a word for government, but grander, with an imperial dash—the whole administration, moved down from the heights in winter, as it did during the British Raj.

But if I were an ordinary Kashmiri, that fact would burn at the back of my mind. A government truly of the people would stay in Srinagar and bear the winter with its citizens. It was the beginning of the question that would not end for me: How did this country hold together? If fear was contagious and congealing, then I had felt it up in the Valley.

We arrived in Jammu, a city the Kashmiris scornfully referred to as 'the city of monkeys', only to switch driver and security officer before setting off north to Rajouri the next day.

chapter sixteen

Unhappy Valleys

The kingdom (of Rajapuri) is about 4000 *li* in circuit; the capital
town is about 10 *li* round. It is naturally very strong, with many
mountains, hills, and river-courses, which cause the arable land to be
contracted. The produce therefore is small . . . The people are quick
and hasty; the country has no independent ruler, but is subject to
Kasmir. There are ten sangharamas, with a very small number of
priests. There is one temple of Devas, with an enormous number of
unbelievers.[1]

&

The government car had switched its plates to a Delhi number,
labelling me an outsider and therefore not a militant target.
Outside the city, we stopped to take off the flashing red lights.
Now it was a totally private vehicle. My new companions were
Hindu, uncomfortable with the idea of the drive, increasingly fearful
as night fell. Lal Singh touched his hands to his ears each time we
passed a temple, an almost self-conscious gesture. Poplar, sareen and
eucalyptus trees lined the roads, which were noisy with cars and
buses. Army convoys too stopped by the roadside, for it was lunchtime.
And here, in the outskirts of Jammu, the atmosphere was warmer
with the soft tones of the Dogri tongue.

We climbed up through soft chir pine forests, thick jungle. The
terrain was hilly with ravines and nullahs everywhere, bushes,
undergrowth. It was ideal territory for infiltration.

'Who knows where they will jump from and where they are hiding,'

Lal Singh said fearfully. I loved my drives through these back roads, no matter how nerve-racking, no matter how my eyes scanned the dusk expecting to see a hunched group of men spring onto the road, arms at the ready, the flash of a gun-barrel in the last light of the day.

My mind folded the possibility of danger, of death, into a wad, stuffed it into a bin and slammed the lid on it. Besides, the monk was hissing in my ear.

'Look around you, open your eyes and look.'

There was heightened pressure in this region. Militants descended further south to this area, for in winter the passes in Kashmir became snowbound, making this the area of choice for infiltrators.

'If a state does not want to be with us, then we could let it go. Is it for the land or the people that we want to hang on to a place? If it's for the land, let's shoot everybody and grab the land. If it's for the people, their hearts are not with us anyway and we should let them go. All this death. For what?'

The sun was setting on the 'Mughal Road', the roads were being widened and dust clouds swelled under tyres so we rolled up the windows. The soft late-dusk sun cast a golden light on the old road and I could smell the wood fires for the evening meal, the sign of night in India.

The light watered down the chir pines to a liquid green and the leaves of the poplars had turned a bright yellow. The Tawi flowed flat on its lonely stone bed. We crossed the bridge over it and entered Rajouri. It was a small hilly place overrun with army-types. The stars were out, the temperature had dropped. Snug amongst the ravines, this was prime militant territory. I learned from my companions that these were old Buddhist areas, that the villages dotting the hills were still known as Buddhal or Buddhkharia, that this was a very porous border because of the terrain. That, in fact, it was an imaginary border.

At a small Rajouri guest house, three women constables waited on me. Each had had one year's training in weaponry. They were terribly young. One was twenty years old and from a neighbouring village; she supported her entire family: two parents, four little sisters and one brother. With the number of men and boys shot and killed, women were being driven into the workforce and large numbers of them joined the police.

One of the police guards had sad eyes that bespoke an education, a depth that surprised me.

'It's inhuman, a man killing a man. Whatever he is, he is human, with a family, with hopes. There is no joy, standing over a man's dead body, a man you have killed. To think that I have dragged a dead man by his feet after shooting him, because there was no other way to get his body out of the jungles . . . Charles de Gaulle said, when a colony becomes more of a burden than a benefit, let it go.'

Was this sub-inspector of police in the middle of absolutely nowhere really quoting Charles de Gaulle?

The night was cold with the distant breath of the Himalaya and the stars clear as they can only be in the hills and in a border town. Outside, armed guards stood their watch in turns, SLRs slung over their shoulders. At the guest house there was a quilt of dubious odour, but I held my nose and pulled it over me. I fell asleep with the light on and a book open on my lap, a book on Kashmiri history apparently banned in India.

There, I'd done it again. Referred to India as another country, as I had China when I was in Kucha. This was what happened when you strayed into a country's periphery.

As the sun rose in the valley, the Ambassador groaned up the hill and from high up in the fort, which had been taken over by the army, there was a view of the valley. Somebody had painted 'Ram Ram Ram' in Hindi all over the fort walls, as though this Hindu invocation alone could scare off the infiltrators. A jawan shouted out at me, 'No pictures allowed here.' Within the fort there was the crackle of radio equipment and turning transmitters.

I had a clear view of Rajouri and, to the north-east, the faraway hint of the Pir Panjals, a white smear of snow dragged against a hazy blue sky and the valley, its ribbon of a river, and the airfield protected by gunmen in trenches. The terraced hills dripped into the valley.

Xuanzang had walked across these mountains from the other side and headed to Poonch. The track is still used by goatherds taking their flocks back and forth to markets for sale and to pasture. 'As a boy I used to walk across in a day,' a local police officer said.

෨

The monk wrote of Poonch:

> This kingdom is about 2000 *li* in circuit, with many mountains and river-courses, so that the arable land is very contracted. There are many sugar-canes but no grapes . . . The climate is warm and damp. The people are brave. They wear ordinary cotton clothing. The disposition of the people is true and upright; they are Buddhists. There are five sangharamas, mostly deserted.[2]

෨

In Poonch, I huddled in a guest house at night, listening to the whine and whump of shells that Pakistan lobbed across the border. The ground shook each time. When evening fell, it was as though the darkness penetrated my pupils and settled on my brain, blanketing everything. It was out of the question to go hunting for Buddhist remains.

At dinner with the local head of police, there were more stories of *fidayeen* attacks. Nobody moved in Poonch after 6 p.m. for fear of shells and bullets. Occasionally, the police chief's radio crackled and he barked into it. 'Okay, go for it. I'll be there.'

He was out for entire nights on end, on patrol, trawling the jungles, as his pretty young wife from Lucknow with creamy skin bit her nails. Once, when a band of eight militants surrendered after an encounter, he accepted their surrender and let them go free. The normal practice was to take no prisoners.

'If the Almighty has seen it fit to let them survive, then who am I to kill them?' he said. His words were whispered in gatherings, amongst locals, in the Kashmiri language.

He got up from dinner to call a friend. 'I'm checking that you got home okay.'

'I've only seen dead militants. There are those militants who *cut* people, chop off bits of them. I have seen things you cannot imagine', he told me.

Villages were divided in half by the Line of Control, houses even, so that the kitchen was in Pakistan and the outhouse in India. Some children needed visas and permits to attend school because it was on the Indian side. Wedding parties needed permissions because the groom's baraat had to go to Pakistan to meet the bride, dodging shells.

Kashmir had been hard on me. I kept having bad dreams, unused to the police escorts, the feeling of being imprisoned by my own guards. The days in the Valley were misty grey deals, thick with cold. But already the bunkers shocked me less. And, always present, the beauty of the Urdu language seduced me. *Yeh bheegi bheegi raat.* This soaking night. Can one live elsewhere? Can one live in Urdu? It was a whole different world, fastidious in its search for exactitude. It was a soaking night, not a wet one.

The cloak of the subcontinent flared on either side of this knot of Kashmir. Pakistan and India. I was tired of Kashmir, tired of war and of guns. The time had come to move into the plains of India, follow the monk's trail into the flatlands, and head to Mathura.

chapter seventeen

Sikander and Porus

Xuanzang came from the mountains into the rich plains of the Punjab, a land watered by five rivers.

Two days out of Rajouri, he crossed the river Chenab. This section of his journey closely followed India's present-day border with Pakistan. In fact, a number of his stops after Rajouri were thought to be in Pakistan, before he veered east, putting the rest of his route well within the Indian border, where I could follow him.

India and its history were wrapping their tentacles around the Chinese monk. He peeled off a layer, only to find another, fact as strange as fairy tale. He tore off a veil and found others that pulled him in deeper and deeper and demanded more investigation. It was like Draupadi's unending sari.

It was from Sakala, possibly in today's Lahore, that Mihirakula, the fifth-century Ephthalite Hun, ruled India. The story interested Xuanzang. He spent some time relating it. The Hun was responsible for a slash-and-burn policy that had resulted in the destruction of much that was Buddhist in India. The Hun had rampaged through Gandhara, or northern Pakistan, and down into Punjab, vanquishing kingdom after kingdom. The trouble was, Xuanzang wrote, Mihirakula had been snubbed when not one single priest came forward to discuss texts on his royal demand, and only an old servant in simple robes responded. The furious Hun, or Huna, as they were called in India, issued a flat, take-no-prisoners order to crush Buddhist priests and monastic establishments across the land.

Shortly after the monk's stop in Sakala, he and his travelling companions entered a great forest of trees east of Narasimha and, to their dismay, walked straight into a band of fifty robbers. It all happened very quickly. The men worked like professionals. Half-wild creatures, they had slipped through the forest in utter silence so that the monks barely heard them. It was as though the trees themselves suddenly took human form and stretched out treacherous branches. The men demanded that the monks hand over their clothes and goods, and then gave chase through the marsh with its thick mass of creepers, tangled and filled with prickles.

The monks ran. The years of travel had made Xuanzang lithe. The outdoors had sharpened his senses. He and his companions spotted a ditch to the south of the marsh and ran towards it, stumbling, listening for their pursuers. Thorns dug into their shins. They stumbled across the ditch and emerged on the south-east, where they found themselves on the outskirts of a village. A Brahmin ploughed his field, following his oxen. Patches of water mirrored the sky.

'Help!' The monks cried. They were dishevelled, out of breath, practically naked. The man straightened, held his hand up to shield his eyes from the sun and peer at this odd apparition.

'Robbers!' The monks panted. It was not the first time. The farmer was frightened, but he knew what to do. The group hurried together to the village. He blew on a conch and beat drums to assemble a group of eighty men. Each picked up a stick, a spear, whatever lay at hand, and marched in the direction of the robbers. At the sight of this determined resistance, the thugs dissolved into the shadows of the forest. The travellers, robbed of their clothes and goods, set up a general wailing. Off to one side, the Chinese monk began to laugh. He held his sides and let out whoops of delight. He leaned against a tree, wiped his eyes. Until, gradually, the others fell silent and turned to their foreign friend in amazement.

The learned priest of China, breathless, his words askew, said, 'It's good to be alive. Who cares about a few clothes and some books?' Then he doubled over in mirth. Perhaps it was the forlorn looks of his naked companions, or perhaps the relief of surviving death.

In the forests in the town of Takka, a day's journey away, Xuanzang met an aged Brahmin who learned the story of his tribulations. In an overwhelming gesture of warmth, the Brahmin sent word to the largely Hindu citizens of Takka, who put aside their religious differences to pool together food and drink and lengths of cotton cloth to replace what the robbers had stolen.

The Chinese monk stayed a month, studying the masters of the Madhyamika school of thought, which had laid the foundations of the Yogacara school of idealism, which Xuanzang hungered to study in its original Sanskrit.

Xuanzang spent fourteen months travelling south of this region. Somewhere in the Punjab was the city known as Chinapati at the time. Scholars still debate its exact location. There, Xuanzang met a priest called Vinitaprabha and studied the *Abhidharma* further with him.

He then ventured east to the kingdom of Jalandhar, its capital still known as such, and settled for four months at the Nagaradhana Monastery where he learned at the feet of Chandravarma, another eminent priest who knew the *Tripitaka* very well indeed. The local king was good to Xuanzang.

ॐ

While Xuanzang studied to his heart's content, I had to turn to Alexander Cunningham for guidance around India. Cunningham was my most concrete bridge to Xuanzang in the subcontinent. To the monk's shadow-outline that I followed here, others were adding themselves, like ghost guests on this peculiar train, a groove of history I'd fallen into.

There was the Buddha himself who started it all. There was the great Indian king, Ashoka, who embraced Buddhism and built stupas all over India—stupas that Xuanzang referred to whenever he saw one. In North India there was Kanishka, the Kushan king who adopted the faith.

And there was Cunningham, who came much later with the British Raj and, reading Xuanzang's words, tramped all over the subcontinent, identifying, logging and checking with military precision the actual sites that Xuanzang mentioned.

The British stumbled on much of India's archaeology because the subcontinent, I learned, didn't much bother with facts and figures of the past. It was a land wedded to myths and sutras. What were mere bricks! And if time yawned and stretched in the vast way it did, why should anybody bother with dates if the stories were so well known?

Britain thought it a duty, as a ruling power, to catalogue its colony's past. There was a certain responsibility to being a colonial master. I found Cunningham when I first arrived in India, in an institution first set up by the British. Almost 150 years ago, he had been appointed archaeological surveyor to the Governor General of India.

The Archaeological Library of the Indian government had shifted to the grounds of the archives buildings, surrounded by green lawns planted with neem trees. In the gentle sun of an autumn afternoon, small groups of men took their shoes off and sat in a circle in the shade and shared lunch from steel tiffin boxes, sloshing with dal and stuffed with chapattis.

Anyone who had ever studied even a shred of Indian history had come across Alexander Cunningham, I imagined. But I was innocent of any such knowledge and made greedier for it by the lack.

From an entrance behind the building, dusty stairs wound up. I stepped over a sleeping pie-dog on the second floor and found the door.

The vast volumes sat in a dusty cupboard: *Archaeological Survey of India: Four reports, made during the years 1862–63–64–65. By Alexander Cunningham. CSI. Major General Royal Engineers (Bengal Retired).*

An 1862 memo said:

It will not be to our credit, as an enlightened ruling power, if we continue to allow such fields of investigation as the remains of the old Buddhist capital in Behar, the vast ruins of Kanouj, the plains around Delhi, studded with ruins more thickly than even the Campagna of Rome, and many others, to remain without more examination than they have hitherto revealed . . . It is impossible not to feel that there are European governments which, if they had held our rule in India, would not have allowed this to be said.

And so it was decided that Colonel Cunningham should receive Rs 450 a month, with Rs 250 extra when in the field, to defray the cost of making surveys and measurements. I came to understand

Cunningham's obsession with crumbling buildings in remote places, with undergrowth and the imprint of rivers that had moved away; a sudden late-blooming passion to find Xuanzang's worlds and see if archaeology might pinpoint them.

Cunningham, at twenty-three, was a confidant of British mint master-turned-historian, James Prinsep. Prinsep died on 22 April 1840, at thirty-nine, in the middle of extraordinary historical discoveries. Perhaps over some *chhota* peg served by a *khansamah* and shared on a veranda, a small flame began to burn in Cunningham.

On the train to Jalandhar from Delhi, I read Cunningham:

> Since the occupation of the plains by the Muhammadans, the ancient kingdom of Jalandhara has been confined almost entirely to its hill territories, which were generally known by the name of Kangra, after its most celebrated fortress . . .
>
> At the time of Hwen Thsang's visit, Jalandhara itself was the capital, which he describes as from 12 to 13 *li*, or upwards of two miles in circuit. Its antiquity is undoubted, as it is mentioned by Ptolemy as Kulindrine or Ktulindrine, which should probably be corrected to Sulundrine as the K and S are frequently interchanged in Greek manuscripts.[1]

Xuanzang was impressed with Jalandhar. There was a sizeable Buddhist community, fifty monasteries, with 2000 priests. Even then, the Punjab's fertile land was, the monk wrote,

> favourable for the cultivation of cereals and it produces much rice . . . The climate is warm and moist, the people brave and impetuous, but their appearance is common and rustic.[2]

I could have sworn he was describing the Punjabis. The train arrived late at night and I checked in at a modest guest house by the station and fell asleep, acutely aware of the surprised question mark in the receptionist's eyes. Nice Indian girls do not check into modest guest houses by railway stations in small Punjabi towns. That too, alone. Still, I smiled, and entered my Delhi address in the register at the counter, asked if there was hot water, pretending that it was the most natural thing for me to be doing. But it *was* so out of the norm that months later two gentlemen in civilian clothing with greasy notepads paid a polite visit to our flat in Delhi.

'Can I see your ID?' I asked sweetly.

To my surprise, they held out wrinkled laminated cards and said they wanted to verify my particulars. Who was I, where did I live, what did I do? Was I married? Did I have children? Had I, in fact, been to Jalandhar? They were checking.

'Yes,' I said. 'It used to be the capital of an old kingdom. Some Buddhist monks used to live there.'

They asked more bemused questions until my father thundered to the door.

'What do you want with my daughter?' he boomed.

'Papa, it's okay,' I muttered, trying to position myself between his bulk and the hapless spooks. The men shut their notebooks and slunk off, leaving small black clouds puffing from my father's ears.

Jalandhar itself was spread out and scattered in the light of the winter morning. I ate a hot paratha for breakfast, a salute to the paratha-mad Punjabis. It was made fresh on the roadside, stuffed with potatoes mashed and sprinkled with chillies. Amazing, that smell of heated wheat eaten with a hunk of mango pickle.

I got directions from a tall Sikh gentleman in an inky turban whose Punjabi language fell like a landslide with rocks clashing. I had no idea what he was saying. He, in turn, simply could not handle Hindi, but he was courteous and the exchange pleased us both.

'So nice, so nice,' he said in English.

'So nice,' I agreed.

The ASI had confirmed there was not much to see by way of Buddhist ruins, no chance of locating the place where Xuanzang spent four months with Chandravarma, studying the *Prakarana-pada-vibasha Shastra*, important commentaries of the same *Abhidharmakosa* that Xuanzang had assimilated in Kashmir. But I was curious. I had never been to Jalandhar before and it was a convenient stop before heading into the hills to Kangra.

Jalandhar also sits on the banks of the Beas, which flows east from the mountains down to Punjab, where it widens and flattens, and it was here, roughly a thousand years before Xuanzang passed through, that the Macedonians under Alexander the Great met their Waterloo. It was the worst kind of defeat, the self-inflicted kind.

Alexander's armies had pushed all the way into Afghanistan, and crossed the Indus River in February 326 BC. He defeated the Indian king Porus by the Jhelum River, further west, though Porus met him with 2000 elephants and a thunderous army. Alexander crossed the flooded river in a surprise night attack and massacred the Indians.

I half-remembered a childhood sing-song rhyme: *Sikandar ne Porus se ki thi larai, se ki thi larai, tho main kya karoon.* Sikander and Porus fought, they fought, so what am *I* supposed to do? In which fold of soft grey brain had that lain in hiding for so long?

I'm supposed to know this.

The victors crossed the strip of land east of the Beas, not far from where I was, and it was on this piece of Indian soil that the Macedonian army revolted against their chief. Alexander begged his men to carry on, invoking his Persian victories. But his general, Coenus, replied equally eloquently on behalf of the soldiers. India, it seemed, had filled their souls with webs and stuffed their heads with sand.

They turned back, and a few years later Alexander died in Babylon.[3]

For me, Jalandhar held the ghosts of fifty monasteries, the shadows of 2000 monks and peaceful sugar cane the height of a man; of wheat planted in neat rows, the Sikhs, turbaned, their tongues thickened with Punjabi so I could hardly understand.

I left for Kangra, the eastern edge of the kingdom of Jalandhar. From Pathankot, I switched to a bus that wound and strained as the sun set over the Kangra hills and their river. In the oblique late light the water flashed coppery, a shiny strip torn and dropped in the valley by some careless minor god.

The hillsides rose dark and steep, the sky yielded the day with regret, and last week's slim moon had fattened by the time I reached Himachal and the foothills of the Himalayas. The bus stopped to let on and off an endless stream of villagers, their hill complexions tinged with fresh air. Each one smiled as they stepped on, such pleasure, such triumph to get on the bus.

There was a sense of familiarity in the way the mountains rose—

to the north-east were the serrated peaks and clefts powdered with snow. I brushed away a thought of Kashmir and the Pir Panjal. Kashmir was still painful, a piece of glass stuck in my heart.

This was the Dhauladhar range. My breath misted up here, where the later kings of the Punjab retreated from their enemies and held fast at Kangra fort. It was late at night when I arrived in Kangra but for some reason, up in the small Himalayan hill towns, I felt safe. The bus stationmaster directed me to a small guest house on the main road which lived at the edge of cleanliness.

chapter eighteen

Kingdom Enclosed by Peaks

From Jalandhar, Xuanzang threaded his way through these hills to Kuluta, or Kullu. He went north-east. He crossed mountains and ravines to arrive at the kingdom enclosed by peaks. Hui Li, the biographer, does not say much about the journey. I had to assume that little of note happened, although Hui's silence irked me.

Before I followed Hui Li's silent trail to Kullu, I thought I would stop at India's densest, most ardent Buddhist community which was not far from Kangra. Perhaps there, among the Tibetan Buddhists in Dharamsala, I might harvest some clues to the monk.

As luck would have it, there was a local bus from Kangra to Dharamsala, a packed affair which wound through stunning mountain vistas and Himalayan villages. For the journey's final leg, in the taxi-bus up to McLeod Ganj, I squashed in beside a Tibetan monk, a big, dirty man in filthy robes. He closed his eyes and as the Gypsy climbed up the slopes, he started chanting 'Om Mani Padme Hum' faster and faster till it became a long drone that rose and fell. Maybe it was the vibrations, but I began to feel immediately and intensely sleepy. An odd warmth flooded through me, a sense of safety and well-being.

The Tibetan Library of Works and Archives would be an ideal place—indeed, one of the few places in India—to try and bone up on my non-existent Buddhist philosophy. At least, that's what my brother suggested by e-mail. Kranti had worked with the Tibetan government-in-exile during his student days. He was a student of philosophy, far better suited to Buddhist musings than I was. I signed up for Geshe

Sonam Rinchen's class on the Seven Points for Mind Training. I had only missed a few sessions.

Cushions were spread on the floor, there was a framed picture of the Dalai Lama on the wall, a tanka and an electric candle. The Geshe sat on a chair, more a throne, with a peaked back and the ubiquitous white silk strip draped over it.

The class consisted almost entirely of foreigners, but this was a relative term. Who was foreign in Dharamsala? The sole Indian in a Tibetan community? The Tibetan community in India? And if all these visitors from the West had gathered to study Buddhism, then isn't the foreigner the one who isn't actually studying Buddhism?

The class rose to its feet and bowed, hands joined, and as I scrambled to keep pace, the assembly dropped to its knees and touched its forehead to the ground, up and down, up and down, three times.

My own family was not religious, barely Hindu. Our home never had a puja room, my parents never went to temples. Only my dadi, whom we called Ammi, worshipped eclectic gods. She had a statue of Hanuman on her writing table. She had a psalm written in paint on a slab of wood that hung on a wall 'The Lord is my shepherd . . .' In her kitchen, on a shelf, were bright pictures of other gods. Was it Lakshmi? Or Ganesha on his rat? I could not recall clearly.

In Geshe Sonam Rinchen's class, I focussed on his sculptured nose with its fine nostrils and a gash that scarred the right side of the forehead. He had a straight, well-drawn mouth and a deep funnel between his nose and upper lip.

Lightly joining his two hands at their fingertips, he began in his even voice, in Tibetan. He shifted a little in his seat, settling in. As he spoke, he rocked ever so slightly back and forth. He paused to let Ruth, his translator, turn it into English.

'You must recognize the preciousness of human life and freedom, and the theme of impermanence and death, where you see that the preciousness of human life and freedom is not going to last forever.'

Ruth, who was English and had washed up in Dharamsala many years ago, had a thin, reedy voice which was oddly hypnotic. She had wide eyes and grey hair. She spoke fluent Tibetan.

'You must realize the disadvantages of psychic existence and the connection between action and suffering. This body and mind are examples of pervasive suffering, of conditioning. If you have a boil, it may not be painful, but if anything touches it the pain may flare up. Like matches, the flame is ready to burst; like a flint, if you strike it, fire flares.'

The Geshe's belief in this system of thought was absolute. It was not a faith, it was some cosmic law, like you need to breathe to stay alive; a law, he felt, that would become clear to those who thought about it even briefly.

I thought I'd stay a few more days. I also signed up for a class on the Perfection of Wisdom taught by Geshe Dawa. The *Prajnaparamita* texts were a foundation of Mahayana Buddhism and Xuanzang translated this enormous work from Sanskrit into Chinese, presented often as a dialogue between a disciple and a guru asking questions and then answering them. Tibetan monks very commonly recited the Perfection of Wisdom, the very heart of Buddhist teachings, the most profound. *Form is emptiness and emptiness is form.*

As Xuanzang translated from the *Mahaprajnaparamita*'s facsimile, 532, Chapter 29 (retranslated into English):

Conditions are brought together which create the supposition that something exists. But actually there is nothing that can be laid hand upon. It is as when a master of magic or his disciple at a crossroads magically creates the four kinds of army—that is to say, an elephant army, a cavalry army, a chariot army and an army of foot soldiers, or again magically creates other kinds of form, complete with their various characteristics. Such things seem to exist, but have no reality. Consciousness is also like this, and cannot really be laid hand upon.[1]

I hoped Geshe Dawa might enlighten me. He was wrinkled, wizened, with large ears and a mound of a stomach under his robes; he looked like a Chinese Laughing Buddha statue. He consulted long strips of paper, sutras which he held in his left hand and pointed to with his right hand, at the sentence, at the air.

He too spoke through a translator.

'Shariputra asks how a son or daughter of noble birth should follow the practice of Perfection of Wisdom, to see that form is empty, *sunyata*, emptiness is form. When defining "emptiness", it's a lack of inherent existence of phenomenon or person.'

I bit my lip. My mind felt like a lump of metal, incapable of subtle acrobatics. Who? What? My stuffed nose and aching limbs felt real enough.

'The mind perceives X, but all phenomena exist within the mind, no phenomenon exists outside the mind. The table and pillar: they are of one nature. There is a non-duality of subject and object: this is explained as emptiness.'

I stifled a sigh.

Geshe Dawa added crossly that when studying Buddhism, one should stick to one school because the four main Buddhist schools, all had different interpretations and one could GET CONFUSED.

I nodded vigorously in agreement, sitting cross-legged on my cushion. Geshe Dawa then yawned hugely and rubbed his face. It was time for the final prayer and we bowed. As he walked out, he shook an index finger at a girl called Carol who had not changed the clock battery and so it was ten minutes slow.

There was a stir in the little community. Sogyal Rinpoche (known as 'Soggy' to some) was in town and was to give a speech. The small crowd gathered on the roof of the Tibetan Library of Works and Archives, which afforded a magnificent view. To the south, the valleys of the plains tilted and rolled, shades of blue-grey, painted with water and a dash of colour. Etched against this, eagles circled in the blue sky. I felt a sudden flash of what a bird might see: a great nothingness below it. The thought gave me vertigo.

Form is emptiness.

Sogyal Rinpoche was a monk grown tubby. I listened half-heartedly to his jokes. It was, it struck me, a masterful, practised way of connecting with his audience. He mentioned the Americans, the British, the Germans, the French. All in a slightly humorous, fun-poking way, the underlying message being, hey, this Rinpoche is cool, man, he speaks our language, he knows our culture.

But he never mentioned the Indians or the Tibetans until right at the end, when he said as an afterthought—he was almost leaving, he turned back and waved his chubby arms—'I have something else to tell you. I feel so pleased when the Tibetans come, the young ones. Please can the westerners bring the Tibetans to these gatherings?'

An obvious point to make, one supposes, in the face of this overwhelmingly foreign gathering. It was a performance. Hollywood had crept in and it bored me. It was karma pre-chewed so infants could digest it.

Below, I could see the Nechang Cafe where monks in their maroon wraps sipped tea.

Why was I put off by the youth of those studying here, the posturing, the dreadlocks, the Indian clothes, this earnest search for wisdom and answers? After all, wasn't that exactly my reason for being here? I was getting old and cranky. I suppose one must be tolerant and pray for the happiness of all sentient beings. But I only managed to feel cynical and cross.

Buddhism was such a grim faith, it struck me again and again, grim and cold in its esotericism.

'The disadvantages of psychic existence.' A black phrase indeed. Were there any advantages? Blue skies and birds and the beauty of mountains? I was so enamoured of mountains, I found it hard to believe in a dark future. I wanted drunken, if necessary self-destructive inspiration.

Buddhism had partly found such a well of support in ancient India because people were fed up with Hinduism's extremes. Enough. Of the Brahmins, the bells, the rituals. More sober things were welcomed—an equality-based, thought-based system, of logic, reason. But Buddhism died out in India, while the Brahmins and the bells and the rituals remained, and what did *that* mean?

I dropped in to see Geshe Sonam Rinchen to discuss the Buddhist texts that Xuanzang so loved.[2] The Geshe sat on his bed, cross-legged, in a small room. I sat on the floor on a small cushion, facing him, leaning against the wall, for my legs ached when I sat cross-legged for too long. Ruth sat on the side, translating.

'When we first came to India, we went looking for all these places, towns called Vaisali, for example. We went to all the places, but sometimes we couldn't find them! Long, long before, in Tibet, we learned the names of places in India by heart. We knew them all— Banaras, Lumbini, Vaisali—we were taught them, their importance in Buddhist history. I remember being beaten by my teachers for not at first remembering the names. They were hard to pronounce.'

'How did you end up in India?' I asked him, needing the full story.

'I came at gunpoint from China,' he laughed, 'not on pilgrimage, not thinking India was the sacred land of pilgrimage.'

He launched into a tale that began in 1959, that traced his difficult journey through Assam, the shock of a new country, the illness.

'From the border, when we walked for ten days we reached an army post. Then another ten days and another army post where planes flew to it. It took ten people at a time and flew them down, but there were too many—500 in small groups. At these army encampments, we were given rice and dal to cook and we were given tea.'

Ruth took a deep breath. The Geshe's story had created its own stir in the air. Scenes from his past floated in the room, it was as though I could reach out and touch them.

'I spent nearly nine years in Buxaduar in West Bengal in an internment camp. It had a river flowing through it, very poor food. The government was providing for us, but the middlemen were taking a chunk and everything was rotting.'

Here, Ruth interjected and corrected.

'They were dying like flies.'

'I was so ill while in the camp.'

Ruth added, on her own, 'There were quite a few suicides, which is very, very unusual for Tibetans, it is a sign of deep distress.'

'In Cooch Behar, in West Bengal, there was a big hospital. Nobody spoke Tibetan. There were two nurses who took pity on me, they were very kind to me. There was a little bus Western people had given to the camp for those who were sick. Two people had to carry me down. When I got to the hospital, there was no bed. So they put me near a door. And then finally I got a bed, I think somebody was evacuated. So I had my own bedding, you're supposed to use hospital bedding, but the nurses allowed me to use my own as well, under the hospital bedding. It was quite dirty.'

The Geshe's tone was almost detached, as though all this had happened to somebody else. He related the story without bitterness, or anger.

At some point in the Geshe's sombre tale, to my own acute embarrassment, I had begun to cry softly. I could not bear it, to hear all this sadness. I tried discreetly to blow my nose. The Geshe was thinking again of the escape from China into India.

'We had to cross swinging rope bridges, huge chasms with rushing water, bamboo rope bridges. It was utterly terrifying. I suffered badly from vertigo. I hated it. There were seven or eight bridges like that when coming through Assam. I could never do that again. It was fear at our heels at the time.'

He shook his head.

'If they said to me today, if they said now you can go back, the Chinese have gone, I couldn't cross those rope bridges again.'

Ruth and I left the Geshe together. The story had affected us both. She invited me to her place, not far away, for hot toddy. The alcohol shook off our malaise. We drank and managed a laugh and it eased the grimness. Ruth lent me an electric heater. I lugged it back to my room, slept soundly and deeply, as though the warmth of the alcohol had soaked my aching back and helped it relax. I only had one bad dream about a Tibetan trying to escape across mountain passes.

Winter was edging into the mountains and all the students' noses were running. Geshe Sonam's class was punctuated by coughs and sniffles and the snorts of nose-blowing. The Tibetan monks still wore only their robes and were bare-armed. I got medicines for my inflamed nostrils and burning sinus. I sneezed at the slightest hint of dust, the cold felt as though it had cast a net of iron over my lungs, my body felt bruised all over and my head was as thick as a bell.

I heard some music one morning, a man's soft voice, singing in Hindi *Na tum jaano na hum* and I thought, thank goodness, there is another world out there. Tibetan music, a horn with its burping noises and the clashing bells, were not aesthetic to my senses.

I was desperate to leave behind the foreigners with dreadlocks or leather jackets or long hair, the older American women looking for nunneries, the Italians studying Shakti, the South Indian woman who had a novel with an agent in New York, the Dutch woman who had a pierced nose and wore salwar kameez, the white-haired American lady with a little Tibetan girl who came late to every single class.

The little girl fidgeted and fiddled and wanted to do headstands. She kicked the blonde woman in the back to get a reaction. 'Stop it,' the woman hissed. 'Stop it.' But she wouldn't stop and the blonde woman, annoyed, shifted her cushion.

All around the camp swirled stories of misery. The Delek Hospital had special departments for tuberculosis and hypertension and treated torture survivors. In between classes, I saw the monk-doctors wearing white masks come out of the tuberculosis ward.

The Dhauladhar peaks, grandiose, rose 4900 metres, topped with snow, right up against your face. I wondered if I had the strength for this, my resolve was leaching out through some fissure. India had sunk its hooks in me, slowing me down by the gut, dragging me to another level where there were no buffers, nothing between me and me.

∞

What did the monk make of the Himalayan kingdoms he passed through? He was succinct, as usual, and left few clues about the nature of his days. The realm of Kullu, he called it Kuluta, was surrounded by the 'Snowy Mountains', he said. Here he found about twenty Buddhist monasteries and some 1000 priests.

> Being contiguous to the Snowy Mountains, there are found here many medicinal [roots] of much value. Gold, silver, and copper are found here . . . The climate is unusually cold, and hail or snow continuously falls. The people are coarse and common in appearance, and are much afflicted with goitre and tumours; their nature is hard and fierce; they greatly regard justice and bravery. There are about twenty sangharamas and 1000 priests or so.[3]

It took a whole day by bus through the hills, the roads winding gently, to Kullu. Deodars were sprinkled along the tops of hills like the remaining shreds of hair on an old man's head. The hill station of Kullu had settled in for winter, the Indian tourists had cleared out. There was an empty, curled-up feel about the town.

The temperature had dropped and I could barely feel my hands in the morning, or my nose. In the evening, a mist fell and blurred the mountainside. There were orange flashes from evening fires, men wrapped in their blankets huddled close, and the setting sun tinged the top of the Himalaya pink, just the edges.

I stayed a night and visited a ninth-century Hindu temple, for in the neighbourhood there were no Buddhist ruins to be found, at least none the tourist bureau knew of, although there was a monastery further north—many, in fact—in the Lahaul Valley, to which the monk referred although he himself went no further than Kuluta.

The scooter-wala who took me to the Hindu temple knew everybody in town. He leaned out and called to them as we rattled by.

'Oi fatty.'

'Oi Chaddah Sahib' to a man who walked along staring at the road and did not look up.

'Oi *fauji* . . .'

'Oi *daku* Mangal Singh' to the policeman at the checkpoint.

We stopped to give a ride to a young man holding a newborn baby. He sat in the scooter beside me and tenderly rearranged the baby's woollen hat.

The Basesvara Mahadeva Temple was dedicated to Shiva. It was, the sign said, one of the tiniest and most ancient shrines in the Kullu valley. In the heart of the temple sat an enormous Shiva lingam. When I peeked into the gloom, I saw a bright yellow sunflower on a stone in a corner. There were ornate pilasters, with Ganga and Yamuna in relief, naga couples. Ganesha, not yet podgy, sat to the south. He had quite a slender torso, and ears.

'Who's this?' a little girl with looped plaits and a knitted yellow dress asked her mother, tugging at her hand, looking back at me.

'An aunty,' her mother said.

It was freezing. I slept in a small hotel up a mountainside with three quilts piled on top of me and promised to leave the Himalaya the very next morning. I loved the hills, I had since I was a child. But my body was on strike. It protested every step of the way and demanded attention.

I left Kullu as the sun came up over the hills and swept the eastern flanks with a gold light. The town was still asleep but the bus adda was active, with people stamping their feet, the hiss of the gas stove, brisk cups of tea and hot parathas for breakfast.

An old man got on the bus after me, muttering, invoking all the gods. *Hanuman-ji ki jai, Panjvir-ji ki jai, Shiv-ji ki jai, Mata-ji ki jai*. And he didn't stop till he got off.

Seven hours later, we had wound our way back into the warmer plains of Punjab, with its irrigation canals slicing through the fields, where the sugar cane was nearly ready and the winter wheat was shin-high. Minutes after crossing a state border in India, it was as though the page turned and everybody changed their dress, their habits, their language, and obediently looked to other rules to make it simple for historians and anthropologists. Immediately, in Punjab, there were swords everywhere, a flash of a figure leaning against a door-jamb with a skirted tunic and a sword hanging from his waist, an orange turban. And later, a man in a white turban with a short dagger strapped to it, right above his forehead. It was like a children's book with pictures of Eskimos in igloos or figures with different dress, with bubbles speaking different tongues dotted across a map.

chapter nineteen

Tree Nymphs

From Kullu the monk went south, about 700 *li*, he wrote. He passed a great mountain, crossed a wide river and came to the country of She-to-t'u-lo, which scholars have translated as Satadru. There, the monk noted with his usual precision, cereals grew abundantly in the warm, moist climate. Gold and silver and precious stones could be found easily. People wore bright silks. The place he described was of a vast, lazy prosperity. People believed in and respected the law of the Buddha, but the halls of the few monasteries he did find around the royal city were cold and deserted. There were hardly any priests.

Where was Xuanzang's Satadru?

Cunninghum played with a mathematical triangle, made measurements with a ruler on maps, calculated distances, hemmed and hawed and finally placed Satadru at the city of Sirhind, between Chandigarh and Sanghol. He wrote:

Taking this corrected distance from Bairat and the recorded distance of 117 miles south from Kullu, the position of Satadru will correspond almost exactly with the large city of Sarhind, which both history and tradition affirm to be the oldest place in this part of the world . . . This conclusion is strengthened by the pilgrim's statement that the country produced gold, which, so far as I know, can only apply to the lower hills lying to the north of Sarhind, where gold is still found in some of the smaller effluents of the Satlej . . . [1]

B.R. Mani, the archaeologist in Jammu, had insisted I visit Sanghol after Kullu. And in the absence of any better ideas, I followed his instructions. We had pored over my map together and in his slow manner he presented me with valuable guidance. How much more lost I would have been without him.

The bus from Kullu arrived in Chandigarh, the nearest big town, after dark. I felt nervous and foolish for underestimating how long it took to cover what looked like short distances on a map. I never really had a proper plan about where to stay once I arrived. I showed up in a city and trusted the local scooter-wala to take me to some respectable establishment.

Inevitably, I was fine. But there was always the temporary, sharp fear that this would be the moment I would be led off to a back alley. Ensconced in a Chandigarh guest house used by travelling Indian businessmen, I phoned my family in New Delhi, for reassurance that went both ways.

'You're in Chandigarh?' My father was delighted. 'I used to go to Chandigarh all the time. Fine people, the Punjabis. The best farmers. People of the soil.'

'How on earth did you understand what they said?' I could feel the giggles come on at my incomprehension.

'When are you coming home to Delhi, darling?' Ma asked, on the extension. I could sense that the journey pulled me away from them, into unexplored territory.

The next morning, I made a seventy-kilometre drive in a hired car, west of Punjab's capital, Chandigarh, through a verdant countryside filled with fields of eggplant and sugar cane to the ruins of the kingdom of Satadru.

Cunningham's calculations were very close, but not quite correct. It was only in the early 1930s, much after Cunningham, that archaeologists in Sanghol—about thirty-five kilometres west of Sirhind—tumbled on a horde of coins and seals of Tormana and Mihirakula, the fiery Huns who marched into India in the fifth century from Central Asia.

At Sanghol, the diggers also found Kushan sculptures, including a fire-worshipping pot, stamped with a flower design on four sides. It was a portable square vessel, blackened inside, a sure signature of the fire-loving Central Asians. This dated Sanghol further back to the first century AD. They found Buddha heads and the bases of stupas and the remains of monastic cells and a plumbing system. There were 117 railings, around two feet high, carved with the voluptuous ancient female fertility figures called *shalabhanjikas*, tree nymphs. The nymphs were said to be so drenched in sexuality, they could make a tree (technically a sal tree) bloom by touching its branches in a particularly seductive posture. They were carved in red stone, imported, archaeologists think, from Mathura. From here it was just a hop to their association with the Buddha's mother, Maya, who it is said reached up and grasped a sal tree as she felt the first birth pangs.

The railing posts had been found intact, lying side by side in a neat pile, buried as though somebody had dismantled them to hide them—perhaps Buddhist monks when they heard of the Huns advancing towards their peaceful establishment by the Sutlej River.

It turned out, when archaeologists dug further, that there were bits of pottery from Harappan times, 2000 BC. This was a very old spot indeed.

Astonishingly, amidst the wheat fields of eastern Punjab, there was a museum, and it turned out that Dr Sharma, a senior historian, lived in the village nearby after retiring from the ASI.

On the way to meeting him, amidst the fields, the Maruti van I had hired broke down. The driver and I clambered out.

'This will take time, madam,' he said, apologetically.

I shrugged and looked into the fields, as though a solution would emerge from there. And it did—a young farmer passing by offered me a lift on his bicycle. He was going the same way. Dr Sharma's house was in the village ahead. He was well known in the neighbourhood. I balanced on the back of the bicycle, gripping the edge of the seat, and with the farmer's help found Dr Sharma's house while the driver fiddled with the Maruti.

'Cunningham was wrong,' he gleefully informed me, as his elderly wife fetched tea. 'There is evidence of very ancient civilizations here, we found a full-fledged stupa, there is absolutely no doubt.'

The river Xuanzang crossed was the Sutlej, which used to flow north of Sanghol, a fact known from the depression in the ground. Over the centuries, the course of the river had moved north.

'Why,' I questioned him, 'would the austere Buddhists choose to carve lovely half-naked women on their stupas?'

'The ease-loving Kushans,' Dr Sharma explained, 'had to be reminded that beauty and pleasure were transient, that it all came to naught.'

The sculptures, now in the museum, were breathtaking, sensual. One figure wrung out her wet hair, another carried flagons of wine. They wore earrings, anklets. From balconies, men gazed at them, lovelorn. There were dangling grapes, rounded hips, cloth sashes, bare breasts, pan pipes. One woman cupped her breast, her yoni lovingly sculpted. How bacchanalian.

The word stuck at the back of my mind, and it would be a few months before a different reason for the sculptures presented itself to me.

Out in the middle of the fields, by the side of the ruins of the stupa, there was a vast warehouse, filled sky-high with jute sacks of wheat and rice. A long line of ants, each one carrying a spilled grain, scurried from the warehouse over the bricks of the monasteries, into the fields.

The foundations of the cells were still visible, the division of each room neatly laid out like an architectural drawing, the circle of a stupa. Fakhir Mohammad, who worked at the archaeological site, fished out his double *bansuri*, an instrument known in ancient Iraq, and in the soft light of the setting sun, began to play a song about a magic stag. It felt like a farewell, a signal to return to my wanderings, head south to Rajasthan, to the kingdom of Paryatra, or Bairat.

chapter twenty

Too Many Women

When the monk reached Bairat, he wrote, 'there is a strange kind of rice grown here which ripens after sixty days.'[1] He had travelled about 400 kilometres to the south. He had left the mountains behind, left Punjab's fertile plains and was at the edge of a desert.

> There are many oxen and sheep, few flowers and fruits. The climate is warm and fiery, the manners of the people are resolute and fierce. They do not esteem learning, and are given to honour the heretics. The king is of the Vaisya caste; he is of a brave and impetuous nature, and very warlike. There are eight sangharamas, mostly ruined, with very few priests, who study the Little Vehicle. There are ten Deva temples, with about 1000 followers of different sects.[2]

࿐

I took the train to Delhi, rested at home a few days with my family. The journey felt hard and brittle and far away. What would stay with me in the end, time with loved ones or this hard-won knowledge? Love and death were the only realities. What I sought felt wraithlike, insubstantial. Was it a fatal flaw that I was caught by facts and forgot the feeling?

Mathura and Bairat were not far from Delhi. I bought a ticket at the railway station. I had stuck on a bindi, arranged my chunni and my kurta, a ring on the third finger of my left hand. The message, I hoped, was clear, but the troubling fact remained. Girls from good families don't travel on their own and I still felt I stuck out like a sore thumb on the Ernakulam Express.

At Mathura, I switched to a local bus to modern Bairat, reaching once again as dusk fell. Much of the road was bad. At each bump the entire bus groaned and shrieked into the air before it crashed back to earth. My teeth were jarred, my back hurt and I had to sit sideways because my knees wouldn't fit into the seat.

A small barefoot boy climbed on and pulled his goat in with him. The animal clambered delicately over my bag. Next to me a flower seller advised, 'If you pray during the month of Kartik, it's better, much, much luckier.' She thought I'd been praying in Mathura. What else could I have been doing there? Here, on this unfamiliar path, the Indians I met travelled enthusiastically to holy places. I was the only one looking for history.

There were fields of wheat and mustard. The mustard, sarson, was thigh-high, with its bright yellow flowers, the wheat still young and green. Away from the mountains, the winter withdrew its sting.

Bairat was within the boundaries of the state of Rajasthan. I was so near the desert that camels abounded, with that glide, that supercilious look. Bairat was barely a village and what a pleasant surprise it was, surrounded by the Aravalli Hills, a range so old that it has been worn down to barely 1000 metres.

I stood in front of the local government dak bungalow. It was my first encounter with this peculiar institution found in places too small for hotels. The bungalow was deserted. The door was latched but not locked and I let myself in, turned on the lights, used the bathroom. A passing man told me the chowkidar had gone to have chai.

In the soft dusk, a sudden northerly breeze sprang up, bringing a crack of rain and the smell of moist earth. I pulled my chunni close around me. A neem tree swished and swayed while two peacocks rustled and fidgeted in the garden. There was a bright bougainvillea creeper at the door.

It struck me again how India's government is still a colonial one, in its mannerisms, its rights and obligations, in the way a government official is a demigod.

But these unlikely spots were precisely what I loved about this journey, the way it picked me up and dropped me into places I had never heard of, where nothing ever happened.

When he finally returned, the chowkidar rented me a cotton-filled quilt for five rupees. It stank. The rooms were large and dusty, they had fireplaces and dressing rooms. The walls were painted blue. It was so empty that when I shot the bolt it echoed like a gunshot and made me jump.

That night in the dak bungalow, I fell asleep with the light on, without dinner, for the shops and the STD telephones were a kilometre away and I was too scared to wander down in the inky blackness. Once again, that half-spooky, half-mind-boggling feeling crept around my gut and tightened. Nobody that I loved knew where I was. If something happened, who would come running?

Like in Kashmir, fear thawed with the morning light. After a quick wash, I dressed in the company of two mice. Black-faced langurs rattled the branches of a tree as I walked past and turned onto a dirt track on the side. India has this fine sand that blows into your each pore. I could feel myself getting grimy. I began to climb, following the directions called out by a man in a dhoti, who stooped to wash under a tap. He seemed not in the least perturbed to find a lone city woman looking for Buddhist remains.

Behind me, a group of women caught up, swinging their skirts, chatting and eating bits of chapatti which they offered me. Santosh, Meena and Sushila.

It was a tumbled, instant conversation, each speaking at once in slightly accented Hindi.

'Here, eat this, have you had breakfast?'

'Are you angrez?'

'She looks angrez.'

'But she speaks Hindi.'

'How old are you? Are you married? Do you have children?' It was India's holy trinity of questions.

'Here, if at thirty-two a woman has no kids, the man gets another wife.'

'We're going into the jungle to collect firewood.'

'I cook on gas, but bajra rotis taste better cooked on wood.'

'She's a big liar.'

'My husband says, I earn so much, why do you need to go collect wood.'

'She's useless, she never listens to her husband.'

'And she, she hasn't been to her in-laws yet, though her husband has come many times to fetch her.'

'There's time, there's time.'

'If you don't serve your husband, who else will you serve, tell me that.'

'She has three sons.'

'She had her tubes tied after two kids. They all bug her about it; two is too few.'

We paused by a well, for water. One woman pulled up a bucket of water and tilted it for the rest of us as we cupped our hands and drank. The water tasted slightly stale.

'See how quickly time passes when we chat on the way.'

'You are off to your duty, we're off to ours.' They used the English 'dooty'.

'Come and have lunch with us, we'll be back at one.'

'When you go to your in-laws, do you cover your head? We have to, till here.' She pointed to her middle.

It was a brisk climb through thorny dhansar bushes that yielded sweet-and-sour red berries. Bulbuls with their black tufts flitted and called.

'See, she's out of breath.'

'Many angrez come here, you know, they take pictures of us when we have bundles of firewood on our heads.'

'They park their cars and come on bicycles.'

'Watch out for the men in this region, they're terrible.'

'They're even worse in Mathura.'

'You should be our friend.'

'Can you get her husband a job in Delhi?'

'I'll come and work in your house for free.'

Our paths diverged. Up a flight of stone steps, to the right, was the Hanuman temple, a vast tipped-over rock and a string of red triangular flags. The women had to go left, deeper into the trees. They paused in a row, looking at me. A brief silence followed.

'Don't forget us.'

'Tell your man you met Sushila and Santosh and Meena in the jungle.'

Facing east to catch the rising sun sat the remains of a Buddhist monastery. There were low rippled hills to the south. It was a brilliant, silent spot. High up, there was the whistle of birds, and far in the distance the sound of a town, the squeal of a horn. From this ridge in the curve of the range, Bairat looked a phantom. A morning mist still laced the mountain tops. This was the site of old Viratnagar, capital of Matsyadesa. It was founded by King Virata, in whose kingdom the five Pandavas spent the thirteenth year of their exile in disguise, the rusty sign read.

I remembered reading about the Pandava brothers of the Mahabharata and their escape from the house of lac as a child. I had loved the phrase 'house of lac'. The five heroic brothers, discovering their wicked cousin Duryodhana had got his men to coat their dwelling with the resin to stage an 'accident' later, set it on fire to fake their death as they escaped through underground tunnels. I was looking for Xuanzang's story and kept bumping into other memories, things that sat at the bottom of my bones, things I had not thought about in years.

I learned again how Indian history relied on its 'traditions' or 'legends' or 'Buddhist scriptures'. Not strict with dates and times, they nevertheless painted a picture of a particular era.

Archaeologists found two Ashokan inscriptions here and, naturally, Buddhist relics. The monastery was a double row of six or seven cells, arranged around an open square courtyard. It was a circular building, with a Mauryan stupa. They found a bowl bearing Mauryan polish and a *chhatra*, or crowning member of the stupa.

It was my first clear sense of how from Hindu traditions Buddhist ideas were nurtured, and how they influenced one another. It was one of the earliest structural temples, the board read, which furnished a model for some of the numerous rock-cut caves of western India.

Other than Xuanzang's own brief description of Bairat, there was nothing further about it in his biography. This was not surprising. The Buddhist monasteries were already abandoned by the time he arrived. There were few monks and certainly no eminent Buddhist teachers. There would be no reason for him to linger.

Down by the bus stand, I washed down dal pakoras and jalebis with some hot tea. The day was alight and filled with people about to travel. Such a strange companionship amongst travellers, I thought, regardless of where they are from.

The question of where I really was from kept simmering. It was time to head to the neighbouring state of Uttar Pradesh, where I was born. I would go to Mathura, the state's westernmost town, and see if I could begin to find some answers.

Mathura for me was a story, the birthplace of Krishna. I remembered shreds of a tale, of a darkened night threatened with storm. A man smuggled a baby boy across the Yamuna River in spate so he could be brought up in safety. I did not remember anything more specific. To that memory I added the knowledge that it was a city that Xuanzang had visited.

Scholars surmised from Buddhist texts that ancient India was densely forested. Xuanzang too refers to such jungles (not least the one he was attacked in). Pockets of such jungle still exist, and if you equate wooded areas to older times, then that is what it must have been like for a monk wandering around India.

The road heading east to Mathura from Bairat cuts through the hills, through the wildlife sanctuary of Sariska. The Sariska forest was nearly 900 square kilometres and had twenty-eight tigers and forty-seven leopards and it lay right across the monk's path. I decided to stay a night in the sanctuary guest house.

Here the protected hills and valleys were thick with date palms and ronge, karchu and hingote—rough thorny scrub trees of Rajasthan. There was the thorn bush kaer, pale pistachio, overgrown and thick, and always the fine sandy tracks of the North Indian soil through the jungle. There was a peepul tree full of migratory green pigeons. Driving through the jungle in an open-air jeep, there were dove chicks, black and flapping by a lake formed from run-off from rainwater. Across it, silhouetted in the afternoon sun, springing off the water, a flock of black storks stood in the water, preening, staring.

Small white egrets dotted the shores and as we moved off into the thick forest, two partridges scurried across the ground, perfectly striped and spotted so as to be invisible if they stopped. The peacocks' tails had shed and shortened post-monsoon but they retained the deep blue neck and crest. Two jackals stopped and stared, their fine pointed noses half-hidden in the grass. Late in the afternoon, with the sun a gold trickle through the trees, a dozen deer and sambar gathered to drink at a pond, their front legs spread so they could bend their heads and sip. At dusk, as the sunset painted the skies a pale even pink, the Aravalli Hills darkened and the new moon rose in the south-west. Three wild boars grunted and trotted into the trees.

I drank it all in. It was like learning a new language, the vocabulary of an Indian landscape. Slowly, I was acquiring a country, a history, making it mine by marching through it, claiming this branch, that road, that casual 1000-year-old brick, these people. Mine, all mine. I felt a little giddy.

෴

'The kingdom of Mo-t'u-lo,' the monk scribbled when he described Mathura further to the east, 'is about 5000 *li* in circuit . . . This country produces a fine species of cotton fabric and also yellow gold. The climate is warm to a degree. The manners of the people are soft and complacent . . . they esteem virtue and honour learning. There are about twenty sangharamas with 2000 priests or so. They study equally the Great and Little Vehicles. There are five Deva temples, in which sectaries of all kinds live.'[3]

In Xuanzang's Mathura, Buddhists and Hindus lived side by side peaceably on the rich soil watered by the Yamuna. The invaders from Afghanistan had yet to come thundering down, bringing destruction in their wake.

Ashoka had built his stupas here too. The monks of Mathura honoured a variety of Buddhist luminaries, including Ananda, the Buddha's right-hand man, and Rahula, his son. On special days they held festivities. Xuanzang described them in vivid detail:

They spread out (display) their jewelled banners; the rich (precious) coverings (parasols) are crowded together as network; the smoke of the incense rises in clouds; and flowers are scattered in every direction like rain; the sun and the moon are concealed as by the clouds which hang over the moist valleys. The king of the country and the great ministers apply themselves to these religious duties with zeal.[4]

A few kilometres east of the city, Xuanzang said, was a mountainside monastery built by Upagupta, with cells carved in it for the priests to meditate in. He said that the Buddha walked here.

Did the great man come often, though? The Buddha is known to have winced at Mathura and said that it had five defects: 'The ground was uneven, it was covered with stones and brick-bats, it abounded with prickly shrubs, the people took solitary meals, and there were too many women.'[5]

Even from the point of view of the ancient Indian monks, Mathura had its problems. According to the Buddhist Anguttara Nikaya, 'The roads were uneven, they were full of dust, there were ferocious dogs, wild animals and demons and the alms were not easily procurable.'[6]

Thomas Watters, who analysed Xuanzang's journey in the early 1900s, doubted if Xuanzang even went to Mathura. 'It is worthy of notice that in his account of Mathura and the surrounding district the pilgrim does not give the name of any hill, or river, or town, or Buddhist establishment in the country. His information about the district is meagre and his remarks about the Buddhist objects of interest in it seem to be confused and to a certain extent second-hand.'[7]

In that case, I thought, tapping my teacup, perhaps he never went to Bairat either, for it was next door to Mathura. From an itinerary viewpoint, his journey would make a lot more sense if he skipped that long southern detour and simply edged gently into the plains from the hills in a more or less straight line. Plenty of roaming monks could have filled him in on the details of both towns.

I shrugged off the debate and watched an early winter morning rise gently above Mathura city. Things had yet to get going in small-town India. At a stall outside the museum, I sipped my tea, made over a hissing stove with the requisite lump of ginger. The tea-boy, not more than fourteen, stirred the steel pot till the milk boiled, frothing at the top. The museum held one of the country's most beautiful sculptures of the Buddha, which I was eager to see, tipped off by my bua who had once photographed it.

The rubbish team came by. It consisted of a buffalo dragging a cart, making slow progress. There was a man in a dhoti with a spade and a rounded scoop for the leaves that were the bowls and plates of yesterday's dinner.

Then it was the milkman's turn, to stop by the chai stall with an earthen pot lashed to the back of his bicycle. He had covered the pot's lip with a square of wax paper and tied it carefully.

Somehow, India held together. Somehow the garbage got collected, somehow there was ginger and milk for tea, somehow the rickety government buses got me to places. I had not worked out how. The sun warmed and tensed. I pushed off to find an Internet place and let S. and my family know where I was.

The day before, I had ridden through the city on a rickshaw, looking for the ruins of a Buddhist stupa and finding the birthplace of Krishna instead.

The cows, laggard in the streets, had looked particularly holy. One splendid pair of oxen had their curved horns painted in stripes, orange and red. They stood by a cart filled with some unidentifiable rural cargo, brought into the city. The village was all around, percolating through the town, blurring boundaries. Men huddled in tea houses dressed in dhotis and discussing politics, a camel pulled a cart, and we careened along by a stall where sugar cane was pressed into a sudsy juice.

The fruit carts, tables on wheels, were piled with guavas, chikus, bananas, anars. The smell of roasting cumin wafted across the street, a sharp jab up my nostrils, and the rickshaw bumped on through the croak of scooter horns and the horse tongas, a prime viewing post.

As it happened, my cycle rickshaw passed by the Krishna *janmabhoomi* where there was the usual garish temple of sandstone, and marble floors bespoke plenty of money. There were high steps and a shoe house where I could leave my footwear safe in exchange for a few coins. Looking up at the cupolas, I spotted a security guard silhouetted against the evening sky, a rifle slung over his shoulder. Leaving Kashmir, I had thought I was leaving the guns behind. There was a security check to enter the temple. Behind it, the sadhus gathered, thin men with knobbly knees, grey caked hair, beards and fine muslin cloths of orange and white draped over their shoulders. They sat in various poses with their steel lotas on tenuous cloths on the ground.

I untied my shoes and leaned across the barrier to hand them over.

'Why is there so much security around?' I asked.

The watchman pointed up at a mosque brushing the back wall of the temple. It had a white onion dome, minarets painted green. There were posts with barbed wire high on the boundary wall. It was a mosque from Aurangzeb's time.

'*They* broke it down, the place where Krishna was born, and built a mosque.' For the second time, I was bumping into the defining story of modern India, how in India's already crowded history, Islam had found a place.

Riding through the old city by-lanes that led to the river, I looked up to see fine balconies, carved in thin stone. Two women in burkhas bought gulab jamuns from the sweet vendor. And finally, we rolled down to Vishram Ghat where the Yamuna at dusk was an oily dark grey. In the last of the fading light, a boatman ferried a load of passengers across the river, leaning on a pole. It was an odd feeling to be here, in the heartland of Uttar Pradesh. The state I hailed from was profoundly familiar in some ways—the Nehru caps, the dhotis, the Hindi, spoken so purely it felt like a row of columns.

My family hailed from Lucknow, although those whom I was close to had shifted to Delhi long ago. Uttar Pradesh, Lucknow especially, was where Hindu and Muslim cultures had mingled and rubbed off on each other the most. The language, Urdu, was common to both in this part of India. Although brought up in a Hindu family, I had referred to my paternal grandmother as 'Ammi', a Muslim term. There lingered still some waft of a UP flavour somewhere behind my memory and Mathura did not feel like a new place.

'What caste are you?' a helpful priest asked.

I pretended I did not understand and smiled instead.

With the evening star in a navy sky the muezzin's call wafted up. This too had been a part of my small life. I watched the first star turn bright in the south-west sky and in the pale rose of the setting sun, flocks of parrots flew south-east, screeching. A sound from my childhood.

But I had no success as far as Buddhist ruins went. I would have to start at the museum after all. So it was that I sat drinking tea

outside the museum the next morning, waiting for it to open, forgetting
that in India things rarely happen before 10 a.m. The museum's most
famous statue came from the Jamalpur mound. Because the roof was
undergoing repairs, the life-size statue rested on its back in a godown.
The keepers kindly unlocked a steel net door to let me edge in through
the debris and crouch by its side.

The Buddha's knees showed through the sculpted robes. There
was the tiniest roll of fat around his hips and his nipples were visible
through the thin cloth. He had the finest symmetrical eyebrows, and
long ear lobes. He held his drapes in his hand and the pleating of the
stone-carved cloth fell in neat, understated ripples. In Gupta times,
the eyelids were lowered more, so as to indicate the Buddha looking
down, inward a bit. It was sculpted by a certain Yasdin. There was a
curious pleasure, in knowing the name of a long-dead artist. All I
knew of him was this statue. Perhaps it was enough. There were
eight more godowns, each crammed with Buddhist artefacts dug up
from around Mathura.

In fact, Mathura was still coughing up Buddhist sculpture. In the
circular building of the museum, there was a garden in the middle
and stone benches. There were bougainvillea bushes at the doors of
offices. The archaeologists had found a hand of Buddha, raised in the
preaching position. The hand was in almost perfect condition, its
fingers gently bent. It was so large that they deduced the whole statue
must have been a good ten feet tall.

Mathura and its school of art flourished under the Kushan king
Kanishka in roughly the middle of the first century AD, setting the
trend for India. And because Kanishka's empire sprawled across
Pakistan and Afghanistan (his winter capital was in Peshawar) he
was also a patron of Gandharan art. Kanishka's Kushan empire lay
between Rome and Tang China, and the trade routes criss-crossed it.
It was most profitable. A Roman, Pliny the Elder, grumbled (VI, 10),
'There is no year in which India does not attract at least 50 million
sesterces.'[8]

Kanishka's court was littered with luminaries: Asvaghosa, who
wrote a life of the Buddha, Vasumitra, Nagarjuna. Kanishka's
decapitated statue still sits in the museum at Mathura, graceful Kushan
lines, the king Kanishka himself still in the Central Asian nomadic

dress—felt boots, a skirted tunic that flares at the bottom. Buddhist yes, but Kanishka leaned too (publicly or privately) towards Mithras, the Zoroastrian god of light and goodness.[9] Leonid's words in Uzbekistan, at the Fayaz Tepa by the Amu Darya, now made perfect sense—Kanishka sensed the mood of the time and felt that protecting the Buddhists, indeed, *becoming* Buddhist, would please many people. Standing here in Mathura, it felt to me that Kanishka's embracing Buddhism was a move aimed directly at his subjects in the Indian subcontinent. It was an instant route to legitimacy.

Increasingly, the Hindu and the Buddhist stories would mingle. It was only natural. Buddhism was born and grew up in a Hindu land. The Buddha had followed the large cities, the population centres, the religious gatherings. How could the two not be entwined?

I flagged down a rickshaw to Govind Nagar and the Katra mound, by the train tracks. Somewhere here, amongst the rooting hairy pigs, across the railway line now closed to let a goods train pass, among the croak and smoke of scooters, I tried hard to imagine through the mists back to the seventh century a very grand constellation of Buddhist monasteries, most likely visited and seen by Xuanzang.

Not long after Mathura, after meandering back north (if indeed he went south) backtracking and zigzagging in a most peculiar manner, Xuanzang was headed to King Harshavardhana's capital at Kanauj. Early in AD 631, he spent three months studying with a sage named Viryasena. He learned the commentaries on the *Maha Vibasha*, the standard text used by Hinayanists. The Mahayana texts he was most drawn to carried critiques of the Hinayana schools. As his Kashmiri instructors had schooled him, if he was to debate the Hinayanists, he had to understand completely the opponent's arguments. Besides, a majority of India was Hinayanist at the time.[10]

In a library's reading room in Mathura, I browsed through Maurice Ettinghausen's *Harse Vardhana, Empereur et Poete* from 1906. Its pages were still uncut at the top, it was so old and so new. Nobody had consulted Ettinghausen. Ganga Ram at the library had to slice the pages apart with a knife, like they did in Jane Austen. I flipped it open, breathing in the smoky smell of old paper.

'*L'Inde n'as pas ecrit son histoire*,' Ettinghausen had written crossly. Of course not, we're an oral culture. *Zaban se sab chalta hai.*

The two brilliant men, the monk and the king, were to meet, but almost a decade later. A great friendship developed between Harshavardhana and Xuanzang. Was it that they were the same age, both cultured men? Was Harshavardhana enamoured of the aura of mystery that the Chinese monk carried, did he admire his chutzpah? Was he a little bit in love?

Harsha ruled from Kanauj or Kanyakubja, a city bordering the Ganga. Xuanzang described it as having a dry ditch around it, with powerful, lofty towers as fortification. It was a gracious city, filled with flowers and woods, lakes and ponds, he said. A wealth of merchandise collected here; presumably it was a flourishing centre of trade and its citizens were well off and contented.

Harshavardhana's clan hailed from Thanesvar, further west, a frontier town poised between the Indus to the west and the Ganga to the east, a town that Harshavardhana's father had defended against the Huns.

Harsha himself had assembled a terrifying army of 5000 elephants, 2000 cavalry and 50,000 foot soldiers and gone on a six-year conquering rampage. Three decades later, his hold on power was complete, there was peace in the land and the king could focus on religion. He delighted in religious debate and had strong Buddhist leanings. The Indian king and the Chinese monk met at exactly the right time in their lives.

I had lunch sitting by the same Mathura tea stall. The paratha man scooped some vegetables into one and rolled it up. He wrapped it in newspaper and carefully put the packet into a plastic bag. Behind me, a man read from a Hindi newspaper. He formed the words, half to himself, half to his friend who held a child.

'Mathura has 10,000 temples. *Arre.*' He looked up. 'Mathura has 10,000 temples.'

His friend shifted the baby. '*Had* 10,000 temples, now where are they?'

The article he was reading went on to describe Harshavardhana's great reign and the subsequent rampage by Mahmud of Ghazni who galloped down from Afghanistan to slash at the plains. I recognized it for another tale of Hindu persecution by Muslim marauders. India, having ignored history, was now all agog with it. In recent years, it had become a tool for more fundamentalist political forces to proclaim Hindu greatness.

Back at the library, three men sat around the reading table, not reading. One was telling a story.

'Got up. I got up, then I got dressed. I got dressed and went to the market. *Achchha*. Went to the market, then I drank some chai-shai.' The others listened with rapt attention.

The truth was, I was enjoying this thoroughly. I was deep inside this country, looking for no other reason than to take a peek. Suddenly, I was used to all this, used to India, used to the travel, used to the hardship, the dust. It felt like I was flying, like a stone skipping over water.

chapter twenty-one

Holy Confluence

It was already the middle of January.

If I wanted to catch the Maha Kumbh Mela, the Festival of the Great Pitcher, which lay smack on Xuanzang's route, I had to immediately join the massive flow of bodies towards Allahabad, or Prayag, the city where I was born, where the Ganga meets the Yamuna, where there was a third river, subterranean and lost.

It meant I had to skip a section of Xuanzang's route in Uttar Pradesh and, to my disappointment, forgo a visit to Kanauj the capital of the great king Harshavardhana. It also meant I would go first to Allahabad and then to Ayodhya, instead of the other way round like the Chinese pilgrim.

Eager to see the Maha Kumbh Mela, I was willing to make the sacrifice. As the monk wrote, Po-lo-ke-ya, or Prayag, was about 5000 *li* in circuit. The capital lay between two branches of the river and was blessed with a warm, agreeable climate. Its people were gentle.

> To the east of the enclosure of charity, at the confluence of the two rivers, every day there are many hundreds of men who bathe themselves and die. The people of this country consider that whoever wishes to be born in heaven ought to fast to a grain of rice, and then drown himself in the waters. By bathing in this water (they say) all the pollution of sin is washed away and destroyed . . .[1]

Even now, every twelve years, the stars align and millions of Hindus believe that pulses from the moon and Jupiter make bathing in the Ganga at this precise moment especially effective. It washes away the dead flies that line your brain, cleanses you of your sins.

Nonsense, part of me thought. I had the westernized urban Indian's wincing disdain of any religious display. It embarrassed me. My mother had her own views. 'Well, Indians are religious because they have no safety nets, no social security,' she said briskly. 'Nobody is safe from enormous tragedy.'

My mother was educated in a girls' convent by Irish missionary nuns on a steady diet of Hail Marys, Shakespeare and Irish ditties. That, combined with her pure Brahmin genes, made her queenly and snappish and, to some extent, disconnected with India's masses. Many thinkers, including the Irish nuns, had tried over the ages to fight the superstitious aspects of Hinduism. Their work had borne fruit to some extent, at least as far as my mother was concerned.

'That's also why we read a lot of fiction. It's our way of escaping the suffering around us.'

'Andh vishwas,' Daddy, my paternal grandfather, muttered from his hospital bed. He called Hinduism a blind faith. Maybe it was. My grandfather claimed loyalty to the Arya Samaj. It was a more austere, egalitarian version of Hinduism. He half-closed his eyes, thinking perhaps of Allahabad. Arya Samajists did not think much of bathing in rivers.

But I was beginning to envy this faith.

The town of Allahabad was lodged inside me, between one breath and another; its small bumpy roads, the traffic roundabouts, the policemen with their hard hats directing a thin trickle of traffic and the occasional cow. But most of all, Allahabad had always been about Ammi and Daddy, my paternal grandparents.

One of my earliest memories is of Daddy, the railway engineer in his white cotton pyjamas, holding me in his arms. How tall he seemed, how small I must have been. We stood on a bridge and watched the steam locomotive puff and chug and howl below. I listened to the grind of wheels and smelled the piles of coal. Perhaps it was that day, that moment, that filtered through the bottom of my bare feet to feed an eternal restlessness.

At some point in her life, Ammi had painted dark oils of trees, still life images of vases filled with flowers. They hung on the walls of the house. When the painting stopped, her moods darkened. She sank into some enormous sea of sadness. I only remember whispers, as we, the children were ushered into other parts of the house to play.

'It's Ammi's nap time.'

She needed so much sleep at such odd hours. For me, the little girl who visited in summer, it was only a part of the mystery of Allahabad. When Ammi died, Daddy took a boat to the middle of the Ganga at Allahabad and slipped her ashes, everything that was left of his companion of over fifty years, into the quiet waters of the river. I wasn't there that day, but I can see it in my mind's eye—the ashes sinking, the bubbles on the water, the marigolds left floating on the surface of the river.

People die all the time, after all, snuffed out without a fuss. When Daddy told us about Ammi's cremation, my sister and I sat at his feet and listened in a silence stretched like cotton on a loom between us, we hardly breathed.

'She was dressed like a bride, all in red,' he said. 'We put her in the crematorium. It was a box about this big, and this big.' He gestured with his hands. He was fond of precision.

My own father mourned his mother with an oceanic grief. It was hidden from us, this mountain of pain, but my father chose to die on the first of June, exactly the same day of the year that she had, as summer began, as hope seemed near. But that was later.

I had gone to see Daddy in Allahabad once, after Ammi died. It was winter then. He fed the squirrels and mynahs in the garden with broken bits of chapatti. When he left Allahabad and moved to Delhi to be with his two daughters, I thought I would never see the town again. There was no reason to return.

For me, for the Maha Kumbh Mela, my bua gave up her train ticket to Allahabad. She had planned to go with an old friend of hers, Vasudha, a history professor. Vasudha was taking her mother, Ija. They had booked the tickets a month ahead of time to avoid the rush for second-class sleepers, indeed for any space on the train.

'You take the ticket,' my bua said.

'But what about you?'

She shrugged. 'I'll go next time.'

'The next Maha Kumbh Mela happens twelve years later,' I said. 'So?'

Allahabad had turned inside out.

The sleepy streets I remembered from past visits had filled with people from the villages of India. Thousands were camping in the vast, specially converted grounds, or in the city's side alleys. They had come on rickety buses, entire villages had hired trucks.

Women sat in groups with their families. A man leaned into a razor, his head had been shorn and only the little queue of hair at the back was left. People cooked their evening meals. They squatted by the roadside, dug a pit in the sand or mud, crossed three sticks, set it alight. A pan, oil and puris bubbled under a truck.

In between, they plodded on towards the river, in rubber chappals, worn leather sandals, plastic shoes, barefoot. There was a relentless column, as though it had a mind of its own, this animal, heading as one creature for a dip in the river because the stars were right. There was the faintest touch of hurry. Crossing a road, I mingled briefly with the column, swept along for a moment. It gave me goosebumps. It was a great link, a simple connection of being surrounded by strangers to a town. It was the homeboys who felt put out.

'*Iss mele ne khopri todh di*,' grumbled the rickshaw man as he dismounted and turned before yet another police cordon. He took me home by another route and, pushing through the broken back streets of my birth town, I saw the sign for the Kamala Nehru Hospital, where I was born. There was hardly time to reflect on it then, jostled by a zillion pilgrims.

Months and months later, I found among my father's papers a yellowed typewritten sheet, addressed to his boss. It was a dry request to be granted leave between 3 September and 5 September 1968. I stared at the dates. It was about me. I was born on 3 September 1968.

How typical his note was. It gave nothing away. Not the joy of his first child, not the terror of having to support his young family and not having the means to do it. My father shouldered his own burdens silently and alone.

To the east of the capital, between the two confluents of the river, for the space of 10 *li* or so, the ground is pleasant and upland. The whole is covered with a fine sand. From old time till now, the kings and noble families, whenever they had occasion to distribute their gifts in charity, ever came to this place, and here gave away their goods; hence it is called *the great charity enclosure*.[2]

On the morning of 24 January 2001, Ija said her prayers early. She did not breakfast. It was one of the most auspicious days, and mid-morning was the most favourable time to bathe. Thirty million people were expected to make it into the water.

Vasudha, Ija and I joined the column of walkers, for all roads in a wide radius had been closed to vehicles, even rickshaws. Vasudha and I walked with Ija between us. The three of us clutched each other tightly. It took us one and a half hours to reach the vast river flanks, seen through a thin mist of dust kicked up by sixty million heels, a fine silvery sand that flew up into our eyes, lining the backs of our throats and nostrils.

'*Arre* people come here for dharma, nobody is going to steal your things,' someone remarked. It was a civilized crowd, because it was a family affair. Men, women, children, the bonds of love and duty and faith, reined in any rowdies. The ties were evident in the lost and separated persons announcements over loudspeakers: 'Pratapgarh zile ke Manju Devi/Vijay/Lalla/, aap ka bhatija/chacha/beta/ma/baap is waiting by the Hanuman temple, by the announcement booth, at Sangam. Please come and collect them.'

As we neared the river, we saw women holding up saris, post *snaan*, to dry in the breeze and billow. They lifted tangled damp hair to squeeze the water out. There were bare-chested men switching to dry dhotis. It was the world's largest public changing room.

Closer to the water, there was a wriggling mass of wet bodies, the beast had shed its clothes—mahogany, bronze, chocolate, ebony, toffee, fat, thin, hairy, skinny, men in briefs or shorts, women in saris or sarongs.

The bank dipped towards the water, sandbags held up the sides and hay strewn on the ground helped keep it all together under the weight and trample of millions. There was the river, and the Sangam where the muddy Ganga met the watery blue Yamuna, whipped up by a wind.

For a moment in the shimmer of the day, the scene was framed. The brouhaha died and in some ethereal silence, far out in the water, was a fleet of boats filled with people—silhouetted, bobbing where the rivers meet. White gulls and egrets fought the wind, and the shapes of bodies, hundreds, thousands, up to their knees and waists, filled the river.

Without quite knowing how it happened, somebody was holding my things, and I had made it into the water fully clothed, the shock of cold and not-cold, welcoming, somehow, this too a living creature.

We held Ija but she stumbled, a helping hand pulled her up, a man with the sacred thread around his chest held her wrist and encouraged her dips—eighteen in all, one for each child and grandchild. Finally, gasping, she waded out. I pushed her from behind, Vasudha pulled at her arms. We dripped and edged through the crowds. My salwar kameez clung wetly. I was beginning to shiver as I clambered out of the river behind Ija, feeling, dare I say it, sanctified.

සං

Vasubandhu, the fifth-century Buddhist philosopher who was Xuanzang's hero, was particularly scathing about the Hindu practice of bathing in sacred rivers to wash away sins.

> Action is thought.[3] Contrary to what the most primitive thinkers, or even the Jains believed, action is not a material substance; sin is not a fluid, or a sickness which one should wash away through ritual baths in sacred rivers or burn up through penitence or fasting. Action is essentially thought, voluntary and conscious, and as a consequence morally qualifiable as good or bad.[4]

And yet, what was it about this particular spot in Allahabad?

Action was thought and morally qualifiable, but where was Vasubandhu now? What trace had he left, while almost 2000 years later, millions of 'primitive thinkers' still tramped to the river to have their sins washed away?

Even 200-odd years after Vasubandhu, in the time of Xuanzang, ordinary people and great rulers alike felt the quiet, magnetic pulse of the riverbank. It was in 'the great charity enclosure' that King Harshavardhana, or Siladitya, Son of Virtue, in a single day distributed the wealth of five years, Xuanzang wrote in awe.

Here, Harsha would adorn the statue of Buddha on the first day and offer it the most expensive jewels. Then he would offer charity to the resident priests, then to the priests who had come from afar, after that, to the men of talent, then to the heretics. Finally, the monk wrote, the king bestowed food and wealth on widows and the bereaved, to orphans and the desolate, to the poor and to the mendicants.

The ancient Buddhists scorned Hindu asceticism too, but amidst a head-shaking bemusement the Chinese monk betrayed a hint of admiration at the tactics the sadhus used at this very same river when he walked its banks:

> The heretics who practise asceticism have raised a high column in the middle of the river; when the sun is about to go down they immediately climb up the pillar; then clinging on to the pillar with one hand and one foot, they wonderfully hold themselves out with one foot and one arm; and so they keep themselves stretched out in the air with their eyes fixed on the sun, and their heads turning with it to the right as it sets. When the evening has darkened, then they come down. There are many dozens of ascetics who practise this rite. They hope by these means to escape from birth and death, and many continue to practise this ordeal through several decades of years.[5]

Twenty-ninth January was Basant Panchami, the beginning of spring. The mela would wrap up soon. The streets still milled with thousands of bathers. That morning, by the river, it was the ascetics' turn to take a dip. I returned to the riverbank to take a look, reluctant to leave the grand spectacle.

From the shadows, between the fencing, came the columns of god-men. Their chariots were pulled by tractors. These men in orange turbans and beards sat surrounded by sycophants with joined hands and rosaries, who held umbrellas over the swamis' heads in the manner of India's ancient rulers. From makeshift wooden towers, foreign cameramen leaned with lenses for the best agency shot. One sadhu half-rose from his throne to wave to the photographers.

Policemen on horses directed the crowd flow. Keep moving, keep moving. The sadhus had caused trouble in the past, in the rush to be in the water first. As the procession of sadhus reached the riverbank, sections broke away from the column to run into the water. The naked nagas with ash-smeared bodies and woolly heads were done quickly. For them, there was nothing to dry off, nothing to change into. They splashed into the river and then ran up the bank, each man's penis dangling from a bed of dark pubic hair. Some men had garlands and tridents. One had pierced his member with a sword.

There was a peculiar, likeable honesty about this sect, for how can you fake grandeur or a hotline to god when your most wrinkly, knobbly parts are open to scrutiny? One ashy naga walked to the Ganga on his hands, his legs bent and spread for balance; he was making good progress.

'They are not wearing any clothes,' a woman behind me remarked helpfully.

The sun deepened, echoed the saffron orange of sadhus' turbans, and now at a height, it poured a coppery light onto the water, setting, it seemed, a narrow strip of the Ganga on fire.

If seventy million people bathe and seventy million fill up plastic jerry cans with the soupy sacred broth to cart home, does the level of a river drop?

chapter twenty-two

Schism in the Sangha

From Allahabad, when the monk turned south-west towards Kausambi, he had to backtrack around sixty kilometres outside Allahabad through a great forest. He said it was infested with herds of savage beasts and wild elephants that attacked travellers and that it was not possible to pass this way unless large numbers of people banded together.

Somebody had, perhaps, warned Xuanzang of the jungle and led him to a group of merchants heading on to Kausambi the very next day. For me, it was an easy day trip. I hired a van and driver from Maharanidin, my grandfather's old chauffeur. After Daddy retired, Maharanidin had started his own car business. He looked much the same as he had when I was a little girl, except for a few more grey hairs. He stood with his hands behind his back, and when he nodded it was still just an incline of his head to one side.

We swerved off to a side road, through the pastel green of wheat fields and the yellow sarson flowers and peas, which in this season were putting forth delicate cream blossoms. There were fields of arhar dal and chana, and mango orchards dense with leaves. The winter sun fell through the trees planted on either side of the road—sisam, babul, chiwil. Soon enough, we passed through harsher landscape. It was wilder, the road wound through ravines. There were no villages here. The driver cleared his throat. He shifted to a lower gear.

Yeh to bahut bara jungle hai.

Can a vanished forest leave a ghost, an imprint in the air, a dimming of the day, which indicates that here, once, stood a dense jungle filled with wild beasts that growled and prowled at night?

At Kausambi, Xuanzang found mostly ruins of the Buddha's story. There were only a few hundred Buddhist monks in the monasteries who, disappointingly, followed the Hinayana school. In thriving contrast, there were around fifty Hindu temples and an enormous number of Hindu worshippers.

King Udayana ruled over Kausambi in the sixth century BC. The city was a hub of the region at the time. Early Buddhist texts often mention the Ghositarama Monastery of Kausambi, built by Ghosita, a leading banker. It was a place for the Buddha and his followers to lodge, a place filled with simsapa trees. It was here, in the ninth rainy season after his enlightenment, that the Buddha, with a handful of simsapa leaves, had warned his disciples not to get entangled in philosophical hair-splitting. The number of leaves in the simsapa forest was much greater than the number of leaves in the Buddha's hand.

'What I see is much greater than what I teach. Why? Because I teach only those things that are truly necessary and helpful in attaining the Way,' he said.[1]

There were some fragments of that story left for Xuanzang to find. He reported to Hui Li:

> Within the city, is an old (or, ruined) palace (i.e. palace precinct), in which is a large Vihara about sixty feet high, in which is a sandalwood figure of Buddha, surmounted by a stone canopy, made by King Udayana.[2]

When he returned to China, Xuanzang carried with him a figure of the Buddha carved out of sandalwood, perhaps to remind him of this very moment in Kausambi. He also wrote that

> Within the city, at the south-east angle of it, is an old habitation, the ruins of which only exist. This is the house of Ghoshira the nobleman. In the middle is a vihara of Buddha, and a stupa containing hair and nail relics. There are also ruins of Tathagata's bathing house.[3]

From the modern village of Kosam, the site of the ancient city lay among the fields nearby. An Ashokan pillar stood at the junction of two very old roads, now crumbled with disuse. The foundations of the houses were left in neat rows. It was a residential area, the archaeologists thought, distinct from the monastic establishments of the royal palace.

Archaeologists, looking at the ruins of the Ghositarama Monastery, as I was now, could tell it had chapels with verandas and that pillars resting on stone bases surrounded a courtyard dominated by a giant stupa. The monastery was destroyed by the Hunas under Tormana.[4]

The only thing left now was a few broken stones in pits in the shadow of a hill. On the horizon, migratory storks flapped south-east with unhurried wing strokes and my mind grappled with the fact that I was standing in an ancient kingdom where the Buddha had once rested and preached. There was the distant thock-thock-thock of a pump pulling water from the Yamuna. The sun had climbed to noon and carried a threat.

Here too, a terrible schism erupted in the monks' community. One monk forgot to clean a wash basin. Another monk accused him of violating a precept of community living. The offender declared himself innocent—it had not been intentional. The argument escalated. Monks took sides. Insults flew like poisoned arrows.

The Buddha asked them to return to the practice, to not become victims of pride and anger. But one of the monks said, 'Master, please do not involve yourself in this matter . . . we are adults and capable of resolving this on our own.'[5]

The Buddha silently walked to the town of Kausambi, begged for his meal and kept walking till he reached the next hamlet.

'Sometimes it is more pleasant to live alone than with many people,'[6] he remarked to his disciple Bhagu whom he met in the town of Balakalonakaragama.

A boy showed me the way through the chana fields, up an incline where the ancient boundary walls of the palace followed the crest of the hills. Enormous ramparts were still extant. The Yamuna River spread out far below, an unfurling satin sheet. To the west there was a half-turret of Udayana's palace.

The boy plucked a few pods of chana and offered me one to taste.

'It's not ripe yet,' he said, biting into his. 'It's not ripe yet. In a few months it'll be ripe.'

He seemed more upset by this than necessary. It was as though the earth, the seasons, the fields had let him down as he offered his visitor the only thing he could think of.

chapter twenty-three

Sarkari Intezam

 Before picking up the monk's route northwards to Nepal, to where the Buddha was born, I decided to stop in Xuanzang's earlier tracks at Ayodhya.

'I really have to leave,' I said to Chandra-di, back in Allahabad. When Vasudha and Ija left, they had deposited me with a widowed relative and her grandson, Kunal. The pair folded me into their little household with much warmth.

Chandra-di fussed and protested and listed innumerable reasons why leaving was an impractical and ridiculous idea.

I sighed with equal regret, stuffed things into my backpack and said goodbye to Kunal. I had grown fond of the bright little boy who introduced me to the more colourful characters of the World Wrestling Federation on Star TV.

The state bus to Faizabad from Allahabad was a pain-filled ride. As always, the seats were narrow and hard, no cushion against the violent bumps of the road. It was only 160 kilometres, but it took six hours, plus another, squashed into a mini bus, for Ayodhya.

The state bus kept stopping to let people on and off, to let trains pass, and for no obvious reasons. I gritted my teeth, took deep breaths to practise endurance.

Still, the mustard fields were blossoming in clouds of yellow lace, the sugar cane was high, and young wheat spread soft and green. I drank in the Uttar Pradesh countryside, these villages made from mud and, always, the milch buffalo with its shiny dark flanks. I let the conversation wash over and around me, and savoured the language of what used to be the kingdom of Avadh.

A long argument over seats was settled peaceably in the end. There was a post mortem, of the mela, of the recent earthquake in Gujarat, of everything.

'They said they could predict the earthquake. All these people are now saying they knew it was going to happen; well, why didn't they say so earlier?'

'How clean things were at the Kumbh. *Sarkari intezam.* If a jamadar didn't come and clean the toilets every two hours he was dragged by the ear to his job. How well-organized it was.' *Sarkari intezam.* Yes, the government had done quite a thorough job of the arrangements.

'The prices in Bihar are much cheaper. If it's four annas here, it's three annas there.'

'*Bus khul gai.*' The bus has opened. It was a peculiar expression for the bus that had started off.

'We're crossing the *darya*,' somebody commented. A flash of Central Asia.

Uttar Pradesh was going bankrupt. It was a state gently rotting from the inside, its skin flaking off before it finally collapsed on itself. In Ayodhya, there were piles of garbage in alleys. Buildings crumbled in slow motion; there was dust everywhere, like on an abandoned person who no longer bathes but skulks and scowls, gets filthier by the day and eventually goes mad.

According to Xuanzang, there was an old monastery where Vasubandhu had composed his brilliant treatises. Through Vasubandhu, I encountered the Sautantrika, the Sarvastivadin and other schools of Buddhist thought. Almost from the beginning, Buddhists were the world's best thinkers and therefore the world's best arguers. They dissected, they debated, they mulled, and they expanded the Buddha's original teachings.

Each generation added a layer of interpretation so that by the time Vasubandhu grew up, almost 1000 years after the Buddha, the time was ripe for a work that clarified all the interpretations of the Buddhist dharma.

'Visible matter is colour and shape. Colour is fourfold: blue, red, yellow and white; other colours proceed from out of these four colours.

Shape is eightfold; long, short, square, round, high, low, even, uneven,'[1] explained the methodical Vasubandhu.

Some say that in the endless arguments of Buddhist sects, Vasubandhu refused debate. He folded his hands, turned away and declared, 'I am now already old. You may do as you please.'[2]

Other legends say that in the depth of the Indian nights by the river at Ayodhya, the Peshawar-born Vasubandhu was converted to Mahayana Buddhism by his brother Asangha. Vasubandhu sliced off his own tongue to punish it for not speaking the Mahayana truth earlier.

The Chinese monk also noted that it was about five or six *li* south-west of here that the great philosopher Asangha spirited himself to heaven and asked Maitreya, a future incarnation of the Buddha, his questions on existence and consciousness. The next day, Asangha descended and preached the Law.

Maitreya was useful to the early Mahayanists, fumbling for an unbroken oral link to the Buddha like the one the Hinayanists claimed. The answer they found was simple. There *were* valid, holy writings, the Mahayanists said. The books were inspired—or dictated—by Maitreya, awaiting his time on earth. It simply required great Mahayanist philosophers to make numerous trips to heaven for consultations with him.

As for the problem of consciousness which so preoccupied Xuanzang, the Buddha had touched on it very early on, admitting that it was a difficult concept. He explained it to his faithful, handsome disciple Ananda once, following a particularly difficult lecture given in the Bhesakala Park in the hamlet of Sumsumaragiri.

He held up a clay bowl filled with water, then emptied it. But it was not exactly waterless, the teacher said.

'Ananda, among the interwoven elements that have given rise to the bowl, do you see water?'

'Yes, Lord. Without water, the potter would not have been able to mix the clay he used to fashion the bowl,' Ananda replied.

The Buddha's point had become clear. Ananda's words tumbled forth, like a man who has found out he can swim.

'I see the air. Without air, the fire could not have burned and the potter could not have lived. I see the potter and his skilful hands. I see his consciousness. I see the kiln and the wood stacked in the kiln. I see the trees the wood came from. I see the rain, sun and earth which enabled the trees to grow. Lord, I can see thousands of interpenetrating elements which gave rise to this bowl.'[3]

'Without this, that is not. The basic meaning of emptiness (sunyata) is "this is because that is".'

The universe is a mental construct.

One can only surmise that the revolutionary philosophy stated by the Buddha begged questions that proved too irresistible for the Indian mind with its affinity for knotty metaphysics: If there was no self, then how did karma transmigrate?

Meanwhile, any Buddhist remains in the city of Ayodhya had long vanished. There was no sign of the great Buddhist monastery with its 200-foot high central stupa by the river built by King Ashoka to commemorate the spot where the Buddha once preached for three months.

In present-day Ayodhya, the people were preoccupied with the birthplace of the Hindu god Ram and how the Babari Masjid, or mosque of Babur, had allegedly been built on top of it. It fuelled anger among the Hindus to think that foreign Muslim rulers, mere Central Asians, had thus insulted a Hindu god. He was a mythological legend but real enough, for how else would he have a specific birthplace?

What birthplace, what mosque? others argued.

The great Buddhist debates on the nature of consciousness had dispersed. Ayodhya's grand decrepitude was the site of a smug, absurd fight. Indians choose the most extraordinary battles and I, the visitor, had utterly failed to understand.

At night in Ayodhya, over loudspeakers, the Muslim azan competed with Hindu bhajans, the spring moon hung like a curved dagger and stars dotted the night. Monkeys crawled all over the dry grass around the tourist bungalow. The railway station was just metres away. Already I disliked the town.

I brushed up my fourth-grade Hindi. The receptionist at the government guest house had placed me in a second as foreign-returned. But I had him pegged too, as a man from South India and therefore not of these parts either.

'Madam, have you lived abroad? Why is your Hindi so odd?'
You should talk, I thought.

My Hindi *was* still rusty, I put my finger under words still, spelled them out, learned how the vernacular press spoke a different pulse.

Nothing was printed in English here, in the heart of the country. I turned to local Hindi papers for distraction. In the *Dainik Jagaran* of 31 January 2001, I deciphered the words of our prime minister. '*Atal ne yeh bhi kaha: "Maine dharamsansad ka faisla note kar liya hai. Bus, isse zyada iss pur kuchh nahin boloonga. Isse lekar mujhe aur mat puchhieh."* ' I said it out loud. I liked how it sounded. Balanced, firm, musical, although the man sounded weary and tired of words.

I spread open the newspaper with a gecko for company. *Chhipkali.* This word too I remembered from my childhood. And the electric wires, and shreds of caught kites threaded and shredded, flapping against lilac skies with the call of the azan—*Allah ho Akbar*—this too was somewhere in my blood.

Soon, I gave up on Buddhist remains to take in the morning rituals of Ayodhya. To my delight, at their front doors, the women of Ayodhya hung large wire cages containing their pet green parrots. The birds hopped and preened with their bright beaks. Even caged birds get to eat some sun. It pulled out of some hole an ancient memory, a story I'd read in Hindi as a child, a story of two such green parrots, Mithoo and Mithee. I could not recall their fate. But remembering Mithoo and Mithee felt like a small brick installed in a house of the past. Later, in Banaras, I saw paintings of doorways with wire cages on either side and I knew the origins.

I wandered into the nawab's palace in Ayodhya, with its double-fish emblem. It reminded me of Lucknow, a part of Avadh. 'An Avadhi princess married Korean royalty,' said Aparna Misra, descended from royalty—it showed in her delicate hands, her fairish skin, freckled nose and thick lashes. We sat in the sunny garden of the vast frayed palace. In a maidan at the back, a cow grazed and a flock of ducks quacked and preened in a dry fountain.

A princess of Ayodhya had sailed to Kimhae in South Korea some 2000 years ago and married Prince Kim Su Ro to found a dynasty. Kimhae, the city named after the princess, and Ayodhya were becoming sister cities, renewing their ties.

'She had a dream in which her father told her to get on a ship and leave. She ended up in Korea, and married the prince Su Ro. A Korean delegation came last year to tell us this.'

Aparna and I nibbled on jalebis and cakes. She fetched her Ph.D thesis and opened up the page. 'See, we are descended from these eighteen Brahmins, Scythian sun-worshippers called Mag. They came flying on a garuda and one of them was called Garg. You see, Krishna cursed his own son Samb with leprosy and then brought these Brahmins to cure him.'

She smiled at me and asked if I was married. I replied, half-distracted, my heart leaping at the Scythian references. There were all these links we had with Central Asia. Even the Buddhist thinkers Asangha and Vasubandhu were from Peshawar.

'No? I'm not married either.'

I focussed on unmarried Aparna. Without saying a word, a world of understanding and sympathy cracked open between us, that of unmarried Indian women. The burden, in this country, of not having a man by our side. We were freaks.

Aparna showed me through the rooms of the rajas. Stuffed tigers and leopards, a bear—the hunting had been rich, clearly. There were gifts from the Koreans, old photographs, a certificate signed by the viceroy and the Governor General of India on 16 February 1887 in Calcutta. It hung framed on a wall, faint brown ink.

'Raja Pertab Narain Singh of Merdaura, Fyzabad, District Oudh. Hereby confer upon you the title of Maharaja as personal distinction.'

It was a snatched glimpse of British machinations, lobbying for loyalty, rewards in power games. I yearned to know more of this other, more recently bygone world, but I would have to save it for another time. We wished each other well and bid warm goodbyes.

The noon sun was fiercer as I headed to what used to be the Babari Masjid. Sometimes, the past I was seeking vanished and forced me into the present. I had to look at it in the eye, this ugliness. Metal pipes welded to vertical bars made a crude caged corridor and forced a single file. Outside, armed guards lounged with their guns. Watchtowers stood at the corners of the field, with floodlights at their base.

This spot, here in this humiliating hutch, was India at her worst—

an overpopulated, beggarly, threadbare state, a town forsaken by gods, preoccupied with fundamentalist sloganeering, as unschooled children played naked by open drains full of human waste.

Where was religion in all this? December 1992 stayed imprinted on the nation as cameras beamed pictures of maddened Hindus climbing up the mosque and tearing it down until there was just a mound of grass left.

The Ayodhya Tulsi Smarak Bhavan was a library where they kindly let me wander around the bookshelves. Looking for Buddhist sites, I was dismayed and disturbed by Ayodhya. I flipped through a booklet written by a certain Ajay Nath. Nath was a Hindu, passionate, upset by all this. He wrote:

> We have three generations' friendship with the Muslims. My grandmother used to tell interesting tales of my grandfather's Muslim friends . . . I remember the pre-partition days of Agra when the Hindus and Muslims lived together in the same *mohalla*s, *katra*s, *kucha*s, *tola*s and *gali*s with perfect amity and harmony . . . Myself and my bosom friend Ayaz were class-fellows in BA in 1952–54 at St John's College, Agra. We have stood together for the last four decades through all thicks and thins and I have no hesitation in accepting that his friendship has been one of my most precious possessions.[4]

Mr Gaud at the library told me in his office (he took off his glasses), 'They are building the Ram temple at another site. It's almost ready, the politicians will declare it a done deal, the courts will pass it, and it will be built.'

His staff had already made discreet inquiries about my marital status.

'You're not married? How interesting. Neither is our sir.'

'Where are all the Muslims? What happened to the mosques?' I asked my main source of information, the rickshaw-wala. He crossed the road and took me straight to a shop where Ahmed Mian sat. Ahmed Mian had one tooth and thick glasses. But his mind gleamed. I unlaced my shoes and stepped up into his shop to sit cross-legged.

'They won't let Muslims build anything here,' he said. 'They pull out the *mians* from mosques and build a temple. They behead cows and leave them in front of temples and say the *mian-log* did it. They've opened our graves. They've renamed all the ghats. It used to be Rahman Ghat, Rahim Ghat, Akbari Ghat, Babari Ghat. This is Nowgazi Muhallah, even in the government records, but they want to call it Shastri Nagar. All the Muslims are leaving this town and moving elsewhere. They don't want us here. They want to wipe out Muslims and masjids. *Mita dena chahte hain*. They want to make a Hindu raj.'

'When Babur came, it was a jungle, there was not a single temple. There will be more *jhagda*,' he predicted. '*In logon ki badmashi*. I'm fighting eleven *mukadme*. But what to do. I cannot take up cudgels. Weak men knock on government doors. *Ayodhya mein mussalman bhuke mar rahen hain*. And when we go to the Arabs, they say you are Hindustani, go back, you're not real Muslims. We'd like a place where we can just be.'

I listened, it was all I could do.

The rickshaw-wala huffed up a back alley of Ayodhya, diving into a narrow lane off the ghats where a few men bathed in the river. He dismounted and pulled the rickshaw.

'See, only local rickshaw drivers know where these places are. Otherwise, the Hindu newcomers only know where the temples are. I was born here, and there has always been peace between Hindus and Muslims.'

'Mosques,' he huffed, 'yes there are mosques, it will take you all day to see the mosques in Ayodhya.'

And up a short hill sat the shrine of Hazrat Saiyad Shah Mohammad Ibrahim, a Sufi saint from Tashkent (Uzbekistan!), visited by both Hindus and Muslims.

'He listens to all,' the keeper there said. 'Mostly to women who want children.' Wishes to be fulfilled were held in a knot tied to the fenced-off grave. Scarf, rope, thread, ribbon, anonymous, secret desires told to a mystic from Uzbekistan.

Opposite the shrine rose a mosque; and in the southern garden a bel tree hung with ripe fruit. In a clear blue sky, four kites hung motionless by their strings. I looked over my shoulder at the imam who sat facing Mecca, with his white cap on in the dusk, at this solitary man in a broken-down mosque.

Was it idealizing a past to think of a time when Sufi mystics catered to both Hindu and Muslim needs, when Hindus and Muslims rubbed shoulders in peace, when their cultures intertwined so much, it hardly mattered which was which? The Indian government, not much better than the British before it, was still dividing, still ruling. All this was layered atop a Buddhist history, particularly in Uttar Pradesh.

I was ready to hit the road again, head still further north in Uttar Pradesh, towards the Nepal border and the Buddha's birthplace.

chapter twenty-four

Wrong Kind of Love

From Ayodhya, the Chinese monk headed south to Allahabad on the river, along with about eighty other travellers. Suddenly, ten pirate boats swung to the middle of the river, powered by quick oar strokes. They had been hiding amidst the dense foliage on either side of the river, unseen by anybody. Screaming in panic and fear, passengers on the ferry began to jump into the water. The pirates seized the boat with the Chinese pilgrim and the remaining passengers still on it, and towed it towards the bank.

'Strip,' they ordered the men. There was a hunt for jewels and precious stones. But that was not all. The pirates were worshippers of Durga, a goddess thirsty for the blood of a good-looking man. The pirates circled the handsome Chinese priest, smiling nastily. Xuanzang mumbled that he had come a long distance to pay reverence to the Buddha and to study the sacred books. He had yet to complete his task, he said. It was not the first time the monk had faced brigands, and he refused to lose his head.

'. . . if you, my noble benefactors (danapatis) kill this body of mine, I fear it will bring you misfortune (instead of good fortune),'[1] Hui Li quoted him in the biography.

The remaining passengers set up a clamour. 'Spare the visiting priest. Take us instead.'

The chief pirate set his jaw. 'Make an altar. Draw your knives. Tie him up. Kill him,' he snarled.

The unruly gang crowded around the Chinese monk. Xuanzang pleaded, but without fear. It was best not to show fear to thugs.

'Please give me some time,' he said. 'Let me with a joyous mind take my departure.'

And then, closing his eyes, for he was prepared to die, the monk prayed to be reborn in the Tushita Heaven, in the presence of the Maitreya Buddha so that he could, like Asangha, receive the *Yogacarabhumi Shastra* and then be reborn to instruct and convert these very murderers. He prayed. He focussed his mind. It was a rapture. He was floating high above Mount Sumeru, climbing through heavens, surrounded by the gods . . .

Suddenly, a black tempest smashed from the four corners of the sky. Sand veiled the scene and the river rose with a roar. The boats bobbed wild. The thieves dropped to their knees, their voices cracking with fear.

'Who is this man? Repent! Confess!'

A pirate's hand brushed the praying monk by accident, and he shook himself to reality.

'What, is it already time to die?'

But the terror-struck dacoits were prostrate, contrite. And, according to Hui Li, there and then the bandits took the Buddhist vows of lay believers.

After this, the monk continued uneventfully on to Allahabad and then to Kausambi, then swung north to Sravasti, once again finding only ruins to illustrate the old drama of the Buddha's life. There must have been at least a twinge of disappointment when the monk had to write:

The kingdom of Sravasti (Shi-lo-fu-shi-ti) is about 6000 *li* in circuit. The chief town is desert and ruined. There is no record as to its exact limits (area). The ruins of the walls encompassing the royal precincts give a circuit of about 20 *li*. Though mostly in ruins, still there are a few inhabitants . . .[2]

৯০

I took a bus to Balrampur, from where it was an easy hop to Sravasti. I felt I was in a trance, I drifted along with ease and took things in. Perhaps it was the weather, a sort of enchanted spring, where the sun was slow and cool and the light fell gold and the wheat fields turned a deeper pastel green. Maybe it was being in this ancient kingdom of Kosal, where the Buddha walked. The sugar cane had ripened and was lush; much of it had already been harvested here in the north.

Sravasti was the last capital of the kingdom of Kosal. It was a prosperous and sprawling realm, with the Ganga on its southern border and the Himalaya to the north. The city stood on an ancient highway that connected the key hubs of Buddhist India: Rajagriha in the east, Taxila to the north-west, Pratisthana to the south. The Buddha spent around twenty-five rainy seasons here, teaching his philosophy.

Bumping into the Buddha preaching in eastern India, the newly converted householder Anathapindika had taken to the Dhamma vision like a clean cloth without black specks that easily soaks up dye, the *Vinaya Pitaka* tells us. Inspired, aflame with new insight, he begged the Buddha to grace his hometown Sravasti with his presence and preach to the people there. Straightaway, he himself set out for Sravasti and searched for a resting place for the Lord. Perhaps he stroked his chin as he strolled, wondering, 'Now, where could the Lord stay that would be neither too far from a village nor too near, suitable for coming and going, accessible to people whenever they want, not crowded by day, having little noise at night, little sound, without folks' breath, secluded from people, fitting for meditation?'[3]

Prince Jeta's pleasure grove fit the bill exactly, but Anathapindika had first to spread 100,000 gold coins over the grounds till Prince Jeta saw that this was no ordinary businessman with an ordinary purpose and relented.

Anathapindika ordered the building of dwellings, attendance halls, privies, places for pacing up and down, wells, lotus ponds and sheds, all for the use of the Buddha and the shaven monks of his sangha. No wonder the Buddha returned here again and again, to this pleasant spot at the ankles of the mountains, when the rains made it too hard to travel.

The Chinese monk wandered the ruins of the king's palace, as the stories rose in his mind's eye. This was where a Brahmachari heretic had murdered a woman and accused the Buddha of the crime.

To the east of the ruined king's palace rose a stupa to mark the spot of a grand preaching hall that King Prasenajita had built for the

Buddha's use. The monarch too had become a disciple of the Buddha, but first, the ruler had scorned the teacher's youth. The Buddha was unruffled.

'A prince may be young but he possesses the characteristics and destiny of a king. A small poisonous snake can kill a grown man in an instant. One spark of fire can cause an entire forest or a large city to burn to ash. And a young monk can attain total enlightenment!'[4] he said.

Here was the spot where the Buddha argued with the heretics. Fearing the Buddha's growing popularity and the threat to their own livelihood, the ascetics had challenged the Buddha, calling upon King Prasenajita to act as mediator. To silence them, legend has it, the Buddha performed the famous twin miracle, rising into the air and shooting water streams and flames from his body.

It was here too that the Buddha had told the intrigued king about love. 'Life has a great need for the presence of love, but not the sort of love that is based on lust, passion, attachment, discrimination, and prejudice. Majesty, there is another kind of love, sorely needed, which consists of loving kindness and compassion . . .'[5]

စာ

The bus to Balrampur slowed and honked impatiently behind ox carts laden with *ganna* inching north to the refinery. Little boys ran behind the carts and snatched loose sticks to peel and chew. There was a depth to the air here, a sort of quiet, as though, nearly 2500 years later, the wind still vibrated with what had happened. Or perhaps it was a subtle shift in the nature of a place as I moved north, nearer the Himalaya again; it was barely fifty kilometres to the Nepal border and I could see the first bumps of the Dundwa range. There had been a thousand kindnesses from anonymous people who stepped out of the crowds to check on me.

'Did you get your change?'
'The bus to Balrampur is here.'
'Sit here.'
'It's this way.'
'Keep an eye on your bag.'

'Here's your ticket.'

Everybody noticed my every move. They were discreet, yet everybody seemed to know, somehow, without appearing to look. Small-town ways of seeing. The sotto voce comments told me many thought I was from Pakistan. Why else would I look more or less subcontinental and yet so foreign and have a reason to be here? The only reason they could think of was to visit relatives from across the border.

But mine was another journey.

To my relief, the government tourist bungalow at Balrampur offered hot water, and a clean room for a few hundred rupees. A waiter brought up a delicious omelette, and tea. I slept soundly under the blankets, and the next morning the staff showed me where jeeps left for Sravasti.

As we neared Sravasti, flying by in quick succession were temples and monasteries put up by the Japanese, Thais, Koreans, Sri Lankans and, further back, the Burmese. If Xuanzang found the place in ruins, there was even less left now, nearly 1400 years later. There were the bases of stupas, knee-high constructions which indicated the lines of a room, monastic dwellings.

The main stupa, where the Buddha spent two dozen rainy seasons meditating, sat at the south of the gardens planted with gulmohar, bel, peepul and mango trees. It was still a pleasant garden, even though winter had dried up a small waterway. How lush it must be when whipped and washed by the monsoons. The rains would be nearly spent by the time they reached here, where the Himalaya refused them passage further north.

For some reason I found myself thinking of M. and the boundaries of love. I had not thought of him in a long time. Perhaps it was the rarefied mountain air which brought sudden moments of clarity, to look back and think of how I died a kind of death when it ended, when we parted.

I thought of how one can live and yet not live, year after year. I saw him a few times after that, but it was too late, we looked at each other across a gulf. He cried one time and said he had squandered things and that I was hard-hearted.

I looked at him and was afraid of the magnitude of what we had lost. That made me a brisk, distant woman. But I had run out of hiding places this spring, in this very old city at the foot of a mountain range. Like the Buddha said, I had been full of attachment, not compassion.

The sun was higher, hotter. It oozed into bones, a laze-inducing heat. At a small stupa, two elderly malis stretched out on the lawns, half in the shade and half out, between a bottlebrush and lagerstroemia. One raised his head on an elbow, his handlebar moustache grey. Two men, eating the sun, lying on the grounds of a history over 2500 years old.

'When Buddh-bhagwan went out to preach, his disciples wanted something of him here, so this tree was planted,' one of the malis proclaimed. He had risen from the lawn and edged over to inspect the foreign-looking stranger. 'It was grown from a cutting of the main nirvana peepul. We found huge pots of bones and ashes.'

The bricks of the main stupa's floors were wavy, as though the architect had hiccupped and the pencil slipped, but this was merely a sign of great age in buildings, of the earth's falling and rising again. And to the east stood a well that the Buddha had apparently drunk from.

৯

The stupas, the gardens, the stories. Xuanzang was delighted. He wrote, with no trace of scepticism:

A mysterious sense of awe surrounds the precincts of the place; many miracles are manifested also. Sometimes heavenly music is heard, at other times divine odours perceived . . .[6]

He had to tear himself away from Sravasti to go to Kapilavastu, the Buddha's hometown. He went south-east, a distance of about 500 *li*, he said. Once again, he found nothing but ruins.

There are some ten desert cities in this country, wholly desolate and ruined. The capital is overthrown and in ruins. Its circuit cannot be accurately measured. The royal precincts within the city measure some 14 or 15 *li* round. They were all built of brick. The foundation walls are still strong and high. It has long been deserted. The peopled villages are few and waste.[7]

Still, at Kapilavastu, Xuanzang felt his excitement build. This was it, this was the heart of the matter, what he had come to see. Like a blind man feeling the face of a beloved grown child after a parting of many years, letting his fingertips read each feature to match or correct the image in his heart.

These were abandoned ruins, collapsed bricks and piles of rubble. But this was where the young Siddhartha grew up, where he came to see he had to leave all this and find a new way. The Chinese monk's lips moved, telling himself the story. He trailed a hand over the stones, squatted to turn a brick over, as though somewhere in the silent landscape there were clues to his Master. Xuanzang sat under a tree and surveyed the debris. He gazed and gazed, as though the force of his longing could revive a scene from the past. But nothing happened. There was just the screech of parrots flying home in indigo skies.

He walked around the desolate ruins and named each stupa. Here, the Bodhisattva descended (spiritually, he was careful to add) into his mother's womb. Here is where Asita the rishi foretold the great life of the young prince, much to King Suddhodana's despair. The king wanted an heir to his kingdom and was determined to keep his precious son.

The prince married, his wife gave birth to a boy, Rahula. Siddhartha lived three sheltered decades. One day, heading to the pleasure grounds, he left Kapilavastu by the east gate on a chariot with his groom and saw, to his horror, a toothless man bent with age, with sparse, grey hair. Another time, leaving by the south gate of the city, the increasingly agitated prince sighted a hideously diseased man, feverish, covered with his own filth and panting for breath. It disturbed him. The third time, exiting from Kapilavastu's western gate, Siddhartha came across a funeral procession, the kind that are still seen on Indian roads, with a corpse covered in a shroud on a makeshift wooden raft carried by male relatives to a pyre usually by a ghat on a river. During a fourth outing from Kapilavastu, the devastated prince found a mendicant with his eyes to the ground, his whole bearing filled with peace, and here was foreshadowing for the way ahead.[8]

It was getting too dark for Xuanzang to see. Amidst the desolate ruins of Kapilavastu, there was still a monastery with monks studying texts of the old Hinayana school. Perhaps they offered the visiting monk shelter. Perhaps he tossed and turned in the dark, unable to sleep, filled with visions of the Buddha's story.

છ

What does one do when the lights go out in the middle of a village in northern Uttar Pradesh?

There was a power failure. It was dark in the Sakya kingdom. Now it was a Muslim village, with pigeons and dovecotes, the smell of kerosene, and my own thoughts.

Nobody knew I was here. In the villages near Kapilavastu, they bred doves and pigeons. Every other dwelling carried a baked-mud dovecote, flocks of the birds circled and came flapping back.

'They make good eating,' the caretaker informed me. 'There are ducks here too, they're good to eat.' He pronounced it *batakh*, with a back-of-the-throat sound at the 'kh'.

The government had bought up the land around to build an art gallery, but I had failed to spot any signs of busy construction. Here too, bubbled a first-rate controversy. We spent our lives fighting over history. Amazing, for a nation so apparently indifferent to it.

The stories still lived, but the remains of Buddhist cities lay dusty and forgotten, buried under creeping jungle. British civil servants like Cunningham, armed with Xuanzang's records, began to uncover the sites. After independence, Indian archaeologists continued the work. In Delhi, I had gone to see the man behind this excavation.

K.M. Srivastava, a retired government servant, was quiet, diminutive, in his starched white pyjamas and kurta and a sleeveless olive wool jacket. His mouth had softened with lack of teeth and he was seventy-four years old when I saw him. He had a careful manner but there was still a flash of the old excitement and stubbornness.

'When I was clearing the periphery of a stupa, I came across a *pradakshinapath*. So I said, there must be earlier relics and they must be the original relics received by the Sakyas, when the Buddha's body was cremated and his relics were divided into eight.'

Srivastava found relic caskets containing charred bones, and deduced that since the Sakyas of Kapilavastu received one share, these were the relics and this must be the location of Kapilavastu. In the monastery, the team found thirty-eight seals with inscriptions and that clinched it.

'*Om devaputra vihare, Kapilavastu, bhikku sangasa*,' Srivastava said it slowly, for my benefit. '"Om devaputra" is the Kushan king who patronized Buddhism. He just enlarged that monastery. "Vihare" is monastery, "Kapilavastu"—of Kapil. They are well-burnt clay seals, in the local dialect of Pali.' He waved his hands. 'Hmmm. Kapilavastu. You can very well view the Himalayan peaks when the sun rises. How can I describe how I felt?'

The ASI had published his book of findings, but they changed the title to avoid embarrassment. They would not call it *The Discovery of Kapilavastu*, but limited it to *Excavations at Piprahwa and Ganwaria*.

The Nepalese, Dr Srivastava felt, were keen on United Nations support to develop these sites of global importance. If Kapilavastu lay in Nepal, there would be tourists, shops, trade, income for the surrounding villages.

He shook his head. 'Tilaurakot will have to wait for any claims to Kapilavastu until the discovery of Buddha's relics and seals.'

Bah, the Nepalese had scoffed. Any monk could have carried the seals to that site. It was hardly conclusive evidence. Meanwhile, the relics were now on display in the Indian Museum at Kolkata on a cushion of cotton wool in a glass dish under a glass case in a wooden copy of the casket—one piece of the relic was shaped a little like a lozenge. It was two bits of bone stuck together, barely one square centimetre. The other piece of the Buddha's remains was a more irregular shape.

Casket model in wood, original in steatite, displayed relics of the Lord inside the casket original found at Piprahwa, Kapilavastu, Sakya Clan.

I was looking at what archaeologists thought were the physical remains of the Buddha himself. There was a neon light. Funny, I had thought there would be more drama.

ॐ

The Uttar Pradesh tourist bungalow at Kapilavastu was hideous. It stood in the middle of a desolate field. Like the rest of the state, the place was weeping for a sweeping, a dusting and a shine. The dustbin in the room was still full of rubbish from the previous tenant, the paint was flaking off. There were cobwebs in the window sill, grass grew between the cobblestones. The curtains were thick with dirt and hung askew. Cows wandered the courtyard. The bathroom was lined with grime. There was no bread because the tourists who came brought their own noodles. They tossed the styrofoam containers with Korean or Japanese letters into the bin, for visitors from Buddhist countries were the only ones who came, shuttled through in tourist coaches. Worst of all, the tea in Kapilavastu's guest house was weak and bland. The cook was genial and friendly, but he couldn't quite compensate.

A powerful kingdom sunk this low. It was sad indeed.

To the north-east stood a mosque, across the road there were a few ruins of the Sakya kingdom. The Muslim man who helped excavate the site walked me around the ruins. The river was too far to see. There were two excavated mounds, the thin bricks I had come to recognize, the low walls and demarcated rooms, two dozen or so at Piprahwa, with a gateway on its eastern side.

Further to the north-east sat the Ganwaria mound and in-between lay a square depression—ghosts of other buildings, monasteries perhaps—and at least three other phantom constructions. I picked my way through bricks sticking up unevenly from the ground, where the structures had crumbled on themselves, who knows when or how.

If this was indeed the kingdom where the Buddha grew up, it was also the place he left in secret. His father, King Suddhodana, had placed hundreds of guards at each gate. The hinges of the enormous palace gates creaked terribly. The hooves of the horse, Kanthaka, would pound the ground. How could Siddhartha leave without raising a din?

Luckily, the legend says, the gods puts all the inhabitants of Kapilavastu into a deep sleep. Jinns held Kanthaka's hooves in their hands to dampen the noise, and the palace doors swung open silently.[9]

The city's descendents—and King Ashoka—had built temples and stupas commemorating each of these events, so that Xuanzang, visiting 1000 years later, wrote pensively:

> To the south-east angle of the city is a vihara in which is the figure of the royal prince riding a white and high-prancing horse; this was the place where he left the city . . .[10]

It was to Kapilavastu that the Buddha returned years later at the request of his father. He spent the night at the Nigrodha Park outside Kapilavastu and entered the city to beg the next morning, with his group of 300 silent monks, all in saffron robes with shaven heads. His father hurried to the site, delighted and dismayed all at the same time. A Kashmiri poet tells it thus:

> The father speaks: 'You who spent delightful nights in beds glistening with the high-lights of silks, on the terrace of a crystal palace, how can you now sleep on the bare forest ground with the rough half-grazed grass stubs left by the deer's tooth?'[11]

The Buddha's family wept with happiness to see him again. His son, Rahula, bounded up to greet him, so did his wife, Yashodhara, and his adoptive mother. King Ashoka had built a stupa marking the meeting, Xuanzang said. Also to the south-east, the Chinese monk noted a stupa containing relics of the Buddha, relics distributed amongst kings after he died and was cremated. In front of the stupa stood a stone pillar, thirty feet high, topped by the distinctively carved lion of King Ashoka.

Perhaps these were the very relics dug up by Dr Srivastava. None of the grandeur was left, the landscape was low and flat and hazy. A crowd of kids formed quickly, trotting behind us. They had names like Zohra and Aslam. One little boy shouted out in a high piping voice, jumping up and down.

'My name is Saddam Hussein and this boy is Dawood Ibrahim.'

I laughed out loud.

chapter twenty-five

Labour Pains

 From Kapilavastu, the monk turned towards Lumbini, where the Buddha was born. It was just a stone's throw from the outskirts of Kapilavastu. He wrote:

> To the north-east of the arrow-well about 80 or 90 *li*, we come to the Lumbini (Lavani) garden. Here is the bathing tank of the Sakyas, the water of which is bright and clear as a mirror, and the surface covered with a mixture of flowers.
>
> To the north of this 24 or 25 paces there is an Asoka-flower tree, which is now decayed; this is the place where Bodhisattva was born on the eighth day of the second half of the month called Vaisakha, which corresponds with us to the eighth day of the third month.[1]

෨෩

It was a perfectly straight road through the terai's wide open flatness and I crossed Asia's most lackadaisical border into Nepal. I was crammed into a jeep with eighteen adults and six children, thinly built women with their heads covered, going for medicines, or errands, in their glass bangles, gold nose rings, saris.

The car stank, the rank odours of insufficiency.

At Nepalese immigration, a blue-clad officer peeked into the jeep and wandered off when I said I was Indian. The main road continued through the terai, mosquito-infested, with its own dry, sickly feel about it.

I switched to a bus, which broke down shortly thereafter so that passengers had to file out and find alternative transport. I heaved my backpack onto my shoulders and walked in the now burning sun to the main road where other jeeps were making the short run to Lumbini.

Queen Maya had not gone very far from Kapilavastu when her baby was born. She stepped out of her palanquin, on her way to her mother's home to give birth. She was pregnant for ten full months, poor woman. The Lumbini grove at the time was wooded with sal trees in full bloom. Perhaps her back ached. She felt the labour pains and gasped, reaching up to a tree for support. That pose became fixed and immortalized in countless statues across the subcontinent.

Lumbini today sits in shabby grounds, built up with monasteries funded by Buddhist countries. Sitting on a rickshaw, balancing my backpack beside me, I made the rounds of the bewildering array and wondered what to do about lodgings.

I saw a man painting a sign on a yellow board. It had enough information on it to tell me that it was a Burmese monastery and that I could do a course on vipassana. It looked pleasant enough. It was not a bad idea, I thought, to give vipassana a shot.

Contemplating the body, the mind, emotion, was the way, the Buddha said, to overcome sorrow and grief, to conquer suffering, to control coveting and dejection in the world. Yes, it was certainly worth trying.

The Burmese nuns welcomed me and told me that the only rules were that I could not talk and that I could give a donation if I felt like it. 'Vipassana meditators must maintain a strict silence and keep writing, reading, socializing to a minimum,' a notice said sternly.

I found a bed in the women's dormitory, curious about meditation. It would be my first attempt. There was a little time to look around Lumbini before the sessions began.

At Runmindei, or Lumbini, King Ashoka had erected a pillar, parts of which were still there, and inscribed it. Xuanzang had described it as a great stone pillar on the top of which was a horse. The inscription read: *King Piyadasi (Ashoka). The beloved of devas, in the twentieth reign of the coronation, himself made a royal visit. Buddha Sakyamuni having been born here a stone railing was built and a stone pillar erected the bhagvan having been born here, Lummini was tax reduced and entitled to the eighth part only.*

For a long time Lumbini had existed only in the stories, the site itself forgotten and covered in jungle. There were other tales of a filthy sadhu who worshipped the Ashokan pillar, who perhaps made animal noises and growled and loped around shouting when the men with their notebooks finally arrived. He would not let the archaeologists through, but finally he died and in 1899 P.C. Mukherjee, an archaeologist, excavated in the area.[2]

To the east of the pillar was the spot where the Buddha was born, covered at the moment by gold cloths, roped off from the public and sheltered by a vast corrugated roof patched together and welded, a makeshift edifice while the Japanese Buddhist Federation and UNESCO tug-of-warred over a temple design. It was festooned with Tibetan prayer flags, as pilgrims had hung strings of them in the Buddhist colours—blue, yellow, red, white, orange. It was good to see the Tibetans again, after Dharamsala.

By the pillar spread the sacred pond where Queen Maya bathed before giving birth. The square tank of water had stone steps leading into it; the water was stagnant and small bits of debris floated in it. Three Tibetan boy-monks poked round in a corner of the pool. Others played cricket outside the temple enclosure with wickets of piled stones, their bare brown shoulders taut, robes flying out, swirling as the bat swung skywards.

Legend says the gods were standing by to receive the Buddha, Hindu gods, as it happened—Indra, Brahma. Lotuses blossomed under the infant's feet as he walked, fully upright, according to the legend describing his birth. The Jataka Nidanakatha told it with flair. He was born standing, and as soon as he was born, he looked east, south, west, up, down, in all ten directions. He looked north and took seven steps and with every step he walked, one lotus flower appeared on the ground. He said in a loud, fearsome voice,

Foremost am I in the world.
Seniormost am I in the world
Best am I in the world
This is my last birth
No more am I to be born.

The earth quaked, the air ceased to blow, birds hid in their nests, trees bore fruit, flowers bloomed. Peace and silence reigned all over.[3]

The Maya Devi Temple was right by the tank. The front of a statue inside had been hacked off—only an outline was left, smudged, as though the ink had smeared, but I could make out the form of a child emerging from the hip. Inside the temple there were smaller sculptures; candles and diyas flickered as pilgrims passed through and around and in and out.

Archaeologists had found the Maya Devi Temple. Over the centuries, the focus had shifted from the Buddha to Maya (the divine feminine again) and local villagers thought the shrine sacred even after the sadhu who had begun worshipping the pillar died. They brought blood sacrifices to her as a Hindu devi, goats and hens to slaughter in front of the temple. The hill dwellers, Paharis, in the neighbouring villages expected the goddess to grant their wishes.

At the Burmese vipassana centre, I was making horrific discoveries in the Theravada tradition, the Hinayanists Xuanzang kept bumping into. In this older, purer, stringent, Pali-based system, closer to the Buddha's teachings, it was all about mind control.

'Focus on your pain,' said the head monk, Sayadaw Vivekananda. He was born as Rudolf. Theravada was bad enough, but I grappled weakly with this new phenomenon—an eastern tradition taught by a blue-eyed monk of German heritage, fluent in Burmese.

I had trouble with the most basic orders of the Buddha—sitting cross-legged and concentrating on my breath. My knees ached. So did my ankles and hips.

'Describe the pain, be precise,' Sayadaw Vivekananda said in a distinctly German accent. 'The location, the duration, does the pain travel, is it sharp, or dull, does it come and go or is it constant. Pay attention to it.'

'Er, yes.'

'Slow down,' he said to me. 'When you slow down, you see things.'

I nodded, feeling hopeless.

'Then go back to your abdomen as it moves with your breath. Think of nothing but the next breath. And of your abdomen. Rising, rising, falling, falling.'

The wake-up gong rang at 4 a.m., a soft boom through the dark and the final chill of winter. In silence we rose, dressed for the walking meditation and the first pre-breakfast sitting meditation at 5 a.m. Rising, rising, falling, falling.

My mind protested in the dawn, amongst the silent shapes of people meditating around me. It begged for release, for other thoughts, it refused the tedium of rising and falling. It clattered, it planned, it imagined, it riffled memories, pulling up file after file to examine and toss. It jabbered and chattered, muscular, simian, leering, luring, beyond reach.

The noise inside my head filled the vast hall. It was so loud I looked around to see if the others could hear. Nobody ate after noon, so that the evenings were the hardest time, food conjured up by that same demonic mind, creating mounds of steaming rice. I remembered with clarity biting into the lamb in Delhi, cooked *dum pukht* to perfection in saffron rice, and had to swat away the images. Another rose to replace it. Steaming dosa, hot rasam, swallowed and followed by a warm gulab jamun. I longed for a conversation, but talking was forbidden. It was perfectly clear that I was not made for the life of a Buddhist monk.

The roses in the small garden of the monastery were light pink, almost white. They were the same shade as the thin transparent cotton slips the nuns tied over their clothes. Thirty-six roses I was forbidden to look at. It seemed cruel to plant them and then instruct you not to look.

The venerable Burmese teacher U Pandita arrived in Lumbini to address us. He flew in from Rangoon on—what else—Buddha Air, dressed in swathes of cloth in varying shades of brown. It was inevitable to encounter the Hinayana tradition as one travelled around the Buddhist sites in India. No wonder the Chinese monk, who started out a frank Mahayanist, made sure he learned everything the Hinayanists had to offer. It was, after all, the basis for later developments. It had a pleasing simplicity.

I bumped into Shantum Seth, whom I had met briefly once on a holiday from college almost fifteen years ago.

'How are you?' he said, not particularly surprised to see me there. I told him I was having trouble keeping my eyes off the beautiful roses.

'Oh, don't worry about that,' he said, knowledgeable and confident in such matters. 'My master Thich Nhat Hanh says it's perfectly all right to meditate on anything, even the beauty of roses.' I was going to explain that I wasn't exactly *meditating* on the roses, just looking at them admiringly, but it felt too complicated.

Shantum, a real Buddhist, offered an explanation as to how Xuanzang's distances were so accurate. 'He was a monk,' Shantum said. 'He would have been meditating with his rosary as he walked.' There was a very precise link, it turned out, between the time it took to say a certain number of prayers and how far a man walked in that time. The Tibetans in the mountains still used that method to measure the distances they covered.

chapter twenty-six

Fatal Mushrooms

From this going north-east through a great forest, along a dangerous and difficult road, where wild oxen and herds of elephants and robbers and hunters cause incessant trouble to travellers, after leaving the forest we come to the kingdom of Kiu-shi-na-k'ie-lo (Kusinagara).[1]

The Buddha came to Kushinagar to die. It was an ignominious death, caused by an attack of dysentery following a meal. In a hamlet not far from Kushinagar, the meal was served by a blacksmith's son, Cunda, who, with his wife, tended to the party of almost 300 monks who travelled with the Buddha. The couple had picked mushrooms from a sandalwood tree and made a dish called *sukara maddava*. They meant well, but the food was fatal. So, plagued by cramps, stopping repeatedly to rest, the Buddha finally reached a forest of sal trees at the entrance to Kushinagar.

In between two sal trees, his head facing north, the Buddha lay on his side. He admired the lush forest, the sal trees thick with red flowers. He noted with pleasure the setting sun, and remarked on the breeze sighing through the branches.[2]

The Chinese monk naturally had to see the spot.

He found Kushinagar in ruins, its towns and villages wasted and desolate. The brick foundations of the old capital were still visible, however, although the town's avenues were deserted, Xuanzang noted.

The spot where the Buddha died was marked by a grove of sal trees, which Xuanzang compared to the huh tree of his native China, with a greenish white bark and smooth, glistening leaves. There was a great monastery, with the figure of the Buddha lying on his side, his head to the north, the Chinese monk saw. Next to it was a stupa built by Ashoka, in a ruined state, although it was still some 200 feet high, he noted.

Perhaps as he settled by the river to escape the noon heat, Xuanzang wrote:

> According to the general tradition, Tathagata was eighty years old when, on the 15th day of the second half of the month Vaisakha, he entered Nirvana. This corresponds to the 15th day of the 3rd month with us. The different schools calculate variously from the death of Buddha. Some say it is 1200 years and more since then. Others say, 1300 years and more. Others say, 1500 years and more.[3]

ॐ

In modern India, Kushinagar is about sixty kilometres east of Gorakhpur. From Lumbini to Gorakhpur, I found a rarity—the Express Seva, a faster, smaller bus, that travelled a better road as it gunned along in the breeze. The same cassette played again and again and again until the tune had somehow ingrained itself in the tyres and the grimy windows. *Chalte chalte kabhi ruk jata hun mein*, the song all of Uttar Pradesh was glued to in the month of Phagun the year I went home.

I felt I was floating through stories and centuries with ease. There was the story of the Buddha that I followed in these spots away from the usual tourist centres. There was the Chinese monk, whose experience felt close.

I arrived in Kushinagar at night. The full moon hung low and buttery above the Vietnamese Linh Son Monastery, its name scribbled on a scrap of paper on the advice of Shantum when he discovered that I had no idea where I was staying either at Kushinagar or at my next destination, Banaras. I was tired and dusty and a little scared. I had mistimed the distances. I made the bus journey from Gorakhpur in the dark. As often, I was the only woman on the bus. I felt apprehensive at first, but gradually relaxed and tuned into a long discussion about *mukadma*. All of Uttar Pradesh bonded over litigation. *Mukadma chal raha hai.*

Like New Yorkers have shrinks, UP-ites have their decade-long court cases. A conversation unfolded in the cottony darkness of a road, between the filth of Gorakhpur and Kushinagar.

'So how does the law work?' an elderly man leaned over the seat to ask another.

'You have lawyers,' the man answered peaceably. *Vakil.*

'But who argues the case?'

'Lawyers of the two sides get together.'

'But it's been fourteen years and nothing has happened.'

Bits of the story fell out for the bus to hear, others joined in. It was an old injustice, a peasant framed, a counterfeit note slipped across at a bank, an undeserved spell in jail.

'Do you still have the banknote?'

'No.'

'Do you have the photographs of the note, the number, the evidence?'

'No.'

'You'll have to tell the judge you were framed.'

'You should get another lawyer. This one is a scoundrel!' *Badmaash hai.*

'There's one in Basti district, he's a man of honesty.' *Imandar hai.*

The street in Kushinagar, for it was a one-street settlement, was deserted, and the stars shone bright. At the monastery gate, already closed, I banged the lock against the iron bars. Beyond, a ghostly Guanyin stood on her pedestal with candles flickering at her feet.

The stolid nun who ran the centre, the Reverend T.N. Tri Thuan, belonged to the Vietnamese Linh Son Monastery. She had studied in Paris and had made India her home. She ladled out rice and vegetables for me and sat with me while I ate hungrily.

Tri's speech fell like raindrops on a tin roof. I tried to catch each drop. She was busy with expansions to the temple.

'Be nice, then everything okay people selfish I help all the Muslim Hindu only I wan respeck that they don cheat me I afrai they go the wrong way have problem another life.'

She paused for a moment. She tossed her words out like a careless waterfall and I splashed around looking for the break in the sentences. She told me that a group of Sri Lankan nuns was expected to visit the next day. The Buddhist sangha was still making its rounds, only this time it travelled in buses or coaches, not on foot.

'I forty years but I look eighteen.' She sighed. '*Na mo a yi da fat.*'

Ananda, the Buddha's devoted disciple, begged his master not to die in this strange little town in the middle of the jungle. He sobbed, preparing himself for desolation, as his Master lay on his deathbed.

The Buddha scolded him gently.

'Enough, Ananda! Do not let yourself be troubled, do not weep. Have I not already told you, on former occasions, that it is the very nature of all things most near and dear unto us that we must divide ourselves from them, leave them, sever ourselves from them? How then Ananda can this be possible—whereas anything whatever born . . . contains within itself the inherent necessity of dissolution—how then can it be possible that such a being should not be dissolved?'[4]

When my own father died unexpectedly, a year after my travels, I realized that in some utterly tangential way, my journey had been a sort of preparation. I did not know it in Kushinagar, but in the sea of grief to come I would remember the Buddha's words to Ananda and they would provide a fragile raft of consolation to cling to.

The next morning, I borrowed a bicycle and sailed to the end of the road to the Ramabhar Stupa, which archaeologists believe to be the cremation spot of the Buddha. The eastern side of the stupa had blackened as though the sun had baked it harder. Mustard fields spread to the east, beyond the stupa. A row of Ashoka trees were planted at the entrance and young amorous couples lay close to each other under them, the vast stupa affording some privacy. It was a gentle garden, filled with the call of spring.

The Mahaparinirvana Stupa was not far. I cycled to it and hopped off, wheeling my bike. Inside, the Buddha lay on his right side, his right hand under his head. He was covered with some gold-fringed cloth in gold leaf. His feet stuck out at the bottom, I had an absurd wish to pull the covers lower, over his bare feet.

I felt achy. Although it was somebody else's death, somebody else's drama, it somehow curled behind my eyelids. How could I know that, soon enough, it would become mine?

chapter twenty-seven

Deer Park

[Banaras] is about 4000 *li* in circuit. The capital borders (on its western side) the Ganges river . . . it's inner gates are like a small-toothed comb; it is densely populated. The families are very rich, and in the dwellings are objects of rare value. The disposition of the people is soft and humane, and they are earnestly given to study. They are mostly unbelievers, a few reverence the law of the Buddha . . . There are about thirty sangharamas and 3000 priests. They study the Little Vehicle according to the Sammatiya school.[1]

 It was natural for the Buddha to find his way to the outskirts of big cities, soon after he reached enlightenment in Bodh Gaya.

Banaras lies about 200 kilometres west of Gaya, but the texts suggest that the Buddha, after his enlightenment, first walked north, crossed the Ganga at Pataligrama, the village where the capital of Magadha would be built, and then turned west on the highway that hugged the Ganga's northern shore.

These cities were natural magnets for a preacher. As required, the Buddha waited until the morning outside the city gates. Then he went begging for food. He bathed and ate the meal of the day. Finally, he walked to the hermitage on the city's outskirts.

The Chinese monk followed the Buddha's footsteps to the hamlet of Sarnath.

To the north-east of the river Varana about 10 *li* or so, we come to the Sangharama of Lu-ye . . . Its precincts are divided into eight portions (sections), connected by a surrounding wall. The storeyed towers with projecting eaves and the balconies are of very superior work.[2]

Five men who had previously disagreed with the Buddha conspired to ignore him. But as he approached, they found themselves rising, taking his cloak and alms bowl, bringing him a seat and water to wash his feet.

Night fell. It was clear, filled with moonlight. During the first watch, the Buddha remained silent. During the second watch, he conversed in a friendly manner. As the third watch began, the Buddha began his first sermon, setting the wheel of law in motion. It was the beginning of a new moral order.

'My brothers, there are two extremes that a person on the path should avoid. One is to plunge oneself into sensual pleasures, and the other is to practice austerities which deprive the body of its needs. Both of these extremes lead to failure. The path I have discovered is the Middle Way.'[3]

But plenty of Hindus in the region ignored the Buddha's words, as the Chinese monk noted even in the seventh century:

> There are a hundred or so Deva temples with about 10,000 sectaries. They honour principally Mahesvara (Ta-tseu-tsai). Some cut their hair off, others tie their hair in a knot, and go naked, without clothes (Nirgranthas); they cover their body with ashes (Pasupatas), and by the practice of all sorts of austerities they seek to escape from birth and death.[4]

∞

At the Deer Park in Sarnath, the awesome Dhameka Stupa, a great silent monolith, dominated, as though its very presence could mark the colossal words uttered here. Around me, Tibetan monks and nuns prostrated themselves full length on the ground, bumped their heads on the ground, raised joined palms, got up, walked a few steps and did it again, all around the Dhameka Stupa.

A few nuns sported dirty spots on their foreheads. One monk

wrapped a white silk scarf around a stone and tossed it up to a niche on the vast structure in the hope that it would catch on a ledge and stay. It took a few tries. The bottom, more reachable, was dabbed with gold leaf. There was knobbly brickwork on top, uneven, and at the bottom, larger, finer, stone carvings, scrolled leaves and flowers. A geometrical band circled the stupa.

Xuanzang may have strolled through the same park, possibly stopping to meditate like the cross-legged monks who sat there now. He noted the washing tank where the Buddha had washed his clothes and rinsed his begging bowl.

When he stopped at Sarnath, there was still a sizeable community of monks. Around 1500 priests still lived and meditated according to the Hinayana school. And perhaps the visitor from faraway China once again swallowed his Mahayana views for a while, to accept a light meal and a bed for the night.

The site was equally holy to the Jains, for it was the venue of the austerities and the death of Sreyansanatha, the eleventh Tirthankara. In fact, wandering around the park in Sarnath were several naked Jains, wearing nothing but the white loin cloth, as though they had stepped straight out of Xuanzang's seventh-century description.

The place was cluttered with the remains of monasteries, stupas, temples, inscriptions and sculptures from the third century BC to the twelfth century AD. But the Dhameka Stupa seemed to throb with a silent energy all its own, drawing all eyes to it, surreptitiously, at intervals, as though the mass of stone had spoken in a human voice, but discreetly, so that each thought he had misheard.

Further north, amongst still leafless trees, was a fenced-off park— used in the loosest sense of the word as the ground was pebbly—and six disconsolate deer that nosed up to the wire in the hope of something green. Such long lashes, dewy dark eyes.

In the greener lawns around the stupas, paired off at the foot of monastic ruins, leaning against old stones, sat young Indian lovers. There were so many that I almost tripped over them, some talking or holding hands, one pair in a passionate embrace, another man lay with his eyes closed, his head on his lover's lap—all these youngsters driven to public places that were far more private than their own homes. It reminded me of China's public garden benches at dusk, similarly occupied for identical reasons.

At the museum in Sarnath I stopped in front of a sixth-century Bodhisattva Maitreya. His hair was looped and tied in a topknot, cascading around his shoulders, his feet had broken off at some point, but the right leg pushed ahead, as though he were taking a step forward. It rang a bell. The Chinese monk had written of a promenade of about fifty paces, with stepping stones composed of piles of blue stones. 'Above it is a figure of Tathagatha in the attitude of walking. It is of a singular dignity and beauty. From the flesh-knot on the top of the head there flows wonderfully a braid of hair.'[5]

It was, to my mind, entirely possible that I was staring, open-mouthed, at the very same statue that had so impressed Xuanzang. In comment of appreciation from this man of metaphysics, the word 'beauty' actually escaped his pen. The dutiful monk was relaxing and beginning to respond to things other than Buddhist philosophy. Perhaps India was seeping into him, shaking him from his esoteric tree.

All of a sudden the broken-off lintels, the dug-up head of deer, the stucco Gupta bits, the carved bricks, became a shattered, exploded version of a whole that Xuanzang saw.

As in a cartoon, I could see the pieces fly back together, reassemble into a seventh-century reality. But in fact the pieces were mounted behind glass windows and labelled, the ensemble, as the builders created it, dead forever.

Nobody would ever know.

In Banaras, on Assi Ghat by the Ganga, the afternoon receded, the river lay still, its pale waters reflecting a washed sky. The sandbank across was a beige smear, and beyond lay a light green band of fields. Against this clear watercolour, sharp, dark crow wings. A flock flapped and vanished into the upper branches of the peepul tree. Below, sadhus lit the first evening lamps. The river hung heavy and silent.

I had awoken that morning to Sanskrit chanting and the light grace of bells. The river I had bathed in at Allahabad, further upstream, mesmerized me here. Dawn rose over the Ganga like a sigh, the lightest of exhalations. Krishna the boatman pulled against flat oars, plashing, the water rippled silk.

But were there other Buddhist remains in Banaras itself? I hunted for them within the city, up near Bakaria Kund, near Langar Masjid. I clambered up the stairs to the mosque and Sami Ullah with his *paan*-stained teeth and cap invited me to have a look around. My Hindu rickshaw-wala said he'd wait outside, and Sami Ullah did not protest.

This was the tomb of Qutub Wali Shah, in whose enclosure lightning came flashing down, twirled around his body and vanished again without burning anything.

'From up there,' Sami Ullah pointed to an opening near the ceiling.

We walked beyond, into the Muslim quarter behind the mosque, a small settlement given to the sari industry, where bolts of silk thread hung ready to be dyed in vats of heated colour. Two men twisted a skein around wooden sticks amid the steam from hot dyes, to wring out the excess liquid. Wherever there was space the fine silk threads wound and stretched across the yard, brick red, preparing for hand weaving, gleaming in the sun and soaking in the dust and days of the mohalla so that each sari carried something of the city that made it.

In front of the mosque, off the main street, looms clattered and shifted, taut with magenta, sea green, purple and gold, the triangular peaks of a design coded by holes punched into cardboard; and from the clashing and muttering of the looms dug into the ground saris inched into existence. There. I had gotten so distracted again, I'd quite forgotten to look for the Buddhist remains and only remembered halfway back what I had gone there for.

The city had addled my brain, or was it the light that glittered in the month of Phagun? I was dragged to the bottom of a liquid gold bubble. I tumbled out of bed to watch the sun rise over the water, and Sambhu the boatman walked over and squatted on haunches. How thin he was. We had tea and looked at the river in easy silence.

'See, god has come out,' he said eventually. *Dekho, bhagwan nikal aaya hai.*

The sun had edged up, half visible in the mist. The sky was a pale lilac silk shot through with the faintest rose, a grey smudged line of clouds across the horizon.

I could not know it in Banaras, but this was the image that would float through my mind on the day we cremated my father in Lausanne. It was the Vedic hymns, perhaps, that conjured up the river that morning, and I felt my face damp with tears.

My father's body lay in a foreign country, ice-cold. He lay surrounded by flowers, dressed in a kurta meant for a birthday he would not have. One by one, we laid flowers over him. My vibrant, larger-than-life father was about to become a jar of ashes.

Wooden oars dipped into the river as we rowed down to Manikaran Ghat where flames tensed and jumped transparent from funeral pyres. Piles of chopped wood lay stacked, ready for use, dogs ran in and around the burning bodies, mud and ashes and death and flames, again and again.

A family stood by with solemn faces, the men's shoulders draped in shawls and kurtas, while a boy poured ghee and spices on the flames. That would be us, only we did not know it then. All that time, the journey was trying to show me, to tell me. Be ready.

But I wasn't.

chapter twenty-eight

Buddhist Ivy League

The kingdom of Magadh sat on the banks of the majestic Ganga near the eastern edge of India. From the air it glittered in the afternoon across the wideness of the plains as three riverine prongs met at Patna before flowing into the Bay of Bengal.

From Banaras, the Chinese monk travelled east directly to Vaisali, an independent city state where the Buddha preached and foretold his own death. Then Xuanzang veered south to Pataliputra (Patna), Gaya and Nalanda. In the Buddha's time Patna was a small village, and by the time Xuanzang came by, its status as a grand capital had faded and the city had crumpled.

At a Delhi dinner party, the idea of my going to Bihar produced amusement and the usual round of Bihar jokes. Nobody took the decrepit state or its comic, playing-to-the-galleries ruler Laloo Prasad Yadav seriously.

'Pakistan is welcome to take Kashmir as long as they take Bihar too.'

'Wait, I have another one,' somebody piped up.

'A Japanese prime minister came to visit Bihar. He said give me Bihar for a week and I'll make it into Japan. Laloo replied, give me Japan for a week and I'll make it into Bihar.'

Laughter erupted around the table.

I landed in Patna and was immediately enchanted by the tall silk cotton trees in bloom. Red flowers with their great crimson waxy petals dropped out of the trees. There was a sibilant undertone to the land, a feeling of approaching something older. Perhaps it was the flaring cobra's hood worshipped at the foot of a tree by the roadside. The ancient, primeval religions felt more open here. Before there was Buddhism in India, before there were even gods in India, there were trees and snakes and the mother goddess.

A friend of a friend had an empty house in Patna where I could stay. From there, I would chart my tour of the Chinese monk's sojourn in Bihar. All I had of Bihar was a childhood memory of Shanti Amma's sing-song Hindi which now filled the air around me. Shanti Amma was a Christian woman from Bihar who bathed and fed us when we were small. Her front teeth stuck out so her lips didn't quite close around them and she wore her hair oiled and in a single braid. We adored her. Over dinner, when my parents had gone out, she told us stories of Jesus ('Jissoo') hauling his cross up the hill. It made her cry and, watching her helpless tears, we all began to cry too.

Bihar betrayed its Buddhist antecedents, its name a derivative of vihara, or monastery.

I headed straight to the ASI office in Patna where, naturally, I interrupted an archaeological conference. Superintending archaeologist K.K. Mohammad kindly took some time out from the proceedings to offer me tea and fill me in on the local history. He was a short man, with precise movements. Without my asking, he offered concrete help in the shape of transport and even an escort.

'Some of the visiting archaeologists are going to Nalanda and Rajgir. You can go with them in the jeep,' he said. I was delighted, but the tales of Bihar's thieves and bandits still spooked me. Xuanzang's itinerary would, once more, take some tweaking to fit the favours or disfavours that arose.

'Nalanda is the biggest-ever excavated university in the world,' Mohammad said, enthusiastic. 'In the fifth century AD, it was mainly for Buddhism and Brahminism. Think of the Sorbonne in Paris, thirteenth century, and Oxford, twelfth century—they were also first established for theological studies.'

He warmed up to his topic. 'Hindu and Buddhist architecture used bricks, not stones, so most is lost. The attack on Nalanda [of that time by invaders from Central Asia] was the prime factor in its destruction. Still, if you know how to look, each and every brick will start speaking. You will see.'

K.K. Mohammad said that two visiting Gujarati archaeologists would also like to see the remains of old Pataliputra, and he could arrange a car to the site and send a man with us. I gladly accepted this second kindness.

The archaeologists and I set off as the heat firmed. We drove around ten kilometres south of Patna where lay the remains of Ashoka's old capital. The river had moved. There were no gorges to contain it, and the Ganga ruled the plain, shifting as it wished. When Xuanzang passed through, the city had already faded into the past. He wrote in his records:

> To the south of the river Ganges there is an old city, about 70 *li* round. Although it has been long deserted, its foundation walls still survive. Formerly, when men's lives were incalculably long, it was called Kusumapura (K'u-su-mo-pu-lo), so called because the palace of the king had many flowers. Afterwards, when men's age reached several thousands of years, then its name was changed to Pataliputra (Po-ch'a-li-tsu-ch'ing).[1]

The place was flooded after the first month of summer and the first month of autumn, and all communication took place by boats, he wrote.

ಜಾ

On a bridge over the Ganga, we stood by Gai Ghat and leaned over the railing to watch the churning waters and the flat-bottomed boats. Buses ground by behind us, making the bridge tremble.

It may have been somewhere here that the Buddha had to cross in the other direction, on his way to Banaras from Gaya, after his enlightenment. One legend has it that the ferryman declined to carry the anonymous penniless monk, so the Buddha was obliged to use his magical powers and leap over the river to the other bank.

Xuanzang would have boarded a ferry across this river to get to Pataliputra. In Mauryan times, 800 years before him, Pataliputra was a prosperous city, a centre of learning and trade. It fell into disuse as dynasties evaporated and centres of power shifted away.

Pataliputra's remains were in a closed-off garden filled with

Ashoka trees. Archaeologists found some eighty stone pillars in Chunar sandstone so favoured by Mauryan builders. They found cracked, thick beams of sal trees that possibly made up the roof. All these remains were now underwater, hidden in a stagnant tank. One pillar in the middle poked out, forlorn. This was once a magnificent assembly hall of Ashoka, the warrior-turned-Buddhist.

By Xuanzang's account, King Ashoka was at first a horrid man. He had custom-built torture chambers that he enclosed in high walls. There were furnaces of molten metal, ugly sharp instruments. Every criminal in the land was consigned to this compound, all who crossed its threshold had to die.

One day, the guards grabbed a novice monk who ventured too close to the hell-gates as he begged for alms. They threatened to kill him. He asked for a few minutes to pray, and as he knelt, he saw a man, tied, struggling, surrounded by guards, enter the prison. They cut off the prisoner's hands, sliced off his feet and, Xuanzang said, 'pounded his body in a mortar, till all the members of his body were mashed up together in confusion'.[2]

The novice monk saw in a flash the impermanence of things. He became an Arhat, free from the power of birth and death. So when they cast him into a boiling cauldron, it felt to him like a cool lake and he sat on a lotus flower that appeared.

Ashoka rushed to the site when news reached him. The guards would have killed the king himself, for he had breached the gates of hell. But the king ordered the chief torturer seized and drowned in the boiling pots. Where had that happened? Somewhere nearby?

Now only a few leaves floated on the tank's murky surface, wind rippled the water. The hall was referred to by Megasthenes, an ambassador in Chandragupta Maurya's court. Perhaps this was where Ashoka issued his edicts, his orders to erect the memorable pillars across the land, the pillars I kept coming across. It was midday. From the mosque opposite the road, the faint chant of 'Allah ho Akbar' rose across the ruins of the city, once again slicing the day into a neat section, a rigorous reminder that the day had progressed and that I had paid the barest attention to time. I had been travelling for almost ten months. The season was advancing, for the mango trees were now covered with feathery yellow-beige flowers.

Xuanzang came too early to appreciate the Pala rulers who founded a powerful dynasty in the eighth century in East India and were great patrons of Mahayana Buddhism and its art. But the museum in Patna was crammed with work from the tenth and the eleventh centuries. There was a relaxed, fluid Avalokiteshvara, lines etched like water. His left hand rested on his left thigh, leg bent, foot up, right leg folded so his foot rested against his crotch. It was the pose of a shopkeeper in Ayodhya.

Sculptors here used the black basalt stone of these parts or grey sandstone to carve the Bodhisattvas or the Tara deities. Tara became the popular female counterpart, or Shakti, of the Avalokiteshvara Buddha. Not content to wait out the goddess-less philosophies of Buddhism, Tara edged her way back into people's lives by standing beside the Buddha. To my mind, the cult of Tara made perfect sense in this part of India. It would simply be a new Buddhist version of the older religions.

Mulling this over, I returned to my kind friend's home, where the cook, Asha, made me tea and offered me biscuits.

Travelling around India like this, looking for the past was profoundly satisfying, but it was lonely. There was no backpacker crowd to talk to. Archaeologists were interesting on their topic, but otherwise mostly dull. I was not fuelled by Buddhist fervour and I watched pilgrims from a slight distance. I yearned for a drink, for a cigarette. Conversation—any conversation—was welcome. I chatted with Asha, who talked in that Bihari sing-song way. She was a plump, short creature and leaned against the door as I sat at the table and ate the food she'd made.

'So, didi, what are you doing here?'

I ventured to explain to her the history, the travel, but it seemed abstract and unimportant. What a luxury it was, I thought, not for the first time, to worry about the past.

ॐ

In the late autumn of AD 631, four monks from Nalanda University arrived in Bodh Gaya to escort Xuanzang to Nalanda. Reluctantly, the monk of China left Bodh Gaya, looking over his shoulder, as though he was being dragged from the presence of his Master. He had been there nine full days.

Word of his arrival at Nalanda spread. People whispered about his journey. He entered the university surrounded by around 200 monks and thousands of lay people. They carried standards, umbrellas to shield him from the sun, and threw flowers on the road. Incense swirled. A head priest sounded a *ghanta* and proclaimed that while the great Chinese visitor lived in Nalanda all his needs would be met. Thus Xuanzang was admitted into the walls of the university. He was awed by his impressive surroundings. It was an Indian Ivy League of the seventh century, and the Chinese monk had entered with a full fellowship. He described it to Hui Li, and so we know that

> . . . the whole establishment is surrounded by a brick wall, which encloses the entire convent from without. One gate opens into the great college, from which are separated eight other halls, standing in the middle (of the sangharama). The richly adorned towers, and the fairy-like turrets, like pointed hill-tops, are congregated together. The observatories seem to be lost in the vapours (of the morning), and the upper rooms tower above the clouds. From the windows one may see how the winds and the clouds (produce new forms), and above the soaring eaves the conjunctions of the sun and moon (may be observed).[3]

There were ponds filled with blue lotus flowers, mingled with deep red kanaka flowers, and the grounds were covered in groves of amra trees. It was India's grandest monastery, the Chinese monk told his biographer.

೫

The visiting archaeologists, two from Tamil Nadu and one from Maharashtra, were ready to leave for Nalanda University. As K.K. Mohammad had promised, I tagged along, tossing a daypack into the back seat of the jeep. There was desultory talk about Bihar's lawlessness. The Tamil visitors addressed me in English and spoke Tamil with each other, which I did not understand. But the Tamil was so interspersed with English that I understood much of what they said, including their disapproval of various archaeological colleagues.

Nalanda University was thought to have been founded shortly after AD 411 when Fa Xian, another Chinese monk who had travelled to India before Xuanzang, left the subcontinent, for there are no records of Nalanda in his work. Scholars suggest it was the brainchild of Kumaragupta (AD 413–55), and had grown into a vast, internationally known centre of Buddhist studies by the time Xuanzang visited between AD 631 and 635. The cultured King Harshavardhana patronized the university.

The ruins of the university where the Chinese monk stayed took my breath away, even 1400 years after its heyday. Nalanda had been a sprawling campus. There were the remains of monasteries and massive dormitories. Each monastery had its own well. On the southernmost shrine was an arched roof. There were brick corridors and monastic cells, restored now, but empty.

Cobwebs trembled in the slight breeze and dragonflies paused on the ancient sun-warmed bricks. The ghosts of monks who met and argued the finer points of Buddhist metaphysics lingered and then vanished. Korean tourists walked down steps, umbrellas held up, exclaiming amongst themselves.

There would have been room after room of monks, debating, listening, reciting, chanting. In a corner room, there was an empty niche, perhaps it had contained a shrine.

There were shadowy remains of Buddha statues in niches on two opposing walls. The bricks were deformed into clumps, which spoke of a very high heat, as did the dark, burnt patches on the corners where fire must have raged for days after Central Asian invaders sacked the university in 1197. I pressed against a wall to let a group edge by. It was a troop of local tourists, listening intently to the guide talk about Xuanzang in Hindi.

'Hiuen Tsiang wrote about Nalanda, that's how they knew it was here, they cleared it up and pulled it out of the jungle.'

જ

The 10,000 priests and scholars at Nalanda followed the Mahayana school of Buddhism, but they also studied the Hindu Vedas and a multitude of other texts, the visiting monk said.

Twenty priestly scholars escorted the Chinese monk to his first meeting with the head priest Silabhadra, a renowned Buddhist scholar, the man who would become a dear friend.

'What brings you here, honourable guest?'

'I am come from the country of China, desiring to learn from your instruction the principles of the Yoga-Sastra,'[4] Xuanzang said.

His words caused a small stir. Silabhadra's nephew and disciple Buddhabhadra burst into tears. Sniffing and wiping his eyes, blowing his nose, he recounted a dream of an ailing Silabhadra. The chancellor of Nalanda University was so ill he wanted to die. But in a dream filled with gold and silver, the Avalokiteshvara Buddha, the Maitreya Buddha and the Manjusri Buddha came to the venerable priest and sternly told him to banish all thoughts of dying.

Teach the *Yoga Shastra*, Manjusri said. Your body will heal. Besides, Manjusri added, 'Do not overlook that there is a priest of the country of China who delights in examining the great Law and is desirous to study with you: you ought to instruct him carefully.'[5]

'How long have you travelled, my friend?' Silabhadra asked.

'Three years,' Xuanzang said quietly.

Outwardly, the monk was composed, dignified. Inside, he exulted. He bowed his head and perhaps allowed the tiniest of smiles to pull at one side of his mouth. Buddhabhadra led him to his own quarters, a tall building with four storeys where Xuanzang stayed for a week before he moved into his own dwelling.

Each day he received 120 jambiras, a kind of fruit, twenty areca nuts, twenty nutmegs, a tael of camphor, butter and other necessities, and a peck of Mahasali rice, a special fat grain that cooked into a shining aromatic heap and was only available in Magadh and only offered to kings or distinguished priests. Every month he was given three measures of oil. He was also gifted an elephant to ride on and two attendants were assigned to take care of his every need.

The university had an endowment of 100 villages, and every day 200 householders contributed rice, butter and milk as supplies for the university students. There was a gatekeeper, an admissions officer of sorts who tested the knowledge of those who sought to enter. If they failed to answer properly and display their foundation, they had to retire. The university admitted a mere twenty per cent of all applicants.

Through all the newness, Xuanzang felt the old discipline kick in. He watched, observed, noted. At night, by the flickering lamps, when the day's studies were over, he scribbled.

> The priests, to the number of several thousands, are men of the highest ability and talent. The rules of this convent are severe, and all the priests are bound to observe them. The day is not sufficient for asking and answering profound questions. From morning till night they engage in discussion . . . Those who cannot discuss questions out of the *Tripitaka* are little esteemed, and are obliged to hide themselves for shame.[6]

Over the next few years, Silabhadra expounded on the enormous *Yogacarabhumi* texts three times in private teaching sessions. The *Yogacarabhumi*, an encyclopaedic work, is one of the root texts of the early Yogacara school and details the thinking that only the mind exists, that there are no objects external to the mind, and that as a result of Yogic practice it is possible to see the world as a manifestation of the internal mind. This was the crux, the reason for Xuanzang's journey.

He studied a brand new work, the *Pramanasamuccaya*, the most important work in Buddhist logic and epistemology, penned by the sage Dignaga. It is a discussion of the valid means of knowledge; it explains that two of these valid means are perception and inference. The work is lost to us in the twenty-first century. Only two rather rough Tibetan translations exist, dating from the eleventh and thirteenth centuries. There is nothing left in Sanskrit and not a word in Chinese.[7]

At Nalanda, Xuanzang asked questions to clarify several passages in the key Buddhist texts. He also cemented his knowledge of the Vedic classics, Sanskrit and other Indian languages. In his records, Xuanzang added an essay on the intricacies of Sanskrit, perhaps to prove how well he had mastered the tough conjugations, declensions and inflections. But, for the time being, newly arrived at Nalanda, Xuanzang watched the yellow firelight flicker off the walls of his cell. He savoured the sense of destination, of destiny. And then he made an extraordinary discovery—he was restless. He was well looked after, but he had yet to visit Rajgir, an ancient capital where the Buddha spent much time meditating and teaching.

chapter twenty-nine

Vulture's Peak

The rocky hills of Rajgir, not far from Nalanda, provided a natural bowl of protection. Our group made the short drive to Rajgir from Nalanda before heading back north to Patna. This, the locals told us, was prime dacoit territory. The valleys were overgrown with thorny acacia trees and straggly shrubs, excellent hideouts for bandits and Naxalites. Perhaps it was the watery afternoon light, but my spine tingled as though unseen eyes watched us.

The city of King Bimbisara, a friend and devotee of the Buddha, had crumbled to a wayside village with a few long-distance buses running through it and a maidan with desultory cows.

The prince Siddhartha left his hometown of Kapilavastu and wandered here in search of a teacher, for Magadha was renowned for its spiritual guides. One day, he went out begging in the capital of Rajgir. People stopped to watch the ascetic glide about calmly and majestically like a lion in a mountain forest. King Bimbisara of Magadha, who was passing in his carriage, happened to see him too and later sought him out.

'This is too harsh a life,' the king told the mendicant. 'You have no bed, no attendant to assist you. If you agree to come with me, I will give you your own palace. Please return with me to teach.'

'Great king, palace life is not well suited to me. I am endeavouring to find a path of liberation to free myself and all beings from suffering. Palace life is not compatible with the heart's quest of this monk,'[1] Siddhartha said.

But Siddhartha promised to return when he had found the path. When he came back, it was as the Buddha, followed by 1250 monks.

The Buddha and his contingent were received by King Bimbisara at the palace and fed hospitably. The king offered the young sangha its first plot of land for a monastery in the Bamboo Forest, outside the capital.

The Buddha admitted gratefully that the monsoon season was not a good time for wandering monks to travel. 'The bhikkus need a place to study and practice together during the rains. Having a place like this will help the community avoid illness from exposure to the elements and also avoid stepping on the many worms and insects that are washed up on the ground during the rainy season.'[2]

After the Buddha died at Kushinagar, King Bimbisara's son, Ajatasatru, took his share of relics to Rajgir and built a stupa. Ashoka rebuilt the stupa, developed it. Here, on this old and lonely road through Rajgir, was a party of archaeologists who were excavating what they thought was the Ajatasatru mound. Xuanzang's biographer mentioned the mound too. 'To the east of the garden is a stupa, which was built by Ajatasatru raja.'[3]

Digging was well under way. History has a way of surfacing, no matter what. What a coincidence that they should be excavating the very story I followed. Or was it? The Tamil archaeologists dived into the fray, leaving me to my own devices. I wandered around the site peering at the diggers hard at work.

There was a small buzz at the main stupa. The Tamilians had found, with a certain satisfaction, that an outer wall being restored by the Patna archaeological circle was a few centimetres crooked. They pointed and repeated this, so everybody knew they had spotted the discrepancy. The group huddled, skipping over debris and a half-uncovered mound, stretching tape measures, shaking heads and jotting notes.

Rajgir lay in the lap of granite mountains. This was inhospitable country now; perhaps it had been greener when it was the capital of Magadha in the Buddha's time, when King Bimbisara ruled. The Bamboo Forest was said to be lush, with nearly 100 acres of thriving groves. At the centre lay Kalandaka Lake where the monks could wash their clothes, bathe and practise walking meditation along the shores.

Further out, Xuanzang mentioned kanaka trees, which burst into

blossoms in spring, and fields of a sweet grass. The boundary wall of
the old city climbed up and down, following the natural humps of the
hills. The remains showed it was a rough-hewn wall, with towers
and turrets. These were such ominous hills, even in the soft afternoon
light there was a harshness about the landscape.

Still nervous about the Naxalites, I asked a student archaeologist,
'Do they ever come here? To this spot, where you are digging?'

'All the men here are labourers, what will they get from us?'

The men who were digging had skins as dark and shiny as
seasoned mahogany, as though the light were all absorbed and reflected
the bare minimum. Their lungis were pulled and tied around their
waists and the hems lifted, tucked in so it seemed they wore miniskirts.
Their heads were bound in a cotton cloth and they were grumbling
amongst each other. The sun was setting and the day's work was
done. The wag in the group put his scoop down and, hips wiggling
like a drag queen, walked to the tent. 'Everyone wants to do the
aaram ka kaam, nobody wants to do *puraan ka kaam*.' It was 5 p.m.
sharp. The group began to put away the digging tools, the brushes,
the containers of earth, and line up for the daily wage of fifty-eight
rupees and sixty paise.

It was true. It was not much of a haul for a Naxalite.

A short drive away, as the archaeologists squatted to examine
wheel tracks frozen in the stony ground, I looked up to see Vulture's
Peak, Gridhrakuta, the spot where the Buddha preached for many
years. King Bimbisara had levelled the valleys and, with the stones,
fashioned a staircase, 2500 years ago. He ordered two stupas to be
built, one called 'dismounting from the chariot' and the other 'sending
back the crowds', for this is how royalty approached the great teacher:
on foot and alone, stripped of all but good deeds and bad deeds, the
sum of a man.

Xuanzang's notes here acquire a hushed quality:

Touching the southern slope of the northern mountain,
[Gridhrakuta] rises as a solitary peak to a great height, on which
vultures make their abode. It appears like a high tower on which the
azure tints of the sky are reflected, the colours of the mountain and
the heaven being commingled.[4]

Before he converted to Buddhism, Ajatasatru had put his father under house arrest. King Bimbisara died aged sixty-seven, having reigned for over half a century. He died alone, imprisoned, with his eyes turned towards Vulture's Peak where the Buddha preached.

Mahayanists, seeking direct claims to the Buddha, said that Vulture's Peak was where the Buddha preached the Perfection of Wisdom sutras, the *Prajnaparamita Sutras*, to an elite audience of enlightened beings. This would have been of special interest to Xuanzang, who translated them into Chinese.

'Shall we climb up?' I suggested to the Tamilians, reluctant to peel off on my own in the fading light, possibly surrounded by Naxalites who in my mind were preparing an ambush as we spoke.

'Oh no, oh no,' they protested. 'It's very far.'

'How far is it?'

'It will be at least one kilometre. Half an hour, one hour it will take.'

So that was that.

chapter thirty

Peepul Leaf and Perfect Wisdom

As Buddha, whilst sitting beneath this tree, reached perfect wisdom (anuttara Bodhi), it is therefore called the Bodhi tree. The bark is of a yellowish white colour, and its leaves of a shining green; it retains its leaves through the autumn and winter; only, when the day of Buddha's Nirvana comes, the leaves all fall off, but when the day has passed, they all grow again.[1]

৯০

From Patna, the bus to Bodh Gaya wound through fields and right through villages where elections were in progress and the local candidate celebrated victory. A group of men by the roadside had smeared themselves with pink powder as though it were already Holi, their eyes rolling with bhang. They jerked their shoulders, arms raised, and whirled and turned along with a musical band on a cart.

The mud huts here, further south, had patterns in white paint on a khaki canvas—a fern with leaves curling. The walls were attractive amidst the green of fields. In the markets, there were piles of chana since it was time for the harvest now. There was a faintly tribal feel about these faces—narrower foreheads, eyes deeper in their sockets, thick shocks of hair. Along the road, mountains of straw, piled as circular huts. But then the bus juddered to a halt. I had a spasm of fear and a memory of Kashmir, but it passed, and after a one-hour delay we rolled into Bodh Gaya well after dark. It had taken nearly six hours to cover 114 kilometres.

At the tourist bungalow, every morning, a dove sat on the parapet and fluttered and let out a soft 'kuk-koo koook'. Its pale neck was ringed with an inky brush stroke, as though, in a hurry, the painter didn't close the circle before dotting an eye and sitting back to examine the effect.

Bodh Gaya, like Lumbini, hosted the monasteries of all the Buddhist countries in the region. The Royal Bhutanese Monastery took Chinese temple kitsch to new heights. They had painted a sign: 'Touching of wall statues, spreading out legs and sleeping in the temple is prohibited.' A young monk sat and chanted in Bhutanese, his face obscured by a drum. A group of sixty Japanese tourists walked by in a stately column, waving off eager hawkers.

Not far from Bodh Gaya, outside the village of Uruvela, lies a stark, hilly area, filled with large rocks and fissures that widen into caves. Prince Siddhartha, not yet a Buddha, sat and meditated here for six years, hardly eating, wasting away so much that he could reach for his stomach and touch his spine.

He sat in the classic posture, with his head and torso straight, his legs crossed in the lotus position, his hands with the palms upturned meeting in his lap. His will conquered his body, mastering fear in the depths of Bihar's nights. When an approaching deer rustled the grass, his fear rose sharply to tell him it was demons coming to kill him. But the Buddha did not budge. He went on a frightening fast, eating a single grain of jujube each day, then only one grain of rice and, finally, just a grain of millet. Then he stopped eating altogether. His bodily functions ceased. His shrivelled head was like a withered gourd and his eyes like stars reflected at the bottom of an almost dried well. But he found no peace.

I decided to start from the beginning. Early in the morning light, I drove in a hired van to the foot of a cliff-like mountain. It was a short, stiff walk up to the cave where he sat for his austerities.

The local priest, Dev Kumar Mishra, was Hindu, the third generation to work at the cave. As I climbed further to enter this dark hole, I glanced back and stopped for the view facing north-west, the fields spread out below and beyond that the river bed.

With a carpet of jungle and the water roaring not far away, what a pleasant spot this must have been. The mountain was named after

its goddess, Dhungeshwari Devi, and inside the cave I first saw at the
back a seated figure of Prince Siddhartha, the wasted, rib-showing,
drawn-skin version hardly ever portrayed in sculpture. There were
dabs of gold paint. To his left, a short, squat figure against the cave,
sat Kali. And next to her, Dhungeshwari Ma.

'Who was this Dhungeshwari Ma, that mountains were named
after her?' I asked the priest.

'I don't know, madam. Actually there are nine sisters.' He started
to count them off on his fingers. 'Let's see. Mangla Ma, Dhungeshwari
Ma, Bageshwari Ma, Rajrappa Ma.' He paused. 'I can't remember
the others.'

Meditating, Siddhartha shared the cave with the goddesses. In all
likelihood, the goddess is an ancient one, possibly mutated from some
prehistoric matriarchal figure. Once more, the thread of an even
older story, a story much before Buddhism, reared its intriguing head.
Further down the mountain, at a separate temple, the Tibetans had
followed suit and built a Tibetan Kali, Maha Kala, so frightening
that the case in which she was installed was covered and she was
hardly visible. 'Om Mani Padme Hum' somebody had carved on the
rock.

On my way down, I crossed a couple of Thai monks slightly out
of breath from the climb. We nodded greetings.

A local youth fell into step with me. He was a teenager.

'Aunty-ji, take me to Delhi with you,' he said, after we'd exchanged
a few pleasantries and I'd answered the usual questions.

'And what will you do in Delhi?'

'Anything. Everything. There's nothing here for me. I have to
guard the temple since two years ago when a statue of Buddha was
stolen; they came in the jeep at night and made off with it, it was
worth one lakh rupees.'

I was silent, used now to being seen as a city visitor. Used to
being seen carrying vast powers, opportunity, future possibilities.
And here was a young man, eager and energetic, who would, if
nothing else came along, have to guard the statue for the rest of his
life, fading into old age, marrying a village woman, pumping her
full of children and then, one day, dying.

'Please, find me some work in Delhi,' he persisted.

'Why don't you ask your precious Laloo Yadav to do something?'

'He won't listen to my sorrows. *Woh mere dukh nahin sunenge.* He's with the netas and the Jatis.'

Suddenly I was irritated with Laloo and his gimmickry and empty promises. What was he but an entertainer who performed for the people and thus offered solace? For when life gets rough, even entertainment has value. One could be fooled into thinking that something was being done. And Laloo had fooled all of Bihar for well over a decade now.

One day, the fasting Siddhartha saw that austerities were not the way to contentment. He was so weak he could barely stand. His robe, worn and thin, simply disintegrated, and the naked prince had to borrow the cloth covering the dead body of a servant. With slow movements, he washed the brick-coloured fabric in the river, spread it in the sun to dry, and then, wrapping it around his body, began to walk to Uruvela. But his strength failed him finally and he collapsed.

The driver took me to Bakror village.

Over a mound of earth where buffaloes sat, and through the potato and wheat fields behind the village, the dew of the wheat stalks brushing against my calves, I balanced on the narrow berms of earth that divided each field. Two village tots trotted along on their short legs and bare feet, hurrying to keep up, and managing to exude a steady stream in their high voices.

'Gall pen, aunty, gall pen.' They meant ball pen. The whole of India seemed to need a pen, as though everyone had urgent letters to write. The morning was still cool. By the dry river bed, by a banyan tree, was the spot where the emaciated prince had collapsed. From the Dhungeshwari Mountain, Siddhartha would have walked down to the river, a most natural trajectory, to bathe in its clear waters. He would have walked westwards, perhaps following the setting sun. Still, it was roughly twenty kilometres or so, a considerable hike for a man who had barely eaten in six years.

'How did he make it?' I asked the local priest.

'It's like the rishis, their bodies are weak from all that penance, but they're full of shakti, they haven't eaten but they can walk for miles.'

The banyan tree was the fifth generation descendant of the banyan the prince sat under, according to the Hindu priest. Buddhist pilgrims had wound the tree about with their prayer flags, but this tree was also where the women from Bakror village still came to pray for a husband's longevity, where they came before a wedding and plucked three or four leaves for the big night. They had possibly been visiting the spot long before Siddhartha sat here and relished a meal. And that's perhaps what thirteen-year-old Sujata was doing at this spot, 2500 years ago, when she saw this strange, thin fellow and ran back home to fetch some khir.

Only in India could such an old story be so completely and utterly present.

From the Sujata Mandir, if you stand by the river and look across it, the top of the Mahabodhi Temple is clearly visible. The enormous temple sprang up right beside the tree under which Siddhartha saw the Way. The man-made structure dwarfs the peepul tree, but the tree is the reason pilgrims still visit. It made perfect sense that this was Siddhartha's next stop. Refreshed from the khir and the bath, he stopped at this bank where the buffalo-boy Svasti offered him khas grass to sit on.

Siddhartha made his way to the peepul tree where he sat, the branches of which are now supported by metal forks. At the time, he would have had a clear view of the Nairanjana River. The original peepul tree here was destroyed, the current one is said to have descended from a sprig in Sri Lanka, which in turn was taken from the original tree.

This is the holiest place for Buddhist pilgrims, the spot where Siddhartha reached Enlightenment, meditating on mind and body, on how each cell held the universe's entire wisdom. There was no such thing as a separate self.

He looked up at a peepul leaf fluttering in the wind and in the leaf, he could see the sun and the stars, how the leaf could not have grown without warmth and light, how without clouds there would be no moisture to feed the leaf. Indeed, the whole universe was present in the leaf.

One night, Siddhartha settled down to meditate as usual. Soothing forest sounds hushed around him; in the distance the river swirled its usual eddies. In the first hour of the night's first watch, he saw that 'organic and inorganic beings, minerals, mosses and grasses, insects, animals and people were all within him . . . He felt all the joys and sorrows of every living being'.[2]

By the second watch, he understood that birth and death were not real, that life was like the sea—while billions of waves keep rising and falling on the sea's surface, the sea itself is not changed by this. A great storm broke, soaking Siddhartha, but he ignored it.

During the third watch, Siddhartha saw that love and understanding were the same thing, that without understanding there was no love. The deluded mind divided reality into birth and death, into self and others, into non-existence and existence.[3]

'All beings contain within themselves the seeds of Enlightenment, and yet we drown in the ocean of birth and death for so many thousands of lifetimes!'[4] he exclaimed.

After years of torment and austerities and searching, Siddhartha had found the Way. He was at peace. According to one school, Prince Siddhartha attained Enlightenment in Vaisakh, one full moon in 623 BC.

එ

Xuanzang was quite overwhelmed. He looked into the branches of the tree and felt his eyes fill with tears, but a small part of him continued observing and noting so that he was able to record that kings and magistrates assembled under the tree to bathe its roots in milk, light lamps and scatter flowers.

A tear dripped down his cheek, and then Xuanzang was unable to hold himself in check. Perhaps he finally let out the pent-up emotions of his years of travel, of being metaphysically inadequate, or perhaps it was the simpler strain of being a stranger, a foreigner. He could, for a moment, be weak and vulnerable, drop his carapace of strength.

The hardship welled up, he thought of home, of China, and began to cry in earnest. Had it been worth it, to come this far and find himself wanting? He sobbed helplessly, his face pressed to the ground. As though from far away, he heard his own rasping and saw that his tears had dampened the ground. It was a rare moment of self-revelation to Hui Li.

> At the time when Buddha perfected himself in wisdom, I know not in what condition I was, in the troublous whirl of birth and death; but now, in this latter time of image (worship), having come to this spot and reflecting on the depth and weight of the body of my evil deeds, I am grieved at heart, and my eyes filled with tears.[5]

It was too hard, he wept. Too hard, to be kind and just and live moderately and well, to not grasp after things, after comfort. He was filled with self-doubt. And how on earth was he going to make it back home?

People were beginning to stare. A class of priests finishing a retreat stopped to watch the sorrowful Chinese monk. At length, one bent down and offered him a hand. Wiping his nose on his robe, drying his eyes, Xuanzang stumbled to his feet.

&

Candles burned. Monks sat at nooks and murmured prayers. It was silent and quiet around the tree and I sat cross-legged to watch. The trunk was flecked in gold paint, the main trunk wrapped in ochre cloth, girdled by a gold railing donated by Sri Lanka.

Along the lower branches there hung a garland of plastic flowers and the white silk scarves that the Tibetans had thrown up had got caught amongst peepul leaves. The railing was practically hidden under layers and layers of prayer flags of all persuasions.

A couple of Sri Lankan pilgrims, in white lungis and shirts, walked around the tree in silence, touching the lower boughs or bending to pick up fallen leaves. Since it was forbidden to tear off leaves or take mud from between the roots or climb onto the base of the tree, people waited for leaves to drop.

To the east of the tree, the Diamond Throne that was built by Ashoka now carried a gold statue of the Buddha facing the wall of the massive Mahabodhi Temple.

In this quiet, a Tibetan monk knelt and bowed his head before the

Diamond Throne to murmur prayers, his voice a strangled whisper; he rubbed his rosary against the plinth and trailed it over the Buddhist statue, hoping perhaps for enlightenment by osmosis.

ಲ

From Nalanda, Xuanzang went across the lower Bengal Delta, through land made swampy from the Ganga splitting into a web of waterways before spilling into the Bay of Bengal. He went down India's eastern coast, all the way through Orissa and Andhra Pradesh, swung up north to Maharashtra, round Gujarat and finally ended up full circle at Nalanda, only to have his teacher, Silabhadra, once more urge him eastwards to visit the insistent king of Assam.

In his narrative, Xuanzang writes about Assam exactly here, between Nalanda University and the ancient port of Tamralipta, now Tamluk. I would follow the same order.

chapter thirty-one

Land of the Eastern Light

Xuanzang's final journey in India was a journey to the east. The afternoon sun softened the outlines of the room in the monastery at Xian where the monk and his biographer sat. Dust motes bounced and settled in the beams of light. The small space was crowded with papers, piles and piles of parchments in orderly and disorderly towers. The journey had been pinned down, held to the written word. It had a new form, a physical shape.

Xuanzang came to Assam under duress. He was back in Nalanda after his long travels through India, studying further. He leaned into the rhythm of the days, the challenge of Nalanda's vast libraries, the sparks from his colleagues' minds. Ensconced in his philosophies, sated with India, he had no desire to be on the move. For once, the impetus to travel came from outside. It was Silabhadra who insisted on Assam. And, beloved teacher that he was, Xuanzang could refuse him nothing.

Bhaskaravarman, king of Kamrupa, as Assam was then called, bachelor, worshipper of Shiva, skipped a stone across the river's flat waters and tried to contain his curiosity. Word had travelled fast to the east, across the great river. Traders and travellers whispered of a priest of China with wondrous intellectual powers, a graceful lilt to his Sanskrit, not bad-looking either, who was staying in the kingdom of Magadha, at Nalanda University. Bhaskaravarman sent messengers bearing a sealed invitation for the monk, carefully worded, addressed to the head of the university, Silabhadra.

Years later, archaeologists found seals of Bhaskaravarman while digging at the site where the university used to be. The seals bore an elephant on the upper part and a genealogy below, minute things, witnesses to a long-ago correspondence.

The elderly chancellor of Nalanda was in a dilemma. He had already broached a debate with the Hinayanists, starring Xuanzang, at the court of King Harsha. If Harsha agreed to Silabhadra's debate and Xuanzang were unavailable, Nalanda University would be caught in a bind.

Silabhadra dismissed the Assamese messengers, but kindly. It was easier to offend a far-off king than one in his backyard. But he had not counted on Bhaskaravarman's temper. The king of Kamrupa wrote back firm words.

'If necessary then I will equip my army and elephants, and like the clouds sweep down on and trample to the very dust that monastery of Nalanda,'[1] the furious king wrote. Silabhadra's shrewd old eyes narrowed. He put it to his pupil in a way that the Chinese man would not be able to refuse.

'You desire to show your gratitude to Buddha, then you should propagate the true law. This is your duty,' Silabhadra said.

Xuanzang wanted to finish his work. And then, more than anything, he wanted to go home to China. But he could not refuse a call to Buddhist duty, and the possibility of converting a heretical king. He bit back a plea and prepared to leave for Assam. He packed, said fond farewells to his colleagues in Nalanda and reminded himself that Assam had been foretold.

Not long before, a naked Jain disciple called Vajra had burst into the monk's room.

Xuanzang asked him to read his horoscope.

The whites of the man's eyes stood out starkly against his smooth dark body. With a piece of chalk, he drew on the ground, cast lots. He walked around and stared at the priest. Then he began to laugh.

Xuanzang exhaled and said, 'I have to go back, but I have an enormous number of books and images, how will I carry it all back to China?'

The fortune teller stretched, yawned and scratched his belly.

'Do not be anxious,' the man said. King Harsha and the Assamese ruler would themselves send escorts. The Master would reach home without incident.

Xuanzang resigned himself to this new long journey, across a great river, to this land where Hindus dominated, where there were few Buddhists and even they prayed in secret.

࿇

I boarded a plane from Kolkata to Guwahati, looking down from the plane window to see the Brahmaputra whip and dive and curve far below across the vast alluvial plain of this riverine land. One swipe of the river's arm could eat a whole city.

Somewhere below these sands and these waters Xuanzang had his conversation with Bhaskaravarman in the Land of the Eastern Light. Somewhere in this plentiful valley covered in banana trees, coconut trees, yellow trumpet flowers amidst their slim leaves, Xuanzang spoke to Bhaskaravarman with a sudden deep longing for home, a realization that all he had to do was cross the mountains of Arunachal Pradesh and he would be in Sichuan, the kingdom of Shuh.

It was as if his malaise slid across the centuries and infected me with lethargy. I felt depleted. How big this country was, what distances. For a moment, it felt as though I had dragged myself through molasses. It was as though, with each step I took, a bit of flesh caught on a thorn and I had to yank at it to move on. But each fresh discovery kept me going, the knowledge was the prize. The way the pieces kept falling into place, each pained brush-stroke, filled out a picture. And there was some nameless momentum that bowled me along.

Besides, knowing these things brought peace. Learning these things about my country, I could move on. I had pulled this land close to me by its collar, stared it in the eye and now I could set it down and walk away.

࿇

Xuanzang bowed to the king of Assam. To his surprise Bhaskaravarman, king of Kamrupa, rose from his throne, approached the monk and spoke to him directly, as though they were strolling in a garden and the entire court had vanished into thin air.

'Although I am without talents myself, I have always been fond of men of conspicuous learning,'[2] the Assamese king said.

Was this the usual polite talk? Xuanzang looked up in surprise and found himself liking the man. There was a warmth in his eyes, a refusal to hide behind titles and crowns, a curiosity about other lands. The monk searched for the right words. And when they tumbled out, he believed them fervently.

'I have only moderate wisdom, and I am confused to think that you should have heard of my poor reputation.'[3]

Bhaskaravarman tried not to stare at the tall stranger. A hundred questions pounded at his throat. What is it like to wander unfettered by royal duties, to walk without courtiers stumbling underfoot? The king turned his gaze, afraid his eyes would reveal a sudden jealousy of such an unimaginable freedom. But the monk understood and the two men smiled at each other. For a short, wordless moment, there were no barriers.

∽

I began my search for the seventh century behind the Archaeological Office on Guwahati's main street. There was a forgotten maidan, overgrown with grass, a patch of land between two neighbours' houses. But it had been excavated in neatly dug square pits, and leaning into them were low boundary walls, corners, rooms, indicating superimposed buildings, six or seven phases.

I felt rested. A good night's sleep had restored my spirits. Lunch with Atanoo Barua cheered me up no end. He was an Assamese tea master and took me under his wing with impeccable hospitality. My hosts in Kolkata had instructed me to contact him. He was fiftyish, with a trimmed grey beard, a slight paunch, fair-skinned. His crackling intelligence delighted me. I never asked a question he could not answer.

It was Atanoo who guided me through the subtleties of Assamese cooking. Look, he said, as we sat down to lunch, how everything is perfectly balanced between acid and alkaline dishes. We discussed a short history of Assam, over a meal of tenga fish of the carp family, fried in a spot of mustard oil and then simmered in a tomato-based gravy till the flesh flaked off the bones. There was khara, green papaya chopped and stir-fried in the barest hint of mustard oil, water added till it was pulpy, and it left me with a curiously contented feeling. Atanoo also told me about the archaeological site at Ambari, where I was now nosing around for Xuanzang's traces, in the company of the local archaeologist, Dr Dutta.

'Many geographical kingdoms were developing at that stage,' Dr Dutta told me, also peering into the pits, although he must have seen them hundreds of times. 'No paramount kingdom, no inscriptions were found,' he said. Was this a place of habitation? It was not clear. Archaeologists found a number of sandstone statues lying in neat horizontal rows. It could have been a production centre, perhaps a sculptors' colony, patronized by a rich king.

The Brahmaputra flowed nearby so the water level was high and it was difficult to excavate much deeper. But the earliest level they found was of the eighth century AD.

What if there wasn't anything before the eighth century? If this was the case, it meant the city would have developed after the Chinese monk came by and so perhaps I had to find his tracks elsewhere.

At the museum, I learned that the site was found quite by accident when the Reserve Bank of India was digging foundations for a Guwahati office. They found bricks and dressed, decorated stone blocks. Residential areas were protected by boundary walls. Over three metres remained submerged. Charcoal samples from a depth of 1.2 metres dated from about AD 1030. A vast quantity of antiques was found—carved stone images and, amongst other things, Chinese celadon pottery.

Later trade links, it looked like.

At the museum, there was also a stone pillar: serpents entwined, tails as ballast and heads meeting as though lightly kissing, which could not fail to remind me of China's Nu Wa and Fu Xi, that old creation legend, head of a woman, body of a serpent. I had seen a similar painting in the museum at New Delhi, in the Central Asian collection. My mind zigzagged over the connections, here, again, even in China, the link between women and snakes echoed thinly on this stone pillar in Assam.

The archaeologists suggested I backtrack four hours west of

Guwahati and have a look at Goalpara, an older site. And, in fact, one of their men was going that very day and could show me the site. Why not, I thought, there was nothing to lose.

But it was a rough drive on the narrow roads to Goalpara. I was badly battered in the van's back seat, clenching my teeth against each bump. The ASI camp was set in the middle of a village. We arrived after dark, to the light of only kerosene lamps. Palm trees rose against a silky sky, the stars a pointille.

Assam in spring had a particular aroma at dusk, as though punctuating the change in the day. Before and after sunset the air became redolent, perfumed, a mixture of dried tea leaves, woodsmoke, dampness, flowers and something else. I shut my eyes and searched, reached for a memory but it vanished, a crab in damp sand. Diaphanous, moody Assam.

I soaked in my drives through these back roads like a precious gift. Who knew when I would be back, in this corner of my so very diverse country. Sometimes I thought it held together through inertia. Woodsmoke rose straight up in the windless dusk. Dried banana leaves hung over poles, making a curtain and, along the road, fishermen by a river dangled silvery fish, the fresh catch of the day. By a railroad track, men cracked open mounds of young coconut for their sweet milk.

In a mud compound in Goalpara, the archaeologists had tamped the earth and fashioned an enclosure. Somebody had split ikora reeds and made a gate that swung on hinges. It would at most keep the village goats out, but it provided a magic circle of sorts, a *lakshman rekha*.

The Assamese village women dished up deep-fried fish, dal and tenga fish cooked on woodfire stoves in the narrow kitchen of bamboo and mud. One had a little girl who dribbled and smiled and waved her pudgy hands. The grandmother walked out, bare-breasted, and smiled a toothless smile. I grinned back at her.

At night, I slept in a spare room under a mosquito net and tried to ignore the cockroaches. The lizard inching across the ceiling I did not mind. I had watched lizards since I was a little girl, flashing behind pictures hanging on walls.

Bimal Sinha, the archaeologist on site, was precise, and under his tutelage the next morning my eyes began to pick out bricks of other sizes—smaller, added, made bigger—and an old path covered over by a new building. See, he said, how they raised the boundary wall and made a *garbhagriha*.

There were two stages, Bimal informed me, as we stepped across the low walls, one during the seventh and eighth centuries, and the other during the ninth to twelfth centuries. There were no inscriptions. But maybe, he said, it was built by Bhaskaravarman. He was a very prosperous king, he used many bricks. If there was a settlement by this temple complex, it has been washed away, he said.

So perhaps here, then, stood Xuanzang and the king of Assam, discussing China.

Bimal Sinha was anxious to show me the one clear sign of Buddhism: several black granite stupas on the hill, like upside down tea cups, cut from the rock itself. They were crude and therefore imposing. Smaller votive stupas were scattered around the hillside, simply carved atop boulders where they lodged as though some ancient rockslide had halted at this valley, presenting a sculptor with the perfect setting.

The site dated from the first century BC to the first century AD. I guessed it had died out by the time the monk came by, for he says there were few monks and those that existed practised in secret. Why the secrecy, if Bhaskaravarman was as tolerant as history paints him to be?

I was satisfied with my Buddhist sighting. Not much was left, even by Xuanzang's account, and the scholars themselves were still vague about the exact site.

∞

'On the east . . .' Xuanzang began to write. His heart thudded like a pebble being shaken in a gourd. Excitement and disappointment mingled, and a fleeting possibility of home. He could not abandon the idea. He sketched maps, measured distances and paced the floor. In Kamrupa his ties to India loosened, he missed Silabhadra, but less. His feet itched and he was shocked at how badly he wanted to go home.

He wrote:

On inquiry I ascertained that after a two months' journey we reach
the south-western frontiers of the province of Sz'chuen (Shuh). But
the mountains and rivers present obstacles, and the pestilential air,
the poisonous vapours, the fatal snakes, the destructive vegetation,
all these causes of death prevail . . .[4]

It was not to be.

ಀ

Assam intrigued me, the way it was India and yet not. Atanoo had
smarted over Assam's isolation.

'We are a part of India, but we have always been neglected,' he
grumbled. 'It's too far from Delhi. Finally, in 1962, Delhi built a
bridge over the Brahmaputra. Until then, they did nothing for Assam.'

Would New Delhi even defend Assam? Atanoo had his doubts.
'The Chinese in 1962 came right up to Tezpur. Jawaharlal Nehru
reputedly said my heart goes out to the people of Assam, but essentially
he was not going to do anything about it.' Nehru was long dead, but
India's border states were still upset with him.

'Okay, Assam is insular, it's fertile, people have tended to stay
here, it's humid, yes, we do become a little lazy,' Atanoo said, sipping
water.

Assam was lush and lovely in spring. In the south-east spread the
tea plantations where elephants still ran wild. It was odd that the
monk did not mention the one-horned rhinos. I twirled a pen and
thought of Kaziranga, where the one-horned rhino flourished.

Travelling through Assam in the seventh century, I imagined,
would have been much like a walk through Kaziranga. So I went,
because I love forest noises. The heart of ancient India, I feel, still
beats in these pockets of relative wilderness, even though they are
always hemmed in by the press of people at their edges.

A few days later I sat happily, snug between a mahout and a park
ranger on an elephant, on the lookout for rhinos. We plashed through
a river, through the elephant grass clumps, past male buffaloes, their

horns making a crescent over their heads. And within minutes, we spotted a one-horned rhino, a male that shifted its armoured bulk through the tall grasses, turned and vanished, its thick plates wrinkled and sagging at the back, a comic sight.

It had flicked its big ears, blinked small piggy eyes set in a misshapen head. There were great piles of rhino scat, perfect globes, deposited in the same place every day, for they are neat animals.

Wind rustled through the plains and the grass whispered back. There were wild buffaloes further into the plains, one a mother who lowered her head and waggled horns threateningly. She was getting ready to charge the strangers who approached her calf. The elephant backed off, short steps, raising its head. The ranger half-lifted his shotgun, ready to blank-fire. A jungle fowl called the arrival of a full-fledged morning.

I was enthralled. I wanted it to go on forever. Did Xuanzang ever pause in one of India's forests and take in these extraordinary moments?

A rhino had waded into the coolness of a lake. A spot-billed pelican glided and flapped its wings, settling on the water surface. Termite hills rose along the dirt track; in the undergrowth the wings of a pheasant flashed.

This was the tune of my journey: I learned of the things that fell across my path, nothing more, nothing less. Particular facts clung to me like barnacles on a rock, random creatures that clung and aged until the rock assumed another shape.

An irresponsible approach to history, perhaps, but no matter how hard one tried, was there any other approach than the entirely subjective?

chapter thirty-two

Reunited

I yanked myself out of this soft-focus dream and flew back to Kolkata, thinking again of my monk, missing him, flipping through my book to find him.

'Welcome back,' he grinned through the smoke of centuries. 'You have a long way to go.' Then, abruptly, he turned with his hands behind him, and strolled to the window. Vanished.

After this detour to Assam, to Xuanzang's future, I would head to the ancient port city of Tamralipta in Bengal.

S. flew into Kolkata. He had quit the job that kept him tied to the United States of America, at the end of long-distance phones in dozens of cities on my path. We both knew that his leaving the US threw open many doors for a future together. It left me a little tremulous.

Enough of separation, I thought.

'You're late, as usual,' he grinned at me at the airport.

'It's not my fault,' I said happily. 'The taxi broke down, the traffic was horrible. Welcome back.'

Welcome back to India, to me. To us. I stretched into the comfort of his presence. It felt like a beginning. He was tanned from his travels in South America. He had gone diving in Belize. In his gentle manner, he settled into the journey comfortably, adapting to the days and rhythms. And it felt as though he belonged there.

March was drawing to an end. The humidity settled like some creature in the air; in minutes we were sweating and hot, the ruffled air didn't help.

After Xuanzang left Nalanda he undertook a vast tour of India, heading down the country's eastern coast, stopping in the port of Tamluk.

Tamluk was a good eighty kilometres south-west of Kolkata, a rough drive swerving around trucks laden with goods. 'The Bengalis here, they're the kind that start *eenta-patthar* (riots) at the slightest provocation,' the Bihari driver told us.

We crossed another large river, boats floating on it. We turned off onto a feeder road and quickly, thankfully, found ourselves driving through paddy fields and village markets, the roadsides lined with banana trees. The bel fruit was ripe, like small melons. Clothes sticking to our backs, we drove into the village of Tamluk.

ଡ଼

It borders on the sea. The ground is low and rich; it is regularly cultivated, and produces flowers and fruits in abundance. The temperature is hot. The manners of the people are quick and hasty. The men are hardy and brave . . . There are about ten sangharamas, with about 1000 priests. The Deva temples are fifty in number, in which various sectaries dwell mixed together. The coast of this country is formed by (or in) a recess of the sea; the water and the land embracing each other. Wonderful articles of value and gems are collected here in abundance and therefore the people of the country are in general very rich.[1]

ଡ଼

There was a local museum, the usual place to find archaeological information. But a lock hung firmly on the door.

'Look for Proshanto,' a passer-by said. 'Proshanto has the keys but Proshanto has gone to the bank for some work.' At the bank they said Proshanto had gone to the railway station.

We walked right through a cricket game in search of the station. On every corner, shopkeepers' radios crackled with the commentary of the cricket test match. Our search for Proshanto wilted as the sun rose and finally we walked down to the river bank, a logical place for an ancient port. It was steaming. Women swam in tanks of green brackish water to cool off. It was an abandoned bank. Only a few vessels were left now, with double masts made of bamboo, like wide ladders stuck in the middle of a ship. The opposite bank vanished into the noon heat. Somewhere here used to be the buzzing, vast port of Tamluk.

From here somewhere, Fa Xian set sail 200 years before Xuanzang, heading north to Canton. This was the place from where, some accounts have it, a prince and a princess stole away in AD 310, hugging under their robes a sacred tooth relic of the Buddha, boarded a trade ship and sailed in a straight line south to Ceylon, where they knew they'd be safe. (Or was it from Kalinga, as other accounts say?)

'Oi, Thakurdada,' a man digging a ditch called out, seeing S. and I walk through his patch. What is the time? He indicated his wrist.

How foreign we were here! Even I, the Indian, could not speak a word of the language. *Ami Bangla janina.*

chapter thirty-three

Flower Mountain

In a great mountain on the south-west frontiers of the country is a sangharama called Pushpagiri (Pu-se-po-k'I-li); the stone stupa belonging to it exhibits very many spiritual wonders (miracles). On fast-days it emits a bright light. For this cause believers from far and near flock together here and present as offerings beautifully embroidered (flower) canopies (umbrellas) . . .[1]

Xuanzang too had trouble with the language as he pushed even further south, to Ucha, Udra, or Orissa, to where the words and language differed from those of 'Mid-India' as he put it. He said the climate was hot, the people uncivilized, tall of stature and of a yellowish-black complexion.

ೲ

By the time we reached Orissa, the mango trees were bent with green knobs of fruit ripening, already that distinctive shape, pulled out at one end. In sleepy Bhubaneswar, the rickshaw prices inched up as the sun rose higher. Sitting on one, bumping along a back road, we sank into the non-citylike rhythms of Bhubaneswar. The city was dotted with ancient Hindu temples by the roadsides, careless jewels dropped by history. How *small* they were, how scaled to human size. It was a sleepy town where it hardly mattered if you came or went.

I hung around, listened and waited for a clue to the whereabouts of Pushpagiri, letting the town tell its secrets in its own time, just what it wanted me to know. Nothing more, nothing less. In the meantime, we wandered to the Parasuramesvara Temple. S. took photos.

I bent to enter the inner sanctum, so dark that I had to squint to see the Shiva lingam in an enormous yoni, the opening of the cervix, the vagina, facing north. Seven metal serpents, their hoods flared, stood around the Shiva lingam. A plate of flowers balanced on the phallus. My throat constricted, or was it a focusing of energies within this dark womb-temple? Lightning streaked the sky.

Orissa was where I first met the four-armed Chamunda, dating from the eighth century AD. She sat scowling at the museum. Her veins stuck out over a bone-thin body. She wore a skull necklace and held a decapitated head in her hand, by the hair. Her face was sagging flesh, cords stood out on her neck, a serpent coiled around her upper arm, her skull was crowned with flames. The crone's breasts were thin flaps over her ribs. One arm cupped a bowl (or a half-skull) at her chest, filled with blood I should think. The statue was terrifying.

Chamunda was connected with the worship of Saptamatrika, the seven mother goddesses, which was an important aspect of the Shakti cult, the divine feminine power, I learned. The cult embodied the energies and powers of seven famous gods: female counterparts of Brahma, Vishnu, Maheshwar (Shiva), Indra, Kumara, Varaha and Yama. But who came first?

Brahmani, Vaishnavi, Maheshwari, Indrani, Kaumari, Varahi, and here, magnificent, straight from some bloodied nightmare, Chamunda.

There was also a Buddhist statue, found in Khadipada, from the seventh century, cracked in half, the eyes hacked out with a hatchet, long ears. There were pilasters of Buddhist railings, shaped like almonds standing end on end, dating from the first century.

It seemed symbolic of the eventual defeat of Buddhism in India that in these eastern parts Tantra arose, although scholars argue terrifically over where it did, placing it equally convincingly in the south, in Andhra, and in the west. There was little doubt in my mind, though, that this region was the root of magic, where psychic practices twisted into cults of goddesses and gods to give rise to esoteric, secretive schools, where Buddhist sorcerers practised black magic, drowning out sober, monkish habits.

All that was possibly later, much after Xuanzang. At any rate, during his sojourn, the Chinese monk was preoccupied with the tussle between the Hinayanists and Mahayanists. This third, tangential school with its eighty-four mystics, he did not mention.

But what of Xuanzang's monastery at Pushpagiri?

All I had was a name. Dr S.K. Moharana was the author of an article on Buddhism in Orissa, an article I had stumbled on in Delhi at the ASI library.[2] After a number of inquiries at the museum in Bhubaneswar, it emerged that Dr Moharana worked in the state's department of finance by day and wrote on Buddhism by night.

With the help of Mr C.B. Patel at the museum, we obtained a special permit to enter the compound of the Orissa Secretariat, a maze of buildings painted a delicate shade of pink. The window shutters were a bright turquoise. We found Dr Moharana, Section Officer, in the Orissa Secretariat in Hall No. 1 of the finance department, in an office where fans revolved slowly and dusty paper files tied with string leaned atop cupboards.

March was the end of the fiscal year and Orissa's finance department was busy. I waited while he finished scribbling notes on a piece of paper. A small hush fell over the gathering. We drank the sweet tea the peon brought. Dr Moharana cleared away some papers. He was amazed that somebody had read his words in faraway Delhi.

'My work is now outdated,' he said. 'There is a certain Dr Pradhan. He has pinpointed the exact location of Pushpagiri. There is no doubt now that Languripahar is the place where Xuanzang went.' He pronounced it Hooen Tsiang, like all Indians. He waved to a peon for more tea. 'It has yielded some materials that prove it to be Pushpagiri—stones, inscriptions.'

My heart began to thump.

Gripped with excitement, we arranged to meet the archaeologist, Dr Pradhan, at Languripahar, armed with directions. It was not far from Udaigiri and Ratnagiri. The krishnachuda tree was in bloom. We stocked up on biscuits and bottles of Bisleri and drove a couple of hours outside Bhubaneswar in a hired Ambassador. The heat of the sun receded under clouds filled with rain. It was time for Orissa's afternoon storm. Lightning slipped across the sky. Chickens squawked across the road, avoiding tyres, and the saris of women wrapped around their legs as the wind blew up. Through rice fields and coconut palms, we pulled up at the bottom of a hill and walked over to the primary school that doubled as an archaeologists' shack. We leaned over to examine the statues of Buddha that Dr Pradhan had found.

໐ๅ

Was it in one of these monasteries that the Hinayanists lived? The proud Hinayanists who, in a moment of folly, challenged the great King Harshavardhana, defender of the rival Mahayana Buddhism, student of Silabhadra at Nalanda University? Perhaps the Orissan monks had chosen a bad time. Harshavardhana had subjugated Kongada, by Chilka Lake, and was returning through Orissa to the north. Xuanzang had finished his grand tour of India and was back at Nalanda.

Hinayanism was deeply entrenched in Orissa. Early Buddhism had spilled to Burma, Sri Lanka and Thailand through the language of Pali, and Kalinga, an old name for Orissa, played a key missionary role, sending monks in boats to these areas to set up Buddhist settlements.[3]

The Hinayana monks of Orissa scoffed at Mahayanist thinkers at Nalanda University, its 'sky flower' doctrine, which said that all phenomena are like sky flowers: not of the real world, not delivered by the Buddha!

Harshavardhana growled at them: 'What do you mean by these words of reproach?'[4]

The Hinayanist monks presented Harsha with a copy of a work by an old Brahmin teacher, Prajnagupta, who was also an expert in Hinayana Buddhism. He had written a text which demolished the Mahayana arguments in 700 slokas. 'This represents our doctrine,' they said. It was a challenge, to thrash it out in a public debate, to come up with any other school that could refute a single word of it.

Harsha hurried to his capital and immediately dispatched a letter to his friend and mentor Silabhadra at Nalanda. Silabhadra, University Chancellor, no fool, rallied to the battle. He selected three monks, and Xuanzang. But the three Indian monks were losing their nerve. Could it really be that the luminaries of Nalanda were afraid to take on a couple of monks from the seaside? Or was this bombast from Hui Li? Or was it, as some say, the crack into which history pushed a wedge, this diffidence of the Mahayanists a sign of a sickness, a foreshadow of its decline and its twist into the esoteric practices of Tantrayana?[5]

Xuanzang stepped in and offered to go. They were nothing, these priests of Orissa, he insisted, his slender wisdom would be quite enough to defeat them. And if, by chance, they won, it would be the reputation of a foreigner, of a mere Chinese priest, that would suffer. However, as Xuanzang prepared to visit Orissa a second time, another dispatch arrived from Harshavardhana. There was no immediate pressure for his former request, he said.

But Xuanzang was curious about the 700 heretical slokas of the Small Vehicle. He begged a man he had defeated in debate to show it to him. His opponent agreed, but only to do it secretly, in the middle of the night, so that Xuanzang's reputation would not suffer. Xuanzang, hopelessly addicted to debates, immediately refuted Prajnagupta's work in 1600 slokas. He called his efforts 'The Destruction of Heresy'.[6] He pinned it down after several tries, earlier efforts crossed and double-crossed, and sat back to admire his handiwork. This was the man, Xuanzang's secret night tutor, who then went to Assam and told Bhaskaravarman about the Chinese monk.

so

At Pushpagiri's coming storm, already water drops flecked off the sandstone Buddhas, surrounded by terracotta debris of a long-gone people. A north-westerly wind snapped and the smell of damp earth rose to meet the lightning against a grey sky. The tal and date palms whipped around and then rain sheeted down over Pushpagiri, Flower Mountain. It sent us racing for cover into the primary school building.

'This was inaccessible because of a network of rivers; the region becomes waterlogged in the monsoon,' Dr Pradhan said, above the noise of the rain. The whole place was a habitation area, he said, pointing with a sandalled toe to what could have been a monk's mortar stone embedded in the earth. It was used perhaps for grinding medicinal herbs.

Sandstone deepens in colour in the rain. The two Buddhas under their stone hoods got wetter and darker as thunder crackled above. As suddenly as it started, the storm bowed out.

We climbed up the moist mound, with umbrellas held against the last drops of rain. The vast mound of the main stupa was overgrown with grass. Dr Pradhan pointed out an outer and inner boundary wall.

There was an Ashokan stupa. Archaeologists had found twenty-eight railing pillars with the almond-shaped carvings, dating from the third century BC. They found inscriptions, as well as the northern black polished ware associated with the Mauryan period. There was a single entrance to the south.

Further up the hill, a panel dated from the first century AD. There were mridangam dance poses, rock-cut stupas of sandstone. There was a dance scene at the bottom, from Kushan times, as though the artist had carved it in bas-relief and then decided to experiment with perspective, carving smaller ones to give the impression of depth.

Given the ancient date, would Xuanzang not have seen these panels?

The key finding was an inscription that identified the location, carved rudely on a stone still stuck in the ground: *Pushpagiri Kanana (Jungle, vihar) by Prarachabala.* 'Bala' is a title indicating cultivator or farmer.

'The title is used to this day,' Dr Pradhan told us. The man may have donated it, a visible declaration of faith, a purchase of insurance against bad luck in later years or later lives.

There were the ruins of a monastery, a floor paved with stones. Somewhere here, the monk rose and prayed and meditated on Flower Mountain. The hills were now dark blue, threaded with a transparent post-rain mist, and through the clouds the sun shot rays across the fields.

There were five convents, Xuanzang said, five hills around Pushpagiri. Dr Pradhan pointed them out: Kayama, Dhauli, Tarapur, Neulpur and Vajragiri.

To the north-east, the Kimriya or Kelua River flowed. On Kayama, they found an inscription that said 'Sri Sri Buddha', an inscription from the seventh or eighth century AD. The evidence was clear as day.

A silk cotton tree grew on the mound, bearing a single crimson flower. There were even records of donations made to Pushpagiri, according to an inscription from the third century AD. I was so delighted, I could not stop grinning. It was an archaeological jackpot. Who would have imagined, even a year ago, that such an obscure discovery would have brightened my day in this extraordinary manner. I congratulated Dr Pradhan on his work.

S. was as pleased as I was. I caught his eye and smiled.

There was one more stop, to the south of Bhubaneswar, to the rock edict of King Ashoka. It was the First Edict. It was a grandiose statement. But in the depths of the rock lay an anguished man, and the dawning of a realization.

The battle of Kalinga was fought somewhere in this region. What a massive army King Ashoka must have had. The dead were said to be innumerable—there were 100,000 wounded, 150,000 taken prisoner. The king's army must have numbered over 500,000 as it marched south on a highway from the capital Patna to somewhere near Bhubaneswar.[7]

Perhaps one rainy morning, this king of ancient India sat here and wept at the devastation he had wrought, leaning on this rock, perhaps still clad in battle clothes stained with blood as the water ran off his sword and his tears mixed with rain dripping into the ground.

And so the Dhauli rock edict marks a beginning of solemnity, sobriety, for how could there be celebrations ever again, after Kalinga?

> This rescript on morality has been caused to be written on the . . . mountain by King Devanampriya Priyadarsin . . . Here no living being must be killed and sacrificed. And also no festival meeting must be held. For King Devanampriya Priyadarsin sees much evil in festival meetings.

chapter thirty-four

Ocean's Edge

On the south-east frontiers of the country, on the borders of the ocean, is the town Charitra, (Che-li-ta-lo), about 20 *li* round. Here it is merchants depart for distant countries, and strangers come and go and stop here on their way. The walls of the city are strong and lofty. Here are found all sorts of rare and precious articles.[1]

From Pushpagiri, Xuanzang headed further south, down the shores of Chilka Lake, stopping at one tip of the saltwater lagoon. Dr Pradhan thought that at present-day Manikpattan might lie Xuanzang's port city of Che-li-ta-lo or 'port of departure'.

At Manikpattan they had found many Chinese materials, indicating a steady trade with China. There was Kaolin pottery, dating from the second to the third centuries. There were also thousands of pieces of celadon pottery, as well as unfinished pieces. The locals had perhaps tried to copy the fine celadon stuff, but it didn't work, the chemistry of the clay was too different.

Perhaps it was at Manikpattan that Xuanzang stood at the edge of the waves and gazed south one night, towards Sri Lanka. He wrote that he could see the tooth-stupa of the Buddha, shimmering as though a bright torch burned in the air. He was feeling lyrical and the drug of travel was on him. He thought he could go on forever, conquering horizon after horizon. He badly wanted to go to Sri Lanka.

Perhaps he chatted with merchants at the port who told him of sea voyages to Sri Lanka. Orissa and Sri Lanka had a long, friendly history, for if you sat on a boat and the wind blew south, it was a straight line to the northern shore of Ceylon.

Kalinga dwellers travelled the seas in droves to Sri Lanka, to pay homage to the tooth relic there. The royal families intermarried, powerfully linked by the Hinayanist school.[2]

∞

From Bhubaneswar, we took a public bus to the edge of Chilka Lake, along with a group of tourists from Bengal. The bus stopped for darshan at a temple, and the Hindu priests did their rapacious act, the temple firmly in their hands, a sacred dab on the forehead for a solid rupee donation. They glared at S.

'Is he Hindu?'

'No,' I said.

'He can't come in,' they said rudely.

Mournfully, S. noted that he was very familiar with the outside of many Hindu temples. But I was quite unable to contain my happiness. I had happened to point at lush ripe jackfruit hanging from a tree, with its spiky exterior.

'What do you call this?' I asked in Hindi.

'*Panas*,' one of the local tourists said. Which is exactly what Xuanzang calls it.

The bus wound through Orissa's back roads, past Manikpattan, south towards the tip of the lagoon, which here curved inland from the Bay of Bengal, shallow and thick with fish and birds. On its northern edge, dolphins rose and dived again by the tour boat. The Bengali women were dressed for cocktails, in gold earrings, bangles and silk saris. I had forgotten how they pinned up their hair with V-shaped pins and the older ones pulled a hair net over the chignon to keep it all in place.

'The sound of silence,' the guide pleaded in English, both arms out. 'The sound of silence.' And in the distance, I thought I saw the hunched figure of a Chinese monk hurrying south.

We decided to cross to the lagoon's southern edge by boat, a three-hour journey that began early in the morning. The water was so shallow that far into the lagoon, fishermen were still only upto their thighs in water, muscles tight against the current, spreading blue shrimp nets between reeds planted in the soft bottom, pushing

their boats with poles. We saw a pair of Brahmani kites, or garuda.
With their burnt-orange wings, black tips, biggish white heads, they
balanced on top of reeds. It was particularly auspicious to see the
garuda, the mount of Vishnu, gliding, not flapping their wings, not
sitting. People waited for days to spot one on a Thursday.

Our small boat glided into Balagaon, on the other side of the lake
and we hopped a bus south to Kongada, or Ganjam, consulted our
train schedule and found that the Falaknuma Express went straight
from Berhampur to Vijayawada.

I had been on the road nearly a year. The last three weeks with S.
had removed me somewhat from the journey. Solitude is a great
guru, but companionship can be harder. We made love, we fought,
but it was as though we turned a corner and he was softer and kinder,
more loving. There was no carping at each other, a lot of laughing.

The train disgorged us, still sleepy, early one morning, into
Vijayawada, and I drank in the delight of more foreignness, India yet
not-India. It was spotlessly clean, for one thing. There was instant
coffee readily available, for another. There were trash cans chained
to pillars, fruit juice stands. Laburnums, bright yellow, outside, and
the language—a whole new pebbly sound, like fingertips off a tabla.
Telugu, Telugu.

The language was different from mid-India, the monk had
commented too. Xuanzang found his way to Dhanakataka, where he
studied the Buddhist canon further with two monks, Subhuti and Surya,
who explained the *Tripitaka* according to the Mahasanghika school.

In Vijayawada, I dived into a local beauty parlour, for the city
was dotted with parlours for 'Ladies' and 'Gents'. The monk and his
quest receded as Vijayalakshmi slapped ayurvedic creams and
sandalwood paste on my face and then rubbed into my scalp a heated
concoction of coconut oil, castor oil and almond oil until I almost
sobbed with delight.

'You must drink coconut water every day,' she advised, as she
patted with her fingers and tugged and tapped. 'It's cooling and
prevents headaches from the heat. The water of the Krishna River is
sweet.'

'People's tempers here are bad, *gussa aata hai*,' she said, her not-
bad Hindi learned in Delhi. 'The heat makes them sweat and then

they get angry.' How odd to hear the words of a seventh-century monk fall from the mouth of this modern beautician. There was to be no break for me.

'The climate is hot. The complexion of the people is a yellowish-black, and they are by nature fierce and impulsive,'[3] Xuanzang wrote of Dhanakataka.

'Very hysterical place,' Vijayalakshmi said (slap-slap, pat-pat). She meant historical. 'Many ancient things. We live here only and ourselves we don't see.'

The Krishna belt is studded with topes and stupas, a rich Buddhist past. Andhra's oldest monuments were all Buddhist, but here too there were signs of the decay that had set in and begun to weaken the foundations of the sangha. Mahayana Buddhism opened its arms to a plethora of gods and goddesses, Vajrayana Tantrism followed and degenerated into rites of Shakti. One thing led to another, and to this day in Andhra each Buddhist mound is known popularly as Lanjadibba and Bhogandanidibba, or mound of the prostitute.[4]

Scholars identify Xuanzang's Dhanakataka with the ruins of an ancient settlement and important political centre that lies about a mile west of the great stupa of Amaravati. It was a monument of a great age. An inscription dates it to the second century AD. But Mauryan writings, the historical equivalent of 'Ashoka was here' graffiti, push the date back another 400 years, to 200 BC.

It was the last day of March. The heat was a torment. We tried to start early to beat the sun, but no matter how early we left, the day grew fierce and filled with battle. We would head to Amaravati, Xuanzang's Dhanakataka, in our hired Ambassador. Thaadichittoo grew everywhere, a type of fan palm, its spiky leaves dried and spliced to form cool walls. A few women harvested the last of the red chilli bushes, only a few chilli shrubs now hung with hot red exclamation marks. All along, in between villages, were swatches of chilli carpets spread out to dry, being readied to be tossed into curries all over the nation. Farmers piling chillies onto bullock carts made a startling picture: white oxen, bright vermilion chillies and the toffee-coloured earth behind. There were cotton bolls still in fluffs, pulled off the tops of shrubs, and bits of cotton had stuck in the bottom branches of the amla trees that lined the back roads. We rumbled through Mothadaka village and, soon enough, arrived at Dhanakataka. In the monsoon, when the river swelled, you could boat westwards from Vijayawada and moor in at Amaravati. *Why didn't precise, meticulous Xuanzang say anything about a river?*

At the museum in the village, we got a taste of the sculpture, with its waxy look of pale green jade. The paleness of the stone gave the sculpture an ethereal feel, as though if you blinked, it might melt in the heat. There was a standing Buddha in the signature limestone of Amaravati. He had a noticeably broader, flatter nose; these were the features around me. His robe was flung over the crook of his left arm, pleats across his chest, right shoulder bare, thicker lips, lower lip sticking out slightly. It still carried traces of ochre paint.

Outside was a vast circular mound, empty, desolate, overgrown with grass. This was the base of the grandiose monument that once stood 100 feet high. Archaeologists had pieced together the fallen bits of stone and reconstructed in their imagination a massive edifice, surrounded by rails, with four gates at the cardinal points. Believers entered at the gates and circled the stupa, muttering prayers perhaps.

Here too was an unexpected clue to the origins of something I had seen, now so long ago, in China: Guanyin, the Buddhist Goddess of Mercy. An inscription dating from the second century AD referred to the installation of the goddess Bhagavati Pushpatara. Tara was the Shakti of the Avalokiteshvara Buddha, his female counterpart, the name derived from the root *tar*, to cross; Tara as in helping to cross the Ocean of Existence.[5]

From here, it was an easy hop to the female Buddhist Goddess of Mercy who gradually became far more important, indeed, subsumed the very identity of Avalokiteshvara for the Chinese worshippers so many miles away.

We backtracked from Amaravati to Undavalli and looked out over the Krishna River at banana plantations, lush and green. Three sages sat at a rock-cut cave in regal postures, looking out over the river, here a docile narrow stream. There was the sharp ammonia stench of bat guano and the familiar twittering.

It was a Buddhist-style monastery, cells scooped out from the hillside, but filled with Hindu gods, a small detritus of the way the two religions lazily lapped and overlapped, borrowing elements from each other, back and forth, until Buddhism quietly sank back into the Hindu sea that had given birth to it.

I had my own teacher. Not a monk, but a retired archaeologist I had lunch with. It took a long, unplanned detour to Hyderabad to meet this Telugu Brahmin, a red powder tika between his half-closed eyes, a short man with sculptured features, taurine shoulders, a powerful voice, a commanding presence.

Dr I.K. Sharma wore a vest and a crisp white lungi with a red border. He scoffed at dating Amaravati to Ashokan times. It was even earlier.

'You must think of Andhra as a centre of pre-Mauryan Buddhism,' he said. 'In the pre-Ashokan phase, there was nothing so propagandist, it was purely Hinayana monks who went from place to place. At the time there was no question of caves and seats, so they moved, they preached Buddhism in the orthodox manner, so there is no evidence. Not like Ajanta, where they had pillows and caves.'

Ashoka was merely building on what already existed. He was known to have waged war on Kalinga, but nothing was said of Andhra, further south, although he was said to have gone south on a mission and some of the thousands of stupas he had built were situated in Andhra.[6]

'Before Ashoka caused the granite railing at Amaravati to be built, there was already a clay stupa below. Ashoka's was merely the beautification phase. He gave a brick lining to the stupa, added a granite rail, erected an edict.'

Buddhism had reached Andhra very early on. In the early Buddhist texts, there are references to monks from the Andhaka school.[7] But wandering sages were not likely to leave much evidence of their passage.

'What do you think, a Vedic rishi living in a thatched roof who doesn't even have chappals, what evidence will he leave? *Hein*? Archaeology does not mean he has a dining table and a water bottle left for us to dig up. Indian life and the Indian way must be understood through literature. Living on river banks, the rishi will know the Chaturvedas, through recitation.'

He frowned at me.

'Even if he is a Vedic scholar, he has only two cows to his name.'

They found a seal in Kharoshti, he explained, a ship with a bodhi tree on it, dating from the third century AD which was about how a sapling of the sacred tree was sent to Sri Lanka from India, which happened in Ashokan times, hundreds of years earlier.

'The evidence is much later, but the story has not changed, literary stories, you don't give them up. Sculptural confirmation will be there, maybe later, but writing it down is a late affair,' he growled.

I nodded meekly.

Ancient India was not Buddhist, Dr Sharma went on, pushing the bounds of ancient history. Every city had a goddess. It was not the king who was the owner of the city, the goddess owned the city and the king ruled on behalf of the goddess.

'Brahminical, Buddhism, Jainism, whatever nonsense it is, still the goddess reigns supreme. Kanyakumari, Pushkalavati, Vaisali, these are all goddess' names,' he said, sipping his water.

I yearned for clarity. A beginning date, an end date. But history was messy. Things interlaced, entwined, looped back and forth, rubbed off and vanished without a trace, only to reappear in another form, hundreds of years later. 'Buddhism died,' Dr Sharma said, 'for the same reason that many modern projects wilt: the funding ran out, the organization became too hierarchical, an elite group took control, there was infighting, monetary patronage lessened and so there were desertions.'

chapter thirty-five

Hidden Buddhas

[Dravida] is about 6000 *li* in circuit; the capital of the country is called Kanchipura (Kin-chi-pu-lo) and is about 30 *li* round. The soil is fertile and regularly cultivated, and produces abundance of grain. There are also many flowers and fruits . . . The climate is hot; the character of the people courageous. There are some 100 of sangharamas and 10,000 priests . . .[1]

From Dhanakataka, the monk pushed south, through the country of Chola. He found the capital deserted, wild, filled with marshes and jungles. He had to hide from bands of brigands who brazenly wandered the countryside. The people were Jains and Hindus, the Buddhist monasteries lay empty and filthy. He hurried further south through more wild forests, and wrote with distinct relief of arriving in Kanchipuram, the ancient capital of the Pallava dynasty, now about eighty kilometres south-west of Chennai.

The language was similar to that of Middle India, Xuanzang noted. Most importantly, he found about 100 monasteries, and a body of 10,000 priests who studied texts of the Mahayana school of Buddhism.

∞

It had rained in Chennai the night before we arrived, cooling things down, but it was so humid that my hair became instantly wiggly and everything felt sticky. The South felt pleasantly empty after North Indian crowds. There was less pressure on public resources, trains were easily booked off the tourist track. We capitulated to the heat and went for air-conditioned comfort whenever possible.

Despite the humidity, it was a pleasant drive the next day to Kanchipuram, the southernmost spot the monk would hit on the Indian subcontinent. I left S. to write postcards and sleep in, and went alone on the day trip, hoping to find some trace of Xuanzang's 10,000 monks. All I had to guide me was an old article dug up from the ASI library listing the Buddhist remains of Kanchipuram.[2]

It had rained again and the flagstones at Kanchipuram's Kamakshi Temple were still wet. The sellers of strings of mallee phool and pink roses, the bald begging women, sat in a gang outside raising their stumps and mutilated fingers, calling 'Ma, Ma' as I walked in, but I wasn't thinking and had left without the necessary pile of small change to buy flowers for the temple, slip into the bowls of beggars and drop into the priest's brass tray.

I shook off my sandals at the door, relishing the morning cool even more because I knew how brief it was. A small crowd had already gathered for a stop at the temple before school or office. They were still fresh from baths, not yet veiled in that wilted, sweaty summer feel.

'Non-Hindus not allowed,' a priest called to me in English.

I replied, mildly, 'I am Hindu.' The words came out easily now, though I still wasn't sure what they meant.

'Kaunsa gaon?' he shot back in accented Hindi. What village, the ultimate proof of who you are.

Lucknow, I called back. He was satisfied.

Deep in the inner sanctum I could see the goddess, black and dressed up, only her face visible. I watched the outstretched hands, eager and restrained at the same time. People held back an urgency, a need for the priest to dab the tika onto their foreheads, drop the flowers into their hands. Awe and humility registered in their faces. I felt the usual awkwardness and that undefined stir at the base of my throat. It was not the priest, nor the rich flicker from the oil lamp that bounced off his shoulder, shiny with sweat, nor the sacred thread, the red lungi, the upside down U with a tilak through it. It was the expression on people's faces, the complete and utter belief. Nothing in my life had prepared me for this almost embarrassing, naked display. I felt a fraud, a bad actress. Indian, and yet deeply not.

From this point onwards, I would head north. It was a beginning of the end, nearing the last leg of my journey through India, and a consciousness that somewhere along the way, the land had lodged between my ribs, in my bones, where it lay like some prickly realization or half-forgotten dream. And just as I began to know its features and moods, like those of a new lover, I would have to leave and awaken to some flavourless reality. For a flicker, the thought felt unbearable. I breathed in and shook it off.

Somewhere within this temple, they found the seven-foot-tall statue of the Buddha standing on a pedestal, now leaning in a corner of the Chennai museum, his face smudged, the arms broken off, the robe darkened with what—chemicals? Age? It was dated to the late sixth or seventh century AD, which put it very close to the time when Xuanzang arrived in Kanchipuram.

A learned gentleman called T.A. Gopinatha Rao stumbled on the statues at the beginning of the twentieth century, wondering why no Buddhist remnants had been found here, given the wealth of literary references. He decided it was simply because nobody had looked before, and it was time that somebody did.

'In the course of a twelve hours' active search, I came upon no less than five images of Buddha within a radius of half a mile from the famous temple of Kamakshidevi . . .'[3] T.A. Gopinatha Rao was inclined to believe that nobody would heft such a large object too far from its origins. It was far more likely that the temple, or at least a portion of it, had been Buddhist.

The monk perhaps saw this statue, or one like it, in the middle of Buddhist Kanchipuram, smack in the middle of his monasteries and 10,000 Mahayana priests, now vanished except for a few signals. Time killed, but, like every killer, left a trace. And somewhere near here, archaeologists had found evidence of monasteries.[4]

In the sandy front courtyard of the Subbarayamudhali School in a side street near the Kaccapesvara Temple, a group of older boys were engrossed in a morning cricket game before classes began. The younger ones wore uniforms—burgundy trousers and grubby white short-sleeved shirts—and looked on from the sides.

There was a ripple of interest at the stranger walking through their school yard.

'English?' I asked the swarm of little boys that collected in seconds.

'Tamil,' they grinned up at me. Soon, the usual gang of kids was following.

'Teacher?' I said.

A boy with curly hair pointed up to a window. I climbed narrow stairs to a crammed classroom—dust and chalk and an early session of algebra.

'What-what-what?' the teacher asked, impatient at the interruption.

'Er, sorry, is there a Buddha statue somewhere in this school?'

'I'm new here, I don't know.'

The class tittered, echoing their teacher's theatrical 'what-what-what'.

Back down the stairs. I stared at the boys waiting for my return, this unexpected entertainment. 'Headmaster?'

'No. Headmaster, nine o'clock.' They looked delighted.

'Pen?' they countered.

I gave it a last try, hands on hips, addressing the boys.

'Buddha statue?'

Their shiny eyes beckoned: Why didn't you say so earlier?

They led me behind a central podium in the courtyard and there on the ground, amidst the sand and weeds, marked by a rusted lamp, was a seated Buddha statue. The boy with curly hair leaned over and watched as I sketched quickly, the elongated ears, the nose rubbed off with age, a flattish face, almost Mongoloid, right palm turned upward and cradled in left. Feet crossed, upturned.

'No, no, you're doing it wrong,' one boy said, standing on his toes to peek at my notebook. He threw an arm around the statue's neck and patted it companionably. In the hollow where the hands cradled each other, water had collected and turned amber.

I crossed the street to the Kaccapesvara Temple, intrigued by the way Buddhas kept popping up in unexpected places in Kanchipuram. It was still early, I bought some more mallee phool. It took a while to find the Buddhist statues in this temple. The administrator was not too clear.

'Ask him,' he said, pointing to an old man, so withered, his knees were wider than his thighs. He wore thick glasses and when I asked about the Buddhist statues, he pointed wordlessly to the temple's inner sanctum. Inside, on one of the pillars painted lime green, layers had been scratched off and the figure of a *dhyani* Buddha was visible, then another. I smiled, filled with the peculiar satisfaction of a task completed.

Back in Chennai, S. and I ate at Kabul Restaurant—tandoori rotis and roasted meat, food of the north-west. They played Urdu ghazals in a fashion that pressed on my sternum and I recognized a most extraordinary sentiment: I was homesick for North India.

Zindagi . . . sharaab . . . safar . . . mohabbat, the ghazal singer crooned, that obsession with the impossibility of happiness. Language was home, I thought, surrounded by words of another, more familiar geography. The air swirled in the same direction as my blood-flow, in a sudden synchronization with the environment. Home was where you learned the first language you ever spoke.

శ

Xuanzang was unable to continue on to Sri Lanka, a three-day sea journey away from the southern coast. It would have made sense, to visit this ancient stronghold of Hinayana Buddhism, a faith he now knew so well. He had had to learn it inside out to debate it, but can you really study an opposing ideology deeply without inheriting a glimmer of sympathy for it?

Was there anything he might have missed? Xuanzang had to be sure. Perhaps a hint of pride, a natural thoroughness in his reasoning. As it happened, 300 Sri Lankan priests arrived at Kanchipuram. With them were two eminent monks, Bodhimeghesvara and Abhayadanshtra, and the Chinese monk hurried to seek an audience with the new arrivals.

'It is reported that the chief priests of your kingdom are able to explain the Tripitaka according to the Sthivara school, and also the Yoga-sastra. I am anxious to go there and study these books. May I ask why you have come to this place?'[5]

The Sri Lankan monks were agitated. They had bad news and muttered and waved the puzzled Chinese priest off.

The king of our country is dead, and the people are suffering from famine without any resource for help, they told Xuanzang. We heard that Jambudvipa possessed abundance of food and was at peace and settled. This, too, is the place of Buddha's birth, and full of sacred traces of his presence; for this reason we have come.

The monk was bitterly disappointed. He had come this far and it was devastating to think he could not finish what he had set out to do. He would have to settle for the next best thing. So he pressed the monks, other travellers, for descriptions of the magical island. Perhaps he was a tad annoyed too, that his predecessor Fa Xian had managed to make it there hundreds of years earlier. Not to be outdone, he penned an entire section on the country.

As for the sutras he wanted to study, the Sri Lankans said *they* were the eminent priests of the land and the Chinese traveller could ask them whatever he wanted. But none of their explanations were as satisfactory as those given by Silabhadra at Nalanda.

There was nothing further left for Xuanzang to do here. In the company of seventy of the Sri Lankan pilgrim monks, who were heading north anyway to see the sacred Buddhist sites, Xuanzang turned towards India's western coast. He stopped a while in Konkanapura, the coastal kingdom south of Maharashtra, and then travelled through a thick forest, infested with wild animals, till he reached Maharashtra.

80

We took a night train that crossed to the Western Ghats and stopped at the foothills of the Nilgiri Mountains in Uthukuli village for the Tamil new year in the western part of the state. A few days later, we flew to Bombay.

chapter thirty-six

Stone Elephants

'The people of (Maharashtra) despise death, and highly esteem right conduct,'[1] Xuanzang must have told Hui Li, who wrote it down. I could see the younger man, his eyes shining, scribbling down the words of the pilgrim.

The king is of the Kshattriya caste. He is fond of military affairs, and boasts of his arms. In this country, therefore, the troops and cavalry are carefully equipped, and the rules of warfare thoroughly understood and observed. Whenever a general is despatched on a war-like expedition, although he is defeated and his army destroyed, he is not himself subjected to bodily punishment, only he has to exchange his soldier's dress for that of a woman, much to his shame and chagrin . . . The king always supports several thousand men of valour, and several hundred savage elephants. When these are drawn up in battle array, then they give them intoxicating spirits to drink, till they are overpowered with it—and then at a given signal, when in this condition, they excite them to rush against (the enemy). [2]

Even Harsha, so filled with confidence at his skill and success, was unable to defeat this king, wrote Xuanzang.

ᎸᎧ

My sister and her boyfriend picked us up. She told us we had landed in the middle of a city-wide strike. The papers indeed blared disaster.

'City to shut down, left, right, centre' the *Mumbai Age* screamed on 25 April 2001. Flights rescheduled. No public transport. SRPF, CRPF deployed. Maharashtra ground to a standstill, private and government organizations did not function. The streets were utterly deserted. The Maharashtra bandh called by all the major trade unions was to highlight the issues of globalization, privatization, liberalization and the policies which, the unions said, had hit workers badly.

S. and I decided to wait it out. The four of us went to eat excellent, and very expensive, Italian food at one of Bombay's finer restaurants. In our grubby travel clothes, for we had no others, we stepped into dark edgy Bombay bars and watched chic, slender women and attractive men in tight T-shirts splashed with cologne talking earnestly over long colourful drinks. It seemed like a different universe.

The government of Maharashtra had also, the newspapers said, declared a red alert.

Luckily the railways, for which I had a soft spot, said they would continue their services, which meant it was possible for us to travel to Aurangabad and see the Ajanta caves which Xuanzang had mentioned.

On the eastern frontier of the country is a great mountain with towering crags and a continuous stretch of piled up rocks and scarped precipice. In this there is a sangharama constructed, in a dark valley.[3]

The heat had mounted to almost unbearable heights. S. fell sick, lying quiet in the government guest house not far from the Ajanta caves. The village doctor rode up on his motorcycle to take his pulse and prescribe small pink pills. He charged forty rupees for his pains. I felt miserable for S. and his rebellious innards. If he could not savour the experience, neither could I. But he got better and insisted on making the brief, sharp uphill walk to the caves set in the wilderness of the Deccan.

There was a dry filigree of twigs across the plateau, a deep canyon carved by a river, creating a rock face in a horseshoe escarpment. The river bed was dry as bone, but water had collected in stone tanks, there were even fish. The monks thought of everything.

Ajanta took my breath away.

The cave paintings were filled with a delicate richness. There were seated ochre cows, with detailed, delicate horns, always painted with a fine brush, fragments like interrupted speech. Some details jumped out—an anonymous painter who traced with care a woman's pearl necklace. Or a man's curly hair that fell from under a jewelled headband.

The cave walls were filled with turned heads, expressive eyes, quiet conversations amongst pillared halls, a chariot wheel, a curved boat, lowered kohl-lined eyes, a fluttered hand. The hum of life, the buzz of an era that died, yet stayed alive.

It was as though the artists had swept corners of Indian life into a muslin cloth, tied a knot and trudged up to the caves with their brushes and oil lamps. When they got there, they shook open the cloth to spill the paintings and fill the walls.

Here the Jatakas came alive, stories steeped in the pulse of ancient India, shivering into existence long before the Buddhists arrived. Instead of meddling too much with the Buddha's actual life, the stories created a plethora of past lives in which the Buddha lived and relived his destiny, like a hall of mirrors reflecting each other into infinity.

In the dimness of one cave, a painted white elephant facing left was surrounded by a herd of faded elephants. His trunk curved around a tusk and before him a hunter in sandalled feet knelt before a sick queen. It was a story of a doctor who demanded a herbal medicine that required ground elephant tusks. The painter had even made a line of ants crawl up the bark of a tree. The white elephant broke off his own tusks and offered them to the hunter, in an act of great selflessness, for naturally this was no ordinary animal.

Each stone pillar was intricately carved. Some of the paintings were famous, like the young god holding a lotus flower, an ornament on his upper left arm, cloths tied around a slim waist.

There was perhaps one of the loveliest paintings of Rahula, the son of Buddha, flanking a cell. He stood solitary, in an ochre robe, his head slightly tipped, holding out a begging bowl in his right hand, his eyes filled, his hair tied in a topknot. The lines were powerful, the colours clean and light.

In a cave far into the U, there was a magnificent sleeping Buddha, on a cushion made of stone which felt like silk, including the tassel at the end of it.

'Don't touch, don't touch,' the guard said, because for a group of women from Tamil Nadu, the first instinct was to reach out and lay a hand on this carved Buddha reclining on a wall. In the chaitya halls, the artists had begun their work from the top, carving out the caves beginning at the ceiling. The roof was first fashioned, and work was continued downwards by making furrows with sharp picks. The rough work was later finished by painters. The sunlight falling on the chaityas made even more vivid the rich, painted tones while the rows of pillars gave an illusion of depth.[4]

We stared at the vast stupas, with the tall Christmas tree-shaped finial on top. The penny dropped, standing there at Ajanta in the heat, beads of sweat creeping down my temples. It was clear as crystal why a Chinese pagoda was a pagoda. The tree-shaped structure had simply swelled and expanded to Chinese tastes, as the stupa itself shrunk and disappeared.

I sat on a step behind the elephants, in front of the naga deva with the snakes overhead and took a swig of water, flipped through Xuanzang's records to see what he said. But somebody was already discussing it. An Indian voice carried from behind the stone elephants in bas-relief.

'And this is where the Chinese pilgrim came, he refers to these elephants, you know.' I craned my neck to see a guide with four Taiwanese on holiday. And fanned myself with my sun hat, feeling the satisfaction spread along my veins, of beading another pearl on the necklace of this journey.

'On the outside gate of the sangharama,' the monk wrote, 'on the north and south side, at the right and the left, there is a stone elephant.'[5]

In the sun-blasted countryside, with its flat plateau, scrubbed bushes, only the hardy neem trees grew, and every now and again there was the bright splash of a tree filled with orange flowers. A strange momentum had taken over, though the heat made travelling miserable. I told myself I should stop. But it was as though the monk was sticking out a tyrannical finger from behind the millennia and wagging 'NO'.

'I'm not sure I'll make it,' I whispered, but I was talking to myself. I took a deep breath and dived back into the journey.

chapter thirty-seven

Hill of Rishis

As (Surashtra) is on the western sea route, the men all derive their livelihood from the sea and engage in commerce and exchange of commodities. Not far from the city is a mountain called Yuh-chen-to (Ujjanta), on the top of which is a sangharama. The cells and galleries have mostly been excavated from the mountain-side.[1]

From Maharashtra, Xuanzang crossed the Narmada River into the kingdom of Bharoch, on his way to the Gujarat peninsula. The soil was salty, as it still is, wind gusted through the air. The monk found the people here crooked and perverse. They were cold and indifferent, he said, with a handful of Buddhists intermingled with Hindu sects, and he hurried north-west to the kingdom of Malava (Malwa). He liked it much better there, finding the people intelligent and studious and endowed with humanity. Their language, he wrote, was elegant and clear. Sadly, they were inclined to Hindusim, the heretical faith, and society had a mix of both Hindus and Buddhists. People liked to eat biscuits of parched cornflour, he observed.

The monk pressed north-west, through the kingdom of Kachha and then further north, to Valabhi. At Valabhi he swung west, deep into the Gujarat peninsula, and the kingdom at its tip that he called Su-la-ch'a: Saurashtra.

৪৹

The train to Surat rattled through the night, roughly parallel to

Xuanzang's tracks, and before heading to Saurashtra we stopped in a Patel village called Gothan, not far from the train station. We were in sugar cane country, where the harvest was on and streams of labourers from Maharashtra trickled in on caravans of bullock carts, a six-day journey from their hometowns. Whole families, with their belongings and the strength of their hands.

The trucks brought great watermelons from the Konkan coast and the first mangoes had reached the markets, thence to our plates in the form of pulp, served in steel bowls along with dal and dhokla. There was the shock of sweetened dal, the way Gujaratis stir sugar into salty things and sprinkle salt on their fruit.

I savoured the way in which, in the villages of south Gujarat, as the summer swelter ebbed, people sat on the wooden swings on their porches and swayed and talked and swayed, as though liberation from the ground loosened tongues and freed dreams of cooler times.

For me, Gujarat was once again a whole new India, where busy men set up humming cooperatives, where buffalo and cow milk was trucked to a chilling plant, tipped over, tested with lactometres, sent off further for processing. Such business all over the state, such no-nonsense enterprise.

The violent riots in which Hindus and Muslims slaughtered each other were still a year away. I learned how so many Patels come back from the United States to their villages in Gujarat to look for wives. There was such a disjunction between heart and soul. I learned how they lived in the US with a faint distaste, a shield between them and their eyes, a thin veil. Samir became Sam.

They lived with a hairline crack through their minds. Divided worlds, but I knew all about those. There was also a historical tangent I had to follow. The Zoroastrians, long vanished from Central Asia (poor Xuanzang, chased by men brandishing flaming torches), were still alive in this region. Surat was where India's Parsees had first landed from Iran around AD 700, barely fifty years after Xuanzang left India. It was another accident of geography, for if you push off Iran's southern coast and sail east in a straight line you cannot help hitting Gujarat.

South of here, the first Persians stepped off their boat from Iran, fleeing, huddling over their sacred fire. They were a strange bedraggled lot, with their beards and an odd light in their eyes. The king politely, even sadly, said, we have no room for you. And the refugees answered that the cup of milk may be full, but you could still add a spoonful of sugar. Delighted by the metaphor, so the legend goes, the king allowed them to stay. Thirteen centuries later, the fire still lives, housed in a temple last rebuilt in 1765; the sun adorns the gate and the figure of Zarathustra hovers on the wings of an angel.

Godrej, I learned, was the name of a counsellor in an ancient Iranian court. I always thought it was just what we called the steel cupboard with push-down metal handles and formidable locks owned by every Indian housewife. 'The servants, well, they steal . . .'

In the bellies of urban Godrej cupboards lay jewels (those not in the bank safe), silk saris, watches, old photographs, children's drawings. It was the woman's domain, an inviolable space, which nobody trespassed. Once, entrusted with the keys to my mother's Godrej, bought thirty years ago, I packed them into my bag and took them overseas. When my mother finally calmed down after discovering what I had done, she wrote to Godrej with the serial number of the cupboard and they pulled out ancient records and sent her a duplicate key.

I remember how I held my breath one summer when my grandfather and I opened Ammi's Godrej cupboard after she died. My heart thudded though I was a grown woman, and on the shelves, slipped under newspaper lining we found old photographs, a letter I had written her when I was fifteen, in a still-childish hand. The gods she worshipped sat in one neat row. On the bottom shelf there were velvet jewel cases. I opened them, one by one, to empty spaces, indents where her jewels had rested against the scuffed surface, I could still see in my mind's eye the diamonds she wore. There were chiffon saris in delicate pastel shades, for Ammi had been a woman of innate elegance.

I had to pull myself away from this other story that tugged at me, to keep to the path, the original one, looking over my shoulder, not quite ready for the suddenness of that resurfaced summer afternoon when my throat felt as if it might shatter and when my grandfather went quiet, resting his hand on her pile of chiffon saris.

∽

S. left India. He took off from Bombay, back to the United States to pack his things. The tremulous Kolkata beginning had solidified on our swing around India. We decided we would try and live together. After all, if we could stand being together every minute of every day for five weeks, if he could ride out my ferocious temper and I could tackle his stubbornness, we might attempt a life together. Hong Kong would be a logical base. We both had lived there before, and when we returned we would both be starting afresh. When I finished this journey, I promised myself, I would allow myself happiness. With him.

Meanwhile, the archaeologists at Vadodara's MS University advised me I should head to Junagarh to find the mountain Xuanzang referred to as Yuh-Chen-to. It was Girnar Hill, they said. I even found an overnight train called the Girnar Express that rocketed south from Ahmedabad towards my destination.

Here in this ragged town of Junagarh, from my room in the Girnar Hotel, I could see the city's old gates and a triangle of planted palm trees. It used to be a nawab's town; his paraphernalia was arranged in orderly rows in an old palace. There were silver howdahs to place atop elephants, carved with the double lion. In Junagarh they stapled torn, worn-out two-rupee notes between pieces of plastic and increased their circulation life. Some were torn in two, or taped together.

'Will anybody accept these?' I asked the ticket man, holding up one such crippled note.

'Anybody in Junagarh will, madam,' he replied. 'Maybe even in Ahmadabad.'

'Have a seat,' the chai-wala said. I did, and sprang up because the hot metal burnt my bottom.

'Kem-chho,' they called at me, 'hello' in Gujarati, and they addressed me in Gujarati, but I didn't understand it. At the museum, there was a group of short, skinny men all dressed identically: in white cotton jodhpurs, with fitted white shirts. Their ears were pierced, but not the lobes, their conical brass earrings sat higher up, in the inner curve of the auricles.

'Where are they from?' I asked the attendant, who translated into Gujarati.

The little men laughed shyly.

'Where are you from?' they asked me back.

The attendant passed the question on, translating from Gujarati into Hindi, then brought the answer back.

'Lalkot. Near Rajkot. They have come for a wedding.'

'Come to the wedding,' they said through the attendant. 'It's in three days.' Sadly, I had to refuse.

Then, I shocked an entire mountainside. High on Girnar Hill, there were no sounds, just me huffing and puffing up the stairs, an hour's steady climb. There was nothing but a quiet rustle of the bushes dried and emptied of leaves by the summer. In the distance, a few peacocks belted out their mourning. The river had dried up.

'Good morning, madam,' chorused a family from Ahmedabad, on their way down.

A group of village girls pushed by, dressed in their best mirrored, embroidered backless cholis, their patterned skirts and silver anklets. They moved down the mountain like a cloud of butterflies. Their hair was held back with silver pins and the earrings again in the inner pinna.

Suddenly, the fist pushing me up the hill vanished. There was no more momentum. I simply could not take another step. It was hot, I was tired. But this was something deeper. It was as though some engine had sputtered out. I sat down on a rock to reflect, and decided that this was it. I had done what I had to do in India, and it was time to say goodbye and move on. There was a curious liberation to the moment. I wondered what had brought me to this point, whether I was doing this to counteract old age, to cling to youth, to somehow resist the moment of death. Could travel beat a mortal end? As long as I was moving, I felt I could not die. But now, it was as though the wrinkles and knots at the back of my mind had been ironed out. I turned around and headed back down the hill.

Every tea seller knew that I hadn't gone to the top. 'You didn't go to the top,' said the old man swirling tea in a saucer.

'You didn't go to the top,' another shopkeeper said, further down, also swirling tea in a saucer.

'It's hot,' I protested.

'So what?' he snapped back.

The whole mountain was horrified. It was as though I had affronted the entire Hindu faith. Yet again.

'You didn't go to the top,' the monkey man said as I passed by.

If there was a sangharama, it had long been converted to Hinduism, I reasoned.

At the bottom I drank tea to the sound of Sanskrit slokas. A guru sat cross-legged inside an ashram and chanted with closed eyes. Everywhere I saw tridents, small temples. A sadhu sat smoking hash, his body covered in ash, his eyes wild and red, rimmed with black, exactly the way Xuanzang described:

> The mountain is covered with thick jungle and forest trees, whilst streams flow round its limits. Here saints and sages roam and rest, and Rishis endued with spiritual faculties congregate here and stay.[2]

I stopped by the Ashokan rock edict, thinking of faraway Orissa, marvelling once more at the king and feeling that I had seen so much of his handiwork, I practically knew him on a first-name basis.

I was spent. I was approaching my thirty-third birthday. I could still make it to Delhi in time for Nani's seventy-fifth birthday, and May had burst upon the subcontinent.

There was a sense of a task completed, a task set years ago that had come to fruition, the thing I had always needed to do. For the first time in days I slept deeply, soundly, a dream-filled sleep. I dreamed I got a visa to Pakistan.

chapter thirty-eight

Limbo

Since the beginning of my trip over a year ago, I had tried unsuccessfully at regular intervals to get a visa for Pakistan. During my repeated visits to Delhi, I tottered at the periphery of the lives of the Pakistanis who worked there. The pleasant receptionist from Swat, who always wore a long salwar kameez, went to Peshawar for a niece's wedding and came back. Mr Jilani, who was handling my case, flew to Karachi for his mother's operation. Another consular official was transferred back to Islamabad. I caught a picture of High Commissioner Ashraf Qazi in the papers and bumped into his daughter at a party at the Delhi Gymkhana Club.

This was my last chance. Back in Delhi, I went to the Pakistani High Commission and met a consular official, Shah Jamali, who assured me that they were working on my visa to Pakistan. He had a wry, self-deprecating manner that I liked, through my desperation.

'We're bureaucrats, we push paper. We're at the top, leading cushy lives, we're not worried about others.'

'Shall I go to the press?'

'I wouldn't. There is a lot of goodwill for your project. India does the same thing to Pakistanis, you know. It's the law of reciprocity.'

I looked at him blankly. I didn't care. The only thing that mattered was Xuanzang's journey and that I was unable to complete it, and that I felt as though I had stopped in the middle of an inhalation.

I had dinner at my mausi's house. She invited old friends for a soiree and served up her famous kebabs and dal. One of her guests had helped draft India's new national security overhaul.

'Write to Musharraf,' he said later in the evening. 'Copy it to the foreign minister and to the UN's Pakistan representative. When in doubt, go to the top.'

That night, I tapped out feverish letters to President Pervez Musharraf and to Foreign Minister Abdul Sattar and mailed them the next day, standing in line at the local post office.

I received a startled e-mail from somebody in Pakistan's Foreign Office, acknowledging receipt of my letter to Abdul Sattar. 'I am sure your visa will be approved,' it said.

'When?' I tapped back. 'I have waited a year already.' I was edging beyond the bounds of civility. May flipped into June and still nothing happened. I had now been on the move for over a year. I fought an urge to leave. I felt trapped. My mind looped in circles, crashed. The days rolled into one. I smoked too much, then quit, dreamed nothing-dreams. I sweated and flapped at mosquitoes in the dark when the air-conditioning collapsed in the season's most humid nights.

S. phoned from LA to console my terrible limbo.

Some hope came on 23 May, via the newspapers. Indian Prime Minister Atal Behari Vajpayee had invited Pakistan's Chief Executive, General Pervez Musharraf, for talks. I picked up the newspapers from under the door where the delivery man had shoved them through and read the headlines, standing barefoot in my T-shirt, hair askew, eyes half-closed.

The newspaper published the letter, dissected the tone of earlier pronouncements, the mood of Islamabad's initial reaction, pointed out inflections and nuances and then grudgingly said it all depended on the tone of Musharraf's reply.

Musharraf accepted.

I missed my journey terribly. I missed having Xuanzang in hand. I missed tracking and finding his traces. Something made sense when I was on the move.

Of my journey, nothing was left but a few dried saffron flowers from a Kashmiri field. The sound of rain, a dried leaf that fell from the tree in Bodh Gaya, a dried peepul leaf, its tip bent, a link that I bent to pick up and slip in between the pages of a book, a link to that event nearly 3000 years ago. These, a few memories, some words.

Devastated at being denied Pakistan, I packed and left for Hong Kong.

chapter thirty-nine

Pure Land

The things I desire most come when I have ceased to want them. I was already pounding the pavements in Hong Kong, trailing behind brisk property agents, looking for a flat, trying to piece together an exploded life, gazing aghast at my bank balance. I was shell-shocked at Hong Kong's throbbing pace, I converted taxi fares into rupees and shook my head, I gazed up at glass-and-chrome façades as though I had never seen them before.

I picked up S. from the airport. We answered an advertisement for a flat and signed the lease. Both our names. Barely one week later, there was an e-mail from Mr Jilani. 'Your visa to Pakistan has been approved.'

My heart began to pound. I scrambled to leave Hong Kong again, for stasis had felt like death. I was delighted to flee, acknowledge my addiction, it was a secret shame to feel the jail door swing open and reach for the horizon once more.

The great white metal gates at the Pakistani High Commission in Delhi swung open for the last time, the usual pigeons fluttered and the receptionist from Swat waved through the glass partition as I held up my green visitor's tag. The heat hovered, its usual June violence in rein.

Jilani stood up behind his vast table. He wore a beige bush shirt and was finishing a telephone conversation, beaming across the room at me. He put the phone down.

'Now you see, our intentions were sincere.'

'Thank you,' I said. I could think of nothing else to say. It was overwhelming.

'One begins to doubt everything, are these people playing games with me?'

'I was upset.' I allowed him that much.

'I didn't want you to be in a depression,' Mr Jilani said. 'Tell me how it went when you return.'

Between the lines of that brief conversation lived the recognition of our joint battle, fought for nearly a year. Our lives were welded together by telephone exchanges: his reassurances, my frustrations, his refusal to let me give up, my weekly calls to the Pakistan High Commission, his regular calls in turn to the ministry of interior in Islamabad. Mostly, I managed to believe that he was on my side. I had no choice.

I had never fought so hard for anything in my entire life, equipped with only a dogged determination to pursue to its end a dead monk's route. It had wearied me, and, I supposed, Mr Jilani too. Nothing further needed to be said.

Shah Jamal said, 'Here is the document permitting you access to Pakistan.'

It was in a thick file. The document had come as a telex and had scribbles in black felt. I asked to see it. 'It's an internal document,' Jamal said sternly. But his eyes held a glint of humour. He asked for tea and biscuits for me and tapped on his Sony laptop. Even I, a perfect stranger, could tell he was a rising star in the Pakistan Foreign Service. It felt immeasurably sweet, this visa in my pocket. It gave me permission to go to every single city I had requested, including Mingora in the Swat Valley.

The bus to Pakistan left at dawn from the outskirts of old Delhi, as the summer sky lightened one morning. It was the end of June 2001. The vehicle swung out of the gates amidst tight security and after thorough baggage searches. Police had pulled out garments, food packages, boxes of gifts—bangles, books, children's toys—which lay scattered across the concrete floor of the bus terminal, the detritus of our lives.

Somebody had painted the bus with the India and Pakistan flags. The vehicle followed an armed police escort northwards, across the plains of Punjab towards the Pakistan border at the Wagah checkpoint. Inside, the air conditioning worked and then didn't as we listened to songs from old Hindi films.

There was a knot of passengers, mostly from Pakistan, returning home. We got on and off the bus in orderly files, for a tea break, lunch. At Indian immigration at Attari, an Indian official with a yellow sticker promising better service pulled me aside and grilled me. He prodded my damaged passport (the rain in Kyrgyzstan had loosened the plastic lamination). He threatened I'd have to go back to Delhi, that he could not possibly let me out of the country.

'Do you want money? Five hundred rupees?' I said, hardened now in the ways of border crossings. I would die before giving up my passage to Pakistan.

'I'm just doing my job, madam. Do you mind if we speak in Hindi? I have to prove you are who you are. Sometimes educated people are more criminal than others.'

We switched to Hindi.

'Are you married, what does your father do, why do you keep going in and out of Hong Kong?'

I made my voice soothing, I wove stories, I kept talking, I focussed on the fields outside, the vehicles that queued. I had been disappointed so often and had come to think of it as some sort of cruel mental test, to have my hopes raised and then dashed. It would be an exquisite irony if the Pakistanis finally relented, allowed me access all over their country, only for an Indian to slam the door shut.

'Okay,' he snapped the passport shut. But he wanted to know more.

'You are a well-travelled person. How are Indians compared to others?'

'They're more bureaucratic,' I retorted. But he missed the sarcasm.

Through brick gates and barbed wire running through green fields, rose the actual border with Pakistan. An arch carried the Indian flag, followed by a short paved drive, and another arch with the Pakistan flag with its green background, white crescent and single star, wilting in the still air.

'It says Pakistan zindabad,' my neighbour told me, deciphering the Urdu writing bannered across the arch. She had already pulled her chunni over her head. The bus rolled into the Wagah checkpoint and we filed out for the Pakistan checkpoint. Coolies in green salwars crowded around.

'Would you like me to get all your stuff through, quickly, for two hundred rupees?' a man in a salwar kameez walked up and offered. I thanked him and waved him off, but I wanted to yell in happiness— do you know how long it's taken for me to get here so you could ask me this inane question?

Officials scanned passports, checked bags, but did not even open them. How much more paranoid were the Indians! We had tea and egg sandwiches inside a building which proclaimed itself a bank, although there wasn't a single teller inside it. Another man followed me and with great respect explained there wouldn't be any way to change money inside the bank, but luckily he could supply me with Pakistani rupees at an excellent rate. Which he did.

I had entered Pakistan.

And?

And nothing.

Same green fields, same villages, same buffaloes. A man on a donkey. It felt slightly different, it was the flapping long salwars and kameezes each man wore; the women were covered, but that they were in India too. We wound our way to Lahore, a short distance away. The city was bathed in a hazy afternoon light. We drove past the canal, the straight avenues lined with neem and alstonia trees, green and leafy.

A couple of men turned to stare at the bus, the two enemy flags joined for once, frozen on the bus's flanks. They smiled and waved. Those who haven't seen Lahore have not been born, the Lahoris say. So that to see Lahore is a kind of birth, a beginning. For me it was the end of a long wait, I was thirsty to see Pakistan, to follow the thread of my story.

Razia in Delhi had sent an e-mail to her elderly aunt: could a traveller stay with you a few days? Lubna Kazim picked me up at the bus stop.

There were jabs of lightning across grey morning skies, a breeze sighed through the rose creeper and bougainvillea.

'*Allah ki hawah*,' Lubna said, as we sipped tea in her garden. Allah's wind. To be in a foreign country and yet not feel it foreign.

Only North Indians and Pakistanis must feel this oddest of sensations. Another flag, a separate currency, but such a familiar pull. I kept forgetting I was in Pakistan. The bazaars felt the same, the people looked the same, they spoke my tongue, we were a single country interrupted by history.

Lubna Aunty and Anwar Uncle.

I had stepped through a mirror and was looking over my shoulder at myself. I felt heady with the Urdu that swirled in the streets around me, its music a direct link to my heart. I soaked up new words: *mashroof, khwaab, ilfaz.*

How pleased everybody was to see me. For my part, I'd earned every step I took across Pakistan and was uniformly delighted to meet each and every Pakistani. We agreed, again and again, that it was the politicians who divided a people.

Right in the middle of Lahore, not far from Zamzama, Kim's Gun, stood a graceless concrete tower called the Minar-e-Pakistan. It commemorated the 1940 meeting of all Muslims, the spot where the idea of Pak-i-Stan was born. *Pak zameen*, pure land. It was agreed that Muslims needed their own space, although India still has three times the number of Muslims that Pakistan does.

Lahore breathed a jumble of history. I floated across the city, taking in the same Mughal architecture that dotted India's plains, the same British leftovers and names. Charing Cross, a 100-year-old high court, a museum founded in 1864. This too was my heritage, my history, and I felt a curious fury at being denied it for so long. Why were we fed a guillotined past? There were reminders of that truncated time: a fighter jet that Pakistan used in the 1965 war against India was propped up at a roadside. It looked curiously innocuous and *small*.

The Quaid-i-Azam University in Islamabad sent an aide, Imran, to Lahore so I would not have to make the journey to Islamabad alone. I was glad to have him around, though he was about ten years younger than me.

Imran was a Pathan, a youth with a lick of hair that fell across his forehead with careful nonchalance. We would head to Islamabad and meet with Pakistan's eminent archaeologist Dr A.H. Dani, who would help me pinpoint the Buddhist routes across Pakistan. Imran was his assistant. Once in Islamabad, I would also have to get, as soon as possible, a visa to Afghanistan, for my time in Pakistan was limited.

At the Lahore Museum, Anjum Rahmani, the director, was kind enough to see me. A portrait of Jinnah hung on the wall behind him. 'You know, forty per cent of the Lahore Museum went to Chandigarh after Partition and sixty per cent was supposed to come here but it never did.' He stopped. The presence of an Indian in his office seemed to spur other memories. 'In Anarkali, there used to be only two Muslim shops, the rest were all Hindu. *Goron*, the white men, have done this, and they have left us underdeveloped.' Anjum Rahmani gave a short, sad laugh.

What if India and Pakistan simply undid Partition? The thought slid across my mind, a raindrop on a window sill. What if people simply annulled it, called off the border, changed their minds and decided that after all, they wanted to be together, pool all the museum pieces again?

We already shared the history.

I flicked it off, wiper across a windshield. Idiotic musings! The kind only an NRI would have.

Xuanzang's route beckoned. North-west Pakistan, the Peshawar Valley, ancient Gandhara, the narrow swathe of land that linked the old trade routes down from the mountains of Afghanistan, the route that then crossed the Indus River and continued east into the kingdom of Kashmir.

I drank in a whole new history. Lapped it up like a greedy puppy starved of milk by a careless owner, front paws in the bowl, milk spattered all over its face, clumsily tipping the vessel so that the dregs spilt and there were milky footprints all over the floor.

How badly I had needed to know all this. How clear things were becoming. Pakistan was the missing link between Persia and India, the blank rift in my mind.

I was transfixed by the Lahore Museum's Fasting Buddha, though the legend printed on a panel complained that details of the historicity were not correct. My mind tumbled back to the hollow-eyed, sunken-cheeked statue of Chamunda in Orissa.

The Fasting Buddha was from the North-West Frontier Province and dated from Kanishka's time, the second century AD. He was carved of fine-grained bluish schist. There were four folds of slack skin above his navel, to indicate how thin he had gotten in his fast. The neck vertebrae showed through, the sculptor had thought to depict in stone the man's armpit hair. The veins stuck out, hip bones jutted and tendons in the neck stretched.

What an alarming figure this would have been on the banks of Nairanjana in faraway Bihar. It was my introduction to Gandharan art.

My eyes, used to the manners of Indian sculptors, had to learn a new language. They resisted the Greek overtones in the sculpture, the Buddhas with moustaches, the high noses, rich draperies, the thong slippers. India's Buddhas were barefooted.

Because Alexander breezed through quickly, without leaving an administrative structure, strong Greek influences seen in Gandhara were possibly the result of later Graeco-Bactrian colonizing kings whose power extended to the region only 150 years after Alexander.[1] The Graeco-Bactrians were still Iranians, but with a strong Greek polish. They ruled Gandhara for about a century, over a local population possibly speaking East Iranian or Sogdian tongues. They may have occupied powerful posts in a Hellenistic 'old boys' network and planned Greek cities, like at Taxila, and that might be how Gandhara acquired its Greekness.

The trouble is, much of the sculpture dates from much later, from the patronage of the Kushans. Those who came *after* the Graeco-Bactrians squabbled and the region disintegrated into petty fiefdoms, unable, in the end, to resist the eastward march of the Saka nomads, then the Parthians and finally the Kushans.

Meanwhile, I had a Partition errand to run in Lahore for my uncle.

The old house of the Shourie clan, Hindus now living in Delhi, sat at the bottom of Abdul Karim Road. Uncle Shourie, almost ninety now, and his wife had not been back in nearly half a century after they abandoned their ancestral home during Partition and fled to

Delhi with only a bundle of belongings. They had left the house with the milk still boiling on the stove.

In Delhi, they had described it to Nani, who described it to me. 'If you can manage it, could you please look for it?' they had said of this rare occasion to cross the border. The house had an arch across the front, inscribed in English. It was tall and narrow. Nani also gave me an old black-and-white photograph of herself with a school friend who lived in Lahore. They had not met since the two were sixteen, separated by history.

'If you could find her, she's an old woman now, like me.'

It took us the good part of two hours, many tries. We took wrong turns, up and down and around Lahore, backtracking, asking, do you know Abdul Karim Road? And finally we found it, in an old area of the city. It was a small lane with shops that had an aura of age and settlement.

'Shourie Building?' Further down, a hand pointed.

And there it was, Shourie Lal Building, a once elegant narrow mansion, with an arch over the front. It was decrepit now, falling to pieces, paint flaking, bricks missing, columns chipped. There were terraces to watch sunsets and kite festivals, where kite strings were dipped in glass and fliers attached a five-hundred-rupee note to the string, jumping from rooftop to rooftop.

Different families lived there now. On the ground floor was a man who had been born there, his family uprooted in that bloody time. They in turn had run from Amritsar, leaving their home fully furnished. He offered us Pepsi.

'Please, please sit. You are most welcome. *Mehman.*'

How absurd it was that entire families should have switched places like this, occupied each other's houses, used each other's sofas and towels.

For what?

chapter forty

City of Dressed Stone

The land is renowned for its fertility, and produces rich harvests. It is very full of streams and fountains. Flowers and fruits are abundant. The climate is agreeably temperate. The people are lively and courageous, and they honour the three gems. Although there are many sangharamas, they have become ruinous and deserted . . .[1]

Having passed the Kushan kings' winter capital at Peshawar and after crossing the Indus, Xuanzang would have walked straight into the Taxila Valley. When he came through, Taxila, sometimes translated as City of Dressed Stone, had just become a tributary of the nearby kingdom of Kashmir. Previously, it had been subject to the Afghan powers at Kapisa. The royal family had died out, nobles fought for power and the region's numerous Buddhist monasteries were already in a state of decay. There were few priests left, but Xuanzang was doubtless pleased to find they followed the Mahayana faith.

∞

The Daewoo bus to Islamabad was a sleek creature, on a sleek highway, as though the future had sliced through the past. A jostle at the bus terminal obtained two tickets for Imran and me. On the desk a computer screensaver bounced off the edges: BISMILLAH.

The bus headed north through sleepy fields. Pakistan had emptied out as the sun set. After India's crammed scenes, humanity fanning out on every inch, practically crawling over each other, this was an abandoned tableau, as though somebody had tilted the country and shaken all the people out.

We crossed the rivers of Punjab, like rungs on a ladder, or fingers on a hand; rivers that began in India and ended in Pakistan, emptied into the muscled Indus, which emptied into the Arabian Sea once again to lap at India's western shore.

Ravi, Chenab, Jhelum. These waters I had known all my life, names memorized from school books as a little girl in India. Here they ran across the border, for rivers did not stop where men drew boundaries. Not even Nehru and Jinnah could stop the flow, but it only added to my confusion of place.

Imran arranged accommodation for me at the Quaid-i-Azam University guest house. I shared a room with two large lizards, transparent skins, uneven bulges. They lived in the upper folds of the curtain and had grown slow and fat on the plentiful insect population. In the soft green curve of the Margalla Hills, as the ground begins to swell into mountains, the guest house of the Quaid-i-Azam University sat amidst bushes laden with anarkali flowers, deep rich pink. One morning they bowed, drenched by rainwater. Through my sleep and unwieldy dreams I heard thunder, awoke to birdsong and the necklace of hills shrouded in mist.

I met Dr Dani, and was astonished at the wisps of snow-white hair, his cheerful, cherubic face. He sat behind an enormous desk. He had studied in Banaras, he knew an awesome amount. We bent over maps, he put a finger on the Khyber Pass.

'This is a relatively new route from Afghanistan into Pakistan,' he told me. The older trade routes followed the Kabul River, amongst the mountains further north. So when the monk descended from Afghanistan into the lush valleys of Peshawar, Dani thought he would have followed the curves of the Kabul River. From Peshawar, Xuanzang had switched direction and turned sharply north, before swinging back south and resuming his journey to India.

He explained how the net of trade routes in the mountains of northern Pakistan, around Gilgit, were filled with Buddhist carvings on the rocks by the side of roads. He himself had discovered many of them. We flipped through his book on the subject, but that part of Xuanzang's route, the place where he made a detour north before

turning back to the road to India, now lay in Pakistan-Occupied
Kashmir. It was a sensitive area, and certainly no Indian would be
allowed there. I squashed a nugget of disappointment.

Don't be greedy, I chided myself. You have the rest of Pakistan to
look forward to.

ஐ

The ancient settlement of Taxila was barely an hour's drive from
Islamabad.

Taxila was a broad, fertile valley flanked by the Sardar Hills to
the north and the Jaulian Hills to the south. The Haro River and the
Lundi Nala flowed at the bottom of each range framing the valley.

Watered by springs and rivers, with the mountains a natural
defence against marauders and buffers against the winter winds but
open from the west allowing easy passage, it was hardly surprising
that settlers found it an attractive place to put their bundles down,
round up their animals and begin to build. This was combined with
the ample availability of easily quarried and chiselled black stone
from the mountains.

The road linking Islamabad to Taxila passed through the Taxila
Cantonment, filled with the signs of Pakistan's military friendship
with China. I read off the Chinese letters on a concrete panel embedded
in the hillside: *Ba zhong you yi wan sui*. Long live the Pakistan–
China friendship. Even the bus stops had pagoda-like structures.

The Pakistani trucks were jewelled, mirrored, flashing works of
art, with a vast arch over the driver's seat.

For thousands of years people had lived here, building on top of
older settlements, so that the valley was sprinkled with an odd
assortment of historical deposits. Here, then, was the evidence for
the tangled history of Pakistan.

The oldest city of Taxila was the Bhir mound where a Persian
satrap had lived. Despite the heat, I shivered in excitement. My Iranian
missing link. From the mid-sixth to the fourth century BC, Gandhara
was one of the forty-two provinces of the Achaemenian empire of
Persia, I had learned at the museum. Cyrus the Great consolidated
his power in 550 BC and for two centuries the enormous dominions of

the Persian empire extended right through Afghanistan, as far east as the Indus and, after Darius, to some parts of Punjab.[2] The imprint of the fire-worshipping Zoroastrians sank deep into the land, wrote Olaf Caroe, the last British governor of the frontier. The underlying whisper of the Persian spirit united Asia from the Tigris to the Indus.

It was possibly from this period that the stone-cutters learned their work, imitating the highly developed art and architecture of Persepolis. India's Mauryans—led at one point by King Ashoka—were mad for the style; they copied the stone-polishing methods for their palaces and for the Buddhist columns that dotted the Indian subcontinent. Kharoshti, an ancient Indian alphabet, was fashioned from Aramaic, the official alphabet of the Persian state.

After playing such an extraordinary part in much of the subcontinent's history, Taxila's vast grounds now seemed at peace, glistening in the harsh sun.

Alexander the Macedonian, with a flick of his sword and a stomp of his horse, put an end to the Achaemenians. He stormed the Indus Valley in 327 BC, marching from Bactria in Afghanistan, the summer of that year, crossing the Hindu Kush into Alexandria, a city he had founded two years earlier, near Bagram, north of Kabul. Then, as Arrian the military historian wrote centuries later, Alexander advanced to the Cophen River (the Kabul), making a sacrifice to the goddess Athena by Jalalabad and sending emissaries to Taxila, ordering the city's ruler to meet him.

The ruler of Taxila, Omphis or Ambhi, capitulated, and it was not until Alexander crossed the Jhelum River, overstepping the Persian empire's eastern boundary, that he clashed with Porus, ruler of Punjab.[3]

Sikandar ne Porus se ki thi larai, se ki thi larai, to main kya karoon.

The Macedonian's raids did not result in any administrative hold. Alexander left by sea, never to return. I remembered the tired, rebellious soldiers by the Beas in Indian Punjab, near Jalandhar. But when the Greek writers who came with Alexander described Taxila, they included the very Iranian habit of leaving dead bodies to circling vultures.[4] They also mentioned ascetics doing *tapasya* in the blazing sun; they took note of polygamy and sati and how girls who could not afford a dowry were lined up in the marketplace for sale.[5]

In Taxila's next valley to the south, between the Jaulian and Margalla Hills through which the Tamra Nala flows, there was a massive stupa called the Dharmarajika, from 'Dharma Raja', the king of Dharma, or Ashoka, that contrite man who wept in Kalinga as blood ran down his sword and he thought of the violence he had perpetrated.

It was a short walk down into the village. The taxi driver followed me at a polite distance. Across the fields of newly planted ganjam wheat, a chitteree bird called: just that, 'chittereeee'. Up the stone stairs, around a hill, stood the rest of the Chiri Tope, ringed by the Khurram Mountains to the east.

The Dharmarajika was a vast stony mound now overgrown with grass. The delicate leaves of wild pepper trees gave the backdrop a soft feel, the peppercorn bunches turning pink.

The British explorer, Sir John Marshall, had sunk a shaft on the north side of the great stupa and found a large block of flat limestone covering a casket of steatite and a miniature stupa of fine grey limestone. His report from ninety-odd years ago is perfectly deadpan, but at times like this the man must have wanted to shout with triumph.

> Inside this casket was a smaller casket of silvery bronze $1^{3}/_{8}$" high, in the form of a stupa crowned with umbrellas; and in this miniature casket were some calcined bones and ashes and a few gold, agate, pearl and bone beads.[6]

In a pine tree flashed a bright blue neelkanth which I had seen over the Indian plains, its turquoise wings a shock. The Punjabi guide dug out from his pocket a feather it had dropped.

'Very rare,' he said. 'People look and look and don't find them, it's very useful for curing breathing problems. You hang it around your neck. Here, you take it.'

It seemed perfectly natural to be standing on a Buddhist brick mound in a Pakistan valley in summer, discussing the medicinal properties of a bird feather.

Shortly after Alexander left, from 323 to 190 BC or so, the Mauryans stepped in from the Indian plains. Chandragupta Maurya was so well entrenched in Punjab and beyond that when, roughly in

305 BC, Seleucus Nicator, who had fought under Alexander, came back across the Indus in a late attempt to grab the Indian provinces back and wallow in some of Alexander's glory, he bumped noses with the powerful Indian kings. He found himself meekly handing over parts of Gandhara, bits along the Indus, not to mention a niece or daughter in marriage and he got, well, 500 elephants in return.[7]

Ashoka himself spent time at Taxila, ruling as viceroy on behalf of Bindusara, his father, preaching Buddhism, building Buddhist stupas, erecting the same edicts he had all over India, but in Kharoshti, in deference to the local population's tongue.

After Ashoka, his son Kunala continued the Mauryan grip of the region. The final missing bits of history were falling into place, this was the rest of the puzzle. From here, it was not such a far cry to Kucha, in China.

The writings of Megasthenes, ambassador of Seleucus Nicator, describe a trunk road freed up from Pataliputra to Taxila. From there, it went on across the Indus to Peshawar and Kapisa, from where it linked to Bactria in Afghanistan and the West.

A bee buzzed and we stepped away from the mound. From a slight distance, there was a faint impression against the stupa, of an enormous seated Buddha. From deep in the hills came the faint clink of metal against stone. You see, the guide said, *taxila* means stone-working. Down in the main village, old men still chisel bowls from the stone, bowls to grind ginger and garlic in and mix into curries, he informed us.

I jammed my sun hat down on my head, took another swig of water.

The Taxila Museum people offered me lunch, which we chatted over. They did not quite know what to make of me, but were unfailingly polite. I was not a renowned professor, nor was I a famous archaeologist with shattering new theories, there was no list of historical publications. I had simply showed up and asked a few directions.

∞

Back in Islamabad, sated and happy, as such excursions unfailingly made me, I made my first mistake. I thought I would pay my respects to Vijay Nambiar, the Indian high commissioner to Pakistan. He and his wife Malini had hosted me in Beijing right at the beginning when I first began to seek Xuanzang.

It was delightful, as always, to see him. We chatted, and he suggested I join them at their home for dinner. Things had been rough in the past year for Indian diplomats. Indian papers were filled with fury about their mistreatment, how their houses were searched, how one was even roughed up.

Preparations for the India–Pakistan talks were in full swing. Rumours swirled. It was a security nightmare. Both leaders had a considerable trigger-happy lunatic fringe to contend with. If Musharraf simply made it to India, met Vajpayee and returned home without incident, it would be a triumph. Security for India's diplomats in Pakistan had been stepped up to unprecedented levels.

'How silly,' Vijay sighed, 'for nuclear powers to be doing *kutti*.'

After dinner, Malini came in their private car to drop me back to the university. As we pulled out of their driveway, another dark car slipped out from where it had been parked and eased into the traffic behind us.

'There they are,' hissed Malini through gritted teeth. 'They're everywhere. Following us around. Even when I go shopping.'

The car followed us right to the university guest house gates. Later, I heard loud voices and the guest house guard answering in low tones. The next day, Imran was silent and furious.

'They've been here, you know.'

He did not have to explain who.

'They've been nosing around the university, pestering Dr Dani with dozens of questions. They wanted a photocopy of your passport. I warned you not to go see any Indians.'

I was absolutely mortified. Had he warned me? It had flown right out of my mind.

He was beside himself.

'Now they will question me also, and my family.'

'Oh no, Imran,' I wailed. 'This is awful.'

He delivered the final payload.

'I don't think you can stay here any more.'

We were sitting outside Dr Dani's office. The sun was climbing. My hands began to shake.

Imran was stony. He rustled some papers. I pulled out a tissue and blew my nose. I was stunned. I had no idea what to do. I could not turn to my ambassador. I could feel my chin quivering, my nose going red. I blew my nose again. I put on my dark glasses, although inside the office it wasn't at all sunny.

'Oh, stop it,' I told myself. *Think.*

By my elbow, the phone rang.

'It's for you,' Imran said, handing me the instrument.

'Hello,' said a chirpy British male voice. 'I've been trying to track you down.' It was Justin, from Nestlé, a contact my father had given me before I left. Before I knew it, from being a sobbing, weeping wreck in the guest house, stuffing clothes and books into my bag, still wearing dark glasses, blowing my nose, I had been rescued, picked up, lunched, and ensconced in a vast elegant house with a well-tended garden and three dogs. Deus ex machina. My sharpened instincts told me there was no need to divulge my whereabouts to Imran.

'If you need anything, call,' said Justin, as he quite calmly went back to work, as though he rescued travellers in trouble every day of his life, in between selling tins of powdered milk.

Ambareen, Justin's Pakistani wife was roughly my age. She splashed through puddles in her low-slung red convertible, her hair cut stylishly short, clad in jeans and T-shirt, flipping on her mobile. She held a high-profile job in the textile industry. She was bright, efficient. She kept biscuits in her car to give the beggar children, although there weren't many. I accompanied her to Melody Market for a doctor's appointment. The wind whipped through our hair in the roofless car.

'Do you know there is five billion rupees worth of unofficial trade across the border? India sends *paan* leaves, beef, cloth, sugar. Karachi markets overflow with Indian goods. And don't even *mention* the films. *Lagaan* was available here soon after its release in India.'

I had no idea.

'There is this incredible thirst for things Indian, people are dying to go to India, to look around. Look at the bus availability, it's much more crowded going from Pakistan than coming from Delhi.'

In the company of this most hospitable couple, my travails with Imran were forgotten, although I felt mortified that I had gotten the kind Dr Dani and his assistant in trouble through my own foolishness.

Justin and Ambareen took me to a goodbye party for a departing diplomat, where the music—Punjabi, nouveau bhangra—went on much after the guest of honour had slipped away. Assorted other diplomats, dispossessed Afghan royalty, rear admirals, oil men and a couple of lesbians mingled over the mango and ice cream, and the booze flowed out in the suburbs of Islamabad.

'I'm a Pathan first, a Muslim second, a Pakistani last,' one guest leaned over to tell me. He had, in his book collection, Aurel Stein's first editions. He had a passion for the North-West Frontier Province. He got up to turn down the bhangra music. The dispossessed Afghan prince turned it back up. The prince was sweating from dancing, damp patches showed through his satiny shirt.

This was a different Pakistan to the one I saw on the streets. It had the unmistakable patina of money, not discussed and yet ever present. This was the Islamabad smart set, where the women wore sleeveless salwar kameez and off-the-shoulder backless sari blouses, and played golf. The men whipped out cigarettes and spoke in flawless British accents, so perfectly rendered that I thought at first they were English.

They drove giant Lexus Land Cruisers, outfitted with compasses and geosatellite positioners, as though there was a great danger of totally losing one's bearings in Islamabad and of roads collapsing and metamorphosing into a jungle.

We all danced. It was a rocking good time. For days, I carried in my head the music of Junoon, a pop band.

Justin and Ambareen had been extraordinarily kind to me. I hoped I was not overstaying my welcome as I tried to plan my next move. I decided to head to Peshawar before I lost any more time and as it happened, Justin had to go to Peshawar on a work trip and said he could take me on the three-hour drive west, across the Indus River.

chapter forty-one

Mound of the King

The kingdom of Gandhara is about 1000 *li* from east to west, and about 800 *li* from north to south. On the east it borders on the river Sin (Sindh). The capital of the country is called Po-lu-sha-pu-lo; it is about 40 *li* in circuit. The royal family is extinct, and the kingdom is governed by deputies from Kapisa. The towns and villages are deserted, and there are but few inhabitants . . . The country is rich in cereals, and produces a variety of flowers and fruits; it abounds also in sugar-cane, from the juice of which they prepare 'the solid sugar'.[1]

The monk felt a strange mix of excitement and disappointment. This far-flung outpost of India at the bottom of the hills of Afghanistan, had produced the Buddhist thinkers closest to his heart. He thought of them as demigods who had penned the Yogacara texts, the brothers Asangha and Vasubandhu. Besides, the land was breathtakingly lovely, with the mountains in the distance, with its flowers and fruits.

But only a ragged settlement was left of the Kushans' powerful Buddhist civilization, a seedy band of a thousand or so families at the bottom of the royal palace, the Bala Hissar, the *kung shing* or fortified and walled portion of the town. They were like orphans clinging to the skirts of a potentially adoptive mother.

He wandered the markets. At night, he paid for travellers' accommodation, mingling with rough-looking traders who eyed him with curiosity. It was not particularly clean and he had to hunt the stalls for vegetarian food. He did not feel much like fraternizing. The reach of the king of Gaochang did not extend this far, there were no monks to fuss over him. A thousand monasteries were scattered across the region, but they were just skeletons, overgrown with wild grass and filled with loneliness.

Instead, he retired to his quarters in the market and wrote by the light of candles, trying to bite back a feeling of having been let down by Gandhara. He resolved to visit the important Buddhist sites, or what was left of them, and then he would press on as soon as he could.

ॐ

One hot day in Peshawar, almost in the middle of July, I set out to look at the spots Xuanzang mentions in his records: Kanishka's stupa was the main one. Peshawar was the winter capital of the Kushans, who came down from Kapisa in Afghanistan to the gentler weather here. Kanishka had built a magnificent stupa and interred the Buddha's ashes under it.

Modern Peshawar had an unsettled feel to it, as though its present shape might not last long, as though anything could rip through the town and alter its destiny. On the drive here, we had passed the Armour and Weaponry Factory and an air force base heralded by a great marble eagle. The North-West Frontier Province bristled with arms and artillery schools that taught people how to use them.

Black cloths fluttered at the backs of buses with their slightly bulging windows—the full chador and burkhas, shuttlecock burkhas they were called, I learned, because the shape was so like one. Here, in camps dotted outside the city, the Americans trained the Taliban in the early 1990s in another of the CIA's typical games.

A small familiarity had percolated into my ears in the surnames of the region. I began to recognize them—Yousufzai, Afridi. I hired a small yellow taxi, driven by a sensitive Pathan who had no idea where the Kushan stupa was. But he turned up the ineffectual air conditioning in his car and said he knew the *ziarat* I had mentioned as a landmark—the shrine of Akhund Darweza Baba—that the University of Peshawar's history department had kindly pointed me to.

We drove south-east of Peshawar, past what used to be the Ganj gate, past boys on donkeys, piles of melons for sale in the streets, fat and ripe, stripy green or long and yellow; past bearded men in round white caps pushing carts filled with onions. Outside the city, past two armed policemen who turned to watch the taxi, we bumped through a massive grassy graveyard covered in pebbled mounds, reaching a section of the city where many Afghan refugees lived.

We stopped by the two shrines, by the Hazarkhwani graveyard, near the grave of the poet Abdur Rahman Baba and the shrine of Akhund Darweza Baba, a Sufi saint of the Chishtiyya order whose ancestors hailed from Afghanistan. I stopped to ask at the shrine.

'Do you know where Shah Ji Ki Dheri is?'

The boys had no idea. They went in to ask the mullah, then, scampering back, they invited me in. That's when I saw the paler yellow taxi with two men inside it parked not far down the road. They watched patiently.

I gesticulated at the boys, trying to explain what I was after. I waved and spoke in Urdu, but these were all Pushto speakers. No, they had not heard of Shah Ji Ki Dheri.

'It's around here, somewhere nearby,' I insisted.

The boys looked interested.

A bearded man got out of the parked yellow taxi. I recognized him—he had been sitting back in the Pathan guest house, reading a paper for what seemed like ages. He had ordered dinner as I stood in the lobby making plans. The penny dropped. By that time, two other armed policemen turned up. They were grizzled and wrinkled, uniformed, bearded, but the Kalashnikovs were real enough. The two intelligence cops talked to the two local guards in the blaze of the midday sun. They shook hands, conferred in low voices, four heads leaning towards each other in the middle of the road. The armed guards left.

The bearded man said politely, in (thank goodness) Urdu, 'What exactly are you looking for, madam?'

The little boys in the shrine stuck their heads out to watch the commotion.

I explained as best I could.

A look of understanding crept across the man's face.

'This way, madam, please watch the stones.'

He led me to the back of the graveyard, to another domed tomb. There was an ancient keeper, with eyes lined with kohl, called Multan. These grounds, he said, were indeed the site of the massive Kushan stupa and its legend that Xuanzang told of in his records.

80

The powerful king Kanishka was still a man of loose morals, believing in neither right nor wrong. One day, like Alice in Wonderland, he followed a white hare across swampy grounds and came across a boy who was building a stupa. The boy delivered a prophecy that urged Kanishka to build his own stupa; he decided to surpass the boy's smaller structure. But the boy's stupa kept growing and the king had to keep adding to his to surpass it.

The structure the king built was 400 feet in height and the base was one and a half *li*. It was five storeys high. On top, Kanishka raised five circlets of gilded copper on a staff. But the little stupa intervened. Disturbed, Kanishka knocked off a couple of levels of his stupa.

'These two stupas are still visible. In aggravated sickness, if a cure is sought, people burn incense and offer flowers, and with a sincere faith pay their devotions. In many cases, a remedy is found,'[2] Xuanzang noted.

He added that, to the south-west there was a figure of the Buddha in white stone, eighteen feet high. It diffused a white light. Around it were 100 little stupas, arranged as regularly as the scales of fish. The air was perfumed and musical sounds emanated, conjured up by visiting saints and sages. Lately, a band of robbers had wanted to loot the precincts, the monk reported. The Buddha figure loomed in front of the robbers who scattered in fright.

To the west of the great stupa there is an old sangharama which was built by King Kanishka. Its double towers, connected terraces, storeyed piles, and deep chambers bear testimony to the eminence of the great priests who have here formed their illustrious characters (gained distinction). Although now somewhat decayed, it yet gives evidence of its wonderful construction.[3]

Only a few priests lived there, but the Chinese monk was delighted, because in the third tower was an old construction in which Vasubandhu had prepared the *O-pi-ta-mo-ku-she-lun* (*Abhidharmakosha Shastra*), the very text he was after! There was a commemorative tablet at that spot. The old priests had pointed it out to the visiting Chinese monk.

∽

Centuries later, D.B. Spooner excavated the spot and found not only evidence of the stupa, but the bronze reliquary which held three fragments of bone thought to be the relics of the Buddha. The Governor General of India, Lord Curzon, presented these relics to the Buddhists of Burma. The identification was made thanks to a slave who could not resist signing the object in Kharoshti, before having it buried.

> *dasa agisala navakarmi (k)aniskasa*
> *vihara mahasenasa sangharame*
> ('The slave Agisalaos, the superintendent of works at the vihara of
> Kanishka in the monastery of Mahasena.')[4]

I sighed in happiness, oblivious of the sun beating down in the middle of the day. We headed back towards the old city, to pinpoint the rest of Xuanzang's story. The intelligence man abandoned all pretence of covertness and followed close behind. He was intrigued. I stood by the Sar Asia Gate to sketch it, one of the few gates still standing from the old brick wall that threaded around the ancient city of Peshawar, followed by the cops solicitous of my safety. I gazed up at the ancient brickwork again. How compact and small old buildings used to be, more to a human scale, more comfortable, like a second skin.

Through the winding streets of the old city, there was hardly enough room for the car. There were birds being sold in cages: kala titar, trained to speak, and then competitions were held to see which was most eloquent. The owner unrolled an announcement of an upcoming competition to see if it would interest me.

Bird merchants, cloth merchants. It was as though a polluted, grimy flap of the city had lifted to reveal some tight ancient order, trading systems in place for thousands of years.

The wind lifted a wisp of cotton from a bale. I walked past the merchants who sold tea from China and Bengal, the nuts and dry fruit sellers, piles of powdered henna in dishes, walnuts from Afghanistan, dals, balls of gur, all jammed into a few small old streets. It was out of some Arabian Nights story, and it was everything I had wanted Peshawar to be. With a whiff of Kashgar and Shahrisabz, the structure of this old trading town reminded me that in its bones, Peshawar held the imprint of Central Asia.

I turned a corner left, then right at the end of the street to Pipal Mandi, where there was still a peepul tree, its spreading branches shading the little lane crammed with shops. I doubted it was *the* peepul tree Xuanzang had mentioned. But still.

It was Friday, and along the main chowk men had placed themselves along the mosque, on the pavement, lines and lines of them spilling outside the mosque, touching foreheads to the ground. The names that trellised the old city rang in my ears. Namakmandi, for salt, Bazazan for cloth, Misgaran for bronze. Fil-khana, elephant line. Shuter-khana, camel line. Dhakki Nalbandi, place for fixing horseshoes. [5]

Followed by the secret service men and the driver, I backtracked east past the Afghan money-changers, past the Cunningham Clock Tower—at the base of which stood a vast chicken coop—through old cobbled streets with ancient house fronts with carved wood balconies, with narrow bridges connecting one house to another on the upper floors, up an incline to the Ghor Khattri, the site where the Buddha's bowl had once been buried.

It was a high spot on the eastern side of the old city, where there used to be a tower. Apparently the bowl used by the Buddha was once buried here before being moved to Persia. Here Xuanzang found a ruined foundation.

A young Afghan joined our small party: the taxi driver, the intelligence men and me. He pointed out sites of interest, said he was studying information technology and worked as a guide. We paused to rest in the shade. I bought a round of lassis, though not without the little drama that precedes such things. First they declined, and I, now well versed in the ways of the subcontinent, insisted.

'Oh no, no, no, no,' they said.

'Please, you must,' I replied.

'Okay then,' they capitulated, as expected. 'Salty is better than sweet,' they remarked quickly. We sampled a Multani mango, in good humour, although the sun was getting to everybody. Our little band was wilting, but I was jubilant.

A few days later, I sat in one of Peshawar's few family restaurants, Shiraz. It was divided into two parts: one for the men and one where the ladies or men with their families could sit, where they played music. Indian, filmi. *Tu pyar hai kisi aur ki, tujhe chaahta koi aur hai.*

Justin had kindly arranged for his Peshawar colleague, Mian Tauquir, to take me north, up into the Swat Valley as Mian had to go anyway to check on his distributors. I was meeting Mian's wife, Homaira, as well as another colleague, a Punjabi, after they had discussed the sale of milk powder. Mian was a stubby, fair-skinned Pathan.

'Why don't we all go,' I suggested to Mian. 'You, your wife, the kids, me, make a holiday of it. You get your work done, I get my journey.'

This would also, I thought, draw less attention to me, dilute the awkwardness of a single woman travelling alone with a male she was not related to in these very conservative Muslim parts. This was no Islamabad. Even Ambareen would cover up here.

Mian's wife, a good Pathan woman, kept her own head covered with her voluminous scarf, as did I. On the streets of Peshawar, of the few women that were visible, I was the only one not in a burkha or full chador.

හ

To the north-east of the sangharama of Kanishka raja about 50 *li*, we cross a great river and arrive at the town of Pushkalavati (Po-shi-kie-lo-fa-ti) . . . To the north of the town 4 or 5 *li* is an old sangharama, of which the halls are deserted and cold. There are very few priests in it, and all of them follow the teaching of the Little Vehicle.[6]

Next to it, the monk wrote, there were the remains of an Ashokan stupa, several hundred feet high, carved in wood and inlaid with stone. Xuanzang was miserable. Would all of India be like this? Ruins of a past Buddhist glory? Had he made his journey in vain?

The monk had to invest it with a grandeur pulled from his imagination. At least there was compassion on an unimaginable scale. He told the story to Hui Li, who faithfully jotted it down.

... it was here that Sakya Buddha when formerly living (acting) as a Bodhisattva, delighted in performing deeds of charity. For a thousand births he was born as king of this country, and here, during these births, he plucked out his eyes (and gave them in charity). Of all these acts there are innumerable holy traces.[7]

chapter forty-two

Lotus City

From Peshawar, we swung north towards Charsadda or ancient Pushkalavati, Lotus City. Charsadda, 'four roads', sat around forty kilometres north-east of Peshawar. It had rained. The thunderstorm left muddy roads and swollen drains.

The children were quiet in the car, in the presence of a stranger, and I thought, when they relax, the ice will have broken. The children had such poetic names. Saman: chameli flower; Haseeb: Allah's name; Maneeb: Begum Ara's name, the prophet's youngest wife. Maneeb, four years old, had on spectacles, gold-rimmed and without any power, but he had refused to get in the car without them and so the little party got delayed.

Spring waters were running down the fertile valley in muddy streams. Sugar cane fields were thick, lush green. Gur is well known in Charsadda. Poplar trees lined the roads, sparkling in the dappled morning sunlight.

We stopped to ask directions to the Bala Hisar, a massive ancient city, reduced to clayey bumps in the earth, an ancient quiet city worn down to a stump, but still with a silent presence. This was all that was left of the major Gandharan town.

Archaeologists found evidence of twenty-five centuries of occupation. One and a half kilometres north-east of this sat Shaikhan Dheri, built by Menandar, one of the Hellenized kings who marched into Punjab from Kabul around 160 BC. It was a city typical of that time: straight streets, right angles. He was a great patron of Buddhism and at the centre of his city he placed a giant stupa.[1]

Was it here somewhere that the wise Menandar conversed with a

Buddhist philosopher called Nagasena about the nature of the faith? It would have been a clever move on Menandar's part, at least to be seen to be supporting the Sangha. It was, at the time, possibly the most widely spread religious group in the Gandhara and Punjab.

The whole family was jolted around the car as we turned off main roads and bumped along the fields. The children were silent, in the way they get when they pay attention; it was as though we had gone underwater, moving in slow motion, a taut moment before we hit a Xuanzang spot.

On a slight mound, Shaikhan Dheri had become an empty compound scattered with bits of pottery, in the middle of a Pakistani village. Somebody jumped into an old trench dug by archaeologists a long while ago and handed me a couple of coins, rusted over. I pushed a piece of a pot over with my toe. On cue, the little village children gathered. An elder invited us for sherbet. I hesitated. I would have liked to, but I was not making the decisions.

'*This* is what you wanted to see?' It was making less and less sense to Mian. He shook his head. 'At least take a picture.'

I had tried again to explain my objective to Mian.

'But have you done a market survey to see if anybody is interested in this?' he asked, perplexed.

'You're right,' I laughed. That would have been the wise thing to do.

It was Xuanzang's habit, Hui Li said, when he arrived at a great tower or monastery, to donate a portion of the silver and silks which he had received from the king of Gaochang. So somewhere here, in this little Pakistani village, 1400 years ago, Xuanzang made the offerings as per his custom and then turned northwards, passing over mountains, through valleys, going around 600 *li* till he arrived at the country of U-chang-na (Udyana), high in the Swat Valley. Its ancient capital is thought to be at the present-day city of Mingora.

We piled back into the car and reversed in a burst of sand and mud, passing three camels padding down the village lane. 'Ca-mel,' shouted Maneeb in English, twisting to look back. A man held a shovel over his shoulder, a boy pushed a kid on a tricycle. It was so like India that I forgot for a moment, once again, that I was in Pakistan.

We pressed north, through tobacco fields, past orange groves and piles of melons on the side of the road. There were horsemen, horses tied to each other with ropes, fine flashing flanks in the sun. They cantered by the roadside, a brief memory of Kyrgyzstan, and I remembered again that this was not that far away from Central Asia. The road curved through a marketplace, and further onto the next stop, before the Malakand Pass into the Swat Valley. It was one of the loveliest parts of Pakistan. I could say that now, relishing the words, everything it meant for me to be here.

Xuanzang did not say anything about Takht-i-Bai, but perhaps he passed there, stopped for a night. Perhaps not. But there it was, right on the route into the Swat Valley, and I reckoned it was impossible to miss.

We huffed and puffed and panted up the steep hill to Takht-i-Bai, or 'spring on flat surface of hill', a monastic settlement from the second century BC to the fifth century AD. It had been excavated by Spooner between 1907 and 1909 and was one of the best-preserved monasteries of that period on the subcontinent.

First, the monks' cells, two-storeyed. The walls were still high. Up here the Huns didn't do much damage; possibly it was too far from the main course, removed from the route they torched their way through.

The valley spread to the south, mountains rose all around, the landscape sat in an extraordinary silence. We stooped into the meditation cells in a darkened corridor. A bat flew out, startling us all. It was a room with only a niche to let in a ray of light, conducive to meditation.

Up on a ledge, near the assembly hall, the guide pointed—there, the Malakand Pass leading to Swat to the north, Afghanistan to the west, Taxila to the east.

There was a tower across the hill. We could see the steps going up to the top, circling. A watchtower perhaps, to tell of approaching travellers. The stairs had crumbled but there was enough to imagine a monk scurrying down with news of an approaching caravan. Maybe a fire was lit for signalling.

By now the sun was blazing hot. Sweat flew off us. We sat on a charpoy under a sisam tree. An iron grid buttress held up one wall of the assembly hall which tilted slightly due to its great age. There were steps cut into the hillside to facilitate coming and going from one peak to another. The valley stretched far to the south, blurred in the heat of the day.

The children were quiet, awed by the height and the ancient bricks.

From the Lotus City, Xuanzang had travelled to Po-lu-sha, but we would skip that and see it later, on our way back, when we stopped to visit Mian's brother who lived close to it.

The road to Swat cut into the hillside. The river flowed below to our west, the valley was already lush and filled with orange and pear orchards, and under the trees it was time to harvest onions. In the warm sunlight, there were onions everywhere in their pale purple skins, heaped by the roadside, carpeted under the trees for sorting, spilling out of jute sacks, loaded onto trucks. There were verdant rice fields in the valley and the mountains rose on either side, rocky but not yet forbidding. The river here rushed swiftly, stumbling and foaming over rocks.

We lunched at an Afghan roadside eatery that served fresh Kabuli pulao, and for me it was a delicious return to Central Asia, for this is how they cooked it in Uzbekistan—with tender chunks of mutton and sprinkled with julienned carrots, served with a raita and naan fresh from the tandoor. The river was irresistible, so we kicked off our shoes and waded in, the cool water banishing heat. Maneeb sat in the water, squealing with happiness, and then lay down flat like a tadpole, waving his arms. Haseeb went in deeper, to his knees, already less childish, more restrained, as though creeping adulthood lashed his tongue in chains and forbade joyish expression.

Homaira and I maintained a womanly decorum, keeping our heads covered, only wetting our ankles, although I would dearly have loved to follow Maneeb's example. Mian lurked on the edges and managed to look pleased.

There was a group of tourists from Punjab—even I could tell they were not locals—the women insouciant about their uncovered heads, a girl in jeans and T-shirt. To my eyes, so accustomed now to purdah, it looked vulgar, their heads seemed naked. Had I been in Peshawar too long? Had I adapted to Pathan mores, or was it the deep survival instinct of those who learn to blend in, chameleon-like, and so hide a vast abyss of difference?

We made a brief detour west, to my surprise at Mian's suggestion, to Chakdara near Dir, for the museum. The entire Swat Valley was filled with Buddhist remains, it was hard not to bump into them at every turn. It was a dusty old spot, shut for lunch, but they brought out the keys and opened it especially for us, waiving the one-rupee entrance fee.

Dir I remembered from my conversations with Q. in Peshawar. Q. was a soft-spoken, educated Pathan who worked for one of the agencies in Peshawar. I leaned heavily on his understanding of the region. *Mazhab ka patta*, Q. had said. The card of religion, which trumps all others. This was a deeply fundamentalist area, where the Muslim clergy appealed powerfully to the people.

'Don't forget, the clergy has regular access to the public—to men,' Q. had said in his gentle, steady way. 'They are highly influential political leaders. Think about it. NGOs spend $50,000 to get people together for a conference. These guys meet every Friday anyway. It's natural. They sit there and they target women. How easily it works, naturally the men react to anything the imam says.

'On one hand we're opening up, with TV and radio, and on the other hand the clergy is closing people's minds.' Q. looked down at his food. 'You know, when I was younger and the US was around training the Taliban to fight the Russians, the towns were filled with their stuff. US jackets—we used to buy them in the markets—books, ballpoint pens, there would be exhibitions, we'd go and buy. But we never saw Kashmir jihad posters. In my own backward little village, we now see these posters, urging people to go to Kashmir to fight the jihad.'

I listened in silence.

'Tanzeem-e-Nifaz-e-Shariat-e-Mohammadi—this group is calling for Islamic law to be imposed in the Malakand district, they started their campaign in 1994, even before the Taliban took over Kabul. They destroyed public buildings, people were killed, government troops and these activists. These guys said they will start Kazi courts—Islamic courts—in this area.'

But in Chakdara, Dir, I was after an even older story.

Once more the Buddhist past was collapsed in heaps, but bits of it had been dug up and saved in the local museum. It was another excellent collection, to my adapting eyes. The monsters were particularly striking: a marine horse with upraised wings and the tail of a demon, caught in a stone triangle; a winged beast with a ram's head, its tail curling, corkscrewing off the back. Another creature had a crocodile mouth, the sign said, but it looked exactly like a Chinese dragon, an influence from far across the Pamirs.

And a rare sight: an unusually lively panel of five monks standing in a row, their figures spaced, undamaged, their hair curling slightly, half-turned towards each other, looking up at what must have been a preaching Buddha. It was beautifully executed, the sculpture exuding movement.

My journey had become its own creature, and it demanded completion. I was into my second summer of travel and I was unable to quit, even when I should have stopped and gone home. It was an absurd urgency to have my dotted lines on the map meet.

I recalled idle conversations in Peshawar, aid workers who gathered at the American Club (where neither Pakistanis nor Muslims are allowed, ostensibly because they serve alcohol) and their stories were set only in doomed places. Aid workers whose marriages dissolved, who cracked under the strain, who turned to god.

'I last bumped into John at Sarajevo . . .'

'When I was in Rwanda . . .'

'This is nothing compared to Liberia . . .'

'I got kicked out by . . .'

And a roving doctor who was trying to sneak into Afghanistan spoke a line that I couldn't forget: 'Show me where the suffering is . . .'

What drove these people to areas of great suffering when, if the Buddhists are to be believed, one only needed to look in the mirror to find endless pain?

chapter forty-three

Silk Road Graffiti

 The monk bent over his notes, soothed by the natural beauty that enveloped him.

The country of U-chang-na is about 5000 *li* in circuit; the mountains and valleys are continuously connected, and the valleys and marshes alternate with a succession of high plateaux. Though various kinds of grain are sown, yet the crops are not rich. The grape is abundant, the sugar-cane scarce. The earth produces gold and iron, and is favourable to the cultivation of the scented (shrub) called Yo-kin (turmeric).

   The forests are thick and shady, the fruits and flowers abundant. The cold and the heat are agreeably tempered, the wind and rain come in their season. The people are soft and effeminate, and in disposition are somewhat sly and crafty. They love learning and yet have no application. They practise the art of using charms (religious sentences as charms). Their clothing is white cotton, and they wear little else. Their language, though different in some points, yet greatly resembles that of India.[1]

He settled for the night, adjusting his head on the bundled clothes he used as a pillow. For a while the sound of rushing water filled his head and then he slipped into a dreamless sleep.

ॐ

It was early in the morning in Mingora, the ancient capital of the kingdom of U-chang-na. Somewhere here, the monk had rested. There was the sound of the rushing river and the valley was a swathe of velvet, green and draped. The river itself, busy and torrential, burst over stones. Packhorses walked into its middle so the owners could shovel sand from the bottom, load it into sacks hung from the horses and sell it for a few rupees. Horsemen cantered smartly along the road, with the theatre of the river. The mountains rose beyond, a sort of silent witness to this morning ritual.

As usual, the Buddhists knew the best spots. Swat, they say, used to ring with the sound of bells from Buddhist monasteries. But that was before the Huns came through, flattening it, chasing the monks out. The less lucky ones died as buildings burnt, and by the time Xuanzang came along, things were decayed beyond repair. His heart ached at the destruction.

'On both sides of the river Su-po-fa-su-tu, there are some 1400 sangharamas. They are now generally waste and desolate,'[2] he said. The mighty body of 18,000 priests had withered into a thin handful. The Chinese monk approached some of the local priests, not far from the monastery. They were searching for wood to cook the evening meal. They were Mahayana Buddhists, it turned out, they meditated, recited the texts, but honestly speaking, did not understand them in any meaningful way.

At the Swat Museum there was a foot imprint, giant, gentle as though made in sand, a sign that the Buddha walked here, so that a nearby village was called Qadam. There was a garland-bearer, nude, with small wings. This was new to me, a nude worshipper of the Buddha, the strongest Greek echo yet. Flakes of gold on another panel hinted that it used to be covered with gold leaf. Here, I remembered the *shalabhanjika* carvings in Punjab, and the bacchanalian tinge they carried that I now thought could possibly have filtered down from here.

Up here in the Swat Valley, there were several remains of old Buddhist monasteries. One such site was called Butkara III, the monastery and courtyard resting off the main road, with the hill rising behind and the river further below. Butkara III must have been a magnificent building, resplendent with gilded statues, lapis lazuli from Afghanistan fashioned into tiles that shone in the sun, bits of them still visible. There was a water tank for ablutions. There were two stone lions, badly damaged, but it was still possible to discern the symbols of Ashoka. The elephant statue was beheaded by Mahmud of Ghazni, the guide told us.

To see a final Buddhist reminder in this region, I drove further north, in the company of Haseeb in his white salwar kameez, the guide from the museum and the driver. We turned east towards Jehanabad, a small valley that opened onto the main Swat Valley. We got out of the car at Shakori village and walked up a goat track, through the fields, straight up the shaded hillside. We paused to catch our breath under a chinar tree, its branches filled with prickly chestnuts, reaching high above the undergrowth, filtering sunlight.

It was a good forty-minute climb, in silence. Enormous glaciers had receded, it seemed, leaving behind giant lumps of rock. And finally, at the top of the hill, we sank down on the grass and stared up at the Buddha carved on the upper boulder in bas-relief.

'They must have stayed for days up here, brought their tools and everything,' Haseeb said. 'Maybe they stood on ladders.'

I looked at the little boy with surprised pleasure. It sounded exactly right.

Up here the breeze was cool, the birds sang and the rice fields spilled far below, I could see how this smaller valley gave way to the main Swat Valley. I sketched the carved Buddha, his eyes downcast, sitting cross-legged, his robe spilling over his knees a little.

Further north, the route continued on to Gilgit, to the magnificent Karakoram range and Buddhist symbols etched on rocks along the entire route. I had to let go of it. For an Indian it was near impossible to get permits. Besides, rain had washed out the mountain roads, blocking it with landslides. It was 'Azad Kashmir' or 'Pakistan-Occupied Kashmir', depending on who spoke. Disputed territory. I knew exactly why Xuanzang went on, away from his path, following the excitement of seeing what was around the corner, answering the pull of the mountains.

The roads are craggy and steep. The mountains and the valleys are dark and gloomy. Sometimes we have to cross by ropes, sometimes by iron chains stretched (across the gorges). There are foot-bridges (or covered ways) suspended in the air, and flying bridges across the chasms, with wooden steps let into the ground for climbing the steep embankments . . .[3]

Back in Mingora, our small party lunched with Mian's distributor. It was a local Swat family who observed the strictest purdah. The women ate in a separate room. Our hosts spread a cloth on the floor. We sat cross-legged and ate chicken curry, mutton curry and some sort of vegetable. Then we had cold drinks followed by sweet mangoes and apricots.

They spoke only Pushto, not even the most basic Urdu, but I chatted with them through Homaira. The mother's fingertips were dipped in henna—because strict Muslims don't wear nail polish during namaz. The Pathan customs were stricter than they used to be in pre-Taliban Afghanistan. I began to get an inkling of Taliban culture, right here in the North-West Frontier Province.

We communicated through gestures and smiles. Homaira translated from Pushto to Urdu. I tried on a shuttlecock burkha for the first time as the women giggled and covered their mouths. It was made of some satiny stuff, a pale beige colour. I fitted it over my head, the top like a cap, and adjusted the wire mesh across my eyes, dropped the front flap which reached my thighs. The back flowed to my ankles.

What a surprise not to be able to see your feet with your peripheral vision. It created an unbalanced feel. I walked a few unsteady steps. The women could barely contain themselves. In fact, I realized, all peripheral vision was wiped out. I looked in a mirror. In an instant I had been erased, like a ghost. It was a most unsettling feeling, to see nothing but this shroud with a dark shadow where my eyes used to be. At the same time, to my astonishment, I sensed the power of concealment, the power of only revealing what is absolutely necessary.

Women who wander around alone, their heads barely covered by a scarf—that is, me—were shocking. I could see this from the other side of the burkha. It spoke of a certain breeding and status, to have men look after you. Upper-class women stayed inside.

An incident in the PCO in Peshawar's Sadar Bazaar stuck in my mind. I had stopped at a public place to make a phone call. It was a perfectly ordinary gesture for me, one I had made a hundred times in India. But here, I unwittingly produced a small cataclysm.

The men scattered to the other side of the room. An elderly man put his hand on his chest and bowed. The shopkeeper hurried to drag a curtain across the telephone booth and create the privacy of purdah. In some perfectly unexpected way, I felt honoured by all the fuss.

Time slowed up in Swat. I longed to stay, enchanted by the echoes of Central Asia, wrapped in the mountain light and the sound of water, the pleasant weather. But Mian had finished his work, so had I, and our last stop in Mingora was a little further down the valley: we got out to look at a vast rock behind a small village at Udegram, a little up the hill. On it were carved pack animals: ancient horses, goats, a donkey—Silk Road graffiti. Some merchant, thousands of years ago, by the flicker of a night fire, picked his teeth clean and then, kneeling by a rock, chiselled for posterity the things that made up his life. On cue, a laden donkey trotted by with his master. It was as though life had blown through the carving, as if it had stepped off the rock onto the road.

The visiting monk did not say much about Shahbaz Garhi, the site of the Ashokan edict. It would make perfect sense for the Buddhist king of India to carve it here, on a major artery, roughly halfway from Charsadda to Taxila.[4] It was a billboard on a 2000-year-old highway.

For Xuanzang, it was the spot that housed the story of Prince Visvantara, another incarnation of Buddha, or perhaps an older folk tale that the Buddhist simply incorporated. At any rate, the Chinese monk related in great detail how the Prince gave away his magical elephant that brought prosperity to the land. The neighbouring country was in drought and needed it more.

Mian promised to drive me to the Ashokan edict after lunch, which we ate sitting cross-legged on the floor at Mian's brother's house. A cloth was spread out and dishes placed on it. The women, sisters-in-law, were delighted to see each other. The pile of hot naan from outside (they take their own dough and the man makes it in the oven) was complemented with vegetarian dishes, kofta, a kind of raita. Since we were so close to the family's home village, we did a whole round of visits in the village of Pathans. Mangoes were brought out, sliced, sherbet mixed and tea made each time.

Homaira lent me a chador to cross from one house to another. 'Keep your hands under it,' she said. This was not a forgiving place.

Her cousin had married her brother, so they all still lived next door to each other. I bent before her mother, an old woman, though she was only around fifty. She took my face in both hands and kissed my forehead lightly.

'Come back soon.'

Over many conversations in Peshawar with Q., who turned out to be a more sensitive and cultured man than I had realized, I began to understand the Pathans a little better.

'Why did such close cousins marry each other?' I asked.

'It's obvious,' he said. 'Men and women in families are exposed to each other. You live near your cousins. It's easy access, love affairs are easy. You know only your cousins, because external exposure is minimal.'

Talaq, divorce, was taboo in Pathan society, even though it is allowed by Islam. I saw how new Islam had been superimposed on these old tribal societies.

At Shahbaz Garhi, the guard, white beard shaking slightly, slept on his charpoy, one arm flung over his head, a bicycle pushed under a leafy zanda tree. Homaira and I crept past him to climb up to the rock. Higher up, the birds twittered in the silent flanks. It was an unhampered view of the plains. Mian's interest was flagging by now and he stayed at the bottom, by the car. The edict was carved on two boulders, dated at 258–7 BC, all in Kharoshti. I ran my fingers over the rock lightly.

'I can't read this,' Homaira said, surprised.

If Xuanzang tried to read the inscription, he did not mention it. He simply said that there was a stupa built by 'Asoka-raja', related a few legends and left it at that.

To the north-east of Po-lu-sha city about 20 *li* or so we come to Mount Dantaloka. Above a ridge of that mountain is a stupa built by Asoka-raja . . . At the present time the shrubs and trees are all of deep red colour.[5]

Poplars rustled, a long-tailed drongo flitted and perched in the branches. The fields spread out in a muted green. One flank of the hill was overgrown with cactus. The sun had softened by now. And back at the bottom of the hill, we stared at a sharp-tailed sabsara, a swipe from which could slice your calves. It looked like a miniature komodo lizard that flicked its tongue and kicked its legs out to walk up.

The rice fields shimmered with water. They grow the chaff here, for buffaloes.

My tour with the Tauquirs ended here. I was reluctant to leave, I wanted to dig my heels in, whine and whimper as Maneeb might have done. Too short, too short.

chapter forty-four

Listening Post

Peshawar, which we rolled into late at night, which had so recently seemed like a frontier town, now felt like an international metropolis. The journey with the Tauquir family felt frozen in time. I hoped the intelligence police would not be after them, for back in Peshawar the spooks asked to interview me.

A., the head of the secret service in the region, and I agreed on a time. We sat in the guest house lobby and sipped green tea.

He flipped open his notebook and took out a pen. He wore a long salwar kameez and had a dark moustache. After my initial shock at the Quaid-i-Azam University at being followed by intelligence men, and its disastrous consequences, Peshawar had taught me to shake off the fear. Sharing lassis in the old town with my minder had helped. So when I had to meet the head, I was quite prepared, indeed, chatty.

'You have not registered with the police,' he said sternly.

'I'm not required to, my visa is exempt from police registration,' I said, handing him my passport.

He cleared his throat.

'We knew you were in town,' he said, a trifle pleased with himself. 'We got the information from the Islamabad police.'

'It's your job,' I said kindly.

We went through the paces.

'Why are you here? What are you doing? Who were you staying with, why were you visiting the American diplomat in Peshawar?'

'He's quite knowledgeable about Afghanistan,' I replied easily.

'Really?' A.'s ears pricked up. 'What did he say?'

'Oh, this and that, his impressions of the place.'

I wanted to say, crossly, surely you know that Peshawar has long been a listening post for the Americans and I suspect he's a spy. I volunteered more information instead.

'I'm visiting the aid agencies for the same reason. They are the ones who travel to Afghanistan and can tell me what the situation is like there.'

'Yes,' he sighed, 'things are very bad in Afghanistan. We get a lot of spillover from the problems there,' he confided.

'Really?' It was my turn to prick my ears up, but he was already back on his guard.

'Will you come back to Peshawar?'

'If I get a visa to Afghanistan, I will have to come back,' I said.

He asked to search my room. He looked through a pile of books. Dr Dani's book on Peshawar's history. Pathan poetry. Xuanzang's works. A pamphlet on Taxila.

There was nothing there that interested him.

'I have one request,' I said.

'*Farmaiyeh*,' he said.

'Please do not trouble the people I speak to or spend time with. They are helping me. If you have questions, come to me, but leave them alone,' I said.

'We have to do our job,' he said, almost sadly. 'But we are professionals.'

'I know,' I said.

They had indeed kept track of me quite closely, although I'm almost certain they had lost me in the Swat Valley.

'Be careful,' A. said. 'Look after yourself and good luck with your work.'

I went into a bank to change money and one of the managers rose from his desk.

'Ms Saran! How are you?' he said.

He was the owner of the guest house where I had stayed the last time, where the secret service man had ordered dinner while keeping an eye on me. It was he who had recited to me:

Kya boodh badh poochcho, ho purab ke sakino
Humko gharib jaan ke has has pukar ke

Dilli jo shahr tha, alam meh bemisal
Aye hue hain hum, ussi ujde dayar se

(What can I ask of our abode, O Eastern sages?
Knowing us to be poor, you laughingly address us.
Delhi was once a city incomparable in the world,
We too came from that uprooted garden.)

Peshawar was a small town, after all.

The India–Pakistan summit finished, disastrously, and Kashmir was on everybody's lips. At the hotel a sorrowful Pathan moaned, 'Eighty per cent of our budget spent on Kashmir . . .'

I tossed and turned at night until at 4 a.m. the azan rang out, *Allah ho Akbar.* The man's voice was particularly fine. I could hear him tap the mike, clear his throat, the slight muffle and crackle before he launched into his call. His voice demanded attention. I lay in my bed, sleepless, and as I followed the thread of his prayer, a knot unwound.

Justin was due back in Peshawar, and not only agreed to ferry me back to Islamabad, but volunteered to help me find Hund, the old crossing of the Indus River.

To return to Islamabad we had to cross the Indus anyway, but Hund was a few kilometres upriver from the usual crossing at Attock. It would mean a detour and I was uncertain about the exact directions.

What a relief it was to climb into Justin's nice air-conditioned car. He played British comedy tapes which kept me laughing, yanking me firmly back into the twenty-first century.

We learned the location of the Hund Fort after stopping several times to ask the way from locals. We turned off at Jehangirpur and went upriver to Ambar village, turned towards the Indus, through mud tracks, squeezing past a convoy of vans filled with police, waiting out the buffalo herd. The bumps scraped the bottom of the car on a pile of pebbles till we got to the low remains of the Hund Fort. It was barely waist-high now, the bricks were thin, but the turrets were still visible, bulging outwards at regular intervals.

A rusted board informed the visitor that Alexander the Great, the

Scythians, the Kushans, the Chinese pilgrims, Mahmud of Ghazni, Shahabuddin Ghori, Timur, Babur, and many other invaders who wished to cross the Indus through the Peshawar valley came here.

Such illustrious footsteps on this sunny afternoon, through this narrow village road, past the village mosque and right at the amluk tree where a goatherd squatted, chewing on a twig. The hush of the Indus rose, the broad river lacerated and divided by banks of mud, but swift and deep and powerful, even here, where it was supposed to be fordable, as it swept towards the Arabian Sea. It was not hard to imagine the clink of armour and the splashing of horses foaming at the mouth with effort, the yells of Macedonian foot soldiers as an army forded the river in the fourth century before the birth of Christ.

Alexander's army numbered 10,000 men and came with vast herds of animals that had to be shepherded across the river on a bridge made of linked boats. The weak ruler of Taxila obsequiously sent envoys laden with lavish gifts: 3000 oxen for sacrifices, 10,000 sheep, 200 talents of silver.[1]

And then the Chinese monk, nearly 1000 years later, hurrying to India. In a boat perhaps, poled across by the boatman to reach the plains of Punjab, or pulled by the ferryman.

A herd of goats trotted across a pebbly embankment, their hooves clicking.

Not far from here, Panini, the great Indian grammarian, was born. The Rishi Panini, as he is called, fascinated the Chinese monk. Xuanzang devoted long passages to describing how Panini collected a multitude of words and organized them into a book of letters that contained 1000 slokas, each sloka of thirty-two syllables. How satisfying the Chinese found order, and how seldom they found it on the subcontinent!

The Indus was an extraordinary river, muscular and endless, a guardian of thousands and thousands of years. I was glad to have seen it. It would be here long after I stepped away from its shores, long after I died and was cremated and had my own ashes sprinkled in some river. For the Mughals, it was the grand gateway to India. Darwaz-e-Hind, the river that gave India her name.

The river is about 3 or 4 *li* in width, and flows south-west. Its waters are pure and clear as a mirror as they roll along with impetuous flow. Poisonous Nagas and hurtful beasts occupy the caverns and clefts along its sides. If a man tries to cross the river carrying with him valuable goods or gems or rare kinds of fruits or flowers, or especially relics of Buddha, the boat is frequently engulphed by the waves.[2]

The Chinese monk would remember this river. Perhaps he even wrote this passage afterwards, after the accident happened on his way back, years later, when he crossed astride an elephant.

It was as if the waters flowed in unnatural directions, clashed headlong so that waves rose towards the sky. He hardly felt the elephant lose its footing, but he instantly knew something was wrong when the great beast swayed and, as if in slow motion, went leaning into the rippled river, trumpeting in dismay. Screams went up the convoy. The monk felt the water close over his head and then hands were reaching for him, he felt nails dig into his wrists as they hauled him back up. He gasped and sneezed, his eyes watered. He was fine, his mount had recovered.

But the boat in front, laden with books, images, the flower seeds of India and fellow travellers soared, its prow pointed towards the heavens, the boatman lurching through the air, the passengers tumbling.

The sutras, he shouted. Save the sutras. But it was too late, the packages bobbed downstream, loosened from their ties, soggy, already swallowed by the depths, a river hungry for a sutra. The frightened dripping bunch scrambled onto the other bank. They had managed to fish out the boatman, save much of their belongings. But the flower seeds were gone. And fifty manuscript copies of the sutras.

Later, when the monk was back in Afghanistan, the king of Kapisa shook his head. It was the seeds, he said. The flower seeds you were not supposed to cross the river with. With the king's help, the monk dispatched a few people to Udyana, so they could copy out again the *Tripitaka* of the Kasyapiya school.

ॐ

It was almost the end of July. I was back in Islamabad. My time in Pakistan would run out soon. Somehow I had to find a way to Afghanistan.

A morning dawned still and lonely—I awoke and thought to myself, what will come of all this, where will my tired body end? The shadows at the back of my mind threatened. The great house was quiet. Justin was at work; Ambareen had returned to Lahore, to her job. I missed them both.

Jack the German Shepherd nosed at my leg. He stuck his muzzle behind my knee, as if to say, don't be sad. And then he parked himself next to me, protective. We liked each other's presence. A companionable sort of silence.

I needed an extension of my visa in Pakistan.

I dropped in to see Hasan at Islamabad's ministry of interior. We had spoken on the phone from Delhi, when I had phoned him once directly to plead for my visa. Now I needed his help again with a visa extension for Pakistan, which would give me enough time for Afghanistan. Jinnah's handsome features looked down on us.

Hasan was a Lahori. We sipped tea and discussed Lahore's excellent food. He had a pile of files in front of him and staring at them I remarked how similar our two bureaucracies were.

'So,' Hasan asked, 'do we have the same files?'

'Yes,' I said. 'The same paperwork, the same punched holes with the little bit of string eyelets tied together.' Hasan arranged a visa extension for me within hours and delivered it with a friendly warning to be careful in Afghanistan.

chapter forty-five

Inshallah

As it happened, the embassy of the Islamic Emirate of Afghanistan was a few steps down the road from Justin's house. I tried to get advice from the people who go frequently. Journalists.

'*Islamabad est une cloche,*' said Jean-Claude Chapon, the bureau chief of Agence France-Presse in the capital. Islamabad was like a bell jar, an artificially created space to protect foreigners. Chapon was ready to leave the country, his term up. He had his photo of the Bamiyan Buddhas and two dots at the bottom that were, on closer inspection, men squatting. It was a photograph flooded with a warm sunlight, firmly set in the past. The Buddhas no longer existed. The Taliban had bombed them to smithereens early that summer. Chapon was a tall burly man with a beard streaked with grey. He was the first person who did not meet my question with horror, disbelief or scorn.

'Watch out for the mines,' he said. Particularly off the beaten track. '*Le Taliban est un reve pour un journaliste,*' he said. Honesty is rare among hacks, who never acknowledge to what extent the industry feeds off other people's misery, natural catastrophes and political extremes. There is a peculiar shiver, almost sexual, about protest and vast disaster; it draws witnesses, wire-service reporters and writers like flies to honey. I sipped the tea he offered and fought tears. His easy optimism was overwhelming, after days of coming up against brick walls.

'You can go to Afghanistan.'

The truth was I had no idea what I was doing. I was out of my depth. Despite Chapon's encouragement, I was a far cry (although constantly near tears) from toughened war correspondents who knew the area like the back of their hands. They had contacts on the ground, cars with four-wheel drive, multilingual local drivers, interpreters, fixers, satellite phones, organizations behind them, digital cameras, US dollar expense accounts. They had the weight of history.

If anything happened to them, they would be flown out on helicopters, their embassies would be alerted, their presidents would issue a statement, international press bodies would hold meetings and condemn repressive Asian regimes.

It was a male domain—the officials, the press pack, not to mention the Taliban across the border. Only the aid agencies seemed to teem with serious, competent women, their mouths imprinted with the effort of doing good, the belief that they were making a difference.

I would have to find my own way, hitch rides, rely on the kindness of strangers. I peered in from the outside, a soloist with a backpack, a split life and a yen for history. But hadn't I been exactly that all my life? I had to ignore, with terror, the indirect message discreetly passed on from a senior member of the Indian Cabinet: Do not go to Afghanistan, on any account.

I reviewed my strategy. For Afghanistan, I decided to dig up my journalist's hat. I had learned well, by now, the lesson of non-identity. Those shorn of obvious frames and not armed with multi-sheeted letters on gilt letterheads were suspect.

The Taliban's visa office was a small room in a side lane off a main Islamabad street, not far from the UNHCR office. The women's side was walled off and they had covered the entrance with a straw mat. It had a corrugated tin roof with a fan. The line of men stayed behind the mat, and a handful of women sat with their heads covered and stared as I spoke in Urdu.

A trickle of men, black turbans wound around their head, the edge left long and loose, hooked noses, beards, filed into the offices. My first glimpse of the Taliban.

'I have an appointment with Zahid Hussain,' I said to the bearded man behind the grill. He looked decidedly Persian.

'You've come now?' he said. 'It's time for namaz,' he said in Urdu.

'Not yet. You have another fifteen minutes. I need less than ten,' I replied, also in Urdu.

Somebody unlocked and unbolted a side door to the narrow room where Zahid Hussain sat. He wore the same black turban and sat behind a wide desk, a black and white flag with Arabic inscriptions sat on his desk. He smiled, or was it a grimace, revealing sharp teeth. Broad shoulders. A warrior–administrator. Fearsome. I wasn't even anywhere near getting to Afghanistan and I was petrified. Zahir, the junior fellow, handed me the form in English and in Urdu.

Here, fill this in. I looked over the form.

NAME.

SON OF.

There was no box for 'Daughter of'. Already, Pakistan officials felt like bleeding-heart liberals with wide-open minds. I filled the Taliban visa form, wrote a letter by hand, attached a photocopy of my passport along with two pictures. They said they would do it urgently, I should return in a few days.

Back at the house, I switched on the air conditioner and then passed out for the entire afternoon, dreaming disturbed dreams.

The rains came with a vengeance. It poured 620 mm in one day, the heaviest rainfall in a century. It had to mean something, a change of pace, a shift in mood, an end to deadlock. My sandals got soaked in the short walk to the Afghan embassy, my salwar clinging to my legs, damp tendrils of hair from under the dupatta.

The Afghan women still sat it out, faces that changed from Mongolian to Pathan, fair and dark, one slow large woman who could have been a Peruvian Indian. The smiles across the language barrier and something stamped in their eyes. Perhaps it was suffering.

One woman pointed with her chin to an empty spot on a bench, we smiled at each other, I stepped across the huddle. They were here to attest marriage certificates, notarize documents, apply for passports from the Taliban government. But there was no news from Kabul.

I was edgy. I was spending precious, hard-earned days in Pakistan trying to arrange a visa to Afghanistan. There was no choice. Currently, the only way into Afghanistan was through Pakistan. Either that, or return to Delhi, fly to Tehran and try from the Iranian side.

In the meantime I spent my days dropping into people's offices, trying to glean as much information about Afghanistan as I could for the article I was supposed to write for a newspaper in Hong Kong in return for an official letter attaching me to the organization. It was a relief to have a role I knew, for a change. I slipped it on comfortably for my meetings with aid officials.

They sat in gleaming lavish offices and reminded me of the paradoxes of foreign aid. How well they lived and worked. The streets of Islamabad were filled with massive white Toyotas, painted with the blue UN insignia, the rubbery antennae flickering on bonnets. The aid workers churned out thick reports, printed on glossy paper with soft-focus pictures of misery. Always, at the bottom, the almost accidental request, slipped in carefully, quickly, for donors to send more money, more money, or the starving would die and the wounded would not survive. It seemed absurd, this talk of starvation and death, coming from the aura of wealth that susurrated from these fattened offices.

I wanted to close my eyes and shove my fingers into my ears. How could I think this, how churlish of me to doubt the do-gooders. Hadn't millions of Afghans been saved, hadn't the UN injected humanity into the carcass of Afghanistan, Jesus-like, saving a country from ruin?

I met Karim, a short, bearded Afghan who had studied engineering in Roorkee, Uttaranchal, and so developed his taste for Hindi films. His left eye wandered, as though it could not bear to look at the things he had to see, a silent floating protest. He translated from Urdu to Pushto, and from Pushto to Urdu, he had read and translated Premchand's short stories. Now he helped with the work of press liaison of the United Nations, for Pakistan and Afghanistan. Karim alerted me to the possibility of going to Kabul with a UNHCR convoy of repatriating refugees. I stored the information in the back of my mind.

Visiting journalists turn to local journalists for a view of the world. Sometimes they quote them. In the basement of the offices of the *Statesman* newspaper, I met the bureau chief, Sikandar Hyat, a serious elderly man with spectacles who said that, in essence, the Taliban had restored a modicum of peace to a battered land. And they had been unfairly treated by the Western media.

We were sitting in the office of one of the reporters. They had ordered round after round of tea for me and I was taking very small sips. I swallowed and nodded.

It was my very first encounter with the confusion that would envelop my entire notion of Afghanistan, an utter bewilderment born from my media-acquired idea of how evil the Taliban was and how the reality turned out to be far more complex. Things were beginning to turn upside down, like a sand hourglass. The feeling of time trickling by beyond my reach was almost unbearable. Was this getting absurd, my following in the monk's footsteps? Did I need to take things to such an extreme? I was too small for such enormities.

Finally, one morning, I met Suhail Shaheen, the Taliban's second in command. But not until I insisted and was told he was in a meeting with the Chinese ambassador. A whole string of diplomatic plates lined up to see the Taliban. Everybody, it seemed, kept up unofficial contacts with them, alongside the public rhetoric condemning them.

Pakistan felt no need for covertness. The Taliban had been useful to Pakistan, a small country developing cracks in it, wedged between the vastness of India and the mountains of Afghanistan. It would be good for Pakistan to have a Muslim ally in Kabul.

Suhail Shaheen was a large Pushtoon. By now I was used to the fierce black turbans and the feral beards. The men were polite. The Taliban peons produced cups of green tea, *chai-sabz*.

'Because of the sanctions, many people have been sacked from work,' he said, in his careful English. 'About 200 foreign and local investors were to invest in Afghanistan. After sanctions, they are not ready to invest. International banks are not ready to give them credit. As a result, there is unemployment among young people.'

My scepticism about UN and aid agencies began to grow, a small canker in the corner of my brain. I fought it. I tried hard to ignore it, I refused to admit it was possible for an ideal to have rotted from the inside, to have become fattened and ineffectual, shovelling donor dollars into its mouth like a greedy fishwife.

Shaheen promised to chase up on the Afghan visa. He needed approval from Kabul.

But when I went a few days later, waiting outside the Afghan embassy, there was still no news from Kabul and Suhail Shaheen was in a meeting. An almost Mongolian-looking girl chatted with me in English. She was fluent, the words tripped out as though she had been waiting a long time to say the things she felt.

'My papa says if you speak one language you are one person. If you speak several languages you can be several people.'

My thoughts exactly. I smiled down at her.

'Suhail Shaheen is coming in ten minutes, inshallah. He's in a meeting with the Japanese consul general,' one Taliban official said.

This frequent use of 'inshallah' alarmed me. It was a constant reminder that the most common, most ordinary things depended on the will of god—a person's arrival, a flight's departure, the approval of a visa. On that score, I was in total agreement: visas in this region really did require divine intervention.

It was Dr Christobel who did it, but she too said it was the will of god. That day at the Afghan embassy, the heavyweights were off preparing a press conference, the place was empty though it was not Friday.

The good doctor ('It's Christ-oh-bee-ee-el') bounced in, curly greying hair, warm eyes. She was an American citizen, an Indian woman who had quit her dental practice in the US to freelance as a humanitarian. She told me she went to where the poor needed her help. She had been to a number of war zones, and Palestine was the worst.

'I like war zones. Money means nothing there. It brings out the best and the worst in people. You help your brother. I have no fear,' she said. 'I tell armed soldiers, you want to shoot me, go ahead.'

'Pray,' she said. 'Just pray. God puts up a wall if you're going straight because he wants you to turn right or left.'

'Hello,' she said cheerfully to the Taliban staff, as though they were her own grown-up boys.

They stopped looking crossly at me and smiled at her instead.

'She's my friend,' Dr Christobel said to them happily. 'You must help her. She's a good person. Give her a visa.'

The most amazing thing happened.

They did.

chapter forty-six

Sacrifice Country

For the third time, tagging along on Justin's work trip, I made the three-hour highway run linking Islamabad to Peshawar. From there, I had to find a way across the Khyber Pass and further up into Kabul and, inshallah, up to the southern banks of the Amu Darya to complete the circlet of my journey.

I pulled my dupatta over my head. The peculiar vacuum I felt was the absence of fear in Peshawar. After my trip with the Tauquirs, coming back here was a bit like coming home. I had a sense of the land, I was gaining a sense of the people. I noticed a welling abstract affection for the Pathans, perhaps because they seemed outsiders to the rest of Pakistan, it was a natural empathy between outcastes. Armed with my visa, I went to visit Afghanistan expert Nancy Hatch Dupree in Peshawar's University Town. She was a frail American woman in a salwar kameez. She had pinned her pale-grey hair up on her head. From under her coiffure, sharp blue eyes scanned me. She spoke the way older, upper-class Americans do, enunciating, the way John F. Kennedy sounds on tinny records of his speeches.

'Archaeologists have always been accused of being spies,' Nancy said at her office. She knew the veins of Afghanistan's past like those on the back of her hand. I needed her advice on seventh-century Afghanistan, which route the monk might have taken, how I should plan it.

'I wish I could come with you,' she said. I smiled at her. I would have loved her company. Nancy's eyes softened into the past, almost forty years ago. She began to tell me a story. She was a young diplomat's wife in Kabul in the mid-1960s, when Kabul was urban, urbane. One evening, she confronted an Afghan official at a cocktail party. She told him she was indignant at the lack of literature on the Buddhist treasures of Bamiyan. And as a result of the outburst, she found herself assigned to the task.

'Anyway, I finished my manuscript on Bamiyan and left it with this great archaeologist, Louis Dupree, so he could go through it. I didn't hear anything for ages and ages and finally I got a call and went to see him and he had written nothing on it. Just a line on top.'

She held up a piece of paper from her desk and tapped with her index the upper left corner.

'He had written, "Adequate but nothing original".'

'I was furious,' Nancy said. 'I said, of course there's nothing original, it's a *guidebook*. I was marching out.'

'He crooked his finger and said, "Wait, come back".'

I waited, listening. Nancy smiled.

'I married him.'

I understood suddenly that Louis Dupree was no longer alive, that she missed him and needed to say his name, that the mountains west of Peshawar held the memories of her husband and his life's work on Afghan history, that after he died, all she was left with was the land of Afghanistan. And that she would never leave its foothills.

For the present, there were other worries, ancient artefacts to save, somehow. Two decades of war had badly damaged Afghanistan's heritage, there were illegal pits at the famous site of Ai Khanoum, there were cracks in Samanid mosques. In 1988, the Minar-e-Chakra the third- or fourth-century Buddhist pillar, fell.

'One of the Taliban's agendas is to convince Afghans they have no heritage before Islam. They want to deny all that, the Kanishkas, the Alexanders.' She said this matter-of-factly, as though the pain of it had deadened now, that she was used to the destruction of her life's work and that of her husband.

I left with Nancy's guidebooks under my arm, her good wishes around me like a protective cloud. Across the generation gap, across our cultures, she held out a helping hand and her staunchness anchored me.

Afghanistan loomed and I battled daily with a terrible sense of inadequacy to cope with it. I needed more courage, more strength. I wished I were more resourceful, more observant. If somebody were shot in front of me, I would not have the faintest notion of what to do. What if something happened to me? Who would find out, who would rescue me? Who would knock on my parents' door to say, 'We believe these are the mangled remains of your daughter. Sorry we couldn't find the head.'

The UNHCR was taking a convoy of Afghan refugees to be repatriated, across the Khyber Pass. They agreed to give me a ride. But for the tribal areas surrounding the Khyber Pass, more permits were needed and it was taking more time. These were regions in which Islamabad's control faltered, where Pathan tribes armed to the teeth fought out clan feuds and killed each other for brief bursts of power.

Meanwhile, there was nothing I could do but bury myself in Nancy's 1977 guidebook, try and learn as much as possible about Afghanistan and preserve my frayed nerves. It was delightfully written, I drank in her light touch, acute observations, an Afghanistan of another time preserved in her words.

Q. and I met for dinner and once again I appreciated his insights into Afghanistan. It was good to see him again. At least he was my age, intelligent, and I did not feel threatened or uneasy with him.

Soon, I told myself, all this will be over. I will be back in Hong Kong, in a flat. I will have a lover, a job, friends. We will all meet for drinks in the evening and go to movies. I will read novels and water my plants. I will get married, have children, get old and, one day, quietly die in my bed watching the sun set.

When the phone rang one evening and a male voice said in Urdu, 'Hello, it's me,' I did not need to ask who it was. But the head of intelligence wanted to clarify. 'It's the person you met before. We knew you were back in town.'

'Yes, good work,' I said, trying to keep the sarcasm out of my voice.

'Do you mind if we meet again?' he said.

I thought it inappropriate and unnecessary, but could I really refuse?

He dropped in at the guest house for tea.

'I got a visa to Afghanistan,' I told him. I showed him my passport, with its lime-green stamp from the Islamic Emirate of Afghanistan. 'So I'm back in Peshawar. I'm waiting for the permits through the Khyber Pass.'

'Who did you have dinner with last night?'

I raised my eyebrows and innocently asked, 'You don't know?'

'Well,' he coughed, 'we need to check.'

I told him, but not precisely. I knew Q. could look after himself.

'Why were you meeting him?'

'He's extremely knowledgeable about Afghanistan,' I said. 'I know nothing about the place. I need to be as prepared as possible to complete my journey.'

It seemed to satisfy him.

'Please be careful,' he said. 'Afghanistan is a dangerous place.'

'No need to pester my friend,' I reminded him.

'*Khuda hafiz.*'

ಌ

One hot morning in August, I climbed into the white Toyota Land Cruiser with the UN repatriation officer who scowled into her portable radio. It crackled and snapped. She made the Afghan driver stop and buy her bananas. We were accompanying a convoy of trucks taking Afghan refugees back to their country.

The refugee camp of Nasir Bagh was to be demolished. The Pakistanis were sick of having the Afghans there, taking over Peshawar, using the water and electricity, overrunning the streets. I remembered Homaira's disgust at Afghan refugees. '*Unhone sab ganda kar diya hai.*' They have spoiled everything.

The women spread cloth on the top of the open truck against the burning heat, all along the jolting ride. I clambered onto the ladder on the tall side of the truck and peered in. They had packed such meagre belongings. I couldn't understand a word and had to smile instead. Their faces mirrored the expressions of their menfolk.

A little Afghan boy, naked to the waist, danced on top of the truck, waving to anybody watching. He strutted his bony frame, jutting out one thin shoulder, and then the other. In the cloud of dust raised by two dozen trucks turning into the road, the boy danced in the sunlight.

There was a dentist's sign: a painted set of false teeth showing in a ghastly grin in the doorway. It was one of the last sights the refugees saw as they left the place where some of them had lived for two decades. It seemed appropriate enough.

The convoy of trucks was followed by the UN cars, the Toyota Land Cruiser painted with the blue UN sign with me in it, along with the repatriation officer and the Afghan driver. We passed World Food Program trucks, painted blue and white. The Afghan drivers waved at each other. We drove by the Warsak Canal: little kids took running jumps from the sides of the canal embankment. August was steaming here. The donkey carts, the melons, the dusty boys.

At Takhatabeg, the first checkpoint of the Khyber Agency, a small open truck swerved past, men crouching in it with the tips of their guns visible between their knees. There were charpoys, mud huts, bundles of grass in an arid landscape. The foothills of the Safed Koh rose in the distance; stony, friable roads looped in hairpin bends through barren hills. This region was famous for gur, tea and guns.

'They don't have planes and tanks, but they have everything else,' the Afghan driver told me in Urdu, looking over his shoulder. 'They have gun factories everywhere. No licences needed here. The British said guns were the honour of the Pathan man and now the big guys have amassed huge amounts of arms.'

By the side of the road, was the rusted old railway track once laid by the British. On a gravelled hillside, 'Khyber Rifles welcomes you. Raised in 1878' was spelled out in white stones stuck on the mountainside. On the stony mountain face rested hundreds of plaques where battles were fought. Below, in the valley, small villages had low walls the same dun colour as the mountains.

From Jamrud to Torkham, the actual border with Afghanistan, lay a winding road, a journey of about forty-two kilometres. Babur had crossed here in 1507.

'The Taliban believe this is not real life, on earth. If you have a bitter life on earth, you have a good life in heaven,' the driver said.

In front of us, an Afghan girl leaned over the back of her refugee truck and vomited over the side. At the Landikotal Bazaar, men balanced guns on laps; they sat atop buses, rifles slung across shoulders. There was not a woman in sight. Swat had prepared me for that.

The old ghost tracks of the British train, paved over with tarmac in places, wove through the grim hills. At one point the rusted rails hung in mid-air between two cliffs amidst a bleak rocky landscape. There were old forts on mountainsides and in the river beds, a forest of cement cones to stop any tanks rolling further. At the border crossing of Torkham there were lines of trucks filled with sacks of flour, construction material, iron scaffolding, all trickling along the battered roads.

At the border between Pakistan and Afghanistan, the heat was held in by the wall of mountains. The police held taped-up lead pipes to beat back the refugees on the other side of the gates, a poverty-stricken lot carrying bags and belongings on their backs, begging by the roadside, feet covered in dust. They had walked a long way to get to this point.

The Pakistani police at the Torkham border interrogated me, politely but pointedly. They brought out a box of mango juice, offered tea.

'Who did you stay with in Islamabad? What are you going to do in Afghanistan?'

But my papers were in impeccable order and I was no longer unnerved by police questioning. I had learned to take slow deep breaths, smile a lot, stay focussed on the monk, the history, and not betray a flicker of relief when the officers shrugged and reached for a stamp. I was attached to that sweet sound, the clunky metal stamp at the borders of the subcontinent, crashing down in slow motion on the pages of my passport.

I squeezed in with four vast, bearded Afghans who worked with the UN in Jalalabad, and savoured the small surprises of a new country. Afghanistan was a right-hand drive. And the Pushto pronunciation of Taliban was more a solemn 'Tolibohn', with a slight elongation of the 'o's. *So that's how they say it.* I had entered the Islamic Emirate of Afghanistan, if the great signboard was to be believed.

OH FAITHFUL PEOPLE WITH STRONG DECISION ENTRY AFGHANISTAN THE SACRIFICE COUNTRY HEARTILY WELCOMES YOU WITH PIESES. IN

THE NAME OF ALLAH THE TOST, THE MOST MERCIFUL THERE IS NO
GOD (NO ONE IS WORTHY OF WORSHIP AND OBEDIENCE) SAVE ONE
GOD AND MOHAMMAD (PBUH) IS HIS APOSTLE.

I was in.

Thoughts blurred in my head. Somehow, I had to find Xuanzang's route; simultaneously, I noted that around me, there was an immediate increase in the level of poverty, in the number of beggars.

The UN Afghans were in a good mood. They popped in a tape into the car's cassette player as we zoomed through plains of maize fields and potato before Jalalabad. On the cassette, Hindi film songs played—*Tere haathon mein sapneh ki dori hai*. They turned down the music at Taliban checkposts and then turned it up again when we drove by, unchecked. Groups of men in black turbans, guns slung across their shoulders, eyed the car. I kept my head well covered.

'The Taliban is on its way out,' my Afghan companions joked. 'Their project isn't sustainable.' The carload erupted in raucous laughter.

'Er, isn't music banned?' I asked nervously.

'Yes, but we'll tell them we have this Indian girl with us and it's her cassette.' More hilarity. I grinned and began to relax the tiniest bit. We rounded a rocky outcrop and came upon the Kabul River, spilling into the plains. It was 42°C. The driver pressed the accelerator. The refugee trucks had already reached Jalalabad. The road to Jalalabad was littered with rusting Russian tanks and blown-up buildings. We flew like the wind. If the Taliban didn't get me, I was quite prepared to die in a road accident.

'This is nothing. Wait till you see Kabul,' the Afghans chimed in, as I exclaimed at the tanks, the debris of war, a whole different archaeology. And in the car, under the Afghans' bonhomie, there was the acrid tinge of failure, of missed chances, of injustice, battered pride, shattered lives.

'If they had jobs, not one Afghan would stay in Pakistan,' Karim said. He was the oldest, his beard flecked with white. 'Afghans are treated badly, but they're not voluntarily coming back, Pakistan is simply destroying camps. If we find a good government, we don't need any help. We just need to improve our irrigation.'

I wanted to believe him. It seemed such a noble, pure thought, that all problems could be solved by improved irrigation.

'The people live in fear,' he said, the jokes evaporating. 'If a child turns up the radio, somebody runs to turn it down.' But Karim felt there was no alternative to the Taliban. Zahir Shah was twelve when he became king, but now he was eighty-five and still wanted to be king.

His voice held bitterness.

'Practically, it is not possible for Zahir Shah to come back. He doesn't know what it's like any more. The staff around him are Europeans. Do you think those people can live in this dusty country?'

'It's only dreaming, for the Afghans living in Europe. It's only dreaming, to talk of coming back.'

We raced along. The road here was not too bad. Outside Jalalabad, on the other bank of the Kabul River, there were caves in the cliff, I could see them from the road, in the shape of a Buddha. It was a fertile valley, with rocky mountains all around, as the monk found it.

ॐ

The country of Nagarahara (Na-kie-lo-ho) is about 600 *li* from east to west, and 250 or 260 *li* from north to south. It is surrounded on four sides by overhanging precipices and natural barriers. The capital is 20 *li* or so in circuit. It has no chief ruler; the commandant and his subordinates come from Kapisa. The country is rich in cereals, and produces a great quantity of flowers and fruits. The climate is moist and warm. Their manners are simple and honest, their disposition ardent and courageous. They think lightly of wealth and love learning. They cultivate the religion of Buddha, and few believe in other doctrines. The sangharamas are many, but yet the priests are few; the stupas are desolate and ruined.[1]

The monk didn't care. He didn't care at all that the priests were few, that the stupas were desolate. He yawned and stretched and put down his brush, folded the paper. As far as he was concerned, he had crossed the Hindu Kush Mountains without fatal mishaps and was at the frontier of North India.

He smiled to himself. The sun still softened the edges of dusk. His feet ached. He carefully felt a persistent blister on his heel, still not swollen enough to burst. The horses were watered and fed and tied. His travel companions dozed in the firelight. The nearby villages had offered food and fodder for the whole caravan in exchange for bolts of silk.

India! If he were a little younger, he might have done a cartwheel.

Many years later, when he had gathered piles of notes from his travels around India, he would write a chapter on the country, its habits, its mores, place it here, before Jalalabad, which he considered the start of India. From his account, he carefully wiped out all traces of the excitement of discovery, the ecstasy of novelty. How could he express that after years of tramping across the land he felt synonymous with it? There were no words for it.

India had percolated into his bones and once, leaning over a well, he jumped back in shock to see his Chinese features. In his mind, he was Indian. He wrote in Sanskrit, he dreamed in the local language, he spoke it. He ate food with his fingers. Nothing about India surprised him any longer. Wordlessly, he knew each of its features. When the time came, he was sick with longing for China, and sick at leaving India. His mind was like a sheet of paper, torn in two with a terrible rustle. It was the price he paid for his journey, a sort of mental purgatory in which he belonged neither here nor there.

So he focussed on the task ahead. How do you pinpoint a continent, impose a frame on the boundless? With words. Be fair, he told himself, dipping his brush into ink. He organized it into sections and placed it here, right before Jalalabad, Nagarahara, so that, entering India with him, his reader would carry some friable sense of the place. Names of India. Measures of length. Astronomy, the Calendar. Towns and Buildings. Dress, Habits. Writing, Language, Books, the Vedas, Study. The Buddhist Schools, Books, Discussions, Discipline. Royal Family, Troops, Weapons. Manners, Administration of Law, Ordeals. Forms of Politeness.

And I, flipping through the monk's anthropological compilation, yelped in delighted recognition 1400 years later, pulling up, like projections on a wall, images that popped up to match his.

They are very particular in their personal cleanliness and allow no remissness in this particular. All wash themselves before eating; they never use that which has been left over (from a former meal); they do not pass the dishes . . . After eating they cleanse their teeth with a willow stick, and wash their hands and mouth . . . They have many vessels of dried clay; they seldom use red copper vessels; they eat from one vessel, mixing all sorts of condiments together, which they take up with their fingers. They have no spoons or cups, and in short, no sort of chopstick.[2]

I was looking at my countrymen over a thousand years ago, but little had changed.

છ૭

The refugee convoy had arrived in Jalalabad, a poor, sleepy rural town, with the UN as its biggest presence. There were rutted roads, trees and an unnatural quiet, because there were hardly any cars and very few people were visible. It was little more than a village, speckled with aid agency houses.

The newly returned Afghan refugees, accustomed to the relative peace of Pakistan, had to be educated about mines. There were nail mines, Russian PMN1 mines, mines like sugar pots, and Iranian M19 mines, mines shaped like a watch, *sat manan*. And I, urban ignoramus, stared at the mines set out on a table as a demonstration, looking at these weapons of destruction for the first time in my life.

I was in trouble, too.

The Afghans were not, in fact, going to Kabul, although the UN in Peshawar had said I was fine for a ride all the way to Kabul. Seeing my perturbed face Karim kindly said that some of the aid agencies might be driving to Kabul the next day and I could get a lift with them. They would put out a call on the UN radio system to see if anybody, maybe from the Red Cross, was going.

Also, it turned out I needed written permission to stay at the UN guest house; there was a fee, payable in dollars. I began to quail. The UN spokeswoman in Islamabad had made it sound like a breeze, the easy extension of UN help to journalists, the use of aid agency guest houses. For the moment, I had nowhere to sleep in Jalalabad and no prospects for a ride.

I took a deep breath, sat down by my bag in Karim's office. I would just sit and wait for something to happen. It was all I could do. It was either that, or break into hysteria.

Karim sent in a plate of cut melon, creamy and sweet. I bit into a slice and noticed that outside the windowpanes, the summer afternoon light in Afghanistan was of a soft, peculiar beauty. I leaned against my inner wall of panic, to keep it from sweeping me away.

Arrangements were made, after radio crackles back and forth. The Red Cross kindly agreed to shelter me for the night, against their rules. I began to feel increasingly silly, with my absurd idea of following some dead Chinese monk. These were serious people doing serious jobs, they dealt in death and mines and refugees. Did I even have a right to be here, if I wasn't engaged in any of the above?

Karim had sat with me for a while, as his radio snapped and he shifted and contacted people. Perhaps he felt like talking, for my offhand remarks seemed to shake loose words blocked in his belly.

'The Taliban have not the knowledge of ruling this country,' he said, in his flawless English with its Pushto lilt. 'They cannot use national resources.' He said he chose to stay in Afghanistan, even though he could have gone to Sweden.

'If I go and another goes and another goes, who will work for this poor country? I will have a good life there. But there, I am not an Afghan. If I am not in Afghanistan, I lose everything.'

It was a land forsaken by its people.

The radio whimpered, and Karim mumbled into it in Pushto. He stroked his beard and looked thoughtfully at me.

'This group, the Taliban, is too difficult to live with. But they are better than the previous mujahideen. This Islam is too difficult. They can't practise it themselves. Nobody can do it.' The words seemed to push from his trachea, past his tonsils, and gather at the back of his teeth.

'The solution,' Karim said, 'is to improve the Taliban, for there to be a very small coup inside the Taliban. Change the big shot at the top. The world is trying to keep the Taliban away, to give more power to the Opposition. But the Opposition has one province. Think.

By the time they take over the other twenty-eight provinces, how much time is this war going to carry on for? There is too much killing, too much destruction.'

He warmed to a theme he had thought about. Nobody liked the Taliban, but the alternatives were too horrible to contemplate. I stared at him, wide-eyed. It had never occurred to me that Afghans might think the Taliban was a viable option.

Karim was no longer addressing me. It was some internal dialogue he was having, some passionate debate, it was something he went over again and again, in his head. He made a list, checking unsuitable names off.

'Massoud would ignore the majority, the Taliban group. He is too narrow-minded. Sayyaf and Rabbani: they were in power for four years. You will see all the destruction in Kabul. These two gentlemen were responsible for that. They are all enemies, they come together only forced by the Taliban. So they are not eligible to rule the country.'

He remembered that I still sat there, as the shadows lengthened. I wanted to quiet my awful doubts. Tentatively I said, well, isn't it wonderful how so many aid agencies operate here, surely they are helping the people with the rebuilding of Afghanistan?

That started Karim off again.

'Do you know there are 180 local and international aid organizations? Aid is one of the purposes. Another side is our own business of making money. The effect of the work is very low. Look around you, twenty years of aid organizations, and what do you see?'

His words rolled out like a row of tanks taking a city.

'And if you look at the files of the Swedish community, Afghanistan is like a European country and everything was built by the Swedes. Billions of dollars were coming to Afghanistan, for rehabilitation because of Russian fighting: but only zero point zero zero zero zero one per cent actually reaches Afghanistan, it's all got stuck in Pakistan. Before, the military there had ancient British rifles, now they all have shiny new Russian Kalashnikovs.

'We're fed up with the situation. We are fed up with Pakistanis. We hate them. They should leave us alone to die here. They trained the leaders who come here and destroy our country.'

The elderly Afghan was so upset he got up and left the room.

ℂ

To the south-east of the city 30 *li* or so is the town of Hi-lo (Hidda);
it is about 4 or 5 *li* in circuit; it is high in situation and strong by
natural declivities. It has flowers and woods, and lakes whose waters
are bright as a mirror. The people of this city are simple, honest and
upright. There is here a two-storied tower; the beams are painted
and the columns coloured red.[3]

There was, Xuanzang continued, on the second storey, a small stupa
of one foot and two inches. It contained the Buddha's skull bone, the
spots for hair follicles were distinct, it was of a whitish-yellow colour.
Another small stupa, with the Buddha's eyeball in it, bright and clear,
deposited in a sealed precious casket. And on top of all that, the
Buddha's robe, made of fine cotton and of a yellow-red colour, as
well as his staff, ringed with white iron. A king had tried to capture
the sacred items, but they magically returned to their original spots.[4]

ℂ

That evening, under a gibbous moon, there was a party in one of the
aid agency residence gardens. Somebody had hung up paper cut-out
streamers in the lawn and spread out carpets and cushions. Michael,
of the Red Cross, invited me to join them. I marvelled at how peaceful
things seemed.

'Don't forget this is a war zone,' Michael warned. 'It's easy to
think it's peaceful, until something happens and there is no redress.'

We kicked off our shoes and slippers and sat on the ground. The
weather had relented and an almost cool breeze rustled the fruit trees
as the moon rose. It was an assortment of people working for aid
agencies—Dutch, German, French, Swiss, a Canadian and a group
of Sudanese working for the Islamic Relief Agency. Many were young.

There had been a de-mining conference, with a pair of Swedish
and Swiss consultants. How much, I wondered crossly, were they
getting paid? Why should white men in peaceful rich countries get
paid enormous amounts to compensate them for the risk of coming to
countries where thousands of brown people lived with the risk every

day? Who was paying the brown people a risk premium?

I wanted to feel sympathetic, because the poor Swede was only trying to help. For a fee. He had worked in the Balkans and knew the region well. He and a Kosovan recently out of the Balkans discussed forgiveness.

'How can you forgive, in the wake of a bloody war?'

'I have suffered,' the Kosovan told the Swede. He was a tall lanky man with the sweetest of smiles.

'How odd to come to Afghanistan and find somebody who knows my region.' The two men fell briefly silent, mulling the coincidence, the meeting. The talk turned to de-mining again, the scatology of war.

'The technology stinks, essentially it's a metal detector. It's not worth the money for the big businesses to develop proper de-mining equipment,' the Swede explained to me. 'In a battlefield after a war, you have a lot of metal. Shrapnel, mines, not to mention the historic metal deposits from older civilizations. You go in there with the detector and it starts screaming. We need something that can differentiate between a Coke can and a mine.'

The German passed drinks around, Cokes and Pepsis stored in blocks of ice since alcohol was illegal. Somebody put on Youssou N'Dour, *Seven Seconds* threaded thinly through the garden.

'I do it for the money,' the German said bluntly. He put down the bucket of drinks and squatted beside me. 'Well, not so much for the money, but I don't pay taxes and I save almost everything. It's a good deal.'

'And how do people know the money is being spent as it should be?'

He began to laugh. 'You know, if you dig 200 wells in villages across Afghanistan, who the hell is going to come and check that you actually built 200 wells in villages across Afghanistan? Do you know how hard it is for somebody to fly in and check things?'

It was looking worse and worse, in terms of logic, at least to my feeble mind.

Why on earth, I asked him, didn't this plethora of aid agencies at least cooperate, you know, pool resources?

'Do Toyota and Ford cooperate?'

'They're businesses,' I said.

'And what do you think this is?'

It began to make sense. The money flows in in great floods, gets sucked up in the great funnel of overheads and staff salaries, and finally a trickle reaches a sunburned Afghan boy in a field, hobbling along on crutches because his foot blew off when he stepped on a Russian mine.

'Afghanistan, it is attractive and repulsive, sometimes both in the same day, but you cannot be indifferent to it,' one of the French aid workers said. 'It gets inside your body.' He pronounced it 'buddy'. And 'World Bonk', which sort of summarized it all.

I finally plucked up the courage to ask about Xuanzang. Had anybody been to Hadda, the historic Buddhist site not far from here? People looked blank. Then it turned out that one aid worker one day had toured the area nearby in a jeep. There was nothing left to see, he said. Besides, the whole place was mined, he would not recommend going.

Mine seemed the most inane, irrelevant question of the day.

chapter forty-seven

Sad Secrets

The road from Jalalabad to Kabul had been torn up by years of tank traffic and military trucks rumbling up and down, and lack of maintenance. It was presently 224 kilometres of nightmarish rock and gravel, bumpy, potholed. Exploded tyres were a matter of course. Every so often, battered cars had stopped by the roadside and Afghans knelt in the morning light to try and repair the shattered axles or tyres.

The UN radio system had crackled all around Jalalabad and it emerged that the de-mining group was going to Kabul in UN cars and yes, certainly, they could accommodate me. But when I showed up at the guest house, the Australian ex-soldier in charge, a short stocky man, was furious.

'Who approved this?' he barked. 'Nobody travels in a UN car without my approval. It's the regulation. It's too dangerous. If the cars get stopped, we need the permissions.'

I explained that I did not know about any form, that Syed—from his own office—had said it was okay, and that I would be happy to do the paperwork needed. I was astonished. If people in one single UN office in Jalalabad—not a huge place—were working at cross-purposes, how on earth did anything big get done, like saving Afghanistan? The de-mining men, including the Swede from the previous night, shuffled their feet and looked sadly at me.

'So, shall I fill out the form now?' I said sweetly to the snappy Australian. But I could tell the real problem was that his authority had been undermined by his Afghan colleague and that some random Asian woman had slipped through the cracks in the system. It made

him look bad. I could tell he was not going to let the incident pass
and that I would suffer the consequences.

'You cannot travel in the UN car, that's for sure,' he said in an
Australian accent, in the breathless way people have when they are
holding in anger. 'You'll have to take public transport. They do have
buses and things here.'

I'd seen the buses. I thought about travelling alone on a public
bus and, as my knees weakened, I sat down on a veranda chair. It
wasn't the public buses. I had taken enough of those all over the
subcontinent. It was the fear of travelling alone in Afghanistan where
I did not speak Pushto and had no guide. I felt my morning optimism
unravel. How foolish I was to have thought things were going to
work out.

How far away my conversation with the UN spokeswoman in
Islamabad seemed, in the air-conditioned office where she said my
route would be smoothed and eased by helpful international agencies
with their enlightened staff and efficient cars. The de-mining men
muttered amongst themselves.

Finally, an elderly, bearded man spoke up. He had a north England
accent. His beard hinted to me that he had been in Afghanistan a
long time and was wise enough to adapt to the prevailing winds. He
looked at me kindly, and in his eyes I could see him process the
situation and come to his own conclusions.

He said, 'I'll take you. I'm not from the UN, so I don't need
forms. Come on, young lady, hop in the back of the truck. It won't be
comfortable, but you'll get there.'

In my usual mature response, I felt tears sting the back of my
eyes. I felt alone and vulnerable. I was so upset, so rattled and shaken
like a single peppercorn in a teapot on that road, so scared that I
couldn't even remember my bearded benefactor's name and was too
embarrassed to ask. He was kind, the way vets are with hurt animals.

I clung to the back of the truck for dear life, held my bag, tried
not to vomit on the bumps and could barely move when we stopped
for breaks. The UN Toyotas raced on ahead on supernatural suspension.

The road was still littered, in strategic military defence spots,
with the rusting carcasses of Russian tanks and 75-mm guns. The
convoy rounded a corner; there was a T-55 tank with a rounded

hood and its gun raised, pointing at the mountains in some ghost war. Rusted and abandoned, not even worth the scrap.

And, at least in one place, there was a minefield right beside the road, marked off with red paint by surveyors. The de-miners stopped to examine it, estimated it would take another ten years to clear Afghanistan of all mines. It was slow work, they explained, with a known risk: for every 5000 mines cleared, there would be one life lost and two severe injuries.

It was a stark, deserted landscape, the Kabul River a smear at the bottom of the valley, green on either side, dotted with low mud houses. Not far from the Sarobi dam, it was a moonscape, the mountain painted with streaks of silver. Behind me rose a blood-coloured rock and, below, the river flowed jade green.

Sick with the road, I almost wept in relief when we stopped at a roadside stall that sold drinks. In my salwar kameez, with my head covered with a dupatta and my subcontinental features, I must have looked Pakistani. The Afghan shopkeeper said to me in Urdu, looking at the UN insignia, his voice terse, 'Tell the UN to lift sanctions.'

For a fleeting moment I was mighty glad I was not in a UN car, though they had better tyres.

'The United Nations is out of touch with Afghanistan,' the refrain went. It seemed to me the aid agencies had failed to claim Afghan hearts, although they had claimed the Afghan landscape, pasting their insignia everywhere. The UNHCR had pasted its logo on a bridge, a Canadian agency had set up a roadside toilet. The rubbish heaps held plastic bags stamped with the UN insignia, but the roads were in shambles and there was no infrastructure to speak of. It felt as though the organization had become arrogant, over-powerful, under-monitored, out of touch with reality, and people were far too concerned with their bloated salaries.

In Islamabad, where profitable multinationals like Nestlé rented rooms in more modest Blue Area offices, the UN rented floor after floor of the Saudi-Pak Building, one of the most expensive pieces of real estate in Islamabad. If funding for a programme was cut, the UN stopped the work, but salaries had to be paid regardless.

We had a flat tyre and stopped by the roadside to fix it, right beside a building shot with bullet holes.

The road to Kabul glistened in the sun, heat shimmering off it in waves. That's it, I thought, in a flicker of heat and tiredness. The United Nations was like one of those vast Chinese state-owned enterprises people bemoaned. And even those were shaping up, streamlining, listing on the stock market. Yes, the UN needed to list on the stock market. It would have to comply with transparency regulations, provide accounts, pay attention to the bottom line. Like everybody else, it would have to fire staff when times got tough. But that summer, outside Kabul, when the car broke down and the tyre had to be fixed, Enron had not yet happened, proving yet again that if you have enough money and power, you can dispense with accountability.

It was a breathtaking approach to Kabul, a steep climb around a gorge to the pass that led to the valley and to the city. The cars groaned up and up. The landscape was arid, with a stark loveliness. How brilliantly defended it was. It seemed that a lone, armed man, strategically placed, could pick off an entire battalion down below, hold off whole armies, or at least that's what the bearded Englishman turned around to tell me. What the Russians couldn't do in months and months, the Taliban did in weeks, one Afghan had said about taking Kabul. Not without some pride.

My own woes were not over. The UN guest house in Kabul was singularly unwelcoming.

'Sorry, but we have better things to do than cater to journalists,' a man with a portable radio said. 'That's not what your Islamabad office told me,' I snapped at him. Furious now, I felt misled, unprepared. 'They told me they would radio ahead and tell you I was coming.'

He shrugged. 'We are a bumbling bureaucracy, welcome to the UN way of doing things. Sorry, but this is what we live with every day. You'll have to stay in a hotel.'

I felt tears threaten. I wished angrily that my instant response to everything was not to burst into tears. I did not even know there were hotels in Kabul. Vaguely I remembered Kate, the BBC correspondent in Peshawar, who had kindly said, stay at the Ariana if you can. I had not really registered the import of it. The UN man was right. I had only myself to blame. My lack of knowledge about the region, my foolishness in coming here in the first place, my inexperience. All those years of journalism, and I had utterly failed to spot the polished piece of public relations fed to me by the nice lady in Islamabad. Sitting in her office, reassuring visions of being handed like a parcel from aid agency to aid agency across Afghanistan had floated before my mind's eye. What did I expect? A guided tour, for goodness' sake?

My bearded English saint stood quietly in a corner of the UN club, listening to my conversation with the UN staff. 'Let me take you to a hotel,' he said, saving me for a second time that day. 'The Ariana is nearby, and the Intercontinental across town. In the end you will have to stay at the Intercontinental, that's where the Taliban put all journalists.'

The Ariana Hotel was of an old Soviet style familiar to me, for most of Beijing's older buildings were similar. In the lobby stood about eight elderly Afghans, all with long beards and the black turban. They did not appear to be having a busy day.

Through my panic and fury, through the tears that bubbled behind my eyes, the doughy fear that rose at my throat, through my gratitude for the bearded man who kept saving me, I detected, finally, a flicker of excitement at being in a whole new universe.

I filled in a hotel logbook as the seven bearded Afghan men looked on in silence and one, with great ceremony, opened a long register with lines in it. Everything, except for my entry, was written in the Persian script and the date there was 12/5/1422. They followed the Muslim *anno Hegirae*.

The Ariana had vast rooms, the toilets were still perched on a wooden pedestal, the taps were large and old but the water was always hot, the halls were strewn with long Afghan rugs and they placed fresh flowers from the garden on the tables. From my window I could see the hills that ringed Kabul.

Oddly enough, surrounded by the Afghans in the lobby, I felt safe. I breathed and slowed down enough to notice that the days in Kabul were a delightful 30°C, that after the burning heat of Jalalabad and Peshawar, the Kabul sky was a pale silky blue.

Elderly Abdul Majid fussed over me. He showed me how to keep my dupatta over my head, so none of my long hair showed. He brought me pulao for lunch, took away my clothes for washing. If he was anything like the Indians, he was lobbying for a tip, I knew that by now.

My terror ebbed in the welter of arranging small details. The locks looked good, the bed comfortable. Okay, I thought. Okay. Okay.

I was to meet the bearded Englishman later in the day. He was acquiring a god-like status in my eyes. He dropped me off to see Ashraf, an Afghan contact a journalist at another wire service had e-mailed me about. The Taliban offices would open only on Monday and so I had a day or so, unregistered, unchaperoned, to wander the city.

The afternoon was wearing on, a golden light sloshed through the city and Ashraf sat me down, offered me tea. I was depleted. I fished for something to say to this nice Afghan with impeccable English, and failed to think of a single coherent sentence.

Where to begin? It was as though I had to throw everything I had ever learned off the edge of a mountain and watch it spin through the air, scatter into pieces and blow away with the wind. Ashraf was unperturbed. He smiled, or maybe he pursed his mouth, it was hard to tell under the beard.

'We don't know what is happening to our country, you know. What a city Kabul used to be! With educated, trained people. And now, seventy per cent gets bread from the World Food Program.'

'The city seems empty,' I mumbled. 'Where is everybody?'

'Kabul has emptied out, people have left in droves because of the war.' He paused.

'So. You're Indian.' This time, it was definitely a smile. 'It was winter when I went to Delhi. I love India, very much.'

I smiled back at him. Yet another Afghan with a passion for India.

'Many, many Afghans were trained in India. Doctors, telecommunications experts. All sixteen of Kabul's cinemas showed Indian films.'

That explained why so many Afghans spoke Hindi or Urdu. Ashraf gave me a few survival tips. 'At around 1 p.m. and 5 p.m., the ministry to fight vice and promote virtue patrols the city,' he said. 'That's the time to be careful.'

That was what kept Kabulis cowed, their eyes filled with fear, men and women. This old and gracious city stank of fear.

'My barber trimmed my beard, but too much. I told him, you idiot, I'm too scared to go out now.' Men as much as women felt the pressure of strictures imposed by the Taliban.

Tolibohn.

A semblance of calm drifted back into my head, but in thin layers. The Taliban brought peace, Ashraf said. Kabul was so divided among the fighters, divided by ethnic rule. We sipped our tea and chatted, but soon I wanted to take his leave and lie in my bed with the sheets over my head. It was a lot to digest.

'Come,' Ashraf said kindly. 'Let me drop you back, I will show you around Kabul. We'll say I'm a taxi driver. Actually, I did used to drive a taxi. You sit in the back so they don't stop us, because men and women don't sit together.'

As the afternoon faded into evening, we drove around Kabul. Ashraf pointed out from the front seat of his battered yellow car the old Indian embassy, the fortified Iranian one, the Turkish—all gone, all emptied out, locked up behind high walls. We drove by the Kabul Hotel where a bomb had, two weeks ago, smashed a wall in, so that a pile of rubble descended onto the pavement. Was it the opposition? A discontented Taliban faction? Nobody knew. The front line was once again just forty kilometres north of Kabul.

Ashraf harked back to 1994–5, when the two sides fought over Kabul, when shells rang across the city and the inhabitants crumpled in their homes.

'Here is the office of the justice minister, he's a hardliner,' Ashraf lowered his voice. 'Here's the office of the finance minister, he's also a hardliner.'

As we drew up at the Ariana Hotel gate, he pointed to the traffic circle ahead: 'That's where Najibullah was hanged from.' My stomach lurched. There was so much I did not know, but I did know that in 1996 the world saw images of a mutilated President Najibullah hanging from a traffic post, that Najibullah's widow had fled to New Delhi and still lived there. I tried not to look at the traffic circle, though it was empty and perfectly innocuous. It's as though places where violence happened bore their traces. Nothing much, only that at dusk that spot was a darker shade of grey. The weekend trickled by. Ensconced in the Ariana, one afternoon, I simply decided not to be afraid. It was crippling me. I had come to Kabul pulling a truckload of inherited fear up the mountains with me. I had come in full mental armour, my mind clogged with walls of it. It was as though, expecting the worst, I had found a few butterflies, a rose garden and some bird droppings.

'I need to telephone,' I said to the man in the lobby, mimicking a phone, holding a fist to my ear with thumb and pinkie held out. In Urdu, we made arrangements to go to the public phone booth in the market. One of the Afghans from the hotel would escort me.

I phoned S. in Hong Kong. His voice quickened with worry.

'I'm okay,' I said. 'I'm in Kabul. I'm staying at the Ariana Hotel.'

I got used to broken-down, beaten-up Kabul. I could banish the fear, but not the sadness. I felt wretched all the time, for this country, for the Afghan children who came up, fair, with pointed chins and clear eyes, to beg. They were tiny, their hair mussed and caked. The children, old men and women and sometimes a woman in a burkha lurched towards me, hands held out, whispering. I couldn't see their eyes, dark behind the lilac net. But I could sense the desperation.

Unlike the Indians, who imbue their begging with a certain professionalism, even humour, these were not people used to supplication. An old woman hobbled up to me, palm held out. I handed her a bag of apples I had bought. She gestured, no.

'What is she saying?' I asked the driver.

'She has no teeth, she says she can't eat the apples.'

'Oh.' I took the apples back and gave her the peaches instead.

'Come to our home and watch the Sony TV,' a taxi driver offered.

'Isn't it banned?'

'Yes, well.'

I declined. I was aching for a conversation, for normal human contact, but the city was still a stranger to me. I did not have a sense yet of the permissible and the forbidden. I did not know my way around.

Afghanistan was like some sad secret, filled with people tied to their mountains. A proud people, who fought but loved pleasure. Music, roast mutton, the bountiful fruit of summer. They came back to these mountains, they always came back. No wonder Babur asked to be buried here.

'I was in Pakistan for fifteen years,' an Afghan at the hotel told me. 'I got tired of it. So tired of it. I didn't like it. It's not our place. I went to fight the jihad in Kashmir. I killed people. And then I stopped. I wanted to come back.'

His beard was still black, he was young. He indicated a wound in his leg. 'The Taliban are good people,' he said, looking me straight in the eye.

The Taliban, on Monday, assigned me a car, a driver, a translator. I sat in a vast hall, filled with stuffed chairs, a grand table and elaborate Koranic calligraphy, carved in expensive-looking wood at the Taliban government offices.

I asked the man in charge of foreign journalists if, instead of charging the usual whack of dollars, they could give me a good price, because I was a freelance writer.

'I'm not American,' I said several times, and pulled out my Indian passport. The Taliban official, a slight man who spoke good English, with the Pushto lilt I was beginning to recognize, agreed.

I met my translator, Mirza Gul Yawar, his eyes fluid with age. He was, or had been, a professor at Kabul University. He was elderly, bony and had a certain insistence that got us around and got us interviews. I learned how people bowed to his status as a professor. Ustad, the younger ones called him; it was a word I knew.

He did not feel like a stranger, for he too had been to India. I later learned the Taliban had assigned me an elderly man for the most delicate of reasons: it was more appropriate for a young woman to have an escort who could be her grandfather.

Yawar was meticulous in his work, but sometimes he was hard to read. In between showing me around, protecting me from myself, he showed flashes of honesty. I could not tell his affiliations. From Yawar and his attitude towards his country, this much I learned: the Afghans do not take kindly to authority. Of any kind.

From the day we met, we spent practically every waking minute together. He did not let me out of his sight for a moment. He was my minder, but with him I felt bolder, I felt safe. I had transport, I had an escort, I had a translator. I had access to government officials, I could talk to people.

To follow Xuanzang's route, I needed to head north, to the banks of the Amu Darya which separated Afghanistan and Uzbekistan. That is where I had stood, almost exactly a year ago, on the other side, with Leonid, staring at Afghanistan, wondering what the soil there, here, held. I even checked, there were domestic Ariana Afghan Airlines flights linking Kabul to Mazar-i-Sharif and Kunduz. But in my talks with the Taliban officials, it became clear that they hesitated to let me out of Kabul. After a few days of humming and hawing, the official who was dealing with me said firmly, we cannot allow you to go. It's too dangerous for a woman, alone.

And by then, I had run out of chutzpah. For a brief moment, I flirted with the idea of sneaking off, I could easily pass for an Afghan woman. But under Yawar's watchful eye nothing like that was possible and I was secretly glad of it.

I had had to transfer to the vast, more expensive, more official, deserted Intercontinental Hotel. In the evenings, I lay in my hotel bed with nothing else to do. The hotel was empty, there was nobody to talk to. The moon rose over Kabul, full and fat, to the sound of the 8.30 p.m. azan. Its silver beams glanced off Sher Darwaza, the rocky hill, Lion's Gate. Evening lights were switched on and glittered on the side of the mountain, the guns were silent now.

The realization came on like a headache: this city was where my journey would flounder, a beached whale with dimming eyes. This is where I would have to bid the monk farewell, my circle left open, the Hindu Kush uncrossed.

The monk floated up behind my lids.

'Let go of it,' he whispered.

On his way back from India, laden with 657 volumes of the precious Buddhist manuscripts on twenty horses, as well as with statues and souvenirs and good wishes from his Buddhist friends, the monk crossed the Pamirs in Afghanistan's north-east corner. He arrived in Kashgar and then took the route south of the Taklamakan desert, arriving at the outskirts of Xian one fine spring day in AD 645. News of his arrival, of his extraordinary adventure, had spread far and wide through the city, and people gathered in such numbers that he could not advance because of the crush. He had to spend the night outside the capital.

By AD 661, he had completed the translation of the *Maha Prajnaparamita Sutra*, 600 chapters in 102 volumes, working steadily, in between his monastic duties. His health declined slowly in his seventh decade and on the thirteenth day of the tenth month of AD 664, he died quietly, having recited a few verses to Maitreya.

As for me, I was stuck in Kabul, struggling with the present. In this bombed-out city, the present had trampled the past to death. I had come face to face with days that demanded my attention. Perhaps the monk had brought me upto here, and no further, for some reason of his own.

I leaned a chair against my door, placed the tin rubbish bin in front of it, and fell asleep thinking of the first law of journalism: both sides of the story. I turned to troubled dreams.

The days fell into a steady routine. Yawar and the driver would pick me up at the hotel on the hill early in the morning. We would start early to pack in a meeting or two before Kabul wound up for namaz and before the worst of the heat hit around noon. The day was punctuated by prayers. Entire neighbourhoods stopped to kick their shoes off and bow before Allah together. It patterned the day with crests and hollows, and filled it with quiet moments.

We would first drive to the Taliban headquarters and get written permissions from the central command to interview officials. I sat docilely, having directed Yawar, and waited for him to do the necessary paperwork. The Taliban ministry that dealt with journalists was usually, by eight in the morning, sitting around the vast room, reading newspapers. Many glared as I walked in behind Yawar every day. But others nodded in recognition and left me alone.

Then, armed with the precious letters folded and slipped into the breast pocket of his kameez, Yawar would adjust his turban and off we would drive, to the ministry of planning, to the ministry of refugees and martyrs, to the ministry of public health, the ministry of commerce.

It was a fully formed government, getting to its feet, learning the ways of administration, trying to get things going in its own way. It came as a shock to me that they felt aggrieved and misunderstood by the world; that, mostly, they received me with courtesy.

The strangeness wore off, that I spent my mornings with these vast, bearded mountains of men, alarming at first. But there was much talk of *mehman*. I could understand bits and pieces of conversation. I drank cups of *chai-sabz*. They brought it in glass cups and saucers, with sweets or toffee wrapped in coloured or silver paper. Sometimes they brought a plate of almonds and raisins, peanuts covered in white sugar balls. To sweeten the tea, I had to sip the clear liquid and pop a sugar-coated peanut into my mouth.

That summer, Afghanistan was doubly crippled by war and drought. The Taliban was furiously bitter at the UN, which with one hand imposed economic sanctions on their country and with the other dispensed humanitarian aid. It was a theme that came up again and again in those nine days. The sanctions were suffocating the country, they were unfair.

Maulvi Said Ahmadullah at the ministry of planning said it the way people do when they're following the party line. 'Many people die because of these difficulties. If you focus attention on unilateral UN sanctions, it shows it directly affects people.'

Yawar translated. It was clear that the UN had achieved only a public relations disaster with the government they had to work with. The view had trickled down to the people—or had been propagated—that 'the international community should ask the UN why they are imposing sanctions on these needy people; they should put pressure on the UN to lift sanctions.'

The pressure, the hammer blow, would come sooner than anyone knew. Eleventh September 2001 was barely a month away.

How surreal the days were here, these drives through bombed-out Kabul, a city gutted and burned to the ground with small signs of life in-between, the squeal of school children. I could see the tops of their heads through the holes in the school building torn out by rockets.

Alhaj Sher Mohammad Abbas Stanikzai had sharp features, accented by the black turban. He was the administrative deputy minister of the Taliban's ministry of public health, but I rather suspected this had been a lateral move for him, away from a much more public, articulate post, for he spoke fluent English. There was no need for Yawar to translate. What internecine squabble had placed Stanikzai here?

He sat behind a desk cleared of papers, with the Taliban flag in a corner, the one I had seen at the embassy in Islamabad: black Arabic script on a white cloth. Stanikzai began with a recitation from the Koran, but in a way that made me think he was making an Islamic point for my benefit, not particularly invoking Allah. He had a subtle, but instantly detectable showman's gloss, a veneer that people who communicate well with large foreign audiences acquire.

He went over a few preliminaries about malaria and polio and how the Taliban's allotment for public health was not sufficient; even with supplements from NGOs and the UN it only provided fifty to sixty per cent of the country's total requirements. The UN sanctions had badly affected the ministry of public health, he said.

There was a brief silence. 'It is the UN policy to not support this government. We are importing each and every thing from foreign countries. Medicines are sensitive to temperature, they used to be imported by Ariana and when Ariana was banned from international flights, they could not bring in vaccines. There is no direct route out of Afghanistan, you have to get a Pakistan visa.'

Stanikzai paused for breath.

'The Americans want to pressurize us,' he said. International firms had already registered with the Taliban's ministry of public health to supply medicines to Afghanistan, like Glaxo Wellcome, who had subsidiary offices in Pakistan and Dubai.

'Their medicine sales manager was warned off by US authorities,' Stanikzai said.

'Are you sure about this?' I asked him.

'I met him, he told me himself,' the Taliban official said simply.

There was a Kuwaiti Red Crescent Society branch office in Afghanistan, providing artificial arms, prosthetics for mine victims. The Sudanese director received a letter from the government of Pakistan, Stanikzai said. It was a subtle warning, the United States had objections. His voice trailed off.

'With the grace of the Almighty, we are bearing our problems. Afghans will have no problems in resisting the Americans. We will put more pressure on the US. We are an independent nation and we do not take orders from superpowers.'

I would soon remember these words. Did the UN know how detested they and their infernal sanctions were? Did they know what a disaster it was? It was impossible to miss the palpable hatred that hung in the air whenever the UN came up, and it came up often. Everybody felt the sanctions were driven by the United States of America.

'What about the whole business about schools for girls?' I asked.

'You are from India,' Stanikzai said. 'Think of your own problems with schooling for girls. Even King Zahir Shah, forty years ago, could not establish schools for girls in Afghanistan, now everybody is asking why there are no schools for girls. The war has destroyed everything, college professors have left, qualified people are gone, there is nobody in Afghanistan. Five years back the life of a normal man in Afghanistan was not safe, because of the killing. First you require peace. When life is safe, you can look after health, social welfare, education.'

They were not against schools for girls, he said, but thought that girls should be educated according to Islamic values.

Was it at all strange, was it the mountain air, was it the surreality of Kabul that I was sitting in this Taliban official's office thinking, well, he must be much cleverer than I, because I could not find anything terribly objectionable in what he was saying? China's education system had for a long time propagated Marxist values, the Soviets too.

The Afghan countryside was traditional, Pathan, Stanikzai said. It was a *shame* to have girls go out to work. This Pathan tradition I had seen with my own eyes in Swat in Pakistan.

It dawned on me that the real problem the Taliban had was with westernized, urban, urbane Kabul, where women had worn short skirts and done as they pleased. It was a clash of citified people and traditional mullahs from the villages. Perhaps it was reductionist of me, but I felt that was the key to all the Taliban's problems. They had not thought to leave Kabul and Kabul's forward-thinking populace alone. In the villages, nothing much had changed since the Taliban.

'We should not be blamed for the problems, we have brought peace,' Stanikzai said.

With the Taliban in control of much of Afghanistan, it was certainly hard to argue against the fact that, for the first time in years, a shaky peace had settled over the country like a frightened dove, ready to flap away at the slightest bang.

I decided to push for a few details. 'Where,' I asked him, 'does the Taliban get their arms from?'

'We have resources, we have a budget, we can buy it also.'

'From where?'

'From Central Asian countries, previous Russian generals. The Russian ex-generals would sell the USSR away, so why not guns?' He was scornful. They would sell their grandmothers, the tilt of his chin seemed to say. 'Russian military aircraft are sold in Dubai—how do you think the Chechens are fighting, where do you think the Tajik and Uzbek resistance get their arms from? They are all purchasing from Russian generals.'

This was way beyond me. I decided to quiz him about my own pet disillusionment—the aid agencies in Afghanistan. 'Ah yes, you have all these umbrellas, red, white, blue, green umbrellas put by different nations, whatever they are doing, helping, but sixty per cent are intelligence people,' he said.

He explained how four years ago, AVICEN, a French NGO registered with the ministry was actually found to be in daily wireless contact with the Opposition.

'We followed those people, we found fifteen kilos of explosives, two sniper rifles, you know, big rifles firing single bullets, of the kind the USA gave to Afghan mujahideen, binoculars, four or five Russian Kalashnikovs, the names of the Taliban military commanders.'

He shook his head, scornful.

'When the donor, poor man, tries to come and see how his money is being used, he is told, "Oh, don't bother coming, it's so hard in Afghanistan, there's fighting, there's kidnapping, Osama Bin Laden is there." But if the donor ever came and saw the state of development projects he would wonder where his money had gone.'

Stanikzai added that the United Nations staff were supposed to work on the ground, but they lived in luxury in Pakistan, spending hundreds of dollars on flights to Afghanistan. All from the budget allotted to Afghanistan.

It was exhausting. There was too much to take in. I had not expected this clarity, this erudition, this disdain from this exceptionally articulate man. He was no fool. He did not come across as a zealot. I *agreed* with much of what he was saying.

Possibly the only thing to do in Kabul at night was to hang out at the UN club, as much as I hated it. Afghans were not generally allowed in. I insisted Yawar go home to his daughters, have his dinner. But he would not listen to me.

'I will wait,' he said gently. 'You are my responsibility. You go and relax. I will sit in the car.'

Grateful, guilty, I sat at the bar, smoking too much, drinking too many gin-and-tonics. Wrung out, shaken, I still took mental notes, surrounded by aid workers from the plethora of agencies that operated all over the country. I met up with K., a European man who worked at one of the UN agencies. He was wry and detached from the people around him. He told me he read obscure novels to pass the numbing time in Kabul. He seemed bent on feeding my growing cynicism. Since he offered me Marlboro Lights, I lit up with him.

Sanctions. What else to talk about when they hovered in the air, like djinns in flowing black, darkening the skies? He took a drag and shook the ice in his drink so that it tinkled.

'These sanctions, they will not contribute to peace. It contributes to intensified fighting and is totally against our humanitarian goals.'

He stared into the middle distance. He had a wife and a young child in Islamabad. Kabul was not a family posting. He spoke, half to himself.

'You see them, in −10°C walking in their socks, eating garbage. I saw a woman holding a baby, they were looking in the garbage for something to eat.'

I can't help noticing, I told him, how severe the differences are, between the garbage-foraging Kabulis and the plush lives of UN workers with their pneumatic Toyotas equipped with radio antennae, the houses covered in bougainvillea creepers, tended gardens behind high walls with armed guards.

He took a swig of his drink.

'I know,' he said. 'It has a name, the vehicle thing. It's called the white-car syndrome. Osama Bin Laden is the target of the sanctions, but they'll create a thousand more Osama Bin Ladens.'

Yawar was waiting outside, when I finally came out. The streets were dark and quiet, the stars twinkled.

chapter forty-eight

Flea in Your Clothes

I was tired of being the only woman surrounded by men, whether it was aid workers, the Taliban, the men on the streets. Afghan women were non-existent, brushed-out phantoms under lilac burkhas. I saw shoes, painted toenails, high heels, a bright red salwar, excessively baggy for fashion. What story was hers, under the lilac pleated tent?

The only time I looked women in the face was at the telephone booths, where I stopped to call S. in Hong Kong, his voice fading— What? What did you say? I'm okay. Everything's fine.

I wrote the number on a piece of paper and handed it to the telephone operators who sat cross-legged behind a booth. I retired to the zenana, behind a grimy curtain, to wait for the call to be transferred. There the women had lifted their burkhas over their faces. They relaxed in each other's company. It was the one place Yawar could not follow me to, though he waited outside, fingers loosely interlaced, watchful, servile and yet not.

Where are you phoning to, the women asked me. We exchanged histories as inevitably somebody or the other spoke Urdu.

One woman said she lived in Peshawar. 'I came to visit family. They live in the refugee camps there. I'm a doctor. There is no work here. They took my job. Now I'm a teacher. I'm from Mazar. What about your chador?'

'I'm from India,' I explained. 'I wear a scarf.'

'They're animals,' one woman hissed.

There was no need to clarify who.

'Come to our house for dinner.'

'You'll get into trouble.'

It cost me much to refuse these warm-hearted, spontaneous invitations from complete strangers. I yearned for easy, informal contact, not conducted as an interview, to see their lives. But I could not risk it. It would not be fair. I felt the strain of being in this country, constantly followed by Yawar, though he was discreet, though he was kind and agreed to my every request. Sometimes I had to be more stubborn than him, force my hand a little, hungry to see the city, eat in its tea houses. Then I sensed Yawar was annoyed, but he said nothing and I pretended not to notice.

I was delighted with the sight of Kabuli men in vast turbans sitting on low seats lined against the windows, eating *pollov* with their fingers. It was a breath of a different world, of ordinary Afghans breaking for lunch.

They must have been horrified at my presence in this male domain, but each one looked decorously at his *pollov*. Which allowed *me* to stare. Once, in a chaikhana, a youth with silky hair curling from under his turban asked, 'Who is she?' He jerked his chin at me. There was something steely about him, his stance, his cruel eyes, but he was so terribly young. In one hand he carried a curled-up notebook. I guessed he was from the ministry to fight vice and promote virtue. Ashraf had warned me.

The chaikhana owner hurried to reassure him, she's foreign, from Hindustan. I noted his sycophantic bent, his hands joined, not even consciously. When the official left, taking his chill with him, the chaikhana owner came to our table and told me that once six American women had come to eat in his chaikhana, and they liked it very much.

Yawar took me to see the tomb of Zahir Shah's father. We walked around the broken mausoleum, the pillars eroded by rocket fire, the roof falling in. It was poised on top of a hill overlooking a tomb, a vast graveyard of Muslim martyrs. They were young, they didn't know, Yawar said. The setting sun cast a pale golden light over Kabul. Squinting, I could see the road vanish into the distance, the hills around the city. The wind blew my dupatta off my head, leaving it uncovered. And a man walked up, military, from the provinces. He spoke to Yawar, who translated politely, but I knew from the words *mehman* and *kanoon* and the gesture to cover my head that the military man was saying I was a guest here, I should cover my head.

Yawar said, they're from the provinces. It's different in the city.

'I don't like those people,' he muttered. 'I don't like them.'

The wind blew through the gaps in the mortar and concrete, twisted wire curling from concrete blocks, the metal sheath on the dome loosened, the nails gone, the flaps groaning and creaking and banging in the wind like some pained sprite.

Like Afghanistan.

Issa Khan Tassal was editor-in-chief of the English-language *Kabul Times*. He worked in a building by the old printing press that had caved in completely because of a rocket attack. The paper was more of a rag, badly printed, their office rooms dusty and small. But they crowded into the small room and sat in a circle on chairs. I mimicked the forms of courtesy, right hand across my chest, head bowed. They brought more green tea to sip.

Tassal said that the prevailing peace was clear-cut proof that Amir-ul-Mominin, Mullah Mohammad Omar Mujahid, was the ruler of all Muslims and legitimately elected.

'He is elected by 1500 ulemas or scholars, representatives of the Afghan people. Every mosque in Afghanistan has a mullah, we listen to him, we respect him. They are benign scholars, they know the code of life, they are well educated. It means the majority of the people respect the rules and recognize the Taliban.'

It was one way to look at it, I supposed.

'With one decree of Mullah Omar, they disarmed everybody, collected the weapons.'

Then he told me a story of Mullah Nasiruddin, the fabled, clever, funny, mythical, mystical man, a Sufi saint, who wandered the world. Everybody in that part of the world referred to him as though they knew him personally, as though they had met him yesterday, and caught up with him, as with a favourite uncle. 'Once, when Mullah Nasiruddin . . .'

Tassal's story was about Mullah Nasiruddin who was once on a horse, going very fast. Why is the horse going fast, somebody asked. Ask the horse, the mullah said. But either Yawar's translation got garbled or I missed the point. I had no idea what he meant.

Driving around the city, I noticed the gestures of affection between men, how they stroked each other's beard. One evening, I had watched from the Ariana Hotel window as three men sat on the lush grass on the traffic island. A fourth man joined them, walking slowly, with effort. They greeted each other, hands clasped for the briefest second, a delicate gesture. Then they leaned into each other, cheeks touching, stopping for a moment. The newcomer dropped his newspaper onto the grass and then settled himself on it. Just friends, meeting in the park as the sun set behind Kabul's mountains painting the sky a dusty pink. I clung to the ordinary moment.

Finally, one of Kabul's senior UN officials had time to see me, briefly, in between appointments, the radio crackling non-stop. I wanted some information on budgets. On UN budgets.

'The funding for Afghanistan, in 2000–1 for various UN agencies, was 250 million US dollars,' he said. 'We got around forty-eight per cent of that. This year there is more, because of a lot of publicity and sanctions. It's a top story for journalists.'

Yes, I said. But how is it spent? Overheads, salaries, per diems, transport, breakdowns? It shocked me to hear that a highly placed UN official had no idea how the budget was spent. I wanted badly to be proved wrong. I wanted to know the facts, I wanted to believe the best about the United Nations and the World Food Program types. Later, the World Food people told me that budgets are tracked in Islamabad, so I should check there.

But they themselves were embroiled in a controversy about the UN guest house in Kabul, because it had recently emerged that millions of unaccounted US dollars were washing around in *that* enterprise. I could not find any evidence to disprove that the UN was not much more than a money-making machine.

The next statement managed to stop me in my tracks. It did not sound particularly humanitarian.

'But I hope the fight lasts. If the hardliners win, the Afghans will suffer more and more. We will be pushed out and replaced by extremist Islamic NGOs funded by the Gulf states. This will not help the future of Afghanistan. Unfortunately, if the Afghans don't take their future in their own hands, we westerners will try and push them to one side or the other.'

I thanked the senior UN official and rose to leave.

Yawar was making his own suggestions now of whom I should see, who might help me understand Afghanistan. I began to trust his judgement and so we went to see Sabir Latifi, an energetic businessman, my age, but he seemed so much more worldly and *capable*, whereas I seemed to spend my time wringing my hands and doubting myself. He was mild-mannered, gestured exuberantly and filled the room with his big dreams.

'Handouts from the international community are destroying the economy, it's not good for the future, it's turning us into beggars, and we are not a beggar society,' he said, in his perfect English tinged with an American accent. He described in detail his dream of building an irrigation canal: it would irrigate tens of thousands of hectares of land, feed thousands of families. Another Afghan with irrigation dreams.

Latifi used to work with Bridas Corporation, the oil consortium that had tossed political correctness out of the window and courted the Taliban for contracts. Bridas had left Afghanistan in September 2000. Latifi stayed and looked after the house they had acquired in case things got better, in case there was peace, in case there was a pipeline and Bridas came back. They had found twenty-seven trillion cubic feet of gas in Turkmenistan. Everything depended on the pipeline through Afghanistan. He was trying to keep the project alive.

Latifi called himself the last Afghan businessman.

80

I desperately needed a change from all this talk. I missed the seventh century. I missed the monk and his Buddhist trail. I had tried to swallow my disappointment at not being able to cross the Hindu Kush, but it rose in waves, like bile. Perhaps more than the ruins and the route through Afghanistan, I had wanted to see the mountains. I thought of fabled Balkh, of the cities I had not seen.

I begged Yawar to take me to see the Kabul Museum instead;

perhaps there would be a glimpse of what was left of Xuanzang's journey.

The museum was a symbol, a collection of gracious buildings with pillars in the front arches, housing the collection, now pitted by bullets and rockets, roofs fallen in, emptied of their treasures. This is not the first time that war has destroyed historical treasures.

The museum president was a petulant twenty-five-year-old called Raza Mohammad Pirozi, who knew not much about ancient history but a lot about Islam. The old museum head, Najibullah Popol, had long gone. I had seen a photo of him on the Internet, months and months ago, squatting amidst the debris of a shattered building.

The main door was bolted, a lock through the iron loops. The paint on the door was peeling and after some effort, they pushed the key, with a brick. Finally, the doors swung open. The corridors were dark, the windows were sheeted plastic and most of the rooms were locked.

There was a slab of limestone from Surkh Kotal, written in the Bactrian language using the Greek alphabet, dating from the second century AD. A brief spill of joy.

Is there anything Buddhist left, I asked. They had apparently put everything in a big safe but I would not be able to see it.

Can a week in Afghanistan change you? A few days spent in a war-torn country licking its wounds and I felt far away from everything. I inhabited a surreal, weird zone, as if the circle of mountains locked in the craziness. Like a prisoner of some sort, I longed to escape, I felt suffocated and longed to wander the bazaars. Tomorrow, I promised myself. A day of break, to rest and do nothing. I was tired.

Little boys waved on the roads, slapping one hand on a calf, again and again, leaning on a shovel. The game was that they had filled in the potholes with mud, and that they should be paid at least something. And so we tossed cash out of the windows, small dirty notes, Afghanis worth nothing. The boys scrambled after them with delight.

I was tired of being alone. I was tired of getting old, the strands of hair at my temples grew whiter by the day and my head filled with difficult things. I kept meaning to be young and have fun, and be not serious. Something dogged pushed me on. Since I was stuck in Kabul,

I had to do *something*. I had not sought this situation. Or had I? Whatever the case, I was unable to rest.

The Taliban Deputy Minister of Commerce Molavi Fazall Mohammad Fizan sat behind a vast glossy table. I could smell the money. This was not the grubby squat of the folks over at planning. Dissatisfied with political talk, I sought refuge in the details, there was often much to be learned when you followed the money and the movement of goods.

Fizan was, as they were all, gracious and polite, and tried to answer my questions in Pushto, pausing to think as Yawar translated into English. There was the usual blurb I was coming to recognize, about the annihilation of Afghanistan's economic structure after twenty-one years of war, the department of highways, the infrastructure.

The Taliban, Fizan said, had started rehabilitation of roads. They were working on a digital telephone system, the reconstruction of factories. Afghan businessmen were coming back. One was setting up a vegetable oil factory, one was setting up a silo for bread production, with Pakistan's help. I wanted to check on the pipeline.

'We are ready to implement the pipeline. It's not a small project. Anyone who wants to can invest. Only US traders are not allowed to invest in Afghanistan, we have no problem with other companies.'

'Are you talking to other companies?' I asked.

'We are holding talks,' he said.

And this, to me, in hindsight, was the crux of the matter. The Taliban were willing to talk to anybody but US traders. So that while the Taliban was in power, there was no hope for US oil companies to snag the juicy contract. In months to come I would remember these conversations with a sharp jolt.

Molavi Fizan's voice became stormy. I waited for Yawar's translation.

'They imposed sanctions because of Osama Bin Laden; the whole nation suffers, this is oppression and a tyranny on the people of Afghanistan.'

He gave a short laugh.

'We say that a person who is very foolish will throw all his clothes in the fire because of one flea. This is the policy of the USA in Afghanistan.'

chapter forty-nine

Tooti-phooti Afghanistan

My Afghan visa was about to run out. Remembering Karim's words in Jalalabad on the bitter landmarks of the Afghan capital, I asked Yawar for a drive through western Kabul.

The road through western Kabul had been the site of ugly factional fighting, Massoud's forces on top of this mountain and the Hazaras defending the bottom. The result of the conflict was still there: factories and schools on the outskirts of the town were in ruins, private buildings, the Polish embassy gutted; not far, the carcass of a Russian tank, its side blown open, tilted into a ditch. A building corner crumpled, as though a giant fist had smashed that spot. The Rabia Balkhi Girls' School emptied out. Entire neighbourhoods vanished into the rubble.

We drove by what used to be a music school, then a polytechnic, a boys' school, cars overturned, burned. From a pump nearby, a man filled a sea of containers. The whole history of what a city used to be was now a lurching ghost lacerated with bullet holes. Children played with a dirty football amid the bombed-out ruins, the building skeletons, the few walls left pitted by bullets. Their faces were covered in sores, their clothes were tattered. Yawar gestured to the driver who stopped the car. We both got out.

'This is my house.'

Yawar pointed at an empty ruin by the roadside in a residential area. The front of the small house had been blown off. The floor caved in dangerously, the doors were gone, the roof damaged.

'I picked mulberries from this tree,' he said, pointing to a stump of a tree. He stepped over a mound to a shallow hole in the ground. 'From this well we got water.'

Yawar's family fled the fighting when the front line moved to his front veranda.

'When we came back, there was nothing left. Everything was destroyed, looted. Next door, we could hear the screams of people being tortured. My wife cried and cried all night and then at 8 a.m. she died of a heart attack.'

Over the days, little things Yawar did sent violent jags through me, how he saved things—anything—for his girls to read. Pamphlets we got from the Red Cross, survey materials from the statistics office, a page of a newspaper from the *Kabul Times* office.

Once I bought him a drink, and he tried to puncture the can of Mirinda with a fork instead of popping open the loop. For some reason, it flattened me that he did not know how to open a fizzy drink can. Ustad.

In front of the ruins of his house, Yawar perhaps felt he could begin to open up a little. I was not here for much longer.

He had his own views. 'The people of Afghanistan are suffering a lot, we lost a lot. Now we are happy, there are no rockets over Kabul. The worst was trying to get from one place to another, each street was like a kingdom, the gunmen could do anything. The city was divided between seven kings. They'd stop people, snatch money from their pockets.'

'People were going crazy, we had a very bad time for four and a half years. It stopped in 1996. At least we can sleep at night, our daughters and sisters are safe. My beard has grown white because of the fighting. Over 60,000 people were killed in factional fighting.'

I believed him. It was hard not to believe a man when you were standing in front of his blown-up home and staring at the ruins of his life. Whatever the story was, this was his truth.

I was too obsessed with the history of the subcontinent to miss a visit to the tomb of the Mughal emperor Babur. Or Babor, as they called him here, and he was Bobor in Uzbekistan.

Bagh-e-Babor, Babor's garden, faced south-west, a well-chosen spot at this height, the garden spreading below. Behind him towered the grandeur of the mountain. The gate was a crunch of metal twisted beyond recognition, filled with bullet holes. It took a while to get the keeper; it meant clanging on the metal gates for a good quarter of an hour as a small crowd of children collected, their faces expressionless, unchildlike. They surrounded Yawar and me. A little boy wriggled under the gate and ran off to get the caretaker. When he came to open the gate, the keeper shooed off the children. As we were walking down the path, I felt a stone graze my shin.

The tiles on the roof above Babur's grave had broken and fallen, the pillars cracked. Thorny weeds overgrew the paths. At the bottom there was a restaurant, and a view of the valley. A vast swimming pool had kept its diving board stand, but the pool itself was empty, the bottom filled with rubble. Zahiruddin Mohammad Babur Shah would have been sad indeed to see his beloved Kabul so torn and broken. He died in Agra aged forty-nine, and had asked for his grave to be transferred to these cooler climes.

Yeh tooti-phooti Afghanistan.

8⊃

One morning, Kabul was tenser than usual. There were rumours. I had breakfasted with a Pakistani 'fixer' for a Western journalist at the hotel. He was a Pathan and had offered to help when I was back in Peshawar, for which I thanked him kindly. He was obviously thick with the Taliban—the Pathan connection—and was amazed that I had no such fixer. They charged hefty amounts in Islamabad. He told me that the Taliban had caught four men and hanged them for treason, so ran the sibilant word on the street.

You pick up quite a lot of information over breakfast at the Intercontinental, where the number of guests had swelled to four, including an Arab in a djellabah. So I was not surprised on that fine day in August when right on the roadside I saw four hanged men.

They were dangling by yellow plastic string from the same traffic post where Najibullah was hanged, the symbolism lost on nobody. Some Afghan traffic posts were constructions, a concrete pillar with a ladder and, on top, a small enclosed platform with a roof, where a policeman can stand and direct traffic. The platform also came in handy to display the hanged bodies of traitors. It was the only elevated place. Around this quiet circle, by the Ariana Hotel, the same circle where the Afghan men had greeted each other on the velvet grass, the four men swung in a light breeze.

At first I saw only two dead men, dangling from a rope. They seemed smaller than they should be. A couple of roads leading to the circle had been closed off; a stream of men walked or bicycled towards the traffic circle. The boys had dressed up, stalls selling drinks had been set up. There was an almost festive atmosphere.

Below the dangling bodies, Afghan men clustered, propping up bicycles, staring up at death. One man's neck had snapped, his head lolled to the right. The hair on the back of his neck was neatly trimmed. His eyes were shut, his tongue stuck out of his mouth, blackened. Rigor mortis had set in rapidly. His salwar kameez flapped in the wind, his body swayed. His legs were stiff, his hands and feet turning purplish as the blood settled with no heart to pump it. A few flies buzzed. Somebody had stuck Afghan banknotes into his nostrils and ears, pushed more in between his toes and fingers. This was to indicate that he had accepted money for his crime. A streamer of pink toilet paper was tied at the bottom of his salwar, flying out in the wind, like a celebration of this punishment.

He looked so very young. It struck me that this body was just a case, a clever imitation of life, as though a particularly skilled mannequin maker had been commissioned to hang these dull, sad dolls from a string. The make-up was impeccable, the hair down to a T. Then I saw the other two bodies.

Around the circle, two military trucks were parked, equipped with a long wrench and hook, possibly for towing tanks or other artillery. On this hook swung one man. On the other truck hung another body. A trickle of dried blood hung from his nose. He was thin.

I felt sick.

The military police squad squatted under a shady tree in the middle of the traffic circle. The chief sat on rugs and cushions, surrounded by a group of his boys. They were a rough-looking lot. Wild faces under black turbans. One rearranged a loaded machine gun on its tripod so it pointed straight at me. They were armed to the teeth. Not just Kalashnikovs, but bazookas and rocket launchers. This then, was the crowd that Kabul citizens referred to as animals.

'Taliban intelligence found out that these men were planning to lay mines, they found documents, they found the equipment, everything,' the chief said. Yawar stood right beside me, translating. Four had been hanged, the other nine got life imprisonment.

My knees were shaking. I fought a rising nausea.

I had my exit permit and only a few more days to go. In a panic, I began to look for a way to leave Kabul. It would have to be through one of the aid agencies. Yawar helped with filling out permission forms and driving back and forth from the Red Cross which flew journalists for free, but only if there was space and on certain days, and they stopped in other Afghan cities for hours.

In the end, I coughed up US $230 for a ticket on a direct UN plane to Islamabad. How ironic, I thought, that the UN charges for flights out but they won't allow Ariana to operate. I would rather have taken Ariana.

But when the UN flight, a Beechcraft leased from the Danes, landed in Kabul, it could not pick up passengers for some unexplained reason. It dropped off a high-level official. Then took off again, leaving a handful of disgruntled World Food Program workers, two Pakistanis who were computer technicians and me stranded. There was a grumble, a rush to arrange cars and race down to the Pakistani border at Torkham before it closed for the day. This time, somebody found a spot in a UN Toyota for me, but I think it was because a Pathan was on hand to help.

I weakly tried to claim my US $230 back. Translated into Afghanis, it was a horrendous sum of money, and a vast amount of rupees, a calculation which I did constantly. But we were bundled into the cars and the Afghan drivers pressed the accelerators. You can get a refund in Islamabad, an official said, but I knew it would not materialize. I kissed it goodbye and notched it up to another atom in the vast sea of unaccounted money pooling in UN banks.

§

When I left Afghanistan, I felt like a different person. Crossing the border back into Pakistan, my dupatta covering my head, my dark glasses hid tears. I wound the cloth around my mouth and felt hot tears and snot soak the covering as I sobbed among people busy with passports and customs.

Incredibly, having scrutinized my every move, it now seemed the Pakistanis had lost interest in me. Nobody batted an eyelid as I zoomed through Torkham and boarded a flight from Islamabad to Delhi, nobody complained even though I was supposed to leave the country exactly the way I came, via Lahore. I felt aged, as though I left with a great burden. I understood less, not more. I had failed to come up with watertight conclusions about anything, I had acquired this *sadness*.

Somewhere in the heights of Afghanistan, through those drives criss-crossing Kabul, I had lost a fundamental belief in the goodness of humanity. I was drenched in cynicism, I saw hidden motives everywhere, I had suspended belief in everything, every printed word, every official statement. I felt stripped of safety and thought I felt a softening at the edges of my mind.

I had long ago lost the monk. Afghanistan had taken him from me. And perhaps it was better this way.

chapter fifty

Afterwards

 My journey in the steps of the monk lived in me, huddled against my ribs like a net of fireflies throwing off a faint light, coating the insides of my mind.

My life would slowly settle, like a soaring bald eagle landing, clumsy, shuffling, folding its wings. My father's death had changed my whole landscape. I dreamed that he came back, that his absence had all been a mistake. I wept in my sleep, able only to shed tears in my dreams. I was left with nothing but the words to say it with, and even those I could not fully believe. Somehow I stumbled through the days and through the words. Time shrank and swelled. The monk and his quest were the background against which I struggled to understand the incomprehensible.

I wanted to bask in the things I had learned; I was afraid of the knowledge flying away, like a web of spider-spit torn loose from its moorings, floating into the bluest of skies. In the shadow of the monk I had learned a necessary past. I felt anchored in the adventures that jostled across the vast lands I had travelled, and was aware of how I had only grazed the tip.

I settled into the shaky peace of a life with S. We got married, we paid the rent, we went to the cinema, met friends for drinks. With him I felt buoyed and held up, held in the safety of his hands, caught in the net of his caring. His presence filled my life like a dark silent forest I could lean on and sink into.

And yet, at times, the shifting light of our days felt as fragile as a dream, or a mirage, or the moonlight reflected on water. And remembering the monk's lessons, I wondered if I had imagined it all.

Acknowledgements

The Mary Elivra Stevens Traveling Fellowship from my alma mater, Wellesley College in the United States, and a grant from the Hong Kong Arts Development Council funded the travel. I thank both institutions for their support.

A special thanks to my family, and to Scott Keller, my partner in the biggest journey of all.

Thanks also to Nandini Mehta and Poulomi Chatterjee of Penguin Books India for their fine work on the manuscript.

A great many people, scattered across the world helped make this book—archaeologists, diplomats, colleagues, friends, historians, officials, relatives, and perfect strangers rolled up their sleeves in ways big and small to nudge the research and travel along. People gave freely of their time and advice, dipped into networks, wrote helpful letters, shared their expertise, opened their homes, bought me lunch, gave me a ride or looked after my affairs. Without their inputs this book could not have happened.

In the US: Paul Cohen, my university professor who first sparked and stoked this eagerness for history.

In China: Vijay and Malini Nambiar, and Huang Xinchuan of the Chinese Academy of Social Sciences in Beijing; Luoyang; Xu Jinxing; Zeng Qin Fa Shi and Wang Yarong in Xian; Li Qunyuan and the Anxi Museum in Anxi.

In Hong Kong: the University of Hong Kong's Centre for Asian Studies admitted me as an honorary research fellow from 2000 to 2005 which gave me valuable access to an excellent library; thanks also to Yao Zhihua at the university's Centre for Buddhist Studies;

Jennifer and Sasha Atepolikhine; Philip Segal; Hugo Restall; Steven Weeks; Norma Connolly; Michael Somers; Ron Thompson.

In Kyrgyzstan: Thanks to the Indian embassy in Bishkek; Stalina and Tahmina Bekeeva; Michael Westerbjerg Andersen and his Danish tour group; Sasha and Luba Danichkin.

In Uzbekistan: Bhaskar Mitra and his staff at the Indian embassy went far beyond the call of duty; thanks to Edvard Rtveladze and Leonid Sverchkov and the Institute of Archaeology in Samarkand; and Qamar Rais.

In Pakistan: I am indebted to A.H. Dani; Imran Khan; Azra Raza; Justin and Ambareen Thompson; Kazi Afaq Hossain; Mian Tauquir and family; Sudhir Vyas; Nancy Hatch Dupree; Nafees Takkar; Farooq Swati; Nidaullah Seherai; Anwar and Lubna Kazim in Lahore; and to UN staff in Islamabad and Peshawar.

In Afghanistan: I am grateful to the Red Cross in Jalalabad and Mirza Gul Yawar in Kabul.

In India: Warm thanks to Arun Shourie, Arjun Mahey, Shalini Saran, Malini Saran, Ajit Saran, Nandini Mehta, Razia and Satish Grover, Suman Dubey, Ashraf Qazi, Jalil Abbas Jilani in New Delhi; Farooq Ahmed and B.R. Mani in Kashmir; Girish Prasad of the Mathura Government Museum in Mathura; Kranti Saran, Geshe Sonam Rinchen and Ruth Sonam in Dharamsala; R.G. Sharma of the Archeological Survey of India in Sanghol; Dr C. Pant and Vasudha Pande in Allahabad; P.K. Gaur of the Tulsi Smarak Bhavan in Ayodhya; Shantum Seth in Lumbini; K.K. Mohammad, Zeenat Ahmed, Ambika Menon and R.S. Sharma in Patna; Tini and Vinay Soi, Rupa and Vivek Atal, and Dev Thapar in Calcutta; Lourdu Swami, Atanoo Barua, H.S. Deka, Bimal Sinha, Baldev Singh, and Hema and Nirudh Singh in Assam; Rohit and Shankhalina Mull, Mitali Saran, Hari Menon and M.N. Deshpande in Maharashtra; C.B.Patel, S.K. Moharana and D.R. Pradhan in Bhubaneswar; I.K. Sharma in Hyderabad; Velli, Seetha and M.V. Subbiah, K.T. Narasimhan and P.V. Rajan in Chennai; Iftiqar Ahmed, V.H. Sonawane and V.S. Parekh in Gujarat.

I am solely responsible for any errors that may have crept into my writing.

Notes

Chapter 2: Journey to the West

1. Shaman Hwui Li, *The Life of Hiuen-Tsiang*, trans. Samuel Beal (1911; reprint, New Delhi: Asian Educational Services, 1998), 3.
2. William John Francis Jenner, *Memories of Loyang: Yang Hsuan-chih and the Lost Capital (493-534)* (Oxford: Clarendon Press, 1981), 135.
3. Mei-chin Chen, 'The Eminent Chinese Monk Hsuan-Tsang: His Contribution to Buddhist Scripture Translation and to the Propagation of Buddhism in China' (Ph.D diss., University of Wisconsin, Madison, 1992), 230–1.
4. Hwui Li, 4.
5. Edward Conze, ed., *Buddhist Texts through the Ages* (Oxford: Bruno Cassirer, 1954), 194.
6. Karl Heinz Ranitzch, *The Army of Tang China* (Stockport: Montvert Publications, 1995), 59.
7. Conze, 216.
8. Paul Griffiths, *On Being Mindless: Buddhist Meditation and the Mind–Body Problem* (La Salle, Illinois: Open Court Publishing Company, 1986), 76.
9. C.P. Fitzgerald, 'Son of Heaven', in *Perspectives on the T'ang*, eds. Aruthur F. Wright and Dennis Twichett (London and New Haven: Yale University Press, 1973), 4 (introduction), 124.
10. Hwui Li, 10.
11. Victor Cunrui Xiong, *Sui-Tang Chang'an: A Study in the Urban History of Medieval China* (Ann Arbor: Center for Chinese Studies, University of Michigan, 2000), 7.
12. Xiong, 10.

Chapter 3: City of the Flying Horse

1. Hwui Li, 12.

Chapter 4: The Jade Gates

1. Hwui Li, 14.
2. Hwui Li, 16.
3. Hwui Li, 16.

Chapter 5: River of Sand

1. Hwui Li, 27.

Chapter 6: Fire City

1. Thomas Watters, *On Yuan Chwang's Travels in India* (1904–5; reprint, Delhi: Munshiram Manoharlal Publishers Pvt. Ltd, 1973), 46–7.
2. Hsuan-tsang, *Si-yu-ki: Buddhist Records of the Western World*, translated by Samuel Beal (1884; reprint, Delhi: Munshiram Manoharlal Publishers Pvt. Ltd, 1994), 18.
3. Watters, 48.

Chapter 7: Twin Convents

1. Hsuan-tsang, 19.
2. Inspired by Eduared Chavannes, 'Wu K'ung', (790), *Journal Asiatique*, 2 (1895): 364, quoted in Rene Grousset, *In the Footsteps of the Buddha*, translated by Marietta Leon (London: George Routledge and Sons, 1932), 54.
3. Hsuan-tsang, 21.
4. Hsuan-tsang, 21.
5. Watters, 59.
6. Hwui Li, 39.

Chapter 9: Heavenly Mountains
1. Hwui Li, p. 42.
2. A display legend in Bishkek's Kyrgyz History Museum says the Juan-juan, about whom not much is known, were based in Siberia.
3. Luc Kwanten, *Imperial Nomads: A History of Central Asia, 500–1500* (Philadelphia: University of Pennsylvania Press, 1979), 19.
4. Richard N. Frye, *The Heritage of Central Asia from Antiquity to the Turkish Expansion* (Princeton: Markus Wiener Publishers, 1996), 180.
5. D. Sinor and S.G. Klyashtorny, 'The Türk Empire', in *History of Civilizations of Central Asia*, Volume 3, edited by B.A. Litvinsky et al. (1996; reprint, Delhi: Motilal Banarsidass Publishers Pvt. Ltd, 1999), 334.
6. Hwui Li, 43.
7. Hwui Li, 44.
8. Kwanten, p. 32.
9. Hwui Li, p. 43.
10. Hwui Li, p. 44.

Chapter 10: Perpetual Snows
1. Hwui Li, 41.
2. Hsuan-tsang, 26.
3. Hwui Li, 41.

Chapter 11: Nine *Lepioshkas*
1. Hsuan-tsang, 25.

Chapter 12: Sogdiana
1. Frye, 90.
2. Frye, 102.
3. Frye, 101.
4. Frye, 205.
5. Frye, 216.
6. Frye, 221.
7. Frye, 228.
8. *Cambridge History of Iran.* Cambridge: Cambridge University Press, 1968–91.
9. Hsuan-tsang, 30.
10. Frye, 194.
11. Frye, 195.

Chapter 13: River of Gold
1. Hsuan-tsang, 31.
2. Hsuan-tsang, 32.
3. B.I. Marshak and N.N. Negmatov, 'Sogdiana', in *History of Civilizations of Central Asia*, Volume 3, edited by B.A. Litvinsky. (1996; reprint, Delhi: Motilal Banarsidass Publishers Pvt. Ltd, 1999), 278.
4. Hsuan-tsang, Book I, 32.
5. To put it more technically, here's what Negmatov says about Ferghana in *History of Civilizations of Central Asia*, 276. 'In palaeo-anthropological terms, the population now belonged to the mesocranial and brachycranial Europoid group, with only a small percentage of dolicranial Europoids very sparsely interspersed with Mongoloid admixtures.' Lovely.
6. Hwui Li, 45.

Chapter 14: Crossing the River
1. Hsuan-tsang, 36.
2. Hsuan-tsang, 39.
3. A.H. Dani and B.A. Litvinsky, 'The Kushano-Sassanian Kingdom', in *History of Civilizations of Central Asia*, Volume 3, edited by B.A. Litvinsky (1996; reprint, Delhi: Motilal Banarsidass Publishers Pvt. Ltd, 1999), 111.
4. Frye, 228.

Chapter 15: Locking the Sea in a Box
1. Hsuan-tsang, 148.
2. Hwui Li, 69.
3. Arthur Waley, *The Real Tripitaka and Other Pieces* (London: George Allen and Unwin, 1952), 30.
4. Hwui Li, 69.
5. Hwui Li, 70.
6. Ram Chandra Kak, *Ancient Monuments of Kashmir* (London: The Indian Society, 1933; reprint New Delhi: Sagar Publications, 1971), 111.
7. Kak, 111.
8. G.M.D. Sufi, *Kashir: Being a History of Kashmir from the Earliest Times to Our Own* (1948–9; reprint, Lucknow: Light and Life Publishers, 1974), 80.
9. Mirza Muhammad Haidar Dughlat, *A History of the Mughals of Central Asia Being the Tarikh-I-Rashidi*, translated by E. Denison Ross (London: Curzon, 1898), 463, quoted in Sufi, 19.
10. Hsuan-tsang, 148.
11. Hsuan-tsang, 160.
12. Kak, 108.

Chapter 16: Unhappy Valleys
1. Hsuan-tsang, 163.
2. Hsuan-tsang, 163.

Chapter 17: Sikander and Porus
1. Alexander Cunningham, *The Ancient Geography of India*, Volume 1, *Buddhist Period* (1871; reprint, New Delhi: Low Price Publications, 1996), 115–6.
2. Hsuan-tsang, 176.
3. Hermann Kulke and Dietmar Rothermund, *A History of India* (New York: Routledge, 1998), 58.

Chapter 18: Kingdom Enclosed by Peaks
1. Conze, 157.
2. Xuanzang's Translations (Ken Ch'en, and addendas by Geshe Sonam Rinchen).
3. Hsuan-tsang, 177.

Chapter 19: Tree Nymphs
1. Cunningham, 122–4.

Chapter 20: Too Many Women
1. Hsuan-tsang, 179.
2. Hsuan-tsang, 179.
3. Hsuan-tsang, 180.
4. Hsuan-tsang, 181.
5. Watters, 312.
6. Quoted in Bimala Churn Law, *Historical Geography of Ancient India* (Paris: Societe Asiatique de Paris, 1954), 108.
7. Watters, 312.
8. Kulke and Rothermund, 76.
9. Kulke and Rothermund, 77.
10. Waley, 38.

Chapter 21: Holy Confluence
1. Hsuan-tsang, 233.
2. Hsuan-tsang, 233.
3. Vasubandhu, *Karmasiddhiprakarana: The Treatise on Action*, translated by Etienne Lamotte, English translation by Leo M. Pruden (Berkeley: Asian Humanities Press, 1988), 15.
4. Vasubandhu, 15.
5. Hsuan-tsang, 234.

Chapter 22: Schism in the Sangha

1. Thich Nhat Hanh, *Old Path White Clouds* (1991; reprint, New Delhi: Full Circle, 1998), 299.
2. Hwui Li, 91.
3. Hsuan-tsang, 235.
4. G.R. Sharma, *Allahabad through the Ages* (Allahabad: The Indian Press Pvt. Ltd, 1965).
5. Thich Nhat Hanh, 302.
6. Thich Nhat Hanh, 302.

Chapter 23: *Sarkari Intezam*

1. Vasubandhu, *Abhidharmakosabhasyam Volume 1*, translated by Louis de La Vallee Poussain, English translation by Leo M. Pruden (Berkeley: Asian Humanities Press, 1988–90), 16.
2. Pruden, 16.
3. Thich Nhat Hanh, 440.
4. Ajay Nath, *The Baburi Masjid* (Jaipur: The Historical Research Documentation Programme, 1991), 54–5.

Chapter 24: Wrong Kind of Love

1. Hwui Li, 87.
2. Hsuan-tsang, 2.
3. Conze, 19.
4. Thich Nhat Hanh, 272.
5. Thich Nhat Hanh, 272.
6. Hsuan-tsang, 7.
7. Hsuan-tsang, 14.
8. Alfred Foucher, *The Life of the Buddha: According to the Ancient Texts and Monuments of India*, abridged translation by Simone Brangier Boas (Connecticut: Wesleyan University Press, 1963), 70–1.
9. Foucher, 77.
10. Hsuan-tsang, 18.
11. Foucher, 175.

Chapter 25: Labour Pains

1. Hsuan-tsang, 24.
2. Henry Falk, 'The Discovery of Lumbini', Lumbini International Research Institute, Occasional Papers, 1, 21–2.
3. Pradhan, Bhuwan Lal, *Lumbini Kapilwastu Dewadaha*, Nepal: Research Centre for Nepal and Asian Studies, Tribhuvan University, 16.

Chapter 26: Fatal Mushrooms

1. Hsuan-tsang, 31.
2. Thich Nhat Hanh, 553–8.
3. Hsuan-tsang, 33.
4. Rhys David (trans.), *Mahaparinibanna Sutta*, in *The Life of the Buddha: According to the Ancient Texts and Monuments of India* by A. Foucher, abridged translation by Boas, 236.

Chapter 27: Deer Park

1. Hsuan-tsang, 44.
2. Hsuan-tsang, 45.
3. Thich Nhat Hanh, 146.
4. Hsuan-tsang, 44.
5. Hsuan-tsang, 48.

Chapter 28: Buddhist Ivy League

1. Hsuan-tsang, 83.
2. Hsuan-tsang, 86.
3. Hwui Li, 111.

4.   Hwui Li, 107.
5.   Hwui Li, 108.
6.   Hsuan-tsang, 170.
7.   For his explanation of what Xuanzang studied at Nalanda, and other parts of India, I am grateful to Dr Yao Zhihua at the Hong Kong University's Centre of Buddhist Studies.

Chapter 29: Vulture's Peak
1.   Thich Nhat Hanh, 98.
2.   Thich Nhat Hanh, 202.
3.   Hwui Li, 115.
4.   Hsuan-tsang, 152.

Chapter 30: Peepul Leaf and Perfect Wisdom
1.   Hwui Li, 104.
2.   Thich Nhat Hanh, 118.
3.   Thich Nhat Hanh, 121.
4.   Thich Nhat Hanh, 122.
5.   Hwui Li, 105.

Chapter 31: Land of the Eastern Light
1.   Hwui Li, 171.
2.   Hsuan-tsang, 197.
3.   Hsuan-tsang, 197.
4.   Hsuan-tsang, 198–9.

Chapter 32: Reunited
1.   Hsuan-tsang, 200–1.

Chapter 33: Flower Mountain
1.   Hsuan-tsang, 205.
2.   Surendra Kumar Moharana, 'Buddhism in Orissa: A Historical Survey', in *Journal of the Institute of Asian Studies*, 10, no. 2.
3.   N.K. Sahu, *Buddhism in Orissa* (Bhubaneswar: Utkala University, 1958), 38.
4.   Hwui Li, 159.
5.   N.K. Sahu, 'Hinayana Buddhism in Eastern India in the Seventh Century', *The Orissa Historical Research Journal* 4, nos. 1, 2 (1955), 33.
6.   Hwui Li, 165.
7.   P. Acharya, 'Ancient Routes in Orissa', *The Orissa Historical Research Journal* 4, nos. 3, 4 (1955), 44.

Chapter 34: Ocean's Edge
1.   Hsuan-tsang, 205.
2.   Sahu, *Buddhism in Orissa*, 42.
3.   Hsuan-tsang, 221.
4.   K.S. Subramanian, *Buddhist Remains in South India and Early Andhra History 225 AD to 610 AD* (1927; reprint, New Delhi: Cosmo Publications, 1981), 30.
5.   I.K. Sharma, 'Buddhism in South India', *Suhrullekha*, July–September 1999, 35.
6.   Subramanian, 4.
7.   Subramanian, 4.

Chapter 35: Hidden Buddhas
1.   Hsuan-tsang, 229.
2.   K. Sivaramalingam, 'Tracing Buddhist Vestiges in Tontaimantalam', *Journal of the Institute of Asian Studies*, 10, no. 2.
3.   T.A. Gopinatha Rao, *The Indian Antiquary*, volume 44, June (1915), 128.
4.   Sivaramalingam, 55.
5.   Hwui Li, 139.

Chapter 36: Stone Elephants
1.   Hwui Li, 146.
2.   Hwui Li, 147.
3.   Hsuan-tsang, 257.
4.   M.R. Acharekar, *Buddhist Chaitya Hall at Karla in Pencil Drawings*, (Bombay: Rekha Publication).
5.   Hsuan-tsang, 259.

Chapter 37: Hill of Rishis
1.   Hsuan-tsang, 269.
2.   Hsuan-tsang, 269.

Chapter 39: Pure Land
1.   Olaf Caroe, *The Pathans* (1958; reprint, Karachi: Oxford University Press, 2001), 44.

Chapter 40: City of Dressed Stone
1.   Hsuan-tsang, 137.
2.   Caroe, 26.
3.   Caroe, 47.
4.   John Marshall, *Taxila: An Illustrated Account of Archeological Excavations Carried out at Taxila under the Orders of the Government of India between the Years 1913 and 1934* (1951; reprint, Delhi: Bhartiya Publishing House, 1975), 16.
5.   Marshall, 19.
6.   Archaeological Survey of India, *Annual Report 1914–15*, edited by Sir John Marshall (Calcutta: Superintendent, Government Press, 1917).
7.   Marshall, 20.

Chapter 41: Mound of the King
1.   Hsuan-tsang, 98.
2.   Hsuan-tsang, 101.
3.   Hsuan-tsang, 104.
4.   Ibrahim Shah, 'A Brief Account of Archaeological Remains in Hazarkhwani Graveyard, Peshawar', *Journal of Central Asia* 20 (July 1997), 96.
5.   A.H. Dani, *Peshawar: Historic City of the Frontier* (Lahore: Sang-e-Meel Publications, 1995), 28.
6.   Hsuan-tsang, 109.
7.   Hwui Li, 64.

Chapter 42: Lotus City
1.   Nancy Hatch Dupree, *Gandhara: An Instant Guide to Pakistan's Heritage* (Karachi: Elite Publishers), 11.

Chapter 43: Silk Road Graffiti
1.   Hsuan-tsang, 120.
2.   Hsuan-tsang, 120.
3.   Hsuan-tsang, 133.
4.   Dupree, *Gandhara*, 16.
5.   Hsuan-tsang, 112.

Chapter 44: Listening Post
1.   Dupree, *Gandhara*, 17.
2.   Hsuan-tsang, 136.

Chapter 46: Sacrifice Country
1.   Hsuan-tsang, 91.
2.   Hsuan-tsang, 77.
3.   Hsuan-tsang, 95.
4.   Hsuan-tsang, 96.

Bibliography

Acharya, P. 'Ancient Routes in Orissa'. *The Orissa Historical Research Journal* 4, nos. 3, 4.

Ali, Salim. *The Book of Indian Birds*. 11th ed. New Delhi: Oxford University Press, 1988.

Archaeological Survey of India, *Annual Report 1914–15*. Edited by John Marshall. Calcutta: Superintendent, Government Press, 1917.

Barnett, Lionel D. *Antiquities of India: An Account of the History and Culture of Ancient Hindustan*. London: Philip Lee Warner, 1913. Reprint, New Delhi: Asian Education Services, 1994.

Barpujari, H.K., ed. *The Comprehensive History of Assam*. Volume 1. Guwahati: Publication Board, 1990.

Bawa, Kanaklal. *Early History of Assam: A Collection of Papers Published in Research Journals on Aspects of the History and Culture of Assam*. Edited by Dr Maheshwar Neog. Guwahati: Asam Sahitya Sabha, 1973.

Bechert, Heinz, and Richard Gombrich, eds. *The World of Buddhism: Buddhist Monks and Nuns in Society and Culture*. London: Thames and Hudson Ltd, 1984.

Bose, Ayodhya Chandra. *Sun Worship in Indo-Aryan Religion and Mythology*. Delhi: Indian Book Gallery, 1984.

Cambridge History of Iran. Cambridge: Cambridge University Press, 1968–91.

Caroe, Olaf. *The Pathans*. 1958. Reprint, Karachi: Oxford University Press. 2001.

Chavannes, Eduard. 'Wu K'ung', (790). *Journal Asiatique*, 2 (1895): 364. Quoted in Rene Grousset, *In the Footsteps of the Buddha*, translated by Marietta Leon. London: George Routledge and Sons, 1932.

Conze, Edward, ed. In collaboration with I.B. Horner, D. Snellgrove, A. Waley. *Buddhist Texts through the Ages*. Oxford: Bruno Cassirer, 1954.

Coomaraswamy, Ananda. *The Dance of Shiva*. New York: The Sunwise Turn, 1918. Reprint, New Delhi: Munshiram Manoharlal Publishers Pvt. Ltd, 1999.

Cunningham, Alexander. *The Ancient Geography of India*. Volume 1, *Buddhist Period*. 1871. Reprint, New Delhi: Low Price Publications, 1996.

Dani, Ahmad Hasan. *Peshawar: Historic City of the Frontier*. Lahore: Sang-e-Meel Publications, 1995.

———, and B.A. Litvinsky. 'The Kushano-Sassanian Kingdom'. In *History of Civilizations of Central Asia*, Volume 3, edited by B.A. Litvinsky. 1996. Reprint, Delhi: Motilal Banarsidass Publishers Pvt. Ltd, 1999.

Dupree, Nancy Hatch. *An Historic Guide to Afghanistan*. Afghan Tourist Organisation Publication, 1971.

———. *Gandhara: An Instant Guide to Pakistan's Heritage*. Karachi: Elite Publishers.

Dutta, Arup Kumar. *Cha Garam! The Tea Story*. Guwahati: Paloma Publications, 1992.

Eliade, Mircea, ed. *The Encyclopedia of Religion*. New York: Collier Macmillan, 1987.

Ettinghauser, Maurice. 'Harsa Vardhana, Empereur et Poete de L'Inde Septentrionale (606-648 AD) Etude Sur Sa Vie Et Son Temps'. Ph.D. diss., Universite De Paris. Paris. 1906.

Falk, Henry. 'The Discovery of Lumbini'. Lumbini International Research Institute, Occasional Papers, 1.

Fitzgerald, C.P. 'Son of Heaven'. In *Perspectives on the T'ang*, edited by Aruthur F. Wright and Dennis Twichett. London and New Haven: Yale University Press, 1973.

Foucher, Alfred. *Notes on the Ancient Geography of Gandhara: A Commentary on a Chapter of Hiuan Tsang*. Translated by H. Hargreaves. Varanasi: Bhartiya Publishing House, 1974.

———. *The Life of the Buddha: According to the Ancient Texts and Monuments of India*. Abridged translation by Simone Brangier Boas. Connecticut: Wesleyan University Press, 1963.

Frye, Richard Nelson. *The Heritage of Central Asia from Antiquity to the Turkish Expansion*.

Princeton: Markus Wiener Publishers, 1996.

Gait, Edward. *A History of Assam*. Guwahati, India: Lawyer's Book Stall, 1992.

Gethin, Rupert. *The Foundations of Buddhism*. New York: Oxford University Press, 1998.

Gombrich, Richard. *Theravada Buddhism: A Social History from Ancient Benares to Modern Colombo*. London and New York: Routledge and Kegan Paul, 1988.

Griffiths, Paul. *On Being Mindless: Buddhist Meditation and the Mind–Body Problem*. La Salle, Illinois: Open Court Publishing Company, 1986.

Grousset, Rene. *In the Footsteps of the Buddha*. Translated by Marietta Leon. London: George Routledge and Sons, 1932.

Grover, Satish. *The Architecture of India: Buddhist and Hindu*. Ghaziabad:Vikas Publishers, 1980.

Harmatta, Janos, ed. *History of Civilizations of Central Asia*. Volume 2. 1994. Reprint, New Delhi: Motilal Banarsidass Publishers Pvt. Ltd, 1999.

Hazarika, Sanjoy. *Strangers of the Mist: Tales of War and Peace from India's Northeast*. New Delhi: Viking, 1994.

Hsuan-tsang. *Si-yu-ki: Buddhist Records of the Western World*. Translated by Samuel Beal. 1884. Reprint, Delhi: Munshiram Manoharlal Publishers Pvt. Ltd, 1994.

Hwui Li. *The Life of Hiuen-Tsiang*. Translated by Samuel Beal. 1911. Reprint, New Delhi: Asian Educational Services, 1998.

Jenner, William John Francis. *Memories of Loyang: Yang Hsuan-chih and the Lost Capital (493-534)*. Oxford: Clarendon Press, 1981.

Kak, Ram Chandra. *Ancient Monuments of Kashmir*. London: The India Society, 1933. Reprint. New Delhi: Sagar Publications, 1971.

Kanakasabhai, V. *The Tamils Eighteen Hundred Years Ago*. Tirunelveli: The South India Saiva Siddhanta Works Publishing Society, 1956.

Kenneth Ch'en. *Buddhism in China: A Historical Survey*. Princeton: Princeton University Press, 1973.

Kitagawa, Joseph M., and Mark D. Cummings, ed. *Buddhism in Asian History*. New York: Macmillan Publishing Company, 1989.

Kulke, Hermann, and Dietmar Rothermund. *A History of India*. New York: Routledge, 1998.

Kwanten, Luc. *Imperial Nomads: A History of Central Asia, 500–1500*. Philadelphia: University of Pennsylvania Press, 1979.

Law, Bimala Churn. *Historical Geography of Ancient India*. Paris: Societe Asiatique de Paris, 1954.

Mangalam, S.J. *Historical Geography and Toponomy of Andhra Pradesh*. New Delhi: Sundeep Prakashan, 1986.

Marshak, B.I., and N.N. Negmatov. 'Sogdiana'. In *History of Civilizations of Central Asia*, Volume 3, edited by B.A. Litvinsky. 1996. Reprint, Delhi: Motilal Banarsidass Publishers Pvt. Ltd, 1999.

Marshall, John. *Taxila: An Illustrated Account of Archeological Excavations Carried out at Taxila under the Orders of the Government of India between the Years 1913 and 1934*. 1951. Reprint, Delhi: Bhartiya Publishing House, 1975.

Mei-chin Chen. 'The Eminent Chinese Monk Hsuan-Tsang: His Contribution to Buddhist Scripture Translation and to the Propagation of Buddhism in China'. Ph.D diss., University of Wisconsin, Madison, 1992.

Moharana, Surendra Kumar. 'Buddhism in Orissa: A Historical Survey'. *Journal of The Institute of Asian Studies* 10, no. 2.

Nath, Ajay. *The Baburi Masjid*. Jaipur: The Historical Research Documentation Programme, 1991.

Palmer, Martin, Jay Ramsay and Man-Ho Kwok. *Kuan Yin*. London: Thorsons, 1995.

Pradhan, Bhuwan Lal. *Lumbini Kapilwastu Dewadaha*. Nepal: Research Centre for Nepal and Asian Studies, Tribhuvan University.

Ranitzch, Karl Heinz. *The Army of Tang China*. Stockport: Montvert Publications, 1995.

Rao, M. Rama. *Glimpses of Dakkan History*. Madras: Orient Longman Ltd, 1951.

Rao, T.A. Gopinatha. *The Indian Antiquary*. Volume 44. Tamil Nadu, June (1915):128.

Rastogi, Naresh Prasad. 'Inscription of Asoka'. In *Chowkhamba Sanskrit Studies*. 103, Varanasi, 1990.

Rea, Alexander. *Pallava Architecture*. Archeological Survey of India, New Imperial Series, volume 44. Madras: Superintendent, Government Press, 1909.

Rhys Davids, T.W. *Buddhist India*. Reprint, Delhi: Motilal Banarsidass Publishers Pvt. Ltd, 1997.

S. Dhammika. *Middle Land, Middle Way: A Pilgrim's Guide to the Buddha's India*. Kandy: Buddhist Publication Society, 1992.

Sahu, N.K. 'Hinayana Buddhism in Eastern India in the Seventh Century'. *The Orissa Historical Research Journal* 4, nos. 1, 2 (1955): 33.

———. *Buddhism in Orissa*. Bhubaneswar: Utkala University, 1958.

Shah, Ibrahim. 'A Brief Account of Archaeological Remains in Hazarkhwani Graveyard, Peshawar'. *Journal of Central Asia* 20 (July 1997): 96.

Sharma, G.R. *Allahabad through the Ages*. Allahabad: The Indian Press Pvt. Ltd, 1965.

Sharma, I.K. 'Buddhism in South India'. *Suhrullekha*, July–September 1999: 34.

Sharma, R.C. *Buddhist Art of Mathura*. Delhi: Agam Kala Prakashan, 1984.

Sherring, M.A. *Benares: The Sacred City of the Hindus in Ancient and Modern Times*. Reprint, New Delhi: Rupa & Co., 2001.

Sinor, D., and S.G. Klyashtorny. 'The Türk Empire'. In *History of Civilizations of Central Asia*, Volume 3, edited by B.A. Litvinsky. 1996. Reprint, Delhi: Motilal Banarsidass Publishers Pvt. Ltd, 1999.

Sivaramalingam, K. 'Tracing Buddhist Vestiges in Tontaimantalam'. *Journal of the Institute of Asian Studies*, 10, nos 2, 55.

Smith, V.A. *The Early History of India: From 600 BC to the Muhammadan Conquest, Including the Invasion of Alexander the Great*. Oxford: Clarendon Press, 1908.

Srinivasan, C.R. *Kancipuram through the Ages*. Delhi: Agam Kala Prakashan, 1979.

Srivastava, Balram. *Trade and Commerce in Ancient India from the Earliest Times to c. AD 300*. Varanasi: The Chowkhamba Sanskrit Series Office, 1968.

Subramanian, K.S. *Buddhist Remains in South India and Early Andhra History 225 AD to 610 AD*. 1927. Reprint, New Delhi: Cosmo Publications, 1981.

Sufi, G.M.D. *Kashir: Being a History of Kashmir from the Earliest Times to Our Own*. 1948–9. Reprint, Lucknow: Light and Life Publishers, 1974.

Thich Nhat Hanh. *Old Path White Clouds*. 1991. Reprint, New Delhi: Full Circle, 1998.

Upadhyaya, Jagannath. 'Sramana Vidya'. In *Sramana Vidya: A Collection of Twenty-three Articles [in Hindi]*. Volume 2. Edited by R.S. Tripathi. Varanasi: Central Institute of Higher Tibetan Studies, 1988.

Vasubandhu. *Abhidharmakosabhasyam Volume 1*. Translated by Louis de la Vallee Poussin and Leo M. Pruden. Berkeley: Asian Humanities Press, 1991.

———. *Karmasiddhiprakarana: The Treatise on Action*. Translated by Etienne Lamotte. English translation by Leo M. Pruden. Berkeley: Asian Humanities Press, 1988.

Victor Cunrui Xiong. *Sui-Tang Chang'an: A Study in the Urban History of Medieval China*. Ann Arbor: Center for Chinese Studies, University of Michigan, 2000.

Waley, Arthur. *The Real Tripitaka and Other Pieces*. London: George Allen and Unwin, 1952.

Watters, Thomas. *On Yuan Chwang's Travels in India*. 1904–5. Reprint, Delhi: Munshiram Manoharlal Publishers Pvt. Ltd, 1973.

Wriggins, Sally Hovey. *Xuanzang: Buddhist Pilgrim on the Silk Road*. Boulder: WestviewPress, 1996.

Wright, Arthur F. *Buddhism in Chinese History*. Stanford: Stanford University Press, 1985.

Index

Abhidharmakosa, 21, 167, 189, 192, 236, 358
Achaemenian empire of Persia, Achaemenians, 129, 347–48
Afghanistan, 161–62, 354–56; civil war, 137; Taliban regime, 405–28; United Nations' action, 402–3, 405–6, 413–17, 421–22, 429
Ajanta caves, Aurangabad, 316, 325–27
Ajatasatru, 281, 283
Aksu, 84–87, 92
Alexander the Great, 101, 129–30, 192–93, 343, 348, 350, 377–78, 388
Al-Khakim-at-Termezi, 160–1
Allahabad, 223, 228, 231, 244
Amaravati, 314–16
Ambhi, *see* Omphis
Amu Darya (Oxus), 130, 136, 137, 159, 160–2, 162, 164, 219, 411
Ananda, 237, 264
Andhaka school, 316
anuttara Bodhi (Perfect Wisdom), 284
Anxi, 40–41, 46, 47, 50
Arhat(s), 175, 274
Asangha, 11, 12, 21, 237, 240, 245, 354; *see also* Vasubandhu
Ashoka, emperor, 73, 167, 175, 189, 213, 215, 238, 253–54, 256–57, 262, 264, 273–74, 281, 290, 309–10, 314, 316–17, 348, 349–50, 361, 370, 372, 373
Asita, the rishi, 250
Assam, *see* Kamrupa
Avadh (Ayodhya), 235–37, 238–40, 244; Muslims' influence, 241–42
Avalokiteshvara Buddha, 18, 275, 278, 315
Avesta, 146

Bactria, 129, 159, 348, 350
Bai, king of Kucha, 70
Bairat, 209–10, 213, 214, 216
Bakror village, 287–88
Bala Hisar, 354, 362
Bamiyan Buddhas, 163, 381, 388
Banaras, 199, 268–70, 271
Basesvara Mahadeva Temple, 203
Bedel Pass, 84, 86, 92, 110, 190
Bhagu, 233
Bharoch, 329
Bhaskaravarman, king of Kamrupa, 292–95, 298, 308
Bhubaneswar, Orissa, 304, 310, 312
Bimbisara, king, 280–83
Binaket, 143–44, 146
Bindusara, 350
Binyang caves, 19
Bishkek, 89, 94, 97, 98–106, 119–130, 133

Bodh Gaya, 265, 271, 273, 275, 284–85
Bodhi tree, 284, 317
Bodhiruci, Indian monk, 11
Bodhisattvas, 250, 254, 275, 361
Brahmaputra, 296, 299
Brahmins, Brahmanism, 199, 240, 272
Buddha, 14–15, 78–79, 205–7, 219–20, 232–33, 235–38, 244, 246–49, 253–54, 255–58, 261–62, 265–67, 280–5, 326–27, 357–59, 369–70
Buddhism, Buddhist(s), 16–18, 57–58, 172–73, 198, 236–38, 306–8, 316–17; doctrines, 4, 107; monasteries, temples, 11, 22, 65, 72–73, 151, 238, 318; scriptures and texts, 21, 73, 213, 316–17

Ceylon, *see* Sri Lanka
Chach, *see* Tashkent
Chakdara, 366
Chandragupta Maurya, 274, 350
Chang An (Xian), 3–4, 14, 20, 22, 23–24, 28, 29, 30, 31, 34, 38, 40, 43, 46, 57, 59, 65, 77, 96, 102, 129, 292
Charitra, *see* Manikpattan
Charsadda, *see* Pushkalavati
Chau-hu-li monastery, 71
Chen River, 10, 13
Chenab River, 187, 346
Chengdu, 21
Chilka Lake, Orissa, 307, 311–12
Chinachket, *see* Chinoz
Chinapati, 189
Ching-Sung, 21
Chinoz (Chinachket), 142
Chuy River valley, 101, 105–6
Confucian, 16
consciousness, 21, 197, 237–38
conversions to Buddhism, 73; to Islam, 172
Cunda, 261

Dalai Lama, 196
Dasasilam (ten precepts), 103
The Destruction of Heresy, 308
Dhameka stupa, 266–67
dhamma, 246
Dhanakataka, 313–15, 318
Dharamsala, 195
Dharmarajika, 349
Diamond Sutra, 11
Diamond Throne, 290–91
Dunhuang, 58, 66
Durlabhavardhana, king of Kashmir, 167

emptiness (sunyata), 4, 16, 198, 238
Enlightenment, 22, 247, 265, 288–89, 291

Fa Xian, 23, 25, 276, 303, 323
Fen River, 20
Feng Xian cave, 20
fire worship, sacrifice, 66, 106, 108, 152, 159, 206

Gandhara, 164, 187, 219, 342, 343, 347, 350, 354–55, 362
Ganga River, 3, 136, 203, 221, 223, 224–25, 228, 246, 265, 268–69, 271, 273, 291
Gansu province, 34–35, 46
Gaochang, 54–58, 62, 71, 92, 102, 103, 144, 355, 363
Gaya, see Bodh Gaya
Ghor Khattri, 359
Ghositarama Monastery, Kausambi, 232–33
Girnar Hill, 332–33
Great Vehicle, see Mahayana
Great Wall, 29, 32, 39
Gridhrakuta (Vulture's Peak), 282–83
Guanyin, the Buddhist Goddess of Mercy, 18–19, 49, 92, 315

Hadda, 399–401
Hami, 41
Han dynasty, Hans, 23, 29, 56, 71, 79, 81
Han Mingdi, emperor, 16
haoma cult, 145, 152; see also fire worship
Harshavardhana, king, 220–1, 223, 229, 277, 293, 307–8, 324
Harwan, 176–77
Himalayas, 7, 202–3, 246
Hinayana school of Buddhism, 220, 232, 237, 251, 258, 259, 265, 267, 293, 306, 307–8, 312, 316, 361
Hindu(s), Hinduism, 172, 199, 215, 218, 220, 224, 228, 232, 238, 241–43, 266, 294, 312, 318–19, 329–30, 334, 343
Hindu Kush Mountains, 129, 131, 164, 348, 395, 411
Hui Li, 10, 20, 22, 23, 33, 62–64, 67, 70–1, 74–75, 96, 100, 103, 111, 147–48, 151–52, 167, 195, 232, 244, 245–47, 276, 290, 308–9, 324, 361, 363
Huns (Huna), 187, 206, 207, 221, 233, 369
Hunza Valley, 164
Hushkara, 164, 168, 173
Huvishka, Kushan king, 168

I-Gu, 45, 53–54
Indus River, 131, 164, 193, 342, 348, 350, 353, 377–79
Iran, Iranians, 101, 107, 173, 343
Islam, 48, 57–58, 77, 99, 133, 152, 160, 172–73, 218, 388, 397
Islamabad, 335–341, 342, 346, 350–353
Jainism, Jains, 228, 267, 317–18
Jalalabad, 348, 395, 402, 406
Jalandhar, Punjab, 189, 191–94, 195, 348
Jataka Nidankatha, 257
Jatakas, 78, 326

Jeta, prince, 246
Jhelum River, 164, 193, 346, 348

Kabul, 131, 348, 362
Kaccapesvara Temple, 320–1
Kalinga, 303, 307, 310, 312, 316, 349
Kamakshi Temple, Kanchipuram, 319–20
Kamrupa (Assam), 291–99, 308
Kanauj, see Kanyakubja
Kanchipuram, 318–22
Kang, see Samarkand
Kangra, 191–94
Kanishka, 159, 175, 177, 189, 219, 220, 343, 355, 357, 360, 388
Kanka, 142–43
Kanyakubja (Kanauj), 190, 220–1, 223
Kapilavastu, 249–54, 255–56, 280
Kapisa, 345, 350, 354–55, 379
Karakoram range, 155, 370
karma, 199, 238
Kashgar, 58, 87–88, 93, 176, 359, 411
Kashka Darya (Kashka River), 154–55
Kashmir, 166–86, 345, 347
Kasyapiya school, 379
Kausambi, 231–33, 245
Kayama, 309
Kesh, 142, 153–55
Khadipada, 305
Khanabad (Nujkend), 141
Khas Khan dynasty, 58
Khavast, Uzbekistan, 146–47
Khyber Pass, 387, 389, 390
Kimriya (Kelua River), 309
Kizil caves, 76–79
Konkanapura, 323
Kosal, 246
Krishna River, 314–15
Kucha, 67, 68–71, 73–80, 84–85, 350
Kullu (Kuluta), 195, 202–3, 205
Kumaragupta (AD 413–55), 277
Kumarajiva (AD 344–413), 17
Kunala, 73, 350
Kushans, 158, 161, 175, 177, 189, 206–7, 309, 343, 345, 354, 355, 357, 377; see also Kanishka
Kushinagar, 261–64, 281
Kusumapura, 273
Kwa-chow, see Suoyang Cheng
Kyrgyzstan, 60, 98–100, 110, 143, 364

Lahaul Valley, 203
Lahore, 342
Languripahar, 306
Lanjadibba, 314
Lankavatara Sutra, 11
Lavani, see Lumbini
Li Daliang, governor of Liangzhou, 37
Li Yuan, duke of Tang, 20
Liang dynasty (AD 502–549), 12
Liangzhou, see Wuwei
Little Vehicle, see Hinayana

Lotus Sutra, 18
Lumbini (Lavani), 199, 256–57, 285
Lung-Tuk'ichi, king of 'O-ki-ni, 65
Luo River, 16
Luoshi Temple, 34–35
Luoyang, 10–2, 16, 19

Madhyamika school of thought, 189
Magadha, 265, 271, 278, 280–81, 292
Maha Vibhasha, 220
Mahabodhi Monastery, 22
Mahabodhi Temple, Bihar, 288, 290
Mahaparinirvana Stupa, 264
Maharashtra, 291, 323, 324, 329
Mahasanghika school, 313
Mahayana school of Buddhism, 12, 18, 197,
    220, 237, 259, 267, 277, 283, 306–8, 314,
    318, 320, 345
Maha Kumbh Mela, 225–230
Maitreya, 237, 245, 278, 412
Malwa (Malava), 329
Manikpattan (Charitra), 311–12
Manjusri Buddha, 278
Marco Polo, 114
Mathura, 177, 186, 207, 209–10, 214–20
Matsyadesa, 231
Mauryan(s), 213, 273–74, 309, 314, 348, 350
Maya, queen, 207, 256–58
Middle Way, 78
Mihirakula, 187, 206
Ming dynasty, 31
Mingora, 368–69
Mithras, Zoroastrian god, 219
Mokshagupta, 70, 74–75, 167
Mongolia, Mongolians, 29, 101
Mothadaka, 315
Mughal dynasty, Mughals, 131, 180, 378
Muslims, Muslim invaders, 160–1, 241–43

Nagarahara, 394–95
Nagardhana Monastery, 189
Nagarjuna, 177, 219, 310
Nagasena, 362
Nairanjana River, 288
Nalanda, Nalanda University, 271–72, 275–
    80, 291–93, 301, 307–8, 323
Narmada River, 329
Navarikat, 105
Neulpur, 309
Nirvana, 78, 262, 284
Northern Wei dynasty (AD 500-553), 19
Nyaya-anusara Shastra, 167

'O-ki-ni (Yanqi), 60, 61–65, 67
Omphis (Ambhi), ruler of Taxila, 348
Orissa (Ucha, Udra), 291, 304–5, 308, 311,
    334
O-she-li-ni temple, 74

Pakistan, 219, 346
Pamirs, 155, 367, 411

panchvarsha, 73
Panini, 378
Paramartha, an Indian Brahmin, 12, 21
Parasuramesvara Temple, 305
Pataligrama, 265
Pataliputra (Patna), 271–73, 275, 280–1, 284,
    310, 350
Persepolis, 101, 129, 348
Persia, 135, 177, 359
Peshawar, 219, 342, 346, 354–56, 358, 365,
    373, 376–77
Pih-li, 54
Pipal Mandi, Peshawar, 359
Poonch (Punach), Kashmir, 180, 184–85
Porus, ruler of Punjab, 193, 348
Prajnagupta, 307–8
Prajnaparamita Sutra, 197, 283, 412
Prakarana-pada-vibasha-Shastra, 192
Prasenajita, 246–47
Prayag, 223
Punjab, 187, 189, 191–92, 209, 350, 362
Pushkalavati, 360, 362, 365, 317, 372
Pushpagiri, 304, 306, 308, 310–11

Qadam, 369
Qilian Mountains, 31, 35, 38, 39
Qing dynasty, 31
Qu Wentai, king of Gaochang, 54, 56, 57,
    59–61

Rahula, 215, 250, 254, 326
Rajgir (Rajagriha), 272, 279–81
Rajouri (Rajapuri), 180, 182, 184, 187
Ramabhar stupa, 264
Ratnagiri, 306

Sakala, 187
Sakya Buddha, Sakyamuni, 57, 175, 251, 253,
    255, 361
Samarkand, Kang, 71, 108, 130, 142, 147–55
Sammatiya school, 265
Sangam, 227–228
Sanghol, 206–7
Sariska, 214
Sarnath, 266–67
Sarvastivadin school, 236
Sassanian dynasty, 25, 145, 177
Satadru, 205–6
Saurashtra, 329–30
Sautantrika school, 236
Scythians, 175, 240, 377
Shaikhan Dheri, 362–63
Shahristan, 146
Shahbaz Garhi, 372, 373
Shah Ji Ki Dheri, 356
shalabhanjikas, 207, 369
shamanist tradition, shamanists, 18, 107
Shahrisabz, 151, 153–56, 359
Sichuan, the kingdom of Shuh, 294, 299
Siddhartha, 250, 280, 285–89
Silabhadra, 5, 291, 292–93, 307, 323, 277–79

Silk Road, 29, 61, 88, 90, 94, 100, 108, 129,
    136, 143
Sirhind, 205-6
Sogdians, Sogdiana, 105, 107-8, 129-30, 135-
    36, 144, 343
Song dynasty, 31
Sravasti, 245-46, 248-49
Sri Lanka (Ceylon), 303, 307, 311-12, 317,
    322, 323
Sthivara school, 322
Su Bashi, 71-72
Su-yeh, 96, 100, 104-6, 110
Subbarayamudhali school, 320
Suddhodana, king, 250, 253
Sui dynasty, 11, 20, 24, 31
Sumeru Mount, 245
Sumsumaragiri, 237
Suoyang Cheng (Kwa-chow), 39, 41, 42
Surkhan Darya, 132, 136-37, 157, 159
Sutlej River, 205, 207
Swat Valley, 363-65, 369-70
Syr Darya (Jaxartes), 130, 134, 135, 136,
    142-44, 146, 159

Taizong, Tang emperor, 1, 22, 29, 65
Takht-i-Bai, 364
Tamga, 144
Tamluk (Tamralipta), 291, 301-3
Tamralipta, see Tamluk
Tang dynasty, 1, 14, 22, 24, 28, 30, 31, 41,
    43, 46, 50, 65, 119, 129, 219
Tantrayana, Tantra, 305, 308
Taoist tradition, 18, 22
Tashkent (Chach), 135, 136, 141-42, 143
Tathagata, 232, 262, 268
Taxila, 246, 343, 345-50, 364, 372, 376, 378
Termez, Uzbekistan, 132, 142, 158, 160-1
Theravada, 258, 307, 322
Tian Shan, 64, 66, 69, 72, 73, 84, 101, 114
Tiananmen Square, 79
Tibetans, 195-97, 199-201, 260, 286, 290
Tigris River, 348
Tokharistan, 156-57
To-Kiu, governor of Kwa-chow, 39-40
Tokmak, 100, 106
Tormana, 206, 233
Tripitaka, 189, 279, 313, 322, 379
Tsing-tu Monastery, 19
Turfan, 55, 56, 58, 61, 77
Turkestan, 46, 142, 147
Turks, 29, 65, 71, 84, 100-8, 127, 136

Udaigiri, 306
Udyana, 232, 233, 363, 368, 379
Udra, see Orissa
Ujjanta, 329, 332
ulemas, 172, 420
Undavalli, 315
ushnisha, 44
Uruvela, 287
Ustrushana, 142, 143, 146-7
Uzbekistan, 131-9, 142, 154, 157, 162

Vaisali, 199, 271, 317
Vajragiri, 309
Vasubandhu, 11, 12, 21, 167, 228-29, 236-
    37, 240, 354, 358
Vijayawada, 315
Vinaya Pitaka, 246
vipassana, 256, 258
Virat, king of Matsyadesa, 213
Viratnagar, 213
Viryasena, 220
Visvantara, 372

White Horse Temple, 16
Wu, emperor, Liang dynasty (AD 502-549), 12
Wuwei (Liangzhou), 31-33, 37, 43

Xian, see Chang An
Xuanzang, born, 1, 10, 11; childhood, 11-12,
    16; parents, 13-14; religious conference,
    37; returned to China from India, 3, 6, 22

Yamuna River, 203, 214-15, 218, 223, 228, 233
Yang Di, last Sui emperor, 11, 20
Yanqi, see 'O-ki-ni
Yarkand, 176-77
Yasht, 145
Yeh Hu, Khan of Turks, 60, 100-3, 105, 108-9
Yellow River, 10, 23, 31
Yogacara school, 11-12, 21, 74, 189, 354
Yogacarabhumi Shastra, 21, 23, 245, 279
Yoga Shastra, 74-75, 278, 322
Yuh-men, Jade Gate, 46, 48
Yuan dynasty, 31
Yung-ning Monastery, 11

Zarathustra, 331
Zerafshan River, 130, 142, 153
Zhang Liang, Han adviser, 23
Zoroastrianism, 66, 108, 135, 145, 219, 330,
    348

It doesn't have to be

Like This

It doesn't have to be

Like This

Global economics: a new way forward

Margaret Legum

WILD GOOSE PUBLICATIONS

Contents

Foreword by Andrea Westall   7

Introduction   11

CHAPTER 1
Old Economics: what went wrong?   17

Myths of globalisation - one   56
Myths of globalisation - two   58

CHAPTER 2
The dearth of purchasing power   59

Myths of globalisation - three   80
Myths of globalisation - four   82
Myths of globalisation - five   84

CHAPTER 3
Alternative sources of government revenue   85

Myths of globalisation - six   112
Myths of globalisation - seven   114
Myths of globalisation - eight   115

CHAPTER 4
Taming the tiger: bringing capital down to earth   117

Myths of globalisation - nine   139
Myths of globalisation - ten   140

CHAPTER 5
Localising globally   141

Myths of globalisation - eleven   171
Myths of globalisation - twelve   173
Myths of globalisation - thirteen   174

Story of a kibbutz   175

CHAPTER 6
The road to New Economics   177

Myths of globalisation - fourteen   208
Myths of globalisation - fifteen   210
Myths of globalisation - sixteen   211

CHAPTER 7
The heart and soul of economics   213

Myths of globalisation - seventeen   222

Bibliography   225

Explanation of acronyms   231

Foreword

For too long politicians, media commentators and all the people who chat away in pubs and shops, have recognised inequalities in the world and the impacts of a global economic system that seems too hard to understand and under no one's control. Political thinkers have bemoaned the loss of policy control with increased globalisation as though there is no option but to do the best you can.

But, as Margaret Legum says, 'it doesn't have to be like this'. Perhaps there is no inevitability about current ways of doing things. Perhaps there really are ways of making the economic system create the kind of world that most people, when they really stop to think about it, would like to see.

This book has done something very special. With passion and clarity Margaret Legum has succeeded in cutting through the complexities and presenting a compelling picture of an economic and financial system that is not working. At the same time she has set out some very practical examples of what could be changed and how.

But this is not an anti-capitalist book. Far from it. Markets can work well but they have their place and are sometimes inappropriate or need to be channelled. In fact, one of the most startling wake-up calls in this book is the recognition of how the money market, supposedly there to grease the wheels of productive investment in goods and services, has in fact sucked money away from real economic activity and creates virtually nothing. It also takes opportunities away from areas and from people that are the most in need of generating their own livelihoods. This means that the mantra of foreign direct investment as a means of development is meaningless if that money just leaves again in profits or with the vagaries of speculation. It is even more useless if, at the same time, available investment from inside the country goes in search of higher returns elsewhere rather than being ploughed back to generate more jobs and growth.

Struggling local economies in Britain and other parts of the world suffer from precisely that same loss of money and resources that prevent them from creating enterprises and jobs that meet the needs of local people. Or think of the waste that is generated as the UK exports just as much milk as it imports, with all the impacts on the environment from excessive use of transport. These are not arguments for protectionism but for encouraging markets to work at the right level to create viable communities across a country and to minimise environmental impacts.

The New Economics Foundation is a sister organisation to South African New Economics (SANE) and both exist to raise awareness of these kinds of issues and to try to create change. Every part of this book, whilst written primarily for a South African audience, also has much resonance for the UK and elsewhere. Ultimately, new economics is itself quite simple – it is about putting people and the environment first. If you see economics as a tool rather than an end in itself, then you reconnect it with values and with real choices about how things can be different.

When you read this book, you will come away inspired to think more about what is happening and how it might alter. To realise that we are financing the US debt and its standards of living or that we tax all the productive things in life but don't touch the activities that make things worse, makes you understand how fundamental some of the changes will need to be. But you will also see how easy it is to change elements of the way we live our own lives. You don't have to be like this either.

Andrea Westall
Acting Director
New Economics Foundation
August 2003

It doe$n't have to be

£ike Thi$

Introduction

This book is based upon a set of lectures given at the Summer School of the University of Cape Town in January 2001. They were prompted by the growing understanding that South Africa, in common with most of the rest of the world, is suffering an economic decline not of its own making. Our famous political 'miracle' is in danger of being undermined by our dependence on world economic factors over which we have little or no control. In other words, we South Africans cannot determine our own economic policies unless we understand the global free market and take steps to protect ourselves from its toxic effects.

That understanding, and those steps, are internationally relevant. Although the immediate audience for the lectures was South African, the book addresses the problems of people everywhere, because we are all victims of the current global ideology. It contains an exposition of the damage being done worldwide; and also ideas about how we can change the management of national and international economies. Many of these ideas are new, although many are being researched in Britain and elsewhere; all arise from the need to define a post-global vision of development. They are not about returning to the communist-versus-capitalist arguments of the past. They are firmly seated within the principles of the free market as a means of pricing goods and services; but they draw upon new processes for pricing and regulation; and they redefine the role of government.

The lectures, and this book, are designed to interest people with no expertise in the discipline of economics, but who want an understanding of economic issues – if only to cast an intelligent vote. As an economist I am convinced that economics is as accessible to non-experts as any other discipline. Physicists whose work affects the rest of us are expected to explain what they are doing in terms we can understand – even though their conversations with each other may seem to us gobbledegook. The same is true for engineers and doctors and biologists. But economists have been notorious for obfuscating issues that are essential for people to grasp.

One purpose of the lectures was therefore to convey the idea that anyone who is reasonably intelligent can understand economics; and to encourage the layperson confidently to query the conclusions economists mysteriously arrive at on their own. In doing this, economists who question the current ideologies have been accused of oversimplifying great matters, even of not quite understanding what they are talking about. They advise us to leave it to 'the experts'. That is like handing over our votes to them, for without an understanding of economic issues, voting is unintelligent. What should we vote on, if not how the government is managing the relationship of people to each other in terms of work, the allocation of resources and the effects on our planet of the way we use the environment?

But there was another reason for presenting these lectures. In common with most people that I know, I am outraged by the effects of the current economic system. Those effects are particularly dire in Africa. It is as if traditional economics and economists are disconnected from the real world – as though they do not know the effects of their theories on real human beings. They seem to have missed the fact that even people who mistakenly think the present system is inevitable and positive in some ways are unhappy about its effects – appalling poverty in the midst of unbelievable wealth and potential plenty for everyone; the degradation of the planet on which our survival depends; and the vast international rise in crime and conflict and cruel suffering.

It has been said that there is nothing so practical as a good theory. When things fall apart we have to ask ourselves whether our theory is consistent with the facts – whether our theory is producing the results we expect from it.

Considering the state of the world – its people and the planet itself – the answer must surely be that it is not. The question is, can it be changed? The answer given by the New Economics movement is yes. We can produce new theory which is consistent with the ethical objectives which, at heart, all human beings espouse and expect – the right to prosperity and security for everyone, fairness in distribution of wealth, a stake for everyone in the economy to which they belong, communities that work for their members. If these things are being undermined by the present dispensation, we are basing it on the wrong theory.

As a South African addressing a South African audience, I felt the aim of the lectures was to influence the political agenda here. But it is not possible to discuss any economy except in the context of the world economic system. The rest of Africa, and indeed the whole of the developing world, and the millions of poor people in rich countries, are closely involved in the analysis given here. My own hope, along with that of millions of others, is that South Africa will join with the rest of the continent in moving to a new dispensation that has the potential to make a reality of the African Renaissance *within a post-global economic dispensation for the world.*

In the past year or two we have experienced the events of September 11 in New York and the American government's strong-arm response against a generalised enemy called 'terrorism'. It has shown virtually no sensitivity to the factors that create the anger behind terrorism, many of which lie in the economic system.

And we have also experienced the World Summit on Sustainable Development held in our own country. There will be no going back from that event. For the first time the opponents of the enforced globalisation of capital and trade received as much or more sympathetic attention from the public and the media as its proponents. For the first time the divide has been not between

North and South, but between those who accept the *status quo*, and those who want it superseded. New Economics now has the ear of the world in expounding viable, sustainable and compassionate alternatives — rooted in the real lives of real people in the real world. This book is about those alternatives.

Margaret Legum

CHAPTER ONE

Old Economics: what went wrong?

At Cambridge University, the story did the rounds about an economics student who discovered that each year the exam papers asked the same questions. She challenged her tutor: 'Don't you know that we have access to old papers?' The lecturer answered: 'Don't you know that in economics the questions are always the same? It's the answers that change.'

Economics is about how people relate to each other around resources and work. Essentially it is about the needs of people in relation to those things. If the system doesn't serve people, we can change it. Economics is not about the logic of a system: it is about people and how they are being served by whatever system we are using. The point needs making not because it is easy to design economic systems that meet the needs of people, but because discussion of economics in recent years has been bedevilled by the carefully fostered idea that what is happening now is inevitable. The term 'There Is No Alternative' (TINA) entered the vocabulary of economists, politicians and the media during the era of Thatcher and Reagan, and succeeded in truncating discussion of alternatives.

According to TINA the 'fathers' of economics like John Stuart Mill and his colleagues laid down some immutable laws which, whether we like it or not, determine how the world of goods and services, money and people interact. That is not so. Mill and his successors described their work as 'political economy', and very much part of an ethical system in the service of humanity. In other words, economics was thought of as a branch of moral science. Students of economics up to the middle years of the 20th century thought of the subject as a branch, and a servant, of politics and the welfare of people. The aberration was TINA. Thatcherite economics took over from politics in deciding how people should live.

Post-modern New Economics is returning to the idea that economics is a human science and a servant of humanity's development. The South African economists Heather Couzyn and Ronnie Lessem are building on the principles of natural science to produce a book called *Principles of Natural Economics: Economics for an Evolving Planet.* They quote leading biologists to show that 'not competition but cooperation between molecules, genes, cells and organisms is what makes life possible … Life did not take over the globe by combat but by networking.'

This is especially relevant to the steady deterioration of our planet's capacity to sustain human life – and how that is affected by the fact that the present system is rooted explicitly and exclusively in competition between people, communities and nations.

This book examines the modern alternatives being researched and advocated worldwide. There is a focus on South Africa, as part of the continent of Africa, because that is where I live. But because we live in a world economy that has deliberately been closely interlinked, neither analysis nor solutions can be effective unless considered in the world context. However Africa wants to decide its economic future it cannot ignore the present system. Solutions are not in its hands alone. It is the contention of this book that the current world system is largely toxic for Africa in particular; and can be changed. But because we are all connected in economic terms, that change involves analysing the world situation as well as local dynamics. This chapter in particular examines what has gone wrong in the world system of economics.

By the end of the 1950s it seemed to many of us that the economist John Maynard Keynes had made the kind of theoretical – and hence practical – breakthrough that would enable politicians to control economic relationships in order to effect the various political purposes for which they were elected. It was thought that Keynes had shown us how to achieve a stable macro-economic framework for the production of goods and services within which we could make decisions about distribution of wealth. So people who were essentially interested in social justice threw their weight into the political arena where values and ends were being discussed – in the confidence that the economic means were available to effect the political ends chosen by the electorate. Economics was seen as value-based, not value-free.

It was only the radical conservatism of Thatcher that brought human helplessness into the picture. Her ideology was based on the premise that the only economic system that works is one in which all people on the planet must compete with all others to produce and sell goods and services. Faced with the result of her policies in Britain – a decimated industrial base; grossly inflated incomes for some and deepening poverty for others; new levels of long-term unemployment, homelessness and crime; a rise in the rate of bankruptcies, home repossessions, family breakdown, TB and infant mortality – faced in other words with the evidence that her policies had left British people less and not more happy and prosperous, Thatcher and her supporters claimed that humanity is in fact the inevitable victim of economic laws deriving from the 'unforgiving markets'.

Her medicine, she implied, was essential for future economic health in conditions over which politicians had little control – the extension to the entire globe of competitive economic activity. The process that Thatcher put the British people through, followed in other parts of Europe, was what later became known as Structural Adjustment when it was applied by the World Bank/IMF nexus to all developing countries as well.

Of course, Thatcherism did not arise in a vacuum. British industry had become complacent, introverted and inefficient by comparison with its rivals in Europe, the United States and Japan. Why this happened will be debated over time. I tend to the theory that the linked psychological issues of profoundly entrenched classism and the need to accept the end of Empire demoralised the British people, and produced a culture of internal blaming and internecine struggle that allowed foreign competitors to overtake the British almost unnoticed.

Generally, the European and Japanese management systems that gave employees a voice in policy-making had always been seen by the British middle and upper classes − consciously or not − as giving away management power to inferiors; while trade union attitudes to management were therefore implacably suspicious and hostile. This struggle undermined the kind of co-operation that other nations adopted as a *sine qua non* for successful industry. One 'side' saw itself as the only one capable of ideas, planning and control; the other as inevitable victims unless they were constantly engaged in a class struggle. British − especially English − classism has as profoundly destructive an effect on the way people see each other as racism in South Africa.

Thatcher saw her prescriptions as essential to shake up both sides of industry, but especially to limit the power of the trade unions by giving advantage to capital. No doubt that would have produced some effects on the balance of power within industry. But there were other deeper factors at work that together led to the world's plunge into a globalised market, forcing all nations to compete in the same market place, and savagely punishing the failures.

Keynesian theory had shown itself inadequate, especially in dealing with two unexpected factors: the sudden traumatic rise in the international price of oil in 1973; and the exponential rate of technological advance − the electronic revolution. Together they created the condition of 'stagflation' − unemployment and inflation at the same time: a circumstance for which Keynesian theory had no ready answer.

The first of these might have been digested in time. But the second – the electronic revolution – means that, unlike during the first Industrial Revolution, machines now inevitably lose more jobs than they create. The illusion that full employment will return, that the current situation is a function of the transition to full globalisation, is simply that – an illusion. Much of this chapter will demonstrate that fact, including dealing with the false idea that the American economy works well and proves it can be done.

Worldwide, when modern technology sheds employment, it creates fewer jobs, and the great majority of those are low-paid, casualised and insecure. That means, in turn, a fall in effective purchasing power. Machines don't go shopping, while at the same time they produce a lot of goods and services. More and more people, being redundant from their previous work, have to take work for lower pay and longer hours in order to stay employed at all. The fact is that purchasing power – that is, people's ability to spend as a result of their work – relative to potential output has fallen steadily. It reached a point where new thinking was needed, since the Keynesian theory seemed to have failed.

There was another factor: the American trade deficit. From the 1970s the US began to buy far more than it sold because it was not competitive with the low-wage economies of emerging markets. Its high living standards would have had to be drastically reduced to bring it back into balance. It would have needed a structural adjustment, along the lines of that which took place in Britain, to make it globally competitive. Indeed, had it been a poor country seeking international finance, it would have been forced so to do. Instead, being powerful enough to make its own policy, it chose to finance its debt by borrowing indefinitely from the rest of the world. By the end of 2002, America was borrowing $4 billion a day. That is, every day $4 billion of other countries' savings financed the American debt.

But that was possible only if the world's capital markets were opened – if savings were available globally. The US could not have had access to European, Asian and African savings if their governments controlled their capital markets. Thatcher's Britain came to the rescue. It facilitated the creation of a Eurodollar market, in which European banks were persuaded to hold low-interest dollars. This, together with OPEC's decision to sell oil in dollars only, led to the 'dollarisation' of world currency markets with the result that all countries now needed to hold reserves in dollars. In effect the dollar, which had been artificially strengthened, became a latter-day gold standard.

For a detailed account of how this happened, and its effects today, see *The US as a highly indebted prosperous country* by Ann Pettifor and Romilly Greenhill, published by the New Economics Foundation in London. (See www.jubileeplus.org)

There were a number of paths the world could have taken when Keynesian theory did not provide all the answers. Not surprisingly the new thinking that prevailed reflected the interests of the people currently running the show. The obvious fact was that business needed new markets, as national markets shrank. These, it was thought, could be found in an unregulated competitive global market, in which the already technologically advanced large markets and politically powerful governments would clearly have massive advantage. But what began as a way for developed countries to maintain their living standards through continued growth came to be seen as good for everyone. In effect a new ideology was created.

This declared that the whole world is necessarily one global market, in which all countries and regions and all producers of all goods and services must compete, thus giving consumers the best deal worldwide. This idea, and its outworking, became known as the Washington Consensus. The international competitive market was put forward as the engine for spreading trade, capital and prosperity from the developed North to the poorer South. The inefficiencies of the command economies of the Soviet block gave some support to that theory.

The Washington Consensus colonised the policies and practices of the international financial institutions including the World Bank and the IMF, as well as forming the basis of government policies in the US, Europe, Japan and the Pacific Rim. Helped by the fall of the Soviet empire, the designers of this new ideology fell for an illusion as old as humanity – that the forces of history, fickle as they sometimes seem, were at last demonstrating alignment with themselves. This had the advantage of freeing them from the accusation that the new ideology was a cover for the promotion of their own interests. If there was no alternative, there was no shame in profiting from it.

Ironically the most recent previous proponents of this illusion had been the Marxists of the twentieth century. Their demise provoked a triumphalism in the Conservative West that found its apogee in *The end of history*, by the Japanese-American economist Francis Fukuyama. (Now repentant, he predicts in his new book, *Our post-human future: consequences of the biotechnology revolution*, the de-stabilisation of human society through unregulated technological revolutions.)

It could be said, of course, that the relative prosperity of the rich countries of the North demonstrates the correctness of the Washington Consensus theory. Britain and other European countries that adopted Adjustment measures came out of the recession of the '80s earlier than countries that did not. They became 'leaner and fitter' and so more competitive. In fact, of course, what it proved was that the system suited them – in that it allowed their more technically advanced economies a massive advantage over less developed countries. The rest of the world became available as markets for them, and were unable or less prepared to compete in the markets of the rich.

Even so, it must be remembered that poverty on a significant scale has returned to these rich European countries. In these countries one in six children – 47 million – live below the poverty line. Who would have thought that

TB and rickets would be found once again in the economically deprived areas of Britain? Between 1979 and 1997 (the Conservative years) the percentage of British children living in poverty rose from 9% to 25% – from 5 million to 14.3 million. It is true they do not starve, but their mortality rates are significantly higher than those outside that category, and so are rates of addiction, crime and illiteracy. They are also significantly less healthy and less educated.

In the US, the percentage of children in poverty is the highest in the developed world. Americans who work full time without being able to support a family in decent health now constitute a new official category – 'the working poor' – their number increasing annually. Many Americans have to find more than one job to reach previous income levels. Only thirty years ago it was the norm for most families in developed countries to be supported by one breadwinner, while the other cared for children. Now it is nearly impossible – not because people are greedier, but because one working or middle-class income will not pay basic bills.

Nor can we comfort ourselves with the idea that 'poverty' these days means a lack of a variety of modern luxuries. International research reveals the serious sacrifices – of a healthy varied diet, holidays, social life, birthday presents and reading matter – made by families living on one income. The lowest percentile of poor families in Europe and America go without warm winter clothing, shoes that fit, a health-sustaining diet and access to effective health services. It is an amazing fact that one in seven American children are functionally illiterate and innumerate.

The effect on the rest of the world as a whole has of course been much worse. Between 1960 and 2000 the disparity in income more than tripled. Over 600 million children live on less than $1 a day. Over 80 countries now have per capita incomes lower than they were a decade ago. The biggest decline since 1990 has been in 55 countries, mostly in sub-Saharan Africa,

Eastern Europe and the former Soviet Union. The richest fifth of the world's population accounts for 86% of the income, while the lowest fifth share 1%. The assets of the world's three top billionaires are more than the combined GDP of 600 million people living in poor countries.

The story of Africa is particularly tragic. Between 1960 (when many countries moved to independence) and 1980, sub-Saharan Africa's income per person grew by 36%. Since 1980, when structural adjustment policies started to bite, their income has fallen by 13%. The continent's share of world trade is now only 2%, and for sub-Saharan Africa it is only 1.6%. Without South Africa that figure falls to 1.2%. This is a result of, not despite, a decade or more of ruthless structural adjustment.

Both the investment and the savings rate in Africa have fallen since the late 1970s – the only continent in which that has happened. Immunisation cover has decreased, and major killers such as cholera and malaria are increasing, as is malnutrition. The human consequences are horrifying, as children are sold into prostitution or slavery to keep them alive: this traffic is believed to involve some 30 million children. Child labour and child soldiers are other manifestations of extreme destitution.

All this is happening at a time of a once unimaginable increase in the world's capacity to produce wealth. The worse it gets for people at the bottom, the more galactic become the sums 'earned' by people at the top. As the value of the South African rand plummeted in 2001/2 – creating huge increases in the prices of food and other necessities, and bringing interest rate hikes, our gold industry earnings doubled and even tripled in one quarter. Profit margins widened by 30% to 45%, according to an article in *Business Report* on January 22, 2002.

Let us imagine for a moment an alternative to the unfettered global market. It is not difficult. For a while it filled our imagination. Remember the fifties and sixties when the older among us first grasped the significance of the radiant blossoming of technology? Tiny, silent, clean machines would take over the work, take the grease and sweat out of labour, and produce unimaginable abundance. Not all of us would be needed to operate the machines; so we should divide up that work. Three-day weeks seemed within our grasp. The major challenges would be the distribution of wealth and the use of leisure time: people would have to be educated to be creative and useful when not employed to produce goods and services for sale.

Alternatively, we thought, five-day weeks would continue, but with a decreasing proportion of us operating machines making goods and services. We would transfer some of the surplus created by the machines to employing the rest of us in activities using our humanity to expand a civilised society – teaching, counselling, nurturing, child care, social work, writing, healing, home gardening, painting, thinking, visioning, inventing – which machines don't do.

Put differently, economics would be about distributing the abundant fruits of technology, because production was now assured. For the first time in history, it seemed, economics was not about scarcity, but about distributing jobs and incomes. The dilemma would be how to get purchasing power into the hands of people rendered unemployed by technology – and people living in poor countries, who would have to be enabled to buy the cornucopia of what could be produced.

At first the service sector seemed to be one answer – at least to the employment problem in the production sector; but even there technology sheds jobs hand over fist. So how could we transfer resources from the profit sectors to the public arena? How could we enlarge the human 'commons' – the public spaces, public services and amenities that address community needs? How could we create more of the things that social democrats thought should come to us by virtue of our citizenship and regardless of our income – public education, public health, public transport, the arts, social services and welfare, and security via the police and the defence forces? As we got richer, there would be more surplus for those things, we thought. And that would produce more civilised, more human, more sharing, more artistic societies.

But that focus on distribution of material wealth, and enlargement of the 'commons', was not to be. On the contrary. A visitor from Mars today might assume that our planet had suffered an appalling catastrophe that had destroyed our resources, leaving us in the grip of scarcity – desperately starting from scratch, and therefore focusing above all on labour productivity. The Martian would notice that, far from expanding, public services and the arts had been contracted everywhere. They would be told we could no longer afford them. They would be amazed to find that those of us who have formal employment are forced to work all the hours that God made to increase our productivity. If we don't, we join the growing millions without a regular livelihood. They would notice the millions of people living and dying in absolute poverty – destitute and starving.

So what happened to what we might call the technology dividend so optimistically anticipated in the sixties? The simple answer is that, in the absence of political action for redistribution, the whole of that dividend went into the private sector – above all as a reward for capital, and to bring about the relative cheapening of consumer goods. To be able to compete, all businesses must offer better value to the consumer for less money. The search for price competitiveness in the global market became the major economic driving force, unmitigated by other considerations such as employment, education and health services, and the quality of community life for which governments had in the past legislated.

If a company did not make it in the cheapness stakes, it went under. The world market held and delivered the promise of higher labour productivity in the production of consumer goods – because of vast economies of scale, and huge availability of cheap labour. Distribution of income was assumed to follow with the spread of prosperity – an assumption grossly wide of the mark because the new generation of technology, unlike the earlier mechanical ones, loses more jobs than it creates.

If the current system were to continue to work even for those who benefit by it, two things would have to happen. First, economies would have to continue to expand. There is no such thing as a steady state or plateau of growth: there must be expanding markets. That is because, second, technology must be continuously updated. Machines must replace people. You can be wiped out as an entrepreneur if your competitors employ more modern machines and fewer workers than you do. So, to stay in business, you must 'downsize' in terms of workers and find expanding numbers of buyers to keep your machines at work. You cannot afford to fall behind or to experience shrinking markets.

What that means is the steady enlargement of enterprises. Huge eats big, big eats medium, medium eats small, small eats tiny. Mergers and acquisitions, along with the shedding of labour, at the global multinational level are the inevitable result of the global market. In the past decade these have created much of the 'shareholder value' at the top – despite entailing job losses and often also reduced business. That is the way you survive in global business.

Consider the significance of this process for small business on which we are expected to pin our hopes. The theory is that as technology destroys jobs in large enterprise, small businesses will create new jobs. The South African government, in common with virtually every other, has espoused that idea and embodied it in government institutions to finance small business. One of these is Khula Enterprise Finance, which targets the small, medium and micro-enterprise sector as 'the engine for the eradication of unemployment'. Its 2000 report tabled in Parliament shows losses close to R26m. It attributes this to lack of business and managerial skills as well as corruption. It is true that in the current economy it takes entrepreneurial skill of an exceptional nature to keep afloat. But the sad truth is that small business cannot provide the answer to unemployment: it is too vulnerable, too exposed and too small to compete with medium-sized and large businesses.

Humanity has certainly seen some benefits from these developments, notably wider choice of cheaper consumer goods. There were good reasons to think, simplistically, that global competition could bring to the poor what it had brought to the rich – that there was a natural progression and that wealth would trickle down. Free-enterprise competitive markets certainly do serve consumers better than systems that rely on human decisions at every level – like the command economies under communism. Of course, some elements of human activity have been globalised to very good effect. The spread of knowledge, information and the arts is beneficial everywhere; international travel is a universal ideal. Moreover, some production must be global because of the nature of the product. The car industry, shipbuilding, steel-making, mining and others must compete internationally, because they are on too large a scale to compete nationally. They need a global arena to maintain efficiency.

The same is not true, however, for apples and shoes and textiles and toys and furniture and pet food. All of these have perfectly healthy national or local competitive mechanisms to keep them on their toes. The fact that they may not be internationally competitive must be offset by the fact that they provide employment and incomes.

The Washington Consensus: how it works

In South Africa we achieved our liberation at the height of the reign of the Washington Consensus. The diagram overleaf shows how that model worked, and how it affects all of Africa and other developing countries through the structural adjustment regimes.

Structural adjustment comprises four policy injunctions:

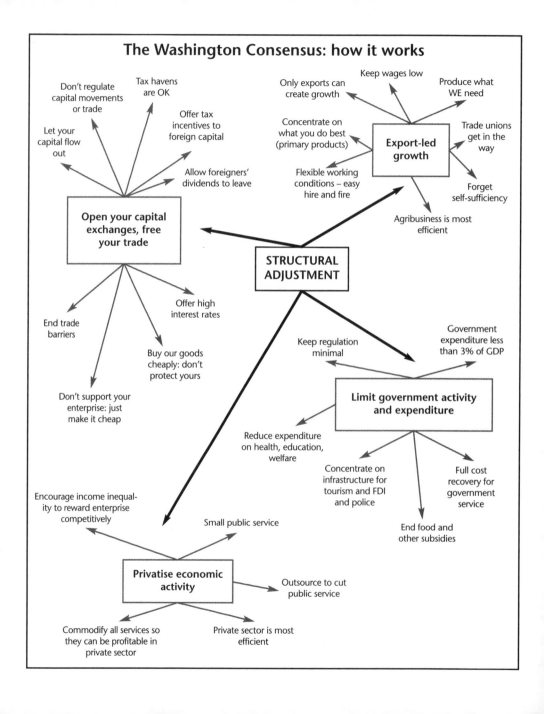

The Washington Consensus: how it works

Open your capital exchanges, free your trade

- Don't regulate capital movements or trade
- Tax havens are OK
- Offer tax incentives to foreign capital
- Let your capital flow out
- Allow foreigners' dividends to leave
- End trade barriers
- Offer high interest rates
- Buy our goods cheaply: don't protect yours
- Don't support your enterprise: just make it cheap

Export-led growth

- Only exports can create growth
- Keep wages low
- Produce what WE need
- Concentrate on what you do best (primary products)
- Trade unions get in the way
- Flexible working conditions – easy hire and fire
- Forget self-sufficiency
- Agribusiness is most efficient

STRUCTURAL ADJUSTMENT

Limit government activity and expenditure

- Keep regulation minimal
- Government expenditure less than 3% of GDP
- Reduce expenditure on health, education, welfare
- Concentrate on infrastructure for tourism and FDI and police
- Full cost recovery for government service
- End food and other subsidies

Privatise economic activity

- Encourage income inequality to reward enterprise competitively
- Small public service
- Outsource to cut public service
- Commodify all services so they can be profitable in private sector
- Private sector is most efficient

- **Open your currency exchanges and free your trade.** All your policies must be designed to make your production internationally competitive and to attract foreign investment. So allow capital, including your own, to move in and out freely. Cut taxes and keep interest rates high. Allow our goods freely into your markets. In time, we will do the same for yours in our markets. Self-sufficiency and protection are bad for you. That includes measures to protect your environment and sustain your natural resources. Such measures are barriers to trade and investment, you cannot afford them, and there are international rules against those barriers.

- **Export-led growth is the modern way.** Make what we need. Compete with all other countries by price. Sell what you make most cost-effectively, and buy the rest cheaply from us. Agribusiness is the cheapest way to produce exportable primary products. We can sell you the necessary inputs. We can also be persuaded to invest in land for agribusiness. Keep wages low, limit trade union activity and ensure people can be hired and fired without too much difficulty. Remember that what you offer the international market is primarily low labour costs. Remember also we are your richest trading partners.

- **Reduce government expenditure.** Government competing for resources with the private sector is inefficient. Governments are a necessary evil: keep their activities minimal and focused on attracting capital. Cut the civil service. Do not subsidise anything, including food. Make all services to the public pay the full cost of delivery, including water, health and education. But subsidise public infrastructure that attracts foreign private capital and tourism and call it investment.

- **Privatise.** All economic activity can be commodified and made subject to the market. Outsource as much as possible of government functions: let private enterprises bid against each other to produce the service, so you can choose the cheapest. Sell off all former parastatal enterprise, including utilities: the private sector always does it better. You can hire our entrepreneurs and know-how. Encourage your entrepreneurship by paying successful people internationally competitive salaries. Measures to achieve equality are bad for you.

What has been the effect of this in the African continent? Here is something to think about:

> *'Why have you failed?' a World Bank expert asked Julius Nyerere, the former President of Tanzania, at a Washington meeting.*
>
> *He replied, 'The British Empire left us a country with 85% illiterates, two engineers and 12 doctors. When I left office in 1985, we had 9% illiterates and thousands of engineers and doctors. At that point our income per capita was twice what it is today – after the Structural Adjustment programme. We now have one third less children in our schools, and public health and social services are in ruins. During those years, Tanzania has done everything that the World Bank and the IMF have demanded.*
>
> *'So I ask you: Why have you failed?'*

The usually forgotten fact is that for a decade or more after independence African standards of living rose. Then came the debt crisis and the collapse of the prices of most of their exports. African states were forced to seek help. Usually forgotten also is the origin of the debt crisis. Its roots lie in the 1970s and 1980s when Western banks were desperately seeking outlets for the huge liquid reserves placed with them by OPEC countries, which could not spend the profits of the huge oil price hikes. Those banks persuaded poor countries to take loans – at the then prevailing low interest rates. It seemed a wonderful opportunity for all concerned. With time, the loans were mostly rolled over – and of course, interest rose at compound rates, as global mobile capital became apparently scarcer. Hence the debt trap.

Poor countries have since become increasingly indebted, despite having paid back many multiples of what they originally borrowed. The extent of the expectations put on them is nicely illustrated by an extrapolation by Ed Mayo of London's New Economics Foundation, when he described what would have to happen in Britain if it were forced to service a debt comparable to that of Guyana in the Caribbean – whose debt service percentage was 40%. Britons would have to lose over a million students in higher education, ban all non-emergency operations in the health service, tolls would be charged on all roads, there would have to be a two-thirds cut in the defence budget, and a third off the law and order budget; while public housing provision would come to an end. Those are the kinds of cuts needed to service the debts of poor countries.

What should have happened, of course, is what happens when you and I get into debt that we can't pay back. There is a procedure for bankruptcy. Debt gets written off in a way that enables the debtor to make a new start. The lender bears part of the cost for having made a poor investment – a risk that interest rates are supposed to cover. The New Economics Foundation has now published a proposal for an international bankruptcy process. The IMF is showing interest in the idea, having become fed up with bailing out banks and other lenders who have continued to make loans with impunity.

But until now there has been no such procedure. In desperation poor countries called in the IMF, which is supposed to exist to tide countries over a payment crisis. In exchange for loans, structural adjustment programmes were required under the instruction of the World Bank and the IMF. These two institutions have in effect managed the economies of most African states. Their governments have not had a free hand in terms of their policies and implementation.

It is said: 'By their fruits shall ye know them.' The fruits of the structural adjustment policies in Africa are plain for all to see; but they are consistently blamed on the victims – the African states themselves. Some African governments have, of course, made mistakes: corruption, inefficiency and military rule among them. There have also been clean, democratic and efficient governments. Nyerere's was one. They have all fared the same. Many that were held up as examples of the success of structural adjustment were unelected and far from free of corruption. Without exception – even those considered showcases for structural adjustment because their GDP has risen – they have lost employment. Even when growth rates have gone up the fruits have gone to capital, not labour.

Mozambique is only the latest to admit the failure of IMF-imposed programmes. *Business Report* of January 11, 2001 revealed that eight years into the 'reforms', far from increasing employment, over 35,000 jobs have been lost; that dependence on outside donors has increased; that inflation is 21.5%; that two-thirds of Mozambicans now live in absolute poverty; that the monthly minimum wage is now sufficient only to buy 29% of basic family needs, which exclude clothing, healthcare, education, energy and transport.

It is widely acknowledged that the South African government has done extremely well in the eyes of the Washington Consensus. Finance Minister Trevor Manuel is the darling of the international economic establishment. In an article entitled 'Economy Cleared for Take-Off', Reg Lumley, then of *The Mail and Guardian* (a South African weekly), pointed out that our government had put everything in place to ensure we are 'poised to perform'. Our deficit is below 3%; we have low government expenditure, low and declining taxation, a high rate of interest, tariff reductions ahead of those demanded under international agreements and open exchanges – 'prudent fiscal management' in other words.

So what happened? Why are we not getting the foreign investment promised if we obeyed in this way? Manuel confesses himself baffled. Lumley suggests it is politics: Zimbabwe, handling of AIDS policy, capacity to deal with crime and so on. So structural adjustment is not enough. We must also adopt the domestic and foreign political policies that the foreign investors want! Apart from the limitations to our political sovereignty, many of these factors cannot be controlled by our government, including the actions of the Zimbabwe government.

But worse, the fiscal policies themselves create most of the problems. We have lost a million jobs in eight years. In the year 2000 we saw a 3% growth rate, but employment fell by 2.2%, or 126,500 jobs. Virtually all of these were in labour-intensive sectors that were decimated by reducing tariffs – a 61% decline in the footwear industry for instance – or in government-paid jobs that gave way to casualised outsourcing or preparation for privatisation. These are the result of 'old economics' thinking.

They in turn result in the huge crime rate. If you demand that people get their income through employment and then fail to provide it, you will get starvation and – on the part of the enterprising – crime. That is a fact confirmed by international research and experience. South Africans are not uniquely prone to crime.

The situation is not helped by a weakening of the laws upholding labour standards – enabling employers to hire and fire people easily and reduce wages. An ILO study shows that South Africa already has a more 'flexible' market than many of its competitors. Moreover, if you reduce the amount employers have to pay labour, you also reduce internal purchasing power, and force people into jobs that pay them less than they need to live on.

What has changed?

Old Economics has failed – not just South Africa but the world – because new factors have entered the scene that have not been understood or reckoned with.

1. Technology and jobless growth

Technology creates jobless growth internationally. Israel, for instance, has unemployment of some 9%, despite a high and uniquely consistent rate of foreign investment and a growth rate of 5%–6%. Modern technology destroys purchasing power by undermining the capacity of economies to produce 'work' in the way we used to think of it. And conventional economists do not have an answer. Technology that should give us abundance has produced a new kind of scarcity – in which all of us have to work harder in the search for labour productivity, when we already have surplus labour. International research shows that there is now 15%–40% global over-capacity in productive enterprise. Without any more investment we could produce 15–40% more. Over-capacity is another word for under-consumption or shortage of demand. It is not that people don't need what can be produced – they don't have the money to buy it. The growth rate therefore does not necessarily tell us anything about prosperity.

In 2000 all the indicators for growth in South Africa looked excellent. *Business Day* (07/02/2001) reported under the headline 'SA's strong production performance heartening' that the previous year had seen the strongest manufacturing performance in ten years. Production was up, so was GDP growth, and sales and productivity and the value of output. Meanwhile, employment dropped by 125,500. Youth unemployment in South Africa is reckoned by the ILO to be 50%. A South African Graduate Development Association has been formed to unite and promote the interests of unemployed graduates. This gives the lie to the widely accepted shibboleth that in South Africa unemployment is a function of lack of education. Worldwide there are educated and skilled people unemployed. Over a billion people aged 15 to 24 are unemployed, 15% of them in developed countries. Many are educated to graduate level or qualified and experienced artisans.

A *Business Report* story (04/02/2001) shows massive layoffs – well into the tens of thousands – in the US and in Europe across the sectors, from banking to car parts manufacturing to steel-making to utility production to computers, despite the fact of continued 'growth' figures. This was well before the events of September 11. The reasons have to do with profit rates falling below the high rates expected. 'Many of these announcements (of layoffs) are due to changes in corporate governance in Europe that force companies to take steps to boost earnings at the earliest sign of weakness,' according to an economist at Goldman Sachs in Paris quoted in the report.

Since September 11, the situation has worsened within and without the US. General Electric's proposed merger with Honeywell may be blocked by the EU; but Honeywell has already cut 12,000 jobs on a profit warning. Hewlett Packard's purchase of Compaq will cost at least 15,000 jobs; and shareholders are demanding double that. US job losses in October 2001 in 'defensive mergers' was 280,000.

2. Footloose capital

That brings us neatly to the second new factor – the essence of the new globalisation – implications of which have not been grasped by 'old economists'. The factor of production, or the resource, that is now seen as most valuable is capital. Why? Because it is the most mobile. Land and labour are either totally or partially static. Capital can move at the tap of a computer button. It has the power of the coquette: 'If you don't do as I say I can always leave – there are plenty of others begging for my services.' Imagine the change in power relations if a worker in Johannesburg were to say to his boss as he stepped into his space-time capsule: 'I won't be in next week. They are paying more in Bangkok.' Imagine if at the same time, capital were kept at home. As it is, work can be removed from one area to another in search of labour prepared to accept less money; but labour cannot follow it.

Let us get it from the horse's mouth. One member of President Mbeki's International Foreign Direct Investment Council is Percy Barnevik, until recently Chief Executive Officer of the multinational ABB. He retired with a package of $80 million – though the company recorded a loss of $691 million in that year. Asked what he meant by globalisation, he said:

> 'I would define globalisation as the freedom for my group to invest where it pleases, when it pleases, in order to produce what it wants, by getting supplies and selling wherever it wants, supporting as few constraints as possible regarding workers' rights and social conventions.'
>
> (Quoted in *Transnational Corporations Observatory 2002*)

The results of this unique freedom include the galactic sums routinely expected by owners of capital and those who use it most effectively. If you are getting less than 15% on your capital you will be thought to be doing rather badly. I was told in early 2001 that if you get less than 26%, you should change your broker. Yet the rate of growth of the world economy in the past 10 years has been of the order of 2–5%. So where are the rewards for capital coming from? It is true that much of that 'return' is based on speculation with share and currency prices. The fact is that it is not being paid to other factors of production: capital is getting away with the lion's share and totally distorting the market in factors of production. It makes a mockery of the conventional economists' idea of the natural 'market rate' for any factor of production. Mobile capital distorts all market rates.

When there is a take-over battle they make no bones about it. The interests of the shareholders – that is, owners of capital – are paramount. When two banks merge, they tell you how good it will be for the shareholders. They even admit that customers may suffer – probably by closure of branches and fewer staff. Staff redundancies are taken for granted. But, they say, that's the way the cookie crumbles, and we will try to make it up to customers in other ways and try to sack as few employees as possible. Capital is now able to call the shots internationally. Nothing we do must risk offending footloose international capital, including, it seems, our diplomatic policies towards our neighbours with whose economies we are connected.

Ann Crotty's column in *Business Report* (01/01/2001) makes the point:

Until the fall of the Berlin Wall … the global system was run by politicians. Since then it has been run by economists and financiers, rather like a macrocosm of the corporate world … Corporates are not working for a broad range of stake-holders and economies are not working for the populace … For the past thirty years or more, the agenda (of the corporate world) has focused entirely on share-holder return. This inevitably results in an obsession with share prices … The best way to protect the share price is to protect the earnings, and the easiest and fastest way to do that is to cut costs … Companies are gutted beyond recognition and millions of employees sacrificed for a short-term share price boost. This share market monster must be fed regularly. So mergers and acquisitions become an essential part of the corporate repertoire … The notion that the stock price is the be-all and end-all of corporate performance is so ingrained that it seems to have been handed down in stone tablets. In reality it is an outgrowth of the go-go 1980s and '90s. The related notion that shareholders are the only stakeholders with a legitimate claim on the corporation is just as ingrained and just as new.

This is extremely serious for democracy. It means the wishes of the electorate must be secondary to those of the owners of capital – foreign as well as our own. It explains why when governments change, their policies hardly do. Gary Younge, of The Guardian writes: 'The global market has given the invisible hand of the market carte blanche to pick up a democratically elected government by the scruff of the neck and slap it around if it attempts to put the needs of its electorate above the interests of international capital.'

It is also very serious for the sense of dependence that we all suffer. If my job in Bloemfontein depends on what is happening in Caracas or Birmingham, that is extremely bad for my sense of responsibility. It creates at worst frustration and rage, at best despair and irresponsibility.

3. De-linked money

One of the worst effects of footloose capital is that much of it is not being used for productive enterprise. Something like $2 trillion a day is traded internationally on the foreign exchange markets. Of that, over 90% – some say 98% – is purely speculative. It does not finance trade or investment. It simply flies around the globe in a virtual economy of its own. It skims profits overnight. Some of it is the surplus income of the very rich, who cannot spend their galactic earnings. It also consists of money held in banks, insurance companies, hedge funds and so on, in which many of us have willy-nilly invested our savings and pensions.

If those institutions did not behave like that, they would not be maximising our returns and we would place our money elsewhere. These mobile financial institutions make billions every year, hardly touching the real human economy at all. Twenty years ago the proportions were reversed: 95% of forex (foreign exchange) trading was related to trade and investment, and only 5% was speculative.

Far from 'trickling down' therefore, there is a huge upward suction effect that withdraws from the world economy some of the means of commerce. If you are earning millions every year, you do not buy an umpteenth yacht; you invest it in this virtual economy, paying experts to increase your capital. Another word for that is gambling; and it is a form of gambling that affects us all. You do not bother to invest in real production. Why should you? You have to get involved with labour and sliding exchange rates and natural disasters. And it is much less profitable. So you send your money up there. You send it where it is virtually useless to the rest of us because it is not used to buy anything that the rest of us are selling.

That is why governments 'can't afford' the welfare services, education, healthcare, etc., that we used to take for granted. 'We don't have the money,' they say. Why not? Because it is flying round up there out of reach. It is also very difficult to tax unless it comes down to earth and takes part in the real economy. Tax havens are openly marketed; and the part of our incomes that takes the form of dividends is largely untaxed once it leaves the enterprise.

Therefore wealth does not trickle down. It gets sucked up. The scale of this phenomenon is breathtaking. In 1971 the daily volume of forex trading was $10–20 billion. By 1983, it was $560 billion. In 1995, $1.3 trillion. Now it is over $2 trillion, according to the Bank for International Settlements. This is over 150 times the total international trade in all commodities; 100 times the daily trading in equities; 50 times the daily trading in all goods and services produced in all countries. It grows by 20–25% a year, whereas trade grows by 5%. Twenty banks have twice as much money to move around as there is in the reserves of all central banks. This is the scale of the disassociation of most capital from the real business of economics – production and trading in goods and services.

It can also have serious effects for quite small investors and vulnerable people. By mid-2002, globally invested pension funds were in trouble, because the stock markets in Europe and the US bottomed out. Millions of elderly people are in danger of losing their investment; they will not, you may be sure, be compensated from the incomes of the executives.

Here are quotes from two experts in the theory and practice of capital markets – some fifty years apart:

> 'Speculators may do no harm as bubbles on the steady stream of enterprise. But the position is serious when enterprise becomes the bubble on a whirlpool of speculation. When the capital development of a country becomes the by-product of a casino, the job is likely to be ill-done.'
>
> John Maynard Keynes
> in *General Theory of Employment, Interest and Money*

> 'The international financial system is suffering from systemic breakdown, but we are unwilling to acknowledge it ... The prevailing system of international lending is fundamentally flawed, yet the IMF regards it as its mission to preserve it ... The private sector is ill suited to allocate international credit – it is not concerned with macro-economic balance – The system tends to disequilibrium. It is more dangerous to capitalism than communism ever was.'
>
> George Soros in *The Crisis of Global Capitalism*

4. Work and how it is connected to income

Politicians and economists everywhere know or suspect that we shall never achieve full employment again. But they cannot say it, because the implications are so awful until we can come up with alternatives. Almost universally the solution stated by economists and politicians is the growth of small business. But successful small business is always taken over by big business – with the loss of jobs. Big business centralises, employs technology, rationalises and sacks people. The research in South Africa shows that the emphasis on small business is almost entirely useless. Small enterprises are going out of business almost as fast as they are created. Those quoted on the stock markets have registered 2%

negative growth in the past five years. In any case small businesses do not employ many people: they usually rely on family to work semi-paid. If they do succeed, larger business makes them an offer they do not refuse: they sell, and jobs are lost. That is the dynamic.

This is not limited to South Africa. There was never such a high rate of business bankruptcy in Britain as in the Thatcher years. In the US today there are 7000 bankruptcies every hour. These are almost entirely in the small business sector.

So what we need is a way of creating livelihoods. The days when an economy could offer everyone a job working for someone else are past. Seven years ago, the economist Will Hutton (*The State We Are In*) showed that the UK economy comprised one third employed in the old sense – with a permanent contract and rights to holidays, time off and a pension; one third self-employed, casualised or sometimes employed; and the last third living on welfare or operating effectively in the informal economy – making livelihoods outside the system, including the tax system. Bernard Lietaer in *The Future of Money* reckons everything we now produce will require only 10–15% of the population to make it by 2020.

Let's remember there is no shortage of work – of things to do that would be productive and creative. Child-care is now grossly neglected, with horrendous implications for the future of the human race. So is social and community work. The work of artists and writers and thinkers and inventors is vital to humanity, and is now largely unpaid, except in the service of some companies who sponsor the arts as part of their marketing strategy. The question is how do we link that kind of work to incomes, as part of the normal life of a country? Some of the answers to this question are explored in following chapters. They hold the promise that humanity may be released from its bondage to employers and the global harshness of the market – without going back to the grinding poverty of subsistence economics.

5. Limits to growth

One of the shibboleths of current economic thinking is that the solution to poverty is to spread high consumption from the rich to the poor. Consistently ignored is the fact that even if the global market could spread wealth, the planet cannot continue to absorb the toxins that even current levels of consumption produce. Californian lifestyles cannot be applied to poor countries without creating terminal problems for the planet. Gandhi made the point that if every Indian were to demand and be given the right to a 'Western' lifestyle we would require eight Planet Earths to produce the resources.

There are two destructive 'growth' effects at work here, which are sometimes confused:

a)   The blanket of carbon dioxide around the Earth, which is a product of the burning of fossil fuels and other toxic emissions, causes a greenhouse effect, raising the temperature of the atmosphere. The Arctic ice cap has already thinned by 42%, and there is now a mile-wide sea at the North Pole. The effect will be to raise the sea level, threatening many low-lying areas of poor countries like the Maldives, Tuvalu and Bangladesh – but also, for instance, the 11 nuclear power plants in the UK sited on coasts. It could also have the paradoxical effect of severely cooling the British Isles because the Gulf Stream will be overwhelmed. This greenhouse effect is the one that is most likely responsible for the climate changes we are seeing with increasing frequency, including in Southern Africa. The year 2002 saw several ancient European cities, as well as large areas of India and China, overwhelmed by floods, while central Africa is dying of drought. Over the last decade, 'natural disasters' have cost the world $608 billion, as much as in the previous four decades together. Insurance claims due to extreme weather in 1999 were higher in one year than in the whole of the 1960s. And none of that touches people who are uninsured.

b)   The ozone layer that protects us from cancer-inducing ultra-violet light is being depleted as a result of irreversible catalytic reactions caused by free radicals in certain chemicals that we use in the process of industrial activity. We do not know what the ultimate effect of this will be. We do know about skin cancers.

No one denies this. The old comfort zone that 'the scientists will get us out of this' no longer holds water. The scientists are in the forefront of the agitation for urgent action.

The WSSD Conference in Johannesburg saw the launch of an 'Appeal from Scientists to Leaders' by 89 scientists, including 29 Nobel Laureates from the World Institute of Science. It was prefaced by noting 'the unprecedented gravity of the dangers and the suicidal inactivity of our political and economic leaders – in particular their refusal to take the necessary measures to deal with the climate crisis'; and went on to point out that 'for scientists to keep silent would be an act of complicity in a major crime against humanity and the living world as a whole'. The three-page appeal acknowledges the responsibility of science 'for the changes which have taken place during the last 300 years'. The changes now required include preserving genetic diversity between and within species, protecting the biosphere from pollution, and reducing the waste of energy and the use of fossil fuels.

We are unable to move from a conviction that as humans we are the crown and the glory of the Earth community – to a realisation that we are the most destructive and the most dangerous of that community … The crash that faces us is not the crash simply of humans. It is a crash of the bio-systems of the Earth: indeed it is in some manner the crash of the Earth itself.

Astro-physicists Swimme and Berry in *The Universe Story*

But the economics of the unfettered global market makes the destruction of the environment practically inevitable – especially if its purpose is to spread the lifestyles of the rich to the poor. International competition inhibits enterprise from spending resources that might raise costs in limiting environmental destruction and so give advantage to rivals. The argument that shareholders will desert if the profits go down is very powerful. Large, rich corporations have a feeble record in environmental preservation – unless legislative pressure from civil society forces them to take action.

But governments dare not make regulations to protect the environment for fear of offending international capital. The Multilateral Agreement on Investment, which the World Trade Organisation nearly managed to get through two years ago, would have made it illegal for a government to put such barriers in the way of international investment. This would have allowed any company to sue a government for taking any of a number of actions that limited the activities of an investor. These included 'non-tariff barriers' to trade, like laws to protect the environment, to promote equal opportunities, or to support local enterprise.

Fortunately a very effective international civil society movement managed to bring the plans to light and scupper them. The multinational companies and their sponsors have not given up. But that international civil society movement is now alert. It exploded in Seattle in 1999, and has grown in effectiveness and numbers since, despite being exploited by the usual violent hangers-on.

Bernard Lietaer reckons there are four 'Titanics' now bearing down upon four 'ice-floes', any one of which will be enough to sink the world economy. The first two – jobless growth and the destruction of the environment – have been discussed above. The third is the ageing of the population in developed economies. How, he asks, are we to expect a declining proportion of the population to support, in their non-working years, a rising proportion? In the UK it is now one elderly person to seven of working age; and in twenty years' time it will be one to four. Ironically, in view of growing xenophobia in Europe, immigration is beginning to be whispered as a solution.

The fourth is the impending crash on Wall Street. The American economy is the most indebted in the world. Its trade deficit was 4% of GDP in 2001, rising by about 50% a year recently. The 300 million people in the US owe the rest of the world $2.2 trillion – $7,333 each. Five billion people in the developing world owe $2.5 trillion – $500 each.

The $12 trillion market capitalisation of the stock market is 140% of total GDP – a fact that has frequently alarmed Alan Greenspan. According to the Federal Reserve Board, at the end of 1999 there was $25.6 trillion of debt outstanding, having gone up by $2.25 trillion in that year alone. This increase in one year is more than the value of all gold and foreign currency reserves in all countries. It is $8,500 for each American man, woman and child. The sector deepest and most rapidly going into debt is the financial one. Debts owned by real estate trusts rose 502% in that year, according to the Federal Reserve Board. This inherent instability was of course compounded by the events of September 11, 2001.

When that bubble bursts it will affect us all.

The American economy: an example to us all?

The American economy is often quoted as a successful example of the effects of the global market, one that we should follow. There are two issues here: whether we can all become as rich as America within the present global system; and whether in fact we really do want the American economic model for ourselves. On the first of these, the argument is that international competition is not a zero sum game, but one in which we can all win. If the US is doing well, that shows that we can all do well if we follow the same policies. While it is true that one country's success is not necessarily at the expense of others', it can be so. In this case I believe it is. The relative success of the American economy is a function of the global competitive rules, which suit the most advanced, and which positively disadvantage and impoverish others.

The second issue is just as important. How successful in fact is the American economy? How does it work for ordinary Americans? The evidence in terms of inequality of incomes is startling.

Since the mid-1970s the majority of households have lost net worth. One in five of them was at negative or zero net worth in the year 2000. Household debt as a percentage of income rose from 58% to 85% between 1973 and 1998. Average weekly wages in 1998 were 12% below those for 1973. Average hours of work rose by 163 days a year. Since productivity had risen by 33%, all of that new wealth, and more, went to capital, according to a Federal Reserve Survey. The top 1% of Americans now own more than the bottom 95% – up from 90% only a year earlier. Between 1990 and 2000 executive pay in American corporations rose 570%, while tax rates fell to historic lows. In the US, the pay of Chief Executives is now 531 times that of the average worker, according to *Business Day*'s Steven Overell, writing on September 3, 2002.

One sign of such extravagant wealth is the growth of a new 'boutique' or 'concierge' health delivery system for the super-rich. Leading clinics give platinum care to such customers, including queue-jumping as well as massage and sauna treatment.

What is the effect of this on the society as a whole? While there are now 189 American billionaires, one in seven American adults cannot read to grade 5 level – i.e. is functionally illiterate and innumerate. Since George W. Bush was elected, 1.6 million fewer Americans are in formal employment. One in six American children lives in poverty, defined as circumstances leaving them prone to malnutrition, stunted growth, learning difficulties, drug abuse and delinquency, and with insufficient warm clothing. In case our South African stereotyping misleads, there are more white children than black in this 'poverty' category. The divorce rate is the highest in the world.

Americans promote their democracy as a meritocracy. Regardless of inequalities of income, they say, all Americans can reach the top and become beneficiaries of the stratospheric level of income accumulated there. The opposite is the truth. In the past three decades there has been a collapse of social mobility. The chance of American workers in the bottom 20% moving to the top 60% is less than in any other developed country. This is because the rich have become increasingly able to ensure that their children remain at the top. In the past 20 years the proportion of people living on unearned income – the fruits of capital – has risen by 50%. The lack of an inheritance tax, the exclusivity of expensive schools and the use of private educational coaching as well as old boy networks ensure income and capital stay at the top. The idea that it does not matter how much people earn at the top contradicts the possibility of meritocracy. But the persistence of the myth of a meritocracy ensures that those at the top oppose taxes to support services, including education and health, for the 'failures' down below. The society develops a 'let them eat cake' mentality par excellence.

The highly competitive nature of the American economy is reflected throughout the society. It has some extreme effects in terms of how people cope with the increasingly devastating results of failure. An American study shows that people born after 1950 in the US are twenty times more likely to suffer depression. International research shows that the closer a country gets to the American economic model, the higher its rate of mental illness. Highly competitive economies, with a high cost to failure, are factories for mental illness. Schizophrenia, depression, dementia and suicide rates all increase with the approach to American-style capitalism; so do alcoholism, drug abuse and family violence.

In one week the New York Times reported the following stories from around the country about violence in children – a manifestation of mental illness – and how they are treated. A 12-year-old boy who killed a 6-year-old playmate was convicted of first degree murder and sentenced to life imprisonment without parole. A 13-year-old shot and killed a teacher who suspended him from class for throwing water balloons: he was imprisoned for a minimum of 25 years. Both are in adult prisons. A 22-year-old educationally 'sub-normal' woman, homeless and cocaine-addicted, was convicted of homicide when her baby was stillborn, because it was agreed her addiction had caused the baby's death. She got 12 years in prison. An 11-year-old was taken from his classroom in handcuffs for drawing a picture of weapons; and a 13-year-old was strip-searched and suspended for saying of the recent spate of school shooting sprees that she could understand how ostracised students could turn homicidal. There are weekly reports of violence at school sporting events, involving parents as well as pupils and staff.

In a remarkably prescient article – written nine months before the twin towers attack – Mikhail Gorbachev wrote an open letter to President Bush, entitled 'The World Doesn't Want to be American'. Here are some extracts:

I am writing to you as a citizen of our planet, and someone who beholds the last remaining superpower … While America's role is acknowledged throughout the world, her claim to hegemony is not … I hope that you will give up any illusion that the 21st century can or should be 'an American Century' … It is time for America's electorate to be told the blunt truth: that the present situation … is not tenable as long as an enormous portion of the world lives in abject poverty, degradation and backwardness … Instead of seeing an increase in US security, the end of the cold war has seen a decline. Should the United States persist in its policies, the international situation will continue to deteriorate.

And elsewhere?

The US leads the way. The same trend is obvious internationally. Russia is perhaps the most extreme example, having been brutally forced from a command economy with hardly any indigenous private enterprise into an open economy within a few short years. UNICEF reports that the number of Russians living in poverty has risen to 66 million, from 2 million in 1987. By the turn of the century the country had one-tenth of the GDP of the United States. According to Russian economist Dmitry Lvov, by the year 2000 some 15% of the population had become very rich indeed − owning 92% of all private property − the other 85% very poor indeed, and there was no middle-income class. The country's death rate is considerably higher than its birth rate, not only because death rates, including suicide, have risen dramatically, but because people do not want children. It is reckoned that whereas by mid-century America will have 79 million more people, Russia will have 24 million less. Lvov calls his country, in which he still works as an academic economist, a 'catastrophe'.

Of the world's 6 billion people, 2.8 billion − nearly half − live on less than $2 a day and 1.2 billion on less than $1 a day. The trend to deeper impoverishment is continuing in parts of Latin America, South Asia, sub-Saharan Africa, Europe and Central Asia. In Europe and Central Asia − in transition to market economies − the number of people living on less than $1 a day has risen more than twenty-fold in ten years.

In the past year or two Argentina, Brazil and Uruguay have gone into what amounts to free fall, their currencies decimated, their populace in revolt and their economies to all intents and purposes bankrupt. All of them had been wards of the IMF, whose prescriptions turned a bad situation into a nightmare.

The claims by the Bank and its allies that the global market has reduced poverty relate to the mendacious quotation of overall growth statistics, which as we have seen say nothing about the reduction of poverty, since growth in the global market does not trickle down – it siphons up.

Psycho-social effects

In closing, let us refer back to the start. If an economic system is not working for people, it is not working. It is not just about figures for production and numbers of goods. The absolute growth in production, if it doesn't serve people, is not worth having. Here are some effects of the way that the unfettered competitive global market works in the lives of people and communities.

1. Insecurity
In the 'flexible' job market you take what you can get, there being little choice. As wages fall, people have to work longer hours. The break-up of families is constantly bemoaned – not least by the very conservative people who insist that the freedom of global markets is the *sine qua non* for freedom itself. They are whistling in the wind: lecturing families on loving care for children is useless when both parents must work long hours to survive. The plight of single parents without capital will obviously be visited on the children.

The world's street children population rises in all countries. Woman and child abuse is a feature and a function of the destruction of circumstances in which children can be lovingly brought up in a supportive, functioning family. The decline of welfare systems everywhere creates a vicious cycle from generation to generation as the resources to help families are withdrawn. The divorce rate rises everywhere from Nepal to New Brunswick, with America leading the way.

Even in families that remain intact the financial insecurity implicit in the competitive market-dominated economy is a prominent threat to decent relationships. That is the human experience of the past decades. People cannot live equitable lives under constant threat. The perfectly reasonable aim of most family heads is to find a fairly predictable basis for security for themselves and their families. The global market makes that nearly impossible; and then justifies that failure as providing the incentive for innovation. We all know from experience that this is nonsense, except for some of the winners in this brutal race.

2. Delinquency and crime

Destruction of families and communities makes delinquency pretty well inevitable, and that leads on to crime. Children who grow up in physically or verbally violent homes, characterised by stress, fear and competitiveness, tend towards aggression, emotional and intellectual immaturity and dysfunction. It happens in all classes. But in some of our economically deprived areas the behaviour that children learn to survive – essentially getting protection by belonging to a gang – automatically makes it impossible for them later to get the socialisation they need to pass exams, acquire jobs and become creative members of society. South Africa is a classic example but no exception. The Western Cape Minister of Community Safety, speaking in the 2001 Budget debate, told members that 100,000 people belonged to gangs in the province – 5% of the population in the area. The US used to lead the world in terms of crime. But the rest of us are catching up. South Africa's rise in violent crime in the year 2000 – 16% – was matched by that in the UK, while in Portugal it rose by 22%, according to the Report of the International Comparison of Statistics published by the British Home Office.

3. Globalisation of sophisticated crime

International crime syndicates have taken over whole areas of the world. We have seen systems of government and civil service totally degraded by their infiltration. The UN reckons some $750 billion is laundered annually through the official financial systems. Where there is poverty, insecurity and the threat of starvation, crime mafia find a fertile soil for recruitment. Since the destruction of the twin towers in New York the Americans have at last understood the toxic results of allowing money to pass freely round the world, being laundered as it goes. The attempt to control footloose capital may thereby be given a fillip.

4. Neo-nazism and xenophobia

The phenomena of neonazism and xenophobia everywhere follow insecurity, poverty and the widening of the wealth gap. The foreigner is scapegoated – in South Africa, in Austria, in Britain, in Russia, everywhere. Some religious fundamentalism is surely a result of the desperate search for certainty and the longing for a place of safety – which becomes distorted into safety against the infidel. Worse, as political parties become increasingly impotent in terms of what they are able to do in the face of the Washington Consensus, they are tempted to court popularity by stoking up ethnic violence. If a party cannot offer the electorate a change in policy, it seeks other issues to fight over. Ethnicity-based politics is a growing feature of modern nations. It is connected to the dearth of other issues on which governments can have an impact.

5. 'Let them eat cake'

The distance of the wealthy elite from the rest of the population is an extremely unhealthy development. The 'let them eat cake' mentality is a function of that distance, which creates profound ignorance and allows people insulated by their wealth to blame the poor for their poverty and their exclusion. Inevitably the 'let them eat cake' mentality leads to rebellion, nationally and internationally, as we have seen since Seattle. The rich in these societies spend much of their lives desperately seeking seclusion and defence against the increasingly desperate and violent poor. Over a decade ago, Tom Wolfe wrote *The Bonfire of the Vanities*. It was a potent foretaste of how society everywhere would develop. The growth of protected residential complexes; the desire to carry guns, though the risks are known; the denial to the public of parts of our environment through 'no-go' areas; the creation of states of terror and paranoia: these are par for the course and inevitable in societies of great disparity between wealth and poverty.

We cannot go backwards. If the current international economic order is toxic to most of the people in the world, how do we move forward to use the best of the market mechanism for a civilised future in the 21st century? What kind of economies can we build that might be called post-global? The chapters that follow will discuss ideas for change based on New Economics.

POINTS FOR DISCUSSION – CHAPTER ONE

1. Was the Washcon economic order inevitable?

2. How is economics related to power?

3. What dilemmas are created by modern technology?

4. How should the world deal with the American trade deficit?

5. Why did the Russian economy collapse in the 1990s?

MYTHS OF GLOBALISATION – ONE

'Empowerment comes from joining the global market.'

The following are inevitable consequences of participation in the unregulated global market:

● Our success as participants in any productive enterprise depends on what is happening elsewhere in places where we have no influence or control. A decision by a foreign government or corporation to change interest rates, to open a factory, to sell currency – to do anything that affects the *relative* success of our own enterprise – can lead to redundancy, dislocation and distress. And there is nothing we can or could have done about it. Helplessness and insecurity are inevitable life experiences of the great majority of working people in all countries. The only people who are in a position to escape this are the small minority whose wealth and/or skills make them highly mobile: they can follow and profit from success stories wherever they are happening. Unless they are unpartnered and childless – and perhaps even then – they also pay a personal price for that mobility.

● All enterprise that is internationally successful – or even nationally successful – is so because it sheds people in favour of technology. Cost-competitiveness depends on reducing the contribution of labour to the costs of the enterprise. Even the new growth areas – largely information technology and e-commerce – are small employers, and use highly specialised workers: they cannot absorb the thousands of workers discarded from shipbuilding, shoe factories or cotton fields.

● Small business development is no answer, because the global market centralises all activity: only enlargement, mergers and acquisitions ensure the survival of any company, and large companies always eat smaller ones, shedding labour in the process. 'Small business' gets larger by the year, according to official definitions. Small business does not survive the global market.

● The ideal economy in the global market is competitive outward oriented. By definition this ignores local economies – rural and village – which become depopulated. The cities become vast sprawls, as people abandon the dying rural areas to seek work.

● Capital, far from flowing to where it is most needed for development, is attracted to success. Capital flows from the poor to the rich, from the undeveloped to the developed, from lack of structure to infrastructure.

- The result is profound social dislocation, especially in the widening band of people who are casually self-employed. Insecure, fearful, competitive adults make poor parents; they create a new generation of rootless, aggressive-defensive adults, fertile soil for delinquency, promiscuity, disease, addiction, crime and violence. All of this is a feature of every country in the developed and developing worlds, including the US, UK, EU, Japan, Africa, Asia and South America. All of them are doubly applicable to countries which are not internationally competitive for historical reasons, but which have been forced or induced to join the global market, ready or not.

- Refugees and economic migrants. People who live in countries being impoverished by the global market obviously try to seek an alternative living elsewhere. That is exactly why 'the colonies' were populated in past centuries: people from Europe sought their fortunes abroad. They called it being adventurous and pioneering then. But when black people do it they are called illegal immigrants and spongers. In any case all relatively better economies are faced with a flood of migration, which it costs a lot to stem – detention centres, an industry of corrupt illegal immigrant services, policing the false passport industry, court time, lawyers, new legislation – never mind the terrible suffering of the migrants and their families.

- The security industry is the only one growing fast in all countries – people are being trained for a dangerous life killing, or being killed, to protect property.

In the global market everyone with a job works twice as hard as before, and everyone else has no job. It is stressful for everyone

All of this may be accompanied by an increase in the rate of growth of the GDP, so it is seen as economic empowerment. The Asian 'Tigers' experienced huge increases in that growth rate. Most of the wealth stayed at the top. Some poor people became destitute, leading to an increase in child prostitution, suicide, addiction and violent crime. In between, a frenetic insecure middle class developed, vulnerable to the dislocation caused by capital flight. When the currency speculators fled, millions lost jobs, homes, pensions and futures; some lost their lives.

Is this empowerment?

MYTHS OF GLOBALISATION – TWO

'The most important economic objective is the efficient use of labour through raising its productivity and reducing the work force.'

The focus on labour productivity is particularly inappropriate at the present time following the technology revolution. The world has a surplus of labour and a growing shortage of natural resources. We are running out of fossil fuels and other inputs to economic growth. That being so, it would make sense to encourage energy and resource productivity along with labour intensiveness. But we do the opposite. We employ more and more energy and resource-guzzling machines which render labour redundant. We behave as though we are desperately short of labour and everything else is plentiful. We make everyone work twice as hard for less money. Except for the world's top 5 to 10 per cent, everyone is working harder for less. Economic insecurity is the order of the day and everyone lives with huge stress.

That would be understandable if we lived in a world of permanent traumatic scarcity. Instead the exponential increase in technological capacity has doubled the world's output in ten years, from an already high base. All industrial goods are currently at least 30% 'over-produced' – that is, there is no effective demand for them. Unsold factory output abounds; dumping of goods at below cost both nationally and internationally is common practice.

Our problem is not scarcity but how to distribute wealth.

The illogical focus on labour productivity is purely a product of unregulated global competition for markets. Value is measured in short-term cost to enterprise, and that determines market share and profit.

CHAPTER TWO

The dearth of purchasing power

The next four chapters will discuss some new ways of mitigating the effects of South Africa's current entrapment in the global economy. At the same time, of course, we must work with others to create an international economic order that works for people and the planet.

Imagine the scene. One of her children has diarrhoea. The child is vomiting and messing several times a day. She knows she has to clean it up if only because it is infected. There is no running water in the house. There is no regular money or food coming into her shack. She has no work, having been made redundant as a skilled seamstress. She is exhausted. Her best hope is that she and the child will be taken into hospital. But will she be asked to pay? And what will happen to her other children? Her neighbours also live in shacks, on the edge, surviving literally God knows how.

Within a kilometre or two is a street known for its restaurants. They are always full. The waiters scrape the leavings from the vast helpings on the plates into a bin of some sort and it is thrown away. The patrons entering or leaving the building ignore or scowl at the small beggars who ask for help. Conversation among the diners as usual includes the quality of the wine as well as politics. The government is condemned for its failure to deal with poverty, crime, corruption, poor civil service, housing, health, and so on. If the discussion includes economists, opposition politicians and the media – that is, people who reckon they are in the know – they will, however, have praise for Trevor Manuel and his 'sound' fiscal policies. They will condemn COSATU's opposition to Manuel's policies, and condemn the labour laws, which uphold certain minimum standards for the treatment of a workforce. Forgive the caricature.

It is possible that the party will include overseas media and business people. They will leave the country with an impression of apparent consensus that the government is failing in every respect except the one that – in the view of the South African New Economics (SANE) Foundation – upholds and promotes poverty and scarcity in the country. So they will attribute the failure not to Manuel's policies, but to the trade unions and the government's political actions, which are said to offend foreign investors. They will see nothing odd in the idea that a democratically elected government is obliged to tailor its political as well as its economic policies to suit the impressions, correct or not, of foreigners. They will have been reading our papers, listening to our radio and watching our television.

There is virtually no news medium in South Africa that does not at least implicitly uphold the viewpoint of the Washington Consensus. The people who are asked to comment on our economy are drawn from the investment houses, which have a direct interest in maintaining policies derived from that Consensus, including open exchanges. They are biased, yet they are used as objective commentators. It is as though, wanting comment on the failure of a Springbok side, we were to consistently ask the coach of the other side to comment on that failure, even though they have a direct interest in the answer. With a few exceptions – perhaps most notably and occasionally Tim Modise – there is no serious examination of other viewpoints. The print media in particular thunder at any sign of wavering from the ideal of attracting and appeasing foreign investors – by lowering government expenditure, reducing taxation, amending the labour laws, hammering the unions. Some of the papers sometimes publish articles by critics of GEAR – the government policy for Growth, Employment and Redistribution – which incorporates the Washington Consensus. But the editorial line, and hence the tone of the news reporting, is universal support for Old Economics. No contradiction is seen between support for GEAR policies and the government's failure to deal with poverty and all that flows from it.

You do not have to be an old-fashioned Marxist to have noticed that the media everywhere is in the hands of fewer and fewer larger and larger multi-national corporations. They also control booksellers, publishers, public relations companies – everything, in fact, that influences the way we think. Their interest in the democratic and educational outcomes of their publications is secondary by a long way to their interest in the bottom line. The 'will it sell?' imperative makes for uniformity at best, censorship at worst. Moreover, there is not one media person who is not seriously worried about advertising revenue; and on the whole large advertisers have a similar short-term view of their interests in terms of the direction of the economy. The centralisation of media power is part of that centralisation of all economic power which is a feature of the unfettered global market in trade and capital.

Capital is always attracted to where it is most profitable. This is perfectly natural and consistent with classical theory, whose proponents however ignore the implications. The result is that where wealth already exists, wealth will be attracted. That is the basic, though not sufficient, reason why most developing countries have done badly since they were required to compete on an equal footing with the most technologically advanced, skilled and sophisticated economies. If it is necessary for American company X to buy and exploit every technology known to humanity in order to compete against other American companies, how do we expect an African company, lacking all that, to compete with it? And so large enterprise, with the additional benefits of scale, access to capital and partnerships, always competes successfully with small where there is no regulation. Buy-outs are the story of small enterprises that get off the ground. Small business is not the answer to joblessness.

Where has the money gone?

We have already noticed the paradox that a world twelve times richer than it was fifty years ago seems to be operating in a context of scarcity. It is obviously not a scarcity of goods and services. We throw away unsaleable goods, from food to shoes to machines. In desperate attempts to derive some revenue from unsold stock we have seasonal sales, loss leaders, give-away incentives, tele-marketing campaigns – every device an ingenious and mushrooming market-ing industry can invent. Marketers are the highest paid profession. Why? Because the market is shrinking. And that is because the scarcity we have imposed on ourselves is the scarcity of money – the means of exchange of goods and services between people.

That scarcity is the result of a system that leads, inter alia, to the hoarding of money. At a national level, all governments strive for a surplus, being congrat-ulated on building reserves and savings. At the international level, similarly, we all aim for a positive balance of payments – that is, to have earned more than we have spent. Never forget that one country's surplus is, of course, another's deficit. By definition, if I earn more from selling to you, you will have a nega-tive balance. So all governments aim for reserves. Except for the United States, being in international debt is dangerous, because it leads to speculation with your currency. And if you are poor it leads to the application of structural adjustment measures being demanded as the price of a loan to cover the deficit. The reason the US is an exception is that the dollar is used as an inter-national reserve currency – for reasons associated with its relative political, economic and military power since before the Second World War. We shall return to this theme when we discuss trade flows in Chapter Five.

There is another reason why money is disappearing. The centralisation of wealth is such that the minority of very rich people to whom most money gravitates are actually unable to spend their income. They use it to speculate with currency and stock market shares. This money at the top ends up in orbit. It does not trickle down. It attracts other money out of the real economy. It is hoarded in the sense that it does not buy goods and services made by real people on earth.

Paradoxically, it is not a bad thing that it does not all come down at one time. By now it would be highly inflationary if it did. Because of the way that money is created in our economies (see Chapter Three) the world is awash with debt-based money. The following table shows how the money stock grew in fifty years. I have only UK statistics, but it is representative in terms of scale.

UK Total Money Stock	
1948	£ 2.8 billion
1960	£ 5.7 billion
1972	£ 20.3 billion
1984	£163.4 billion
1996	£586.0 billion

Much of that huge inflation of debt-based money is now floating around in space. It probably accounts for the amazing facility with which rich governments are able suddenly to finance wars or other emergencies, having pleaded poverty when it comes to hospitals, schools and so on. It is borrowed from that orbiting stream of gambling chips – at huge cost to taxpayers in the future.

Meanwhile, the dearth of purchasing power – money – means that the real economy shrinks. Over 40% of South Africans, increasingly of all skin colours, are unemployed. Without jobs they have virtually no income except what they can literally beg, borrow or steal. In practice most people with no income live off someone else who is also poor but has some access to income. The remittance figures are very high in South Africa. Few unskilled unemployed people have any real hope of being offered more than occasional casual employment. Technology-driven enterprise needs specific and high quality skills. Throughout the country we have unemployed skilled artisans, matriculants and even graduates: what hope for a person without education or skills. You only have to see the hopelessness on the faces of the men lining the side of the road willing to accept any job, however low-paid – which most will not get. We will never employ them in our country on any serious scale that will make a difference.

The illusion of employment is beautifully captured in Viviane Forrester's book *L'Horreur Économique*, winner of the Prix Medici. I quote from an extract published in *The New Statesman* of May 24, 1999.

We are living in the midst of a deception where artificial policies claim to perpetuate a world that has in fact gone forever. Millions of human lives are devastated and annihilated by this anachronism, which asserts the immutability of our most sacred concept: work … Our concepts of work, and thus employment, around which politics revolve have become an illusion. Our struggles with them are as much of a hallucination as Don Quixote tilting at windmills.

The unemployed today are no longer put aside temporarily or occasionally, and in only some sectors. They are up against a general implosion, a phenomenon resembling those tidal waves, cyclones or tornadoes that don't aim at anyone in particular but that no one can withstand. Yet the jobless are treated and judged by the same criteria as when jobs were abundant. They are made to feel guilty for being jobless, at the same time as they are lulled by deceptive promises that an abundance of jobs will once again be available. They wonder what inadequacies, what aptitude for failure, what ill-will or errors could have led them there …

They feel shame. They undergo work experience and retraining, only to realise more forcefully than ever that they have no real role. They come to realise that there is something worse than being exploited – that is not even to be exploitable.

We pursue some very strange routines. The shortage of jobs is ever increasing, yet we compel every one of the millions of unemployed to search for work that does not exist and to do so every working day of every week, every working month and every year. Is this really a commendable use of time? Aren't such chains of rejection just staged to persuade the jobseekers of their nothingness? So many stifled, crushed, cornered, beaten and falling apart lives, merely tangential to a shrinking society.

People are induced to seek work, beg for it, any work at any price ... Is this not the way one would construct a society of slaves ... ? But why should a society burden itself with slaves if their labour is superfluous?

Surely we recognise that description. Surely all of Africa is familiar with that picture. Do we want that? Do we who have income want to continue to pass by with averted eyes, to sigh with exasperation when the umpteenth beggar comes to our door, to shout at least inwardly, 'I can't help everyone.' Do we want to watch ourselves slowly but surely harden and begin in self-defence to blame them: they don't even look for work, they drink, they are frauds? Or adopt the 'let them eat cake' ignorance of the insulated rich? No, I don't think we want that.

So how shall we give income – purchasing power – to people whose labour is superfluous? In Europe and America, the most obvious and frequently used is some version of the dole. We give people an income if and while there is no work for them. In South Africa some people who fall into unemployment can get a temporary unemployment payment, but they are a small minority of unemployed people. That is partly because of the way the means test inevitably operates.

The dole has huge disadvantages. Here I want to mention only one – the regulations and the bureaucracy it takes to assess whether or not a claimant is legitimate. Using a means test is a tricky and unpleasant task for the bureaucrat and a humiliating one for the claimant, for whom lying is a constant temptation and an advantage. How do you assess, let alone prove, a person's assiduity in seeking work? Means testing of their income is even more fraught with the possibility of corruption and error. Very poor people seldom have the 'proofs' that are required to qualify for the benefit.

In all countries millions in welfare benefits are unclaimed because the documentation needed to claim it is difficult to obtain for all but the experienced scrounger. In all countries it is recognised that targeted benefits are problematic to administer. They also lead to the notorious 'welfare trap' in which people cannot afford to lose benefits by taking a low-paid job, and so spend their lives idle and dependent on welfare.

How, in any case, should we define 'work' in South Africa? If a woman makes R10 a day selling chips outside the station, is she 'employed'? We do not have a situation in South Africa where people are mostly in jobs and need to be tided over between jobs. We have a huge informal sector. We have lost a million jobs in ten years: there is more poverty now than when we achieved democracy. It is getting worse, not better.

New Economics suggests by contrast to a dole a Basic Income Grant (BIG), sometimes called a Citizens' Income. This is an income paid from cradle to grave, unconditionally, to all citizens, as individuals, without a means test or work requirement. It is a right of citizenship. It represents a person's entitlement to a small part of the fruits of the society in which they live; and their stake in its success. It could be age-related: children getting least, adults more and the elderly most. The BIG of children is paid to the principal carer, usually the mother. It is paid by the most convenient method – electronically through a bank account or in cash through a public outlet like a post office. To receive it the beneficiary needs only to show an ID of some sort. In that sense it is exactly like the old age pension.

How much should it be? In principle it should be enough to allow people to keep body and soul together, but not enough to discourage them from seeking other income. These are vague terms, and will be differently interpreted. Amazing as it seems, hundreds of thousands of Africans live on R540 a month and share it with many people. In large parts of our rural areas pensions are the only source of cash income for the whole community. Recent detailed research shows that children who live with a grandmother in receipt of a pension are noticeably heavier and healthier than those who don't. The same is not true, however, for children who live with grandfathers.

Two widely respected international economists – whose views on the political economy of the world are radically different – both support the idea of a BIG. They are John Kenneth Galbraith, that great economist-populiser-activist, who has done more than anyone to make plain the issues of economics; and Milton Friedman, Thatcherite/Reaganite guru and pillar of the right.

The advantages of a BIG especially, but not exclusively, in South Africa are:

1.   With no means test, the bureaucracy involved in distribution is minimal. Nor is there large scope for corruption as there is when assessment is involved. This is a vital consideration in our country at this time. Our public service is appallingly disabled by our history. Even in a country like Britain, which has had a stable and sophisticated public welfare service for many decades, the experience of dealing with officials to claim benefit is painful, frustrating, time-consuming and dispiriting. I know this from having sat in a queue for the best part of a day to establish my right to a pension a couple of years ago. Had I been desperately

poor and apprehensive, had I the care of small fractious children, I know the experience would have stretched my stress-tolerance to its limits.

2. It deals with chronic destitution, where people have literally no alternative to begging or stealing.

3. It is an agent of compassion. In South Africa at present only some 23% of welfare benefits are taken up. If everyone received the benefits to which they are entitled, we would still address only 36% of people now living in poverty – meaning living with an income of less than R400 a month per household. Most poor households do not include a potential welfare beneficiary. A BIG is the most efficient way to address poverty

4. It ends the state of cashlessness in which many of our communities live. They cannot activate their skills because no one has any cash to buy anything from them. So it can begin a benign circle of local regeneration: employment is created as small amounts of money begin to circulate. An accelerator effect begins to operate.

5. It can create employment and growth on a wider scale too. In order even to look for work, people need a small cushion of cash. Not only for fares, for clean clothes and a CV equivalent, but also to enable them to take risks. If you have no money you cannot risk borrowing any for a job interview. Other risks may be taken – spending money on training for instance – if it is known that the grant will be regular.

6. Because it is regular it allows poor people to plan to change and uplift their lives, in a way that one-off payments cannot do. Those of us who have regular incomes, no matter how small, find it hard to understand the disorienting effect of unpredictable income. There is nothing more likely to incline people to fecklessness than the idea that the money now in their hands may be the last for some time. Basic security represents the possibility of responsibility and the ability to plan. It is the *sine qua*

non of the freedom to be an individual.

7. It allows people to take jobs at lower rates of pay if, for instance, a job offers training or other advantages that make the low pay worth it.

8. By contrast, it allows people to resist exploitative rates of pay and conditions.

9. It encourages labour-intensive local production, because people on small incomes support that kind of enterprise.

10. It does not involve the shame associated with means-tested welfare payments and the inquisition that goes with it. It makes sense of the rights of citizenship.

11. It reduces the strain on people in employment who have to share their income with so many destitute relatives. We forget that poverty represents a tax on the poor, who must support on their tiny incomes people who have none. We need to shift the burden of that tax to the rich.

12. It treats people equally. Therefore it narrows inequities of gender, youth or age.

13. The advantage to the rich is that it is likely to cut crime, although deprivation for several generations has probably led to some cultures in which that is unlikely immediately. For some of us it is also an advantage not to have our hearts and our pockets wrung by people who we know have no alternative but to appeal to us.

14. Since we know that nutrition in children is a massive determinant of a person's capacity to contribute in adult life and of her/his call on medical services, a BIG would have a benign effect on the economy in the next generation. We have millions of people in South Africa whose intelligence has been stunted for ever by malnutrition in childhood.

15. In time it would increase tax revenues as it encourages economic growth. There is plenty of research to show how people who escape

poverty contribute to economic growth.

16.   It would allow citizens to afford services like water and electricity, now literally impossible for people without cash. Our government has focused on provision of new services, including water, electricity, education and health. But the poor cannot access these services. Their failure to pay is condemned as deriving from 'a culture of non-payment and entitlement'. Research shows that this is largely untrue. The result is that these new services risk being expensive failures. Our health budget is a good example. We spend something like 400% more on health than we did under apartheid, but the results are disappointing, because poor health is largely the result of chronic poverty. Education is another example: people without income cannot send their children to school, even if the service is there.

17.   People who save are not penalised, because the BIG is paid to everyone without a means test.

18.   A BIG only gives the poor what taxpayers already get. Tax allowances amount to a government subsidy to people with incomes.

The objections to the BIG, with responses, are:

1.   *It is bad for people to get handouts. People shouldn't get something for nothing. There should be some reciprocity.*
      Some of us get handouts all our lives – from our parents, our privileged access and our inherited positions – and it helps us to make something of our lives. Of course, some of us get handouts and fall to pieces. But we don't stop rich people giving their children handouts. Many of us are constantly getting something for nothing. Moreover, in the matter of 'handouts' there is always an implied obligation as a result of a sense of belonging. It is precisely this sense of belonging that very poor

people lack, and that would make their citizenship feel real, perhaps for the first time.

2. *It will cause people to stop looking for jobs. There will be a labour shortage and employers will have to pay too much and become uncompetitive.*

   Research from the University of Cape Town's SALDRU suggests otherwise. People not only look for jobs more when they are above the destitution level, but they also succeed more. Let's remember, too, that there are currently millions more people than jobs. We want to end the humiliation of people having to look for jobs that aren't there. Perhaps we should be grateful to those people who are content to live on the small BIG and leave the jobs to the rest of us.

3. *They will drink the BIG away or spend it on the Lotto. The beneficiaries will be the drug barons and the liquor stores. And the men will beat up the women to get their BIG.*

   When the child allowance was first introduced in the UK, the same objection was made to it. Some parents, though few mothers, fulfilled the prophecy. The great majority used it to the benefit of their children. Thus also in South Africa some people will probably abuse the benefit. Should we refuse a right to the most vulnerable because a few abuse it? We know that addicted people have usually encountered deprivation or trauma somewhere in their lives. Moralistic attitudes are not helpful.

4. *Rich people don't need it, why give it to them?*

   The reasons for the universality are important. They are both practical – the lack of bureaucracy – and in principle, as a right of citizenship and a mark of inclusivity. But there are reasons in South Africa to accept that the rich should not benefit. Some people think it should be seen as a 'Solidarity Grant' paid by the rich to the poor. The BIG could easily be clawed back in the income tax of people who pay taxes: the full amount could be added to the calculated tax, so it all returns to the Treasury. That practice was latterly used in the UK in relation to the child allowance.

5.   *People will have more and more children just to get the BIG.*

Again that objection was used against the UK child allowance and proved groundless. It is a mistake to make laws on the basis of the possibility of abuse by a few. The fact is that the BIG would not give the parents a profit on a child. People have 'too many children' for a variety of reasons, mostly by mistake, hardly ever to do with the bottom line.

6.   *It will put civil servants out of a job.*

No. It will enable good civil servants to be moved to other jobs that desperately need doing. There is no shortage of work for good public servants.

7.   *The administration would not work. Already we are seeing the pension distribution falling apart.*

In fact the pension distribution is improving, and it is vital that we continue to improve it. If the whole country were to have a stake in such a system it would no doubt be totally overhauled. It is the kind of thing that might benefit by outsourcing to the private sector or to NGOs because it is easily monitored and does not involve policy judgement.

Paying for the BIG

Broadly speaking, there are two ways of paying for a BIG. The first is out of regular taxation and the second is to include an alternative system of taxes, which has a great many advantages in itself. These alternative taxes will be discussed in Chapter Three. Here we examine the work of Prof. Mike Samson, Director of the Cape Town-based Economic Policy Research Institute, and also a professor at the Williams Centre for Development Economics in the

United States. Professor Samson is one of several researchers who have been examining the cost and revenue implications of a BIG, using the present system of taxation.

Professor Samson shows that South Africa is currently under-taxed compared with similar economies. The myth of over-taxation is assiduously spread in all countries by the exponents of the Washington Consensus, who usually persuade people everywhere that they are more heavily taxed than their peers elsewhere.

Cross-country Government Revenue Comparison

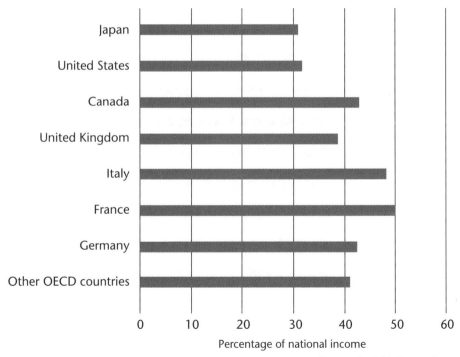

Percentage of national income

(Source: Prof. M. Samson)

The graph compares South Africa's average tax rate (total tax revenue as a percentage of national income) to those countries in comparable stages of development. South Africa's government revenue (relative to national income) is less than two-thirds the average calculated for those countries.

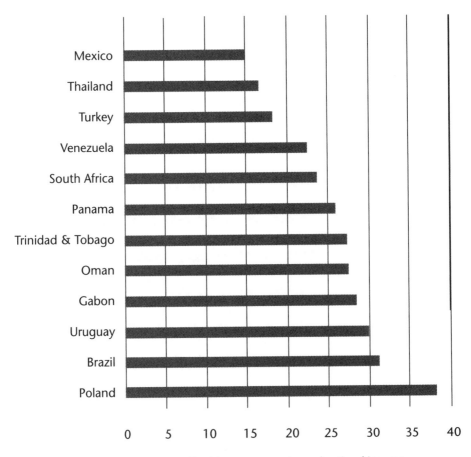

Total tax as a percentage of national income

(Source: Prof. M. Samson)

Econometric studies that control for individual country characteristics have found South Africa's average tax rate to be significantly less than that which would be predicted given the country's economic profile. South Africa could mobilise an additional R25 billion per year without undermining international competitiveness.

Thus these two charts show that South Africa is not comparatively over-taxed. The first looks at the taxation regimes of the most developed countries, with whom we might be thought to compete for investment capital. It is clear that even if investors chose to invest only on the basis of taxation levels we would be doing fine. We are under-taxed compared to many other countries. The second chart compares us with countries of comparable states of industrialisation, where we come fifth out of twelve.

It is probably true that the middle and lower income earners are over-taxed in South Africa, while the rich are grossly under-taxed. That is an argument for shifting the burden to the top, both in terms of income and corporation tax, and through creating a higher VAT on luxury goods.

Cost of BIG of R100 monthly

The BIG that is being suggested for South Africa is R100 a month. This amount was proposed by the Taylor Committee of Inquiry into a Comprehensive Social Security System, whose report was completed in 2001 and published in April 2002. It is acknowledged that the amount is less than is needed to support decent life; but with an average household of five people it would go some way to alleviating absolute poverty.

The price of a universal untaxed grant of R100 a month would be R53 billion annually. If it were clawed back from taxpayers, it would cost R28 billion.

This is how it would work. I quote from Professor Samson:

Every South African is given a tax-free income grant of R1200 per year. The primary income tax rebate is eliminated. The marginal tax rate is increased to 10% for the first R10,000 of income, 20% on the next R10,000, and 30% on income up to R60,000, and then follows the existing tax structure. This proposed tax structure eliminates the 'poverty trap' found in some means-tested schemes that impose high effective marginal tax rates on potential workers, reducing the incentive to work. Low-wage entrants into the labour force face only a 10% marginal tax rate.

The net cost of the BIG, while substantial, is clearly affordable. Research shows that South Africa has considerable additional taxable capacity – of the order of approximately five percent of national income. Potential revenue sources include making income tax more progressive, which could yield R7–12 billion; reducing private sector medical aid tax subsidies to raise R2–3 billion; taxing the proceeds from capital gains, which would produce R9–14 billion; an increase in value-added tax to raise R4–7 billion or a higher value-added tax rate on luxury goods to yield R3–5 billion; and/or tapping the 'hidden surplus' indicated by consistent over-attainment of tax revenue targets which amount to R5–6 billion. Moreover, saving would be made from other welfare programmes of the order of R3–4 billion. Between 33 and 51 billion rands of potential resources are available.

The South African government is currently looking very seriously at this possibility. Minister Skwiyia, shocked when he took office at what he described as 'the breakdown of society' due to poverty, introduced a two-year study by an interdepartmental task team – welfare, finance, labour, transport and health. That led to the Taylor Committee of Inquiry, which took evidence throughout 2001. The idea was to look for a welfare system that would replace or incorporate child support, pensions, disability benefit, unemployment insurance, workmen's compensation, accident insurance and national medical insurance. The BIG has the potential, with some adaptation, to meet that requirement.

Professor Samson's extremely modest scenario should be seen in relation to the fact that in 1999/2000 South African company tax rate changes gave away R1.5 billion. The next year the government gave taxpayers another bonus – R9.9 billion. Those earning over R200,000 a year got relief of R1,375 a month; those earning R50,000 got a cut of R80 a month, while those earning R30,000 a year benefited by only R7.50 a month. And the 2002 Budget reduced taxes by another R13 billion. Compare these figures to the monthly R100 proposed by Prof. Samson. The three years' tax giveaway could have produced most of the cost of a BIG if it were clawed back from the rich. Notice also taxpayers' subsidies in the form of tax rebates. The only people the existing tax system does not benefit are the very poor.

And while all these figures are being scrutinised, we must constantly bear in mind the costs of not providing a BIG. The minute-by-minute stress and suffering of half our population. The waste of lives. The hunger of children and their parents. The desperate resort to violence, drugs, prostitution. The resources lying fallow because our people cannot develop or access them. The anger. The loss of self-respect. The waste of our resources in ambulance work, in picking up the pieces. The loss of confidence in our country. This is a small part of the price we are paying now.

What we need is the courage to go for something new – to overcome the inertia of the familiar. The alternative of providing vast schemes of 'make-work' public works would be very much more expensive if it were to address the whole unemployed population, and it would require management capacity which our public service currently lacks. Above all, we must eschew the route of targeted benefits, however improved in terms of amount and spread. That will cost us far more in the end. The BIG will encourage economic growth effected by people taken out of poverty to create livelihoods, and contributing to the fiscus.

Chapter Three will examine alternative taxes – new and original sources of government revenue that could be used to finance a BIG as well as a great deal else.

Towards the end of 2001 a BIG Coalition was formed to campaign for a BIG. It comprised heavyweights like COSATU, the Black Sash, the SA Council of Churches, and the Catholic Bishops' Conference, as well as individual trade unions, church bodies and smaller NGOs like SANE, the Gender Advocacy Programme, the Community Law Centre and the Earth Centre. Its members agreed to campaign for a universal grant of R100 a month, which should not replace other existing benefits, but leave recipients at least as well off as before. It should be paid out of existing taxation.

International experience

In the UK a similar campaign group, the Basic Income Research Group (BIRG), was started at the London School of Economics. It is linked to the European BIEN (Basic Income European Network) Federation of groups proposing and researching Basic Income. They exist in Holland, Ireland, Spain, Sweden, France, Germany, New Zealand, Australia, Brazil, Canada and the US. BIEN's 2002 Congress had the backing of the ILO, in whose offices it was held.

New Basic Income groups are constantly in formation. Information is available at bien@etes.ucl.ac.be. Perhaps the current debate most relevant to South Africa is that taking place in the Canadian Supreme Court. Like South Africa, the state of Quebec includes social and economic rights in its human rights legislation. The recent case of Gosselin v. Quebec (Attorney General) 2002 involved a welfare claimant who pleaded that she should receive a consistent and adequate level of social assistance that cannot be cut, because it is a human right. In effect that is a claim to a BIG. In the event, the case was narrowly defeated, but it is interesting to note that, in one of their rulings, the judges almost unanimously agreed that there was a possibility that in the future the law could be interpreted to include positive obligations on the government to provide a minimum standard of living.

Brazil is out in front. Some municipalities are already paying something like a BIG. It is a monthly payment to households, not individuals. Following a campaign by Senator Eduardo Suplicy, an economics professor elected for the Workers' Party, the idea is catching on and spreading. Research shows that where the household grant is in place, employment rises and crime drops.

In Japan, the government's response to the collapse of purchasing power after the Asian Crash was to try to stimulate the economy in a direct way by giving everyone money to spend. In January 1999 children and low-income elderly people were given shopping vouchers for use in the shops in a particular area. This was designed not only to stimulate the economy but also to regenerate certain local economies. It was a one-off rather than a regular payment.

Thus there is a large international movement in favour of a Basic Income Grant. Imagine if South Africa once again gave a lead by introducing a measure based in compassion, as well as having massive practical benefits. From the viewpoint of business the imperative is to get money – purchasing power – into the hands of potential consumers. The BIG is an essential part of that process: it distributes income to people from whom the current economic system removes it. Nothing would so quickly and directly get to the root of poverty. But it is not the whole story. Public funding for badly needed 'commons' and infrastructure will be a vital part of the growth of a newly civilised society. And that means public finance – the topic of the next chapter.

POINTS FOR DISCUSSION – CHAPTER TWO

1. What creates scarcity for some people, abundance for others?

2. How should the productivity of labour be distributed?

3. What should be available as national 'commons'?

4. What should be available as international 'commons'?

5. How should 'commons' be provided?

MYTHS OF GLOBALISATION – THREE

'Admittedly the global market has created some disruption and some people have suffered. But this is a product of transition. When painful adjustments have been made, everyone will benefit.'

The first Thatcher government – and the second – and the third – and her successors – repeatedly offered this assurance, and still do. Governments everywhere that follow global market imperatives repeat it. But poor people and communities have benefited nowhere, after a quarter of a century of this 'transition'. Wealth has indeed increased but only at the top, and always at the expense of people at the bottom, who are systematically excluded from the fruits of growth. We now have, in all the formerly great European, American and Asian rich democracies, an 'underclass' of people, over generations unemployed, under-educated, criminalised and alienated from the mainstream economy. Those people are now stigmatised as responsible for their own failure by being intrinsically inferior. Recovery will be very difficult.

That pattern has been imposed between countries as well, because the unregulated global market in capital always concentrates wealth with the already successful. Racism infuses the description of Africa as 'a basket case'; its failure ascribed to colour and culture. Even the staunchest proponents of the global market will not claim that Africa has benefited, but they ascribe that to the feebleness of Africans. A great injustice is inherent in this myth, with its opponents regarded as whingers.

Even its proponents admit that the system is set up to promote the interests of those in the best position to compete. Competition is the driving value. That means that the victory will always go to the strongest, and the relatively weaker will be sacrificed. Logically, the developed countries and the most resourced individuals are bound to overcome the others in that race. The system automatically creates a steeply graded playing field in favour of the rich.

In that process the values of human solidarity, human equality and intrinsic human rights find no place. The idea that there is something fine and humane in a society of equals is inevitably seen as sentimental and inefficient. Periodic acts of charity replace intrinsic justice as a means to ameliorate the fate of excluded people. The Christian promotion of Jesus's 'bias to the poor' finds no place in official policies.

This is not about humanity having mutated in some mysterious way. It is a system that undermines human solidarity – or what we call in South Africa 'ubuntu'. The global system has, however, created new, harder values that people have had to adopt as survival mechanisms.

MYTHS OF GLOBALISATION – FOUR

'Trade is the engine of growth and development. Africa is failing economically because its involvement in world trade is too little, not too much.'

This statement, which implicitly blames Africa, is rooted in a number of illusions. The first of these is that trade is always beneficial to both parties. It is obviously not so, because it depends on the relative power of both parties, and therefore the terms of trade. Any child who has 'traded' with a bully knows that. The terms of trade between Africa and the rest of the world, especially the US, the EU and Japan, are profoundly disadvantageous to Africa – a fact well documented – which has resulted in Africa's share of trade falling in the last twenty years to half what it was in the 1970s. So have the benefits of that trade. Africa remains dependent largely on primary commodities, which are notoriously unpredictable in price, and upon low-wage, labour-intensive enterprise with little value added. There is no evidence of a positive connection between trade and income growth.

The World Trade Organisation's trade rules, which are set by the most powerful countries, favour rich countries' exports at the expense of those of poor countries. The most notorious example of this allows, despite the rules, the subsidisation of agricultural products in developed countries, so that poor countries, notably Africa, cannot compete in either their own markets or abroad. They must see their home agriculture suffer, without being able to compete overseas.

These facts are now accepted universally. The rich countries' answer is a vague assurance that in time they will end their subsidies and reduce their barriers to poor countries' goods. This is another illusion. In close-fought elections in developed countries leaders show no willingness to sacrifice their own people's secure livelihoods – whether in agriculture or manufacture – in the interests of poor people elsewhere. Nor is there any realistic prospect that they will do so in the future. As those leaders will admit when pressed, 'I am elected to advance the interests of (the American people).' For 'the American people' we may reliably substitute those of any other country.

The focus on trade as a solution to economic stagnation – a focus that suits rich countries' interest in finding foreign markets – has removed attention from internal market expansionist mechanisms that would enable poor countries to grow. 'Export-led growth' has been the unquestioned mantra of the Washcon. Poor countries have sought its benefits in vain. It is a myth.

MYTHS OF GLOBALISATION – FIVE

'The global market may not have distributed its benefits equally, but it is the only way to develop.'

American researchers have produced a scorecard comparing the periods 1960–80 with 1980–2000. In the first period, national governments regulated their economies, sometimes with tariffs, to grow their own enterprise. In the second period we had the global market ideology. During the first, per capita income in Latin America grew by 73%; that in Africa by 34%. In the second period, Latin American growth fell to virtually nil and incomes increased by only 6% over the whole period; while African incomes fell by 23%. More than eighty countries now have per capita incomes lower than they were in 1980, according to the UN Development Programme. The UNDP points out that 'it is often the countries that are becoming even more marginal which are highly integrated into the global economy'. In Africa the higher the proportion of GDP that is exported, the higher the number of people living in poverty.

Life expectancy, which had grown worldwide by nearly 10 years in the first period, dropped in African countries during the second period. Only the rich countries slightly increased life expectancy.

It is clear that countries that have done well have successfully dropped tariff barriers as they became richer. Integration into the world market is successful if it is controlled; disastrous if it is forced upon poor countries.

Globalisation puts pressure on wages as well as jobs, because mobile capital moves investment where wages are lowest and the pool of unemployed largest. The per capita income of workers even in rich countries has fallen under this pressure. The arrival of China in the world trading system has already created unemployment elsewhere, while also rendering some hundred million Chinese unemployed by means of even cheaper imports from other countries – including subsidised agricultural products from the US and EU.

CHAPTER THREE

Alternative sources of government revenue

If one ironic result of our new riches is scarcity of purchasing power, another is falling government revenues. Governments can now 'afford' less in the way of public service, common infrastructure and redistributive measures than they could when Gross Domestic Product was a tenth of what it is now. Why is this? There are four main reasons.

First, expenditure by government is frowned on by the powerful international arbiters of policy – the owners of capital and the very large transnational corporations (TNCs) who are the main drivers, beneficiaries and architects of globalising the market. They believe that governments should not compete with the private sector for resources – labour and investment capital. If there were ever any doubt about the power of these coalitions of interest, we have only to refer to the similarity between the policies of democratically elected governments worldwide, despite the massive differences in their electorates, social and economic conditions and other elements that should produce variety in governmental priorities and policies. There is one tune when it comes to government expenditure, and it is a tune to which all governments must dance.

The anti-public sector ideology was so extreme in the '80s that some structurally adjusted countries had hardly any government service at all. Later it was recognised that some things must be provided by government – law and the legal system, roads and other transport, defence and some public education and health – and that government must hold the ring while competition happens within it. So the attitude has softened. But basically government is considered a necessary evil, and is expected to be minimal and to make very little call on resources. Everything that can be produced in the private sector should be made and sold there. Thereby government revenues will be kept small.

This is justified on the basis that without the profit motive governments are inevitably inefficient in terms of the delivery of goods and services. Private enterprise, driven by the search for profit, knows how to produce competitively to the benefit of consumers and shareholders alike. This is the theory behind the drive for privatisation of what used to be seen as government services. If services are produced by the private sector, taxation is relieved of their costs.

For that to happen, everything, including education, prisons, public utilities and health, must be commodified and costed, in the same way as bananas and radios and hats, and the full cost of production plus profit paid by the consumer. The international privatisation movement now expects to include in the private sector most of what used to be taken for granted as a government service or responsibility.

This change represents something very important in principle. It is not only about what works best. The concept of government service has its roots in the idea that a society as a whole benefits from all its citizens adopting and having access to certain standards – typically education, health, housing and public order. These form the basis of a society's 'commons' – things that are accessible to everyone, of all ages, regardless of willingness or ability to pay for them. The theory is that everyone benefits if everyone else is healthier, better educated and so on; and that no person or group should be able to deprive others of these things for their own gain. This is basic to social and Christian democracy, Ubuntu, humanism, liberation theology and other political philosophies with roots miles away from communism.

Taken to its extremes the privatisation movement contradicts all that. It asserts that the private sector – by its nature, because it uses profit to measure and motivate effectiveness – is always not only more efficient but also healthier for humanity. There is some truth in the efficiency argument – as the contrast between the command and the free market economies demonstrates – but only if we ignore the value of social 'commons'.

The problem is that not everything produced has only the one purpose of efficient allocation of resources in terms of monetary value. Take clean water – a basic requisite for health. If people don't get it they die one way or another. The profit motive for water distribution ignores this fact. Private enterprise distributes water efficiently to people who can pay for it, not to anyone else. Government services used to be considered essential for basics like this. Water was seen as a right, without which a person would not only become ill but would also become a danger to the rest of the community. The provision of such a service was seen, therefore, as of benefit not only to the direct recipients, but also to the standards of life for everyone.

The WSSD Conference clearly demonstrated the divide. Government after government spoke of water provision as a basic right. But those who supported privatisation spoke of water as a basic need. If something is a right, it is obviously wrong to deprive people of it because they cannot afford to buy it; whereas a need is something you satisfy if you can afford it, but not otherwise. Such semantic distinctions extended to describing the thorny issue of people's being unable to buy water as 'demand management'.

Governments have always wrestled with this issue. What should people get as a right? Shelter? Food? Education? And if it is a right, how should it be provided to those – like children – who cannot get it for themselves? What is clear is that a platform of good education and health is basic to all growing economies and social stability. The social democratic Mauritian government of the 1960s and 1970s pulled the country out of chronic dependence on a single crop, widespread poverty and an out-of-control population growth by a sharp focus on three government-funded areas – education, health and family planning. Of course, in those days governments were supposed to be active and its currency was under its own control. That story is worth study.

Privatisation should not be a matter of principle. While most activities are handled better by the private sector – the administration of the BIG described in Chapter Two may be one of them – many are not. Privatised railways, for instance, have been shown to be a disaster everywhere, while nationalised railways on the whole work well. Compare those in Britain with those in France, for example. Water and electricity privatisation are now regretted in many places as bad for the consumer and the taxpayer. Make no mistake – privatised former utilities cost the taxpayer millions.

Nor is privatisation good for education, where controversy as to objective and process is inherent, and where the profit motive may be seriously damaging. In the US, there are schools sponsored by Coke and Pepsi. Guess what drinks are on offer where. What next? Prozac? Cigarettes? Oil companies? Media corporations? Might that distort decisions about the curriculum?

One reason why privatised public service is opposed by trade unions is that by its nature private tendering creates the need for cost cutting in the interests of competitiveness. This, unless regulated, always leads to exploitative labour practices. And regulation is another dirty word as far as the private sector and capital investors are concerned. It is recognised in Britain for instance that the outsourcing (privatisation) of the more manual functions of the health service – cleaning, laundry, catering – has lowered standards dangerously, and this seriously undermines the functioning of hospitals. Cleaning in a hospital is a specialist skill, integral to its core functions. You cannot run a good hospital that is dirty and accumulates laundry even temporarily; and that may well happen where casualised labour is employed. The process in the UK lost thousands of jobs, and created far fewer jobs in inferior conditions of work that resulted in a demoralised and unstable work-force, high turnover of staff and dangerous conditions in hospitals.

Second, the implication of the general anti-government movement is that you must have a very low tax regime and very little regulation. Wages and conditions of work, hiring and firing and exploitation of the environment must be left to the operation of the free market. A Multilateral Agreement on Investment (MAI), threatened in the mid-'90s, would have made it illegal for any government to take any action that got in the way of free access on equal terms of any enterprise to any market. It would have been illegal – a barrier to trade – to legislate in favour of local or small enterprise, to create equal opportunity laws or to protect the natural environment. The MAI was scuppered by international civil society objection. But it illustrates a trend that is still dominant. Governments are getting this kind of pressure constantly from the potential suppliers of overseas and local capital. That is why when governments change, policies don't very much. And it is why governments are always setting tax reduction as a priority.

Third, e-commerce depletes government revenues. Internet trading will make it increasingly hard for governments to collect VAT, customs duties and other sales levies.

Fourth, ageing populations make it necessary for governments to collect revenue from the increasingly few to supply pensions to the increasingly many. Conventional taxation will find it hard to meet the bill.

In addition to these constraints on governments' sources of public revenue, we must recognise that current taxes are perverse. We tax the value that people add – incomes, profits and VAT – all the things that people do that are productive. We also tax employment, although we are short of jobs. And we provide incentives for people to use the earth's scarce resources and to capital-intensify. By contrast, we do not tax value subtracted. As societies we expect to pick up the bill for the results of destructive and polluting activity, including health and environmental destruction. We do not, in other words, make the producers and consumers of things that have toxic side-effects pay the full cost of that production.

Taxes should be about two things. Government revenue is only one. The other should be to use the price mechanism, which incorporates taxes, to encourage the activities and conditions that we want and discourage those we don't want.

Taxes should *encourage*:
- Social inclusion
- Social equity
- Economic efficiency
- Environmental sustainability.

Taxes should *discourage*:
- Use of non-renewable resources
- Monopoly of God-given common resources
- Pollution and waste.

Therefore *we should not tax the value that people add*, as we do now through:
- VAT
- Personal income tax
- Company tax

We should tax the value that they subtract, for example through:
- Green taxes
- Taxes on value created by society
- Site value taxation on land
- Taxes on speculative currency transactions

Existing taxes are perverse. They:

- reduce employment by taxing employment and value added
- reduce employment by subsidising capital-intensive production and energy to increase competitiveness
- encourage polluting and waste because the state funds measures to restore health and cope with waste
- encourage inefficient land use and speculation
- encourage currency speculation
- encourage inefficient use of resources, and pollution, by subsidising long-distance transport using fossil fuels
- deepen social exclusion by means testing benefits
- fall most heavily on poor people, especially VAT
- create poverty and welfare traps.

New Economics taxation would replace income, company and value added taxes with taxes that encourage the activities we want and discourage those that cause damage. They do that not by clumsy regulations but by using the price mechanism. Taxation has the power to make some things relatively cheaper and some things more expensive, and that is the way consumption patterns can be influenced. Some of these taxes are broadly known as green taxes, because a major feature is that they protect and promote the natural environment. Global market forces, left to themselves, destroy it.

Why new taxes?

We have to redefine the search for productivity. We now have an excess of labour and a growing crisis in the use of natural resources. Therefore we need to encourage the use of the former and discourage the use of the latter. A good exposition of this case is given in a book called *Factor Four: Doubling Wealth,*

Halving Resource Use by Von Weizacher and Lovins.

We now consume as much oil in a year as it takes nature a million years to create. In 2000 the world consumed 28 billion barrels of oil, costing a total of $756 billion. By burning this and other fossil fuels we have increased carbon dioxide in the atmosphere from 285 parts per million to 365 since 1850. Americans spend $500 billion on energy every year – their average per capita consumption being some five times that of any other nation.

Oil is among the natural resources that are running out. We know that Western sources will run out in the foreseeable future. We don't know for sure the situation in the OPEC countries; and we have become complacent as a result of past false alarms. What is clear is that the production of fossil fuels will probably peak within the next decade, but we are acting as though oil and gas supplies will continue to be cheap and abundant for ever. We have no idea how dependent we are on oil until we hit a crisis, as we did over the sudden price hikes in 2001. In parts of Europe commerce was nearly brought to a halt by the public demand that government take action in the form of subsidies. Much the same applies to our forests, seas and clean air. We behave as though their continued exploitation is not a problem, though we know that is not true.

In fact we actually subsidise the destruction of the environment, of communities and of poorer areas. Helena Norberg-Hodge's wonderfully illus-trated little book *Small is Beautiful, Big is Subsidized* shows, inter alia, that:

1. *Long-distance transport, especially by air – used most profitably by big companies – is subsidised by governments.*

   Planes are the most polluting form of transport: they create twelve times more greenhouse gases than trains and four times more than cars, as well as noise and air pollution. Hence for instance the modern epidemic of asthma. Yet there is no tax on aviation fuel. Air traffic has grown by 250% since 1960, partly because it is becoming progressively cheaper – by 42% in the last 10 years. Each year air travel creates 750 tons of pollutants. Taxpayers subsidise air travel in other ways too. They build new airports and the roads and other infrastructure that serve them. There is no VAT on airline tickets or new planes. You can buy duty-free at airports and on planes. It is reckoned that the UK Exchequer could make £5 billion annually if it ended these subsidies and tax exemptions. For Europe the figure is £30 billion.

The way we could deal with all this would be either to tax aviation fuel or to tax emissions. Both would raise revenue, discourage flying and make the industry pay the full cost of its operation. New electronic communications technology makes it possible for business to operate without so much air travel. Tourism would become more local.

The criss-crossing of the skies by identical products – an amazingly inefficient use of resources – would also be discouraged. The UK, for instance, exports 250 million litres of milk a year, and imports 226 million litres of milk. The same proportions apply to butter and milk powders as well as meat. The economist Colin Hines has reckoned that 'fresh' food landed at Heathrow will have used ten times as much energy as it will give out when eaten.

The argument that poor countries are especially dependent on air travel – because of the contribution of tourism and the export of high value crops – applies only if we imagine that local and national production for local and national consumption is not a possible substitute. That is not so. Our dependence in Africa on tourism and overseas markets is our Achilles' heel. It can collapse overnight, as it has in other places. It is also unnecessary. Chapter Five will examine the value of localisation.

2. *Long-distance road travel is also subsidised by taxpayers.*
The multinational enterprises that use huge lorries to transport goods pay in road fund taxes only a tiny proportion of the cost of providing the roads

and of the damage they do to them. If they were to pay the full cost, it would be very expensive indeed to take goods over long distances. Rail traffic and local production would be the beneficiaries. We might think it is cheaper to transport, say, beans from the Lowveld to Cape Town, because they can be sold cheaper than beans from Philippi. But that is because we taxpayers have subsidised the travel. If we were similarly to subsidise rail traffic we could shift a great deal of traffic from roads to rail to the benefit of all. Currently, with a poor railway system, we have created a vicious circle in which the road system is over-used and the railways neglected.

The odd thing is that when this point is put to policy-makers they say that roads and airports are an investment, which will recover the costs in growth and hence employment. Why do we not say that about railways? More to the point, what about education and health, housing and utilities? Are they not investments? Sadly, they are regarded as something govern-ments have to do *for* people, as a kind of welfare subsidy. And the present economic thinking is that people ought to pay for these things: it is wrong to give people water and electricity and schools and clinics. Whereas, according to these ideas, those who use our roads and airports should have them subsidised by the taxpayer. Why? What is the difference?

3. *Energy is also subsidised.*

It, too, is seen as an investment. The full costs are not passed on, especially to the bringers of new foreign direct investment. Considering the subsidies which governments put into energy utilities to 'get them ready' for privati-sation, it is very clear how much taxpayers underpin the energy industry.

4. *American and European industrial agriculture or agribusiness is heavily subsidised by governments around the world, including that of South Africa.*

All of these companies use artificial fertilisers, pesticides and herbicides, which are dangerous to our health when eaten, or breathed in the air. The subsidies are not only direct, but also indirect. Governments and affected individuals pick up the bill for the health consequences – the respiratory diseases and the creeping effects on human immune systems. We are now seeing some particularly hideous ill-effects, financial as well as moral, of coping with diseases like new variant CJD ('mad cow') that arise from practices instigated by ill-researched attempts to cheapen output. Agribusiness worldwide is subsidised also by long-distance transport. And governments' diplomatic services offer 'aid' agreements that include subsidies to encourage farmers to use the chemicals and seeds, some of them genetically modified, patented by large agribusiness corporations.

5. *Governments subsidise their large-scale private sector to take risks in foreign countries, so as to create and exploit new markets.*
    Very often this new market penetration comes on the back of 'aid/loan' projects that involve dams, roads, power stations, arms deals, etc., later shown to have serious side-effects for the local population

6. *The following subsidies and incentives were given in the 2000 budget in South Africa:*
    *   R380 million to manufacturing; R50 million as tax holidays; R162 million in various start-up grants; R230 million in interest subsidies;
    *   R121 million in the export development programme; and
    *   R300 million in technology enhancement for industry.
    Meanwhile there was no grant for research on labour-intensive production, out of a total research budget of R517 million. Only some 4% of the Trade and Industry budget was for small and medium business development. In South Africa, as elsewhere, big is subsidised compared to small.

Make no mistake: we do not have a level playing field. Apart from the advantages of scale, big capital-intensive enterprise is subsidised as compared with small, labour-intensive and local production. That is why it seems cheaper. It is touted as being efficient. On the contrary, it is extremely wasteful of the Earth's resources.

Green taxes

The most obvious forms of green tax are levied on:
- Carbon in fuels
- Car/truck/airline emissions
- Industrial pollution
- Municipal solid waste
- Fertilisers, herbicides, pesticides
- Cut timber, unless replaced
- Harvested fish, unless stocks can regenerate
- Wasteful water use – evaporation
- Noise pollution. Think of jet aircraft – Concorde!

All have the advantage of internalising in all products the full cost to society of producing and consuming them. This is called 'full cost accounting'. At present many activities have toxic side-effects that have to be borne by everyone – whether or not they are involved in the making or consuming of them. There is nothing new about this idea. We have taxed smoking and liquor for years already, despite the huge interests vested in those industries. And recognising that smoking is not only bad for the smoker, we are also taking strong regulatory measures to prevent it affecting the rest of us. Green taxes raise the price of producing less acceptable products, and so discourage their use. They do not necessarily exclude regulation as well.

1. Carbon in fuels is best taxed upstream – where the product leaves the earth.

That needs international cooperation, so for the time being it may be applied at the point of entry to the country. Clearly the effect could be regressive. There is a case for subsidy where that is so.

2. Car, truck and airline emissions may also be discouraged by taxation at the point of sale.

3. Industrial pollution taxes can be traded between companies: those who continue to pollute can buy limited rights to do so from others who are cleaner.

4. Municipal solid waste is already fairly heavily taxed in many European and American cities.

5. Fertilisers, herbicides and pesticides should be taxed to cover the cost of repairing the health of people affected by these chemicals, both directly and indirectly. These taxes would privilege organic methods of food production.

6. Cut timber should be taxed unless it is replaced.

7. Water use can be assessed for its wastefulness in terms of how much is allowed to evaporate.

8. Fish harvesting should be taxed if it uses methods that deplete stocks.

9. Noise pollution can be evaluated and taxed to discourage it: there is currently no disincentive to creating noise.

Some very detailed work has been done on all these taxes. A comprehensive 'organisers' kit' has been produced by an American organisation called Sustainable America. It addresses itself to all these and other taxes directed to enhancing the environment, urban as well as rural. The kit describes for each of the taxes:

- The problem that needs to be solved
- What should be taxed to help solve it
- Who should pay the tax
- How the revenues should be used
- How the tax will change behaviour
- How people and communities will be affected
- Who is using these policies today
- Where you can get more information.

We need similar research in South Africa. But already there are examples of the successful use of green taxes. The EU Environmental Agency's 2001 Report on Recent Development in the Use of Environmental Taxes shows that eight members already levy carbon taxes, nine waste disposal taxes. Another EU report, Environmental-Energy Taxation and Employment Creation has some startling things to say about how employment can be boosted by harmonised energy taxes. The costs of labour would be relatively cheapened, as energy costs rise, and about 120,000 jobs would be created by 2010. It reckons emissions would fall by some 20%. It describes these measures as 'correcting market failures'. A similar detailed sector-by-sector study by the forecasting group Cambridge Econometrics in the UK shows how, apart from the revenue raised, employment could be created and emissions reduced through the introduction of these taxes. We need similar research for South Africa and our continental neighbours.

At an international level there is one further 'tax' that could promote the replacement of destructive with benign activity. Known as 'contraction and convergence', it has been worked out by the Global Commons Institute in London. The idea is similar to the trading of emissions rights between companies referred to above. It is the proposed trading of emissions rights between nations. Like its national equivalent, it is designed to give an incentive to rich nations to reduce the dangerous emissions their industry produces. The idea is to divide the total emissions that the planet can endure by the world's population. Each nation would be entitled to a certain emission level according to its population. The United States, Europe and Japan are clearly way over their allocation – up to 90%. So they would be required to reduce their emissions drastically.

In the meantime, and to provide them with a solid incentive to reduce, they would be required to buy other nations' rights. The sellers of emissions rights would be poorer countries, and this would provide a useful incentive for them to avoid the emissions route to development. It would also constitute a massive transfer of resources from rich to poor countries. Indeed, the UN Environment Programme's Klaus Topfer has calculated that the G7 countries were at the turn of the millennium running up annual emissions 'debts' to the tune of $13 trillion. This is three times the size of the combined international debt of the Highly Indebted Poor Countries (HIPCs), which we are being asked to 'forgive'.

This scheme is attracting interest in the rich countries, as an alternative to the apparently politically impossible task of inducing Americans and Europeans to vote in large enough numbers for politicians espousing drastic curtailment of their use of fossil fuels, air travel, industrial pollutants – hence their standards of living. Of course, some within the ecology movement oppose emissions trading, because it seems to postpone the day when emission levels come down. I personally believe it will have the opposite effect.

We are stuck at present in the whole area of how to deal with the emissions that are causing climate change. The US government in particular, apparently seeing no way of inducing Americans to change their way of life so as to reduce the emissions they create, seems to stick its head in the sand. It has virtually scuppered the Kyoto Agreement on Climate Change, preferring to leave the Bonn Conference rather than face its role in perpetuating the problem. The United States insists that no binding regulations be made in international law to deal with climate change: all should remain voluntary and aspirational.

Meanwhile the UN Environmental Programme estimates that the extra economic costs of disasters attributable to climate change are running at more than $300 billion annually. This has led the New Economics Foundation in London to propose legal action. 'One of the most basic principles in law is that, if you do someone damage, first you should stop what you are doing, and second you should compensate the injured party,' says NEF's Andrew Simms. 'As the evidence of harm from global warming is growing – especially in poor countries that pollute relatively little – and since the US is the largest single polluter … It should be possible to take legal action.' The first step would be to ask the UN General Assembly to request an advisory opinion from the International Court of Justice. The USA's cheap energy policy could also be challenged as an insidious subsidy at the World Trade Organisation.

Total Economic Activity Levy (TEAL)

The purpose of green taxes is not primarily to raise revenue; and to the extent that their environmental purpose is achieved – producing a healthier environment – revenues would fall over time. We should not exaggerate that, however. Sweden raises 6% of its budget from green taxes. People will always smoke and drink, it seems; and if people want to use vast gas-guzzling cars or eat mangoes in Scotland in January, they will at least be paying the full cost to society of producing and transporting them.

But there are other proposed New Economics taxes that also would have the effect of raising a sustainable revenue. The first, a total economic activity levy (TEAL), has the additional advantage of preventing the vast waste of resources represented by the professions of tax evasion/avoidance lawyers and tax evasion/avoidance government inspectors. This is a tax that cannot be evaded or avoided. It is a homegrown South African alternative tax suggestion, and has the principal virtue of being a very simple and comparatively painless way of collecting revenue.

This is the idea. A small tax – say 0.5% – is levied on both sides of all transactions that are routed through financial institutions. For example, if a R100 cheque is passed from one person to another through a bank, the seller is credited with R99.95, and the buyer will pay an extra R.05. Both will go directly to the Reserve Bank from the bank or other financial institution that has made the transaction.

In South Africa, the current annual value of transactions outside the bond market is some R25 trillion. A tax of 0.65% – six and a half cents in each hundred rand – would bring the government something like R280 billion. This would be enough to end the need for all other taxes at current rates of government expenditure. We would have to levy no other taxation. You can work out for yourself your total tax liability. Take your annual income and double it, because you pay the TEAL both on receiving and on spending money. Then take 0.65% of that; and that is your total tax. No VAT. No income tax. No company tax. And no fuss with tax accountants and revenue forms.

If we brought the bond market into TEAL the rate could be even lower and yet replace all other taxes.

The advantages are huge. Tax collection would be immediate, unavoidable, continuous and predictable, allowing the government to budget more accurately. Tax lawyers and accountants could be redeployed to more productive activities such as introducing systems to foil corruption. And government revenues would be produced at much lower cost. The TEAL would be extremely difficult to evade – short of risking being mugged by carrying all one's money around in suitcases. Available purchasing power would increase with the ending of VAT. With no employment taxes or PAYE, it would be cheaper to give people jobs at the same rates. Goods and services would immediately become cheaper. For example a professional who now needs to earn say R100 net must charge her client R182, to include VAT plus income tax at 37%, amounting to R82. Under a TEAL system of taxation she would charge only R102.

The tax would be progressive. People with most money would pay more than those with less. But wealthy businesspeople who have been approached with the TEAL idea have found it attractive because their customers would be considerably better off, while their own tax-related costs would disappear altogether, and they would pay no tax on their personal income.

Sounds too good to be true? You can contact TEAL on the e-mail address teal@worldonline.co.za

Land Value Tax

The philosophy behind this tax – originally the brainchild of Henry George in the 1930s – is that all members of a society should have a stake in and a dividend from the common inheritance of that society. We should all benefit from the value that is added to a product by the society as a whole.

Taxation should be related to how much we use of resources inherited from nature and how much value we create ourselves. Thus land value taxation makes the distinction between value that is created by people as a result of their own work or investment, and value that is created either by nature itself or by the activities of society as a whole. A barren hectare in the Karoo is worth less than one covering an oil field – not because the owner of the latter has created anything, but because of what nature has given. A plot in Adderley

Street in central Cape Town is more valuable than one in an isolated fishing village only because, unlike the latter, it is surrounded by many other streets and a large population and is served by roads, railways and airlines. Its value is created by the rest of society. The building of a new road can double or halve the value of a piece of land, regardless of what its owner has done. Land value taxation plans to tax the value of the land without the buildings or other infrastructure created on it by its owners.

This would have a number of beneficial effects. It would discourage the practice of holding land out of use for speculative purposes, because its current value would be the subject of the tax, regardless of whether it is used or not. It would encourage the bringing of derelict land into use, as well as improvements to the resource itself. It would make renting and building relatively more affordable by not penalising building itself.

The creation of money

Finally, a very obvious way for the government to raise its revenue is to put itself back in control of the creation of money. This is an old idea – not surprisingly scuppered constantly by the banking industry – that is now putting its head over the parapet once again. It formed the basis of James Robertson's 'Alternative Mansion House Speech' in 2000. A full, detailed account of how this would work is to be found in *Creating New Money: A Monetary Reform for the Information Age* by James Robertson, independent economist and former banker, and Joseph Huber of the Institut für Soziologie in Berlin. The idea is also explored in depth in Michael Rowbotham's two recent books: *The Grip of Death* and *Goodbye America*, the latter launched on his 1999 trip to South Africa; and in the writings of Richard Douthwaite.

The way money is at present created is both inequitable and extremely dangerous, John Kenneth Galbraith says: *'The process by which banks create money is so simple the mind is repelled ... Where something so important is involved, a deeper mystery seems only decent.'*

Money is not intrinsically valuable. It is a means of exchange and a store of value. It is vital that it properly serves those functions. If there is too little or too much money to facilitate the exchange of goods and services, you get inflation or deflation; and if you have inflation, money loses part of its value. That means that at any one time the amount by which the stock of money is increased to allow the creation and exchange of new goods and services is extremely important. If there is not enough money in circulation, people and resources are left unemployed. Thus this is a vital decision that some person or body has to make. It cannot be left to 'the market', because supply and demand does not apply to something that has no intrinsic value.

So how should we decide how much money should be created? At present the central or Reserve Bank, with the government, makes that calculation. But you may be surprised to hear that they do not themselves create or withdraw money. They try to influence the amount of money in circulation by setting a rate of interest by which all other banks can borrow from them. This interest rate filters into the system and affects indirectly and imperfectly the amount of money that people borrow from the commercial banks – because, amazingly, it is in fact the commercial banks that create money.

Banks create money by giving people loans, and they do that on the basis of what they regard as creditworthiness. They are required by law to cover with their reserves only a small proportion of the amount they lend, their reserves being the deposits of other people. That proportion varies in each country between 5% and 20%.

This 'fractional reserve banking', as it is called, works like this. A person asks for a loan; and collateral security and interest are agreed. It is then written into the equivalent of a ledger in their name, and they can start spending it. It is called a 'sight deposit'. *It is made out of thin air.* The bank has not been to another customer and told them they cannot use that part of their money because it has been lent to someone else. It is not money that the bank has borrowed from someone else. The bank is obliged by law only to respect the fractional reserve: that is, they may not lend more than *80 to 95 times the sum of their deposits.*

But notice that the fractional reserve is no real inhibitor of banks' activity in creating money. When the customer starts spending the loan, most of it will be deposited into other people's accounts. Then *their* deposits become part of the fractional reserve of that or another bank, and another multiple of its value may be created into existence in the form of a loan. These sight deposits – also called checking or money deposits – are described in the bank's own credit account as a claim on the customer, and described in the current account of the customer as a cash liability to the bank. When the loan is repaid, both the capital and the interest *become part of the assets of the bank* – and can be recycled to form the basis of new loans. If it is not repaid, the bank collects the customer's collateral security, which had been offered to cover the loan. As James Robertson has noted, *'Don't let anyone tell you there is no such thing as a free lunch: banks have free lunches every day.'*

One caveat to that process: Governments do also create money, but only the coins and notes that are used in the economy – at present between 3% and 8% in most countries. This is all that is left of what used to be known as the government's seigniorage: originally the right of the monarch in Europe to create coin. It is hardly worth saying that seigniorage is highly valuable. Whoever has the power to create the money supply has a valuable asset. It now lies – all but 3–8% – with commercial banks.

Notice four vital aspects to this process:

First, what the government spends into the economy in the form of coins and notes comes interest free: they simply create it and spend it. They do not create a loan by creating the money.

Second, all the rest of new money is created by banks *in the form of debt*. The more money there is, the more debt there is. As the money supply increases, so does the nation's indebtedness.

Third, the banks do not put into circulation the money to cover the interest on the loans. So everyone who has a loan competes with everyone else to get hold of enough money to pay the interest. Inevitably some lose. Hence bankruptcies. This is less important in times of expansion because this year's borrowers can use the extra money put into the economy by next year's borrowers. But in the end there is a reckoning. And then the cycle changes and recession arrives, fewer loans are made and bankruptcies are compounded. This system of creating money is inevitably unstable. In times of expansion, banks give out more loans, because more people are seen as creditworthy; in times of recession they restrict their loans. So they exacerbate the cycles of boom and bust. The creation of money should do the opposite.

Fourth, money created in this way is not linked – theoretically or practically – to real resource use or potential, or to the amount of goods and services in the nation. It is created on the banks' assessment of individuals' ability to repay. It has only the faintest connection with savings; so it is not in the conventional sense 'capital'. The table on page 109 shows the growth of total money supply; it illustrates how this system has created a debt-based potential monster. David Boyle's book *Funny Money* explains in detail.

Money has become an industry, run by the banks, that has taken over our economies. The financial sector, whose size is a function and a symptom of 'funny money', provides the largest taxable surplus in South Africa – and probably many other countries as well. It grew by just under 50% between 1993 and 2001, while the economy as a whole grew by 24%. Its power gives weight to its vested interest in the globalisation of money, in the relative scarcity of money and therefore in the preservation of the Washington Consensus about how to run the world's economic affairs.

The only control the government has over this process is its indirect influence via the rate of interest of the Reserve Bank. This can influence how many people want to take out loans. But the government's control is indirect, inefficient, unpredictable and slow to take effect. Also a high rate of interest to control the process is a clumsy instrument, being extremely bad for small business, homeowners and others.

Now imagine something equally simple. Suppose that, in an orderly way, the government removed the right to create money from commercial banks. They could still act as moneylenders, but only to lend out the money they had borrowed. Then suppose the government allowed the Reserve Bank – politically independent – to decide what the annual flow of new money should be, given the potential flow of new goods and services via existing underemployed labour and resources. Then the Reserve Bank would credit that amount of money to the government's Treasury as public revenue. Interest free. The government would then put it into circulation as public spending. Debt free. In other words, the government's seigniorage would extend to electronic money as well as notes and coins as now. Just as it now spends the notes and coins into the economy free of charge it could be the source of electronic money as well. In deciding how much money to create in this way, the Reserve Bank would be expected to operate with a high degree of independence from the political authority or government to prevent populist decisions.

The advantages of such reform were given in a paper by Joseph Huber to the Forum for Stable Currencies at the House of Lords in London in June 2001. They are worth summarising.

1. It represents an obvious next step in the evolution of the monetary system. It is not about overthrowing or doing away with what exists. It is just a slight but important restructuring of long-established institutions and practices.

2. There are obvious benefits to government budgets. This will leave the taxpayer more of their income, making individuals and small business better off. The government would not have to tax people to pay interest on loans needed for public finance.

3. The sight deposits in money accounts would be completely safe for the first time, and not subject to the possibility of a commercial bank failing in a financial crisis.

4. The stock of money in circulation would be stable, and not subject to commercial banks' decisions about creditworthiness – now the only criterion banks use in deciding whether to create new money through issuing loans. It would be stable or continuous, transmitting itself into stabilising effects on the real economy.

5. The quantity of the stock of currency would be fully under the control of the issuing monetary authority – the central or reserve bank. This would keep inflation under control for the first time: central banks have lost control over the quantity of money in circulation, which is now decided by commercial banks based on narrow commercial principles.

I would add that such a system would enable governments to write off the loans of poor countries. Compound rates of interest – responsible for the endlessness of the loan repayment process – would be a thing of the past. It is an extraordinary thought that the present system enables private commercial banks to create money out of thin air for their customers, but not to release poor countries from the yoke of unpayable debt.

The only people who would be disadvantaged by this system would be the large commercial banks, who would lose that aspect of their profits that comes from creating the national money supply. Banks would retain their present functions of borrowing money from depositors and lending it to borrowers; currency exchange; account management and investment advice. We are not talking about nationalising banks, only nationalising the creation of new money.

In fact it is not so long ago that governments were creating some new money by issuing a far larger proportion of the money stock in the form of notes and coins. The table that follows illustrates this clearly:

UK Total Money Stock		% created by government
1948	£ 2.8 billion	1.3 billion = 46%
1960	£ 5.7 billion	2.3 billion = 40%
1972	£ 20.3 billion	4.4 billion = 21.7%
1984	£163.4 billion	12.6 billion = 7.7%
1996	£586.0 billion	22.4 billion = 3.8%

No wonder debt has become such a massive problem in the past twenty years or so. In such a short time all but 5% of the new money supply has become debt-based in the UK, which is typical of most countries.

If our government were to take this action, it would save billions of rand annually in interest payments for which taxed money has to be found. It would never have to borrow money again. We as citizens would have our taxes reduced by the amount of the interest we now pay on borrowed money, plus the amount commercial banks would have created in the form of sight deposits. The question, 'Where will the money come from?' would not be asked in the same way again. All the Reserve Bank would have to ask is: Do we have the resources, physical and human, to create this? That is, what kind of expansion is feasible here? And then it would credit the government with the money needed to effect that expansion.

In the words of James Robertson in the Alternative Mansion House Speech: *'This reform will restore the prerogative of the State to issue money, and to capture as public revenue the income that arises from issuing it.'*

Notice also that the fact that the dollar is used as an international currency acts in the same way in favour of the US. In the eight-year period 1992–2000 an additional $800 billion were taken up and held by non-US banks around the world. This amounts to the creation of money out of nothing by the US. It has in consequence been able to buy $800 billion of goods without having to pay for them. And this huge sum is only a part of the increase in the dollars in circulation outside the US during that period.

To sum up, there is a variety of ways the government could both increase its own revenue and create an economy in which, in our interests as consumers, we would be contributing to a cleaner environment and a more equitable society. All of this needs research as to exactly how it would apply in particular countries and by how much their populations would benefit.

Note: For more information on this subject, see the book *Creating New Money*, by James Robertson, published by The New Economics Foundation, UK, and obtainable from their website: www.neweconomics.org

POINTS FOR DISCUSSION – CHAPTER THREE

1. What should be in the private sector, what in the public? Why?
2. What should be available as national 'commons', and how should they be financed.
3. Can a government introduce 'green taxes' nationally?
4. How could benign activity be encouraged and toxic behaviour be discouraged?
5. What is the best way to put new money into an economy?

MYTHS OF GLOBALISATION – SIX

'Capitalism is the most efficient way of allocating resources because people compete to supply the best quality at the lowest price. Any regulation of it reduces efficiency.'

Here are some of the costs of unregulated capitalism, writ large by the global market

- Where competition is the driver, some people will lose. Unless they are provided for they will die or continue to live by begging, borrowing and/or stealing. Crime, sophisticated over time, loses its stigma for many, and corrupts, terrifies and destroys increasing areas of society. Crime goes with drug-abuse, which destroys people. It requires money to be spent on prisons, police services, social services, counselling, drying-out centres and other social and psychological ambulance work.

- Competition to deliver low cost goods entails labour exploitation – people working for less than they need to live – unless there is regulation of labour practices.

- The need to compete by cost means identical goods crossing the skies and the continents to get to markets that import and export the same products. The transport pollutes the air and gobbles up scarce energy resources. By the time food has arrived at a European destination from a developing country it will have used over a hundred times the amount of energy it will provide when eaten.

- The marketing and public relations industries are products of the competitive market, which is shrinking in relation to output. They threaten to exceed in value the products they are seeking to sell. The American catalogue industry alone used 3.35 million tons of paper in 1998, one-twelfth of the output of the US paper industry.

- It is more profitable for people with spare money to speculate with it on the currency markets and stock exchanges than to invest it in productive enterprise.

- Unregulated, growth-driven capitalism produces waste on an unimaginable scale. The disposal of this waste is an unproductive industry. It also results in disastrous pollution events like oil spillage, regulations to prevent which are stigmatised as bureaucratic. The damage limitation is unproductive, restricted and usually leaves the poorest people worse off.

- Competition, unless limited, leaves the toughest in control, and breeds an aspiration to toughness. It creates a dehumanising 'let them eat cake' mentality.

- What else? Add to the list.

MYTHS OF GLOBALISATION – SEVEN

'The way to create employment is to cut company taxes, so that companies can spend more on job-rich investment. Multinational companies in particular must be wooed with low taxes, otherwise they will move their job-creation elsewhere.'

Research shows no benign connection between cutting taxes and investment by either local or multinational companies. Very high taxation in the Scandinavian countries accompanied high investment by local companies. South Africa's Finance Minister has cut taxes for companies every year since 1999. There has been little increase in investment; none has been attributed to causes other than unrelated confidence in market growth. Companies invest because they see the chance of profits, and that is influenced by a buoyant market, price and exchange rate stability and expansion. None of those is necessarily linked to tax cuts; on the contrary, to the extent that tax cuts lead to lower public expenditure, it reduces local demand and the growth of the economy.

Nor is there an automatic connection between higher investment and more jobs. Investment in machinery and technology is as likely to cut jobs as to increase them.

Multinational companies are especially prone to reduce employment wherever they invest. They are highly capital-intensive, and put out of business small enterprise currently employing more people, which cannot compete on cost grounds. The arrival of a multinational company that produces, say, shoes bankrupts thousands of small shoemakers in underdeveloped regions. That pattern is universal. The larger the company the more 'rationalisation' (cutting) of labour is introduced. All mergers and acquisitions are followed by job losses. Unemployment, not employment, is the result of attracting multinational companies – by low taxation or anything else. It may grow the GDP, but it is jobless growth.

This myth of globalisation is a self-serving product of those with a personal and institutional stake in promoting it.

MYTHS OF GLOBALISATION – EIGHT

'Trade unions who represent workers in bargaining for pay and conditions should be more responsible, considering the dangers of inflation.'

This exhortation contradicts the ethos that provides managers with their rationale – that the market does and should determine rewards. If trade unions may not use their clout, why is it OK for managers to do so? Here 'responsible pay bargaining' implies that pay bargaining should always be unsuccessful.

It is the wages of low-paid people that tend to be blamed for inflation. Yet rich people are far more likely to bid up prices, especially for the basic necessities of life. Unlike poor people they also create a demand for imports, so they strain the balance of payments. The arrival of tourists in a poor area, for instance, invariably inflates the price of foodstuffs, and leads to imports. A salary increase of £5,000 a month for executives is more inflationary than a 5% increase in the poverty pay of hotel workers.

CHAPTER FOUR

Taming the tiger:
Bringing capital down to earth

The lynchpin of the global market is the freedom of capital to move internationally. At first sight that process would seem obviously benign, and especially for poor countries. Let capital flow from where it is abundant to where it is sought, from where it is least productive to where it is most effective, and surely everyone will benefit.

In practice the opposite is largely true. Capital flows to where it makes the most profit; and that is not necessarily where it benefits most people. It is usually where it is already doing well because markets are large, technology available and human capital highly skilled. More important, because capital is mobile, and other resources of production – labour and natural resources – are not, capital can always demand higher returns than anyone else. The 17% that South African investors earned on average in 2001 from unit trusts was widely regarded as disappointing. Compare the profit margins and yields on capital quoted daily in your news media with increases in wages or rents to see the proportion that capital routinely expects. And what it expects, it can demand – because it can desert.

Even more important, if capital can be used for purely speculative purposes, it can often do best and minimise its risks by profit-taking on buying and selling currencies and shares of various kinds. It need never get involved in the hassles of employing people, building factories, supplying goods and services or transferring technologies – all of which are supposed to be the positive outcome of the movement of capital. Because it is so easy to make money by speculation, 90% to 98% of the capital that moves around the world today is purely speculative. The same applies to funds 'invested' in stock markets. In 1960 only 10% of shares on Wall Street changed hands each year; by 1990 it was 50%; by 2000 78%. The fecklessness of capital is extremely destabilising to the economies and the enterprises in which it operates. Internationally, it has been devastating. It can flood or abandon an economy at the tap of a computer button. And when, as a result, currency rates collapse, it can have drastic effects on the lives of ordinary people: employment falls, public services may have to be slashed and food may become scarce. People may die.

Even at those times the world's richest people become richer and the poor poorer. A joint study by Merrill Lynch and Cap Gemini Ernst and Young in the year 2000 showed that the world's richest people escaped the stock market falls by selling out of equities or using sophisticated hedging techniques. Small investors lost when stock markets fell, but the rich saw their wealth rise by 6% to $27 trillion. Over 180,000 people joined the ranks of the high net worth individuals (HNWIs) – those with at least $1 million of liquid assets, not including property. That took the HNWIs to 7.2 million – 2.3 million in Europe, 2.5 million in North America and 1.7 million in Asia. Some 57,000 had liquid assets over $30 million. But all that was small beer compared to the previous year when HNWIs gained 18%. Their success was the result of booming corporate profits and bonuses – and the fact that these individuals employed the best techniques for diversification when markets fell. Hedge funds earned an average of 11% in 2000, and venture capital funds an average of 41%

The process of capital mobility from which these people benefit increases the uncertainties within which all individuals and governments must operate. We know to our cost in South Africa that our government can obey all the rules that have been recommended to create a solid basis for investment. But literally overnight something can happen elsewhere, which in some un-predictable way derails our own capital markets. It can be particularly rapid growth in some other continent. Or the opposite – a decline or collapse else-where. A neighbouring country may behave badly, causing jitters around investment in the whole region. Even political events that are perfectly normal in a democracy can have an effect, like a demonstration of strength by trade unions. Any of these circumstances, which are outside the control of the government, can create havoc with its plans.

Finance Minister Trevor Manuel told Parliament in March 2001 that the capital flight of rich South Africans in the previous year had doubled. Between the inception of the investment allowance in July 1997 and the end of 2000 R17.4 billion had left the country. By the end of 2001 the situation was even worse. J.P. Morgan reported that the net dividend outflow in 2001 was some R20 billion on the current account alone. South Africans had invested nearly R57 billion in offshore foreign funds over the previous three years. And an annualised R45 billion left the country in the third quarter of the year, because of the profits and dividends sent overseas by the local companies that had listed in London. Incidentally, the reason given for allowing the overseas listing was explicitly that it would give our companies access to capital; no one said anything about losing capital.

Publicly Manuel and his deputy, Maria Ramos, put on a brave face. Volatile capital flows were something the country had to accept. 'If you liberalise your capital, there will be outflows and inflows … a normal part of what happens in an open economy,' Ramos said, pointing out that this was 'portfolio diver-sification by investors'. This is what you have to say if you accept the capital globalisation package. You are warned by the international investing fraternity that you must not only open your capital markets; you must also avoid giving any indication that you might be having doubts. Behind the scenes, despite

Treasury denials, there was some tightening of exchange controls. But publicly the government had to avoid saying anything to cast doubt on its continued espousal of the free exchange ideal.

The ugly truth is that internationally mobile capital has resulted in massive flows of capital and income from poor countries to rich ones since capital was 'deregulated' in the late 1970s. The American economy is the world's largest importer of capital. Africa has lost capital consistently in the last twenty years as structural adjustment programmes have taken hold. South Africa is only the most recent victim of the mobility of capital.

This in turn has had its effect on the value of currencies, which in turn means countries must struggle to export more to pay for imports. When the rand loses 50% of its value, which it has, we need to export 50% more to pay for the same imports. When we lose capital, we are effectively exporting our savings and our growth. The rich countries consistently gain, the poor consistently lose.

The Zambian government – under even greater pressure than South Africa from a rapidly falling currency – publicly confronted business over capital desertion. President Chiluba chastised the business community, at a meeting in January 2001, for taking advantage of the lack of exchange controls. He said the economy was sluggish because capital was being taken out of the country. *Business Day* (15/1/2002) reported: 'He appeared to have back-pedalled on his government's policy of a liberalised economy with open markets by seeking to reintroduce protective measures … He said he did not believe in exchange control regulations, but the lack of such controls could not be seen as giving businessmen free license to operate outside Zambian laws.'

Unfortunately lack of exchange controls does precisely give people the right to take their money out wherever and whenever it suits them; and blaming individuals looks like a futile exercise. Chiluba's desperate attempts to protect his country's currency while not antagonising the source of capital looks like ending in tears.

Meanwhile the noted senior South African banker Iraj Abedien, group economist for Standard Bank, also proposes an attack on individuals rather than the system. He publicly advised the South African government to penalise banks that receive government business and also speculate against the rand. He said (*Business Times*, 16/2/2001) that rumours which had lowered the value of the rand had emanated from financial institutions in London and New York that were beneficiaries of government business. 'It is right in a free market to say that unless you comply with good corporate ethics you won't do business with us.' These institutions with large currency holdings had used them to bet against the rand on rumours of possible changes in the government. He recommended that heavy penalties be placed on such institutions.

His suspicions were later apparently confirmed when the SA Chamber of Business claimed they had evidence of illegal activities in manipulating the value of the rand; and an official inquiry was set up to examine the claims. Whatever it reported, the fact is that the system operates to suck wealth from the poor countries to the rich. Crooks only take advantage of that fact.

An unusually frank article was published by *Business Day* on January 16, 2002, written by Michael Power, doctoral economist student at the University of Cape Town, and now at Investec in Cape Town, with the impeccable Old Economics credentials of having worked for Baring Asset Management in London. It is worth quoting at length for its confirmation of the systemic toxicity of global capital flows for poor countries.

> *Argentina's agony is plain for all to see. Less visible are the ruined reputations of countless economists who concocted the ideal economy and called it the Latin Miracle. Their cocktail mixed the standard ingredients of the Washington Consensus …*

Argentina drank this depth charger and guess what happened: it exploded …

Not only has (South Africa) failed to attract long-term capital; it is haemor-rhaging it … The mounting evidence shows that net capital flows are massively in the direction of poor countries to rich … The US, UK and euro-zone countries collectively run an annual current account deficit of almost $500 billion, of which only about $140 billion is matched by the surpluses elsewhere in the developed world … This means that $360 billion must come from outside the developed core if balance of payments are to balance … Last year the poorest countries of the world contributed a net $260 billion to global capital account flows. These more than 100 countries represented only 17% of GDP, yet lost an average of 4% of their GDP in capital outflows to the developed world core. If there is a giant sucking sound to be heard in the world … it is a net $450 billion of longer-term capital being drawn into the US.

My own economic biases are rooted firmly in the free market tradition, but it is hard not to conclude that a form of financial Darwinism is seeing owners of capital naturally deselecting developing countries … The corporations involved (are) just trying to preserve their capital in dollar terms … It is this duty – of preserving and ideally growing shareholder capital – that is driving currencies in a globalised world. The harsh reality is that most owners of mobile capital would rather graze their capital in the greener pastures of the developed world today …

Mainstream economics as yet has no rebuff to these uncomfortable facts, facts that should shame advocates of free trade and globalisation – myself included – into providing answers. Until then, perhaps such facts should instead shame us into silence.

Power's honestly expressed sense of helplessness derives from his previous conventional acceptance that it is impossible to control capital – that *'there is something innately mobile about currencies'*. In fact, mobile capital and unregulated currencies are a relatively new phenomenon in the modern world. John Maynard Keynes wrote, in his book *The General Theory of Employment, Interest and Money*:

> *I would sympathise with those who would minimise rather than those who would maximise, economic entanglements between nations. Ideas, knowledge, art, hospitality, travel — these are the things that should of their nature be international. But let goods be homespun wherever it is reasonable and conveniently possible, and above all let finance be primarily national.*

There was another period during the 20th century when capital was globalised – from the early 1920s to the not-unconnected Great Crash of the 1930s. During that time, as now, the banking and financial services sector was in control. And because money is their 'product', and because they want to maintain the value of that product, deflation was the order of the day. If you want to maintain value, keep it scarce – everyone knows that. People were sacked, notably civil servants, budgets were 'balanced', and the end result was the financial crash, from which the world recovered only as a result of the war.

It is an ironic fact that the Bretton Woods Institutions – the World Bank and the IMF – were set up at the end of the war as part of a determination to end the tyranny of footloose capital. Future security and stability, it was realised, depended on governments' restoring their control over capital and ending their reliance on 'self-regulating' market mechanisms. This accounts for the general upliftment of the per capita standards of living worldwide during the '50s, '60s and early '70s. During that time governments, responsive to their electorates, created an increasingly egalitarian order, welfare states and expanding access to prosperity. It is ironic because those very institutions have, since the mid-'70s, presided over, and implemented, a return to the reign of unaccountable capital dominance. For an in-depth analysis of that history, see

Ann Pettifor's writing on the website www.jubileeplus.org. The cause of governments' wariness in dealing with international financial operators is of course the unreasonable power that the present system gives to footloose capital. That is because it has become an article of faith among Old Economists – and hence our government – that we must attract foreign direct investment (FDI), because we do not have enough savings at home, and because it brings with it badly needed technology transfers. But, as we have already seen, capital is no longer a function of savings. Moreover, common sense will tell us that South Africa can create its own capital. Indeed, as we know, we have the kind of capital liquidity that enables us without collapse to export tens of billions of rand a year. If we could have used that capital effectively at home, where is the need to import capital?

But common sense is not widely respected among economists. The IMF may be a better authority. A research paper it put out in October 2001 shows that South Africa has an abundance of capital; and is now a net exporter of capital-intensive goods, even to rich countries. We do not need to import technology: we are exporting it. The implication is that South Africa should go for a high wage, high capital economy as part of its competitive strategy. Kevin Wakeford, former MD of the South African Chamber of Business, who is hardly a revolutionary, is reported in *Business Day* (23/1/2002) as saying 'Just because we are at the bottom tip of Africa does not mean we should be a source of slave labour.' He disputes the idea that cheap labour is what we should be offering.

Therefore a strategy to build our own capital instead of trying to attract it from outside should give us more confidence in dealing with footloose capital to suit our own economy. How can we begin to ride the tiger of footloose capital, instead of appeasing it? There is no shortage of ideas, some of which are already in operation.

The Tobin Tax

In the late 1970s, Prof. James Tobin, who became the 1981 Nobel Laureate for Economics, designed a scheme for, as he put it, 'throwing some sand into the wheels of the foreign exchange markets'. Even then it had become clear that speculation on the currency markets could be dangerous. So he proposed a small tax to be imposed on the value of all forex transactions. The purpose was to rein in market volatility, raise revenue and restore some national sovereignty over monetary policy.

Since then, of course, the dangers have become infinitely worse. Today most currency dealing has nothing to do with investment or trade. It is about people betting on what other people are going to be doing. The Asian Tiger crash was not about lack of information or transparency or 'crony capitalism', as rationalised by a red-faced IMF and other such figures – who had been lauding these economies as an example to all developing countries. The crash was about panic, about herd behaviour. The fact that the banks in those countries were over-borrowed was widely known; but then so are many large enterprises everywhere. It only mattered to investors when they began to panic en masse.

As we know, the Asian crash led to speculation against other currencies, including the rand. And we had to listen to po-faced commentators telling us it was natural that other 'middle income' countries, like ourselves, should come in for the same treatment, even though our 'economic fundamentals' are fine. So what's natural about it? Their attempts at explanation were confirmation that that kind of currency transaction is not about rational investment, only about betting.

The Asian crash was followed in 1999–2000 by the near collapse in the currency markets of Brazil and others, notably Russia. And in 2001–2002 we saw the agony of Argentina – once considered 'the Switzerland of Latin America'. That country's free-fall was followed by much the same story in Uruguay and, once again, Brazil. All had been obediently following IMF prescriptions. For a more detailed account, see the website of the SA New Economics Foundation (www.sane.org.za) on which appears an article by myself called 'Latin America: Graveyard of Structural Adjustment'.

It was that kind of thing that led George Soros to write, in his book called *The Crisis of Global Capitalism*: 'The international financial system is suffering from systematic breakdown, but we are unwilling to acknowledge it … The private sector is ill-suited to allocate international credit – it is not concerned with macro-economic balance … The system tends to disequilibrium. It is more dangerous to capitalism than communism ever was.'

The financial panic in the late '90s has brought the international community to the point of looking for more fluent alternatives. If, for instance, the US economy were to be among the next to come in for panic selling, the rest of us could not be insulated from it. The Asian crash could be partly ring-fenced; not so one affecting the American economy.

The most widely canvassed idea to counteract such dangers as well as to raise revenue is the Tobin tax. It would be levied on all foreign exchange transactions, including spot and forward transactions, hedge funds and even derivatives. It could be varied in size according to how long the funds remained in one place; this would privilege funds used to buy currency for genuine trade or investment.

The rate recommended by the international movement for a Tobin tax is 0.25%, which would discourage all speculation at profits of less than 0.3%. It would therefore have a relatively calming effect. Even this small tax would raise, on the current daily transactions of around $2 trillion, some $250 billion every year. Compare this with the $160 billion that Jubilee 2000 reckons to be the cost of wiping out the unpayable debt of Southern countries. It could also address the $80 million the UNDP estimates would be needed to eliminate the worst forms of poverty. A Tobin tax would net that amount each year. If the tax served the purpose of reducing speculative transactions, then the take from the tax would of course decline. This could be offset by raising the tax, depending on the relative expectations from it.

Opinions vary as to who should administer the tax. The countries in which the transactions take place could use it. Or it could become the property of the international community as a whole. The only international organisation that represents all nations at present is the United Nations and its specialised agencies. The tax would have to be collected nationally, backed perhaps by the Continuous Linking Settlement Bank, newly established in 2000 to track all international deals round the clock. Evasion is a possibility with all taxes, but perhaps least of all where it is international. Heavy penalties for evasion could apply.

The international campaign for a Tobin tax has made considerable headway. At the June 2000 Social Summit in Geneva, the Canadian government – the first government to have committed itself to promoting a Tobin tax – achieved agreement that the UN host a study on 'a currency transactions tax'. All 160 governments represented agreed to the study.

Meanwhile, in 2000 over 200 members of the European Parliament narrowly missed achieving a majority in favour of a Tobin tax, voting 225 to 229. And a supporting motion in the British Parliament received over 100 signatures from MPs of all six parties. The Belgian, French and German governments have all indicated their intention to study the implications of a Tobin tax. The French Parliament adopted the proposal in principle in November 2001, noting that at their proposed maximum rate of 0.1%, the return on a tax on the Paris Bourse would be 50 million euros a day. Even the

US Congress is facing a motion by Congressman Peter de Fazio proposing a comprehensive Tobin tax resolution.

The British Chancellor of the Exchequer is not enthusiastic. Appearing before a House of Lords economic affairs committee, Gordon Brown said the Tobin tax had 'big problems attached to it'. Most of these appeared to be about enforcement – as though the problem of evasion had ever discouraged governments from imposing taxes that they believe in! Interestingly, though, Brown's chief economic adviser, Ed Balls, commenting on the possibility that a Tobin tax might limit the destabilising effect of currency speculation said: 'Well-designed, short-term capital controls could actually be more effective.' Quite so. Here perhaps is a chink in the armour of footloose capital. As a matter of fact, a Tobin tax and capital controls are not mutually contradictory. It depends how much you want or need to please the owners of capital.

At the international level governments are talking – largely behind closed doors – about 'a new financial architecture'. Indications are that the ideas so far generated fall within current parameters, with modified rules being set for a body like the IMF still to wield power over the way that countries behave, and perhaps more influence being given to the poorer countries. This is nowhere near radical enough to deal with the systemic problems.

Successors to the Bretton Woods Agreements

But there is also a revival of some ideas of the British economist John Maynard Keynes put forward at the first Bretton Woods Conference in 1944. That conference, faced with post-depression and post-war financial and trade chaos, was convened to establish what we would now call a new 'financial architecture' for the conduct of trading relations between nations. It was from this conference that the World Bank and later the IMF emerged. What happened there is well described in Michael Rowbotham's book *Goodbye America* (Jon Carpenter Publishing, UK). I quote:

> *In the months leading up to the conference the two major world powers, America and Britain, each tabled proposals … They were fundamentally different in character. The British prepared a proposal, largely the work of John Maynard Keynes, for a system of trade accountancy that Keynes called 'The International Clearing Union' … The American proposal was for an 'International Stabilisation Fund' (which is) reflected in the … World Bank and the IMF … The American delegation won the day.*
>
> *Fundamental to Keynes' thinking was the importance of fostering a balance of trade between nations and avoiding the scenario in which some nations became 'creditors' and others 'debtors' through their trade accounts … Imbalances in trade tended to become self-perpetuating and compounding in effect. Debtor nations, who needed to export more to redress the balance of trade, were thrust into recession. Their output, competitiveness and exports tended to decline …*
>
> *The trouble at root, Keynes observed, was that creditor nations, having gained surplus revenues from an excess of exports over imports, simply failed to spend this money back in debtor nation economies. (He) argued that it was fundamental to a constructive framework of international trade that there be a mechanism to ensure … that imbalances of trade between nations were redressed.*
>
> *The key feature of Keynes' proposal was that it placed an equal obligation on creditor and debtor nations to maintain a balance of trade … Nations that imported more than they exported would pay a small interest charge to the Clearing Union … Equally nations that ran an aggressive trade policy and exported more than they imported would be charged by the Clearing Union for their surplus account.*

Unfortunately the Americans blocked the Clearing Union idea; and the

World Bank and IMF were set up in effect to cope with the results of imbalances that could have been self-righting. We are now at another crossroads, and the Bretton Woods agreements are being revisited. No doubt we shall hear some more about the Keynesian idea – but not if it is left only to the governments of the rich countries, notably the United States.

Keynes also proposed that currencies should be aligned and valued according to a basket of commodities that are globally traded. This would mean that all currencies had much the same value in terms of those commodities. Thus today, for instance, wheat grown in a country with a badly devalued currency costs a fraction of wheat grown in another country; and hence is heavily exported regardless of whether the wheat is needed at home or whether it can be grown more cheaply, in terms of real cost, in other countries. And when currency values change – say, due to speculation – so does the pattern of trade in wheat. This is highly destabilising and has no reference to where wheat is best grown in terms of real costs relating to climate, soils and so on.

Keynes' ideas were not accepted at Bretton Woods, basically because they did not suit the then perceived interests of the US. The same may still be true, but only if 'interests' continue to be defined in a very short-term sense.

Bucking the system

Meanwhile, in the absence of international systemic reform, some individual governments have taken steps to limit the damaging effects of mobile global capital. We are repeatedly warned that it is impossible to buck the system: the 'unforgiving markets' will punish us if we are not faithful in following the global rules for opening economies. It is not necessarily so.

Chile's 'speed bumps'

Following a period of instability, and in order to discourage volatile, short-term speculative capital inflows, as well as to avoid contagion risks from other countries, the government of Chile introduced in 1991 an 'unremunerated reserve requirement'. This meant that anyone who wanted to invest in Chile had to put an amount equal to 20% of the capital investment into the Central Bank for a one-year period. The purpose was to increase the cost to foreigners of short-term investing in Chile; this gave an advantage to local financiers. The amount was increased to 30% in the next year, then gradually reduced to 0% by 1999.

The Chilean government also introduced a 'minimum-term requirement' for foreign direct investment and portfolio flows, which meant foreign investors had to wait at least three years to repatriate capital. This too had the aim of encouraging local capital. The results of both measures were as good as expected. GDP growth averaged some 8% between 1990 and 1997. Inflation fell from 27% to 6%. The government's current account deficit averaged 3%. Foreign reserves rose from $4.7 billion to $17.8 billion. Capital did not desert.

The effect of these measures was to change the composition of capital flows to favour equity and long-term investment. This enabled the government to defend the currency when it came under attack along with others during the Asian crisis. Maria Elena Ovalle, board member of Chile's Central Bank, told a conference in South Africa in August 1999 that 'financial freedom presents problems in a small country like Chile. An emerging country should advance cautiously in the liberalisation of its capital account.'

Other ideas

In Colombia foreign investors are allowed to invest directly but may not buy into corporate equity or 'debt instruments'. This makes it impossible for foreigners to exit en masse and collapse the economy.

An idea still to be tried out is that of 'waiting at the gate'. The brainchild of Denver University's Ilena Grabel, this means that if the ratio of foreign to domestic capital investment reaches a certain point, foreigners have to 'wait at the gate' before they can buy local assets.

Meanwhile Hong Kong has in effect nationalised its Stock Market in order to fend off the speculators. India and China have never liberalised their currency exchanges. They avoided the Asian crash.

The saga of Malaysia

A story worth telling is that of how Malaysia defied the Washington Consensus and got away with it. It is an important antidote to the current belief that conformity is in effect a *sine qua non* of survival. That belief paralyses not only action but also the ability even to think about alternatives.

On September 1, 1998, Mahathir Mohamed, Prime Minister of Malaysia, made a very angry broadcast. He announced that the ringgit (Malaysia's currency) would no longer circulate outside the country. Any then held in banks abroad would have one month to get home, after which it would be worthless. The government would fix the exchange rate – later set at 3.8 ringgit to one US dollar. He also restricted the repatriation of profits made by foreigners from trading shares. Non-residents would have restricted access to the ringgit. Investments abroad by residents for non-trade purposes would require permission. In other words, he put out of bounds speculation in the value of the Malaysian currency. He also reinforced measures to expand the economy by means of low interest rates, increased government expenditure and help for the banks stricken by the panic.

As a solution to Malaysia's problems this was greeted with derision by all Western governments, financial institutions and media pundits. All of Malaysia's equally ravaged neighbours – Japan, Korea, Indonesia, Thailand – were obediently and painfully following IMF prescriptions about how to recover. They used tight fiscal and monetary controls, and free trade and capital flows. Malaysia had done the same for the first year after the crash. The result had been continued depreciation of all their currencies. The ringgit had fallen by 35% and the Kuala Lumpur Stock Exchange Composite Index by 52%.

Mahathir had had enough. His heresy was heard with disbelief and predicted to lead to disaster.

Three years on, what had happened? Perhaps the most convincing evidence comes from the IMF itself. In July 2000 it concluded an 'Article IV Consultation' with Malaysia. This is a summary of what it acknowledged.

The Malaysian economy had recovered from the 'sharp decline' of 1998. Real GDP growth was over 5.5%, while manufacturing sector growth was 13%. Capacity utilisation in many industries had reached pre-crisis levels. Inflation was below 2%. 'Directors broadly agreed that the regime of capital controls – which was intended by the authorities to be temporary – had produced more positive results than many observers had initially expected.' Foreign inward investment had resumed. 'The Kuala Lumpur Stock Composite Index recovered by 39% during 1999, and rose further by 10% this year, *while most neighbouring countries' indices fell*' (my emphasis).

In other words, Malaysia had fully regained the confidence of the investing fraternity. This is a major lesson of this story. People who want to invest capital on the ground – as opposed to speculatively – are suited by a stable currency and stable government policies. Malaysia's recovery has been led by its domestic investors who had been confined to the home market when the exchange was closed. They make up some 97% of new investment; and they are pulling in international capital behind them.

The truth is that there is no evidence that economic growth is a product of foreign investment. Foreign investment does not initiate growth; it is not a charity. Only capital in the form of grant aid can do that. Foreign capital goes where the economy is already working and the prospects of low-risk profit are good. The measures taken by the Malaysian authorities provided that environment while discouraging speculative capital. That is the best of both worlds for the economy; and it was welcomed by investors who wanted to create wealth by getting on to a flourishing bandwagon.

Restore the Financial Rand

Finally, here is a proposal especially designed to suit South Africa, but applicable elsewhere. It comes from the economist Richard Douthwaite, who has studied the South African situation. He suggests we should have two separate rates of exchange for the rand. One would be for the movement of things and people – imports and exports and tourism – for which we need an exchange of currencies. This is in effect the current account and would be called the commercial rand. The other would be for capital flows – the money people want to take in or out as investment – in effect the financial rand. If the two were separated, they would each find their own separate level of value. For instance the value of exports would be equal to the value of imports, because the commercial rand value would adjust to the flows. Similarly the inflows and outflows of capital would adjust the financial rand price so as to get a balance. But the two rates would not, as now, adversely influence each other.

If, say, the value of the financial rand increases because of a large inflow of capital, that would not, as now, make things difficult for exporters – because exporters would be using the commercial rand, valued by the relationship of imports to exports. Conversely, and more relevant today, if there is a large outflow of capital, this would lower the value of the financial rand, without affecting the activities of importers and exporters.

This is not an ideal solution, because administratively it is hard to keep the two separate. But it is at least second best. The current situation puts every South African in a state of permanent insecurity – except those who live entirely by moving capital around, contributing little to economic development in the country.

This would release the South African government from having to look over its shoulder at the effect of its policies on potential investors.

Prospects

So there are a number of ways in which our government could take some control over our own capital, even before there is international agreement on controlling the malign effects of footloose capital. Because the interests vested in a continuation of the present system remain so powerful, individual governments will have to give the lead in taking some relatively small but brave steps. It is possible to call the bluff of international and corporate power, even in the face of its threats. The governments who have done so in a planned and coherent way have shown it is possible to generate capital at home and diminish dependence on the global market.

But more radical proposals were put to an Asian regional meeting of the UN in Jakarta in August 2000. A statement by Martin Khor, Director of the Third World Network, included the following. After noting that the IMF had made the Asian crisis worse by even further financial liberalisation that converted a financial debt problem into a structural economic recession, he recommended actions at the international level to avoid new policies or agreements that would 'lock in' financial liberalisation.

- The IMF should not have powers over capital account convertibility which enable it to force developing countries to open their capital account and markets.

- The OECD countries should give up the idea of a Multilateral Agreement on Investment, which would give extreme powers to mobile capital to dictate the terms of its investment everywhere. When the MAI was proposed in 1998, it was defeated by an international coalition of civil society and governments.

- The WTO should not pursue an enforceable investment agreement that would pressurise developing countries towards liberalisation.

- The WTO should review its financial services agreement in the light of lessons learnt about the negative effects of liberalisation.

(The clauses relating to the WTO are explained in Chapter Five.)

Khor also recommended measures that should be put in place to avoid the effects of liberalisation. They included:

- Once a crisis has broken out there should be measures to manage debt including a system that divides the costs and burden between debtors and creditors.

- Countries should be allowed and encouraged to control inflow and outflow of funds, especially speculative.

- Countries that are the source of mobile funds should regulate their financial institutions to prevent their causing volatility abroad.

- International regulation of highly leveraged funds, including hedge funds, offshore centres, currency markets and trade derivatives.

- An international system of stable currencies, including possible return to fixed exchange rates or rates that move within a narrow band.

- Reform of the decision-making system in international institutions to give developing countries a fairer voice.

- A change in the set of conditionalities that accompany IMF/World Bank loans to allow recipient countries wider options on financial, monetary, fiscal, trade and other macroeconomic policies.

In the absence of such reforms, Khor says, countries will have to take the necessary domestic action to protect their economies and promote development. They should examine the appropriateness of trade liberalisation policies, many of which have caused loss of employment and foreign earnings. They should consider selective capital controls and stabilising their currency rates to give them greater freedom in macroeconomic policies, such as lower interest rates and budget expansion. In particular they should regulate foreign loans, restricting them to projects that have the capacity to repay in foreign currency. They should treat foreign direct investment in a selective way – as only one of a number of options.

Chapter Five will discuss the ways in which a new focus can be given to the global economy to enable it to regenerate local economies.

POINTS FOR DISCUSSION – CHAPTER FOUR

1. Why did globalisation of capital and trade not spread prosperity worldwide?
2. Is the world short of capital? Why is it so well rewarded?
3. How could the Bretton Woods institutions be improved?
4. Why do diverse elected governments implement similar policies?
5. Why did Malaysia get away with its defiance? Could others do the same?

MYTHS OF GLOBALISATION – NINE

'State activities are parasitic. They don't add value and have to be carried by the private sector.'

This belief stems from the idea that any activity that does not command a direct cash reward out of profits is not productive. So a doctor who has cash put into her hand by her patient adds value, but one who works in a hospital where patients are treated free does not. It is part of the ideology that governments are favoured by socialists and are by nature both authoritarian and inefficient; whereas capitalists favour the private sector and run it efficiently.

The extraordinary implication is that public education does not add value; nor do health services, or roads or police services or Parliament and other democratic institutions. Perhaps we should simply appoint a State Chief Executive Officer to run the country, and make him find sponsorship for his fellow directors and the civil service. That would do away with the expense of elections.

As for efficiency, public service is efficient to the extent that it is well paid, well resourced and well managed. In a democracy people get the civil service they deserve, according to the value they put on it.

Private enterprise can be efficient to the extent that it is not monopolistic and is well regulated. If not, it can be corrupt, wasteful and abusive, as recent examples have shown. The current anti-public ideology has reduced public standards worldwide, and provided a field day for the abuse of power in the private sector.

MYTHS OF GLOBALISATION – TEN

'The way to create employment is through a "flexible" labour force which is not protected by legislation: employers should be free to hire and fire and offer whatever conditions they can afford. Regulation of labour conditions discourages employment. This is the cause of South Africa's unemployment, for instance.'

(You can substitute almost any other country that suffers unemployment.)

The ILO's 1999 country report on the effects of globalisation on South Africa suggests that the low rate of domestic investment – 17% of GDP – and not the labour laws is at the root of unemployment. It said that, if anything, the labour market was too flexible. Lack of regulation leads to extremely low rates of pay, lack of training, high staff turnover, falling purchasing power and a low wage/low cost/low productivity economy. It means some people – in South Africa, 60% of the employed – are unable to make a living though working full time. That makes it essentially unproductive and internationally uncompetitive.

Countries such as the US and the EU which recommend 'flexible' labour policies for poor countries have minimum wage regulation and laws to prevent labour exploitation – because they know that is the basis for strong internal market growth.

CHAPTER FIVE

Localising globally

Chapters Two, Three and Four dealt with coping with the unfettered global market – managing within it to minimise its destructive effects. But the ideas developed were more than that. They have intrinsic value – even were the global market to be regulated in the interests of the world's population.

Thus the basic income grant is needed in a world where technology sheds labour: it is designed to offset the destruction of purchasing power. The various forms of alternative tax, which create new sources of revenue for governments, have the advantage of widening the base of revenue in a way that will have benign effects on the environment and make collection easier and more equitable. Both of these mechanisms cope with inevitable long-term trends in the modern world, regardless of the unfettered global capitalist market. The BIG will be necessary in any case as a way of distributing the fruits of technology. And alternative forms of taxation will be needed to penalise toxic forms of production and consumption and to privilege the benign, as well as to create government revenue.

This chapter looks at a more profound reorientation of the global economy. Aspects of it are already happening internationally in the movement for local economic development (LED), but they are being hampered by the consistently centralising dynamic of the unfettered global market. The most complete expression of it is set out in Helena Norberg-Hodge's book *Bringing the Food Economy Home*, and in Colin Hines' book *Localisation: A Global Manifesto,* both published in 2000 by Earthscan Publications Ltd.

Hines distinguishes between globalisation and internationalism. The first, he says, is 'in essence the systematic reduction of protective barriers to the flow of goods and money by international trade rules … It pits country against country, community against community and workers against workers.' A striking example of that is demonstrated in a report in *Business Day* (25/1/2001) to the effect that American steelworkers are up in arms against the closure of steel mills – thirteen so far and another three on the way. The American government has already threatened South Africa and other countries with sanctions for what it reckons is 'dumping' steel in US markets. If that succeeds we shall lose jobs. Meanwhile, under pressure from American steelworkers, the Bush administration is proposing substantial new tariffs on steel imports. But American workers in industries that use steel are fighting the steelworkers to preserve the international profitability of their products. Everyone is being pitted against everyone else within shrinking markets.

This issue now threatens a trade war between the US and the EU. The EU is already taking the Americans to the World Trade Organisation for a compulsory ruling against the higher tariffs. They are claiming a $2.7 billion package of sanctions to be imposed against the US. Britain supports the claim, since its five steel companies, employing 18,000 people, are threatened by the US proposals for steel tariffs. The EU has already achieved a ruling by the WTO that it is entitled to impose several billions of sanctions against America for its support, through taxation grants, to some of its large corporations.

Going back to Colin Hines, he says internationalism (as opposed to globalisation) is 'the (global) flow of ideas, technology, information, culture, money and goods with the end goal of protecting and rebuilding local economies worldwide. Its goal is maximum local trade, within diversified, sustainable local economies and minimum long-distance trade.'

If that seems like a return to self-sufficient insularity, that is not what is meant, nor is it possible. Re-localisation is about changing direction – away from centralisation of economic forces towards decentralisation, using modern technologies and global support to do so. It is not about going backwards.

Just to recap the facts about centralisation, today eight companies own more than does half the world's population. Fifty-one of the world's largest economies are transnational corporations (TNCs). Five hundred companies control two-thirds of world trade and half of all productive assets. In the UK, for instance, the nine largest supermarkets now account for 97.9% of grocery sales – up from 59% as recently as 1990.

In the second 'Alternative Mansion House Speech', Andrew Simms of the New Economics Foundation in London comments: 'This trend (to concentrating corporate power) ridicules the theoretical argument for a purely free market economy. It is almost embarrassing that governments still make policy on the foundations of competitive general equilibrium theory – of which one of the many bizarre assumptions is that there is an infinite number of small companies and that none has power over the market.'

People sometimes think the one good thing you can say about the TNCs is that they create employment. That is why governments woo them with all the incentives that we have noted. A threat to TNCs is sometime seen as a threat to jobs. The reverse is the truth. Although the combined sales of the 200 largest TNCs exceed the combined economies of all but nine countries, they in fact employ only 18.8 million workers, less than 0.75% of the world's total. Between 1993 and 1995, global turnover of the top one hundred TNCs increased by more than 25%, but during that period they cut 4% of their workforce. Meanwhile these huge technology-based companies put labour-intensive rivals out of business. In the UK for instance the number of grocery stores fell between 1960 and 1997 from 147,000 to 27,000. Local organic box schemes in the UK, through which organic farmers sell to local people, create twice as many jobs as supermarkets by value of produce. Small business is threatened, not helped, by large business.

That process of business enlargement also homogenises: the biggest is able to provide the cheapest, and variety is lost. Britain is losing its famous apple diversity as supermarkets stock only four or five mass-produced varieties. Other varieties cannot find the outlets and distribution channels that will take smaller quantities; so even if the demand is there, it cannot find expression. That is a tiny example of the loss of diversity, which is replicated all over the world and in every product that can be mass-produced.

Cultural variety is also on its way out. Helena Norberg-Hodge's book *Ancient Futures* gives an account of how one hitherto successful and harmonious local culture – that of the Ladakhis – was undermined and made to feel stupid and shameful as a result of the impact of consumer culture when the much-vaunted tourism entered their area of 'Little Tibet'. We all know how Western, and especially American, culture takes over our lives and those of our children. That is not surprising. A few mega media corporations control newspapers, television and radio, publishers, bookshop chains and even the advertising and PR industries – everything that influences the way we think. Uniformity in that respect is hardly good for democracy.

And while it irons out the expression of dissenting opinions, it also loses jobs. *Business Day* (25/1/2001) reports that the latest merger that produced the new AOL media giant has caused the Time Warner element to lose more than two thousand jobs, the CNN division having already announced it was sacking four hundred. It was part of the belt-tightening drive to make good on a promise to investors that the merger would deliver a major boost to earnings: this is the smooth explanation of the MDs of AOL. As a result, the price of shares rose 31 cents on the New York Stock Exchange. So the merger was 'a success'.

To look at how to change direction, we need to see what keeps the current system in place. The global market in goods is the result of a long process to free markets via a negotiating forum called the General Agreement on Tariffs and Trade (GATT). Over the past 30 years it has had several 'rounds', designed to agree rules that open every economy to every other. The last round, in Uruguay in 1994, created the World Trade Organisation (WTO), charged with enforcing the agreed rules. It can and does invoke sanctions against governments that flout the rules.

In principle all governments may take part in its meetings as they did in the GATT rounds. In practice the Group of Eight (G8) dominant countries, which can afford large permanent delegations and legal help, are in an inner circle and make the decisions. After the Battle of Seattle – of which more in Chapter Six – the WTO and its allies had to admit that most poorer governments had in practice been marginalised in all its processes. Their voices in the speed of the globalisation process did not prevail, while those of the rich countries did.

Here is an obvious example. Pascal Lamy, the French EU Trade Commissioner told an SA Institute of International Affairs seminar on June 22, 2000:

> *The EU has taken a deliberate decision to keep its farmers on the land, whether or not they are internationally competitive. We will be left with farmers in the EU who are not as competitive as the African standard … If we are fully competitive, employment in the farm sector will drop from seven million farmers to just one million. This is politically unacceptable. The question is whether market rules should apply to everything. Important to EU decision-makers is rural life, landscape, environment; and these justify the continuation of its costly and inefficient farming strategy.*

That sounds sensible, doesn't it? Why shouldn't a people and a government decide that they want to put such considerations above price competitiveness and efficiency and export effectiveness? Why, then, should we South Africans not decide, for instance, that we would rather have high employment in the footwear industry than access to marginally cheaper imported shoes and boots? The answer is that we have not had the clout in the international forums to insist on that right, whereas countries in the EU have. Countries that have a relatively small market can have their economy wiped out by sanctions from a large one, whereas our sanctions would be a fleabite to them.

Another example: The Americans and the Japanese very nearly engaged in a WTO-sanctioned trade war a few years back, because Japan refused to abolish its tariffs on cars in blatant defiance of WTO rules. This was because the Japanese economy was in trouble. And while Japanese cars were fully competitive with American ones, its people had a predilection for American cars. This was a drain on foreign currency so the Japanese protected their industry with tariffs. In the end they had to give in to American pressure. This relatively harmless standoff happened because the two countries are more or less equal in strength. South Africa, on the other hand – let alone, say, Niger or Lesotho – can in theory be snuffed out and the smoke hardly noticed. These are not minor imperfections to be gradually ironed out in the global market; they are the outcome of a system in which the rules can be made to favour the powerful and bent when they are harmful to the interests of the rich.

One more current example: It has been decided at the WTO that tariff rates should be allowed to increase on goods as value is added to them. This means that primary products like those exported by most of Africa can have relatively free access to rich countries, but if those primary products are processed, instead of being sold raw, the tariff rate rises. This ensures that Africa continues to produce raw materials and the more profitable job of adding value remains with the richer countries.

The result is that the LDCs (least developed countries) are worse off under the WTO regime than they were before. Twenty years ago the ratio of income in LDCs to that in the OECD was 1 to 87. Today it is 1 to 98. With 11% of the world's population, the LDCs account for 0.5% of its income. As tariffs have come down under WTO rules, those tariffs against LDC exports remain high – in sectors like agriculture, textiles and other labour-intensive manufacturing. LDC exports to industrialised countries are three times as likely to face tariff peaks over 11% than goods traded between industrialised countries themselves. The World Bank itself estimates that LDCs lose about $2.5 billion a year because of market access restrictions

Mainstream economists are beginning to understand the situation. Michael Power, academic and investment manager, was quoted in Chapter Three. He describes his own new thinking as a result of his research (*Business Day* 16/01/2002). Net dividend outflows from South Africa in 2001 were 2% of GDP, meaning that South Africa 'effectively exported its economic growth last year'. The same is true of all developing countries. 'Indeed, last year the poorest countries of the world contributed a net $260 billion to global capital account flows. The more than 100 developing countries represent only 17% of global GDP, yet lost an average of 4% of their GDP in capital outflows to the developed world core.'

Most mainstream economists continue to believe that expanding world trade is vital for poor countries. Latterly they have conceded that existing patterns of trade are disadvantageous to developing countries. But they recommend simply that the developed countries adjust their trade policies to level the playing field. This is like whistling in the wind. Are we expecting that an American President, a British or a French Prime Minister or a German Chancellor, courting election as they must, will seriously propose measures that will create local unemployment in the interests of fairness to developing nations? Where is the evidence that this is remotely possible? Pascal Lamy's remarks quoted earlier make it explicitly clear that it is 'politically unacceptable' for a French government to end subsidies to its own farmers.

The subsidies now enjoyed by manufacturers and farmers in the developed countries include $17,000 per farmer in the EU. American farming subsidies amount to $1 million a day. The average import duties on farm products are 40%–50%. Japan's tax on foreign rice is nearly 1,000%. OECD countries spend more on subsidising their farmers each year than the entire GDP of sub-Saharan Africa. The OECD countries have intensified their subsidies to producers from $275 billion in 1988 to $326 billion in 1999. By June 2000 the US had lifted only 13 of the 750 restrictions acknowledged at the Uruguay round of GATT; the EU 14 out of 219, and Canada 29 out of 295.

The truth is that the populations of rich countries are not willing to abandon their own systems of protection. But poor countries are being forced to do so. The result is that poor countries are subsidising rich ones. The promise of 'trickle-down wealth' is not fulfilled, because the only countries that open their markets are the poor ones.

In October 2000 Pascal Lamy made a bold proposal: unrestricted market access for all LDC exports to the EU. 'Everything but arms' was the slogan. The big farm and agribusiness lobby rapidly defeated it. It will be reconsidered in 2006. Comments Kevin Watkins, Oxfam's policy adviser: 'The response of some EU states in placing powerful vested interests before the interests of the world's poor highlights the gulf separating rhetoric and policy … The sheer chutzpah of northern governments in demanding liberalisation in poor countries, while subsidising their own producers to the tune of $1 billion a day defies credulity.' The fact is that the terms of trade have been heavily rigged against poor countries, for no better reason than that the powerful are able to do so. There is nothing fair about it. Nor is there any political mechanism to change the situation.

So we should ignore the pious suggestion that the WTO has been doing no more than making and enforcing rules impartially to suit everyone. Would that it were so, because it is true that a rule-free world is one where the rich gobble up the small with impunity. So we do need rules. But not rules that preserve the privilege of the rich and expand trade for the sake of expanding trade. We need rules that create economies in which the prosperity of each is the prosperity of all. This is not just a pious suggestion, as we shall see later.

The various agreements made and enforced at the WTO are all important to the South African economy. But few of us know about them. The WTO legislates (makes enforceable laws) not only about trade and capital, but also relating to intellectual property protection (patents) and the commodification and privatisation of life forms for research. These rules threaten the preservation of plant diversity and the control of that diversity by poorer countries. They prevent our country among others from buying generic forms of vital medicines in the control of diseases like AIDS. All these agreements and their effects are beautifully set out in a book called *The World Trade Organisation: A Citizen's Guide* by Steven Shrybman, published by the Canadian Centre for Policy Alternatives.

The world narrowly escaped, four years ago, the imposition of the Multilateral Agreement on Investment (MAI). Behind closed doors, with hardly any media comment, an agreement was proposed within the WTO, which would have made explicit what is now implicit. It would have given investors rights to override those of governments. Anything that limited investors' rights or profits in any country would have been illegal, and subject to sanctions through the WTO. That included 'equal opportunities' legislation, protection of local or small business, protection of the environment – or indeed anything that regulated or restricted investors in doing as they pleased in any country.

It is scarcely credible that this measure was the subject of negotiations about which electorates were not informed. Fortunately it leaked, and as a result of civil society protest a number of local and regional authorities declared themselves 'MAI-free' zones, and the proposal was stalled.

Two WTO proposals are the subject of current protest. One is the General

Agreement on Trade in Services (GATS). This would require governments to make available for investment, on a world-wide competitive basis, the delivery of all services – including education, health, transport, water, prisons, even social services – as though they were commodities like bananas and motorbikes.

This pressure to privatise what has been regarded as public service arises from the fact that the American government sees its economy as most competitive in the commercial operation of services. Its huge current account deficit reflects its uncompetitiveness in terms of the export of goods; but it reckons it could compete successfully in the management of services, and hence begin to narrow the trade deficit. If GATS were passed, all public service would be threatened. It could become illegal, for instance, for a government not to open its health and education services to international competition. This means everything would have to be commodified and costed. Naturally it would follow that everyone would have to pay for all services when they receive them, since the private sector is not in the business of welfare. In South Africa we are already seeing the proliferation of water and energy cut-offs, as poor people, newly connected to such services, are unable to pay for them.

The other WTO proposal is the monopolisation, through patents, of the genes of the world's main crops – commercial companies taking ownership of gene plasma. That would be done under a WTO TRIPS agreement – 'Trade in Intellectual Property Rights'. Opposition groups, which include the UN's Food and Agricultural Organisation, have described this practice as bio-piracy and are pressing for a binding global agreement to govern the use of crop seed varieties and genetic resources that underpin food security. They want to ensure that at least thirty main food crops are protected and preserved against sole ownership under intellectual property rights.

Patrick Mulvany of the Intermediate Technology Development Group comments: 'Bio-piracy is rife. Intellectual property rights regimes create private ownership rights which remove locally adapted varieties from communal ownership and exchange ... These resources are our life insurance against future adversity, be it from climate change, war, industrial developments or ecosystem collapse.'

Crops that have sustained people well in the past cannot safely be replaced when lost. The UN Food and Agricultural Organisation (FAO) called on the WSSD to produce an endowment of $260 million to introduce global gene banks that would hold 5.4 million crop samples, lest they be lost in the homogenising of agriculture.

The main support for TRIPS comes from the governments of the United States, supported by Canada, New Zealand and Australia. The following is quoted from representations made by the American agricultural lobby group in support of its government's position:

As one of the most productive industries in the world, US agriculture is charged with the great responsibility to feed and clothe an ever-increasing world population. The World Food Summit in Rome underscored the fact that the US must become ever more efficient if the goal to eliminate hunger is to be accomplished ... Technology must be developed to produce the needed food in a manner that fully utilises our productive capacity in an environmentally conscientious manner. Biotechnology is an important component of that needed technology.

Because trade is so important to American technology and the US food industry (author's emphasis), it is imperative that policy and regulations governing international commerce of genetically modified food and agricultural products are based on sound science and not just emotion ...

Some officials of the EU advocate requirements that could be considered non-tariff trade barriers to the US ... It is critical that the EU understand at the highest level that the US would consider any trade barrier unacceptable and subject to challenge in the WTO.

In other words, if the EU and other countries do not find genetically modified products acceptable, they should be forced, via the WTO, to accept them anyway. What is good for the American agricultural sector is good for the world. And if we don't agree, our objections should be overruled by calling them non-tariff barriers to trade which are illegal under WTO rules.

Food security

Contrary to the position of the American agricultural lobby, there is growing concern that the international trade in food is actually a factor in the spread of hunger. The area where re-localisation would be most beneficial is that of food security. A major effect of the global market is to undermine the food-producing economies of small farmers. The 'export-led growth' ideology means that vast areas of local food-producing agricultural land throughout the world have been given over to export crops. From pineapples in Indonesia to tobacco and export mange-tout in Zimbabwe, from strawberries and roses in Kenya and bananas in the Caribbean and asparagus in Qwa Qwa to tea and coffee, sugar and rubber elsewhere, food-growing land has been taken over by large, mostly foreign, companies producing for export. Farmers have to buy food for themselves.

Second, even where countries are still 'feeding themselves' in the sense that the amount of food grown is theoretically enough for its citizens, this is increasingly being done by agribusinesses on huge farms owned by very few people, sometimes using genetically modified (GM) crops. Some of the food is being exported, because local effective demand is not sufficient. Small farmers and people growing for local consumption are being bought out and lose their livelihood. Income from exports does not reach the small farmers. The nature of food-growing for sale via the large corporations makes it nearly impossible for small farmers to survive. They then join the ranks of the cashless and unemployed in the shanty towns on the margins of cities.

In Britain 200,000 farms disappeared between 1966 and 1995. Since then it has become much worse: the average farm turnover fell in two years, in 1999 and 2000, from £100,000 to £10,000. In the US, farm numbers declined from 6.8 million to 1.9 million – there are now more people in prison than farmers working the land. In the EU the number of farmers fell from 22 million to 7 million between 1957 and 1999. There was a rash of suicides of farmers from India to the UK and the US in the late 1990s.

Agribusiness, especially when combined with genetic modification, drastically reduces employment in the farming sector. New GM developments in coffee are a chilling example. The development agency Action Aid points out that in nature coffee beans don't all ripen at the same time, making mechanised picking inefficient. For that reason 70% of all coffee is grown by small farmers. But a US company, ICTI, is developing GM coffee beans which can be made to ripen all at the same time, by the use of a chemical spray which 'switches them on' together for machine picking. This will make it cheaper to grow coffee on large plantations; and it will put smallholders out of business. Seven million small farmers now grow coffee; and it will not be economical for them to buy the spray.

Lest we imagine that this is a good thing because only a tiny proportion of people are now required to feed us all, think again. Millions of people are at work producing the industrial input to agriculture – from machinery to chemicals. It may well be that the same proportion of people now works in producing food as when farmers did all of it. But the food they produce is less healthy, less varied and less fresh. It gives a good living to a few large farmers and the chemical industries; but is that the purpose of growing food?

Agribusiness is in the control of four or five TNCs. They often own the land and always supply the seed. Much of that seed is genetically modified, or at least adapted, to require high levels of fertiliser (which replaces the organic processes that nature provides), herbicide (which destroys everything except the crop), and pesticide (which destroys natural pollinators and produces superbugs, needing new generations of pesticides). All of them are supplied by the company. And then the company buys the product and sells it internationally. Even when small farmers succeed in buying all that input in one season they are often bankrupted in the second, because the company decides the prices at both ends. Many of the modern seeds are actually modified to prevent their producing their own seeds, which must therefore be bought each season. It is called, spookily, terminator technology.

The use of herbicide and herbicide-resistant crops destroys biodiversity, as it kills everything except the crop. It increases the need for agrichemicals and produces new breeds of resistant 'superweeds'. It promotes soil erosion by destroying cover crops and lowers water tables because the crops require more irrigation.

Each 'high-yield' crop destroys the nutrition that small and subsistence farmers reap from the other products of their soils. The monoculture required by industrial agriculture robs the farmer of a variety of other sources of nutrition, medicines and soil enhancers. The research of Vandana Shiva, Indian scientist and activist, shows that the so-called Green Revolution that introduced large-scale hi-tech agriculture to India, despite giving more grain per unit, reduced the overall nutritional value of the agricultural sector. She reckons that intensive monocultural agriculture yields only six units of energy in food for every fifteen expended in its production. It also needs a lot more water, thus permanently reducing water tables. It is hard to imagine how agribusiness can be called 'efficient' in terms of its use of the earth's resources.

Vandana Shiva concludes that instead of the promised abundance, the Green Revolution strategy left behind diseased or exhausted soils, pest-infested crops, waterlogged areas and deserts, as well as indebted and impoverished farmers.

An alarming story concerning the introduction of genetically engineered cotton in South Africa received almost no attention in the mainstream press. Bt cotton, incorporating the *bacillus thuringiensis* gene, was the first genetically engineered crop grown commercially in South Africa, and it is planted by small farmers as well as large. Bt acts as a pesticide against common South African pests. A study done by Monsanto, the producers, in 1998 showed a 20%–30% increase in yield by the small farmers of the Makhatini district of KwaZulu Natal. The study was done over one season only, with four of the best farmers in the area. The first field trials of this product were started in the previous year, 1997 – the same year as the seeds were sold to farmers: so farmers were being used for the trial – a recognised malpractice.

The environmental NGO Biowatch started a study of the project in 2000. Their published results show:

- Bt farmers are now dealing with pest outbreaks, including stinkbug infestation, that they never encountered before. Therefore, over and above the cost of the licence fee for Bt, they still have the cost of spraying. In some cases a high proportion of the crop has been lost. In American trials stinkbug infestation had been noticed, but local farmers were not warned or protected.

- Small farmers must sign licence contracts that make it illegal to store seed and to exchange it with their neighbours. They did not understand this.

- According to the GMO Act, the legislation that covers commercial release of GE crops, farmers are held liable for any environmental or other damage as a result of planting these crops. Responsibility for genetic pollution or health damage has been passed to farmers, and not the company.

The theory behind the current system is called comparative advantage. It says that countries and regions should do what they do best and import the rest so that we all benefit by specialisation. It has never worked well, partly because some places have so much more advantage than others, who must rely on the 'advantage' of cheap docile labour. The global market has finally reached the end of its credibility, because what specialisation has done in the era of free capital and high technology is to ensure that labour as a factor of production has become increasingly redundant and therefore powerless. All countries must compete in a race to the bottom in terms of labour costs. The demise of small farming carries the implication of the end of food security. Rural areas, instead of remaining as safety nets for urban workers, become depopulated, while cities fester with the rural poor.

Canadian farmers are increasingly regretting their early adoption of genetic modification. One farmer, Percy Schmeiser, had the extraordinary experience of being sued by the GM food giant Monsanto, when some of their GM seeds blew onto his organic farm from neighbouring land, thereby ruining his business. Monsanto claimed that Mr Schmeiser had stolen their patented seed! Even more astonishingly, the Canadian Court found in favour of Monsanto. Such, it seems, is the reach of the corporations. Other Canadian farmers are experiencing hardships coping with the high cost of the accompanying chemicals, with the by-products in the form of super-weeds and insects, and with declining markets abroad. Their advice to Africa at the WSSD Summit was: 'If you don't already have GM crops in your country, keep them out.'

It is very clear that such crops cannot be contained where they are grown. They pollinate easily and affect crops over a wide area. This means that GM-free crops cannot be guaranteed within a wide radius of their production, and so will not be bought where GM is resisted or outlawed. Increasingly that includes the whole of the EU. That is the reason why African governments, seeking food aid as a result of famine, are refusing to take GM food: it would compromise their ability to export in future to lucrative markets in Europe. It is a disgraceful consequence of American attempts to push GM foods that African farmers are being offered GM seeds and technology or nothing.

But the economic effect of the current situation goes deeper than the means of food production. The technology necessarily entails trade in food. Identical types of food criss-cross the skies, the seas and the highways as they seek international markets. Fresh food travels thousands of miles, often arriving unripe, to be artificially ripened for a market on the other side of the world. Meanwhile the air, the waters and the land have been polluted in the process of growing and transporting food that is identical to the local product. Often the 'foreign' version is cheaper than the local because it has been mass-produced and mass-transported. Small producers are ignored by the giant corporations: it is not worth their while to deal with them.

Localising the growth and consumption of food – limiting the trade in food – would solve a heap of problems. Small farmers would be enabled to make a living: a vital matter in the whole of Africa and Asia. Food would be fresher, packaging more limited; and the environment would be spared the pollution of long-distance transport. Food diversity would return. French markets are a joy and a pleasure because their farmers have more successfully than most resisted the impact of the global trade in food; and their local diversity has been relatively preserved. For that, of course, they are generally regarded as stubborn, selfish, nationalist, even fascist. See Helena Norberg-Hodge's *Bringing the Food Economy Home* for details.

Yet the World Bank and Western development agencies are still funding large agribusiness schemes which displace local people and especially small farmers. Many are in 'partnership' with the multinational corporations. The British government is funding a scheme in Andhra Pradesh that will displace some 20 million people. Where will they go? It seems little has been learnt about the failure of these large export-focused schemes which employ relatively few local people and create profits for a few, including the corporations. One such was a Canadian-funded wheat-growing scheme in Tanzania that displaced 40,000 to produce a crop that only the elite eats. The local people are malnourished for the first time.

But an ecological crisis wider than that of food security looms. 'A conservative estimate suggests that the economic costs of natural disasters driven by climate change could equal and pass the value of gross world production in just over sixty years. But depending on how you measure it, it could happen in half that time.' That sobering thought from the New Economics Foundation's Andrew Simms in his Alternative Mansion House Speech is given weight by the floods in Europe, China and India in 2002. It also brings into focus the ecological aspect of Old Economics. Environmental protection runs counter to the imperatives of the unregulated global market. His conclusion is that the only way to meet the challenge is to 'create a vision of an environmental war economy. Our enemy is not another country. It is a hostile climate, and the weapon we have to disarm it is a change in our lifestyles.'

The UN Environmental Programme reckons some three million people have died as a result of extreme and unstable weather conditions. On that basis a case has been taken against the American government by the New Economics Foundation for the USA's refusal to sign the Kyoto Protocols, knowing that climate change stems from polluting emissions and results in death and loss to millions.

The present system is not only destructive but also unsustainable, because in its inevitable search for growth of all kinds, it uses more and more fossil fuels, and employs fewer and fewer people. World oil output could peak in 2005; and by 2050 we could have available only the same amount of oil as we used in

1950. Natural gas will probably peak in 2020. Coal will last longer; but its polluting effects are worse than those of other forms of fuel. Global gas guzzling will become increasingly expensive: all transport costs will go up suddenly and steeply unless we take some steps now. Meanwhile each year the world sheds labour. We need some 3% more fuel-based growth each year just to re-employ the labour being made redundant. World hunger and the inability of poor people to pay for what they need for health are intrinsic aspects of environmental degradation. Richard Douthwaite's *Short Circuit* is invaluable for a detailed exposition of this point.

So it is clear that the global market has some inevitable consequences that must be reversed if we are to regenerate the planet's productiveness, restore the capacity to feed everyone and give people back control over their lives and livelihoods.

How do we do that? The global alternative is very simple in principle. It is to create an international economy in which everything that can sensibly (including competitively) be produced locally should be so produced; and if it cannot be produced locally, we should go national or regional, and only finally global. What we consume should have travelled as little as possible to get to us. We should rely on local competition to make the market operate in the interests of consumers and staff – as well as shareholders. That process should happen globally, and into that global process should go the world's best technology, ingenuity and information. We will be freed from the compulsion to export, because we will not be driven to import. When we do export we will have flourishing markets to sell in.

Consider what might sensibly have been done in the UK during the foot-and-mouth outbreak. As we in Africa know, this disease is not fatal to animals and does not infect humans, who can safely eat the meat. Yet the British government arranged for the compulsory slaughter and burning of over a million animals, the great majority of which were uninfected. The cost to taxpayers ran into millions of pounds. The reason given was that foreign meat importers would not buy infected or potentially infected meat. But the real solution, since Britain imports and exports roughly the same amount of meat, would have been to stop exporting and importing it. The British people could have eaten local produce. The impediment was the rules of the WTO, which do not allow such an interruption to trade. It is true that some farmers would have objected to the (possibly temporary) loss of export markets; but that would surely have been a small price to pay to avoid the economically and emotionally devastating results of the attempt to wipe out the disease – which included an impact on the tourist industry.

The change of direction that would have been involved in such a solution to the foot-and-mouth epidemic is partly one of mind-set, and partly one of managing the interests of different groups in the economy. We need to return to Colin Hines' ideas around global localisation.

There are a number of ways in which governments can encourage local economic development, especially if they are released from the primary obligation to open their markets and exchanges to global trading.

Local Exchange Trading Systems (LETS)

In any advanced economy wealth tends to leak from rural to urban areas, from poorer to richer communities, from villages to towns. During periods of money scarcity – a permanent condition under the present dispensation – that process is speeded up. John Courtneidge of the Fair World Project in England defines five ways in which money leakages happen.

- Money earned locally is spent externally, because large outlets can sell more cheaply.

- External workers come into an area, are paid more than local rates and leave with the money.

- Non-resident ownership of land and other assets extracts profits and rents and spends them elsewhere.

- Local employment by external employers, who pull out when profits fall.

- Loans taken out by local people from lenders outside the area, ensuring that payment of interest goes external.

Part of the leaking process can be addressed by LETS – local currencies that circulate only in a limited area. These parallel or supplementary currencies enable trade and exchange in an area which is short of the national currency and therefore of livelihoods. People's skills can be activated by trading within the area, even though the national currency is in short supply. The system is sometimes compared to a form of barter. But it is much wider than that because the currency allows trading between people who do not want direct exchange. If I am a carpenter in Gugulethu I can build your kitchen for a price in LETS. I can then buy my vegetables from someone else, also in LETS. In cashless areas that transaction would not have happened, unless it were pure barter – direct exchange of carpentry for vegetables.

The currency can take physical form, such as notes or coins – provided they do not look similar to the national legal currency – or transactions can simply be recorded. For instance, Person A gave a service or a product, and so is credited with currency, while Person B received the same and so is debited in the currency.

LETS systems are, of course, entirely without the risk of inflation. The currency comes into existence only when a transaction in the form of a product or a service happens. The currency is limited to the amount of resources, human and natural, available in the community; and it can be expanded as long as resources are idle. It is not interchangeable with the national currency, so it cannot leak out of the community. It simply enables people to trade within a particular area. It has the limitation that it does not allow local people to interact economically outside the area; but it raises living standards within the community in terms of everything that can be created there. Some LETS systems allow transactions partly in the national currency – to cover the costs of materials imported into the area – and partly in the local currency.

There are over 7,000 such schemes running all over the world. In the English West Country alone there are 35 local currencies. South West Australia's LETS systems are so successful that you can pay your tax in the local currency. One American version is called Time Dollars. People accumulate credit for time spent in social services of one kind or another, and are entitled to 'spend' that credit on goods or services of a defined kind. In one scheme ex-offending youths were offered the gift of home computers in exchange for time spent tutoring other youngsters who needed help with schoolwork. Another offers credits for helping elderly people in their communities. Clearly very much more is achieved in those schemes than simply the goods and services exchanged. Community solidarity and mutual understanding is a by-product of these community-restricted currencies.

In South Africa there are four areas that await funding to establish LETS schemes – two in Gauteng, and two in the Western Cape. There is also a proposal that a Basic Income Grant might be paid partly in the form of a parallel currency. This has many advantages. It would make fewer demands on the tax system; and it would remain in the communities in which people live. The complications arise when it comes to administering a benefit in a multitude of local currencies. Somewhat similar is the idea that the Basic Income Grant be paid in the form of vouchers for public services such as health, education and electricity.

Reduce distances between producers and consumers

Keeping production and consumption relatively local clearly counteracts the toxic effects of distance: the pollution, the chemical intensity, the large-scale production and the homogenising, the destruction of small livelihoods and the impersonal callousness of distance trading. Obviously not everything can be produced and sold locally, but lots can. Many local farm stalls and specialist vegetable or health shops sell organic vegetables where and whenever available, but in any case stock only fresh food grown within the local area. Their example is being followed as others discover that consumers find shopping locally a joy and not simply a chore. There are now over 600 farmers' markets operating in England alone, giving farmers a better income and consumers a better product.

Further afield local authorities are encouraging localisation of food and other products. Some American states tax-incentivise supermarkets to stock local and organic foods, and have even passed laws favouring locally owned business in the town centre. Of course this contradicts WTO rules – and Vermont was actually sued by the giant corporate Wal-Mart – but it clearly makes sense to local residents and consumers. That kind of consumer pressure is already foiling corporate attempts to use the WTO to force Europeans to accept genetically modified foods.

Another example: in India most hotels now have a policy of ensuring that all procurement be from within a range of fifty miles, and that the ownership of the hotel should be at least 50% from the community, as defined by those living in the fifty-mile radius. Already the effect is to stimulate local economies throughout the country.

At a macro level, it is for governments to judge when and how their economy should export and import, and what benign incentives are best to produce that result. Many of these mechanisms were used extensively by the so-called Asian Tiger States, in the 1980s and 1990s, when their economies took off. They would be illegal now under WTO rules. But those measures increased productivity without losing employment, essentially by supporting labour-intensive sectors of the economy. They comprised direct long-term government support, and also protection through tariffs until they were ready to compete internationally. In other words each sector entered the global market when they had been thoroughly prepared.

In South Africa the most labour-intensive sectors are clothing, wood products, furniture, footwear and construction. Sadly, we were persuaded to open our borders to trade in these industries long before they were ready, and even before we were obliged to do so under WTO rules – on the grounds that such courageous entry into the competitive world arena would create confidence on the part of the much-sought foreign investor. It did no such thing. It destroyed employment for tens of thousands and decimated in particular the footwear and clothing industries, maybe beyond repair. It still goes on. Weekly we have news of new redundancies, couched of course in smooth euphemisms about restructuring and right-sizing.

'Protection' has a bad name. It means to conventional economists the beggar-my-neighbour, tit-for-tat policies of the desperate thirties, and the 'feather-bedding' of inefficient production. It has become a myth, for instance, that the reason India has not developed is because it has protected its industry. This is a gross over-simplification: the reasons for India's relative under-development in some sectors are legion. Important is the existing semi-feudal ownership of much of India's land, and the hold that rich people and companies have over the economic policies of its government in terms of redistribution. The exception is Kerala, where land has been redistributed under radical state governments, and the economy there has a higher level of prosperity than elsewhere. Kerala is worth studying.

In any case tariff protection does not have to mean perpetual protection; only that governments should have the right to judge when and how protection is applied. There is no exception to the universal rule that no country has taken off industrially except behind some form of protection – tariffs, wars, or in South Africa's case, sanctions. You cannot go from having small capital formation, little entrepreneurial tradition or experience, poor education and health, technological backwardness and so on, straight into direct competition with the world's most advanced. A process is needed, as common sense would dictate.

However, alternative forms of taxation will do some, if not all, of the job for you. If aviation fuel is taxed, if petrol and diesel are relatively expensive, if agribusiness has to pay the full internalised costs of the chemicals it uses, if the large TNCs have to pay the full cost of transporting goods, occupying sites and using energy, then local and organic food growing will be privileged by price. Currently we subsidise size and long-distance travel. If, instead, we taxed travel, local would become more attractive. Judgement would be needed as to how much these green taxes can naturally create local economies, and how much you need more direct intervention as well.

Colin Hines has an idea also for a 'site here to sell here' policy. Government would pass a regulation that if you want to sell your goods and services within its borders you must create the employment involved in making it there as well. You cannot pull your capital out because something, probably labour, is cheaper somewhere else – and retain your market here. In other words you must make where you want to sell. Of course this could not apply to some massive industries like steel and shipbuilding; but would be perfectly easy for the great majority of goods and services.

Much is made of the supposed efficiency of the global market in terms of resource use. This is myth. Let us remind ourselves of the way that the current system subsidises the movement of goods internationally – even as it destroys local employment and natural resources.

Multinational supermarket chains are publicly subsidised by:

- Super-highways built by taxpayers' money
- Shipping terminals built by taxpayers' money
- No tax on aviation fuel
- Air and noise pollution untaxed
- Satellite communication/product of space programmes
- Laser technology/product of military research
- High technology education programmes subsidised by governments
- Government-supported negotiated benefits internationally
- Tax breaks and other subsidies
- Polluting agribusiness cleaned up by taxpayers
- Declining public health.

Capital controls

The present era is the first in which capital has been so mobile. Economists used to warn against it. In the '50s and '60s European countries had strong controls on the movement of capital, and built welfare states on the theory that capital should stay where it is created, unless directly invested or given away as aid. There is no theoretical reason why governments cannot introduce capital controls; many countries have controls in one form of another. We still have some in South Africa but are under constant pressure to reduce them so as to create the elusive 'market confidence'.

Moreover there is no clear evidence that foreign direct investment does in fact contribute to economic development. Munetsi Madakufamba, writing for the Southern Africa Research and Documentation Centre, shows that there is scant link between FDI and poverty alleviation. Zambia, pressurised to sell parastatals to (foreign) private enterprises, incurred huge losses, as the copper mines were sold for a song, to mostly foreign-owned companies. Zimbabwe gave a five-year tax holiday to Australian mining giant Broken Hill Properties to mine platinum. The company also got 100% profit repatriation rights, relaxed environmental and labour standards and the right to export without going through the Minerals Marketing Corporation. After five years the company pulled out, leaving hundreds jobless. In South Africa preparation for privatisation of water has caused its price to rise and payment to be required from often cashless people. This was blamed partly for the cholera outbreak in 2001. Of course, some employment has been created by FDI, but there is no evidence as to whether this is more or less than would have been created by South African capital if it had stayed in the country instead of being allowed to leave in search of offshore profits.

A seminar in Windhoek early in 2001 brought together NGOs and trade unions. It concluded that 'SADEC governments are trying very hard to create the right climate for investment on the advice of experts from the World Bank and IMF … However governments are not putting the right policies in place to ensure that such investments serve a national investment agenda.' The statement says the SADEC governments engage in a 'race to the bottom' as they compete with one another to attract FDI by lower taxes, relaxed standards, repatriation of profits and unlimited imports.

We have to shift the debate. If the name of the international game were to change – if the objective were to build sustainable national economies, we would have an altogether different set of international rules. Let us set down both sets of rules, roughly as defined by Colin Hines.

Globalisation Code: International investment treaties create a broadly defined list of investor rights to conduct business free from government oversight or regulatory control. This is accomplished by explicitly prohibiting an extensive catalogue of government policies, laws and programmes. These treaties also include very powerful legal enforcement mechanisms that can be invoked by any foreign investor.

Alternative Investment Code (AIC): States party to the AIC may not pass laws or adopt regulations that diminish local control of capital or divert investors from giving priority to meeting local needs. States may impose requirements on investors that further the goals of the code, which seeks to stimulate investments that benefit local communities.

Michael Shuman, of the Washington-based Institute for Policy Studies, says in his book, *Going Local:* 'Going local does not mean walling off the outside world. It means nurturing local businesses that use local resources sustainably, that employ local workers at decent wages, and that serve primarily local consumers. It means becoming more self-sufficient and less dependent on imports. Control moves from the boardrooms of distance corporations, and back to the community where it belongs.'

The South African economist and director of Earth Africa, Norman Reynolds, has detailed proposals for balancing a local focus with benign involvement in the global economy. He explains that pure market logic is based on the right to 'exit', inevitably short-term and disloyal, while a 'commitment' logic is essential for local development. He recommends that the government should support, through tax and other interventions, employee and peasant ownership, creating long-term investment in human capital. With his colleague, Professor Johan Van Zyle, Reynolds proposes that local communities should be given 'investment rights' by means of government grants. This treats poor people not as a cost to the State but as a resource for development. Villages would become trust companies, providing an investment vehicle for rural people that rewards both cash and labour inputs. He concludes that the task is to promote South Africa as a nation that puts its people and economy ahead of outsiders; that works hard on structural and poverty issues; and that harnesses the short term to realise long-term goals (*Business Day* 15/1/2002).

We are a long way from that ideal, mostly because we are so terrified of 'market punishment' that we create self-fulfilling prophecies. Opposition politicians and most of our press lecture government on what it has to do to avoid offending 'the markets', meaning foreign investors. Perhaps the most alarming example was an item in the *Business Report* of 4 February 2001, quoting a spokesperson for South African business, which condemned a court judgement in support of striking workers. It warned that this kind of judgement, if not overturned, could discourage investors. So now, it seems, our courts should be concerned not with application of the law but with the effect of upholding the law on the investment decisions of persons abroad.

As we consider how to change direction despite the pressures on us, we should bear in mind that the Malaysian and other unorthodox experiences show that a country acting on its own can defy the Washington Consensus to rebuild its economy. Of course, re-localisation would be most effectively approached by concerted effort regionally or internationally.

South Africa has a great role to play here – if we develop the strength and courage to do so. It seems we have very little to lose. The *Business Report* of January 23, 2002 reported that in 2000 FDI in South Africa 'plummeted' by 42%. Our government has swallowed the hard medicine of the 'markets' to the last drop. Still the investment is elusive. Maybe it is because of Zimbabwe, and maybe it is not. Maybe it is just that other places offer even more craven obedience. Who knows? The point is that all that should not cripple us. We need to re-localise our sovereignty, our right to determine our rates of interest in our own interest, our allocation of resources, our government revenues – our democracy, in fact. Otherwise we can kiss our famous miracle goodbye.

POINTS FOR DISCUSSION – CHAPTER FIVE

1. Should food be traded differently from other commodities? How?

2. How could global localisation help avert climate change?

3. Could public/private partnerships (PPPs) help to localise globally?

4. Could the world move from globalisation to localisation? How?

MYTHS OF GLOBALISATION – ELEVEN

'There have been alarms about the ecosystem before.
Don't worry. The scientists always sort it out.'

Those of us who have inherited the West's confidence that science can do anything easily fall for this. It helps us cope with a sense of impotence about vast climatic events and trends that seem incomprehensible and overwhelming. We tell ourselves there have been Jeremiahs before. Malthus told us the human race was increasing so fast that mass deaths by famine and disease were inevitable. But then we found contraception and new technology which led to a large increase in living standards in the West. So maybe that sort of thing will happen again. This is widely believed in the US, where it may be combined with conservative Christian beliefs about the approaching God-intended end of the world.

But this time it really seems to be different. Scientists themselves are the Jeremiahs, warning that we are reaching several points of no return. In the past forty years the population has doubled. At the same time conservative religions are severely restricting funding to enable women to limit their families.

Worldwide there is a devastating change in climate patterns, producing floods, droughts, cyclones and insurance crises never before encountered by humanity. In all developed countries we are rapidly wiping out species of flora and fauna through using up the remaining rainforests and by industrialised monocultural agriculture. Chemical herbicides and fertilisers destroy the soil's fertility, and pesticides wipe out whole species while creating new immune ones. These practices are spreading across the planet as a diminishing number of corporations control the trade in food.

The effect of this is that the world's remaining areas of biodiversity are to be found in the poor and least developed countries. There is a serious danger that these plants and animals will be controlled and patented by the large science-based food corporations, who were responsible for the research that produced the 'Green Revolution' (the introduction of high-yield food crops produced by agribusiness, intended to feed more people) and who are now engaged in genetic modification. We now know that the Green Revolution, while increasing yields, also led to increased hunger because of its effect on land ownership, income distribution and the trading of food. We now know enough to be on our guard against that kind of science.

MYTHS OF GLOBALISATION – TWELVE

'In the free market people are rightly paid according to the laws of supply and demand, and the freer the market the better that works.'

A post is advertised for a fund manager in an insurance company. The starting salary is £10,000 a month, a company car and share options. Dozens of people apply. Does the company decide to lower the remuneration since the supply clearly exceeds the demand? No, because, says the company, it wants to choose the very best from a large pool of applicants.

A job is advertised for a community worker in an NGO. It pays £800 a month, there are no perks and the job is highly stressful. One person applies. Does the NGO decide to raise the pay? No, it can't afford to pay any more than that.

So what happened to supply and demand? The economics of the profit and the non-profit sectors are very different. The former is directly income-generating; the non-profit sector must be supported by charity or by public funds obtained through taxing the cash surplus generated in the profit sector. Public funds give us roads, health services, schools and universities, social services, governments and civil services. These are infrastructures which cannot make profits but which enable the rest of the economy to function. This is not about supply and demand. It is about how we value skills and how much we are prepared to be taxed for the public good in the public sector. Similarly most community services in poor communities rely on public subscription rather than profit surplus.

MYTHS OF GLOBALISATION – THIRTEEN

'In the free market people are paid according to the value that they add.'

A person plays the share markets on the internet or in an office. In one day he might clear £1,000 – or £10,000 or £100,000. He might also lose, in which case he might commit suicide or even murder. In effect he has been gambling.

Another person spends her life in a hospital, looking after accident casualties, people with hip replacements, incontinent elderly people, others with dementia, dying children. She takes home £1,400 a month.

A third person has just been recruited to the executive board of a major parastatal organisation and is paid £500,000 a year, plus bonuses based on the share price of the soon-to-be-privatised company. As they take their seats the Chairman announces it has been decided to raise their remuneration to £700,000 to bring it into line with equivalent pay for large private companies. The new recruit makes a hash of the job, and is paid to leave with £1.5 million.

A woman tills the soil with a hoe. It is slow work in the heat. She carries a baby on her back. She is growing food for her family. She is paid nothing.

Which of these people adds the most value? Human output can seldom be measured exactly. That which can tends to be in the lowest paid groups – like women paid for piecework at home – and their rates reflect their need for work. The boards of major corporations pay themselves ostensibly by reference to what other boards are paying their members. In the past decades this has produced a prodigious leapfrogging process of competitive hikes. The price of a company's shares tends to be attributed to successful management when they are going up and to poor market conditions when they are going down. Managers who leave an organisation when it fails are often paid huge golden handshakes to leave. This is not a principle often applied to failing workers at humbler grades.

STORY OF A KIBBUTZ

Here is the story of a kibbutz that I know. Forty years ago most of its members worked in the fields to produce fruit for export, food for its dining room, and milk for the local market; while others staffed the kitchens, laundry, children's houses and other services.

Then a member with a marketing nose identified possibilities for a new fruit with a high yield, profitable markets and easily mechanised production. The orchards were given over to this fruit. This gave work to only 50 of the 150 agriculture workers, but brought in enough income to support the whole population at the previous level. Then they found machines to reduce the number of workers needed for services. And calculations showed that it was more efficient to buy food for the dining room. So food was bulk-bought and cold stored. More people became unemployed. Of course they were not homeless or hungry or abandoned. They went on eating and sleeping and living together as they had always done.

So the problem for the kibbutz was not income – that was assured, thanks to technology – nor inequality and poverty. The problem was meaningful work for everyone. That was addressed by giving 'surplus' workers the chance to raise the internal living standards of the kibbutz. Some worked to upgrade housing and sports facilities; some were given training for specialist educational and health professions; others developed their hobbies, becoming artists, scholars, librarians; one became the spiritual director. Some began to grow vegetables and fruit organically. It found a ready market among others who resisted the bulk-bought food in the dining room, and so preferred to eat in their own homes.

The reason the kibbutz managed that outcome is that it has no internal market for labour or for its own output. The economy competes only in its 'export' markets. All members, whatever their jobs, share equally in the fruits of its economy. None is paid more than any other. The replacement of workers by machines does not throw people into poverty or reduce their capacity to consume or produce. It does not deprive them of education or health, so that they become social liabilities. It does not threaten their mortgages or render them homeless, so that they become delinquent, alienated, drug-abusers or otherwise parasitic. The continued consumption of kibbutz members is not inflationary. They continue to be productive and to earn their keep by contributing.

Could a basic income grant have the same effect?

CHAPTER SIX

The road to New Economics

First, let's see what is on our side. For a start, we have beautifully hosted the WSSD in Johannesburg. In terms of the organisation of a highly complex and huge event, we can be proud of ourselves as South Africans.

As a result of that conference the world will never be the same again. During and since that conference Old Economics has been on the defensive. For the first time, the media has reported the opposition to the Washington Consensus in at least as much detail and with at least as much sympathy as they reported the position taken by Western governments. No doubt there will be backsliding. The proprietors of the media will try to take back the initiative on behalf of the unfettered global market. But the genie is out of the bottle – we have heard from the victims that the system is not working – and it will be hard to stuff it back.

This is a result of a huge international civil society movement that has been working separately and together all over the world. The WSSD Conference showcased programmes and projects all over the world that demonstrate how local communities can beat the global concentration of wealth and power to regenerate local economies, and they will be locally and internationally inspirational.

The European consumer movements have already had a considerable effect on political life there. A church in London, for instance, asked all the local supermarkets to stock 'Fair Trade' goods – those imported by development agencies after buying at a price fair to the producers. When they got a polite brush-off from some of the managers, they collected for one month the receipts of parishioners from those shops, to show how much they spent in each supermarket. The very next week they got an appointment and a serious discussion; and very shortly the shelves stocked 'Fair Trade' coffees and teas. None of the large supermarket chains in the UK now stock food containing genetically modified products, because there has been such consumer resistance to it.

Environmental groups internationally now have access to government structures – some of course more than others. Some European Green parties have real political power and all of them seriously influence other political parties' programmes. The New Economics Foundation in London and its allies in Europe are represented in a number of top-level policy forums. The NEF won top prize in a Think Tank of the Year competition in 2002, judged by journalists, academics and political figures.

In the West, and also in South Africa, there are rules about what chemicals can be used in agriculture; and artificial aids to soil fertility and pest control are not as bad for everything else as they used to be. Unfortunately, of course, the chemical companies are still selling the toxic versions wherever they can find unregulated markets in poor countries – and testing new chemicals and pharmaceuticals in those countries. So we are already winning some battles on the environment, but by no means all.

Here is a cheerful success story, taken from Guy Dauncey's publication *EcoNews*.

Sixty-eight thousand people live in the Belgian town of Hasselt; and another 20,000 commute in and out every day. Faced with rising debt and traffic congestion, the mayor decided to abandon plans to build a third ring road round the town. Instead he closed one of the two existing ring roads, planted trees in its space, laid more pedestrian walkways and cycle tracks, increased the frequency and quality of the bus service and announced that public transport would be free of charge. A year later the use of public transport had increased by 800%. The merchants were happy because business had increased, there were fewer accidents, fewer road casualties and an increase in social activity. The same day that the town made transport free, they also cut local taxes. More people are attracted to Hasselt because it is easier to get there, and the extra income has offset the reduction in tax rates. One of the reasons the measures were adopted was a shortage of funds – the city did not have enough money to expand the roads. Free buses were a cheaper alternative to the new road and it worked. The city had been losing population, but since the new measures were adopted the population has been rising 25 times faster than it was shrinking. Hasselt has been showered with prizes for the innovative way it has tackled pollution and congestion.

In South Africa it is clear that the government is having second thoughts about the adequacy of the Growth, Employment and Redistribution policy as a mechanism for growth, let alone equity or redistribution. Economic stagnation and growing tensions within its alliance with COSATU and the Communist Party have opened the way to new thinking. Some within the government claim that GEAR served the purpose of getting inflation and tax collection under control – the 'fiscal fundamentals' – and is now free to move into growth mode. This context opens the way to new thinking.

Here is another fact that should give us hope. There is now repeated longitudinal research evidence that the economies in which incomes are most equal do better in terms of consistent steady growth – and of course social cohesion – than ones with larger differences between the top and bottom incomes. For instance, research from 26 poor countries presented by Harvard's Peter Timmer to the US International Seminar Series on Comparative Development in 1999 showed that the more equal the distribution of income the better the effect and extent of growth.

The Thatcherite idea that inequality of incomes produces growth was a myth. The US and Britain, where there are huge disparities, have had the bumpiest ride over the past 30 years, as well as the worst social indices. Britain has the highest ratio of chief executives' salaries to average workers' pay in Europe and the lowest tax rates. It also has one of the lowest benefits levels, the productivity gap is widening, and public services, including health and education, are much poorer than most in Europe.

The Scandinavian countries and the Netherlands, relatively egalitarian, have been fairly stable and consistent in terms of growth, and their public services are a marvel compared to Britain's. They all have a per capita income close to that of the US. All are technology-driven. The difference is that these countries put half their GDP through the government budget – with a top marginal income tax of at least 60% – and they have excellent welfare systems for old people, the sick and the poor, whereas the US does not. They also have a steadier rate of growth over time.

Despite the Asian crash, the Japanese economy, which is the most egalitarian in terms of income among developed countries, is still among the most successful in the world, as far as standard of living is concerned. Doug Struck of the *Washington Post* Foreign Service noted in an article on 7 February 2001 that the Japanese have higher incomes, more savings, longer lives and better health than Americans. And they work less hard to achieve it. The average working week among manufacturing workers is five hours shorter than in the US. The Japanese also pay lower taxes – less than 12% of their incomes compared to more than 16%. And they get more services. Health care is virtually free. Every local ward in Tokyo has a large public swimming pool and several playgrounds. The public transport system is the most efficient in the world. More Japanese take overseas holidays than Americans. And they still manage to save money. While American workers spent more than they earned in 2000, the average Japanese family put away 13% of its pay cheque in savings.

Above all, Japanese 'stagnation' is relative. Japan's unemployment rate has risen from 4.7% to 6%, after ten years in the doldrums, compared to 4.2% in the US after eight years of roaring boom – and 5.7% since the events of September 11. Every Japanese household has a colour television, nine in ten have a microwave oven, 85% have a car, 40% a computer and 39% a set of golf clubs. The rate of heart attacks is one third of that in the US; the divorce rate is half the American, the crime rate one third and the homicide rate one sixth. Proportionately, more Japanese 18-year-olds go to college than do Americans. Japanese read twice as many books per capita as Americans. There are hardly any homeless Japanese, compared with 700,000 American.

It is true there is achievement-stress in Japan, as there is in all modern countries. That is the nature of the capitalist beast. People commit suicide, because the consequences of failure can be so awful. But it is no worse in Japan.

Doug Struck concludes that the reason for Japan's comparative success lies in the different economic philosophies of the two countries. 'Japan's public and corporate officials have largely resisted the route so often urged by the US to cut their losses, cut their workforces and let companies go bankrupt. Japan baulks at the US model wherein highly paid CEOs rescue a struggling company by throwing thousands of its employees out of work. Instead, workers keep their jobs while the companies limp along. It may be inefficient capitalism, they say, but workers have jobs.'

Here is another startling fact. In the state of Kerala in India there are proportionately more post-graduates than there are in the United States. It is the most literate region in the world. Kerala also uses one-seventieth of resources per capita compared with the US. Kerala's very active democracy produces policy that gives a high priority to public education and health and hence an egalitarian regime. It is governed under the economic theory of Amartya Sen, 1998 Nobel Prize Winner for Economics for his work on the livelihoods and capacities of poor people, and a thorn in the side of the Washington Consensus.

Here is another contradiction of the conventional theory about the way that capital needs to be wooed. Which stock market would you think has offered the best return on capital in the 20th century? New York? London? Hong Kong? No, it is Sweden – socialist Sweden with its apparently ludicrously high taxation, strong trade unions and welfare state. Followed closely by Australia, also with strong trade unions, legal constraints on capital and a welfare state. Sadly, of course, Sweden and Australia have been forced like the rest of us to globalise their economies and many of those indices are beginning to crumble.

Malaysia, Korea and Taiwan succeeded, before they fully entered the global market, in combining a high level of state intervention with the strength of market forces, and produced some of the highest rates of growth with some of the fairest income distribution systems. They used government intervention mostly in deliberately fostering local industry – something the Multilateral Agreement on Investment (MAI) would have outlawed altogether. This should keep us hopeful that both logic and experience teach that humanity can be served by refusing the prescriptions of Old Economics, and by starting to think both rationally and compassionately.

There has also been a change in the terms and the tenor of the debate. The World Bank's World Development Report in 2000 admits that structural adjustment has failed as a cure for poverty. The critique did not go far enough for Bank economist Professor Ravi Kanbur, who resigned because the Bank watered down the analysis of what had gone wrong. The former deputy MD of the IMF, Stanley Fisher, acknowledged the validity of many anti-globalisation protests. The 2001 report of the UN Conference on Trade and Development (UNCTAD) warned that the current global architecture operates in favour of developed countries and contributes to global systemic instability.

London and Washington's financial journals – usually the ones most ardently warning governments of the dangers of flouting 'the markets' – are full of foreboding. *Time* magazine's leader writer, Michael Kinsley, regretted that 'the WTO is despised across the entire political spectrum'. *The Financial Times* of 11 September 2001 (yes, that day) warned that 'as long as the demands of the public and capital are in conflict the politicians will conclude that anti-business populism promises electoral dividends'. Populism is now the dirty word. *Business Week* (06/11/2000) warned that 'unless multinational companies shoulder more of the social costs themselves in countries where governments are weak, street protesters will probably set the rules for them'. And *The Economist* admitted on 23 September 2000 that 'the protesters are right that the most pressing moral, political and economic issue of our time is third-world poverty. And they are right that the tide of globalisation, powerful as the engine driving it may be, can be turned back.' This, it added, was what made the protesters so dangerous. In 2000 the Canadian Security Intelligence Service published a report called 'Anti-Globalisation, A Spreading Phenomenon'.

Jeffrey Sachs, influential Director of the Centre for International Development at Harvard, has become a campaigning opponent of the current operations of Western governments and the direction of the Bank and the IMF. Here are some of his remarks in a speech to the World Bank's annual conference on development economics in April 2000 and a subsequent article in *The Financial Times* of 26 September 2000:

> *The truth is that the Bank and IMF are the instruments of a few rich governments, which hold a majority of the dollar-based votes, and would rather pretend that all is well than ask their tax-payers to address the urgent problems of the poor.*
>
> *When push comes to shove the IMF and World Bank side with the creditor interests of the rich countries ...*
>
> *The IMF has no business trying to run dozens of poor countries: it knows very little about development challenges ...Its policy recommendations (sic) have*

left Africa every bit as dependent on primary commodities as it was 29 years ago ... The World Bank is equally ineffectual. To shield US taxpayers it has pretended for 20 years that public health disasters in Africa should be solved by 'cost recovery' measures.

The truth is that we do not need a public sector bank – directing most of its lending to already creditworthy countries. We need a World Development Agency to help spur technological solutions to the problems of the poor, that would provide grants that would deliver urgently needed healthcare and education.

That comprehensive condemnation of the results of conventional thinking about the benefits of the global market comes from the heart of the arena of the Washington Consensus. And what could be closer to its heart than the CIA? In 2000 it published its prediction of global trends up to 2015 (www.cia.gov/ cia/publications/globaltrends2015/index.html). Here are some of them:

- World population will be 7.2 billion, up from 6.1 billion in 2000.
- There will be enough food produced, but increased hunger – up 20% in sub-Saharan Africa.
- Nearly half the world's population will live in countries that are 'water-stressed'.
- Greenhouse gas emissions will increase substantially.
- AIDS will consume more than 50% of health budgets of the countries affected.

This is a horrifying scenario, which needs desperately serious action. At least now it is out in the open.

George Soros has also become something of an embarrassment to the upholders of the current dispensation. He gave a talk, a draft for a new book, to the Institute for International Economics in Washington on October 25,

2001. He said globalised markets have produced three key imbalances: considerable private wealth but limited public goods; international institutions unable to deliver global public goods; and arrangements that favour established markets at the expense of emerging markets. He added that this was no accident, because the political forces driving globalisation are working to reduce the influence of the state and curb its intervention in the economy. But the state ought to be able to correct the drawbacks of globalisation's benefits.

Soros set out three goals. First, to address unstable financial markets. Second, to level the playing field for emerging markets; and third, to improve governance in the countries lagging in development. Market fundamentalists, he said, would obviously oppose the first two. As to which international institutions are best fitted to take change forward, Soros said the WTO was biased in favour of its dominant country members, and he was especially critical of its involvement in enforcing intellectual property rights. The World Bank had been moved forward considerably by its current president, James Wolfenson, but was crucially constrained by its constitution, with its emphasis on lending rather than grant-giving. The IMF had two asymmetries: disparity in its treatment of debtors and creditors; and a preference for crisis intervention rather than crisis prevention.

Soros proposed an issue of Special Drawing Rights (SDR) by the IMF to which rich countries would donate, but the spending of which would be out of their hands – except as to country of destination. An independent Board would act according to agreed criteria, but implementation would be carried out by recipient countries.

A danger that became obvious during the WSSD is that the Transnational Corporations (TNCs) will seek to maintain their dominance through the widespread institution of public/private partnerships (PPPs). These could become means by which public funds are used in effect to employ the TNCs to implement development programmes. The overt purpose is to use the resources, managerial and financial, of the TNCs to enrich the process of sustainable development. At the Johannesburg Summit ten awards were announced for sustainable development projects – chosen from 120 – that flowed from PPPs. They ranged from the production of organic spices to recycling to electricity production through renewable resources in remote areas. The awards were offered by the International Chamber of Commerce together with the UN Environmental Programme, whose Director, Klaus Topfer, praised the 'triple bottom line' approach of progressive businesses. That approach engages business in seeing profit or the economy as only one aspect of its outcomes – the others being the environment and society as a whole.

It may seem churlish to look with suspicion upon these PPPs. At the Summit the World Business Council for Sustainable Development (WBCSD) actually joined Greenpeace to call on all governments to sign the Kyoto Protocols. And there is a growing movement in business to address the 'triple bottom line', to join the international imperative for sustainable development and to be seen as progressive. Their economic strength means it is impossible to avoid them.

Three factors give reason for caution. The first is, of course, their history. TNCs have been quoted to the effect that poor countries cannot afford pollution control: it is a luxury that must be sacrificed in view of the higher priorities around poverty. Meanwhile, their activities in some countries have seriously contributed to the deepening of poverty, precisely because they have paid no attention to the effect of their activities on the environment on which poor people depend.

Second, they have been great beneficiaries of the activities of the Bretton Woods institutions. The World Bank is reckoned to have paid out $3 to the business sector for every $1 received as aid in the developing countries. And where corporations have funded others – whether NGOs, governments or multilateral organisations like UN agencies – they have exacted a price in terms of support for their view of the world economy – export-led growth, open markets, free exchanges. That is because those policies have privileged their activities. Of course, it may be that they have changed their minds on all that; but they need to convince many of us.

Third, the corporate lobby has operated against regulation of their activities by governments. 'Self-regulation' is their demand, and so far they have prevailed. This seems suspect – on a number of grounds. They demand explicit regulation of others' interests where these might conflict with theirs. They are right behind the WTO in its legal powers to prevent others limiting their rights – and indeed supported the proposed MAI. Yet they require that their own activities be outside the law and subject only to their own conscience. More-over, one would have thought that corporations that intend to raise their own costs by paying attention to the environment would demand regulation so that others would have to bear the same costs. Surely competitiveness would require a level playing field, and regulation would provide that. So why are they not on the side of regulation, if they intend to operate sustainably anyway?

The story on environmental regulation in South Africa is complex and deeply disappointing. (It is contained in an excellent booklet published by Groundwork, called *Partners in Pollution – Voluntary Agreements and Corporate Greenwash*, obtainable from Box 2375, Pietermaritzburg, South Africa.) A two-year process, involving over 100,000 citizens, including the business sector, seemed to be leading to a system of compulsory regulation of business in relation to the environment. But behind-the-scenes lobbying by business produced the National Environmental Management Act which allowed business to negotiate voluntary agreements on a cumbersome industry-by-industry basis. It is a betrayal of the original intention and an ominous portent for a future in which PPPs are the main organs of implementation.

Similarly, the final wording of the Summit's paragraph (111 of Chapter 5) on 'Sustainable Development in a Globalising World' gives in to the corporate demand for self-regulation. It is a significant defeat compared to the text agreed at the preparatory meeting in Bali. That should be linked to the success of the Washington Consensus in removing from the final Statement the 'precautionary principle' as the basis of decisions about what is acceptable in terms of pollution – in favour of 'the ecosystem approach', a much more vague term.

All of this leaves one apprehensive about the effect of giving the corporate sector a large and official role in promoting sustainable development. That sector has hardly enhanced its reputation for honesty, let alone altruism, in the past year. Corporate crime is a major feature of our modern economy. In South Africa, for instance, white-collar crime has increased by 20% a year, and cost the country R40 million in 2002, according to *Business Day*. Of the 60,000 cases reported, less than 7% led to conviction.

The Summit did not have a mandate to deal with global trade matters that fall under the WTO negotiations. But the issues that arise from the unregulated global market were aired.

The chart that follows gives a comprehensive alternative scenario to the one now prevailing. It shows how globalisation can be used for the benefit of humanity as a whole. Knowledge should be global, and so should communication, as well as mutual support and help in all directions. Art should be accessible to everyone everywhere. We have the digital revolution to thank for the fact that we can learn and talk and cooperate internationally; and the means – telecommunications – are getting better and cheaper all the time. But we need also to be very clear about what aspects of globalisation are toxic to vulnerable people and other parts of creation. As intelligent beings we can control this. We are not flotsam on the sea of global forces. This is what we could be doing.

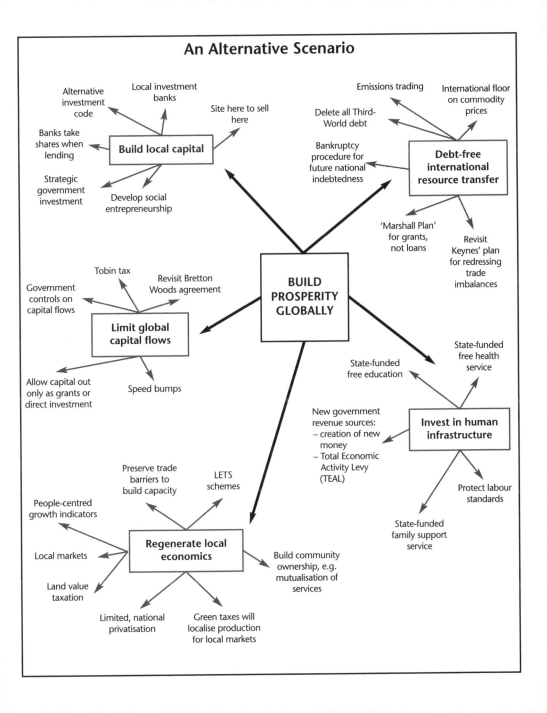

Transfer of resources

Start at the top right-hand corner of the diagram. Internationally we need transfers of resources from the rich to the poor countries in the form of grants, not loans. This is the consistent theme of Jeffrey Sachs, following all his years in international banking and development theory and practice. We could, of course, waste a lot of time and hot air arguing about whether poor countries 'deserve' such treatment, or about why some countries fell behind in the Industrial Revolution. Do we need to wonder whose fault it is that poor countries are poor? Or could we accept that over the past two centuries poor countries have become poor largely as a result of their relationship to rich countries, for example through colonisation? And however well or badly their leaders have coped with that legacy, their people do not 'deserve' the poverty in which they now live. Surely we want a world in which prosperity is shared, however it all started.

Add to that the almost unimaginable facts of the AIDS pandemic. AIDS is killing teachers and middle managers and whole families of helpless poor people. It is leaving children and old people without support. It is fast gobbling up the health budgets of countries across Africa and other parts of the South. AIDS adds a dimension to need in poor countries never before imagined. People with AIDS cannot be expected to pay 'the full costs of recovery' – in the words of the privatisation lobby.

That means we need something like the Marshall Plan that put Europe back on its feet after World War 2, and without which Europe even today could have been a struggling backwater – or indeed could have fallen into the Soviet sphere of interest. We need the equivalent of the Tennessee Valley Authority, which poured resources into a dustbowl and made it flourish. Or the money that has gone annually from overseas supporters into what was the desert of Israel and made it bloom. We need the opposite of current practice.

In 1970 the OECD countries agreed they would all move to providing seven-tenths of one per cent (0.7%) as development assistance. Since then aid has fallen consistently. If it were 0.7%, it would amount to $175 billion – enough to tackle AIDS, provide universal primary education and deal with shortfalls in clean water and sanitation. Instead, all the OECD countries together give a total of 0.22% or $53 billion. The US gives the lowest proportion of its GDP – 0.15% – of any developed country. No country reaches the agreed 0.7% of GDP.

The world needs to forget about loans. It needs to do what any of us would do with a family member who has fallen on hard times, or what we already do within countries when disaster strikes. We give. If we must put it in economic terms, we invest in the future of that person or that area, because they are seen as part of us and of our own future. We do not lend with crippling and unpredictable rates of interest, as the rich countries have done to the third world. That should be the basis of the OECD response to President Mbeki's Millennium Africa Plan, now the New Plan for African Development (NEPAD). Unfortunately the President's plan is couched in the form of investment loans and repayments, because that is the way the thinking of the powerful now operates.

End unpayable debts

The creditor nations should end third-world debt for a start. It does not need to forgive the debt. There is nothing left to forgive. The creditors freely made loans, which became bad for a number of reasons – by no means all the fault of the debtors – and Western banks and other creditors have had back multiples of the original loans, as a result of the compound interest applied to the unpaid capital. The rich North should write off third-world loans as you or I – or commercial banks – would write off other unrepayable loans.

The US Financial Secretary, Paul O'Neill, has tentatively backed the call by the international campaign Jubilee Plus for an international insolvency law that would apply to countries – just as individuals or institutions can file for bankruptcy when they cannot pay their debts. That process is receiving sympathetic attention from the IMF, which has finally become fed up with bailing out banks who have made bad loans. Like domestic bankruptcy procedures, the process would make creditors accept some of the costs of the unpayable debt, and leave the debtor with prospects for recovery. This is a response to the latest eruption in the international financial markets, namely the collapse of the Argentine currency – indeed of its economy. Its debt stood at 27% of GDP in 2001, and represents 322% of export receipts. Talk about unrepayable! Clearly it is bankrupt. But the people of Argentina are expected to starve while they service debts arranged by previous unelected governments. No legitimate court of law would expect that of a domestic debtor.

And when the debt is ended, we should not attach savage conditions laying down what governments may do in their macro-economic fiscal policies. Mozambique's debt was 'forgiven' on condition it privatised municipal water and required consumers to pay for it; and multiplied by five the cost of primary health. How's that for punishment?

These conditions, moreover, flatly contradict what rich countries do when their own economies are in trouble. Joseph Stiglitz's latest book *Globalisation and Its Discontents* (Penguin, UK) shows the contrast between American domestic policies and those they insist poor countries follow. While American governments operate deficit budgets and reduced rates of interest, and allow global commodity cartels as a defence against recession, they insist on balanced budgets, high interest rates and transparent competition rules in poor countries. Those countries able to ignore the IMF prescriptions do markedly better than those forced to comply. 'The contrast between Russia's transition, as engineered by the international economic institutions, and that of China, designed by itself, could not be greater. While in 1990 China's GDP was 60% that of Russia, by the end of the decade the numbers had been reversed.' He shows also how IMF policies directly underwrite currency speculators.

The truth is that if the creditor countries do not end the debt burden, they will lose control. Debtors will simply stop servicing the debt. Already there is an international civil society movement – a Debtors' Union – aimed at doing just that.

As part of the process of transferring resources, we should introduce, on a mandatory basis, emissions trading, which in itself could do the trick. Rich countries would pay poor countries for the right to emit dangerous pollutants – thus providing both with a cash incentive to move to renewable sources of energy. And meanwhile we need to put a floor beneath commodity prices – currently virtually the sole export of many very poor countries, and now subject to the vagaries of the internal markets of rich countries. The entire economies of poor countries are at the mercy of economic trends and inventions over which they have no control.

Invest in human infrastructure

That 'Marshall Plan' resource transfer should be invested mainly in human infrastructure. It should focus on raising literacy and numeracy and technological literacy; on preventive and restorative health; on services for spacing children in families; and on welfare services to break the vicious circle when families break down. Some of these are interconnected. Do you know the social measure that correlates most closely with falling family numbers? It is the level of literacy in women – mothers.

And we should positively encourage governments to protect labour standards. This can be a tricky one. The ICFTU presented a proposal at the 2001 World Economic Forum to uphold labour standards internationally, asking that Transnational Companies (TNCs) should be required to give the same wages and conditions of work to employees wherever they operate. This sounds fair and progressive. In fact it stems from an attempt by workers in rich countries to protect their own standards if necessary at the expense of employment in poor countries. And why should they not? The truth is that labour standards, hard won everywhere, have fallen further in the North than in the South over the past 25 years, because TNCs have moved their operations to places where workers are paid less. The danger of falling employment in poor countries would be less significant to the extent that localisation of the economy takes hold. TNCs are never a reliable source of employment, and often reduce employment, as we have seen.

The fact is that of course labour standards cannot be separated from the wealth of the country where they operate, and cannot be imposed from outside. That is something that a national government has to do, if necessary by protecting the economy. But labour standards have a lot to do with human infrastructure, and if they fall so does the whole level of civilisation of a country, including its health and education. If the human infrastructure is healthy and educated, the natural entrepreneurial wishes and capacity of the people will develop of their own accord. This in turn will help to build local capital.

Build local capital

We need to ground capital: preserve it largely where it is made. It should leave its own country only in the form of Marshall Plan-type grants or as direct investment where it can contribute to wealth and produce dividends.

Governments and peoples should not be at the daily mercy of the mood swings of international financiers, most of whom have no intention of direct investment anyway.

The Archbishop of Cape Town, Njongonkulu Ndungane, in a speech to Anglican Primates in the US in March, called for 'the mobilisation of our own internal development-finance resources, so that we are never dependent upon a dollar, a yen, a D-mark or a Swiss franc for our development needs. After all, why should a rural school in Africa or Latin America be financed with a foreign loan when all the input costs are in a local currency?'

Our current depleting dependence on foreign capital is a continuing source of worry. The Terry Bell column in *Business Day*, 28 January 2000 reports a BusinessMap survey to the effect that for every dollar of investment that flowed into South Africa in 2000, $24 flowed out. Jac Laubscher, Chief Executive of GenSac, points out that it is unreasonable to expect foreign investors to put money into South Africa when local investors are not doing so. 'We should be realistic in expecting to attract FDI and should first concentrate on stimulating domestic investment.'

But when exchanges are open, the whole thing becomes a Catch 22. Governments should restore their right to decide whether and how its citizens may export capital, and it should have transparent rules. The decision to allow South African companies to list overseas cost R56 billion in three years, without offsetting advantages.

Governments should also retain the right to fix exchange rates if floating ones are undermining the economy. The UK's recent strong pound was what really undermined the income of her farmers among others; and only free market ideology and rules — as well as the aspiration to become part of the euro zone — prevented the government fixing the currency at a more realistic level.

The possibility — indeed likelihood — of a crash in the American stock market is another reason to develop our own capital independence. The US trade deficit rose in the month February/March 2001 from $28.86 billion to $31.17 billion – a rise of about $1 billion a day. By January 2002 the trade deficit stood at $445 billion or 4% of GDP. This daily deficit, plus capital outflows, means the US must borrow $4 billion a day. Until June 2002 the dollar remained strong, largely because it is in effect an international currency, and foreign currency holders have an irrational sense that the American economy is an exception and can go on for ever losing trade without its currency losing value. Indeed, the dollar has appreciated by 65% against the euro over the past six years.

But by mid-2002 the dollar began to fall. We do not know when the usual herd behaviour of speculators will kick in. Meanwhile the theoretical base for this flourishing dollar is faltering badly. Investment is down and so are stocks. Alan Greenspan responds with reductions in the interest rate, and that is sensible. But it will not cure the imbalance.

All economies have the capacity to build and put to work their own capital. One way that some countries, notably Japan, do it better than we do is in the practice of their banks and other lending institutions taking shares in any enterprise to which they lend. This means that they have a stake in seeing it work, as opposed to simply the capacity to call in collateral without any loss if the enterprise fails. They support business over a much longer period and offer more than simply credit. They help their clients/partners to build capital.

Credit unions should be encouraged. These use local capital for local communities. There are now over 700 in the UK, up from 327 in 1991. They are growing everywhere. They generally apply ethical criteria and so they raise standards as well as capital. By 1996 American community banks had financed over $2.5 billion worth of economic development. Essentially they invest in 'social capital' – that means people and their skills – and put these to work to restore the physical capital – the buildings, the parks, the homes. The South Shore Bank of Chicago is a fine example, having set up in a virtually derelict part of the city. It now has assets fifteen times what they were when it started 25 years ago.

In South Africa there is an association of credit unions, but they are given much less attention than they deserve.

Social entrepreneurs

Business entrepreneurs are often seen as the most important engines in creating local capital and enterprise. But what about social entrepreneurs? They have the same kinds of skills as business ones. They see something that needs to be done, bring resources to the job, organise it and create new wealth from that combination. But they are not interested in a profit for themselves; they do not fit well with profit-based business plans. What they want is to see a difference on the ground and in the lives of people. We all know them. They are not business entrepreneurs, but they have the same dynamic attitudes. Our NGO sectors are full of them. In the UK research has shown that they produce ten times the number of livelihoods as business entrepreneurs. We should invest at least as much in supporting social entrepreneurs as we do in business entrepreneurs.

Limited, phased-entry participation in the global market

Chapters Three, Four and Five have discussed the measures needed to restore government control over the process of participation in the global market. They include a Tobin tax, and the other 'speed bumps' that inhibit currency speculation. They incorporate alternative taxes that privilege local production, investment and consumption. An alternative investment code would give preference to the growth of local enterprise over attracting foreign direct investment. The 'site here to sell here' policy would ground footloose capital by limiting sales to where production takes place. The Keynesian proposal to make all countries responsible for imbalances in trade is key – so simple and with such huge implications. The Bretton Woods institutions need careful rethinking.

Become more self-sufficient

This is a relative term, but it is at the heart of the new direction. It is linked to all the other boxes in the diagram, of course. It is not only about promoting and regenerating our national economy, but also about protecting ourselves against the vagaries of others' economies. One of the main subjects on the agenda of the recent meetings of the World Economic Forum in Davos has been the downturn in the American economy. If panic develops there, while we are all so interconnected, we are in big trouble. Make no mistake: our interests and those of other poor and developing countries will not be in the forefront of the minds of the international economy fixers.

Becoming more self-sufficient involves regenerating our economy partly through adopting new ways to raise government revenues, so that, for instance, we can revive dead and dying areas. Some of these ideas for revenue will take years to become respectable – and perhaps we in South Africa will have to wait for powerful countries to prove them first. But perhaps we can use the fact of our newness to pioneer as well. If we can take measures to protect our economy in ways that other governments are already doing, there is no reason why we cannot introduce green taxes, TEAL and land value taxation

One of the most radical measures may also require the most courage, because it flies in the face of so much received wisdom. If we want growth to be needs-driven we must remove the creation of money from commercial banks and give it to the Reserve Bank. Commercial banks cannot create money on any criterion other than profit growth. That means that endless economic growth is a necessity to keep the system going and we know that will wreck our planet. The Reserve Bank can tailor the creation of new money to what is needed and what can be produced without putting a strain on resources like fossil fuels and without degrading the environment.

Privatisation really should go into the local capital box: wherever possible outsourcing should go to local capital enterprise. Privatisation should not amount to selling off our assets to foreign companies, however seductive that looks. Privatisation should not be a principle: some things can well be privatised, others not. Experience in Europe and elsewhere shows that railway privatisation, for instance, is mostly disastrous; and that of public utilities much the same. New Zealand had the developed world's longest blackout because the privatised Mercury Energy failed to deal with known flaws to the system, due to the focus on profit. In 2003, the US, Canada, Italy and Sweden suffered similar blackouts. Some of the same considerations explain why the British railways are in such a mess today: chronic failure to deal with infrastructure investment. The City Council of Grenoble has voted to end its water privatisation system. Even California – Reaganland – is considering renationalising its electricity industry, following its failure to deliver at a fair price, and sometimes even to deliver at all.

The South African public service has a lot of work to do to create a culture of competent service, to end decades or more of corruption and to ingest modern methods of large-scale management and strategic planning. In some of this, outsourcing can help. But regulation is needed to protect workers from exploitation in highly competitive markets. Even more important, privatisation cannot operate on the basis that all services must be paid for by the consumer.

People who do not have an income – because the economy excludes them – cannot pay for water and power and education and health. These are basic needs. And therefore basic rights according to the South African constitution. If people don't get them, they may die: certainly they will fall outside the productive economy. The fact that municipalities are owed money is not an indication of 'the culture of non-payment'. Income figures show that it is due to inability to pay. Privatisation policies must be rooted in facts, not theory, and in the compassion that is due to vulnerable people in a civilised society.

Finally, all countries need new indicators of success and wealth. The Gross Domestic Product lumps everything in together. Clearing up an oil spill, and increasing the police service to cope with new crime levels, are counted into the GDP along with mining and apple-growing. We need to calculate and subtract from the total the depletion of our capital stock – just as business accounting does. So from the GDP calculation should be subtracted the use of non-renewable resources and the activities that are toxic. They amount to value subtracted. Above all, we need to assess the quality of life in terms of things like the environment, crime levels and access to sport and the arts. A lot of work is being done here as well as abroad on developing these indicators and measuring economic activity against them.

Threefolding

So how will the process develop? I believe the future is well described in a small book called *Shaping Globalisation: Civil Society, Cultural Power and Three-folding* by the Filipino civic leader, Nicanor Perlas (New Society Publishers).

Perlas has developed the concept of threefolding. It refers to the interaction of the three realms or subsystems of society: politics or government, business or economics, and civil society or culture. What is new, says Perlas, is the equal importance and strength of civil society, which emerged just before and during the Battle of Seattle as a third global force. The world is now tri-polar: business and government can no longer operate without the agreement of civil society. The interaction of the three – and how that unfolds – will determine the quality of societies.

The business or economic sphere is responsible for the efficient running of economic processes of resource use, production and consumption. The political or government sphere relates to the efficient conduct of legal systems and representative institutions. The civil or cultural sphere encompasses the aspirations of humanity – the way people relate in communities and families, their cultural values and spiritual expression. It is concerned with the development of full human capacity and the generation of knowledge, meaning, art, ethics and a sense of the sacred. It is this civil or cultural sphere that is now confronting the unregulated globalised market, while politicians are relatively paralysed. Perlas predicts several phases in which the voice of civil society will come to negotiate, first as opposition, then cooperatively and finally by *including* the political and economic in its sphere.

Social capital, formed by citizens coming together voluntarily, is, as everyone knows, the stuff of life and the basis for stable and functional communities. Robert Putnam's research in the United States shows the effect of the fact that social capital has been draining away since the 1960s. And where that happens children do badly at school, crime rises, violence and mental illness increase, under-employment is high, wages are low. People die young and the political system is discarded or ignored. Authoritarianism develops. In turn this can further reduce social capital. The restoration of a real role for civil society can turn this round.

This is how Perlas describes the present era:

Just in time. Just when the destructive and totalitarian juggernaut of elite global-
isation seemed unstoppable. Just when the unholy alliance of unaccountable and
irresponsible segments of the government and business seemed unbreakable. Just
when the possibility of building a just, free, compassionate, prosperous and
sustainable world seemed unattainable … Just then a powerful global force
emerged. The global force is civil society. In its contemporary form civil society is
the most important social innovation of the 20th century. It ranks in importance
with the invention of the nation state in the 17th century and the creation of the
modern market starting in the 18th century.

The growth of civil society is already having a major impact on the way that the
international instruments of the Washington Consensus are conducting their
business. They know they are now being observed. They know they can no
longer take decisions and expect to implement them in obscurity. Since Seattle,
it has become increasingly difficult for the meetings of the G8, the WTO and
the World Bank/IMF axis to take place at all. Street protests have forced them to
convene in places where they can be insulated by a wide *cordon sanitaire* from the
rest of the world. They still display a lot of bravado about all this – in particular
blaming small violent elements within the protest meetings – but it is very clear
that they and the police protecting them are extremely rattled. They can no
longer behave like a small exclusive club entitled to do their business in private.

For example, these were the agenda items for the WEF meeting in Davos in
February 2001:

1. How globalisation can deliver the goods: the view from the South.
2. The shape of the 21st century corporation: how new technologies affect
    the way we work and interact.
3. The corporation and the public: open for inspection. What changes are
    necessary to regain the public's confidence … and allay their fear about
    corporate power?

4. Addressing the backlash against globalisation.
5. Seizing the global digital opportunity: turning the global digital divide into a global opportunity.
6. Business and NGOs: from diatribe to dialogue … Identifying possible areas for more constructive dialogue.

Those items would not have absorbed the interest of the WEF even at its last meeting, let alone five years ago. The ideology was secure then. The 2002 meeting, held in New York, had an even more inclusive agenda.

Conclusion

So there has been huge movement. But if the complacency of the Washington Consensus is now past, we should not ourselves become complacent. Remember who still owns the media, and what side they are likely to be on. The growth in the public relations industry outstrips the growth in GDP worldwide by a factor of three. The PR industry essentially serves large enterprise and investment houses which are suited by the present dispensation. US firms spend $1 billion a year on anti-environmental PR alone. McDonalds spends $1.8 billion a year on PR. There are always corporate funds available for what I would call propaganda against civil society.

An American book called *Trust Us, We're Experts*, by Sheldon Rampton and John Stauber, gives an account of corporate efforts to use propaganda and PR to manipulate opinion and massage the results of science. It is based on the idea that people cannot be trusted to make political decisions because they are irrational, emotional and illogical. Thus Professor H.W. Lewis, a risk assessor, says that people worry about 'non-problems like nuclear waste and pesticides (sic) because they are irrational and poorly educated'. Therefore 'the common good is ill-served by the democratic process'. A spokesperson for Burson-Marsteller told the Society of Chemical Industry in London in 1989: 'All of this research is helpful in figuring out a strategy for the chemical industry and its products. It suggests that a strategy based on logic and information is probably not going to succeed. We are in the realm of the illogical, and we must respond with the tools that we have for managing the emotional aspects of the human psyche ... The industry must be like the psychiatrist ...'

Corporations spend some $10 billion each year on public relations. It seems to be worth the money. About 40% of the stories that appear in American newspapers have been planted there by the PR industry, The *Columbia Journalism Review* found that half the stories in *The Wall Street Journal* were based solely on press releases, even though a staff reporter is credited. PR experts 'spin' stories for the media, assuming they will not be checked. That 'spin' includes literally buying scientific opinion. For instance in the early 1990s tobacco companies paid $156,000 to scientists to sign their names to letters to respectable journals like *The Lancet* and *The Journal of the American Medical Association*, which are then cited by the tobacco companies in support of their position. Ghostwriters are commissioned for a fee to write medical articles.

In 1996 Sheldon Krimsky examined 789 articles published by 1105 researchers in 14 leading life science and biomedical journals. In 34% of the articles one or more of the authors had an identifiable financial interest connected to the research. Researchers in the mid-1990s found that more than 3,000 researchers had financial ties to corporations. Some 20% admitted they had delayed publication of adverse results to allow patents to be obtained. The authors conclude that 'the behaviour of universities and scientists is sad, shocking and frightening ... They are seduced by industry funding, and frightened that if we don't go along with these gag orders, the money will go to less rigorous institutions.'

As things stand, big business still sees its interests lying in the unfettered global market. Perfect expression of this is given in a document put out by the

European Round Table of Industrialists (ERT), in 2001, supporting the enlargement of the EU. This, it says, will solve the problems of the ERT members, because new member states will be forced to 'reduce their taxes, prevent delays in the privatisation process, remove the restrictions on the purchasing of land by foreign companies and combat the dominance of national players'. The ERT membership remains therefore very clear that the success of Western corporations is economic success. They call their strategy 'The East–West win–win business experience', but they talk about the benefits to themselves. The report cites the case of British American Tobacco, which has invested in Hungary. BAT's problem had been that the Western European market has become 'highly mature'. Competition is intense and margins tight. Growth in profitability and shareholder value must therefore come from the developing markets.' We could hardly have a clearer description of the view that developing markets are good for corporate business in a manner that is surely closer to colonisation than to integration. The whole of Eastern Europe is indeed suffering right now from that attitude and that process.

The question is whether the G8 governments will be compelled by civil society to change direction in time to pre-empt a process in which history is made in the streets. Make no mistake: that is a disastrous prospect. Mob rule is profoundly non-democratic. It also provides cover for increasingly violent repression by police and armies, and increasing isolation of one side from the other. But it will happen, unless serious reforms are made soon.

These are the main reforms needed. (They are further developed in an excellent booklet called *The No Nonsense Guide to Globalisation*, published by New Internationalist Publications, Oxford, UK.)

At international level:

- Reform the IMF, World Bank and WTO so that they represent effectively the needs of poorer countries and so reflect a vision of development rather than market domination.

- Establish new international financial institutions to succeed the processes set up at Bretton Woods. Link currency values to a basket of commodities, and develop an international currency to succeed the dollar.
- Create a new Global Environmental Association to override the WTO, which actually prevents environmental protection.
- Put in place a mechanism for collecting and distributing a Tobin tax to discourage international currency speculation.
- Institute a new international code of practice for capital investment, so that it serves the communities in which it works. This would fulfil the provisions of the 1974 UN Charter on the Economic Rights and Duties of States, which gave governments the responsibility to regulate foreign investment to serve the priorities of development.

At national level:

- Deliver a Basic Income Grant to all citizens. (This should lead to its equivalent at international level, but one thing at a time …)
- Shift the burden of tax from people to activities that subtract value.
- Move the job of creating money from the commercial banks to the Reserve or Central Bank.
- Encourage local parallel currencies to get local economies moving.
- Encourage localisation of organic food production, and consumption of goods and services that have not travelled far.
- Reward recycling, renewable energy source development, environmental protection and cooperative production methods.

Many of these are interconnected; and some can be introduced on their own. All require a mindset that understands the urgency of change.

'We have entered a new age. An age where all of us will have to sign a new compact with our environment … and enter into the larger community of all living beings. A new sense of our communion with planet Earth must enter our minds.'

Klaus Töpfer,
UN Under-Secretary-General and Exec. Director
UN Environment Programme,
address to World Council of Churches, 31 October 1999, Bonn

POINTS FOR DISCUSSION – CHAPTER SIX

1. Why do some people become terrorists?

2. How does that explanation differ from justification?

3. How could the news media be removed from corporate owner ship and control?

4. Which nations are avoiding the worst effects of the global market? Why?

MYTHS OF GLOBALISATION – FOURTEEN

'Foreign-exchange rates are determined by supply and demand based on market fundamentals – the real value of the economic base.'

That suggestion will surprise South Africans. During 2001–2, the rand plummeted – at one stage apparently in free fall – losing a third of its value in months. All conventional measures of market fundamentals were positive: inflation was low, fiscal control was tight, the budget deficit was falling fast, interest rates were high, taxation was coming down, privatisation policies were in place. Searching for an explanation, the pundits blamed President Mbeki's policies regarding Mugabe's Zimbabwe and AIDS; or/and, they suggested, other 'emerging markets' like Turkey, Brazil and Argentina were in trouble, and that affected 'market sentiment' towards South Africa.

Then, lo and behold, the rand started picking up. By January 2003 the rand had recovered much of its losses and was still rising. Why? The policy towards Zimbabwe remained the same, the AIDS policy was still considered inadequate, other 'emerging markets' were still in trouble. Various explanations were sucked out of various conventional economists' thumbs.

The truth is that currency values are determined almost entirely by what currency speculators expect that others of their ilk will be expecting to happen. Well over 90% of currency transactions are speculative, having nothing to do with the kind of economic fundamentals that would affect investment or trade. In other words, most people buying and selling currency are not planning to use the money for trade or investment: they are seeking only to make a profit on the transaction itself. Whether that happens depends only on whether other currency traders are buying or selling.

Add to that the fact that the US dollar is the dominant reserve currency, so not subject to the same considerations as other currencies. Its value has very little to do with the US economy. So, for instance, in 2002 the dollar accounted for 68% of global currency reserves; but the US share of global exports was only 12.3%, and of imports 18.9%. That tells you that the US gobbles up considerably more of the world's goods and services than it provides. It sustains that situation by creating more dollars – which other countries have to buy as a reserve currency in case their own currency is attacked.

The economist Henry C.K. Liu sums it up: 'World trade is now a game in which the US produces dollars and the rest of the world produces things that the rest of the world can buy.' What has that to do with supply and demand and market fundamentals?

MYTHS OF GLOBALISATION – FIFTEEN

'Education, education, education is the answer to unemployment.
Africa is poor because of its poor education.'

This thrice-repeated policy priority was first proposed by aspiring Prime Minister Blair as a response to the effects of Conservative rule in Britain. It has become the mantra of the reformers in the World Bank and other agencies offering advice to Africa. The slogan is as little based in reality in South Africa as it was in Britain.

The fact is that in South Africa – as in Europe – there are unemployed educated people. There are unemployed graduates, not to mention school-leavers. In the past six years, the jobless rate of matriculants in South Africa has doubled to 32%, while that of tertiary-level graduates has trebled to 15%. There are also unemployed computer operatives, skilled and experienced artisans, managers, people retrained and retrained again. Many of them have been successfully employed in the past but have been made redundant by the global market; some are fresh from education. They seek work. They are not uneducated.

Of course education is important – for its own sake. But the answer to unemployment is paid work, not education. The focus on education is a red herring to divert attention from the systemic lack of jobs. While we think the solution is education, we won't realise what is the real problem.

Needless to say, along with this diversion does not go a recommendation for higher taxation to pay for this 'education, education, education'. The ideology is that since the state 'cannot afford' what is necessary, the private sector should get involved. This leads into the argument that all services, including education, should be opened up to the international private market.

MYTHS OF GLOBALISATION – SIXTEEN

*'It is human nature to be greedy, competitive and selfish. That is why
capitalism works and other economic systems do not.'*

The nature of humanity cannot be limited by such a definition. The
way that people treat each other depends on what they are taught
by those they depend on as small children. For example, people who
live by subsistence agriculture and small-scale trading tend to live in
small close communities in which mutual dependence is accepted as
natural and inevitable. Children are cared for by a large number of
people in such an extended society. They also care for each other,
whichever sex they are. Farmers cooperate in the cultivation of the
land. Celebrations are inclusive. Good times and bad times apply to
everyone. Individual 'selfish' behaviour would be practically suicidal,
because its perpetrator would have no place in the economic and
social order. Similarly greed and competitiveness are pointless.

In large modern cities, especially in areas of severe scarcity and
conflict, many children learn very early to look after themselves –
violently if necessary. In many cities in industrialised countries, especially in America, the only skills young people learn are precisely
those that will disqualify them from employment: lying, violence,
self-defence. In those environments people will walk away, apparently callously, from others in distress. Males are hard and unemo-
tional, females manipulative. They are mutually exploitative.

People who live in these opposite environments are all people. They
share human nature. It is probably true to say that all of them were
born with both competitive and cooperative capacities and wishes.
Probably all small children seek above all loving protection, and
whether or not they get it will determine their 'nature' thereafter.

If anything, the 'greedy, competitive and selfish' syndrome is the
deviation, since it arises in societies which are least child-friendly,
and most likely to create distortions.

CHAPTER SEVEN

The heart and soul of economics

This book started with the reminder that economics was originally seen as political economy – therefore as a branch of the study of human society as acted out in the public sphere. We ended the previous chapter with the hope that civil society, which holds the value systems of humanity, may at last be finding its rightful place as the arbiter of political action and the economic systems it creates.

Some economists have let it be thought that only they understand the complicated dynamics that determine how economies run. If that were so, non-economists would be hard-pressed to know what they should vote about. At a deeper level, it is a dangerous idea. Questions around who gets what for what kind of work, and how resources are allocated, are essentially moral and ethical ones. They lie at the root of our very humanity. The spirit that gives us life informs the way we relate to other human beings and the life of the planet that sustains us. Our spiritual growth cannot be limited by handing over to others, however 'expert', questions of right and wrong.

The world's great religions are unambiguous:

When the ruler of a country fails to apportion wealth to those in need, poverty becomes prevalent. Poverty being prevalent, theft becomes prevalent, weapons become prevalent. When weapons become prevalent, killing and maiming become prevalent, lying becomes prevalent ... slander ... sexual infidelity ... abuse and frivolity ... covetousness and jealousy ... wrong understanding becomes prevalent.

THE BUDDHA, 545 BC

The Christian and Jewish scriptures would be virtually non-existent if we were to cut all references to the imperative to income equality and distribution. From the Prophets – notably Isaiah, Jeremiah and Micah – to the teachings of Jesus of Nazareth, the constant refrain is the requirement for human beings to treat one another as though each represents the deity on earth. 'In as much as you did it to the least of these my brethren you did it unto me' implies that poverty in the midst of plenty is a sin against God. The concept of Jubilee, the regular periodic forgiveness of debt, is an explicit recognition that from time to time inequalities must be wiped out and a new start made. The Prophet Mohammed gave the same message.

Most people know this in their deepest being. Readers will have noticed a certain passion running through this book. I remember, when I first discovered the New Economics Foundation in London, being asked why I was present at a particular meeting. I could only say truthfully that I was outraged by what was happening in the world and wanted to find ways to contribute to its demise. An emotional response, but it found echoes in others who were present. If economists stick to econometric models, with no human response to the effects of those models on humanity, they are in the wrong job. If they believe that only they can discuss economic systems, they should be sent packing.

Economics – the way that people relate to each other with regard to resources – matters a great deal. It profoundly affects what kind of a society we have, and therefore how people behave and develop. That is its real importance. The pretence that this is a technical matter that can be dealt with only by 'experts' ignores the fact that we are all affected by our culture, and our culture is much influenced by the prevalent economic system.

In some respects this is similar to the way that theologies are sidelined as though our spiritual lives can be separated from the rest of our existence. Reference to the teachings of the Prophet Mohammed, Jesus Christ, the

Buddha or the prophets from Joshua to Malachi is sanitised into pious moments neatly fenced off from the rest of life. The African philosophy of Ubuntu is a spiritual understanding of the whole of life: 'I am because you are.' Yet our Western generations have felt able to split off these most profound aspects of our existence as human beings from what they call 'real life'. Interpretations of deeper meaning may be heard with sentimental smiling eyes and then patronised with lip service only. And yet our belief systems, including those that are implicit only, profoundly affect our behaviour and indeed our real lives. New Economics, unlike Old Economics, may be described as economics for real life.

I do not expect human beings to become full-time theologians. What is frightening is when a political or economic system that flies in the face of what people claim to know, or at least believe, about morals, ethics and the spiritual life is accepted as inevitable, even though it is clearly human-made. It is one thing to accept that a volcanic eruption will result in the deadly flow of lava; another to acquiesce in a process that leads to suffering when it can be changed by human intervention.

Ah, but can it? I hope this book has shown that the present economic system can be changed: indeed that it must be changed because it is bringing catastrophe. The only question is when and how. Many shoulders will need to be applied to many wheels if the changes are to pre-empt a whole range of disasters. These include rage expressed in anarchistic street rule; collapse of financial systems including pension provision; acceleration of climatic abnormalities with calamitous results for humans; wars over water; the crumbling of human immune systems; pockets of prosperity razored off from seas of famine; crime and epidemics of mental illness; and terrorism and more terrorism – and bigger budgets for the military. A somewhat different picture, you will agree, from the one offered – albeit increasingly nervously – by the proponents of the global market, who see Western prosperity as its sole characteristic, and envision it spreading happily across the globe.

My own belief is that the economic system will change if only because nothing can be inevitable that is so clearly wrong. It is clearly wrong that:

- while there is waste on a huge scale, people scavenge for food on rubbish tips or die quietly in rural destitution
- the population of abandoned street children multiplies annually
- people's lives are dominated by fear of not competing effectively
- the air we breathe, the food we eat, the soil we depend on is remorselessly poisoned without our informed consent
- suicide, mental illness and prison populations increase as societies emulate the United States
- parents are forced to subject their children to prostitution and other kinds of labour in order to survive
- a person's livelihood depends on events and people living way beyond their reach on the other side of the world or in distant boardrooms
- alcohol, drugs, sex and material accumulation dominate the lives of human beings, who some of us believe are born in the image of God
- rural areas and communities are depleted of their substance, becoming helplessly poor, cashless or dormitory/retirement areas for people who work elsewhere
- the world's ancient forests, the lungs of the planet, are destroyed and replaced by agribusiness to cheapen consumer products
- corporations whose prime purpose is profit have extensive influence over the news and opinion-forming media, publishing outlets, and universities, colleges and even schools
- all entertainment is sponsored and has to seek the widest audience, meaning that standards homogenised and the lowest common denominator prevails

• And so on and on. Add your own …

These are inevitable products of a system that undermines the powers of democratically elected governments to regulate the way that business operates; that relentlessly centralises and concentrates wealth and marginalises the poor; in which the competition imperative ruthlessly overrides the needs of the natural environment as well as the human need for community and cooperation; and that has no place for vulnerability of any kind. We should never forget that the very rich are themselves victims of this system – with, as they say, certain compensations. They are trapped in a protected but frenetic environment that they cannot afford to abandon, even if they knew how.

An extraordinary piece of observation recorded by John Schumaker, an American now living in New Zealand, captures the absurd agony of the privileged.

> *Sitting in a shopping mall in Wisconsin above me towered a brutish vending machine, complete with celestial chimes, rotating lights and a steely synthesised voice beckoning the assembly of dupes. A miserable young lad approached, dragging the body of his package-laden mother. He searched her eyes repeatedly until she finally fed the machine, got a Rocket Ranger toy and stuck it out to the child. He slapped it onto the floor and screeched for another selection. Mom stuffed in more bills until finally the boy was out of choices. 'Well, for God's sake, what do you want?' she bellowed. In a confused rage the boy bawled over and over again: 'I want something. I want something. I want something.'*
>
> (ARTICLE FOR NEW INTERNATIONALIST, JULY 2001)

This multi-faceted psychological dysfunction is far more prevalent than we imagine. It is not the way that human beings are meant to live, either singly or together. You do not have to want a return to a non-existent rural idyll to know in your bones that we are meant to be 'members one of another', and that if we let go of that as an ideal we are wandering in a hellish desert of our own making.

But how can we put our relationships first when the market, which ignores everything except monetary value, discards so much. Edgar Cahn, a leader of the Time Dollars movement, puts it like this:

> *Price values what is scarce and what makes money. It does not value what is universal, what every human being has – the ability to care, love, share, rear children, take care of parents, be a good neighbour, be a good citizen striving for a better world. In other words the very core characteristics of our humanity are worthless in market terms. But these enabled us to survive as a species …*

The current test of value is called 'Value Added'. The extent to which a person is said to add value to the output of an enterprise is supposedly reflected in their income. It has very little to do with normally accepted human values. Thus teacher and nurses get low salaries, because that it how 'the market' values what they do; while a person selling and buying currency receives a massive income. Directors of companies are given huge handshakes to leave even when they have made a mess of their job – presumably because it is cheaper to send them out than to keep them in. But 'value' is hardly a normal description of what they have each 'added' in relative terms.

This is not to suggest that the price mechanism is not the right way to exchange goods and services – it is. But because it excludes so much else that is valuable, it must be kept corralled where it is needed. The unfettered market mechanism is what is depriving modern societies of 'commons' – those services (now almost a dirty word) which we used to believe should be available as a right, because a society is gentler and more civilised if it provides them. These include healthcare, clean water, education, clean air, adequate food and shelter, prisons that reform offenders, support when trouble strikes, open spaces for recreation, opportunity to experience the arts, safe public spaces. These 'commons' represent our sharing, our membership of a society. Even at a practical 'selfish' level, of course, a more civilised society is also a much less threatening and more enjoyable one.

So I believe that an economic system that flies in the face of what is satisfying, what is shared, what is fair, cannot prevail. And economic systems in their turn influence the way that human beings develop. Mental health professionals know that altruism is a product of psychological health, while self-obsession is a sign of dysfunction. People who grow up in secure environments, feeling themselves and their vulnerability valued, are likely to mature as socially constructive, peaceable and happy to promote others' interests. Similarly, people who experience violence, fear and abandonment as children hand on all of these in their relationships.

The Dalai Lama puts very simply his formula for society, and the relationship between cause and effect:

> *If you wish to experience peace, provide peace for another. If you wish to know that you are safe, cause (others) to know that they are safe. If you wish to better understand seemingly incomprehensible things, help another to better understand. If you wish to heal your own sadness or anger, seek to heal the sadness or anger of another. These others are waiting for you now ... Most of all they are looking to you for love.*
>
> *My religion is very simple. My religion is kindness.*

That simple philosophy is very well understood in Tibet, where there is very little competition for anything. Our milieu is different, so we may find those words simplistic and soppy. I suggest this is partly because of the way we run our economic relations between people. Here is a contrasting quote from a cleric, Rabbi Lerner, published in *World Faiths Development Dialogue*:

This is a world out of touch with itself, filled with people who have forgotten how to recognise and respond to the sacred in each other, because we are so used to looking at others from the standpoint of what they can do for us, how we can use them towards our own ends. The alternatives are stark: either start caring about the fate of everyone on this planet or be prepared for a slippery slope towards violence that will eventually dominate our daily lives.

I believe that the way people relate as Rabbi Lerner suggests is partly a function of the economic system. I lived for thirty years in Britain, and saw the transition from the social democratic philosophy and practice of the Labour Party to the radical conservatism of Thatcher and her successors. There was a noticeable change in the *character* of the British people. The much admired honesty within commerce, the incorruptibility of public servants, the decency expected between neighbours, the public courtesy and respect for elderly people and children were replaced (of course as stereotypes) by the football hooligan, the lager lout, the public insults and routine cursing, the 'mindless' violence and graffiti and street squalor, as well as the commercial rip-off, and the public representatives and servants caught taking bribes. Clearly there was no change in the genetic make-up of people descending the birth canal in Britain: it had to do with the change in the culture and family life – the financial stress, the drop in public standards, the decline of public service – in effect the despising of the public sector and the commons which Thatcher explicitly espoused.

At the same time, standards of public entertainment – hence the general level of popular awareness and attitudes – dropped sharply when most broadcasting was commercialised. The continued existence of the BBC as a publicly funded service is the only bulwark against the excruciating babble that greets anyone foolish enough to turn on a television or radio set in the United States. No wonder the average American is more ignorant and less tolerant than his/her equivalent in any other comparable country.

I end with two little quotes:

From the war of nature, from famine and death, the production of the higher animals (humans) directly follows.

Charles Darwin

Learn to do good; seek justice, relieve the oppressed, defend the fatherless, plead for the widow.

Isaiah 1, verse 17

Which of these two views of humanity do you think most matches our economies today? And which would you rather see prevail?

We do have a choice.

POINTS FOR DISCUSSION – CHAPTER SEVEN

1. How are values related to economics?
2. How can values be explicitly addressed through an economic system?
3. What is the role of religion in the economic system?
4. What do you think the world will look like in ten years' time?

MYTHS OF GLOBALISATION – SEVENTEEN

'If we are all part of one globalised market, there will be fewer wars.'

There is no doubt that a world order in which people are mutually and beneficially dependent will minimise the tendency to settle disputes by warfare. Since 1945 there has not been a war in Europe, previously a very bloody continent; there have been only NATO-related wars in Asia, side-effects of the Cold War between the US and USSR.

However, there have been dozens of violent civil wars, and wars over boundaries, within and between poor countries. A feature of those wars has been the extent of mutual dependence, which did not limit the conflict but only made it more painful. The most obvious have been in former Yugoslavia and former USSR as well as Rwanda, Burundi, Somalia, Sierra Leone, Liberia, Ivory Coast and Democratic Republic of Congo. If we add periodic outbreaks of ethnic violence, the number of conflicts triples, leaving very few poor countries unaffected.

This is because social upheaval caused by struggles over scarce resources easily becomes projected onto others. Those 'others' are most conveniently categorised by ethnicity, colour, religion or nationality. People who lived happily side by side, welcoming and sharing each other's diversity, change when survival is at stake. Political leaders, constrained by the market from improving the basic economic situation of their followers, fall for the populist device of scapegoating.

Even the most ardent believers in the global village aspiration accept that one of its effects has been extreme disruption and even destruction of the economy in some places and for some people. There is no doubt that the East Timor tragedy had some connection with the decimation of Indonesia's economy during the Asian crash. Similarly no one denies that the great majority of Russians and others in former USSR have suffered extreme privations since its government was induced to fling the country's economy into the global market in one fell swoop.

Africa tells the same story. For the first two decades following independence, African economies slowly expanded: education, health, transport infrastructures, small industry, agriculture all developed slowly but steadily. Following the devastation caused by the fourfold OPEC oil price hike, huge increases in import prices and collapse of raw material prices, African economies needed help. Then, as now, that meant the IMF and structural adjustment. African economies have shrunk as a result. Roads, health, education, agriculture, employment, extension services, social services and income per capita – all have declined.

No wonder conflicts have increased.

Bibliography

Anderson, V., *Alternative economic indicators*. Routledge, 1991.

Anderson, V., *What's radical now? Politics and creation spirituality*. Centre for Creation Spirituality, 2003.

Barlow, M. & Clarke, A., *Blue gold: the battle against corporate theft of the world's water*. Earthscan, 2003.

Batchelor, M. & Brown, K. (eds), *Buddhism and ecology*. Continuum, 1992

Blum, W., *Rogue state: a guide to the world's only superpower*. Zed Books, 2002.

Bond, P., *Against global apartheid – South Africa meets the World Bank, IMF and international finance*. University of Cape Town Press, 2002, and Zed Books, 2003.

Bouma, J.J., *Sustainable banking: the greening of finance*. Greenleaf Publishing, 2001.

Boyle, D., *Funny money: in search of alternative cash*. HarperCollins, 1999.

Breuilly, E. & Palmer, M. (eds), *Christianity and ecology*. Continuum, 1992.

Cahn, E.S., *No more throw-away people: the co-production imperative*. Essential Works (US), 2000.

Camp, J., *Because people matter*. Paraview.com, 2003.

Carmack, P. & Still, B., *The money masters – how international bankers gained control of America*. (Video script in book format) Royalty Productions Co. (US) and Pathway Book Service, 1998.

Chambers, R., *Whose reality counts? Putting the first last*. ITDG Publishing, 1997/2003.

Cheru, F., *African renaissance: roadmaps to the challenge of globalisation*. Zed Books, 2002.

Chomsky, N., *Rogue states: the rule of force in world affairs*. Pluto Press, 2003.

Commission on Population and Quality of Life. Report: *Caring for the future*. Oxford University Press, 1996.

Commission on Global Governance. Report: *Our global neighbourhood*. Oxford University Press, 1995.

Dauncey, G., *EcoNews*. Periodical, formerly UK, now published from Canada. See www.earthfuture.com/econews/

Douthwaite, R., *Short circuit: strengthening local economics for security in an unstable world*.

Lilliput Press, 1996.

Douthwaite, R., *The ecology of money*. Green Books, 1999.

Douthwaite, R., *The growth illusion*. Lilliput Press, 1992; Green Books, 1999.

Ekins, P., *Wealth beyond measure: an atlas of new economics*. Gaia Books.

Ellwood, W., *Globalisation: a no-nonsense guide*. New Internationalist Publications/Verso, 2001.

Fiffer, J (ed)., *Living in hope: people challenging globalisation*. Zed Books.

Forrester, V., *L'horreur économique*. Fayard.

Fukuyama, F., *The end of history and the last man*. Penguin, 1993.

George, S., *The debt boomerang: how third-world debt harms all*. Pluto Press, 1991.

Girardet, H., *Creating sustainable cities*. Green Books, 1999.

Godrej, D., *Climate change: a no-nonsense guide*. New Internationalist Publications/Verso, 2003.

Gore, A., *Earth in the balance*. Earthscan, 2000.

Gray, J., *False dawn: the delusions of global capitalism*. Granta, 1999.

Greco, T., *Money: understanding and creating alternatives to legal tender*. Chelsea Green (US), 2001.

Gupta, J., *Our simmering planet: what to do about global warming?* Zed Books.

Hassed, M., *The prosperity paradox: the economic wisdom of Henry George rediscovered*. Victoria, Australia, Chatsworth Village.

Helleiner, E., *States and the re-emergence of global finance*. Cornell University Press, 1996.

Henderson, H., *Beyond globalization: shaping a sustainable global economy*. Kumarian Press, 2000.

Hertz, N., *The silent takeover: global capitalism and the death of democracy*. Arrow Books, 2002.

Hines, C., *Localisation: a global manifesto*. Earthscan, 2002.

Hopkins, A.G. (ed), *Globalisation in world history*. Pimlico Press, 2002.

Houtart, F. & Polet, F. (eds), *The other Davos: the globalisation of resistance to the world economic system*. Zed Books, 2001.

Huber, J. & Robertson, J., *Creating new money – a monetary reform for the information age*.

New Economics Foundation, 2000.

Hutchinson, F., *What everybody (really) wants to know about money.* Jon Carpenter, 1998.

Hutton, W., *The state we're in.* Cape, 1995; Vintage, 1996.

ILRIG, *An alternative view of economic crisis.* Cape Town, International Labour Resource and Information Group.

Institute of African Alternatives, *New agenda*: South African journal of social and economic policy. Cape Town.

Jacobs, M. (for the Real World Coalition), *The politics of the real world.* Earthscan, 1996.

Jordan, B. et al, *Stumbling towards basic income.* Citizens Income Study Centre, London School of Economics.

Keen, S., *Debunking economics.* Zed Books, 2001.

Keet, D., *Alternatives to the TWTO regime – a discussion paper on tactics and strategies.* Cape Town, AIDC.

Keynes, J.M., *General theory of employment, interest and money.* Macmillan, 1963; Prometheus, 1997.

Khor, M., *Rethinking globalisation.* Zed Books, 2001.

Kingsnorth, P., *One no, many yeses: a journey to the heart of the global resistance movement.* Free Press, 2003.

Klein, N., *No logo: taking aim at the brand bullies.* Flamingo, 2001.

Korten, D., *The post-corporate world: life after capitalism.* Berrett-Koehler (US), 1999/ McGraw-Hill, 2000.

Korten, D., *When corporations rule the world.* Earthscan, 1995.

Lane, R.E., *The market experience.* Cambridge University Press, 1991.

Lang, T. & Hines, C., *The new protectionism.* Earthscan, 1993.

Lietaer, B., *The future of money: creating new wealth, work and a wiser world.* Century, 2002.

Lumley, R., 'Economy cleared for take-off' – article published in *Mail & Guardian*, Johannesburg, South Africa.

MacKenzie, C., *The shareholder action handbook: using shares to make companies accountable.* New Consumer, 1993.

Madeley, J., *Big business, poor peoples.* Zed Books, 1999.

Madeley, J., *Food for all: the need for a new agriculture*. Zed Books, 2002.

McIntosh, A. *Soil and soul*. Aurum Press, 2001.

Mihevc, J., *The market tells them so: the World Bank and economic fundamentalism in Africa*. Zed Books, 1996.

Mofid, C., *Market economy, free trade and globalisation*. Shepheard-Walwyn.

Munck, R., *Globalisation and labour*. Zed Books, 2002.

New Economics Foundation, *Participation works: techniques of community participation for the 21st century*.

New Economics Foundation, *Communities count: a guide to community sustainability indicators*.

Norberg-Hodge, H., *Ancient futures: learning from Ladakh*. University of California Press, 1991;Random House.

Norberg-Hodge, H., *Bringing the food economy home*. Zed Books, 2002.

Norberg-Hodge, H., *Small is beautiful, big is subsidised*. International Society for Ecology and Culture

Novalis Institute, *Sustainable, integrated area development framework towards a South African Civil Society*. Agenda 21, Cape Town.

Nuernberger, K., *Prosperity, poverty and pollution: managing the approaching crisis*. Zed Books, 1999.

Nuernberger, K., *Beyond Marx and market*. Zed Books, 1998.

Palast, G., *The best democracy money can buy*. Constable & Robinson, 2003.

Perlas, N., *Civil society, cultural power and threefolding*. Philippines, Center for Alternative Development Initiatives

Perlas, N., *Shaping globalisation: civil society, cultural power and threefolding*. Kima Global Publishers, 2003.

Pettifor, A. & Greenhill, R., *The United States as a highly indebted prosperous country*. New Economics Foundation.

Prime, R., *Hinduism and ecology*. Continuum, 1992.

Putnam, R., *Bowling alone: the collapse and revival of American community*. Simon & Schuster, 2001.

Rampton, S. & Stauber, J., *Trust us, we're experts: how industry manipulates science and gambles with your future*. Putnam, 2001.

Ransom, D., *Fair trade: a no-nonsense guide*. New Internationalist Publications/Verso, 2001.

Rifkin, J., *The end of work*. Warner, 1995; Tarcher, 1996.

Rist, G., *The history of development* (updated edition). Zed Books, 2002.

Roberts, R. & Kynaston, D., *City state: how the markets came to rule our world*. Profile Books, 2002.

Robertson, J. & Huber, J., *Creating new money: a monetary reform for the information age*. New Economics Foundation, 2000.

Robertson, J., *Benefits and taxes: a radical strategy*. New Economics Foundation.

Robertson, J., *Beyond the dependency culture: people power and responsibility*. Adamantine Press, 1998.

Robertson, J., *Future wealth*. Cassell, 1990.

Robertson, J., *Future work: jobs, self-employment and leisure after the industrial age*. St Martins Press, 1985.

Robertson, J., *The sane alternative*. Bootstrap Press, 1983

Robertson, J., *Transforming economic life: a millennial challenge*. Green Books, 1998.

Rodgers, P., *Losing control: global security in the 21st Century*. Pluto Press, 2002

Rose, A., *Judaism and ecology*. Continuum, 1992.

Rowbotham, M., *The grip of death*. Jon Carpenter, 1998.

Rowbotham, M., *Goodbye America*. Jon Carpenter, 2000.

Rowbotham, M., *Interest-free credit*. Jon Carpenter.

Rowbotham, M., *The drive behind globalisation*. Jon Carpenter.

Rowbotham, M., *The invalidity of Third World debt*. Jon Carpenter.

Rudin, J., *Odious debt*. Cape Town, AIDC.

Samson, M., *Report on research commissioned by the Committee of Inquiry for a Comprehensive Social Security System*.

Schutt, H., *A new democracy: alternatives to a bankrupt world order*. Zed Books.

Schwartz, W. & D., *Living lightly*. Jon Carpenter, 1998.

Shiva, V. D., *Biopiracy: the plunder of nature and knowledge.* Green Books, 1998.

Shiva, V. D., *Protect or plunder? Understanding intellectual property rights.* Zed Books, 2001.

Shrybman, S., *The world trade organisation: a citizen's guide.* Ontario, Canadian Centre for Policy Alternatives.

Shuman, M., *Going local – creating self-reliant communities in a global age.* Routledge, 2000.

Singh, K., *The globalisation of finance: a citizen's guide.* Zed Books, 1999.

Smith, D., *In search of social justice.* New Economics Foundation.

Sogge, D., *Give and take – What's the matter with Foreign Aid.* Zed Books, 2002.

Soros, G., *The crisis of global capitalism.* Little, Brown, 1998

Stiglitz, J., *Globalisation and its discontents.* Penguin, 2003.

Swimme, B. & Berry T., *The universe story.* Arkana, 1994.

Teivainen, T., *Enter economism, exit politics.* Zed Books, 2002.

The environpaedia – environmental encyclopædia and networking directory of Southern Africa. Hillcrest, Eco-logic Environmental.

Turok, B., *Beyond the miracle: development and economy in South Africa.* Cape Town, Fairshare.

UCT Environmental Evaluation Unit. *A pathway to sustainability – local Agenda 21 in South Africa.* Cape Town

Utting, P., *The greening of business in developing countries.* UN Research Institute for Social Development. Zed Books, 2002.

Von Weizsacher, E., Lovins, B., & Lovins, L.H., *Factor four – doubling wealth, halving resource use.* Earthscan, 1997.

Weisbrod, M. & Janoff, S., *Future search – an action guide finding common ground in organisations and communities.* Koehler (USA).

Weissmann, R., & Mokhiber, R., *Corporate predators: the hunt for mega-profits and the attack on democracy.* Common Courage Press (USA), 1999.

Worldwatch Institute, *State of the world* – regular report on progress towards a sustainable society. Earthscan, UK.

Zadek, S. & Evans, R., *Auditing the Market.* 1993.

Explanation of acronyms

AIDS   Acquired Immune Deficiency Syndrome

AOL   America On Line

BCI   Basic citizens' income

BIG   Basic income grant

CBI   Confederation of British Industry

CEO   Chief Executive Officer

CIA   Central Intelligence Agency

CNN   Cable News Network

COSATU   Congress of South African Trade Unions

CJD   Creutzfeldt-Jakob disease

FDI   Foreign direct investment

G7, G8   Group of richest industrialised nations of the world

GATS   General Agreement on Trade in Services

GDP   Gross Domestic Product

GEAR   (South African government policy for) Growth, Employment and
         Redistribution

GMO   Genetically modified organism

ILO   International Labour Organisation

HNWIs   High net worth individuals

HIPCs   Highly indebted poor countries

ICFTU   International Confederation of Free Trade Unions

IMF   International Monetary Fund

LDCs   Least developed countries

LED   Local economic development

MAI   Multilateral Agreement on Investment

NATO   North Atlantic Treaty Organisation

NGO   Non governmental organisation

OECD   Organisation for Economic Cooperation and Development
OPEC   Organisation of Oil-Exporting Countries
PPP   Public-private partnership
SADEC   Southern African Development Community
SALDRU   South African Labour Development Research Unit
SANE   South African New Economics
TEAL   Total economic activity levy
TNC   Transnational corporation
TINA   'There is no alternative'
TRIPS   Trade in intellectual property rights
UNDP   United Nations Development Programme
UNICEF   United Nations Children's Fund
WEF   World Economic Forum
WSSD   World Summit on Sustainable Development
WTO   World Trade Organisation

The Iona Community

The Iona Community, founded in 1938 by the Revd George MacLeod, then a parish minister in Glasgow, is an ecumenical Christian community committed to seeking new ways of living the Gospel in today's world. Initially working to restore part of the medieval abbey on Iona, the Community today remains committed to 'rebuilding the common life' through working for social and political change, striving for the renewal of the church with an ecumenical emphasis, and exploring new, more inclusive approaches to worship, all based on an integrated understanding of spirituality.

The Community now has over 240 Members, about 1500 Associate Members and around 1500 Friends. The Members – women and men from many denominations and backgrounds (lay and ordained), living throughout Britain with a few overseas – are committed to a fivefold Rule of devotional discipline, sharing and accounting for use of time and money, regular meeting, and action for justice and peace.

At the Community's three residential centres – the Abbey and the MacLeod Centre on Iona, and Camas Adventure Camp on the Ross of Mull – guests are welcomed from March to October and over Christmas. Hospitality is provided for over 110 people, along with a unique opportunity, usually through week-long programmes, to extend horizons and forge relationships through sharing an experience of the common life in worship, work, discussion and relaxation. The Community's shop on Iona, just outside the Abbey grounds, carries an attractive range of books and craft goods.

The Community's administrative headquarters are in Glasgow, which also serves as a base for its work with young people, the Wild Goose Resource Group working in the field of worship, a bi-monthly magazine, *Coracle*, and a publishing house, Wild Goose Publications.

For information on the Iona Community contact:
The Iona Community, Fourth Floor, Savoy House, 140 Sauchiehall Street,
Glasgow G2 3DH, UK. Phone: 0141 332 6343
e-mail: ionacomm@gla.iona.org.uk; web: www.iona.org.uk

For enquiries about visiting Iona, please contact:
Iona Abbey, Isle of Iona, Argyll PA76 6SN, UK. Phone: 01681 700404
e-mail: ionacomm@iona.org.uk

Also from Wild Goose Publications ...

Cherish the Earth
Reflections on a living planet
Mary Low

A fine collection of readings, poems, theology and liturgy to help us start rethinking our beliefs as if the rest of nature mattered. Among the poets and authors featured are Chinua Achebe, Alan Spence, Ted Hughes, Derick Thomson, Dorcas Symms, Kenneth C. Steven, Gerard Manley Hopkins, W.H. Davies, Eunice Buchanan, Waldo Williams, John Agard, Kathleen Raine, R.S. Thomas, Satish Kumar, Chaim Potok, Betsy White, Barbara Kingsolver, Leo Tolstoy, Adomnán of Iona, Jonathon Porritt, Albert Schweitzer, Pierre Teilhard de Chardin and others.

ISBN 1 901557 71 5

The Sacred Art of Listening
Forty reflections for cultivating spiritual practice
Kay Lindahl

More than ever we need to embrace the skills and practices of sacred listening. Kay Lindahl guides us through forty practices of sacred listening – to ourselves, to each other and to our Source. In this book we learn to: enhance our capacity to listen to people with different belief systems; heighten our awareness for deep listening; communicate with courage and compassion; speak and listen from our heart. The author shows us how listening releases a creative force that transforms relationships. Kay Lindahl is recognised as an inspiring teacher and spiritual guide to people of all religious backgrounds. She conducts workshops and retreats around the world on the sacred art of listening for religious, spiritual, community and business groups.

ISBN 1 901557 65 0

Also from Wild Goose Publications ...

Exile in Israel
A personal journey with the Palestinians
Dr Runa Mackay

An autobiography covering forty years in the life of a British doctor working in Israel, the Occupied Territories and Lebanon. Runa Mackay shares her behind-the-scenes thoughts, and with her diary-style narrative gives the reader an insight into this major political situation.

ISBN 0 947988 75 0

George MacLeod
A biography of the founder of the Iona Community
Ron Ferguson

Born into a famous ecclesiastical dynasty and working as a young minister in Edinburgh during the 1920s, George MacLeod became disturbed by his increasing awareness of 'two nations', the rich and the poor. He shocked his many admirers by taking a post as a minister in Govan, a depressed area of Glasgow, and during the depression years moved inexorably towards socialism and pacifism.

In 1938, George MacLeod embarked on the imaginative venture of rebuilding part of the ancient abbey on the isle of Iona with unemployed craftsmen and trainee ministers. Out of this was born the often controversial Iona Community, which over the years has trained clergy for work in deprived areas, produced innovative worship for the world church, pleaded for disarmament, inveighed against world hunger and advocated joint ecumenical action on social issues.

ISBN 1 901557 53 7